The Entrepreneurial Adventure

A History of Business in the United States

The Entrepreneurial Adventure

A History of Business in the United States

LARRY SCHWEIKART
University of Dayton

ISBN-13: 978-0-15-508455-1
ISBN-10: 0-15-508455-0

Library of Congress Catalog Card Number:
99-61382

Thomson Higher Education
10 Davis Drive
Belmont, CA 94002-3098
USA

For information about our products, contact us:
Thomson Learning Academic Resource Center
1-800-423-0563
http://www.wadsworth.com

For permission to use material from this text or product,
submit a request online at http://www.thomsonrights.com

Any additional questions about permissions can be
submitted by email to thomsonrights@thomson.com

Printed in the United States of America
12 11 10 9 8 7 6 5 4 3

Dedication

To Peggy Verity: a true stalwart.

THIS BOOK HAD ITS ORIGIN IN AN ARTICLE I PREPARED FOR THE HISTORICAL journal *Continuity,* in which I surveyed the field of texts in American business history.[1] When I looked at the history of American enterprise, I couldn't get away from people—from the Eli Whitneys, the Lydia Pinkhams, the P. T. Barnums, the Bill Gateses, and, every much as important, the less well-known names or the modern entrepreneurs just starting their empires. I was also impressed with the ocean of new scholarship that has confirmed in a myriad of ways that the market works, and that scholarship, whether examining the effects of deregulation, taxation, monopolies, or other topics, has tended to reaffirm the great blessings conferred by free enterprise.[2]

Historians have been intensely critical of business for decades, yet when I surveyed the American past I saw the transportation systems entrepreneurs built, the communications networks they fabricated to tie families together, the constantly rising wages they paid to raise the wealth level of even unskilled workers, and the vast array of products they supplied—many of them far from trivial—that improved every aspect of our daily lives.[3] Contrary to the assertions of some, historians have paid plenty of attention to the *process* associated with enterprise, and now, I suggest, it is time to devote more attention to the people who made the processes possible.[4]

I wanted to present an alternative to recent textbooks that have focused on "business strategies" and "management structures," and instead to analyze, discuss, and even celebrate the men and women who created the enterprises in the first place. I have come to *celebrate* entrepreneurs and the private sector, not to bury them. In that sense, this book does not seek to portray an "objective" history of American business in the sense that it dwells on the shortcomings of entrepreneurs. Seldom do I deal at length with business fiascos, fraud, or deliberate efforts to defy the law, in part because those are recounted extensively in other textbooks, and in part because in the overall scope of American business history the contributions of entrepreneurs so substantially outweigh the flaws that to engage in extended discussions of particular individuals is akin to nit-picking brush strokes on the Mona Lisa or criticizing Michael Jordan for only scoring 30 points in a game. Where relevant, I have included contrasting views and sources, especially where more recent scholarship is involved. But the key is proportion, not equality, and where an entrepreneur's life is dominated by job creation and wealth generation by serving the needs of others, it seems disproportional to deal in the one time he or she passed an orphan on the street

Nor do I begin from a presumption that government "needs" to perform widespread societal functions; of course, national defense and internal security are constitutional mandates of the U.S. government and must be carried out, and the Constitution requires protection of individual (and corporate) rights, the sanctity of contracts, private ownership of property, and other obligations that are stated with precision. Consequently, lest there be any misconception, this is not a "Libertarian" defense of the market, for, as I point out, government is both natural and desirable as a central element of the human character.

My main points are: (1) entrepreneurs shape the future more than they are shaped by the past; (2) individuals, not groups, "classes," social movements, or structures, account for the vast majority of the creation of wealth and economic progress; (3) the central, if not only, characteristic all entrepreneurs have in common is faith in their abilities and/or product, and that faith often—but not always—seems to reflect a deeper, religious, spiritual faith; and (4) currently popular historical interpretations emphasize individuals' contributions too little and the benefits of large-scale organizations, whether corporations or the government, far too much. These four points are straightforward and simple. Yet business, in some ways, *is* remarkably simple; statistics overwhelmingly confirm that those successful in business work hard, save, invest, and get (and stay) married. Competition works. Prices reflect value. People respond to incentives. High taxes destroy productivity. Faith can carry people through situations when, by all logical accounts, they should quit.

As a history, this book surveys the major events in the past of American business. It also offers three special sections interspersed at the end of various chapters. One, "Challenge Your Perceptions," offers new evidence or new perspectives on historical episodes or ideas that have been widely—but perhaps erroneously—held. For example, did frontier bank robberies actually occur? Are monopolies bad? These sections should be stimulating for further discussion and certainly not as the final word on the topics.

The second section that appears, "The Economics of Business," is designed to address a problem common to business history classes, namely the absence of an adequate economics background on the part of students. One of the most frequently asked questions of instructors in such classes is, "How much economics do I have to know?" These sections are intended to present abbreviated discussions of basic economic theory, economic history and historiography, and the use of statistics. They present the latest scholarly consensus on topics such as the cost of shipping and ocean trade in the 1700s, the effect of the Navigation Acts on the American Revolution, the importance of railroads, and the causes of the Great Depression. Although these sections are "equation-free," they offer to students the opportunity to examine historians' evidence and ideas as well as their conclusions.

A third section, called "Tales from the Crypt: Entrepreneurs Who Came Back from the Dead," provides case studies of entrepreneurs who came back from the dead, that is, who survived and recovered from terrible personal circumstances, usually bankruptcy. One of the most surprising facts I learned while producing this work was how many entrepreneurs started after serious personal tragedies or began their careers very late in life, including many who were over fifty and bankrupt.

In addition to providing a historical setting for entrepreneurs, an analysis of scholarship, and background to the economics of business, I have endeavored to use the most recent research available whenever possible. Always alert to the complaint that writers rely on "out-of-date" theories or data, more than 60 percent of my primary citations (i.e., other than "see also"), and 35 percent of my total citations are sources published since 1985. Obviously, I could increase those percentages, but it is necessary to reference a number of classic articles or books that never lose their value. I have made the endnotes extensive and, therefore, excluded any separate bibliography. Finally, the inclusion of several charts and graphs presents material in a much more manageable form than is possible with purely textual discussions.

Several individuals assisted me in preparation of this work, especially Fred Cedoz, who relentlessly searched citations and obtained material. He also read early versions with an editor's eye. David Ulbrich, currently at the history program at Ball State University, did the foundational research for the deficit and debt tables. Sarah Halsall, Eugene Gangl, Leroy Eid, Larry Flockerzie, John Heitmann, Deborah Hirschfield, and several students in my classes read various parts of the manuscript. Lynne Pierson Doti and Burt Folsom, in particular, read and commented on the entire book, and it was improved greatly through their contributions. Cynthia Thomas, Laura Fetsko, Elizabeth Koslik, and Jeaninne Chaffin at the University of Dayton, as well as Jenny Davis, all contributed to the preparation of disks. Jean Lail, my executive assistant, proved a lifesaver on this and other projects. It is my pleasure to thank each and every one of these people for their help. Any errors or interpretations that remain are my sole responsibility. The University of Dayton, and in particular Assistant Provost (now acting Provost) John Geiger provided funding for research materials and student assistance for this book. It is always gratifying to thank the University for its consistent support of research. Finally, this book is the culmination of a process of faith. Paul writes in Hebrews 11:1 that "faith is the substance of things hoped for, the evidence of things not seen." He just as easily could have been describing the inception of this work.

Larry Schweikart
Springboro, Ohio
March 16, 1998

Notes

1. Larry Schweikart, "Lessons of Business History: Evaluating Business History Texts," *Continuity* , 14 (May 1990): 85–99.

2. See the dissertations in the June 1985 *Journal of Economic History,* 45 (June 1985): 452–479.

3. For a sense of this criticism of American business, see the all too typical comments of Louis Galambos, "What Makes Us Think We Can Put Business Back Into American History?" in ed. William J. Hauseman, *Business and Economic History,* 2d series, 20 (1991): 1–11 (quotation on 9).

4. Galambos, "What Makes Us Think . . . ?" 10.

CONTENTS

The Entrepreneurial Adventure

A History of Business in the United States

CHAPTER 1

Entrepreneurs—The Essence of Enterprise

A STRANGE ITEM STARTED TO APPEAR ON PLAYERS IN THE NATIONAL Football league during the 1994–95 season. Several players showed up at games adorned with small, Band-aid-type strips adhered across the bridges of their noses, about halfway between the nostrils and the eyes. Some football stars, of course, are known for their idiosyncratic dressing habits—Joe Namath once wore women's pantyhose beneath his uniform, and kick returners occasionally sport knee-high socks. But when San Francisco 49ers star wide receiver Jerry Rice (hardly known among his peers as a "hot dog") wore the little strip, it had to be more than a sartorial statement. Indeed, it was an incredibly practical, relatively cheap, and radically simple new breathing aid called "Breathe Right." It consisted of little more than an adhesive strip specially designed to pull the nostrils open from the outside to allow more air into the nose. Football players, used to grabbing oxygen masks at the bench between plays to increase their oxygen flow, suddenly had a quick stick-on source of fresh air. Best of all, it reduced the need for chemical nasal sprays and inhalers. For football players—and for anyone with a deviated septum, sinusitis, or nasal congestion—the remarkable little strips were heaven sent.

B. C. Johnson, the man who invented the Breathe Right, himself suffered from a deviated septum and allergies, and had sought any kind of relief, even to the extent that he pushed "small tubes or wire forms into [his] nostrils" to improve his breathing.[1] Then it occurred to him that instead of putting things inside his nose to push them open, he could pull them open from the outside. He also recognized that millions of people had the same breathing problems as he did, and he applied for a patent.

If Breathe Right proves as successful as it initially seems (not a certainty with product-liability lawsuits, or the Food and Drug Administration's requirement of absolute scientific proof that a product performs as it promises *and* has no side effects!), business historians will look back at the introduction of the little strips and ask why they were developed. While the answer may seem obvious to some people, historians often make the obvious complex. For example, despite what B. C. Johnson claimed, did he contrive his personal problems as a justification after the fact? Did vast, sweeping social forces—in this case, the NFL—make it "the right time" for such an invention? Did Johnson perceive great profits, and leave other, unrelated work to create his strip? In short, how does the economy operate—from entrepreneurs upward, or from large invisible forces downward? What is the role of success in creating, and sustaining, business?

Not long after Breathe Right had carved a niche in the health-aids market, a seemingly unrelated set of events in a completely unrelated industry spoke to similar questions from an entirely different angle. In late 1995, one of America's leading telecommunications companies, AT&T, announced that it planned to reduce its white-collar workforce by 40,000 over three years. Although much of that force reduction was anticipated to involve early retirement packages, buyouts of existing employee contracts, and attrition, the reaction in the media was one of horror and criticism. Media coverage focused on negative elements of the policy, stressing the effects on individual midlevel managers, some of whom genuinely would suffer from the layoffs, or on the apparent lack of company loyalty. For all the discussion of the pain and suffering the layoffs would cause, however, one point went unmentioned entirely: Someone, somewhere, had to take a risk to start the company; others, at other times, had invested all they had and lost. Even after AT&T took root, other entrepreneurs had to assume substantial risks to expand the business, and still others, at other times, had to invest their own capital and reputations to sustain AT&T. Each of those individuals was an "entrepreneur," and without any of them it is unlikely that AT&T would have existed.

Another aspect of the AT&T story was completely ignored. During the decades that AT&T had grown and prospered—to the point that it could employ 308,000 people in the first place—dozens, if not hundreds, of other communications businesses had failed, many of them because they were unable to adapt to changing market conditions. Still countless others represented mere flickers of entrepreneurial light before they died in complete obscurity. When one of those companies failed, it produced no news headlines at all, a fact that hardly eased the pain of the individual, the family, or the close group of employees that made up those small businesses. Instead, the firms just vanished, leaving the entrepreneurs to try again or give up and find other, perhaps more secure, employment. It is easy to see why the media, and subsequently historians, have tended to focus on the larger firms with their armies of employees and levels of managers. The real story of entrepreneurs in America is so diverse, with each individual or entrepreneurial firm representing a slightly different blend of circumstances, personalities, and markets, that only the largest businesses command public attention. And if their growth is charted on the business pages, often their failure is reported on the evening news. Consider the example opening this chapter: If B. C. Johnson had not put his "inventor's story" inside the Breathe Right boxes, even he would be essentially unknown by consumers of the product. Yet it is this constant creation and destruction of businesses, and the attendant rise and fall of individuals' dreams, that makes life better for everyone. As astounding as it may seem, the lives of most Americans and many people in other nations will improve as a result of AT&T's actions, and even more shocking to some people, the lives of many of the AT&T employees who were laid off will actually improve!

The AT&T example raises a second set of questions—mirror images, really—of those raised by B. C. Johnson. Did the management at AT&T respond to real economic pressures on the company, or did executives connive after the fact to fix blame for their own failures on the company's midlevel managers? When companies become large, multiunit organizations, do they lose their entrepreneurial character and zest? What is the role of failure in the creation or formation of new businesses? And what is the relationship between an individual and a vast, faceless corporation such as AT&T?

To understand how both success and failure, birth and death, are essential to the entrepreneurial process, it is necessary to ask yet another set of questions. What is it that entrepreneurs do? How do they differ from managers who oversee an existing business? How do other people, even others around the world who have no awareness of entrepreneurs' efforts or specific businesses, benefit from entrepreneurs' successes? Perhaps more important, how do those same people benefit from entrepreneurs' failures?

This book, while tracing the history of American business from its European origins to contemporary times, will examine these questions through a focus on entrepreneurs. To a considerable extent, this is a celebration of entrepreneurs and entrepreneurship. I do not intend to delve deeply into the contributions of labor, or on social forces that shaped labor movements. Instead, the entrepreneur, and those forces that directly affect entrepreneurs, will receive central treatment. At the same time, defining entrepreneurship has proven more difficult for economists and business historians than might appear at first glance, and their definitions expanded or changed over time. I have therefore chosen to examine the context in which the concept of entrepreneurship appeared in a comprehensive framework. It begins, not with a businessman, but with a professor at the University of Glasgow, Adam Smith.

Adam Smith, Economics, and Entrepreneurship

The essence of entrepreneurship is *capitalism,* an economic system elaborated by Adam Smith in his famous book, *An Inquiry into the Nature and Causes of the Wealth of Nations* (1776).[2] Smith did not "invent" capitalism; he only laid out in a systematic form an explanation of economic practices as old as time itself. But Smith is worth examining in detail at this early point for two reasons. First, his theory is as valid today as it was in 1776; challengers still remain, but increasingly they have retreated into debating the effects of capitalism on spiritual grounds, where proof is impossible and faith is essential. Second, Smith's major points have been misrepresented or misunderstood (by defenders as well as critics) to the extent that he has received credit or blame for positions he never took.

Adam Smith concerned himself with an explanation of economic growth, or the process of making products or providing services for personal gain. In that context, aside from those dedicated individuals motivated entirely by religious, ideological, or artistic factors (Mother Teresa or Tibetan monks come to mind), many people, if not most people, operate to a substantial degree out of concern for personal gain. Certainly some individuals crave only power; but usually the trappings of power include most material goods, including houses, transportation, food, and personal assistants. Other people want fame; but fame, too, usually produces wealth as a by-product, making it difficult to separate a desire for one from the other. Whatever the case, a good rule of thumb for life is that when someone says he is "not in it for the money," watch out! He is in it precisely "for the money." Smith understood that self-interest was the most important motivating force in the world under normal conditions (i.e., except during war and revolutions, when ideology or nationalism prevails). More importantly, Smith observed that society as a whole benefited and improved materially as individuals pursued self-interest.

Critics of capitalism have viewed this as a paradox: How can society thrive if the key economic tenet is "selfishness"? Perhaps it cannot; but Smith never equated self-interest with selfishness. Instead, he saw capitalism as a moral system. Smith was a man consumed by moral questions. His previous book, *A Theory of Moral Sentiments,* asked, "Wherein does virtue consist? . . . how and by what means does it

come to pass, that the mind prefers one tenour of conduct to another?[3] Smith emphasized what economists call "macroeconomics"
(the broad spectrum of economic activities), and "microeconomics,"
which investigates individual firms, markets, or sectors of economic
activity. Although Smith sought to explain the overall functioning of
the capitalist system—really, as a capstone to his broader discussion
of morality—he did so through analysis of individual markets and examples. But because he had already written extensively on morality,
Smith assumed that the reader would already have grasped the spiritual elements of his economic theory. Thus, the references in *Wealth
of Nations* to "self-interest" were intended to describe only some aspects of human psychology, not an operational moral framework. In
fact, Smith *presumed* that economic work would necessarily exist in a
minimum condition of justice, because in *A Theory of Moral Sentiments*
he had laid the groundwork for a human propensity to please others.
It is exactly this basis of service that critics of capitalism ignore, and
that defenders fail to explain.

Smith thus began his investigation with the "natural wants" of
people, and noted that the range of human wants made people dependent on the labor of others. This resulted in a *division of labor* that
made capitalism especially vibrant. Any person, he theorized, could
perform almost any labor to one degree or another. The difference,
however, could be literally life and death. (A butcher once told a sur-
geon, "You know, the only difference between us is that I cut with the
grain and you cut against it.") Obviously, some people have vastly different skills or talents than others, and the difference is more than one
of style. To Smith, then, it did not seem logical for every person to try
to do everything (farm, build, philosophize, and so on), but rather to
specialize in what he or she did best to "maximize" the return, allowing others to do those tasks they did better. Division of labor became
more than a phrase associated with capitalism; it represented the fundamental economic difference between capitalism and all socialist systems, which insist that the state can and should direct, limit, or control
human wants. Specialization then spread upward from the individual
to nations, giving one country *comparative advantage* over others (see
"The Economics of Business: Comparative Advantage" p. 22).

But while division of labor was a key element in capitalism, Smith's
theory consisted of far more. He observed that self-interest created
competition between people, either to produce goods and supply services on one side of the equation, or to acquire goods and services on
the other. Human nature suggested that people thought highly of themselves, regardless of religious training or government suasion. Individuals therefore tended to ask as much as possible for their own labor
and sought to purchase goods made by others for as little as possible. Or,
in Smith's vernacular, "sell dear, buy cheap." Smith realized, however,

that everyone could not "sell dear" and "buy cheap" simultaneously. That caused competition to appear, creating a "market" wherein all goods and services would reach a specific *price*.

When explaining "price," Smith did not use the notions of "just price" developed by the Catholic Church.[4] Instead, a price was a piece of information about the availability of a good or service, plus the difficulty in producing it or attaining it, combined with the desire of people to acquire that good or service combined with their ability to pay for it.

As a piece of information, there can be no such thing as a "just price" or a "fair price," any more than there can be a "just" or "fair" report of a basketball score or a cake recipe. Information is information; data is either accurate or not, but it has *no inherent moral value*. It is as absurd to talk about a "fair price" as it is to insist that it is "unfair" that only a Chevrolet car key will start a Corvette, or that an airplane will fly only when it attains greater thrust than it has drag. Smith— again, concerned with morality—instead noted that if a price is "unfair" or "unjust," no one will pay it (excluding, of course, situations where government is able through force to exclude competitors or to restrict supply or where consumers have no genuine choice). As will be seen later, many modern views of "just price" and "fair wage" have their basis in religious doctrine and social criticism, not in economics, but the confusion often affects economic policies. It also should be obvious that, as information, prices cannot be "controlled" by governments. Have governments ever successfully controlled information? Some command economies with access to extensive secret police networks and torture have kept the lid on certain types of information temporarily. However, in the twentieth century, no major state has controlled information *and* maintained a vibrant economy, as the former Soviet Union demonstrated. Even "Communist" China permits widespread operation of the free market in many sectors of its economy, and the Peking government has recently suggested that it will not interfere with the market economy of Hong Kong, which it took over in 1997.

Smith understood that competition among suppliers and competition among buyers occurred simultaneously; that innumerable business decisions stood behind any single transaction (or "exchange," as he called it); and that no single individual or group could possibly have access to all the necessary information about availability or desirability of a particular good or service. Only the market, which represented the cumulative information of all the suppliers and buyers, could reflect that information through a price.

For all its genius, Smith's explanation was unduly dependent in its discussion on large, impersonal forces, such as markets and competition. Although he mentioned the butcher and the baker, Smith de-emphasized—and outright ignored—the role of any single individual entrepreneur. He did not provide a single case study of how one became an entrepreneur or succeeded in a specific business, nor did he attempt to offer a model of business success. But one has to look no further than the latest *Forbes* 400 richest Americans to find "prototype" entrepreneurs. There, we find:

✦ William A. Cook, an ex-cabbie who worked for five years in the medical supply business before spending $1,500 on a blowtorch, soldering iron, and plastic tubing to make cardioscopic catheters. Net worth: $700 million.

✦ Eli Broad, a home builder who borrowed $25,000 from his in-laws to build his first home and sold insurance in down cycles. Net worth: $690 million.

✦ Estée Lauder, who started selling skin creams for her chemist uncle and in 1946 developed her own cosmetics and fragrance lines, including Aramis, Clinique, Origins, and Estée. Family net worth: at least $3 billion.

✦ Leonard Stern, who inherited a small canary and pet business from his father and turned it into Hartz Mountain pet foods and supplier in 1959. Net worth: $825 million.

✦ Frank Ferfitta III, a bellman and blackjack dealer in Las Vegas who acquired a small casino to specialize on bingo. Net worth: $300 million.

✦ H. Wayne Huizenga, a dropout who literally took the garbage jobs by hauling trash, turning it into the largest U.S. waste-disposal company. In 1984 he shifted to video rental stores that became Blockbuster Video and subsequently purchased the Miami Dolphins football team. Net worth: $700 million.

✦ John Stanly, who pumped gas and leased his first Gulf gas station as a student. He went bankrupt, twice. Net worth: $700 million.

Certainly we could find on the *Forbes* list many who inherited wealth. But excluding women (who mostly inherited from their husbands or fathers), the *Forbes* list features many, if not more, super-millionaires who "pulled themselves up by the bootstraps" than it does people who inherited their fortunes. Many declared bankruptcy—some two or three times—and several had no college education. But they all had one thing in common: They took a leap of faith, either on savings or borrowed funds, to pursue a dream. Whether bingo or videos, cat chow or catheters, garbage or great buildings, the fruits of those entrepreneurs have improved all our lives. They also shared another characteristic in that they stepped out on faith with total and complete dedication. That total dedication came at great personal cost; more than a few of the *Forbes* entrepreneurs were divorced, some many times, reflecting the demands of their quest. Others, as we will see in later chapters, clashed with the federal government, occasionally at

the expense of their companies or private fortunes. Still others—
Howard Hughes comes to mind—captivated the public with their exploits but never successfully managed a business. One final quality is
visible in the lives of entrepreneurs, namely, that every businessman
or woman must identify a need or desire on the part of others for that
product. Likewise with service businesses, every service must *serve*
someone. Successful entrepreneurs are better than others at identifying and meeting the needs and desires of others, and it therefore
should be obvious that—far from concentrating on their own needs
and wants—successful entrepreneurs focus on others.

It also should be obvious from the above examples that entrepreneurs come from all walks of life and backgrounds—from Harvard
MBAs to penniless immigrants—and defy any capsule definition. (Certainly Adam Smith did not provide one.) And since the nature of entrepreneurship is service to others—which can take almost any form—
no clear "model" of entrepreneurship or path for entrepreneurial
success exists. Despite the appearance of dozens of courses in entrepreneurship blossoming around the country, business success requires
small doses of talent but large doses of attitude. Indeed, not all entrepreneurial success is related to formal education: A recent "*Forbes
Four Hundred*" featured 10 people who never finished high school and
64 of the 304 who went to college never graduated. Still others attended
school after the fact to enhance their already prospering commercial
ventures.

Lacking a clear model of an entrepreneur makes defining entrepreneurship more difficult. Nevertheless, most theorists have accepted a
definition of the entrepreneur as "one who takes the risk to start a business," a phrase generally attributed to Jean-Baptiste Say, a French
writer who first defined production as a composed of three factors—
land, labor, and capital—and with formulating "Say's law" (supply creates its own demand).[5] After the emergence of the modern corporate
structure in the mid-1800s, some scholars argued that the definition of
an entrepreneur needed to be broadened to include managers or even
executives in nonprofit and government sectors. That approach led economic historians such as Jonathan R. T. Hughes to count as entrepreneurs religious leaders such as William Penn and Brigham Young as
well as employees of the federal bureaucracy in his classic study of business leaders, *The Vital Few.*[6] Further expanding the definitions of
entrepreneurship, the term "intrapreneuring" was coined to describe risk-
taking activities within a corporate framework, suggesting that wage
employees could receive intracorporate resources for their projects.[7]

Individuals within corporations, nonprofit organizations, the military, and government can operate with great independence and
autonomy, but one should not carry this line of thinking too far; entrepreneurship still requires an element of *personal* risk—the individual

must stand to lose or gain financially and personally. Consider the position of a U.S. Air Force officer placed in charge of a procurement program for new aircraft. The air force invests the officer with considerable institutional authority and provides a large budget. The officer might even use cutting-edge managerial techniques or innovative business strategies to acquire the aircraft. Yet if the aircraft program is an abysmal flop, the officer loses none of his own money, although a worse assignment might be in store. In short, little personal capital has been risked. One should not confuse using entrepreneurial methods with entrepreneurship.

For our purposes then, a working definition of an entrepreneur is "the person who takes the risk to create material wealth in the economic realm." For the most part, such a definition excludes individuals such as Lee Iacocca or Walter Wriston because they made their marks as executives within larger corporations. It excludes bureaucrats, such as the former secretary of housing and urban development, Jack Kemp, because no matter how innovative his programs, he personally assumed none of the risk. And it excludes William Penn or Brigham Young, counted as entrepreneurs by Jonathan R. T. Hughes, because they did not concern themselves primarily with creating material wealth in the economic realm. Nor would it include modern ministers such as the "Faithdome" pastor Rev. Frederick K. C. Price, who personally signed for the entire $9 million loan on the Faithdome, because while his messages encourage investment, sacrifice, and other probusiness attitudes, he is not *primarily* concerned with material wealth. But while Penn, Young, or Price have concerned themselves primarily with creating value in the spiritual realm, it is critical to realize that the process of creating material wealth involves the spiritual as much as the physical. George Gilder has argued that for entrepreneurs to develop a business idea, that "creative thought requires an act of faith [for which] commitment can create its own confirmation."[8] Thus, creative activity itself is in a sense spiritual, involving a "personal and psychological drama" that decides whether an entrepreneur will borrow money to launch a new business in the face of statistics that show that close to two-thirds of all new businesses fail within five years.

The Spiritual Side of Capitalism

Gilder's publication of *Wealth and Poverty* (1981) and *Recapturing the Spirit of Enterprise* (1992) brought renewed emphasis to capitalism's spiritual side.[9] With Michael Novak's *The Spirit of Democratic Capitalism* (1982), Gilder provided a desperately needed counter to the almost century-long trend of casting capitalism in a morally negative light.[10] But Gilder's books also unfortunately implied that Adam

Smith had ignored the spiritual aspects of capitalism, suggesting that Smith concerned himself more with technical factors of supply, demand, and price. Such a misperception seeped into the work of writers of all political stripes, resulting in critics of capitalism from the left (Michael Harrington and Robert Heilbroner) and from the right (Irving Kristol and Richard Weaver) charging that material progress occurred only at the expense of individual dignity or of society's spiritual values.[11] Were such claims true?

Smith's weak link in *The Wealth of Nations* arose from his assumption that people had already read his earlier *A Theory of Moral Sentiments,* which explained that individual self-interest required a person individual to *serve* his fellow man to obtain a return. Ultimately, Smith said, not only did individuals have to serve others first to receive material rewards, but people were inclined to do so. Whatever the motivation, the individual must focus on the desires and needs of others, address those needs, and provide a good or service before receiving any recompense. Another way to look at those activities is as service: A person must first serve others before demanding a return. Except in strict barter economies, however, determining how much service has been performed is fraught with problems if one leaves it to an arbitrary source, such as a government board or commission. Market economies typically use money as a measure, or symbol, of how much service one individual has provided to others. Economist Walter Williams has detailed on several occasions how the process works in daily life. A woman sits down in a restaurant and orders a meal (which represents the accumulated efforts of farmers, shippers, meatpackers, the restaurant owner, the waiter, and others); but in order to pay for the meal, she must have money (for the moment, exclude credit from this discussion). The money in her pocketbook represents her own service to others that she has performed in her clothing business, and the value that others have placed on her service to them. Money acts as a type of "accumulated service to others"—proof that the holder has served others, and to what degree.

To see how this works, a typical comment about professional sports salaries is "The ballplayers are *way* overpaid!" That seems accurate enough when one looks at Deion Sanders getting $35 million just to play football (he has also played pro baseball and preaches on Sundays!). But examine this more closely. Ask most football fans, hypothetically, "Would you pay 30 cents a game to watch Deion Sanders?" and the answer from most fans would be, "Thirty cents? Sure that's a deal." Extrapolate that 30 cents a game across the thousands of fans who actually attend the game in the stadiums, then the millions of fans who watch the National Football League on tv; the millions of dollars advertisers pay the NFL to broadcast the games; and so on. It easily computes into $35 million for "Neon Deion," and in reality Sanders may be underpaid based on his performed service to others—in this case, entertainment and advertising value.

With entrepreneurs, the same process is at work, but, of course, with far less publicity. Assume that an entrepreneur starts a hamburger stand. In doing so, he invests time, energy, and talent procuring products, facilities, and employees. Before earning a single dime, he has served others by making these investments of time, talent, and energy. (This process later became the essence of "supply-side economics," which argues that the founding of a new venture itself creates wealth for others.) The entrepreneur still has not received any personal return, which he must do by meeting his customers' culinary needs or desires. What if he provides terrible food? Or what if, although the food is good, he is abusive and crabby to his customers? In either case, he will soon be out of business; he has not served his fellow man, nor has he met any need or fulfilled any desire. Note that *despite simply working hard,* he has not benefited others! Consequently, labor itself is not sufficient as a measure of value. Indeed, unwanted labor is useless in one economic sense, in that it allows a person to consume scarce resources without returning anything to society. Rather, labor that does not serve others (in a market sense) is actually consumption, not production. All economic activity can then be summarized with a question—"How have you served your fellow man?"—and an imperative—"Prove it!"

Smith, surprisingly to some, thought that most people were naturally inclined to such service but that they naturally overestimated the value of their own labor and underestimated that of others. Consequently, the only reliable measure that could adjust for the individual misperceptions of millions of people in the market was the crucial price mechanism. Prices forced on everyone a "reality check," so they could not overestimate their own service or undervalue that of others. For that reason, he warned about any distortions of prices brought about by anything other than the market itself, such as business combinations ("monopolies," in current jargon) or businesses obtaining special privileges from governments.

Indeed, it is important to realize that *any* economic activity not solely derived from market effects can produce negative results. Charity, for example, generates its own economic implications. If individuals, churches, community groups, or governments provide at no cost (or at artificially lower cost) what others in "the market" would charge to provide, that free service will have an impact on the price and affect the market. Labor unions have long resisted efforts to have prisoners perform work, contending that "slave labor" undermines the price of "free labor," and they are correct. If a farmer simply gave food away— for whatever moral motive—it would have the effect of driving down the price of food everywhere, essentially telling other farmers that their service is worth less than it really is. Artists, musicians, writers, and actors have long faced the grim reality that their love of their craft means that they would paint, act, write, or play music if no one paid them, which has had the effect of driving down the price of all art. (Likewise, the fortunate few who succeed can reap phenomenal rewards, with actors who are box-office "draws" receiving millions of dollars per movie as a means of compensating themselves for the time they went without.) In short, all activity—even charity—has economic outcomes that affect prices. Although these effects are often hidden, they nevertheless exist.

A final point alludes to one of our earlier questions, namely, how do others benefit from the *failure* of entrepreneurs? When entrepreneurs fail, they provide critical information about the wants and needs of others. The collapse of a video-game arcade may suggest that the location is wrong (Is it in a retirement community? for example), or that the product is too expensive, or that teenagers have other things to do. (Does the high school have a strong sports program, or do local churches have effective youth programs?) One thing is certain: Other aspiring video-game arcade owners will examine the experience of the failed business before establishing an enterprise of their own at that location.[12] Not only do other businesses benefit from failed enterprises, but consumers profit, too. A bookstore in sharp competition with other similar stores may only be able to stock the best-sellers. But if the competitors fail, and the bookstore can raise prices on its stock, it can also begin to carry more obscure titles. Conversely, what consumers lose in price competition, they can gain from economies of scale when an industry focuses on a single technology. Or vice versa: RCA's videodisc proved an utter flop compared to the videocassette recorder, mainly because it did not offer the taping feature, but as more consumers concentrated in the videocassette market, manufacturers lowered prices by increasing production.

Failures by some businesses can have positive ramifications in other ways as well. The inability of one person to succeed in a business stands out as a challenge to others. Such entrepreneurs usually exude confidence and are convinced that they can succeed where others did not. And, in fact, some of America's greatest success stories resulted form abject failure. Automaker Henry Ford, banker A. P. Giannini, department-store founder Sam Walton, and media personality Rush Limbaugh all either declared bankruptcy, had their first enterprises fail miserably, or were unceremoniously kicked out of companies they created before they attained ultimate success. In other cases, entrepreneurs have made fortunes or founded thriving businesses in services or with products that few would find lucrative. Yet no matter what path a particular entrepreneur took, each had a single characteristic in common: a willingness to take a risk.

The element of risk-taking by entrepreneurs—which, again, constitutes an act of faith and not reason—sets them apart from managers and paid employees. *No* element of business enterprise is risk free, and certainly management and labor have seen periods of mass layoffs (as the AT&T managers or former workers from U.S. Steel well know). Ultimately, the only source of a job is one's own talent and labor: the worker's ability to, in essence, create his own employment demand. But in general, companies in capitalist societies offer a far higher level of income security and, whenever possible, extend employment to managers and employees than typical entrepreneurs ever attain. In most small businesses, employees receive pay even if there is not enough left for the owner at the end of the week. Many small-business owners have reported not taking a paycheck for years, ploughing every cent back into the business. At larger companies (barring the most calamitous circumstances), even when the stock plunges and the stockholders lose huge amounts of money, employees are retained—and paid—until quarterly reports appear and the company can restructure.

Varieties of Business Organization

Capitalism's spiritual side is most clearly seen in the activities of such entrepreneurs, who constantly must act on faith. Ultimately, they must believe that their idea, product, service, or business will find a market. While larger firms also take risks and make investments based on their convictions that a demand exists for their products, the number of managerial "filters" through which decisions must pass weakens and dilutes the connection between action and faith in large corporations. On the other hand, entrepreneurial faith is clearly visible in the almost 14 million sole proprietorships in the United States as of 1995. Sole proprietorships can range in size from an individual working out of a home to a large-scale, unincorporated business that can employ hundreds of people, but the sole proprietorship is most closely identified with what Americans consider "small business." As Stuart Bruchey has pointed out, " 'small' is a relative concept" best examined industry by industry, and some authors have adopted functional approaches that define small business as those firms lacking a layer of management between owners and employees.[13] For those readers intent on attaching a size restriction to the definition, however, the government defines "small" as any business with fewer than 500 employees, and certainly any business with under 20 employees qualifies for practical purposes as a "small business." Equally important, the explosion of home-based businesses created by the revolution in computing and desktop publishing has led to an entirely new category of firm—the "microbusiness" with five or fewer employees.

Most people have daily contact with small businesses—usually grocery stores, bookstores, restaurants, or service businesses—but for much of American history, the most common small business was the family farm. On the fringes of the early frontier, the family farm truly put entrepreneurial faith to the test: If the farmer failed to plant enough, or the right type of crops, or did not take precautions against flooding or fire, he and his family literally faced starvation. Between 1850 and 1900, the urbanization of America shifted the majority of entrepreneurial activity into cities, and typical small businesses included foundries, tool shops, "general stores," and producers of a vast spectrum of other goods and services. The advent of the personal computer and of desktop publishing in the late 1970s and 1980s sparked yet another transition among sole proprietorships, reducing the size of the average small business and making it more mobile. For the first time in American history, many small businesses had a genuine opportunity to tap into national, if not world, markets. Entrepreneurs appreciated the chance that appeared: In 1950, small business start-ups numbered 93,000 annually; the number surged to over 450,000 by 1980; and by 1995 the number of start-ups had almost doubled the 1980 figure, exceeding 800,000. The proportion of failures over that period remained essentially unchanged.

A second form of business organization, the partnership, accounts for fewer than two million of the nation's businesses as of 1995. Partnerships have proven especially effective in professional services, particularly medicine, accounting, and law, where partners share office costs and other overhead expenses but otherwise develop independently their client base and their fees. Obviously, partnerships can succeed in such areas because no central vision or product direction is required, but they would not work in a business that needed a single leader.

More numerous than partnerships but wielding far more economic power than sole proprietorships, corporations constitute more than 3.5 million businesses. Many entities are "Chapter S" corporations that often amount to no more than an individual obtaining a corporate charter for an existing sole proprietorship with no change in capitalization, as seen by the fact that most American corporations have less than $100,000 in assets. Far more influential are the large companies most people identify with the word "corporation": the large, multiunit business enterprise with hundreds (if not thousands) of employees. In 1990, the top five corporations in *Fortune* magazine's list of the 500 top American industrial corporations (General Motors, Exxon, Ford, IBM, and General Electric) had total sales exceeding $428 billion, and General Motors alone had sales of $126 billion, surpassing the gross national product (GNP, or the goods and services a country produces) of many nations in the world. But the influence of the large corporation has waned steadily since 1970, and between 1986 and 1990 the sales of the top five fell from 8 percent of GNP to 2.2 percent of GNP. On an individual basis, although each of the five companies experienced rising sales, four of the five showed a percentage loss in profits since 1988. Put another way, the largest units of business have lost an increasing portion of the marketplace to entrepreneurial small businesses since 1980.

If anything, this recent history suggests that attempts to broaden the definition of entrepreneurs were misguided, and that the corporate form that dominated the period from the Gilded Age to the Great Society has looked increasingly less entrepreneurial than some have argued. Certainly, a vision of the American business scene such as that offered by John Kenneth Galbraith in his *New Industrial State* (1967) has failed to materialize.[14]

Is There an Entrepreneurial Character?

Defining an entrepreneur as "one who assumes the risk" hardly narrows the search for characteristics that identify entrepreneurs. Is there an entrepreneural character one can point to that all businesspeople possess? Do certain cultures, or backgrounds, lend themselves to entrepreneurship? Max Weber thought so. He argued in *The Protestant Ethic and the Spirit of Capitalism* (1904–05) that Protestants, particularly those who derived their teachings from John Calvin, adopted certain practices (frugality, investment, hard work) that they believed reflected their status with the divine.[15] Material prosperity, they assumed, was an indication of heavenly blessings. Rather than wait for such prosperity—which might never come—they instead created it themselves, leading Weber to contend that Protestants substantially accelerated capitalism.

Weber's thesis ignored the phenomenal success by Italian Catholic bankers such as the Medici, the Bardi, and the Frescobaldi, not to mention the entrepreneurial spirit of the great Catholic explorers such as Columbus. Recent studies by "public choice" economists have taken a much more favorable view of the Church's appreciation for the market.[16] Economist Thomas Sowell has detailed the vitality of entrepreneurship among such groups as the Lebanese, Jews, Chinese, and West Indians, often even as those peoples immigrated to other nations as minorities.[17] In South America, Jewish minorities carved out thriving businesses as middlemen; in Malaya, Chinese minorities have dominated commercial business despite government programs designed to impede them at the expense of native Malays.[18] Immigrant experiences of non-Protestants in America have looked much the same. Studies of businesses in Atlanta, Georgia, showed that Lebanese and Koreans achieved inordinate success in retailing and groceries, while Vietnamese immigrants in Texas carved out a share of the fishing industry on the Gulf Coast. Several non-Christian cultures worldwide over time have witnessed pockets of capitalism, and simple entrepreneurship has existed since the earliest stages of human life. Given this evidence, it seems that all Weber managed to do was to identify certain traits of entrepreneurship—thrift, diligence, hard work, honesty—that Protestants happened to share with other entrepreneurs from other faiths and other nations.

Conversely, religion can act as a deterrent to business success. Some Christian denominations, for example, have treated wealth creation and accumulation as evil or sinful, citing passages in the Bible that either imply rich people fell short of heaven or that, conversely, the wealthy gave away their possessions when they took their religion seriously. Christianity is hostile to neither wealth nor entrepreneurship, and there is substantial biblical evidence that Jesus and the disciples were far from being poor, homeless vagabonds.[19] Under Judaism, wealth was an outward sign of God's blessings. God prospered Abraham so much that he and Lot could not graze their herds on the same hills, and when the Jews gave gifts to build the Tabernacle, they provided gold, silver, and precious gems in such vast abundance that Moses had to tell them to stop giving! Clearly Old Testament Jews had wealth in abundance to permit them to give in such quantities. The New Testament Christians maintained that they were the rightful heirs of Abraham and that his blessings were their blessings. Jesus' disciple Matthew held a feast in his house so large that all of the "publicans" (government employees, tax collectors, and, in general, "sinners") in the city could fit inside. Other evidence abounds that many New Testament Christians had productive jobs and material wealth.

In the Middle Ages, the Church possessed exceptional amounts of wealth and land, and many members of the Catholic hierarchy lived in luxury in apparent contradiction to their vows of poverty. At one point, the Church held one-third of all the land in Europe, leaving kings to "raid Church revenues to survive," and financing King John of England's campaigns against Wales, Scotland, and Ireland.[20] The Church's ability to expand its resources at a time when peasants complained about their own deplorable conditions and landlessness constituted a serious challenge to the allegiance of the masses to the Christian religion. Whether deliberate or not, the gradual emergence of an emphasis on "the meek inheriting the Earth" certainly provided theological grounds for the masses to accept their lot in life. Moreover, individuals who deliberately sought wealth—which was a gift from God, given for a moral purpose to improve the welfare of everyone— risked committing the sin of avarice. Or, as Christine Rider summarizes the situation, "Poverty was of divine origin. . . . [And] Wealth was justified: it enabled the wealthy to fulfill the obligations imposed on them by Divine Providence."[21] Commercial activities, however, which involved the active pursuit of wealth, constituted sin and were excorciated from the pulpit.

The Catholic Church had a long philosophical strain that established such concepts as "just price," which in its original use accounted for scarcity and applied centrally to instances of emergency. Over time, however, the notion was secularized and broadened to apply to any "undo" profit. Further interpretations of prices devolved from early variants of the labor theory of value, first formally developed by Robert Owen but made famous later by Karl Marx. Theologians such as Saint Augustine argued that human existence involved man's mixing his labor with land, thus lending value to all work. Prices and wages had to be "just," a concept ultimately left to the definition of the religious or political leader at the time. Any activity that did not involve a visible exchange of goods or services—and thus anything requiring a middleman, due to distance or insufficient funds—represented a potential immoral transaction because it could not be seen, although the Church did allow for clearly documented "transaction costs" to be included in the price. Thus, over a period of 1,000 years, religious interpretations of Scripture related to the material world had substantially inverted the notion that "Faith is the evidence of things not seen" (Heb. 11:1). Economic growth required faith in exactly those things "not seen" because the investment had to appear first—as an act of faith. At any rate, the methods designed by the feudal societies to maintain the social ethic, and in the process regulate the social order, proved impossible to enforce outside of the individual's compliance.

The most infamous of the attempts to restrain capitalistic impulses (or, conversely, to ensure concepts of "just price") came in the form of usury laws. *Usury* was defined as lending money or charging interest above the observable transaction costs. The Church certainly appreciated that all lending was not bad, because monarchs constantly needed financial support in the form of loans. Rather, only interest charged for purely profit motives—and then, only "unjust" profits—received condemnation. Enforcing usury laws involved the attempt to determine "just" interest rates, which officials found entailed assessing risk, character, economic conditions, and a universe of information in every single case, a task they learned they could never accomplish. When rates did appear, they were generically so high that they were unnecessary (but, of course, also "unjust"!).

Is There an Entrepreneurial "Life Pattern"?

Attempting to approach entrepreneurship "scientifically," as Weber or Joseph Schumpeter (*Theory of Economic Development,* 1934) tried to do can produce abject futility when considering the life stories of numerous entrepreneurs. P. T. Barnum did not found the Barnum & Bailey Circus until he was seventy years old. Famous Amos took the recipe for his million-dollar cookie empire from the back of the Nestlé's chocolate bag available to every baker and housewife in the nation. Susan Powter, a fat divorcee, decided that the road to fitness demanded a new sense of self-worth, which she then turned into a product through "infomercials." Frederick Tudor made a fortune by selling the free ice from ponds and lakes around his home. A dentist, Dr. Thomas B. Welch, an ardent opponent of "demon rum," created a nonalcoholic beverage that tasted like wine for use in church communion. Gail Borden spent most of his adult life as a schoolteacher, a newspaper editor, a real estate salesman, a tax collector, and a surveyor who failed miserably to sell his first food product, the unappetizingly named "meat biscuit." Hall of Fame pitcher Albert Spalding is better known today for the special baseball glove he designed and produced. Dr. John Harvey Kellogg, a Seventh-Day Adventist who ran a health sanitarium, provided specialized cereal products for his patients in Battle Creek, Michigan. It was there that a sick cowboy who had lost his fortune in real estate scams, C. W. Post, got the idea for his own (later competing) cereal company.[22]

Perhaps the most amazing thing about these and thousands of other entrepreneurs is that they *have* no life pattern: the old, the young, the idealistic, the pragmatic, the inventors, the innovators, the driven, the greedy, the compassionate—all characterize different entrepreneurs. Every successful entrepreneur, however, does have one characteristic in common with the others. The entrepreneur has faith and vision, in essence a driving motivation that infuses his or her commitment to at least one (often more) idea or product. For the true entrepreneur, challenges represent opportunities. Indeed, it seems that entrepreneurs do not even see challenges in the same way as others. They consciously or subconsciously diminish the size of the hurdle to be cleared, or possibly do not even perceive obstacles as existing at all. Robert Ringer, whose best-selling tongue-in-cheek book, *Winning through Intimidation* (1974) made him a millionaire, spent a chapter or more explaining that entrepreneurs change the language itself, to the point that there are no "problems," only "points to be dealt with," and from discussions of "if" a deal would be done to "when."[23] If anything, the traditional juxtaposition of the "glass half full" and the "glass half empty" does not apply to entrepreneurs at all, in that to them the half-full glass is already full!

Entrepreneurs do recognize serious threats to their concepts or businesses, but they seem to have an innate ability to separate genuine from perceived threats, which leads them to focus always on the most important issues. In turn, they pay little attention to competitors, especially in the early stages of their businesses. Most entrepreneurs concentrate so intently on their own product, idea, or operations that they have no time to worry about the actions of competitors. (Once established, that occasionally changes, but even then true entrepreneurs continually seek product or process improvement.)

Likewise, when getting started, if entrepreneurs seek advice, they go only to successful people. In every activity in life, new entrants will be dissuaded by some who have established positions or markets to protect. While I am not an entrepreneur in the purest sense, my personal background may have some application to this point. When I started work on my certification to teach high school, for example, I was told there were no jobs at all in teaching—that each job had hundreds of applicants. After taking a position teaching reading to seventh-grade children in a migrant farm community in Arizona, I again applied for high school positions, ending up at perhaps the most prestigious college prep school in the state. Then again, after starting work on a Ph.D., I heard the lament that there were no jobs teaching in universities, especially in a field such as American history. That was eleven years ago, and I have been a tenured full professor for three years. In a previous "life," I played drums with a rock band that achieved some success, opening for the major acts of the day in huge arenas. Again, we had heard that there were "a million" rock bands and that it was impossible to get airplay on the major stations. We refused to listen, and our record played on the largest station in Los Angeles, garnering reviews by *Billboard, Cashbox,* and *Record World.*

At some point, virtually every successful person—and certainly every entrepreneur—has been told "You can't," "It won't work," or "There are enough of those already." If Sochiro Honda had listened to the Japanese officials who told him that Japan did not need another car, one of the largest auto companies in the world would not have been born. If Arnold Schwarzenegger had listened to critics who complained that with his accent he could never succeed in acting, some of the biggest box-office hits in the world never would have been made. If Louis L'Amour had heeded any of the first 100 rejection letters he received, he never would have become the best-read western novelist of all time. And if a fourteen-year-old named Jack Daniels had listened to neighbors in Tennessee, where moonshining was a family tradition, one of the best-known names in whiskey never would have existed.

While those people had persistence and determination, more than just hard work or a good idea is required to allow entrepreneurs to achieve. A structural foundation must exist that ensures human liberty and a society based on law. Such notions as property protections, contract enforcement, copyrights, and other mainstays of free capitalist societies made it possible for Honda, Schwarzenegger, Daniels, and virtually all of the other entrepreneurs discussed above to take advantage of their own talents and abilities.

The Foundations of American Capitalism

Several factors permitted entrepreneurship to flourish in America and constitute the foundations of capitalism in this nation. The mainspring of any capitalist system is the presence of private property, or, more specifically, the legal right to own it. This right often serves as an incentive to acquire even more property. Because one can retain the fruits of one's own labors, an individual is motivated to work all the harder.

In the United States, the right to property is so basic that it is formally guaranteed to all in the Constitution. The Fifth Amendment explicitly forbids arbitrary interference from the federal government by the command that no person "be deprived of life, liberty, or property, without due process of law" and that no "private property be taken for public use, without just compensation." Interference by state governments is prohibited both by the Fourteenth Amendment and by the clause in Article I, Section 10, which prevents any state from enacting a "Law impairing the Obligation of Contracts." And the Constitution's property protections even extend to a specific manufactured item, guns.

A second permanent feature of a capitalist system is its economic freedom. It includes freedom of enterprise, the right of individuals and firms to enter any markets they choose and to conduct their own operations as successfully as their abilities, resources, and even luck allow them. Conversely, consumers have the freedom to buy the products they prefer and to reject those they do not, if they have the money to pay for their purchases. Similarly, employees are free to pick the employment they find most suitable, if they are adequately qualified for it and willing to accept the wages offered.

Another element of capitalism is its reliance upon competition instead of government planning as the primary means of allocating resources. This allocation takes place in the marketplace, where the exchange of privately owned goods and/or services occurs. There an economic unit, such as an individual or a firm, offers to supply goods or services in exchange for the products or services of others or, as is more likely in a complex society, for their equivalent value in money, with the monetary value being established by the price (i.e., the information) of the item. Whereas at one time markets involved hand-to-hand transactions, as one might see at a supermarket, modern markets span the globe, involving billions of transactions every hour.

The debate over the proper role and scope of government has staged a resurgence in the 1970s, '80s, and '90s in America, beginning with the deregulation movement, in which government agencies exercised less control than they did earlier over certain activities. Trucking and airlines, for example, were deregulated in the late 1970s and early 1980s; some banking functions were deregulated in the 1980s and early 1990s; and so on. City governments have handed over large segments of work previously done by the private sector, such as garbage collection in Ohio, education in New England, or fire protection in Arizona. The movement to privatize has only started, and in the 1980s cities undertook experiments to contract private education firms to take over floundering public school systems and states contracted prison administration to private firms.[24]

On the national level, however, the U.S. government has moved slowly in yielding power, either to states or to private organizations. By 1985, the U.S. government's expenditures absorbed a whopping 23.9 percent of GNP.[25] The bad news was that that number represented a peacetime high—it had dropped to under 23 percent by 1989 through economic growth—but the good news was that the federal government's share of GNP remained far lower than the share other countries' governments consumed of their national product. In the Netherlands, for example, transfers and subsidies *alone* accounted for 37 percent of the gross domestic product (GDP, a measure equivalent to GNP that measures what is produced in a country, including the output of foreign companies residing in the home country but excluding income earned abroad) in the period 1978–1992! But in America a shift that reduced government's activities in the economy started in the 1980s and accelerated in the 1990s. In 1994, for example, members of the Democratic party, which had created Social Security in 1935 during the New Deal, called for a reconsideration of the program before the Social Security fund went bankrupt. That same year, the Republican party's "Contract with America," signed by all of the victorious Republican members of the House of Representatives (and accepted by several Democrats who switched parties after the election), contained numerous provisions for scaling down government's role in all aspects of American life. And in his 1996 State of the Union message, even Democratic President Bill Clinton admitted "the era of big government is over."

In America's business history, most—if not all—of these characteristics of capitalism were in place when the first colonists arrived, although capitalism as an economic system did not appear until the eighteenth century. But many of the fundamentals of capitalism, especially private property rights, had been well established when the first colonists landed at Jamestown in 1607. Their arrival owed much to economic beliefs prevalent in Europe and England that predated Smith's exposition on capitalism, so that is where our focus will turn.

THE ECONOMICS OF BUSINESS

Comparative Advantage

PERHAPS NONE OF ADAM SMITH'S CONCEPTS was as simple and yet as confusing as the notion of comparative advantage. Rich nations usually enjoyed an *absolute advantage* over others. However, there would be no reason for wealthier nations to trade with poorer nations if not for comparative advantage. In the most simple example, consider an attorney who is also able to type. The attorney earns $150 an hour for his legal expertise, but typists earn only $8.50 an hour. However, the typist has not studied law and cannot perform legal services. Therefore, it would be irrational for the attorney to spend time typing reports and briefs when a typist could do it. By hiring a typist for $8.50, the attorney is gaining $141.50 per hour; but most important, the division of labor allows each person to perform to his highest level of training and expertise.

At the national level, comparative advantage must be measured using a common denominator, which is what makes the concept somewhat tricky, like fractions in math. One way to standardize measurement is to use labor costs. Assume the following labor hours required to produce 1 unit:

	U.S.	INDIA
1 unit of wheat	3	6
1 unit of cloth	6	8

The United States has an absolute advantage in both products—it can grow wheat or make cloth more efficiently than India can. But it takes twice as much labor for the United States to produce cloth instead of wheat (6/3 = 2), while for India it takes only 1 1/3 more labor (8/6 = 4/3 = 1 1/3). Thus, the United States has a comparative advantage in wheat, while India has a comparative advantage in cloth.

When there is no diversification, an inevitable *underutilization* of skills and talents takes place. Return to the attorney/typist analogy: If the attorney did his own typing, he would not be serving his fellow man as well as he could, although he still would be serving to the tune of $8.50 an hour. But that also would deprive a typist—who could not do the attorney's job—of work (or of serving others). By typing himself, the attorney cheats himself of income, robs the typist of work, and deprives society of the service that (in this case) only he can perform. Note that this is true regardless of the motive of the attorney in doing his own typing; others suffer when talents and skills are underutilized.

Notes

1. "Breathe Right: Inventor's Story," inside Breathe Right boxes.

2. Adam Smith, *An Inquiry into the Nature and Causes of the Wealth of Nations,* ed. R. H. Campbell and A. S. Skinner, 2 vols. (1776, reprint, Indianapolis, Ind: Liberty Classics, 1981).

3. Adam Smith, *A Theory of Moral Sentiments,* quoted in ibid., 5.

4. Recent assessment's of the Church's position on "just price" appear in Robert B. Ekelund, Jr., et al., *Sacred Trust: The Medieval Church as an Economic Firm* (New York: Oxford University Press, 1996).

5. Say's theories can be found in Henry W. Spiegel, *The Growth of Economic Thought* (New York: Prentice-Hall, 1971), 260, and in C. Joseph Pusateri, *A History of American Business,* 2d ed. (Arlington Heights, Ill.: Harlan-Davidson, 1988), 6–7.

6. Jonathan R. T. Hughes, *The Vital Few: The Entrepreneurs and American Economic Progress,* 2d ed. (New York: Oxford University Press, 1986).

7. Gifford Pinchot III, *Intrapreneuring: Why You Don't Have to Leave the Corporation to Become an Entrepreneur* (New York: Harper & Row, 1985).

8. George Gilder, *Wealth and Poverty* (New York: Basic Books, 1981), 262.

9. In addition to the above cited *Wealth and Poverty,* see Gilder's *Recapturing the Spirit of Enterprise* (San Francisco: ICS Press, 1992).

10. Michael Novak, *The Spirit of Democratic Capitalism* (New York: American Enterprise Institute, 1982).

11. See, for example, Richard Heilbroner, *The Making of Economic Society,* 8th ed., (Englewood Cliffs, N.J.: Prentice-Hall, 1989); Joseph Scotchie, ed., *The Vision of Richard Weaver* (New Brunswick, N. J.: Transaction, 1995); and Daniel Bell, *The Cultural Contradictions of Capitalism,* 20th anniversary ed. (New York: Basic Books, 1996).

12. The example actually is appropriate: In 1995, most major video-game arcades in the nation experienced substantial losses, with many reporting business down by 15 percent or more. Some of the largest chains went out of business entirely. Even the Prodigy "Video Games Bulletin Board" manager Steve Forbis featured a topic in 1996 called "Trouble in Arcadia." See January and February 1996 issues of *Next Generation* computer magazine for details on the malaise in the industry.

13. Stuart Bruchey's definitions appear in his "Introduction" of his edited volume, *Small Business in American Life* (New York: Columbia University Press, 1980), 4.

14. John Kenneth Galbraith, *The New Industrial State* (Boston: Houghton-Mifflin, 1979 [1967]). Also see his *The Affluent Society,* 3d ed. (Boston: Houghton-Mifflin, 1976).

15. Max Weber, *The Protestant Ethic and the Spirit of Capitalism,* trans. Talcott Parsons (New York: Charles Scribner's Sons, 1958 [1904–05]).

16. Eklund, et al., *Sacred Trust,* passim.

17. Thomas Sowell, *Race and Culture: A World View* (New York: Basic Books, 1994).

18. Ibid., 47 and passim. Also see his *Economics and Politics of Race: An International Perspective* (New York: William Morrow, 1983).

19. Frederick K. C. Price, *High Finance: God's Financial Plan, Tithes and Offerings* (Tulsa, Okla: Harrison House, 1982). Price notes, for example: that as a tax collector Matthew was well off financially; that Peter, James, and John had fishing fleets with employees, that apparently the disciples traveled with a considerable amount of cash on them because they needed a treasurer to hold the "bag"; and that Judas stole from the bag for more than three years without anyone noticing.

20. Paul Johnson, *A History of Christianity* (New York: Athaneum, 1976), 195, 216.

21. Christine Rider, *An Introduction to Economic History* (Cincinnati, Ohio: South-Western Publishing Company, 1995), 37. Again, some of this interpretation is challenged by Ekelund, et al., in *Sacred Trust,* who argue that the Church merely used economic doctrine to maximize its own monopoly status, but that process in turn fostered a heightened level of entrepreneurial activity.

22. References for each of these stories will appear in the more developed sections discussing each individual throughout the book. In general, however, see Joseph J. Fucini and Suzy Fucini, *Entrepreneurs: The Men and Women behind Famous Brand Names and How They Made It* (Boston: G. K. Hall, 1985), as well as Robert Sobel and David B. Sicilia, *Entrepreneurs: An American Adventure* (Boston: Houghton-Mifflin, 1986).

23. Robert Ringer, *Winning through Intimidation* (Los Angeles: Los Angeles Book Corp., 1974).

24. Randall Fitzgerald, *When Government Goes Private: Successful Alternatives to Public Services* (New York: Universe Books, 1988).

25. Several sources discuss these trends, dissecting the data in different ways. See Henry R. Nau, *The Myth of America's Decline* (New York: Oxford University Press, 1992); Ben Wattenberg, *The First Universal Nation* (New York: Free Press, 1991); and Edwin S. Rubenstein, *The Right Data* (New York: National Review, 1994).

CHAPTER 2

European Settlement and Business Enterprise in the New World

CHRISTOPHER COLUMBUS HAS RECEIVED CONSIDERABLE CREDIT FROM historians as a navigator, sailor, captain, and leader. But few writers ever have viewed him as an entrepreneur. Columbus did not risk his own funds, wisely using "OPM" ("other people's money"), but in many other ways Columbus was the quintessential entrepreneur. He had a vision, resting on a faith that lucrative trade routes to China lay due west. He planned a project, then convinced investors to support it—King Ferdinand and Queen Isabella of Spain. Columbus efficiently organized and outfitted an expedition, managed it on the high seas, and produced a decent profit in the process.

The voyages of discovery, highlighted by Columbus's arrival in the New World, sparked an international competition among major European powers for the wealth of the Americas. That competition marked a transition period between the feudal economies of the Middle Ages and the birth of modern capitalism. Starting with the appearance of the "commercial revolution" that surfaced in Venice, Genoa, and other Italian cities as early as A.D. 1000, trade expanded to cities such as Barcelona, Marseilles, and especially Flanders, whose indigenous cloth industry imbued it with substantial advantages over competitors. Cities lured peasants from their back-breaking labor on feudal lands and allowed them to disappear from their lords' view by fading into large populations, then brought them into the commercial economy through guilds. The cities already had started to encourage division of labor and the use of money instead of the barter system found in the countryside. At the same time, the cities provided permanent markets that ended the practice of holding regular "fairs," where goods could be traded. Those two forces—erosion of the feudal control over labor and creation of permanent markets—effectively ended the old systems wherein lords extracted labor without pay. Yet if the nobility lost influence, the appearance of cities would not have been possible without the security provided by increasingly powerful monarchs, who stabilized the economies by ensuring relatively safe trade routes, enforcement of basic property rights, and freedom from invasion. And technology proved as critical as political stability: New productive methods related to introduction of better plows and yokes helped farmers generate surpluses that permitted economic expansion.

Economic Life in Transition

During the 1300s, Europe experienced a succession of famines brought on by poor harvests, while, beginning in 1337, France and England engaged in a hundred-year-long conflict that resulted in each nation strengthening its national unity. As a result, trade suffered. Business activity in Europe also declined due to the Black Death, which swept the continent in midcentury, killing more than one-third of the population. (England witnessed an even sharper decline of almost 40 percent.) The demographic crisis spawned a period of lawlessness, as bandits and pirates inhibited commerce and discouraged investment.

By the 1400s, though, trade revived, and merchants devised new tools for facilitating the exchange of goods and services, not the least of which was the *bill of exchange.* Until bills of exchange appeared, the only money accepted by most merchants, especially at long distances from the purchaser's home, was gold or silver coin. Coin's heavy weight, however, made it difficult and unsafe to carry. In the late 1100s, the Italian trading cities pioneered paper promissory notes called bills of exchange, which the seller accepted from the purchaser and which were convertible into gold or silver upon demand at the purchaser's city. Bills of exchange carried a future date, after which the seller could present the notes for collection. Over time, merchants extended the bills' payment date for a small fee (still hesitating to call it "interest").

Armed with bills of exchange, an early banking establishment emerged in Italian cities, led by families such as the Bardi, Ricardi, Peruzzi, Frescobaldi, and Medici. Italian influence spread as far north as England, with traders following the papal tax collectors to gain a virtual monopoly over the wool trade there by 1300. Italian traders had the benefit of good port cities—particularly Venice—and a central location in the Mediterranean, then the nexus of most seaborne commerce. But Italian merchants, especially in England, also had the good sense to provide generous loans to English royalty, leaving them in a protected position until the Hundred Years' War, when they failed to extend further credit to the king.[1] The Italian merchants also pioneered another business innovation, *dual entry bookkeeping,* developed in the 1300s. The foundation for all modern accounting, wherein transactions are arranged into credits and debits, dual entry bookkeeping owed much to Luca Pacioli, an Italian who wrote one of the earliest texts on accounting in 1494.[2]

When the Crown evicted the Italians from England, English businesses filled the vacuum. In the early 1300s, a group of wool merchants formed the Company of the Staple to compete with the Mediterranean houses. Although lacking in most of the characteristics associated with modern corporations—unlimited life and limited liability—the Company of the Staple illustrated how rapidly European business institutions adapted and innovated. It received a formal monopoly on the wool trade emanating from England for the promise of regular loans to the Crown. Quickly, other English merchants formed consortia, the most significant of which emerged from businessmen in Bristol, who managed to enlist the entire town in their enterprise.

The Bristol merchants rapidly stretched their routes and diversified their products from wool and clothing to fish, coal, wine, and iron. Their connections to Iceland, and the lucrative fishing market they had tapped, led them to examine still other supplies of fish further west, dispatching ships in the 1480s to explore west of Iceland near Newfoundland. The information they brought back proved valuable to other explorers interested in transatlantic trade.

Exploration and Entrepreneurs

Several historical forces combined to make overseas exploration more profitable and desirable. First, new technologies, brought through trade with the Arabs, as well as European breakthroughs led to advances in sailing. Astrolabes—circular devices with a pivoted limb that measured a beam of sunlight through a sight against the horizon, establishing the sun's altitude above the horizon—were introduced in the 800s and soon made their way to Spain.[3] The Vikings introduced new methods of hull construction, enabling the vessels to withstand violent ocean storms. States of the Hanseatic League on the Baltic coast experimented with larger ship designs capable of carrying heavy cargoes and utilizing sternpost rudders for better control; triangular and lateen sails were incorporated after the Crusades, making it possible to sail a vessel at an angle. Improved ships, however, would have had difficulty reaching new destinations without the appearance of accurate maps, generated by the Arabs and Italians—and accelerated by the inquisitive character of the Renaissance.

Second, political changes coincided with the search for treasure and advances in shipbuilding technologies. After ambitious European monarchs had started to consolidate their possessions into cohesive dynastic states, the funding available to expeditions increased, and military protection (in the form of soldiers on board the ships) was provided free to investors. Capital, combined with improved sailing technology, made it possible for Europeans to consider voyages of much longer duration, stimulating a new generation of explorers who found that monarchs would support more expensive undertakings that integrated the monarch's interests with economic reward.[4]

Third, by the 1500s the Protestant Reformation had fostered a fierce, and often bloody, competition between Catholic and Protestant countries, as well as among Protestant countries themselves, for power and territory that reinforced the infant nationalism. England competed for land with Spain, not merely for economic and political reasons but because it was distasteful to consider the possibility that Spain might "Catholicize" non-Christians (and Catholics thought the same of yielding natives to Protestant "heretics"). Therefore, even in the face of marginal economic or political gains for discovery and colonization, strong religious incentives spurred monarchs to open their royal treasuries.

Those three factors explained the sudden burst of exploratory fervor that swept the European nations in the period 1400–1600. Portugal took an early lead, thanks to the efforts of Prince Henry the Navigator, an eccentric who lived as a recluse in Sagres, where he trained navigators and mapmakers.[5] Henry's Portuguese explorers concentrated on finding routes around Africa to the East, unlike the Genoese Columbus, who persuaded Spanish royalty to outfit a three-ship expedition to sail westward in 1492. Columbus embodied the best traits of the new generation of navigators: He had resilience, fearlessness, vision, and the courage to demand obedience when all other leadership skills failed. To be sure, Columbus sought glory, and, as a religious man, he was "earnestly desirous of taking Christianity to heathen lands."[6] Yet Columbus was also an entrepreneur who persuaded investors to support his mission. Risking his reputation as a sailor and even his life at the hands of a mutinous crew, Columbus put on his managerial hat at sea, allocating scarce resources and maintaining efficiency within his small fleet.

Columbus arrived at Watling Island in the Bahamas in October 1492, then continued on to Cuba, where, convinced he had reached Cathay (China), he dispatched emissaries into the interior to contact the Great Kahn! Columbus found none of the spices, jewels, silks, or other evidence of Cathay, and although he received no response from the Kahn, he returned to Spain confident he had found an ocean passage to the Orient.

Over the ensuing fifty years, subsequent Spanish expeditions conquered Mexico and Latin America. They failed to find the legendary "seven cities of gold" but discovered enough wealth in mines to encourage still further exploration. With the mines in operation, a flood of bullion sailed eastward for Spanish vaults, where, uninvested, it entered general circulation, causing inflation. By that time, the English—who trailed Portugal and Spain in overseas exploration—realized that they could take gold directly from the Iberian vessels as easily as they could mine it themselves. A burst of pirate activity enveloped the "Spanish Main" by the mid-1500s, with Sir John Hawkins and Sir Francis Drake gaining repute as looters. And clearly profitable returns existed for such activities: In a single mission lasting from 1577 to 1580, Drake earned 4,500 percent on his investment in ships and sailors.[7]

The piracy against Spain had two effects on the early business history of America. First, it severely curtailed interest among potential Spanish colonists to go to the New World. Over the long term, that constituted a substantial advantage for the English in their attempt to dominate North America. Second, the very fact that they could steal such vast sums meant that the English knew that they had only scratched the tip of the iceberg; they then concluded that their own colonies might produce similar wealth.

Sir Walter Raleigh was among the first English to see the potential returns of colonization. He received a royal charter in 1584 to plant a settlement in Roanoke, North Carolina. Utilizing the marketing methods of the day, Raleigh enlisted Richard Hackloit, whose *Discourse Concerning Western Planting* (1584) lured investors with promises of acquiring the Spanish West Indies trade, eliminating Spanish middlemen. That Raleigh's Roanoke colony, planted in 1587, vanished with only the cryptic message, "Croatoan" carved into a tree, did not deter adventurers from arriving in the New World.

England and the Foundations for Business Success in the New World: A Hypothesis

Even as Raleigh's Roanoke colony failed, England had laid the foundations for business success in the New World. Within fifty years after the first British colonies were planted, they equaled any Spanish, Portuguese, or French colony in the Americas. Why?

What follows is hardly original and is taken from the work of Nathan Rosenberg and L. E. Birdsell, Jack Goldstone, and David Landes. While it is conceivable that English colonies prospered simply due to luck, the dominance of Europe in general and England in particular—a tiny island with few natural resources—suggests that specific factors can be identified as the reasons for the rise of an English-Atlantic civilization, including the appearance of new business practices and structures and the presence of a climate receptive to risk-taking and innovation.

One of the most obvious areas in which England surpassed other nations was in its business practices. The threat of incurring substantial losses during the establishment of the English colonies in the Americas could have strangled most of the early efforts if not for another innovation of business (and law), the *joint-stock company*. Sole proprietorships and partnerships both suffered from a common problem, that of unlimited liability. The individual was liable to creditors for all the debts of the business, even to the extent that personal assets were subject to confiscation by creditors for debts owed. Likewise, even a minor partner was liable for the debts of a majority partner if a business collapsed. In either case, potential investors often shied away from any but the most secure investments, and middle-class investors avoided putting their personal assets at risk in any involvement in a business that might sour. But joint-stock companies had *limited liability,* under which investors stood to lose only what they put into the enterprise. Suddenly, limited liability freed vast new pools of capital, opening risky ventures to middle-class merchants who, though making a living in other endeavors, wanted to put their small amounts of capital to work. In England, the abbreviation "Ltd.," and in America, "Inc." indicated that a company had limited liability as a corporation.

Joint-stock companies also achieved a degree of permanence, because they did not end with the death of the proprietor. Instead, shares of stock simply changed hands. Thus the joint-stock company solved simultaneously the problems overseas expeditions faced of raising capital and ensuring stability over time. A number of joint-stock companies formed between 1500 and 1600, including the Levant Company (1592) and the Dutch East India Company (1600), facilitating a burst of overseas trade and colonization.

A second factor, a climate receptive to risk-taking, contributed to the early success of the West in general and the English colonies in particular. Joel Mokyr has argued that "Political and mental diversity combined to create an ever-changing panorama of technologically creative societies."[8] While that climate permeated all of Europe, it reached its most advanced state in England. It is important to note that key inventions and technologies appeared in non-Western countries first; yet they were seldom, if ever, employed in such a way as to change society dramatically until applied by Western societies. The stirrup, for example, was known as early as A.D. 400–500 in the Middle East. But it took until 730, when Charles Martel's mounted knights used it in cavalry charges, to change combat on a permanent basis.[9] Something other than mere invention was at work. As one economic historian put it, "The West did not overtake the East merely by becoming more efficient at making bridles and stirrups, but by developing steam engines . . . [and] by taking unknown risks on novelty."[10] Stability of the state, the rule of law, and a willingness to accept new or foreign ideas rather than ruthlessly suppress them proved vital to entrepreneurship, invention, and technical innovation. In societies dominated by the state, scientists risked their lives if they arrived at unacceptable answers.

Third, by the 1600s, property rights had become so firmly established as a basis for English economic activities that its rules sifted through to the lowest classes in society. The combination of freedom from royal retribution in science and technology and the right to retain the fruit of one's labor—even intellectual property—gave England a substantial advantage in the colonization process over rivals that had more than a century head start.[11]

Historian William McNeill has suggested that an appreciation for competition played a central role in the drive by various European states to surpass each other. The multitude of small city-states, especially in Italy, led to the adoption of a "free market" of ideas; and any planner or merchant who could improve the lot of the city was rewarded. As economist E. L. Jones notes, "The general explanation of change lies at the intersection of technological change, increasing market size, and the ambitions of a system of nation-states."[12] Jones credits the "organisational change associated with the growth of the market" combined with the nation-states' establishment of "stable conditions necessary for expanding development and growth, for the diffusion of the best practices in technology and commerce, and in several countries for the actual founding of manufactories where there only had been handicrafts."[13] Both concepts—state competition and private markets—had deeply ingrained themselves into the English psyche by the age of colonization.

Mercantilism: The Merger of Business and Government

The rapid appearance of the joint-stock companies, which received charters from the king, fit well with the new economic doctrine of *mercantilism*. Spain and Portugal had practiced mercantilism since the early 1500s, but not until 1620, when Thomas Mun elaborated the theory, was it applied by England. Mercantilism rested on the premise that the individual entrepreneur existed to serve the needs of the state. It contained three basic concepts: (1) all wealth in the world was limited or fixed, because wealth consisted only of gold, silver, and precious gems; (2) for a nation to improve its position among other nations, it had to obtain gold and silver, preferably through a "favorable balance of trade"; and (3) the government should regulate the nation's production and investment through a series of tariffs and subsidies, enforced at ports and harbors by having all goods travel in (in Mun's case) British ships. With wealth fixed, as Mun suggested, all economic activities resulted in a "zero-sum game," with a winner and loser—a concept that made even Mun uncomfortable.

Monarchs, naturally, approved of mercantilism, and where they achieved "total control over the nobility . . . and where the commercial class remained weak, mercantilism remained in its earliest, bullionist phase."[14] Spain and Portugal engaged in little more than resource extraction from Mexico and Latin America. In England and Holland, however, business simply moved beyond the ability of the government to direct all its activities. Although the search for gold and silver still dominated the agendas of English colonies in the New World, new incentives for exploration in North America appeared, including a rising demand for furs, particularly beaver fur for hats. Eleven English joint-stock companies formed between 1606 and 1630, most of them with the aim of establishing a fur (and, of secondary importance, fish) trade in Canada and the northeastern North American seaboard.

English Business in Colonial America

The most significant of the English joint-stock companies in the New World, the Virginia Company, was established in 1606 after receiving a grant from James I for land in North America. Two subsidiary companies emerged: the London Company, based in Bristol, and the Plymouth Company, located in Plymouth, each with its own grant of land from the Virginia Company. Territory under the grant to the London Company received the name "Virginia" in honor of Queen Elizabeth (the "Virgin Queen"), while the Plymouth Company's grant encompassed New England. The London Company organized its expedition first, sending three ships and 144 settlers to establish a trading colony designed to live off the land and extract wealth for shipment back to England. In April 1607 twenty-six-year-old captain John Smith piloted the fleet 50 miles up the James River, where the settlers established the triangle-shaped "James Forte," or Jamestown, on low-lying, swampy land.

Jamestown's investors—who had stayed in England—quickly learned that they had misread the opportunities for business in America. Rather than producing profits, the colony produced starvation. It had few of the advantages found in the established Asian port cities, which had served as the model for the London investors, and none of the Far Eastern existing markets for trade. Worse, the settlers had come from the ranks of adventurers, who drifted into endless searches for precious metals and refused any agricultural work until provisions dwindled. By then it was too late. Fewer than 40 of the 120 settlers saw the second winter, and so few survived that Smith noted the living "were scarce able to bury the dead." Smith, burdened with soldiers and gold seekers, pleaded with the London Company to send "30 carpenters, husbandmen, gardeners, fishermen, blacksmiths, masons and diggers up of trees . . . [instead of] a thousand of such as we have. . . ."[15] Smith saved the colony by imposing military-style discipline, issuing the biblical edict, "he who will not work will not eat," with the resulting society briefly resembling a regiment more than a commune.

Had tobacco not come along, Jamestown would have disappeared. Instead, the colony stumbled onto perhaps the single product—perfectly suited to the climate—that it could grow in mass quantities. A market already existed. Columbus had reported Cuban natives rolling tobacco leaves, lighting them on fire, and sticking them in a nostril. By 1612, when John Rolfe cured tobacco, the English had refined the custom by using a pipe or smoking the tobacco directly by mouth. Characterized by King James as a "vile and stinking . . . custom," tobacco smoking gained still wider popularity in England through the promotions of Walter Raleigh. Jamestown, and the London Company, had a product and a market. What they did not have was a labor force.

After the "starving time" of 1609–1610, when the colonists, barricaded within James Forte, ate dogs, cats, rats, toadstools, horsehides, and even human corpses, a new influx of settlers arrived. Many of them had received stock from the company as an incentive to migrate to Virginia. Free passage, in the form of "indentures," awaited anyone willing to work for seven years upon reaching the New World. By 1617, however, the London Company needed still more laborers, and it offered a grant of 100 acres of land to any freeman who would migrate to America. The company also shipped over 100 young women to the colony as potential wives, seeking to make the men "more settled." Within a short time, the policy of giving land to encourage immigration, called *headright,* not only offered every head of a household 50 acres for himself but also an additional 50 acres for every adult family member or servant who came with the male family head.

The headright policy had an ironic effect: Tobacco cultivation encouraged expansion, requiring large numbers of laborers, who were enticed to migrate in return for land. But the land made the immigrants free and left them in a position to demand higher wages. It soon became clear to employers, in Virginia and elsewhere, that unless they paid high wages, a laborer might sing the old Johnny Paycheck song at any time, "Take This Job 'n' Shove It!" Later, that dynamic produced a self-reinforcing cycle for business, but at the time the effect was more immediate. Virginians needed laborers, and they could not pay free workers enough (or simply could not entice enough immigrants to move to America) to supply the needed labor. They turned, therefore, to slaves.

In 1619 a Dutch ship brought some 20 black slaves to Virginia, introducing a status into the American English colonies that previously had not existed. Yet overall, the legal status of the first blacks in America remains murky. Historian Edmund Morgan, in *American Slavery, American Freedom,* contended that the first blacks had the same legal status as white indentured servants.[16] Indeed, the presence of so many new documents around 1800 prohibiting slaves from purchasing their freedom suggests that this status was commonplace. White colonists apparently did not distinguish blacks from other servants in their minds, releasing them at the end of their indentures. Rather than viewing blacks as a source of unlimited labor, English colonists preferred European indentured servants well into the 1670s, even when they came from the ranks of criminals taken from English jails. But by the 1660s, the colonists had altered their attitudes toward blacks dramatically, viewing them as permanent servants. In 1664, slavery was declared hereditary in most southern colonies.

Thus, the abundance of America and the high wages demanded by laborers forced planters (and other businessmen in the South) into an early choice. Instead of restructuring their businesses based on market principles, they invoked the power of government to change the condition of an entire race. Such behavior by businesses was not surprising, and Adam Smith had warned that businessmen—like anyone else— would seek advantages from government whenever possible. But neither the Crown nor Parliament stepped in to enforce the "rights of Englishmen" for the black indentured servants whose status had just been changed. (English planters had settled in the West Indies, where they established large sugar plantations using slaves in the harshest work.)

Both tobacco and rice production required large labor forces, and both products found large European markets by the 1700s. At a penny a pound, rice was almost as profitable as tobacco when shipped in large quantities, but the location of the coastal paddies and its oppressive climate in the summer caused many of the planters to reside further inland and leave the administration of the slaves to overseers. As for tobacco, the monopolies on the English market granted to the colonial planters ensured success and substantial wealth. Production soared, from half a million pounds annually in 1627 to 15 million pounds by 1670. Despite thirty years of stagnant tobacco prices, production of tobacco hovered at approximately 28 million pounds per year in the late 1600s. Then prices took off again, and tobacco accounted for almost half of "the total value of colonial commodity exports in 1750."[17]

Planters constituted the backbone of the early southern economy, although they often had a wide range of businesses beyond agriculture.

Tobacco grower William Byrd, for example, had substantial estates by 1700; but he also had commercial activities, including trade with the Indians, an import/export business, and a labor-supply service that employed a slaver. In 1687, he was appointed auditor of the Public Accounts of Virginia and receiver-general of the colony, which required him to hold funds collected from the quit rents and to collect and hold the tobacco tax. Likewise, Byrd's son, William Byrd II, was not a pure entrepreneur. Well educated, he chose to abandon formal schooling as an apprentice in a Dutch business house, where he studied commercial exchanges and international trade. He inherited his father's estate in 1704 and could have simply retired on the wealth he received had he sold the Virginia properties. Instead, he went to America to run the plantation.

There, he plunged into daily management of the estate, which produced corn, wheat, hay, fruits, vegetables, livestock, and lumber.[18] Byrd's estate, like other early plantations, was self-sufficient. Located on—or close to—rivers, the early tobacco growers received regular visits from merchant ships that bought their products and sold utensils and basic supplies. Byrd, however, did not passively preside over a manor; instead, he worked the business daily, rising at five or six o'clock to start his management rounds, caring for sick slaves, investigating the condition of the crops, testing the soil, and bargaining with tobacco factors or merchants. As his letter books make clear, Byrd knew his business well. But in addition to his estate-related activities, Byrd engaged in land surveying and sales, exploring a tract of territory in North Carolina, eventually acquiring 20,000 acres. In another transaction, he received a grant of 105,000 acres tax free on the condition that he populate it with at least one family per 1,000 acres. Colonists in his territories might, "with the help of Moderate Industry, pass their time very happily. . . . Besides grazing and Tillage, which would abundantly compensate their Labour, they might plant Vineyards upon the Hills," as well as "Hemp, Flax and Cotton, in what quantity they pleas'd." In short, he astutely observed, "every thing will grow plentifully here to supply either the Wants or Wantonness of Man."[19]

Despite their often ostentatious mansions and expansive tracts, some of the southern planters lived on the verge of bankruptcy, dependent on the monopoly-supported price of tobacco, rice, and indigo to sustain them. The plantation culture of the South owed much to early incentives by the English government to tobacco cultivation, and when tobacco prices fell, the planters felt the effects in a number of ways. Had the early tobacco incentives not existed at all, it is possible that the South may have diversified even more.

No area of diversification offered better returns than speculation in land. Land purchase and sale became a common means of gaining quick wealth or experiencing a sudden plunge into poverty. Land-speculating planters were not just looking for new lands on which to raise tobacco but sought large parcels that they could sell rapidly to others at a handsome profit. Between 1743 and 1760, for example, Virginia awarded three million acres of land in its Appalachian West to individual speculators and to others organized in joint-stock companies. Certainly no one epitomized the planter/land speculator better than George Washington, whose Mount Vernon plantation generated a romantic legend but yielded a slight income for its master. Washington, branching out into a variety of activities, was a tobacco factor; exported flour; imported and sold finished goods; ran a fishery; and, of course, bought and sold land in the West. At times, Washington even operated a ferry boat service and a distillery.[20]

Still, for most people land represented a means to an end—tobacco. The "noxious weed's" dominance resulted in yet another development in the southern economy, namely the reliance on middlemen, first, sea captains or agents of English mercantile houses, then later a specialized intermediary called a *factor*. Middlemen often were English or northerners, leaving the planters somewhat dependent on outsiders for transacting sales and distributing their products. In the short term, that probably contributed to the slow development of a strata of southern business professionals; in the long term, it fanned fears of attempts by northern businesses to "subjugate" the South. Those fears were not groundless, but a southern merchant class did develop, although at different rates in different colonies. As two historians of American business observed, "The Carolina merchant, more so than the Virginian, appears to have developed as an entity separate from that of the planter" by the time of the Revolution.[21] Perceptions that the middlemen and factors took more than their "fair share," however, spurred planters to assume the role of factor or middleman whenever possible, leading a number of planters into private banking activities.[22] Agricultural businesses such as indigo and rice production required extensive contacts with intermediaries from other cities, regions, and even abroad. Even as dependence on agriculture steered the South away from traditional lines of commercial development, it nevertheless integrated the southern economy and its entrepreneurs with the rest of the world.

Colonization and Business in the North

A second joint-stock company, the Plymouth Company, formed with a much different purpose than that of the London Company, resulted from the efforts of a group of Scrooby Protestants called Puritans. More than 100 of the separatists had left England for Holland in 1608, where they hoped to practice their religion more freely. Soon, however, they grew dissatisfied with Dutch society and sought to move to the New

World. One of the proprietors of the Virginia Company, Sir Edwin Sandys, gave them a grant to settle on the northernmost boundary of the Virginia grant, near the mouth of the Hudson River. To raise capital, the Puritans—by then called "Pilgrims" because of their wanderings— utilized the joint-stock structure to enlist numerous non-Puritans in their colony. In September 1620 they arrived at Cape Cod Bay, at an area called "Plymouth."

Other Puritans followed, including a group that gained control of the business known as the Massachusetts Bay Company (1629). As with the Plymouth colony, the Massachusetts Bay colony intended to find religious freedom in the New World. It also intended that the colonists, who were stockholders, make a profit. That situation differed starkly from that of the Virginia Company, where the stockholders had remained in England, and it produced enough friction that the early immigrants complained about the interference of English businessmen who did not understand the conditions in North America.[23] Every colonist had an economic stake in the performance of the company. Politically, the transfer of authority from England to Massachusetts had enormous consequences. All governors acted *rex in abstentia,* meaning their edicts carried the authority of the king. But locating the management of the Massachusetts Bay Company in America tied the governor (in that case, John Winthrop) to the New World instead of the Old. Furthermore, it allowed the colonists a framework in which they could govern themselves. And, from a business perspective, the move showed an appreciation for the difficulty of managing a colony from thousands of miles away, especially lacking modern communications technology. Thus, the Massachusetts experience heralded a principle institutionalized after the "managerial revolution" of the mid-1800s, namely that management worked more efficiently as it drew closer to the productive activity of the business.

Also unlike the Virginia settlers, the Puritans prospered at the outset, possibly because they, as stockholders, *were* the entrepreneurs. They took advantage of the area's natural timber, fishing, and abundant furs, as well as, of course, farming. Fishing represented one of the first, and most natural, occupations in colonies along the North Atlantic. In 1631, the Puritan leader and governor of the Massachusetts Bay Colony, John Winthrop, launched the first colonial-made fishing vessel. New England fishermen rapidly established themselves as formidable competitors, developing techniques that allowed them to preserve cod and mackerel with salt for export to Europe. Although the business was seasonal, it produced a reliable source of gold and silver coin, providing a mainstay of American colonial enterprise. By the time of the Revolution, fishing comprised up to 90 percent of Massachusetts' exports to the Continent and represented 10 percent of all American exports.

A similar labor-intensive industry, whaling, developed in New Bedford and Nantucket. Dominated at first by the early Puritan fishermen, whaling eventually became the province of numerous Quakers. Whale oil was the cheapest, and most popular, fuel for interior lamps. Catching the leviathans was not easy, however, as Herman Melville explained in his classic adventure tale, *Moby Dick*. Lacking the powerful harpoon guns of later years, colonial whalers had to approach the mammal in a small boat, heave a harpoon into the animal, and hang on for dear life as the whale ran or flailed about, depending on the accuracy of the throw. Many a New Bedford whaler went on a "Nantucket sleighride," in which a dying whale dragged a tiny boat and a handful of terrified men across the water at breakneck speed, or, if they were unlucky, took them down with a fatal dive.

Maritime enterprises generated a boom in ship construction businesses, making the American maritime fleet the third largest in the world by 1776.[24] British competitors grew alarmed at the sudden rise in the merchant sea power of the colonies, commissioning a study of American shipping after the Revolutionary War called *Observation in the Commerce of the American States* (1784) by John Lord Sheffield. American shipyards, Sheffield maintained, had cut into English marine construction, building in 1769 alone 113 ships with topsails and 274 sloops or schooners. Massachusetts alone launched 40 ships with topsails that year, as well as 97 sloops or schooners.

A prime example of an early fishing entrepreneur was George Cabot, whose father, Joseph, had started from scratch to develop a small business. Given the opportunity to attend Harvard, George instead took to the sea as a cabin boy. Gaining experience on the oceans, Cabot was captain of his own vessel by age nineteen, sailing along the eastern seaboard, then on to Spain, where the family had established business connections. Cabot's ship stopped at the major ports, exchanging, buying, and selling goods at each.

With the expansion in ship construction, seagoing trade expanded, opening other lucrative early business opportunities for the New Englanders. Wood products made up the fourth largest category of exported items by 1768, reflecting the fact that the industry had expanded from simply cutting and shipping trees to making a wide assortment of furniture and finished wooden goods, despite attempts by England to restrict the colonies' ability to make finished products. Skilled artisans appeared in cities and towns, becoming small business owners. To facilitate sales abroad, colonial merchants became adept at international trade in woodcraft, iron works, copper and tin products, and other finished goods. American middlemen learned the foreign markets, identified the most profitable regions and cultivated the best customers, and took note of the most important competitors.

Despite the impressive expansion in maritime activities, most New Englanders earned their living from the land instead of the ocean. As Gerald Gunderson points out, "Falling freight rates made it worthwhile to produce for more distant markets, reducing self-sufficiency."[25] Therefore, even the small farms that represented the dominant business activity in the North looked outside their region, and even their shores, for consumers. Farming on a larger scale dominated the South, but unlike the English who settled in Virginia and the Carolinas, northern immigrants adopted inheritance rules that ensured the continuation of small farms. Pennsylvania, under the proprietorship of William Penn, established rules that, while feudal in nature, extended land ownership to individuals on a liberal basis. His use of "quit rents," in which landowners received their holdings for a payment, after which they were "quit and free" of further obligations to the proprietor, made Penn "history's most enlightened feudal lord."[26] Even so, many colonists resisted even the quit rents, providing evidence that even in the 1600s, Americans had started to view property rights in an entirely new context.

Most northern colonies established traditions of dividing the patriarch's land among the living sons. That meant that an estate of 400 acres would be divided into four 100-acre estates if four sons survived the father. Compare that with the South, where the legal tradition of *primogeniture* prevailed. In that case, the entire estate went to the eldest son upon the father's death, leaving other sons to move or become landless employees of the oldest boy. Most tended to move westward, putting constant pressure on Indian tribes and on colonial authorities to restrain them. But even in the North, there was a limit to the division and subdivision of property—40–50 acres was considered the minimum needed for a self-sufficient family farm—forcing sons with small amounts of land to sell their inheritance and move to cities for employment.

Consequently, each section took on a distinct business culture related in no small measure to the land policies it adopted. Large plantations appeared in the South; smaller farms in the North, with the resulting expansion of northern towns and their hubs of commercial activity and scores of mechanics and artisans. The availability of slaves, the profitability of tobacco, then rice and cotton—large "cash crops" grown in vast quantities—further supported the regional differences between the sections over time. And while southern towns had their share of cobblers, barrel-makers, ironworkers, tinsmiths, and other artisans, they did not exist in comparable numbers or concentrations as in New England towns.

Wherever they conducted their business, however, the artisans (or "mechanics," as they were known) included chandlers, tanners, shipwrights, tailors, and coach makers. We can gain a glimpse into the world of those early small businessmen, thanks to Richard Walsh's essay examining Charleston mechanics. Walsh located an army of painters, glaziers, ironwrights, ropemakers, and other independent businesses in the city, some of which dealt with problems scarcely different than those existing today. Even in the 1760s, it appears, businesses had to cope with government environmental regulation, as Charleston candle makers found themselves presented before grand juries on charges that the noxious fumes of boiling tallow constituted a threat to the health of local residents. Most made living wages, and some grew rich, including a cooper whose business expanded to the point that he employed thirty other workers, and the wills of several tanners, shoemakers, and other entrepreneurs revealed that they attained substantial wealth from their enterprises.[27] Whether cabinetmakers or silversmiths, the careers of the mechanics were characterized by a high degree of mobility—both upward and downward—on the ladder of wealth. Much of that mobility arose from the fact that licenses or other regulations did not inhibit ambitious men from expanding their businesses. Carpenters often entered the ranks of architects; house painters entered teaching and otherwise instructed in art; and so on.

Colonial Merchants: Thomas Hancock and Paul Revere

Alongside the mechanics and artisans, a second business group began to emerge in the 1700s, the colonial merchant. Sometimes the lines between the two groups blurred, as in the case of Paul Revere. At other times, the merchant led a distinctly nonartisanal life, as with Thomas Hancock. Those two men, therefore, serve as examples of the variety of entrepreneurial experience in colonial America.

After the 1690s, England reestablished its authority over New England, which to that point had operated with considerable independence under Puritan governors. Until that time, the clergy represented not only the most respected members of society politically but also the upper strata within the economy. Not surprisingly, then, the quintessential colonial merchant, Thomas Hancock (1703–1764), was the second son of a Lexington, Massachusetts, clergyman named John Hancock. Unable to afford a Harvard education for his younger boy, Reverend Hancock placed Thomas in an apprenticeship in Boston with a bookseller. At age twenty-one, after a seven-year apprenticeship in which he learned printing, book binding, sales, and other business skills, Thomas established his own small business, importing his volumes from England and Europe. To acquire books, he purchased and resold maritime products, particularly whale oil, bone, and related products abroad.

Although he expanded from his book business, Hancock did not ignore it. Instead, he solidified his place in the Boston book trade, selling a diverse mix of wares in his stores, acquiring some products on consignment and others in payment for books or other debts. One could find clothes (which constituted more than half his total sales by the 1750s), knives, buttons, and swords, as well as tea, pepper, salt, and other food items. Bins of coal sat next to reams of paper; cloth jackets were draped near leather belts or fur pelts; and ships' compasses and bells hung above the ever present books. Hancock found that many of his customers needed credit, and as he started to supply other merchants, he routinely offered them goods with up to one year to repay with interest. Hancock and other American shop owners also understood that money—especially gold and silver coin—was scarce, making it imperative that businesses deal in credit, consignment, or barter on a regular basis. Hancock's firm used bills of exchange, which circulated domestically in the colonies to allow merchants to draw funds on a business in another section of the country, and which allowed merchants with limited access to gold or silver to acquire products around the world.[28] As business historian John Dobson has noted, "Although Thomas Hancock appears to have been a remarkably successful merchant, his story is by no means unique. Many other colonists rose from humble origins to positions of wealth and influence."[29] Equally famous, but seldom recognized as an entrepreneur, was Paul Revere.

Revere (1735–1818) made himself into the premier silver- and goldsmith in the colonies. His hardware store bought and sold English and American goods, but with a difference: Paul Revere also manufactured the iron, "hinges of Brass," "Sley Bells," "Truck Bells," copper, and silver products he sold.[30] At age sixty-five, when many working Americans think about retirement, Revere embarked on one of the riskiest ventures of his life. He built a rolling mill to produce sheet copper, calling the project "a great undertaking [that] will require every farthing which I can rake or scrape."[31] Using $25,000 of his own savings (a fortune in modern dollars) and a loan of money and 19,000 pounds of copper from the U.S. government, Revere began making rolled sheet copper to plate the sides of the USS *Constitution* in 1803. "Old Ironsides," which ironically resisted cannonballs because it had green, flexible wood, was coated with copper! One hundred years later, a navy lieutenant, conducting a repair of the *Constitution*, identified the very bolts Revere manufactured and proudly reported that they had been "stretched [so that] the elastic limit of the metal had been reached," but, leaving the obvious unstated, not exceeded. The bolts held.[32]

Revere's casting and foundries were unmatched in their craftsmanship and quality. For that reason, Paul Revere received numerous government contracts for items ranging from plates for money to bells and cannon, while the silver flatware that today bears his name was exceptional in its durability and appearance. His firm, managed by the Revere family, survived him and continues to the present. And while Paul Revere was exceptional, the "career path" he followed was not. Rather than resisting change, colonial artisans themselves had started to change their crafts through innovations and inventions that allowed America to industrialize. Both Hancock and Revere aggressively pursued diversification and innovation. Throughout the northeastern seaboard, especially in cities such as Philadelphia, the promise of social mobility and the prod of economic adversity encouraged local entrepreneurs to adopt new products and strategies whenever possible. In the port cities, "under the insistent, reckless, often ruthless urging of merchants and manufacturers, a backward agricultural economy was pushed into the onrushing currents of the Industrial Revolution."[33]

The Ladder of Wealth

Not only did merchants' relentless competition improve the material conditions of the entire society by propelling it into industrialism, it resulted in a highly stratified merchant community in which new entrants rose quickly to wealth while older, less adaptable traders drifted to the bottom. But traders at the top found they could freeze out new entrepreneurs on the bottom, and therefore to remain successful merchants had to stay on the cutting edge of technology and management. Or, as historian Thomas Doerflinger put it, in port areas "opportunity, enterprise, and adversity reinforced each other. A young businessman could borrow money and move into trade, challenging the commercial position of older, more established merchants. His opportunity was, in effect, their adversity."[34]

Doerflinger has suggested that the major urban merchants and large landholders, who represented perhaps 10 percent of the white population, held as much as 65 percent of the personal wealth. Movement up the ladder was rapid, but conservative merchants could lose their wealth just as suddenly. Much more numerous was the colonial middle class, probably constituting about half the white population, which accounted for about 20 percent of the personal wealth. That group included yeoman farmers, small storekeepers, master craftsmen, and a modest number of urban professionals, such as doctors, lawyers, and ministers. Most of those individuals, for all intents and purposes, "were their own bosses" and gained in business and workplace independence whatever they lacked in pure capital. Recall, also, that for farmers and some craftsmen, children were viewed as net assets—not liabilities—and provided a substantial source of unpaid labor and uncounted capital.

Certainly a portion of the population struggled at the bottom. It is unlikely that any but the tiniest percentage of that group ever achieved great wealth.[35] However, it is also safe to say that homelessness and vagrancy were rare, due to the apprenticeship system and stringent laws against "bums." Availability of land meant that no one had to accept his position for long, and indentures and apprenticeships were temporary conditions.[36]

Overall, however, the colonies on the eve of the Revolution were as wealthy—if not more so, per capita—than the mother country. Gary Walton and James Shepherd, among others, have shown that aggregate income for the colonies grew by an annual average of just over 3.4 percent, or about the same rate as the population growth for the colonial period. But the early years of some of the colonies were so dismal that they substantially affected the growth rates overall; per capita incomes in the 1700s rose by perhaps 1 percent per year. Measured in 1991 dollars, colonial per capita incomes have been estimated at $720, and amount that put the colonists of 200 years ago on a par with the privately held wealth of citizens in modern-day Mexico or Turkey. In sum, even those struggling at the lowest rungs on the economic ladder were vastly better off in America than almost anywhere else in the world at the time; and most people of average means *then* were far better off than the masses of people alive in so-called Third World countries in 1999!

Business and Government: Early Relationships

If large divisions in wealth existed in colonial America, and if mobility upward and downward resulted in a constant churning and frothing, virtually all groups at any given time understood one fundamental fact: They alone were responsible for the generation of wealth. Government has almost nothing to do with creating wealth, and little more to do with distributing it. Occasionally merchants such as Hancock had to deal with British agents or customs officials; artisans such as Paul Revere interacted with royal authorities only if they needed to import or export specific items on the "enumerated" list of products required to be shipped to England for reshipment to other countries. Certain of the enumerated goods were subsidized, and others, bound for the colonies, were taxed. Other than those instances, most Americans never saw a representative of the Crown except at tax time. And excepting those items taxed or subsidized in the mercantilist system, from the 1650s to the 1750s government erected few barriers to most enterprises, especially to small businesses.

Government did play a substantial role in the colonial economy of America, but the few edicts coming from London had little effect on average American enterprises. When taxes grew too onerous, as they did on tea, the colonists simply smuggled tea into the nation in huge quantities. More important, the government made no serious attempt to end the smuggling, giving its tacit approval.

The most commonly used—and abused—tool of the king involved the use of charters. Every colony had received a charter, which included a grant permitting the company to conduct business within certain geographic boundaries in North America. From a business perspective, the grants from the Crown entailed a number of problems. Boundaries from one grant tended to overlap others, a difficulty easily understood given the fact that the grants were made before land was surveyed. But it led to conflicts, nonetheless. Colonists frequently battled each other in courts over boundaries, occasionally identified by little more than phrases such as "eastward to the large rock" or "due north to the treeline."

A more serious problem involved the assumption that the royal charters gave the company a monopoly over trade and land transactions in the grant area. Most monopolies, of course, never existed in a practical sense. Enforcement proved impossible. Nevertheless, the longer-term result of implying that charters included monopoly grants was that some critics came to associate charters of all sorts with "special privilege."

Having handed a charter to a joint-stock company, the king looked to the company's English proprietors to administer the New World lands. Proprietors usually came from well-connected, landed families upon whom the king thought he could rely. Cecilius Calvert had received a grant in 1632 for the area of Maryland, which he hoped to develop as a Catholic colony. He did not ignore the economic realities, however, and constantly sought to address business problems, such as the labor shortage, with other proven tactics, including the use of headright. William Penn, although a religious dissident and a rebellious son, inherited his father's estate and land in America (granted by Charles II in 1681). He intended to make a profit from the land yet also to establish a safe haven for members of his faith, known as the "Quakers" (officially, the Society of Friends). Penn's grant, which extended from New York to Maryland, represented an area larger than England and Wales combined, and unknown to Penn, "contained more valuable soil and minerals than any other province of English America."[37]

Penn, greatly resembling a modern real estate "wheeler-dealer," had to sell land and attract settlers to gain a profit from the grant. To that end, he offered parcels of up to 20,000 acres and advertised heavily in Europe and England. Like modern ads, Penn's promotions emphasized the benefits to the buyer's "lifestyle." An 1683 ad for his colony boasted that "the air is sweet and clear, the heavens serene" in Pennsylvania. In writing about the city of Philadelphia in another advertisement, Penn enticed settlers with the promise of rising property values: "The improvement of the place is best measured by the advance of value upon every man's lot. . . . the worst lot in town, without any improvement upon it, is worth four times more than it was when it was laid out, and the best [,] forty."[38] Although immigrants flocked to Pennsylvania, the colony never produced the profits Penn anticipated, in part because he never spent more than two consecutive years in America to manage his investment. His final days included a stint in an English debtors prison before his death as a pauper in 1718.

Almost all colonists agreed that the proper role of government involved defense, especially protection from French and/or Indian attacks. Settlers on the western frontiers wanted a permanent British presence—forts and soldiers—near the borders of Indian lands. Difficulties with the Indians, both from farmers wanting to expand westward and from new waves of traders filtering into the frontier, placed considerable pressure on the British to control the situation. In 1763, attempting to stem the flow of traders and farmers into western lands, Britain established the Proclamation Line, prohibiting settlement west of the Appalachians. That appeared to favor the fur traders who benefited from government monopolies to operate in Indian territories; but land companies pressured the government to redraw the line in 1768, and in 1774 (following the Boston Tea Party) the Quebec Act reversed the decree yet again, extending the Quebec boundary to Ohio. Once again, the fur traders appeared to have gained a victory over the settlers and land speculators. Britain's inability to define its role as a "policeman" in the West, and its vacillations between courting the favor of land companies on one hand and fur-trading companies on the other, illustrated the difficulties a government faced when it ignored its basic responsibilities and sought to pick winners and losers in the economy.[39]

Government played its most successful role in business enterprise at sea, where, by the late 1680s, the Royal Navy had gained control over the oceans and thus ended or substantially reduced losses to pirates. Control of the seas ensured safe trade lanes to Africa, South America, and the Far East, while denying the use of oceans to continental rivals, especially Spain. Access to the Far Eastern markets and raw materials thus constituted a powerful advantage for British and colonial merchants.

Finally, the English government and its representatives in America maintained British property and contract law. In so doing, the government played its proper role of providing a secure foundation for business enterprise. Jonathan R. T. Hughes has argued, for example, that it takes five parties (not two) to make a market: two buyers, two sellers—for competition—and a government intermediary to enforce contracts and ensure compliance with laws. The place of government in the political economy has been an issue of paramount importance, involving a debate with roots in the Enlightenment.

John Locke, considered by many historians to have had an intense influence on many of the American Revolutionary thinkers, had argued that to return to the "state of nature," man had to create a "civil state" that would ensure his liberty; he added that the state would shrink as liberty grew. That sentiment, echoed by Jefferson as "The government that governs best, governs least," implied that in the state of nature there would be no government at all. Locke's view, however, rested upon the proposition that government was not "natural"—that it was artificial and created by humans. Moreover, Locke's position stood in direct opposition to the classical positions of Plato, Aristotle, and Aquinas that politics constituted the *most* "natural" of human behaviors; and it had to fit with current religious doctrines, particularly those in New England that spoke directly to economic matters.[40]

Misunderstandings over the doctrine of *laissez faire* (so named by a group of French economic theorists called the Physiocrats) led many political economists to develop theories involving "perfect markets" in which no external forces, such as governments, affected supply, demand, or competition. Yet Smith himself never envisioned a "perfect market," nor did he favor complete *laissez faire*. Quite the opposite, the *Wealth of Nations* dealt at length with the *proper* role of government in the economy, not its absence from business affairs. Smith advocated, for example, maintenance of a large navy expressly for the purpose of protecting trade.

In the mercantilist era, government attempted to identify the *objects* of economic activity and occasionally attempted to shape the tools used in economic warfare by business through subsidies and taxes. But since that tended to occur at a distance, it had no immediate impact on the lives of most colonists. The effectiveness of smuggling, the "benign neglect" with which the British enforced many of the laws, and the already crumbling theoretical foundations of mercantilism made it apparent to many Americans that its days were numbered, with or without the British Empire. To the extent that the Revolution can be explained as an economic event, it could be summed up as follows: Americans threw dirt on the casket of mercantilism, while the British still were attempting to perform CPR.

Business as a Revolutionary Force

England had regulated trade within its empire through a series of laws known as the Navigation Acts (officially, the "Acts of Trade and

Navigation"). Based on mercantilist principles of enlisting commercial activities in the interest of the state, the Navigation Acts created a set of colonial goods, including (of course) tobacco, sugar, molasses, and furs, that had to be shipped to England before transmission to other British colonies. Known as "enumerated" goods, the list provided England access to inexpensive raw materials while at the same time providing a market for colonial production. Other acts taxed or indirectly increased prices on goods shipped to the colonies, such as iron, fur hats, wool clothes, or finished products, or on sugar, tea, or rum imported from outside the empire.

In 1650, England established the Council of Trade to oversee the imperial system, although the council deferred to the advice of large British trading companies. An independent body called the Commission on Trade and Plantations (known as the Lords of Trade) soon assumed genuine oversight activities in 1675, after which it "attempted to drastically alter the colonial political structure in order to shape colonial economic development into a mold more amenable to English merchants."[41] Instead, the Lords' meddling generated bitter opposition in the colonies, the depth of which remained so strong that even when the Board of Trade replaced the Lords in 1696, the colonists had started to guard their businesses from interference.

Nettlesome as the Navigation Acts may have been to certain businesses, they hardly constituted a threat to political or economic freedom prior to 1763. The end of the Seven Years' War, however, and the subsequent new borders that resulted from the Treaty of Paris, saddled the British with seemingly endless wooded frontiers to patrol and fortify, and little revenue with which to pay for the task. A series of prime ministers and chancellors of the exchequer thus adopted a string of policies that transformed the acts from regulatory nuisances to direct economic threats.

Such was the Stamp Act of 1765, a measure that required a government stamp be placed on every paper transaction, from marriages to the sale of property to divorces to dice. Of course, obtaining a stamp involved a tax, or fee. Citizens never before affected by Parliament's policies found themselves taxed at every turn in their daily commerce. The colonies responded immediately and resolutely, forming the first intercontinental congress, the Stamp Act Congress, to oppose the measure. Outraged delegates reiterated a principle stated earlier of "no taxation without representation." Having badly misread the colonists' response, Parliament repealed the act in 1766. For the first time, however, merchants perceived that imperial regulations easily could be converted into weapons used to attack business.

After new acts in 1767 further alienated the colonists, Samuel Adams (John's distant cousin), having flopped in private enterprise and having plodded through a string of government jobs, found his calling as a writer and organizer. Adams was no entrepreneur. Yet he had noteworthy skills when it came to assembling teams of writers, publishing their work, and circulating it to colonial state assemblies. He found support in the more than forty colonial newspapers that echoed his basic message, and while the merchant community provided the fuel for the Revolution, newspapers generated the flame.

A brief respite occurred for more than five years. Then, in 1773, British officials passed the Tea Act, which imposed a minor hike in the duties on tea but opened the colonial tea trade to the East India Company, bypassing the English auctions. Conceived as a way to support the East India stockholders, the act was expected to gain a warm reception in America, where tea prices would fall somewhat. However, more than 750,000 pounds of tea entered the colonies through smuggling operations, and the crackdown on smuggling expected to accompany the Tea Act elicited a violent response from Americans. Rhetoricians such as Adams managed to make the illegal tea trade appear a legal "right," but many merchants feared the ease with which the English government had imposed a law that could have destroyed American tea merchants.

The Tea Act shifted the debate from Britain's right to impose taxes to the process by which the government made decisions. Immediate colonial reaction came in the form of attacks on customs officials and, of course, the famous "Tea Party" of December 1773, when a number of merchants—including Paul Revere—dressed as Indians, boarded British ships bearing tea and dumped 45 tons into the waters at Boston harbor. Merchants had emerged as the most unified voice against British policies, but in time they were joined by Virginia planters, Pennsylvania farmers, Connecticut woodsmen, and New England seafarers. First and foremost, however, the Boston Tea Party was a revolt against taxes—not only the burden of taxation but arbitrary implementation of them. England ensured further resistance when it invoked the Intolerable Acts, closing Boston Harbor and requiring colonists to quarter troops.

War broke out in 1775, whereupon the British attempted to establish a blockade. Colonial merchants such as George Cabot converted their fishing fleets into armed blockade runners, taking advantage of the demand for scarce American goods in Europe and for imported items. A business related to blockade running involved privateering, which cost Great Britain 2,000 ships, 12,000 sailors, and $18 million.[42] American privateers made a significant contribution to the war effort by tying up the Royal Navy, destroying British supply lines, and providing colonial consumers with a variety of goods taken from captured vessels.

Nevertheless, there was no question that normal commercial routes were disrupted. With English trade curtailed, America's principal export markets shifted to Spain, France, and Holland. The French, in particular, sought American tobacco, and some even have gone so far as to attribute French intervention in the Revolution to nicotine! That seems unrealistic, given the eagerness with which France greeted any opportunity to fight the English. Nevertheless, France's commitment of troops to the war created a new network of European purchasing agents who replaced the British, though not in nearly the same numbers. Likewise, in some areas where the British army managed to establish control, such as in Philadelphia from 1777 to 1778, trade was temporarily reestablished. Those represented halting, piecemeal, and minor exceptions to the broader loss of trade with England.

Given the reality of the interruption of trade with Britain, American domestic production accelerated to meet the reduction in imports. Military demands alone accounted for an expansion in munitions, shoes, clothing, tents, and food as well as the production associated with harnesses, wagons, and iron. Because of the entrepreneurial skill involved in organizing production, collecting finished goods, and ensuring deliveries, "American merchants . . . were both crucial to the success of the war effort and the principal material beneficiaries of armed conflict."[43]

All, however, did not prosper. Indeed, the overall picture for merchants and business owners was murky; large numbers of Loyalists left for England, while others (mainly involved in trade activities) suffered debilitating losses. Analysis of correspondence books of the Brown family of Rhode Island and Tench Coxe of Philadelphia, comparing the list of correspondents' names before and after the Revolution, reveals that numerous merchant businesses disappeared during the war.[44] The nation recovered from the losses due to the war, but the sudden decline in the foreign sector temporarily outweighed any gains made in new industrial development, small-business manufacturing, or war-related production.[45]

What Were the Costs and Benefits of the Revolution?

America's separation from England did not come cheaply. Thousands were killed or wounded, families were uprooted, property was destroyed, and relations between Canada and America soured for decades. Freedom from arbitrary control by a king or central government exacts a cost. In the case of the United States of America, trade routes temporarily deteriorated and foreign powers did not hesitate to demand tribute from American merchants that no longer had to contend with the superb Royal Navy.

Economic gains from separating from the mother country are discussed in a sidebar on the burden of the Navigation Acts. Neither the losses from remaining in the imperial system nor the small benefits it offered outweighed the perceived injustices to fundamental liberties. More than that, however, Americans took from their separation from England a deep-seated suspicion of government's power. Taxation, always a matter of concern, was targeted for special controls by placing it under the House of Representatives in the new Constitution. States drafted bills of rights reiterating their commitment to property rights, personal liberty, the right to bear arms, religious toleration, and restricted government—all elements that finally became part of the federal Constitution. Finally, a benefit of the Revolution, largely unseen until the early twentieth century, was the orientation toward individual, and not state, effort. Whatever America's heritage of natural resources and land, it is unlikely that its entrepreneurs could have prospered quite as they did if they had been subject to British labor laws and the impositions of its social welfare programs of the late nineteenth century.

During and immediately after the Revolution, however, many of the advantages of being a part of the British Empire were obvious, while some of the benefits of independence were less so. Certainly one area in which the rebellious colonies, then states, suffered was in their lack of a stable money system. Fortunately, America found an individual to meet the challenge.

Robert Morris, Financier of the Revolution

The effects of trade disruption rippled throughout the colonies after the outbreak of hostilities, producing rising prices and a shortage of money. All thirteen states and the Continental Congress printed their own paper money, but often without gold or silver backing. Consequently, the value of currency depended on consumer confidence that the value would remain constant or that the money had some intrinsic value (if, for example, it was receivable for taxes). Colonial presses produced generous sums of money, more than $226 million within a five-year period. Accordingly, the value plummeted with each new issue, plunging to a ratio of 146 continentals to a single silver ounce by 1781.

No one appreciated the dangers of inflation more than Philadelphia merchant Robert Morris, who had seen his own business severely damaged. At age thirteen, Morris had come to Maryland with his family, whereupon he soon accepted an apprenticeship with the commercial firm of Charles Willing. In 1757 he joined in a partnership with Willing and his son, Thomas. Morris—a signer of the Declaration of Independence and a member of the Continental Congress until 1778—continued his business activities after war broke out. His firm received $850,000 of the $2 million that Congress spent from 1775 to 1777, thanks in part to Morris's position on the Committee of Commerce.

Rivals claimed Morris profited unfairly from his "insider" position; yet no criticism of the goods Morris's firm supplied, nor really of the prices it charged, arose at the time. Few of Morris's competitors wanted to admit that, perhaps, Morris's firm met a need that no other could.

After the ratification of the Articles of Confederation in 1781, Congress beseeched Morris to remedy the young nation's financial problems. He assumed the position of superintendent of finance, proposing that the nation charter its first commercial bank, the Bank of North America, founded in Philadelphia in 1782. The bank acted as the fiscal agent for Congress, issued banknotes, and acted as a "national" bank. Its notes circulated as currency and retained their value because the bank redeemed the notes for gold or silver *specie.* Or, in the parlance of banking, the notes retained their *par* (face) value. To appreciate the significance of that fact, recall that the continentals' par value was $1 but their market value was 1/146 of a dollar! The bank made short-term loans to businesses, upon which it collected interest. It was no charity, either, paying stockholders a 14 percent return on their stock.

Morris's financial plan closely paralleled the plan of Alexander Hamilton, the nation's first secretary of the treasury ten years later. Morris insisted that the credit of the nation had to be maintained, regardless of whether it helped or hurt individual groups. The Bank of North America provided a case study for other banking institutions, such as the Bank of Massachusetts and the Bank of New York, which laid the financial groundwork for the new Republic.[46] Those "merchants' banks" typically did not make consumer loans (to buy products) or even loans to farmers, but rather extended short-term credit to merchants to conduct trade. Consequently, several states issued paper money, which often struggled to maintain its par valuation. Merchants tended to blame the Confederation's financial policies for any downturn in business. By 1786, however, most citizens agreed that the Articles had a number of weaknesses that needed correction. To that end, a constitutional convention was called for in May 1787, a meeting at which American business leaders were prominently represented.

The Foundation of Business: The Constitution

A large number of issues related to business and the economy were addressed by the framers of the Constitution—so many that a vigorous historical debate has arisen over the extent to which the Founding Fathers simply institutionalized their own "class" advantages. The document itself includes clauses dealing with each of the following business or economic issues:

- ✦ Taxation
- ✦ Interstate commerce
- ✦ Mails and the post office
- ✦ Patents and copyrights
- ✦ Coinage of money
- ✦ Internal security
- ✦ Import and export tariffs
- ✦ Weights and measures
- ✦ Armies and navies
- ✦ Immigration
- ✦ Contract enforcement
- ✦ Bankruptcy
- ✦ Self-protection and protection of one's business through the right to bear arms

With the exception of slavery—the debate over which the founders postponed—the document created a political and legal climate conducive to economic risk-taking. Inventors had property rights to their ideas; the security and safety of commerce, both internally and externally, was provided for under the clauses allowing the government to raise armies and navies and to maintain domestic order; and states and the federal government were prohibited from penalizing exports. The Constitution encouraged free transit of goods and labor, making the states a giant free-trade zone, since no state could levy internal tariffs. Reserving for itself the regulation of foreign and interstate commerce, the federal government ensured uniformity and consistency, two keys to successful business operations. Although it did not always occur in practice, the concept of providing a federal judiciary that would treat citizens of different states equally also promised to enhance commercial activity.

As important as the powers given to the federal government were, the powers reserved to the states, such as internal police powers and the right to enact rules and laws that, at the time of the framing of the Constitution, comprised licensing, inspection, and similar regulation of business activities, greatly shaped business and the economy. Historians of the Second Amendment suggest that the clause prohibiting Congress from abridging the right to bear arms not only addressed concerns about national government power but also constituted a statement about self-protection against brigands. Protection of commerce abroad fell under the provisions that allowed Congress to raise armies and navies, an authority it exercised periodically. For example, it took only a handful of marines led by William Eaton and Lt. Presley

O'Bannon to end the threat to American trade in the Mediterranean by the Barbary pirates in 1804.

On the other hand, the framers avoided the key decision of the age by postponing any final judgment on whether slaves were people or property. The Constitution also left somewhat clouded the definition of money, since it used the term "coin" at a time when paper money was becoming increasingly popular. Nevertheless, the document proved remarkably flexible and resilient. For almost all areas affecting business, the Constitution reflected the understanding that political freedoms and freedom to innovate in the marketplace were inextricably linked, and that real riches came "from the power of production and supply, not bullion collected through a trade surplus."[47] Rather than seeking to place the state at the center of economic decision making, as had occurred under mercantilist regimes, the Constitution provided a framework of order, sanctity of contracts, and reliable measurements; the founders assumed that the market could handle the rest.

The fact that the Constitution placed such a priority on property rights convinced some, such as Charles Beard, that the delegates had drawn up the document merely to protect their "vested interests." Beard's book, *An Economic Interpretation of the Constitution* (1913), emerged from the author's Marxist perspective, in which all events are reflections of "class struggle."[48] Beard examined the background of the delegates, finding remarkable continuity in their economic status. But in 1958, Forrest McDonald's *We the People: The Economic Origins of the Constitution* challenged Beard's thesis by reexamining the delegates' occupations. McDonald contended that Beard applied a generic term "businessman" to a number of delegates who, in reality, were craftsmen and artisans. But as we have seen in the discussions of colonial artisans, many *were* small business owners or people who straddled the worlds of both labor and capital.[49] A subsequent study, looking at voting behavior on specific issues at the Constitutional Convention, found significant patterns of voting for economic interests but fused with what the study's authors defined as including "constituent interest."[50] Put another way, the delegates voted along certain lines that reflected the desires of their constituencies and communities. While doubtlessly different measures would have been adopted if the makeup of the convention were different—either a heavy dose of back-country farmers or former Tories might have made things interesting— "measures of ideology" remained the only consistent explanation for voting across all the issues.

The members of the Constitutional Convention were both men of substance and men of ideas; and the notion that they could not be the latter if they were the former is itself troubling. It would mean, among other things, that Beard himself must have been incapable of ideas independent of the influence of "class" or wealth, which is both demeaning and untrue of Beard. As for the document itself, its amazing durability and timeless truths suggest that the framers must have done something right.

THE ECONOMICS OF BUSINESS

What Was the Burden of the Navigation Acts on the Colonists?

FOR MANY YEARS, ECONOMISTS HOTLY DIS-cussed the effects of the Navigation Acts as a cause of the American Revolution. If, for example, it could be proved that the Navigation Acts placed such a burden on the colonies that their economic life was at risk, then we could say with confidence that the Navigation Acts "caused" the American Revolution. But if their economic effect was minimal, then other explanations for the Revolution are needed.

Lawrence Harper, in 1942, was the first to attempt an economic analysis of the acts, measuring only the direct burdens on trade. But Robert Thomas, in his famous 1965 article, used a counterfactual model to assess what American economic life would have been like without the acts. Thomas calculated the burden on colonial commerce for exports, such as rice and tobacco, and examined the burdens on imports to arrive at a gross trade burden of $3.1 million in 1770, or about $1.24 per person. However, he acknowledged, the colonists gained from the imperial system

as well, and the benefits of British trade preferences, bounties, and the protection of the English navy came to $885,000, or about $.40 per person. The net loss to the colonists of belonging to the imperial system was approximately $1 million, or less than 1 percent of income. Or, to say as Jeremy Atack and Peter Passell do in their book *A New Economic View of American History* that "The British presence was not a serious financial hardship to the colonists" is an understatement. Thomas's was not the last word on the effects of the imperial system, of course. The most significant subsequent research came from Peter McClelland, who pursued a slightly different path to determine the burden of the Navigation Acts. McClelland computed the burden by analyzing the fraction of national income loss as a result of trade route distortions expressed as a fraction of GNP. He concluded that the upper-bound burden made up about 3 percent of GNP, an amount that, while slightly larger than that derived by Thomas, still represented a minor sum. Ultimately, the research suggests that, in this case at least, no one went to war for economic reasons alone.

Sources: Jeremy Atack and Peter Passell, *A New Economic View of American History,* 2d ed. (New York: W.W. Norton, 1994), quotation on 62; Lawrence Harper, "Mercantilism and the American Revolution," *Canadian Historical Review,* 23 (1942): 1–15; Robert P. Thomas, "A Quantitative Approach to the Study of the Effects of British Imperial Policy on Colonial Welfare," *Journal of Economic History,* 25 (1965): 615–638; and Peter McClelland, "The Cost to America of British Imperial Policy," *American Economic Review,* 59 (1969): 370–381.

Notes

1. W. Elliot Brownlee, *Dynamics of Ascent: A History of the American Economy,* 2d ed. (New York: Alfred A. Knopf, 1979), 8.

2. Pusateri, *History of American Business,* 40.

3. See James Burke, *Connections* (Boston: Little, Brown, 1978), 122–123, and Carlo Cipolla, *Guns, Sails and Empries: Technological Innovations and the Early Phases of European Expansion, 1400–1700* (New York: Pantheon Books, 1965).

4. The best analysis of the "feedback loops" that enabled the city-states of the post-feudal era to evolve is William H. McNeill's *The Pursuit of Power: Technology, Armed Force, and Society Since 1000 A.D.* (Chicago: University of Chicago Press, 1983).

5. An excellent discussion of the explorers of this era appears in Esmond Wright, *The Search for Liberty: From Origins to Independence* (Oxford: Blackwell, 1995), 5.

6. Oliver Perry Chitwood, *A History of Colonial America,* 3d ed. (1931, reprint, New York: Harper & Row, 1961), 24.

7. Brownlee, *Dynamics of Ascent,* 15.

8. Joel Mokyr, *The Lever of Riches* (New York: Oxford, 1990), 302.

9. McNeill, *Pursuit of Power,* passim.

10. Jack A. Goldstone, "Cultural Orthodoxy, Risk, and Innovation: The Divergence of East and West in the Early Modern World," *Sociological Theory* (Fall 1987): 119–135 (quotation on 119).

11. David Landes, *The Unbound Prometheus: Technical Change and Industrial Development in Western Europe from 1750 to the Present* (Cambridge: Cambridge University Press, 1969) provides a classic study of these forces as does Nathan Rosenberg and L. E. Birdsell, *How the West Grew Rich: The Economic Transformation of the Industrial World* (New York: Basic Books, 1969).

12. E. L. Jones. *The European Miracle: Environments, Economics and Geopolitics in the History of Europe and Asia* (Cambridge: Cambridge University Press, 1981), 149.

13. Jones, *European Miracle,* 148–149.

14. Rider, *Introduction to Economic History,* 95.

15. Quoted in Wright, *Search for Liberty,* 119.

16. Edmund S. Morgan, *American Slavery, American Freedom: The Ordeal of Colonial Virginia* (New York: Norton, 1975).

17. See John M. Dobson, *A History of American Enterprise* (Englewood Cliffs, N.J.: 1988), 14. The most thorough discussion of tobacco prices during this period appears in Russell R. Menard, "Farm Prices of Maryland Tobacco, 1659–1710," *Maryland Historical Magazine,* 68 (1973): 80–85; Jacob Price, "The Economic Growth of the Chesapeake and the European Market, 1697–1775," *Journal of Economic History,* 24 (1964): 496-511, and John J. McCusker and Russell R. Menard, *The Economy of British America, 1607–1789* (Chapel Hill: Institute of Early American History and Culture and the University of North Carolina Press, 1985), especially chap. 6.

18. Patricia Irvin Cooper, "Tennessee Places—Cabins and Deerskins: Log Building and the Charles Town Indian Trade," *Tennessee Historical Quarterly,* 53 (Winter 1984): 272–279.

19. Byrd quoted in John Spencer Basset, ed., *The Writings of Colonel William Byrd* (New York: B. Franklin, 1970 [1901]), 207–208; Pierre Marambaud, *William Byrd of Westover, 1674–1744* (Charlottesville: University Press of Virginia, 1971).

20. See James T. Flexner, *George Washington*, 3 vols. (Boston: Little, Brown & Co., 1965–1969).

21. Bryant and Dethloff, *Hisotry of American Business*, 52.

22. See Larry Schweikart, "Antebellum Southern Bankers: Origins and Mobility," in *Business and Economic History* ed. Jeremy Atack (Urbana, Ill.: Bureau of Economic and Business Research, 1985), 79–103, and "Entrepreneurial Aspects of Antebellum Banking," in *American Business History: Case Studies* ed. C. Joseph Pusateri and Henry Dethloff (New York: Harlan-Davidson, 1987), 122–139. Johnston's activities, along with those of many other planters-turned-bankers, are discussed in Schweikart's *Banking in the American South from the Age of Jackson to Reconstruction* (Baton Rouge: Louisiana State University Press, 1987).

23. See Bernard Bailyn, *The New England Merchants in the Seventeenth Century* (1955; reprint, Cambridge, Mass.: Harvard University Press, 1979).

24. Keith L. Bryant Jr. and Henry C. Dethloff, *A History of American Business*, 2d. ed. (Englewood Cliffs, N.J.: Prentice-Hall, 1990), 40.

25. Gerald Gunderson, *The Wealth Creators* (New York: Truman Talley Books, 1989), 37.

26. Jonathan R. R. Hughes, *The Vital Few: The Entrepreneur and American Economic Progress*, expanded ed. (New York: Oxford, 1986), 54.

27. Richard Walsh, "The Revolutionary Charleston Mechanic," in *Small Business in American Life*, ed. Stuart Bruchey (New York: Columbia University Press, 1980), 49–79.

28. Other similar instruments were sight drafts, which were payable when they arrived back at the account on which they were drawn, and time drafts that had a specified pay date on them. For further information, see Larry Schweikart, ed., *The Encyclopedia of American Business History and Biography: Banking and Finance to 1913* (New York: Facts on File, 1990), 64.

29. John M. Dobson, *A History of American Enterprise* (Englewood Cliffs, N.J.: Prentice-Hall, 1988), 24.

30. See "Paul Revere, Pioneer Industrialist," pamphlet by Revere Copper and Brass Incorporated, n.d., circa 1957.

31. Esther Forbes, *Paul Revere and the World He Lived In* (Boston: Houghton Mifflin, 1942; Sentry Edition, 1969), 377–397; 424; and 481n. [Quoted in Bryant & Dethloff, 43]

32. "Paul Revere, Pioneer Industrialist," 5.

33. Thomas M. Doerflinger, *A Vigorous Spirit of Enterprise: Merchants and Economic Development in Revolutionary Philadelphia* (New York: W. W. Norton, 1986), 345.

34. Doerflinger, *Vigorous Spirit of Enterprise*, 351.

35. For a different approach to wealth, based on consumption patterns, see Carole Shammas, *The Preindustrial Consumer in England and America* (Oxford: Clarendon Press, 1990), and Lois Green Carr, Russell R. Menard, and Lorena S. Walsh, *Robert Cole's World: Agriculture and Society in Early Maryland* (Chapel Hill: Institute of Early American History and Culture and University of North

Carolina Press, 1991). Cole's life reflected the fact that temporary conditions often could interrupt even the best entrepreneurs' plans, and that marriage and social patterns affected the accumulation of wealth in important ways.

36. Jeremy Atack and Peter W. Passell, *A New Economic View of American History* 2nd ed.(New York: W.W. Norton, 1994), 40–51; David W. Galenson, "The Market Evaluation of Human Capital: The Case of Indentured Servitude," *Journal of Political Economy,* 89 (1981): 446–467; and his *White Servitude in Colonial America* (New York: Cambridge University Press, 1981); James Henretta, *The Evolution of American Society, 1700–1815: An Interdisciplinary Analysis* (Lexington, Mass.: D.C. Heath, 1973); and Alice Hanson Jones, *Wealth of a Nation to Be: The American Colonies on the Eve of Revolution* (New York: Columbia University Press, 1980).

37. Alan Brinkley, *American History: A Survey,* 9th ed. (New York: McGraw-Hill, 1995), 50.

38. Louis B. Wright, *The Atlantic Frontier: Colonial American Civilization, 1607–1763* (Ithaca, N.Y.: Cornell University Press, 1947), 221. See also the chapter in J. R. T. Hughes, *The Vital Few,* on Penn.

39. Bernard Bailyn portrayed this indecision as a crisis of confidence that contributed directly to the Revolution. See his *The Ideological Origins of the American Revolution* (Cambridge, Mass.: Harvard University Press, 1967).

40. An excellent discussion of these themes appears in Leo Strauss, *Natural Right and History* (Chicago: University of Chicago Press, 1953), as well as Ted V. McAllister, *Revolt Against Modernity: Leo Strauss, Eric Voegelin, and the Search for a Postliberal Order* (Lawrence: University of Kansas Press, 1996.) On the relationship between business and religion at that time, see James D. German, "The Social Utility of Wicked Self-Love: Calvinism, Capitalism, and Public Policy in Revolutionary New England," *Journal of American History,* 82 (December 1995): 965–998.

41. Brownlee, *Dynamics of Ascent,* 94.

42. McCusker and Menard, *The Economy of British America,* 362.

43. Ibid., 364. See also Robert A. East, *Business Enterprise in the American Revolutionary Era* (New York: Columbia University Press, 1938), and John T. Schlebecker, "Agricultural Markets and Marketing in the North, 1774–1777," *Agricultural History,* 50 (1976): 21–36.

44. James B. Hedges, "The Brown Papers: The Record of a Rhode Island Business Family," American Antiquarian Society *Proceedings,* New Series, 51 (1941): 21–36; Jacob E. Cooke, *Tench Coxe and the Early Republic* (Chapel Hill: University of North Carolina Press, 1978).

45. Todd Cooper, "Trial and Triumph: The Impact of the Revolutionary War on the Baltimore Merchants," in ed. Ernest Eller, *Chesapeake Bay in the American Revolution* (Centerville, Md.: Tidewater Publishers, 1981), 282–302.

46. See B.R. Burg, "Robert Morris," in Schweikart, ed., *Encyclopedia of American Business History and Biography: Banking and Finance to 1913;* and Clarence L. Ver Steeg, *Robert Morris, Revolutionary Financier* (Philadelphia: University of Pennsylvania Press, 1954).

47. The quotation is Gilder's, *Wealth and Poverty,* 29, but the concept is Smith's.

48. Charles Beard, *An Economic Interpretation of the Constitution* (New York: Macmillan, 1913).

49. Forrest McDonald, *We the People: The Economic Origins of the Constitution* (Chicago: University of Chicago Press, 1958).

50. Robert A. McGuire and Robert L. Ohsfeldt, "An Economic Model of Voting Behavior over Specific Issues at the Constitutional Convention of 1787," *Journal of Economic History,* 46 (March 1986): 79–111 and their earlier article, "Economic Interests and the American Constitution: A Quantitative Rehabilitation of Charles A. Beard," ibid., 44 (1984): 509–520.

CHAPTER 3

Entrepreneurs in the New Nation, 1787–1840

IT WAS APROPOS THAT ADAM SMITH'S *WEALTH OF NATIONS* APPEARED IN 1776, the same year as the Declaration of Independence. Both heralded the primacy of the individual over the state, marking a new stage in theories of political economy. Not until 1848, with the publication of *The Communist Manifesto* by Karl Marx and Frederich Engels, did thinkers seriously attempt to restore the state to its pre-Smithian position.

For entrepreneurs in America, most of whom had never heard of Adam Smith, business in the new republic simply reflected a commonsense approach to economics. After all, they assumed that they knew more about their abilities, talents, productivity, and markets than some member of the House of Burgesses or a representative of the Continental Congress. During the war and the subsequent period under the Articles of Confederation—with virtually no assistance from government—entrepreneurs had opened entirely new markets. For a time, government involvement in the economy was minimal.

Trade routes, although damaged, were repaired quickly. New York merchants established new contacts with China, shipping ginseng root on the *Empress of China* from Canton in 1784. A burgeoning Far East trade sprang up, and, as business historians Mansel Blackford and Austin Kerr wrote, "Soon wealthy Americans decorated their homes with directly imported Chinese rugs, wore fine silks, and sipped Chinese tea."[1]

Government and Business in the Early Republic

Given the number of business activities that took place with no involvement from the national, state, or even local government, it is inaccurate to maintain as does historian John Dobson that there was a "consensus" that "most Americans felt that government at all levels was responsible for encouraging economic development and enterprise."² It is more appropriate to place the entrepreneurs of the 1770s and 1780s in historical context: Few of them had known anything other than the mercantilist system, and therefore to portray them as "free marketeers" is also inaccurate. Some businessmen wanted subsidies for their goods—as they had been conditioned to receive from the English—and groups battled over which stood to gain the most from the type of banking and financial system the government endorsed. Most adult Americans had grown up with, and gotten comfortable with, a mercantilist view of the state as a "facilitator" of business. At the same time, Americans had started to adopt the Lockean, or restrictive, view of government in things political. Individual liberties were set apart from authority granted to governments, state or national. Gradually, Lockean interpretations of government's role in economic life replaced mercantilist assumptions. By the 1790s, therefore, Americans adopted a view of government as an impartial arbiter and enforcer of contracts. Such activities as road building—taken for granted today as a normal function of government—were carried out almost exclusively by private contractors who constructed turnpikes for a number of years.³

The tension within the dual heritage played out in the arena of politics then spilled over into business, with the very nature of politics polarizing views in such a way as to make the debate a personal struggle between Alexander Hamilton—viewed by some as the advocate of "big government"—and Thomas Jefferson—celebrated by others as the champion of "small government." Of course, neither man saw himself in such terms, and each, to one degree or another, demonstrated mercantilist tendencies on some occasions and a market orientation on others. In truth, both men were nationalists who envisioned America as an expanding nation comprising component states. Jefferson added millions of acres to the map of the United States with his Louisiana Purchase, while Hamilton deliberately strived to create a national economy. They differed primarily over where markets occurred: Hamilton saw a national market developing, and wanted to fashion government institutions to provide the necessary structure for it. Jefferson, on the other hand, remained wedded to notions of local markets, and resisted the nationalization of the American business system. As a result, it is worthwhile to devote some attention to these two "nonentrepreneurs"—in the sense that we study them not for their personal business histories but for their role as builders of the framework for business in America.

Hamilton and the Foundations of Business Enterprise

Arguably, no American shaped the institutional structure—the "playing field"—of American business more than Alexander Hamilton, whom historians have characterized as among the most eloquent defenders of state activism in the economy. Born on the island of Nevis in the British West Indies in 1755, Hamilton, as an illegitimate son, was denied his father's inheritance. Home educated, at the age of thirteen he took a job with a local merchant. Virtually penniless, Hamilton proved a capable and trustworthy employee as well as a talented writer whose account of a hurricane in 1772 led a New Jersey minister to raise enough money to send Hamilton to New York for a more formal education. He freely admitted that he wanted to advance financially: "I condemn the groveling condition of a clerk . . . to which my fortune, etc., condemns me, and would willingly risk my life, *though not my character,* to exalt my station [emphasis mine]."[4] During the Revolution, Hamilton served time in Washington's army, often representing the general at conferences. The problems of supply, organization, and decentralized procurement in times of war convinced Hamilton that national strength demanded centralized authority. Ironically, then, Hamilton, who through hard work, occasional good fortune, and little help from government had raised himself from the direst poverty, came to favor a "planned" approach to economic growth with the government providing much of the planning.

Hamilton's predisposition to having a strong federal government direct aspects of the economy can be traced to his essays in *The Federalist,* especially numbers 6 and 62. In those, Hamilton betrayed his essentially pessimistic view of human nature, and his distrust of the actions of the masses—whether in politics or the economy—led historian Ceclia Kenyon to call Hamilton the "Rousseau of the Right."[5] Neither did Hamilton trust the "invisible hand" to provide all of the nation's needs. He appreciated the fact that in any economy, government would play *some* role and that the national, not local, government had to play an important part in integrating markets. What, however, would that role be? Would it be that of providing stability and security for the economy as a whole, or would it simply be to support the elites and their "interests"?

Hamilton distrusted the economic motives of elites as much as he did the economic impulses of commoners. It was his *political* theory that only the wealthy could support government, and therefore "making [them] reliant on the federal government for redemption of the debts they held would generate greater future support for federal taxation and centralization of financial policy."[6] As Hamilton himself stated, "The only plan that can preserve the currency is one that will make it the *immediate* interest of the moneyed men to cooperate with government [Hamilton's emphasis]."[7] Thus, Hamilton completely inverted the modern basis of the welfare state, which makes (by design or accident) a dependent class of a broad mass of poor people; instead he wanted to make the wealthy dependent on the government so that in the future he could take more of their wealth!

Did that make Hamilton a *redistributionist*—one who wanted to take from one group to give to another? Not really. Hamilton repeatedly supported the sanctity of contracts, which undergirded his entire debt-repayment concept. Contracts in his mind were legal agreements voluntarily arrived at, with each party equal and competent. To Hamilton, no contract signed in good faith could be interpreted as oppression of a weaker party by a stronger. Both participants voluntarily accepted and understood the conditions of an agreement, which then became a moral document. In that context, to Hamilton, the Constitution represented a voluntary contract and the government had a moral obligation to maintain its credit, which he viewed as a variation of a lawful agreement. "The debt of the United States," he wrote, was "the price of liberty." Hamilton stated his concern about the ability of any governmental body to impose taxes that violated the spirit of the original contract, and he distinctly opposed consumption taxes, which tended to favor the wealthy.

In a number of other ways, Hamilton showed an appreciation for the dangers a meddling government posed to business and the economy. For example, his fiscal plan for the nation, taken from the *Report on Public Credit* (1790), had four primary components, some of which would have reduced or limited the ability of government to intrude into the economy. The first component involved "assumption," wherein the federal government would assume the debts incurred by the thirteen states during the Revolution. The creditworthiness of the new nation was at risk if the government ignored the states' debts. While on the surface that component appeared to expand the scope of the federal government's powers in the economy, Hamilton took for granted the nature of the Union as one whole—not fourteen separate entities. Since that single entity stood responsible for a mutually incurred debt, how best to pay it? That comprised the second element of Hamilton's plan, "funding." He developed a two-pronged strategy to pay the debt: (1) give the creditors a "menu" of choices of repayment, including trading old debt (with a 6 percent interest rate, but no stated federal commitment to repay) for new (at 4 percent, but guaranteed), or retaining their existing notes and their higher default rate; and (2) subordinate old debt—the assumed state debts—to new debt, with the old debt retired through scheduled payments in a "sinking fund." The genius of Hamilton's plan was that it rewarded creditors for taking new issues at lower rates, but it also instilled discipline on government, which had to repay the old debt on schedule, whether it issued new debt or not. In subsequent *Reports* (that read much like those of modern-day "deficit hawks"), Hamilton recommended that the nation acquire no debt without simultaneously providing for its retirement.

Thus, while the sinking fund reduced the real value of the creditors' claims—hardly a pro-market approach—Hamilton presented the

note holders with a very promarket mechanism of offering as many options as possible. Politically, the charges that hundreds of speculators
in state notes stood to "get rich" off the war was untenable, and to enlist public support for his plan, "war profiteers" had to incur some
losses.

The third component of Hamilton's fiscal plan, advanced in the
Report on a National Bank (1790), brought out the "mercantilist
Hamilton." Yet again it showed his appreciation for the necessity to
preserve the government's credit. No constitutional provision existed
for the creation of a national bank—but then, neither did a provision
for the creation of the president's cabinet—so Hamilton acted as if the
Constitution did not *prohibit* a bank. He argued that the "necessary
and proper" clause justified the implied powers to carry out expressed
powers. Hamilton reasoned that public monies needed to be retained
somewhere. Since a bank paid the citizens interest, while a government facility simply stored the money, he chose to use the market to
reduce costs to taxpayers, in essence "privatizing" the storage of public funds. Indeed, the Bank of the United States (or BUS), chartered in
1791, was owned four-fifths by private stockholders, but foreign stockholders had no voting rights.

But the BUS's monopoly charter—being the only government
bank—fit perfectly with the mercantilist view of using business in the
service of government. In addition to its "special privilege," the BUS
had other significant advantages in the market, even had there existed
a number of strong private competitors (which there were not, at the
time). Among its obvious advantages, (1) the BUS had a larger capital
than any other bank at the time; (2) it had a huge pool of government
funds on deposit; (3) its profitability increased, because it could make
more, and larger, loans; and (4) it had the power of *interstate branch
banking,* meaning that it could establish branches in any state it
chose. Other banks, in subsequent years, were denied that authority.

The BUS also had significant responsibilities shouldered by no private bank. It had to lend money to the U.S. government, and thus
could not always lend in the private sector at higher rates. Second, it
had to maintain the value of its notes at all branches, which made it
an extremely conservative institution. Finally, it had to retain sufficient reserves to provide the government with its own deposits on demand, further limiting its business flexibility.

The fourth component of Hamilton's financial plan involved the
nation's manufacturing base. In 1791, he issued his *Report on Manufactures,* where he broke entirely with the contemporary political
economists who advocated *laissez faire,* urging a policy of subsidies
and protective tariffs to promote domestic industry.

On the other hand, Hamilton's position in his *Report on the
Establishment of a Mint* (1791) supported the stability of markets

by establishing standards and measurements. Hamilton's background with the English system of banking kept him from perceiving the economic benefits that privately produced money might offer, and thus he stopped well short of a free-market position on money creation. But in other ways he limited the power of government over the money supply. He agreed with Jefferson's suggestion of a decimal currency and wanted the American currency at parity with the Spanish milled dollar. Working together, Hamilton and Jefferson thus deprived Congress of the power to debase specie money, ensuring that business had a stable financial base—no small contribution! To this day, the most popular currency in circulation features Hamilton's or Jefferson's visages, which remain a testament to their contributions to, arguably, the most stable national financial system in the world. In short, Alexander Hamilton, despite his bent for centralization and government activism, nevertheless provided much of the free-market framework for American enterprise. And despite his proposals for government subsidies and tariffs, his more lasting contributions to American business were a sound financial system and a nation focused on keeping its debt low.

Jefferson's Land Policies

Ironically, the man who disagreed with Hamilton as much as anyone, Thomas Jefferson, had made his own contributions to a thriving base of enterprise.[8] More than any other person, Jefferson created a national market in land, authoring, in 1785, a Land Ordinance that laid out the land in divisions of *sections* (640 acres) and *townships* (see Figure 3.1). A six-mile township was divided into 36 sections of 640 acres of 1 square mile each. (Typical farms of the day covered 160 acres, or a quarter section.) Congress agreed to sell the land at $1 per acre, reserving only 5 of 36 sections in a township for itself (one of those was to support a public school, and the other four could be sold by the government or used for other purposes, such as locating armories or storehouses). The government then at an early point determined that land was better off in the hands of the people than the government, which acted as the "auctioneer." Jefferson thought individuals could make better choices than government. Perhaps more important, he "feared the potential abuse of power by the national government and wanted the land, whenever possible, removed from its grasp."[9]

Although the government-established price of land was low, Congress stipulated that the minimum auction purchase be 640 acres, meaning that in reality land companies and speculators bought several of the sections. But since the government could not survey all the land immediately, a market developed for unsurveyed land. Speculation thus allowed owners to adapt the true value of land to demand, revealing

FIGURE 3-1   *Sections of a Township under Ordinance of 1785*

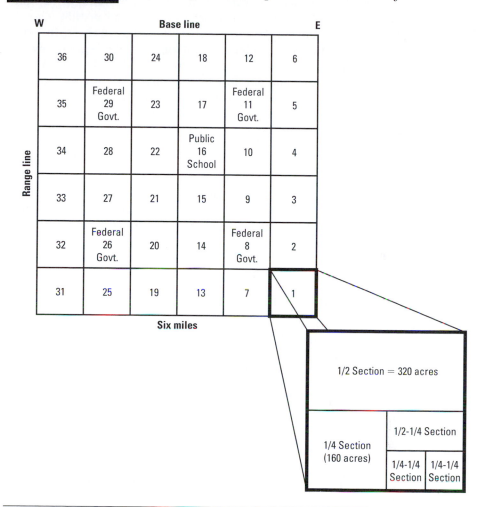

Source: Jeremy Atack and Peter W. Passell, *A New Economic View of American History*, 2nd ed. (New York: W.W. Norton, 1994), p. 255. Copyright © 1994 by Jeremy Atack and Peter W. Passell. Copyright © 1979 by Susan Lee and Peter W. Passell. Reprinted by permission of W. W. Norton & Company, Inc.

again the futility of government's efforts to fix prices. Of course, speculators sought government assistance and attempted to bribe politicians when they could. They also occasionally held large tracts of land unbroken awaiting higher prices, thus impeding development. But speculators provided land to tenants, and even provided credit with which tenants could purchase land. The role of the speculator was not as evil as has been frequently portrayed.

Despite the merits of the land distribution system, it could not provide a farm to everyone who wanted one. But the system was designed to counteract the creation of manorial estates, and in that vein the early courts recognized *preemption,* or "squatter's rights," in which anyone who remained on a piece of land for seven years gained ownership of that parcel. In that way, large landholders could not buy land and "sit" on it: If they did not develop and inspect their land regularly, they stood to lose it. Squatters also found that if they could harvest and market crops before the owners discovered them, they could raise enough money to purchase the land they had squatted on.[10] Further, America evolved a policy of taxation of land, which required that landholders pay taxes whether land was developed or not, which behooved landholders to develop their properties.

Jefferson anticipated that his land policies would create an agrarian republic—not a "rural" nation—with the key difference being that in Jefferson's vision, landowners would be more than self-sufficient small farmers.[11] But somehow the notion has persisted that small farmers, especially in New England, resisted the market and sought to carve out self-sufficient—virtually Amish-type—enclaves.[12] Several recent studies have concluded much the contrary. Farmers of southeastern Pennsylvania deliberately planned excess production to sell in Philadelphia; and Massachusetts farmers "purposefully and consistently produced more than their families could consume and engaged in long-distance and complex searches for markets in which to sell their surpluses."[13] Farmers routinely purchased more land than they needed precisely to sell some of it in difficult times, and most deliberately purchased more than they needed to farm in order to sell some at future dates.[14] In that sense, the simplest farmer became a "speculator."[15]

A second law inspired by Jefferson, the Northwest Ordinance of 1787, permitted settlers to form a territorial government when the population reached 5,000 adult male inhabitants, then to apply for statehood when population exceeded 60,000 "free inhabitants." Jefferson wanted to ensure that no "colonies" developed on the American frontier, while business enterprises on the frontier never had to fear "taxation without representation," further solidifying the institutional setting for enterprise in new territories. Settlers never hesitated to flock to western lands, due in part to the fact that they knew they did not have to forfeit their citizenship. Nor, from the earliest admission of new states, beginning with Vermont in 1791, were citizens in the newly admitted states anything but complete equals, compared to British citizens resideding in India who were disdained by "real" Brits. Politics and business again intertwined, as Jefferson insisted on keeping the states reasonably uniform, under the assumption that the business interests of exceedingly large states would dominate Congress, or, conversely, a coalition of interests from a large number of small states sharing the same economic concerns would control the government.

Jefferson's contributions to the business climate of the nation were extensive, and, while more geared to making America an "agrarian republic," nevertheless displayed vision in critical areas. He did not hesitate to use the federal government's power to acquire land that American citizens could settle, as with the Louisiana Purchase. In 1802–03, he embraced free trade as France and England took a brief respite from their wars, and America's trade with Europe soared. Exports tripled in value between 1793 and 1807, resulting in a business boom in large commercial cities. New York, Philadelphia, Baltimore, and other cities not only expanded but increased their manufacturing base. In a rapidly changing world of commerce, a new generation of entrepreneurs appeared.

John Jacob Astor: Furrier, Shipowner, Speculator

Cutting and delivering meat hardly seemed the most likely starting point for "one of the preeminent businessmen of his day," but John Jacob Astor (1763–1848) learned the essentials of commerce at an early age working for his German father, a butcher.[16] Astor came to America in 1783 after spending four years in London with his brother. During the voyage, the vessel upon which Astor sailed became ice-bound in the Chesapeake Bay for two months, which gave Astor the opportunity to learn the fur trade in exquisite detail from agents of the Hudson Bay Company who were aboard. Astor promptly left for New York—where he worked as a baker's apprentice—but had his vision fixed on the fur trade.

Astor's break came when he took a job with a New York fur merchant, and by 1786 Astor had his own fur-trading business—which did not quite make a profit, requiring Astor to make up the difference by selling musical instruments. But soon, the business achieved a sound footing. Astor's network extended up the Hudson, as far as Montreal, and he maintained business connections with London. Growth remained steady but slow until John Jay signed the unpopular treaty that bore his name in 1794; after that, Astor's furs could be shipped directly from the frontier and forests to New York without making the previously mandated stop in London. As the fur business grew, Astor's personal fortune exceeded $250,000.

On a visit to London, Astor acquired a license to trade in East India Company markets, especially China. In 1801, his first ship returned from Canton, where Astor representatives had traded furs and pelts for silks, tea, spices, porcelain (shipped for ballast with the tea), and sugar. Astor repackaged many of the products for shipment immediately to England and Germany. A single voyage could yield up to $50,000, and Astor did not hesitate to purchase the best ships with ever-larger cargo holds. While he constantly kept his eye on China,

Astor recognized the new opportunities for the extension of his fur-trading business when the Jefferson administration purchased the Louisiana Territory from France in 1803.

Despite the fact that the Mackinac Company, a Canadian enterprise, had control of the fur trade in the upper Mississippi Valley, Astor treated the region as though it were his own. He envisioned New York as the departure point westward for trading operations and eastward for sales operations. In 1808 Astor's company, the American Fur Company, received a charter from the New York legislature, but the establishment of actual trading posts came slowly, with the central outpost, Astoria, founded in 1811 in the Pacific Northwest at the mouth of the Columbia River, only to fall to an Indian uprising.

Nevertheless, Astor established a managerial hierarchy within the fur trade, predating the railroads' "managerial revolution" by fifty years, and largely for the same reason the railroads needed a centralized administration: the challenges of time and distance. John and his son William directed the collection and packaging of furs in New York; William Matthews outfitted traders and set them on their way from Montreal; and a pair of managers administered the Mackinac trading post, which became a business hub itself. A typical post featured office buildings, store houses, sleeping quarters, a store, and facilities for smiths, artisans, and mechanics. An army of boatmen and interpreters annually went into the interior from Montreal and Mackinac to a series of small stations on the frontier in Wisconsin, Illinois, and Michigan. At those posts, traders and trappers brought furs to exchange for goods transported by the boatmen. Since money was scarce, the furs themselves often circulated as currency.[17]

Astor had more than a few undesirable character traits. He became so obsessed with saving pennies that it hurt other elements of his operations, while his notorious examination of the most minute items from each trading outfit's ledger books placed incredible pressure on the post supervisors to pay the lowest possible wages, even to the detriment of productivity. The lowest employees, the *engages,* received minimal wages and yet paid high prices at the early company stores established by Astor. His sophistication in forcing prices down in urban areas pushed him toward uncivil treatment of his most necessary employees, another unwise business practice.

Eventually, of course, the market caught up with him. Competitors—independent traders—lured *engages* into more renumerative employment and obtained pelts from the Indians for higher prices. Over a period of fifteen years, his profits from the fur trade fell. New pioneer traders, such as Jim Bridger, opened the trans-Mississippi West to the Rocky Mountains, making their own connections and freezing out Astor, who sold his fur interests in 1834, a victim of his own poor management skills.[18]

Meanwhile, Astor, beginning with an investment of $80,000, had developed a secondary business in Manhattan real estate. He purchased extensive chunks of New York real estate, which was increasing at astounding rates: In 1813, Astor purchased $30,000 worth of Manhattan property, the value of which by 1819 surpassed $715,000. Among Astor's holdings was a tract of land called Greenwich Village; he sold the lots for $1,000 each, making a profit of 200 percent. In addition to being an astute fur trader, then, Astor was a "marvelous short-term speculator and real estate financier."[19] He further expanded into purchases of large sums of government bonds, often buying the bonds at large (18–20 percent) discounts. Then, in a dramatic burst of investment energy, he poured $1.25 million into Manhattan real estate between 1820 and 1848. Nevertheless, he acquired only a small percentage of his properties by foreclosing on mortgages (70 pieces out of more than 500), and almost all his foreclosures occurred as a result of panic of 1837. Astor recognized value and purchased huge quantities of real estate that had plummeted in price during the panic. He also realized that improving the lots and upgrading the property increased the value of his housing. The concern for consumers paid off. Between 1838 and 1848, Astor's Manhattan lands produced more than $1.25 million in income. Oddly enough, the man who never learned the value of his employees never forgot the value of consumers.

John Jacob Astor represented a new breed of entrepreneur who appeared on the scene in the early 1800s. He understood the necessity for, and role of, management. His cost-cutting in furs, which produced early profits, eventually returned to haunt him, indicating the weaknesses of focusing on the bottom line at the expense of long-term relationships involving production and labor. But apparently he learned, or at least got away from dealing with labor directly, for his real estate business was nothing less than a money machine. Astor also diversified, however, working as a director in two life insurance companies, buying the City Hotel and building the Park Hotel, both in New York, and investing in the Mohawk & Hudson Railroad, the forerunner of the New York Central. Business dominated his life, and his few charitable contributions, totaling half a million dollars, paled in comparison to those of other captains of industry.

While his dealings with subordinates and government officials was characterized by ruthlessness, selfishness, and arrogance, leaving Astor's legacy there would be misleading. One biographer, Kenneth Porter, concluded that Astor played by the rules as they existed, and the tunnel vision with which Astor bored in on commercial activities left him little room for the broader societal picture.[20] But that is the perspective of the twentieth century; in a sense, Astor did not have to "give back to the community" in charitable contributions because he had virtually built Manhattan with his capable real estate ventures. Thousands of renters and buyers lived in housing that would not have been possible without Astor. No one complained when their mortgages were too low, their rents affordable, their conditions amenable, or their apartments well maintained. He provided jobs for thousands of people from Canada to the Dakotas, yet sold his products at a price so low that no one could match it for years.

New Commercial Ventures in the Early Republic

John Jacob Astor's transition from managing a fur-trading operation to real estate and insurance reflected the changing business specialties deemed important in the Jeffersonian era. One of those new areas was insurance, primarily fire and shipping insurance. Early insurance organizations, made famous by Edward Lloyds' London coffeehouse, where merchants pooled their funds to insure cargoes putting to sea, reached America with the creation of Benjamin Franklin's Philadelphia Contributorship for the Insurance of Houses from Loss by Fire (1752). By 1800, thirty-three insurance companies existed, including the Philadelphia-based Insurance Company of North America (or INA, 1790), the Massachusetts Fire and Marine Company (1795), and the Insurance Company of New York (1796). Many, such as the INA, offered life insurance policies, although marine insurance remained the most significant source of revenue. Not until the 1840s did companies concentrate on selling life insurance, which farmers—still the majority of the nation's population—viewed as "downright useless and probably immoral, since it put a price on death."[21]

Both the appearance of insurance and Astor's real estate ventures reflected the impact of urbanization, allowing economies of scale to produce demand for new products and services, putting a premium on land. New York's population grew from 33,000 in 1790 to 313,000 in 1840, and Philadelphia's went from 42,000 to 200,000 over the same period. The entire nation counted only 3.9 million souls in 1790, but by 1820, the "South Atlantic" region alone (as defined by the U.S. Census) exceeded 3 million.[22] But if the nation remained substantially rural, with 13 of 14 people living in rural areas as late as 1810, market influences generated by concentrations of people nevertheless expanded the "urban attitude."

Cities created new opportunities for manufacturers to envision mass production of items previously made by artisans, thanks to broader demand. That led to *economies of scale,* or the ability to maintain a profit by reducing the per unit cost of items through higher production. American entrepreneurs learned to "make it up on volume" early in the nation's history. Urbanization also brought numerous ancillary or support businesses in close proximity to an individual's primary business. Blacksmiths benefited from having a leatherworks close, because consumers with horses could attend to all their riding needs at once. Clothiers and furriers complemented each other. Most businesses utilized banks, and many benefited from having insurance companies nearby. General merchants found that their businesses boomed from supplying other establishments.

Rising populations brought a different type of growth, in which the whole was greater than the sum of the parts; a town of 50 could not support an orchestra, or a theater, or a dance company, or even an art institute, but a larger population could. Such amenities attracted still more people to cities. And a final component of this feedback loop existed, in that governments could raise revenue through taxes, licenses, and fees. As the population and the number of businesses rose, government revenues rose, allowing governments to improve streets, lights, sewers, courts, and harbors, and later involve themselves in building railroads, subways, and other large-scale projects. The feedback loop then completed itself, as better roads, lights, sewers, and courts attracted still more immigrants to the cities. Urbanization also attracted pools of capital that could be tapped for insurance protection.

Expanded production often required more than rising demand and additional funds: It demanded technological and organizational breakthroughs. Such was the case with textiles. Wool-spinning factories already had appeared in New England in the 1790s, and by the early 1800s spinning machines developed by Richard Arkwright had reached America in large numbers. At almost the same time, Henry Maudslay, a locksmith who had walked out of his London job, established his own workshop, which soon took on the task of manufacturing wooden ships' blocks (from block-and-tackle devices), using a moving metal screw to carve the wood. Maudslay's lathe system used a series of belts and pulleys in a mass-production system, based on an idea given to him by a Frenchman, Marc Brunel. Brunel, it seems, had recently gone from America to England, where he had visited musket factories.[23]

Once again, Jefferson played a crucial role. As ambassador to France, he had seen the work of a French gunsmith who conceived the idea of creating identical parts for his weapons so that if one part broke, it could be replaced instantly with another. While Jefferson churned up support for the concept of identical parts with Congress, a young inventor named Eli Whitney had brazenly bid for a government contract to make 12,000 muskets. On Jefferson's advice, Presidents George Washington and John Adams pushed through Congress a contract for Whitney in 1798. How original Whitney's premises were remains in question. Two other gunmakers, John Hall and Simeon North, had started mass producing guns by then. North, who had made farm equipment before switching to gun manufacture, had built the first standardized milling machine that ensured weapons parts built to preset specifications. But Whitney clearly adopted the three-fold process of using *standardized parts* (borrowed from France), *mass production* (borrowed from Arkwright and Maudslay), and *simple design* (which Whitney may have arrived at on his own, based on his opinion of the American workforce). Those elements formed the foundations of the "American system" of manufacturing. Using unskilled labor and working with gauges that standardized dies, Whitney's system turned every worker into a craftsman. Power machinery took care of some aspects of mass production, while the standardization of the parts ensured interchangeability.[24]

Whitney had worked on his father's farm in Connecticut, spending a great deal of his time in the workshop. He produced metal instruments at the forge, earning a reputation as a blacksmith. After gaining a modest education, Whitney enrolled in Yale, from which he graduated in 1792. At Yale, Whitney met Phineas Miller, who managed properties in South Carolina for Catherine Greene. Miller managed to get Whitney a position as a tutor. Whitney—well familiar with farmwork—carefully watched the operations of the plantation, especially the difficulty slaves had separating the seeds from cotton fibers. He devised a machine that featured a feeding bin, a short chute, and two rollers (one with teeth). The teeth strained the fiber through, leaving the seeds to fall below in a box; and a second roller with brush-type teeth swept the cotton fiber from the first, at which point the worker cleaned the cotton off the roller for baling and shipping. Cleaning a single pound of upland cotton required a full day's work; with Whitney's gin, a slave could process fifty times that much. Production of cotton per slave rose from 119 pounds per day in 1810 to 759 by 1860.[25] Unfortunately for Whitney, his machine, though patented, was so easy to copy that he never reaped the fortune he deserved from his invention. He had joined Miller in a partnership, allowing him to return to New Haven to produce the gins, while Miller, who proposed to conduct ginning activities, paid 60 percent of the profit to Whitney. After the copies of his gin proliferated, and after numerous fruitless suits, Whitney turned his attention to meeting a government contract for muskets, which is what led him to the "American system" of manufacturing often incorrectly credited to him.[26] But regardless of the degree to which Whitney invented the American system, it is a fascinating point of history that he was, as much as any individual, personally responsible for the growing differences between North and South. His musket manufacturing embodied the new manufacturing systems that had started to dominate the North, while his cotton gin enabled the South to shift to a single-crop cotton economy.

A revisionist interpretation of Whitney's manufacturing breakthroughs, presented in the works of Merritt Roe Smith and David

Hounshell, contends that the "armory practice" of mass production originated in the public sector—the federal armories—then spread to the private sector through the migration of trained mechanics. Those men transferred the skills and organizational insights they gained in musket manufacturing to sewing machines, reapers, bicycles, and, ultimately, automobiles.[27] In this thesis, "Men left the arms business to set up the machine tool industry and went on from there to carry the principle of uniformity into the manufacture of railroad equipment . . . pocket watches . . . and so on."[28]

Testing this hypothesis would not prove difficult, and doing so involves answering three questions: Who had the ideas first, who had the technological lead, and where were the new products developed? In each case, Donald Hoke's recent study of technology in early America concludes that "The American System is primarily and overwhelmingly a *private sector phenomenon*."[29] Hoke found that the private sector "held the technological lead in America throughout the 19th century . . . [and that it] developed new products, new methods, new materials, new sales and promotion techniques, and new designs without any federal subsidy."[30] In particular, makers of wooden instrument clocks incorporated designs that were to be adjusted in the future as an integral part of the manufacturing process. That feature alone made it possible for entrepreneurs to cut costs by refining the relationships between the parts, not the parts themselves. Clock makers found that they could produce parts with wider ranges of tolerances, then adjust the relative position of the verge and escape wheels instead of the numerous parts within the clocks. Similar innovations characterized work in typewriters and heavy machinery. The entrepreneurs of the early manufacturing revolution, temporarily relegated to a minor position behind the federal armories by historians in the 1970s, thus seem to have rebounded to their once-esteemed place as the pioneers of invention and innovation.

But where the government expressed a desire for a product, enterprising individuals certainly sprang up to fill the demand. A case in point was Samuel Colt, perhaps the most famous gun manufacturer of all time. Colt, like so many other early innovators, hailed from Connecticut and had gone to sea while still a teenager. The story of the invention of the revolving pistol has several versions. In one, Colt, on board a ship bound for China, watched the action of the ship's wheel and deduced that he could design a pistol with a rotating cartridge cylinder, allowing for multiple shots without reloading.[31] After patenting his design in 1836, Colt waited . . . and waited. The orders did not come flooding in; quite the contrary, and Colt, employing hokum later associated with P. T. Barnum, traveled the nation as a chemical expert demonstrating laughing gas (nitrous oxide) for an admission fee of 50 cents per person. He finally obtained support from a cousin to start an arms manufacturing company, but his products did not impress the army at a competition at West Point. By 1842, Colt's factory had closed, deeply in debt.

Actually, though, Colt's "first love" was even more remarkable than the revolver. Under the term "aquatic pyrotechnics," Colt experimented with waterproof cartridges and antiship mines.[32] He worked with concepts developed by Robert Fulton and Samuel Morse to connect underwater explosives with a telemagnetic cable, and in 1844 he blew up a 500-ton schooner sailing down the Potomac, much to the glee of an audience of thousands who gathered for the fireworks. Employing a theatrical touch, Colt even set off two "decoy" or "dummy" mines first, deliberately misleading the crowd into thinking he had failed miserably!

After the western frontier opened, however, settlers and ranchers suddenly realized after several encounters with Plains Indians that they needed a portable weapon for use while on horseback—one that did not require reloading after every shot. The popularity of the Colt five-shot revolvers soared. In 1844, using revolvers purchased before the factory closed, sixteen Texas Rangers fought a battle with Comanches who outnumbered them five to one, yet they emerged victorious. The Rangers sang the praises of Colt's weapon across Texas, making, ultimately, the Colt .45 caliber virtually synonymous with frontier self-defense. Although still in debt at the time of the Mexican War—at which point Colt tried, unsuccessfully, to enlist—the inventor received a contract for 1,000 revolvers. Lacking a factory, he subcontracted to Eli Whitney Jr., who had his father's musket operations, and took a small loan from his uncle, Elisha Colt. The Texas Rangers also put in a special order for a new, larger caliber handgun, which Colt produced as a six-shot .44 called the Walker. Overnight, orders for both weapons streamed in. To fill the orders, he opened a new armory at Hartford, placed under the management of Elisha Root, an expert in mechanical systems.

At the Hartford armory, Colt installed "over a thousand belt-driven machines that allowed him to produce a revolver that was 80 percent machine made."[33] In 1849, after repeated failures, disappointments, part-time jobs, utter poverty, miscues, patent problems, and personal debt, Colt turned his first profit. He also became wealthy. Invited by the British to establish a factory in England, Colt set up an armory on the Thames. (Whitney had declined such an appeal.) Colt, far more attuned to salesmanship than Whitney, even "recognized the euphonic appeal and symbolic potential of his name. 'Sam Colt' has all the snap and crackle of the pop icon he became."[34] The British press referred to him as "Colonel Colt, a Thunderbolt," while Samuel adopted the powerful stallion known as a "rampant" (i.e., a dominant colt) as his trademark. Even before Colt's arrival, though, the English manufacturers had started to recognize that American technology and manufacturing processes had outstripped their own. What better way to acquire expertise than to hire a nineteenth century version of a "management consultant"? In the process, the British hoped to learn American processes firsthand. By then, of course, the companies founded by Colt, Whitney, and dozens of other U.S. manufacturers had incorporated still better technology and improved processes. Those manufacturing techniques spilled over, diffusing to a spectrum of consumer products that further accelerated the rise of the mass market.

Manufacturing Businesses: The Original "Managerial Revolution"

Entrepreneurs broke new ground in product design and manufacture; but they also blazed new paths in managerial techniques and strategies. By 1800, mass-production techniques, powered by steam engines characteristic of the Industrial Revolution, spread throughout America. Several manufacturing industries already had incorporated the acquisition of raw materials, the production of a product, and the distribution of the finished good into a single system. Traditionally, historians have accepted the thesis Alfred Chandler advanced in *The Visible Hand* that vertical integration of that type did not appear until the 1850s, when the "managerial revolution" started with the railroads. Subsequent work, however, has cast doubt on that claim. In at least two major areas, iron production and publishing, signs of vertical integration appeared long before the railroads used that strategy.

Early Iron Manufacturing

In New York, iron production thrived as merchants such as Thomas Brown, who had a cutlery store, expanded their businesses to deal in iron and iron products.[35] Others, such as Philip Livingston Jr., developed sophisticated systems of production, warehousing, transporting, and sales. Livingston began by accepting payment in kind, including rum or molasses—other iron merchants received real estate in exchange for their products—and markets stretched as far away as the West Indies.

Some of the earliest colonial commercial ventures involved digging iron ore and smelting it, with Virginia shipping ore to England as early as 1609. A blast furnace appeared in the 1640s, and by 1776, iron-ore furnaces existed in all the colonies except Georgia. The production of so-called pig iron took place at large forges; then the iron was molded into bars at a smaller forge. From that point, the iron manufacturer sold the iron to blacksmiths or fabricators who made smaller iron parts. By the early 1800s, the iron firms already had incorporated integrated factories and sales of ownership shares to stockholders, making the iron firms among the first to use permanent managers separate from ownership.

Two sectors within the iron industry reflected that managerial change: the Ramapos Mountains ironworks and the iron merchants of New York City. The Ramapos area, bordering New Jersey and New York, was home to several iron manufacturers, including Peter Hasenclever, who came to America as an agent of a group of stockholders who wanted iron-rich property in America. Hasenclever acquired the Ringwood Iron Company, which had been closed in 1764. Hasenclever managed the business, importing 500 German ironworkers and planning a gigantic operation intended to produce 3,500 tons of iron a year. But the English investors removed Hasenclever before he ever started the project, and a succession of managers failed to make enough profit to cover the project's debt. Other producers near New York City had better success. Nearly 200 iron merchants operated in New York City alone by 1800, segmenting into specializations such as makers of pots and kettles, anchor manufacturers, and "hand" or "curling iron" producers. Customers included blacksmiths, masons, cutlers, shipbuilders, and anyone else needing a variety of hardware goods. If the rule of the day was *caveat emptor* ("let the buyer beware"), the merchants stood ready to provide customers with as much information as they desired. Over time, the merchants posted small signs that showed that they dealt in only certain, proven products, while their trademarks, such as the "Gilt Anvil" associated with the store of John Youle, were displayed as symbols of quality at the stores of general merchants.

Sales tactics of the day that emphasized family name, the reputation of products, or generally accepted trademarks all were intended to operate within the legal consumer protection of the day, *caveat emptor*. Originally, the notion constituted an advance in consumer protection. Early European markets offered the customer the liberty to examine goods personally and inspect them for quality. In contrast to the modern view of consumers as incompetent to judge the quality or safety of a product, *caveat emptor* treated consumers with respect, assuming that a person could spot shoddy workmanship. Along with *caveat emptor* went clear laws permitting suits for damage incurred by flawed goods.

Iron production benefited from new marketing strategies, which somewhat offset the industry's allegiance to charcoal instead of coal. The principal sources of bituminous coal, needed to make coke to purify the iron, were found west of the Appalachians. By the 1840s, however, metallurgists found a way to make another type of coal, anthracite coal, productive, and iron productivity swiftly shot up to levels equal to that of textiles.[36] David Thomas (1794–1882), a Welsh iron master, blazed the trail in the use of anthracite coal to make iron, constructing a number of furnaces for the Lehigh Crane Iron Company.[37] He created the Lehigh Fire Brick Works to supply bricks for his blast furnaces, and at the time of his retirement in 1879, he had paved the way in vertically integrating a company.[38]

While mill designs and production innovations in iron traveled from ironmaster to ironmaster by word of mouth, the need for detailed, precise plans increasingly characterized the industry. And while reputation and personal advertising represented the most trusted form of advertising, a new industry contributed heavily to the success of the iron manufacturers by using the printed page to reproduce and circulate designs and aid merchants in selling their product.

The Publishing Industry

A critical part of the iron industry's sales strategy, published advertising, itself depended on a broadening class of literate consumers, and had only recently come on the scene. The early 1800s witnessed a dramatic upsurge in American publishing. Whereas Revolutionary broadsides rolled off hand-cranked presses in the hundreds, by 1840 large newspapers' weekly circulations exceeded 100,000. A decade later, the weekly story paper, *The Ledger,* poured out of a single factory at the rate of 400,000 per week! Book titles only numbered in the hundreds as late as the 1830s, but by 1850 the number neared 80,000. As one scholar noted, "the same individual enterprise at work in building . . . early textile industries operated as well in the world of literature. These publishers and writers, booksellers, periodical dealers, wholesalers—everyone involved in producing the printed word—were speculators on the frontier of economic development."[39]

By the 1850s, book publishers adopted the innovations first used by the ironmasters, organizing integrated factory systems, diversifying their products, developing mass marketing and advertising campaigns, and gaining managerial control over the market. Newspapers subsidized sales by carrying "deadbeat" customers in hopes of eventually expanding circulation, carrying some customers for years. As early as 1825, the firm of John and Sidney Babcock deployed managers to handle a wide variety of supervisory tasks; and two decades later, the large publishing houses of Harper and Brothers in New York and Frederick Gleason in Boston had "brought together in one plant all aspects of book production: editing, printing, binding, storage, shipping, retail and wholesale sales, and, in some cases, even authorship and type founding."[40] In half a dozen different ways, the publishing industry (like the iron industry) predated the "managerial revolution" identified by Chandler.[41] Only in a single area, that of separating ownership from management through the creation of a class of stockholders, did those iron manufacturing and publishing businesses fail to anticipate changes decades later. Indeed, the evolution of American enterprise suggests that those and other early businesses had initiated the changes, and the railroads adopted them at a later date.

Samuel Slater and the Lowell Mills

Ironically, however, the first manufacturing sector to expand hardly used any of the new managerial concepts at all. Textiles, however, took advantage of formidable new technologies that increased an individual laborer's output ten times over. Once again, an immigrant made the most revolutionary contributions to the business.

Samuel Slater, an apprentice in an English textile mill, had gained a detailed knowledge of the operations of textile firms by 1789, when he arrived in the United States. Slater had worked on Arkwright's spinning machines, and he observed that the "perpetual card and spinning" process developed by the Englishman had not yet reached America. Taking a job in a small mill in New York, he learned of Moses Brown, a Providence, Rhode Island, manufacturer who had specialized in candles. Brown and his brothers had capital; Slater had expertise. Assisted by a family of Pawtucket artisans, Slater built a small mill using the Arkwright designs that he memorized while in England. In 1790, the Slater spindle, using water power, started to produce textiles, marking the first mechanical weaving process in the United States. Within twenty years, Slater or his associates controlled half the spinning mills operating in the United States, causing Brown to write to his children, "Our people had 'cotton mill fever.'"[42] At maturity in the 1830s, Slater's mills had over 9,500 spindles, and his business interests spanned several state lines. His companies diversified into wholesaling and marketing, although he carefully limited the variety of his products to a minimal number.

Slater, like Whitney, showed that the first entrepreneur to develop a process did not necessarily know how to run it most efficiently (although Slater accumulated a fortune by 1800s standards). He frequently missed opportunities to install more up-to-date equipment; he remained extensively dependent upon capital from his friends; and his outlook remained rooted in the traditional single-owner business structure, with Slater firmly—and totally—in control.

Consequently, it took another aspiring businessman, Francis Cabot Lowell, to introduce the kinds of inventory controls and distribution systems needed to take advantage of the prodigious output of Slater's mills. Lowell did share one trait with Slater that proved indispensable in gaining access to loom technology—a keen memory. Born into a merchant family, Lowell attended Harvard—which suspended him after he started a bonfire on the university's yard—and he moved into the family's trading business until Jefferson's 1807 trade embargo virtually ended all international trade. But that stimulus led Lowell and other American merchants to develop their own textile manufacturing. After a visit to England, where he absorbed the latest weaving technology, Lowell took advantage of the dearth of foreign products during the War of 1812 to unite with a group of Boston merchants to form the Boston Manufacturing Company in 1813, located at Waltham, Massachusetts. The operation—converted from a paper mill—had double the capitalization of Slater's mills ($300,000), and, more importantly, featured an integrated manufacturing process that incorporated then separate processes for spinning, dying, and printing.

The Waltham mill used water to turn gears and pulleys, running a number of spinning processes at one time. It allowed the flow of production along an organized, steady series of steps. Production was simplified and standardized, as well as measured with a primitive accounting formula devised by Lowell. By 1822, five years after Lowell died, the investors searched for additional sites with abundant water, and found a location on the Merrimack River. Incorporated as the Merrimack Manufacturing Company in 1822, the mill needed large numbers of new employees, which the proprietors found in the labor of young women, most of them from rural areas where the meager production coming from inferior lands had forced the women into domestic manufacturing. Already possessing some independence from the home resulting from their contributions in manufacture, the young women moved into a wider arena of social independence. The Waltham owners, recognizing they had to make the factories attractive places to work, created "a social environment in the mills that was both protective of young women and conducive to the development of intellectual independence from parental authority."[43] In addition to paying good wages and offering a reasonably clean working environment, the Lowell mill boarded the women in dormitory-type arrangements, from which Lowell and his investors anticipated the women would leave after a few years for marriage. The women (called the "Lowell girls") worked ten-hour days, and although the mills were relatively isolated, were under strict supervision to defuse any potential objection from farm families.

By 1845, the Merrimack Company's five cotton mills rolled out a quarter million yards of cloth each week from its 1,300 looms. Its capital had risen to $5 million, making most of its original investors wealthy. More important, the Lowell mills showed that the new organizational gains made in iron and publishing and the technological gains made by Whitney could be translated to yet another industry—one on the brink of explosive growth. The experiment with the "Lowell girls" proved less successful, and soon the mills resorted to hiring recent immigrants. Economists have yet to sort out the exact reasons the mills changed, but whatever the cause, the mills soon found themselves resembling the impoverished English towns Lowell was determined to avoid.

Merchants, Finance, and Commercial Banking

Already the capital demands of businesses such as the Merrimack Company and the Boston Manufacturing Company had started to exceed what friends and families could supply. Stock sales raised initial capital but could not provide the daily "working capital" needed by any enterprise. Instead, merchants and early industrialists needed a way to allow the public to "invest" in their businesses without purchasing stock, in essence lending the entrepreneurs money without formal repayment times or schedules. They accomplished that by creating commercial banks.

As a rule, two types of banks emerged: private and publicly incorporated (or "chartered") banks.[44] Private banks accepted deposits, made loans, and traded in foreign exchange. However, they usually did not issue their own notes—paper money—and did not have to obtain a charter from the state legislature. The absence of a charter did not necessarily constitute a disadvantage, because it also meant that the business did not have to submit to any kind of regulatory oversight. On the other hand, incorporated, or chartered, banks generally issued notes and had to undergo regular (usually annual) examinations and disclose their capital to state officials.[45] The term *private* referred to a bank's unchartered status, not ownership: like "private" banks, all chartered banks were privately owned, except for a handful of banks chartered by states, such as the Bank of Tennessee.

One example of a private banking firm that emerged from primarily mercantile activities was Alexander Brown & Sons, founded in 1800 by a successful Irish auctioneer. Brown and his four sons, who ran the business after his death, carried on an extensive transatlantic trade with English cotton merchants, importing linen and exporting cotton, rice, or any other goods that were in demand. The oldest son, William, moved to England in 1809 to solidify the company's grip on the other side of the ocean. Gradually, the Browns came to emphasize finance over commerce, and by the mid-1800s even moved their headquarters from Baltimore, where Alexander Brown had started, to New York City. Since the bank did not issue its own notes, it could establish offices, or "branches," in a number of locations, including Boston, New Orleans, Philadelphia, and Liverpool, as well as, of course, Baltimore. According to historian Edwin Perkins, the Browns had a reputation as the preeminent banking house financing Anglo-American trade.[46] As Perkins observed, "By conducting business with the Browns an American importer with large sums due overseas could avoid the problem of seeking out and eventually purchasing a whole series of sterling bills [i.e., notes payable in gold] drawn by a number of exporters, in uneven amounts, on different English drawees with varying credit reputations."[47]

Other private bankers came from the ranks of shop owners and, later, railroaders or planters, such as William Johnston of South Carolina.[48] Less common in sheer numbers than the private banks, but better known to history, were the chartered banks. Using the Bank of North America as a model, several state legislatures chartered new institutions in the pre-1800 period, when more than thirty banks existed. Between 1790 and 1830, those businesses increased their capital stock from $3 million to $168 million as major institutions appeared in Boston, Baltimore, New York, and Philadelphia, and the Bank of New York's charter was drafted by no less than Alexander Hamilton. Gradually, the banking boom (in which the number of banks multiplied by a factor of twelve in the first two decades of the 1800s) centered on New England. There, according to statistics collected by J. Van Fenstermaker and his colleagues, growth rates exceeded 20 percent and every town came to expect its own bank.[49]

Early chartered banks received their charter—their "license" to print money—from the state legislatures after drafting a petition in which the owners spelled out the details of their business. Charters still implied "special privilege" and, in many people's minds, monopoly powers; therefore the bank owners had to show that they were providing a public service, not merely making a profit or financing their own activities. Owners put up their own capital, in the form of gold or silver *specie* (that is, coins), then issued notes, which they put into circulation through loans. The specie reserve stood as a guarantee that the notes would be honored, but no specific reserves were required in the charters. A legislature could refuse to grant a charter based on its perception that a bank's capital was inadequate, but once the bank received its charter, the legislature more or less lost control of its activities. Banks regulated their own functions based on the amount of specie they kept in their vaults as a *reserve* against the notes it issued. If a bank issued too many notes, its reserves plunged, creating the danger of failure; and if it did not issue enough, its reserves—and thus, unemployed capital—lingered in the vaults. The trick was to find exactly the proper balance between employed specie and noteholders' demand. That constituted the essence of all modern commercial banking, *fractional reserve banking*, in which banks maintain only a small portion of funds on hand relative to the amount of deposits (or claims against the bank) outstanding at any given time. While charters did not specify the reserve level or *reserve ratio*, a bank's failure to redeem notes in specie could result in the legislature revoking the charter, and some states even allowed flogging the directors of a failed bank!

When many banks experienced "runs," or people lining up to redeem their notes, it was called a "panic." If it appeared that a panic had started, few banks maintained sufficient reserves to redeem all their outstanding notes (based on their practice of fractional reserve banking). Since banks could not pay out sufficient specie during a panic, they *suspended* specie payments, essentially telling customers, "We can't give you gold and silver today, but maybe in a day or two we can." If an individual bank suspended specie payments alone, a panic could spread to solvent or nonsuspended banks. But if all the banks in a city or region suspended together, they could break the runs and end the panic. In such a case, the legislature seldom revoked the charters of all the banks, for then no one would have access to loans or notes. More important, although noteholders—and the public in general—groused about most suspensions, they accepted them as one of the inconveniences of business, much like getting the wrong order at a modern drive-through restaurant. In large part, such an attitude developed because most suspensions were highly localized and/or temporary. But when a panic became national, and banks across the nation suspended, the public grew outraged.

Stephen Girard and the Second BUS

A suspension of that type occurred in 1814, when many banks labored under the credit-generation necessities related to the War of 1812. Americans blamed the chaos on the number of new banks created without "restraint," issuing calls for some degree of control over the financial system. In 1811, Congress allowed the charter of the First BUS to expire. Several factors contributed to the death of the country's first national bank, including concerns about the influence of foreign stockholders, the bank's privileged position, and a sweeping hostility to "elites" that started to surge through the young nation. After the war, those demanding that Congress charter a new national bank to restrain the issues of the state-chartered banks prevailed. In 1816, Congress obliged by chartering the Second Bank of the United States (BUS), again owned four-fifths by private stockholders. It had a capitalization 3.5 times larger than the First BUS, but otherwise resembled the original in structure and special advantages, especially its interstate branching powers.

Stephen Girard of Philadelphia, a French immigrant orphaned at the age of twelve and blind in one eye, played a key role in persuading Congress to create the Second BUS.[50] Girard had made himself into an able captain and ship's pilot by the age of twenty-four, when he started to deliver cargoes from the West Indies to New York. During the Revolution, he docked in Philadelphia, where he turned his efforts to merchandising. By 1807, Girard had ships spread across the ocean and cargoes stretched across Europe. The Napoleonic Wars convinced Girard that he needed to get his merchandise and transports out of harm's way and to repatriate his assets to the United States, either in government bonds or by purchasing shares in the First Bank of the United States.

The demise of the First BUS coincided with the high point of Girard's asset relocation, and by 1812 he had $1 million in cash that cried out for investment. He found it in the office of the defunct national bank, opening his own nonchartered bank under his sole ownership, supplied with a capitalization of $1.5 million. Within two years, the bank's capital doubled. Girard's reputation and influence grew to the point that, like Robert Morris before him and J. P. Morgan after him, he almost singlehandedly bailed out the government from dire financial straits. Washington's sudden drop in tariff revenues left the government precariously close to bankruptcy; Congress requested an $11 million loan, but subscriptions reached only $6 million. Girard and John Jacob Astor rescued the Treasury by forming a syndicate to raise $10 million.

Naturally, when the Madison administration planned its new national bank, Secretary of the Treasury Alexander J. Dallas consulted the Philadelphian on the structure of the institution. Girard was appointed as one of the five commissioners, and when subscriptions fell $3 million short, Girard again headed a syndicate that purchased the remaining shares. In 1817, he resigned as a commissioner, though not as a stockholder.

Despite Girard's feat of twice saving the government from financial embarrassment, he had less in common with J. P. Morgan than he did with Alexander Hamilton. Girard saw a national bank as indispensable to the nation's economic health. He engaged in "political entrepreneurship," in which business supported the government in return for special favors. As a political entrepreneur (a term coined by Burt Folsom), Girard typified a substantial segment of the business community who actively sought to gain market advantage by seeking special privileges, grants, subsidies, or protections from government.[51] A second group, called by Folsom "market entrepreneurs," focused more on producing or marketing a superior product at a low cost to gain market advantage. Many entrepreneurs, failing to enlist government support, became "market entrepreneurs" out of necessity, and, conversely, most businessmen did not hesitate to accept special favors from the national or state government when given the opportunity. But usually a sharp distinction developed between those who labored to gain government support and those who instead focused on making their businesses succeed without outside help.

Again, there is no economy without *some* government involvement. In the area of banking, that involved the granting of charters.
But applicants for charters in most states merely had to show that they
were upstanding business leaders and had the necessary capital to
start a bank. Understandably, then, the first banks were founded by
merchants or mill owners who sought to develop a pool of capital for
their enterprises, and thus an extensive "crossover" between merchants and bank presidents was natural. What modern Americans find
more difficult to appreciate is that the banks *existed* primarily to lend
money to their owners and directors, a practice disdainfully referred
to today as "insider lending" and virtually illegal. For the communities
that deposited money in those early institutions, "insider lending"
posed no threat. Just the opposite, the depositors saw their banking
activities as contributing to the expansion and improvement of the entire local economy.[52] Bankers in New England, for example, financed
textile mills, shoe factories, and basic manufacturing; bankers in
southern states emphasized capital formation for railroads and early
factories.

The New York Stock Exchange and the Securities Market

Financing manufacturing and commerce through pools of local capital
proved adequate for new business and local companies. Entrepreneurs
engaged in larger-scale enterprises needed to sell stock to a wider universe of investors. In 1792, a group of twenty-four New York City merchants and brokers forged an agreement to standardize their commission
fees on the new federal government bonds issued to pay the debts left
from the Revolution.[53] The brokers continued to deal in their securities
on Wall Street, but the activity remained at a low level until after the War
of 1812, when the number of securities issues started to expand. When
the brokers formally organized the New York Stock Exchange (NYSE) in
1817, they adopted a constitution to establish trading and administration rules. Gaining membership in the NYSE required that the trader
operate a brokerage business for a year and win a vote of the existing
members, making the exchange a somewhat restrictive club. Members
met twice daily to buy and sell securities in a "call market," a term taken
from the practice of reading the name of each stock from the podium,
at which time the brokers called out their bids to buy or their orders to
sell. When the president heard two brokers agree on a price, he announced the sale and had the secretary record it. When all the sales of
that particular stock had terminated, the president moved to the next
security.

Until the 1830s, most of the securities traded on the NYSE were
federal, state, and municipal government bonds. That situation changed

with the influx of new railroad, mining, and insurance companies in the 1830s; then, after the Civil War, the number of securities swelled to over 300, mostly coming from railroad companies in need of capital. Of course, the securities of all companies were not traded on the NYSE. Instead, outside on the streets "curbstone brokers" dealt in those stocks not traded inside. Those brokers formed the New York Curb Exchange, and later made up the American Stock Exchange.

Finance for Other Businesses: The Role of Money and Notes

Agriculture and commerce were financed in a much different way, using short-term (six month) credit. Those short-term loans came in the form of paper signed to the borrower. Often, planters in the interior areas endorsed these notes to intermediaries in New Orleans, Mobile, Savannah, or other coastal cities, where they were deposited in the intermediaries' accounts. That allowed planters to purchase seed and implements in the cities, then return to the plantations to raise the crops. Merchants, on the other hand, frequently renewed their notes on a regular basis. To the extent that banks financed daily business activity at all, they did so through note issue, not small-business loans. Consequently, a blizzard of bank and personal notes circulated throughout the United States in the antebellum period.

It might appear that no one could transact business with such a diversity of money instruments. In fact, the system was relatively stable and fairly systematic. Bankers and large merchants maintained a book called *Dillistin's Bank Note Reporter,* which provided up-to-date information about the value of most banknotes in existence. If a note arrived in Baltimore from a bank in New Orleans, the bank teller checked the note against the *Reporter,* which told the teller the *discount.* If a note had a 1 percent discount (considered high for all but the most distant notes), the bank knew that the money was not as valuable as one trading at a .5 percent discount. Distance counted: The further away the source of the note, the greater cost involved in redeeming it, and thus the higher the discount. Needless to say, no bank survived long if its notes traded at discounts of 20 percent! As for personal notes, they acted somewhat like checks, except one person could transmit them to another through endorsements. The owner of the note, say, a cotton purchaser, might endorse a note from a planter to the local merchant. At that point, the reputation of the intermediary, as well as the planter, backed the note. Woe to the planter who found that no one would accept his notes, either due to his own credit history or because his bad notes had the endorsement of a bankrupt intermediary!

Trade Revisited: The Source of American Business Growth

Once the financial structure expanded sufficiently to provide a variety of financial instruments to merchants, industrialists, small business-men, and farmers, American enterprise increasingly found itself able to compete in the international markets. Trade with England and Europe, made possible by American business's unique set of comparative advantages, drove the expansion of the early 1800s in which exports grew at a level of 6–7 percent of GNP. Trade centered on agricultural production or processed food, such as flour, with raw materials and grains comprising two-thirds of U.S. exports, while manufacturing—for all its revolutionary innovation—made up less than one-quarter. Cotton dominated all other exports, and thus financed expansion in other sectors. For all its export growth, the United States did not have a favorable balance of trade from the 1820s to the 1870s, or the period of the greatest growth in the nineteenth century.

Before becoming tunnel-visioned about the importance of textiles, however, it is well to remember that *at the time* a South Carolina planter was more valuable to the economy than Samuel Slater. But textiles have dominated debate in another area of economic history, namely the role and effectiveness of tariffs. Again, though, expanding the perspective beyond American borders brings a much different perspective. Reductions in tariffs, which occurred after the first two decades in the United States and in England in the 1840s, stimulated the growth in trade. It could be argued that the most important factor in American economic growth was the repeal of the Corn Laws in England (1846). Immediately thereafter, U.S. exports, especially of manufactured goods, soared. Cotton, especially, benefited from the relaxed trading policies, and as the cotton frontier spread, the international cotton market steadily expanded.

Nevertheless, a heated debate arose over the role of tariffs (which resurfaced in the late 1970s and again in the 1990s), especially protective tariffs. Of course, Hamilton proposed the tariff in his 1792 *Report on Manufactures,* arguing that "disparities" in the maturity of American industry relative to that of Britain required that the government "protect" U.S. manufacturing. Without protection, infant American companies might be overwhelmed by foreign competitors. It was an appeal that virtually all small or new producers have used ever since: Established companies (or countries) have advantages and reserves that allow them to lower prices and eliminate competitors.

No industry seemed to have a greater claim to protection than early textile manufacturing, which faced the most potent industrial power in the world, England. American cloth (of much lower quality than that made in Britain) sold for 10.17 cents a yard, while English competitors exported linen at 12.77 cents a yard but had to pay a duty of 8.75 cents, making the final price 21.52 cents a yard. American manufacturers had a "cushion" of over 11 cents a yard, but economists have observed that protective tariffs pushed British prices considerably higher than 11 cents. As the authors of *A New Economic View of American History* concluded, had Britain been able to achieve the savings anticipated without the tariff, "the impact would have been catastrophic for the American industry."[54] Still others, most notably Paul David, have argued that the American textile industry "learned by doing."[55] Taking advantage of the learning curve, domestic manufacturers achieved higher productivity and lower costs.

Other economists have substantial reservations about the benefits of the tariff. First, if Britain could have reduced costs by 2.60 cents a yard, why did British manufacturers not go ahead and reduce those costs, undercutting the Americans? Given that England was an intellectual sieve, already allowing its best technology to sail to America, *any* cost reductions the British might have achieved probably would have reached the American producers almost as soon as the technologies or organizational structures were developed. The tariff also harmed large numbers of Americans—consumers—for the benefit of a few, which constituted a subtle form of taxation without representation. Without the tariffs, textiles costs, especially for those in the South, would have fallen and remained consistently lower than was the case.[56] One study found that landowners in the South and western areas suffered wealth reductions of 25 percent by the tariff.[57] A final consideration is this: Absent a textile industry, and all the talent and resources it consumed, is it seriously thought that entrepreneurs and manufacturers would not have flung their energies into something else (and, perhaps, even more productive)? Had textiles not existed, Samuel Slater and Francis Cabot Lowell would have thrived in other ventures. We need look no further than Whitney, who, despite difficulties gaining his proper returns for his cotton gin, picked up, moved on, and gave us the American system. All too often, historians stumble into explanations of the past only as it occurred, without appreciating the numerous paths available at the time crucial events took place. According to this logic, *because* a tariff existed and *because* the textile industry grew as it did, *therefore* the former caused the latter. But we have no studies of the potential impact on the iron industry, or on the shipping industry, or on the countless industries that *never developed* because it was more profitable (thanks to the tariff) to manufacture textiles. Had the government not cleared and paved the road to textile production for them, American entrepreneurs surely would have carved out other paths for themselves—some rougher, some smoother.

Entering a New Era

John Jacob Astor and ice mogul Frederick Tudor (see "Tales From the Crypt . . .") characterized a new type of entrepreneur who greeted a new era in American business. Gradually, market ideas had displaced mercantilist mentalities. The role of the government in the economy had been established—occasionally as a participant, but more often as an umpire—and most entrepreneurs thought in terms of market first, government favors second (if at all). Private-sector advances in clock making, gun manufacture, and textiles placed American business on a plane close to that of England, and in some cases, ahead of European rivals. New managerial innovations in iron production and publishing had initiated sweeping changes that made possible substantial efficiencies and extended business markets.

Entrepreneurs took the progrowth land policies of Jefferson, combined with the stable financial structure founded by Hamilton, and applied American innovation. As a result, pioneers like Slater, Whitney,

---

TALES FROM THE CRYPT: ENTREPRENEURS WHO CAME BACK FROM THE DEAD

Frederick Tudor: The Iceman Cometh

PERHAPS NO ONE BETTER EXEMPLIFIES THE maxim that entrepreneurs carve their own path than did Frederick Tudor, who literally carved a fortune out of ice. Tudor was one of those "rich kids" that everyone envies while growing up; his father was a lawyer, his brothers all went to Harvard, and his family had enough money that Tudor did not have to work in any but the most comfortable surroundings. Tudor, in-stead, left school at age thirteen to take a job as an apprentice with a spice merchant, where he became acquainted with food preservation. In 1805, while at a party, Frederick and his brother discussed the potential for harvesting ice from New England ponds and shipping it south. They explored the demand with merchants in Martinique and other Caribbean islands.

Supported with a small investment from his cousin, Tudor spent $10,000 to carve and ship 130 tons of ice to Martinique. Although he sold much of his stock, Tudor realized that people who had never used ice before would need an introduction to the use of ice in storage and food preparation. He had to educate as well as sell. His inventory melted, leaving him with a $4,000 loss at the time he sailed for Cuba to negotiate still more contracts. Twice he verged on bankruptcy, hiding on the family farm as creditors pursued him. His business had virtually died, and most people would have given up. Not Tudor. After the War of 1812, with connections all but severed to many of his previous customers, Tudor redoubled his efforts

Colt, and Livingston established the basis for manufacturing in the United States, while individuals like Stephen Girard and Alexander Brown provided the capital and commercial ties. In the next three decades, a revolution in transportation brought their efforts together in ways they scarcely could have imagined.

Notes

1. Mansel G. Blackford and K. Austin Kerr, *Business Enterprise in American History,* 2d ed. (Boston: Houghton-Mifflin, 1990), 59.

2. Dobson, *History of American Enterprise,* 50.

3. See Daniel B. Klein and John Majewski, "Economy, Community, and Law: The Turnpike Movement in New York, 1797–1845," *Law and Society Review,* 26 (1992): 469–512.

4. Hamilton, quoted in Charles Calomiris, "Alexander Hamilton," in *Encyclopedia of American Business History and Biography: Banking and Finance to 1913,* ed. Schweikart, 240. Biographies of Hamilton include Broadus Mitchell, *Alexander Hamilton: A Concise Biography* (New York: Oxford University Press, 1976) and Forrest McDonald, *Alexander Hamilton: A Biography* (New York: Norton, 1979).

---

to fashion new markets. He explored demand in the South, traveling through states to demonstrate the value of ice packs to doctors and staging side-by-side comparisons of iced drinks to warm drinks for bar patrons. Indeed, Tudor gleaned that iced drinks would become a national standard, and he envisioned ice as a central component of every saloon. He identified a prominent bar and provided the owner with ice for a year, free, as a way of promoting his product.

By the 1820s, Tudor annually shipped 2,000 tons of ice from the Boston area (two-thirds of the total) for about $.10 per pound. Realizing that it was only a matter of time before a wave of competition caught up to him, he improved the harvesting, delivery, and storage of ice. Efficiencies and cost cutting, he reasoned, could enable him to store additional ice for shipment later. Testing his methods in Havana, Tudor built above-ground insulated sheds, experimenting with everything from wood shavings to sheepskins to maintain cold temperatures. At the same time, he met Nathaniel Wyeth, a hotel owner, who wanted to sell ice in southern regions. Wyeth patented an ice cutter in 1825 that sawed deep trenches in pond ice, allowing manual laborers to finish the harvesting by making the last cuts and prying up the blocks. Tudor and Wyeth negotiated an agreement for Tudor to obtain the patent, giving Wyeth the position as manager of the ice company.

Tudor's markets extended as far as Calcutta by 1838, then on to parts of the Middle East. He not only constructed ice depots but educated local residents in the manufacture of small refrigerators. By 1846, Tudor, who had started harvesting ice at Walden Pond, accounted for much of the 65,000 tons of ice shipped from Boston each year. A number of middle-class Americans had iceboxes in their homes by the time of the Civil War, made possible only by the availability of ice. Frederick Tudor changed the very nature of American consumer culture by altering what people ate and drank—and when they could eat and drink.

Source: Robert Sobel and David B. Sicilia, *The Entrepreneurs: An American Adventure* (Boston: Houghton-Mifflin, 1986), 65–71.

Calomiris's essay, however, is particularly revealing as it is written by an economic historian who specialized in money and banking, and therefore is uniquely attuned to Hamilton's financial positions.

5. Cecilia Kenyon, "Alexander Hamilton, Rousseau of the Right" *Political Science Quarterly,* 73 (June 1958): 161–178. See also Paul Goodman, "The First American Party System," in *The American Pary Systems: Stages of Political Development,* ed. William Nisbet Chambers and Walter Dean Burnham (New York: Oxford University Press, 1967), 56–89.

6. Calomiris, "Hamilton," 244. For a different view, see John Steele Gordon, *Hamilton's Blessing: The Extraordinary Life and Times of Our National Debt* (New York: Penguin, 1998 [1997]).

7. Alexander Hamilton, "To a Member of Congress," in Kenyon's article, reprinted in *The American Past,* ed. Fine and Brown (New York: Macmillan, 1965), 251–265 (quotation on 257).

8. Views on Jefferson range from those seeing him as auguring a wave of individualistic capitalism under the rubric "republicanism," to assessments of Jefferson as a conservative and a restrained student of Jean-Baptiste Say. See Joyce J. Appleby, *Capitalism and a New Social Order: The Republican Vision of the 1790s* (New York: New York University Press, 1984) for the first view and M. L. Burstein, *Understanding Thomas Jefferson: Studies in Economics, Law, and Philosophy* (New York: St. Martin's Press, 1993) for the second. Burstein cites a single letter from Jefferson (February 1, 1804) to Say suggesting that he would never have blocked the natural growth of manufactures, based on the conclusion that nature sometimes permitted manufactures to arise.

9. Jonathan Hughes and Louis P. Cain, *American Economic History,* 4th ed. (New York: HarperCollins, 1994), 87.

10. A recent study of farming in America is David B. Danbom, *Born in the Country: A History of Rural America* (Baltimore, Md.: Johns Hopkins University Press, 1995), esp. 72–73 in this context.

11. Several sources deal with Jefferson's concept of land ownership and development. See, for example, Donald Jackson, *Thomas Jefferson and the Stoney Mountains: Exploring the West from Monticello* (Urbana: University of Illinois Press, 1981); Merrill D. Peterson, *Thomas Jefferson and the New Nation* (New York; Oxford University Press, 1970). Also see Carl Edward Skeen, "Jefferson and the West, 1798–1808," in *Papers on the War of 1812 in the Northwest,* no. 7, Ohio State Museum, 1960.

12. This view was supported by Percy W. Bidwell in his "The Rural Runaway in New England at the Beginning of the Nineteenth Century" (*Transactions of the Connecticut Academy of Arts and Sciences,* 20 [1916]: 241–399), James Henretta ("Families and Farms: Mentalite in Pre-Industrial America," *William and Mary Quarterly,* 35 [1978]: 3–32), and James Lemon's *The Best Poor Man's Country: A Geographical Study of Early Southeastern Pennsylvania* (Baltimore, Md.: Johns Hopkins University Press, 1972).

13. Atack and Passell, *A New Economic View of American History,* 33. Sources on the market orientation of farmers include Winifred Rothenberg, *From Market-Places to a Market Economy: The Transformation of Rural Massachusetts, 1750–1850* (Chicago: University of Chicago Press, 1992), and Duane Ball and Gary M. Walton, "Agricultural Productivity Change in Eighteenth Century Pennsylvania," *Journal of Economic History,* 36 (1976): 102–117. But even Lemon admits the farmers produced more than they needed.

14. Jeremy Atack and Fred Bateman, *To Their Own Soil: Agriculture in the Antebellum North* (Ames: Iowa State University Press, 1987), 124.

15. Puth, *American Economic History,* 71; Edwin Perkins, *The Economy of Colonial America,* 2d ed. (New York: Columbia University Press, 1988). Also see Winifred Rothenberg, "The Market and Massachusetts Farmers, 1750–1855," *Journal of Economic History,* 41 (June 1981): 283–314.

16. Michael F. Konig, "John Jacob Astor," in *Encyclopedia of American Business History and Biography,* ed., Schweikart, 13.

17. See Lewis Davids, "Fur Money and Banking in the West," in *Banking in the West,* ed. Larry Schweikart (Manhattan, Kan.: Sunflower University Press, 1984), reprinted from the April 1984 issue of *Journal of the West.*

18. John D. Haegar, "Business Strategy and Practice in the Early Republic: John Jacob Astor and the American Fur Trade," *Western Historical Quarterly,* 19 (May 1988): 183–202; Hiram M. Chittenden, *The American Fur Trade of the Far West* (3 vols., New York: Francis P. Harper, 1902; 2 vols., Stanford, Calif.: Academic Reprints, 1954).

19. Konig, "Astor," 17.

20. Kenneth W. Porter, *John Jacob Astor, Business Man,* 2 vols. (Cambridge, Mass.: Harvard University Press, 1931). Also see Paul C. Phillips and J. W. Smurr, *The Fur Trade,* 2 vols. (Norman: University of Oklahoma Press, 1961).

21. Bryant and Dethloff, *History of American Business,* 204; Vivana A. Rotman Zelizer, *Morals and Markets: The Development of Life Insurance in the United States* (New York: Columbia University Press, 1979); and George A. Bishop, *Capital Formation through Life Insurance: A Study in the Growth of Life Insurance Services and Investment Activities* (Homewood, Ill.: Richard D. Irwin, 1976).

22. U.S. Bureau of the Census, *Historical Statistics of the United States: Colonial Times to 1970* (Washington, D.C.: Government Printing Office, 1975), 1:22, 23; Puth, *American Economic History,* 133.

23. A provocative interpretation of these events appears in James Burke, *Connections* (Boston: Little, Brown, 1978), 145–151.

24. Robert S. Woodbury, "The Legend of Eli Whitney and Interchangeable Parts," *Technology and Culture,* 2 (Summer 1960): 235–253; Robert A. Lively, "The American System: A Review Article," *Business History Review,* 29 (March 1955): 81–96.

25. Puth, *American Economic History,* 190; Alfred Confrad and John Meyer, "The Economics of Slavery in the Antebellum South," *Journal of Political Economy* (April 1958): 95–130; D. Schaefer, "The Effect of the 1859 Crop Year Upon Relative Productivity in the Antebellum South," *Journal of Economic History* (December 1983): 851–865.

26. Constance McLaughlin Green, *Eli Whitney and the Birth of American Technology* (Boston: Little, Brown, 1956).

27. Merrit Roe Smith, *Harpers Ferry Armory and the New Technology* (Ithaca, N.Y.: Cornell University Press, 1977) and David Hounshell, *From the American System to Mass Production* (Baltimore, Md.: Johns Hopkins University Press, 1984).

28. David F. Noble, "Command Performance: A Perspective on the Social and Economic Consequences of Military Enterprise," in *Military Enterprise and Technological Change: Perspectives on the American Experience,* ed., Merritt Roe Smith (Cambridge, Mass.: MIT Press, 1985), 337.

29. Donald Hoke, "Product Design and Cost Considerations: Clock, Watch, and Typewriter Manufacturing in the 19th Century," in *Business and Economic History,* ed.William J. Hausman, 2d. series, 18 (1989), 119–128 (quotation on 120), and, for a deeper analysis, his book *Ingenious Yankees: The Rise of the American System of Manufactures in the Private Sector* (New York: Columbia University Press, 1989).

30. Hoke, "Product Design," 120.

31. William B. Edwards, *The Story of Colt's Revolver: The Biography of Col. Samuel Colt* (Harrisonburg, Penn.: Stackpole Co., 1953); and Sobel and Sicilia, *Entrepreneurs,* 152.

32. Henry Barnard, *Armsmear: The Home, the Arm, and the Armory of Samuel Colt, a Memorial* (New York: C. A. Alvord, 1866), 276, quoted in William Hosley, *Colt: The Making of an American Legend* (Amherst: University of Massachusetts Press, 1996), 22.

33. Pusateri, *History of American Business,* 157.

34. Hosley, *Colt,* 75.

35. See Allen S. Marber, "America's First Marketers: The New York Iron Merchants," in ed. William Childs, *Essays in Economic and Business History,* 13 (1995): 83–96.

36. Jeremy Atack and Peter Passell, *A New Economic View of American History,* 2d ed. (New York: W.W. Norton, 1994), 189.

37. Material for this section comes from John W. Malsberger, "David Thomas," in *The Encyclopedia of American Business History and Biography: Iron and Steel in the Nineteenth Century,* ed. Paul Pascoff (New York: Facts on File, 1989), 333–336.

38. Samuel Thomas, "Reminiscences of the Early Anthracite-Iron Industry," *Transactions of the American Institute of Mining Engineers,* 29 (1899): 901–928.

39. Ronald Zboray, "Literary Enterprise and the Mass Market: Publishers and Business Innovation in Antebellum America," in Edwin J. Perkins, ed., *Essays in Economic and Business History,* 10 (1992), 168–172 (quotation on 169). Also see his *A Fictive People: Antebellum Economic Development and the American Reading Public* (New York: Oxford University Press, 1992) and "Antebellum Reading and the Ironies of Technological Innovation," *American Quarterly,* 40 (1988): 65–82; as well as John Tebbel, *A History of Book Publishing in the United States: Vol. 1, The Creation of an Industry* (New York: R.R. Bowker, 1972) and Thomas C. Leonard, *News for All: America's Coming of Age with the Press* (New York: Oxford University Press, 1995), 43.

40. Zaboray, "Literary Enterprise and the Mass Market," 170.

41. See, for example, Rosalind Remer, *Printers and Men of Capital: Philadelphia Book Publishers in the New Republic* (Philadelphia: University of Pennsylvania Press, 1996).

42. Moses Brown to T. Rogerson, November 11, 1810, quoted in Barbara M. Tucker, "Forms of Ownership and Management," in *American Business History: Case Studies,* ed. Henry Dethloff and C. Joseph Pusateri (Arlington Heights, Ill.: Harlan-Davidson, 1987), 60. Also see Tucker's book, *Samuel Slater and the Origins of the American Textile Industry, 1790–1860* (Ithaca, N.Y.: Cornell University Press, 1984).

43. Brownlee, *Dynamics of Ascent,* 160.

44. An overview of the structure of banking in this period appears in Schweikart, ed., *Encyclopedia of American Business History: Banking and Finance to 1913,* as

well as Benjamin J. Klebaner, *Commercial Banking in the United States: A History* (Hinsdale, Ill.: Dryden Press, 1974); and for a concise treatment of the historical interpretations and a survey of the literature, see Schweikart, "U.S. Commercial Banking: A Historiographical Survey," *Business History Review,* 65 (Autumn 1991): 606–661.

45. Among the sources dealing with these developments are Vincent P. Carosso, *Investment Banking in America: A History* (Cambridge, Mass.: Harvard University Press, 1975) and Fritz Redlich, *The Molding of American Banking, Men and Ideas,* 2 vols. (1947 reprint, New York: Johnson Reprint Co., 1968), as well as the superb overview of banks and banking by Charles W. Calomiris in the *Encyclopedia Britannica* (forthcoming; currently available as a working paper, University of Illinois, Department of Economics).

46. Edwin J. Perkins, *Financing Anglo-American Trade: The House of Brown, 1800–1880* (Cambridge, Mass.: Harvard University Press, 1975).

47. Perkins, "Alexander Brown," in *Encyclopedia of American Business History and Biography: Banking and Finance to 1913,* ed. Schweikart, 73–80 (quotation on 77). See also Ralph W. Hidy, *The House of Baring in American Trade and Finance: English Merchant Bankers at Work, 1763–1861* (Cambridge, Mass.: Harvard University Press, 1949).

48. See the "Assigned estate William Johnston, 1851," in the William Johnston Papers, South Caroliniana Library, Columbia.

49. J. Van Fenstermaker and John E. Filer, "Impact of the First and Second Bank of the United States and the Suffolk System on New England Money: 1791–1837," *Journal of Money, Credit, and Banking,* 18 (February 1986): 28–40. Also see Fenstermaker's excellent monograph, *The Development of American Commercial Banking* (Kent, Ohio: Kent State University Press, 1965).

50. Donald R. Adams, Jr., *Finance and Enterprise in Early America: A Study of Stephen Girard's Bank, 1812–1831* (Philadelphia: University of Pennsylvania Press, 1978); Harry Emerson Wildes, *Lonely Midas: The Story of Stephen Girard* (New York: Farrar & Rinehart, 1943); and Gregory Hunter's excellent essay, "Stephen Girard," in *Encyclopedia of American Business History and Biography: Banking and Finance to 1913,* ed. Schweikart, 221–224.

51. Burton W. Folsom, Jr., *The Myth of the Robber Barons: A New Look at the Rise of Big Business in America* (Herndon, Va.: Young America's Foundation, 1991). Although Folsom concentrates on the period 1830 to 1900, his descriptions are appropriate for the period prior to 1830 as well.

52. Several new sources have elaborated on this practice, including Naomi Lamoreaux, "Banks, Kinship, and Economic Development: The New England Case," *Journal of Economic History* (September 1986): 647–667 and her book, *Insider Lending: Banks, Personal Connections, and Economic Development in Industrial New England* (Cambridge, Mass.: Cambridge University Press and the National Bureau of Economic Research, 1994); and Larry Schweikart, *Banking in the American South from the Age of Jackson to Reconstruction* (Baton Rouge: Louisiana State University Press, 1987).

53. Steven Wheeler, "New York Stock Exchange," in *Encyclopedia of American Business History and Biography: Banking and Finance to 1913,* ed. Schweikart, 384–385; Robert Sobel, *The Big Board: A History of the New York Stock Market* (New York: Macmillan, 1970); Deborah S. Gardner, *Marketplace: A Brief History of the New York Stock Exchange* (New York: New York Stock Exchange, 1982).

54. Atack and Passell, *A New Economic View,* 134.

55. Paul A. David, "Learning by Doing and Tariff Protection: A Reconsideration of the Case of the Ante-Bellum United States Cotton Textile Industry," *Journal of Economic History,* 30 (September 1970): 521–601; Mark Bils, "Tariff Protection and Production in the Early U.S. Cotton Textile Industry," *Journal of Economic History,* 44 (1984): 1033–1046.

56. Atack and Passell, *New Economic View,* 137–140.

57. C. Knick Harley, "The Antebellum American Tariff: Structure and Welfare," working paper, University of Western Ontario, 1990.

CHAPTER 4

The Entrepreneurial Explosion, 1820–1850

PERHAPS NO AGE IN AMERICAN HISTORY—SAVE THE MODERN—HAS witnessed as explosive growth in business and entrepreneurship as the so-called "Middle Period," or the era from the Missouri Compromise to the end of the Mexican War. Private enterprise, especially small businesses, flourished. Business expansion brought calls for political change and attacks on "special privilege" seen as impediments to the opportunities of the "common man." As a result, citizens demanded the end to the process of petitioning the legislature for a business charter. It was an era in which banks competed freely in note issue and a burgeoning new industry—transportation—fundamentally transfigured the landscape and the market itself.[1]

The changes in transportation represented the application of steam on rivers and rails. As new technologies brought entirely new industries into existence, they also expanded the market in such a way as to make once isolated interior areas functional parts of the economy. Construction of canals and railroads, the manufacture of steamships and locomotives, and the founding of companies to build turnpikes all generated entirely new enterprises. At the same time, the capital demands for those new businesses fueled the financial and insurance sector.

Society was affected by the upheaval in transportation, if for no other reason than that for the first time people could move from a radius of a few miles beyond the nearest town. As late as 1790, "most of the 3.9 million Americans . . . still lived within a hundred miles or so of the Atlantic Coast."[2] More than 200,000 settlers populated Tennessee, Kentucky, and Western Virginia by John Adams's presidency, and by the

Monroe administration at least 1.5 million had crossed the Appalachi-ans to the West. They faced high transportation costs on the one hand and extremely limited localized markets on the other. Settlers, farmers, and merchants all knew that they needed cheaper ways to ship goods to the urbanized areas. The question was, how were the transportation costs to be reduced, and who would do it?

Gallatin's Plan

Jefferson's secretary of the treasury, Albert Gallatin, had an answer: "The General Government can alone remove these obstacles."[3] Gallatin delivered an extensive report to Congress in 1808 on the sta-tus of roads and canals in the United States. He outlined the benefits for the business world of a sophisticated system of internal transpor-tation and the challenges to developing such a network (citing, among other problems, interest rates). Gallatin then made an astonishing proposal, especially from one appointed by the proponent of "small government," Jefferson. The secretary recommended that Congress fund a ten-year, $20 million project in which the federal government would construct roads and canals itself or provide loans for private corporations to do so. He detailed $16 million worth of specific pro-grams, including a canal to connect the Atlantic Coast and the Great Lakes, while he included a $3.4 million allocation for local improve-ments that enhanced the overall plan. By all comparisons, the plan dwarfed anything the government had ever proposed. The entire bud-get for the federal government in 1810 was only $10 million, and Gallatin's ambitious outlays were five times those of the government under Jefferson in 1808.[4]

Indeed, Jefferson had reservations about the government's role in the scheme, and argued that a constitutional amendment might be needed to proceed legally. Ultimately, some elements of Gallatin's plan were enacted, such as the national road from Maryland to Wheeling, Virginia (completed in 1818). But the revenues for the plan had to come from tariffs, which had produced steadily lower returns after the troubles with Britain between 1807 and 1809. Nevertheless, much of the design of Gallatin's project did appear through the efforts of private entrepreneurs.

Roads, Turnpikes, and Entrepreneurs

Modern Americans take for granted that one of government's jobs is to build roads: "No one else would do it" goes the traditional reasoning. Except that in antebellum America, the traditional reasoning is wrong. Individual entrepreneurs and chartered turnpike companies provided many of the early roads, which represented daunting feats of construction in some cases.[5]

Early roads consisted of little more than narrow paths, well-worn Indian trails, or, occasionally, logs laid crossways to traffic to form "corduroy" roads. Flat plank roads were an expensive luxury, and the cost of transportation reflected the difficulty of construction and the problems of maintenance of such roads. Teamsters charged up to $5 to carry barrel-sized cargoes 10 miles over potholes and bogs, pushing road transport to $30 per ton-mile by 1815. Turnpikes, built with solid rock or gravel foundations and flat surfaces flanked by drainage ditches, must have looked like superhighways to early travelers. The Lancaster Turnpike Road, a 62-mile artery linking Philadelphia and Lancaster, Pennsylvania, was the first attempt by private companies to provide better transportation. The company issued $300,000 worth of stock, started construction on the road in 1792, and completed it two years later at a cost of $465,000. Yet even if the road produced strong toll traffic, it would have had to have carried a constant stream of travelers and freight to pay the $7,500-per-mile construction costs. In fact, the road returned dividends of only 2.5 percent to the stockholders. Entrepreneurs, to their chagrin, discovered that potential customers had developed a variety of toll-avoidance maneuvers, including taking side trails called "shunpikes"—short detours around tollhouses. One turnpike president estimated his company's revenue would have been 60 percent higher if not for shunpikes.

Perhaps at first, turnpikes may have held promise for substantial returns if the companies could police the routes and keep construction costs down. Certainly enough were attempted. Northern states witnessed a private construction boom, resulting in more than 400 road corporations chartered in the Northeast by the 1820s. Those companies raised capital through stock sales to the public, anticipating returns from the tolls. To that end, private corporations pumped more than $6 million into New England alone, laying thousands of miles of highway—two-thirds of the nation's total by 1810. Similar levels of activity touched other northern states: Between 1812 and 1840, New York issued charters to more than 130 companies that constructed 1,500 miles of roads, while Pennsylvania chartered more than 80 turnpike corporations that invested nearly $40 million to build 2,000 miles of roads.[6]

When examining only the returns from the roads, few businessmen could have justified their investments. The Salem Turnpike in Massachusetts, for example, paid average annual dividends of only 3.1 percent over sixty years, and it was considered one of the most successful of the road companies. However, measuring profits by such strict definitions of return may not provide an accurate understanding of the motivations for entrepreneurs to build roads and stockholders to invest in them. Usually, the merchant-capitalists who founded the turnpike companies had other business interests that profited from a better road system.[7] Thus, the road itself did not have to turn a profit, only contribute in a systemic way to the overall profitability of the merchant's other activities. By taking the lead in the formation of road-building companies, entrepreneurs of the early 1800s had more in mind than mere tolls—one could say they had faith and vision. And not surprisingly, most of the stock in turnpikes was owned in the towns through which the roads passed.[8] In Kingston, New York, for example, the local newspaper, the *Ulster Palladium,* which served as the medium for business groups to publicize their efforts, argued that bad roads "not only dampen the enterprising spirit of commerce, but would produce the same effect on agriculture and manufacture."[9] Another local paper agreed, suggesting that a turnpike would "add materially to the prosperity of the inhabitants of this village."[10]

As Gerald Gunderson points out, "The value of the turnpike organization was emphasized by state legislatures frequently turning *existing routes* over to private companies in order to improve their condition . . . [and] the improved use of existing resources justified shifting to private management."[11] Moreover, the enthusiastic reception of turnpikes contrasted with the repeated failures to win federal support for funding internal transportation.

Nevertheless, turnpike companies faced a number of challenges. First, charters contained sometimes severe restrictions, and even set tolls. As one authority on turnpikes noted, "While legislators readily sanctioned road provision by private associations, they wrote extensive regulation into company charters."[12] Second, a fundamental "free rider" problem existed, in that once the road was built, excluding nonpayers, who seldom had invested in the turnpike, proved difficult. Organizers of the turnpike companies overcame that problem when the roads were in their infancy by holding stock sales meetings, at which upwards of 100 people attended, thereby involving the majority of townspeople in the enterprise. But when roads needed additional capital, it had to come from outside the towns.

A more insidious threat came concealed in the form of "assistance" by states. Offered the chance to enlist the aid of state taxpayers, many entrepreneurs could hardly resist, especially when the state controlled the charter process. States hoped to stimulate trade, open new lands, and tie together existing markets. Government participation in turnpike or other road ventures commonly involved buying stock directly or guaranteeing bond sales for particular projects. The resulting "mixed enterprise" characterized many of the large construction projects after the 1820s.

Obviously, however, any company—in any industry—to gain such state support first had a tremendous advantage over other existing or potential competitors. Newspapers, for example, were highly politicized businesses because city, state, or national printing contracts could supply them with substantial profits. Washington, D.C., publishers Gales and Seaton relied on federal money from their work on the federal *Register* and other documents printed at federal expense to stay profitable.

Even when federal subsidies did not offer contracts directly to companies, government assistance still provided substantial advantages. Railroad or canal companies acting with state support had greater leverage to obtain land through *eminent domain* (in which the government can take private land for the public good with fair compensation). When necessary, states threatened individuals who would not sell, whereas private companies usually could not make such threats. Gradually, mixed enterprise shifted slowly toward state-run local monopolies. As a result, the purely private toll roads increasingly gave way to government-supported projects, although they "were by no means banished from the stage" entirely.[13]

Evidence that market demand did not exist for most government-initiated road projects can be seen in the paltry profits returned by public turnpike companies. Individual travelers and merchants may have benefited from such roads, but public turnpikes did not generate enough traffic to achieve economies of scale, making it cheaper to ship by water. According to early economic assessments of turnpikes examining comparative savings between waterborne traffic and roads—an admittedly strict form of cost analysis—fewer than 10 percent of New England's 200 turnpike businesses paid even average dividends. By 1815, before steam-powered vessels sailed most water routes, upstream costs for a ton-mile were $6, while shipping goods on a raft downstream cost a mere $1.30, or a tiny fraction of the costs of shipping by road.

Why, then, did roads receive as much support from state governments (and, after 1812, the federal government) as they did? First, and most apparent, roads could go places where rivers did not and/or could connect two bodies of water. Second, recent economists have distinguished between private profits and so-called social rate of return. Some economic activity, such as the construction of new transportation facilities, is more profitable to society as a whole than to the specific entrepreneurs responsible for their operation. Farmers and merchants living in close proximity to a road, for example, benefit from the road even if they did not invest in it.[14] Strong incentives, therefore, existed for states to support large-scale transportation projects. Nevertheless, it must be reiterated that there are moral challenges to forcing some people (through taxes or government-insured bonds) to support projects that only benefit others.

One social benefit seldom mentioned by historians involved not the turnpikes that survived but those that failed. Business failures contribute to the overall knowledge base of all entrepreneurs: By telling people what *not* to build, or what will *not* work, the market distributes information throughout society. Whether America in the early 1800s or Japan in the 1970s, studies have suggested that growing economies generate business failures at very high rates.[15] Indeed, as one recent study concluded, "The reality is that our most successful areas are those with the highest rates of innovation and failure, not the lowest."[16] Economies grow precisely because people attempt new, imaginative projects and often fail, yet society as a whole gains.

Historians agree that the transportation revolution yielded economic benefits to society beyond the direct profits earned by the companies immediately involved, as when the turnpikes opened new markets, facilitated shipping, and encouraged settlement in more remote areas. Economists call those benefits "externalities," meaning that the business could not "internalize" all of the benefits to itself. However, those who celebrated the societal gains at the expense of individual turnpike entrepreneurs, who failed to make profits on private construction, soon learned that externalities had a dark side, too. Companies found ways to shift costs to society as a whole, especially in areas of environmental protection or health care for employees injured on the job.

Ultimately, the issue boiled down to property rights. At what point did an entrepreneur wishing to build a road have to purchase all the land needed without resorting to eminent domain? Such pressures encouraged many otherwise independent businessmen to ally themselves with state and local governments, whereby they could acquire land in the name of "society." And transportation issues became even more clouded after 1812, when the federal government started to construct the National Road to extend from Cumberland, Maryland, to Columbus, Ohio. It represented the largest internal improvement ever undertaken by the government, justified by the need to move troops around the nation for purposes of defense. (Even this—the crown jewel of American highways—hardly qualified as a smooth, even highway in the modern sense: "Contractors building the National Road . . . were permitted to leave any tree stump less than eighteen inches tall in the roadway[!]")[17] Eventually, the National Road carried a steady stream of traffic, convincing states to lobby for federal assistance for their own road projects. Congress relented, after 1803 requiring that 5 percent of the proceeds from the sale of federal land support road construction. Still later, the federal government provided surveys and mapping through the U.S. Army's Corps of Engineers.[18]

The federal government had its own eminent domain powers when it came to large construction projects of any type. Private lands and businesses had to yield to the government in cases of "national interest," which were infrequent in the antebellum period. But the federal and state governments shaped business far more profoundly with their interpretations of laws, especially when it came to property rights.

Property and Law

The entire structure of antebellum property law evolved out of a debate over the conflict between so-called pristine property rights (i.e., untouched land) versus developmental rights and their associated "social return" or "social savings." James Willard Hurst's *Law and the Conditions of Freedom* analyzed that tension through numerous court cases in the early 1800s, especially focusing on cases known as the "Mill Acts."[19] Hurst concluded that American business law favored developmental rights over pristine property rights, and thus a farmer who dammed a river to build a mill—thus flooding the farmers' lands above him and reducing the flow of water to those below him—provided a societal benefit greater than the harms caused the other individual farmers. Characterizing the prevailing legal approach as the "release of energy," Hurst noted that property rights were enforced as long as the property was productive, reiterating the same assumptions underlying the preemption laws and property taxes.

Road and canal building offered prime opportunities for entrepreneurs to enlist the public in their projects by promising social savings, which they usually delivered in the form of greater access to markets, lower costs for shippers, and easier travel to and from remote areas. The hidden burdens were more difficult to measure, whether in the form of losses to bondholders when roads and canals failed or the "paths not taken"—the numerous privately financed projects that might have germinated had public monies not existed. In contrast to Hurst's approach, legal historian Morton Horowitz contended that the "release of energy" simply constituted a ruse to conceal the true costs of public spending, and that the United States should have adopted a more openly redistributionist approach of using taxes to finance development.[20]

American hostility to taxes, however, coincided with the notion that the land existed for the purpose of wealth creation. Thus, American courts supported property development, all the while allowing redress for damage caused by road, canal, or rail companies to occur under liability and negligence laws. While courts tended to dismiss charges against railroads brought by farmers after sparks from the trains' metal wheels burned crops, or refrained from citing slaughterhouses for the smell they produced, they nevertheless granted restitution for genuine harm that occurred when companies "knew the score." The law emphasized intent and foreknowledge and did not penalize businesses for accidents that the owner "should have known about" in an abstract or hypothetical sense. Rather, the claimant had to show proof that the damage was due to more than bad luck; that the claimant was not negligent or his fellow workers not contributory; and that the business could have anticipated the problem by applying common sense.

Competition for the Roads: Canals

Acquiring the property rights to build plank roads or turnpikes often proved less daunting a task than that of mustering sufficient capital. Competition from a new transportation system, canals, made it even more difficult to obtain scarce financing. By comparison, the costs involved in road construction paled next to those of canals, whose expenses reached the millions of dollars. As might be expected, entrepreneurs whenever possible looked to use "other people's money," sending the entrepreneurs to the states to garner support for canal projects more than they had in the case of roads. Between 1817 and 1844 the "canal era" unfolded, bringing together more than ever before the efforts of business and government in "mixed enterprises," producing more than 4,000 miles of canals at a cost of more than $200 million. Mileage only told part of the story, however, since many canals constituted "shortcuts" that circumvented rapids or falls in the rivers or eliminated long U-shapes in rivers.

As with roads, private businesses built many of the early canals. Projects such as the Middlesex Canal in Massachusetts and the Santee and Cooper Canal in South Carolina joined together existing trading areas. The returns from commerce and identifiable markets provided ample incentive for entrepreneurs to invest in short-route canals. But obtaining funds for longer canals or for areas lacking mature markets required other approaches. Those projects tended to link less developed western trading centers with the Atlantic seaboard, or join upcountry farming regions with port cities.

The most famous American waterway, the Erie Canal, connected the Hudson River and Lake Erie, two bodies that served as hubs for further market expansion. Little population resided along the route, but the founders realized their anticipated growth quickly. Demand for such a route was so great that the state of New York—the builder of the canal—collected more than $1 million in tolls before the Erie even opened in 1825. Constructed over eight years, the Erie Canal regained its $9 million investment by 1836, with a net rate of return of 8 percent. By that time, more than 3,000 boats had traversed the canal, bringing food and raw materials to New York City and returning with immigrants headed for the Old Northwest.[21]

An engineering feat, the Erie Canal was 40 feet wide, 4 feet deep, and 363 miles long. It required 83 locks that raised and lowered boats

565 feet, traversing rivers and streams using 18 aqueducts, bordered by towpaths for draft animals needed to pull non-steam-powered vessels along the canal. As impressive as it was, the canal could not handle the volume of traffic that sought to use the route. The Board of Commissioners decided to enlarge the canal in the 1850s, and the Erie Canal finally reached its peak in tonnage in 1880.

No commissioner played a more important role in promoting and financing the "ditch" as DeWitt Clinton (1769–1828), a New York lawyer and politician who served as mayor of New York City. The quintessential "career politician"—Clinton hardly held a job outside of politics until he was over forty—he was capable and talented, and managed to drift between both the major political parties, serving as a Republican senator of New York and running for president as a Federalist. After successfully persuading the New York legislature to build the Erie Canal, he ensured its completion by insisting that construction start in the middle of the route and extend eastward and westward, thus preventing political enemies from killing the project by ensuring that *no* segment would profit from the canal until *all* did. Construction of the canal also benefited from economic disaster. When the Panic of 1819 put hundreds of farmers west of the Seneca River into bankruptcy, they went to work as construction laborers and at reduced wages as the only way to keep their land away from creditors.[22] Clinton epitomized the "political entrepreneur." Winning re-election as governor of New York in 1824, he celebrated the opening of the Erie in 1825 and died three years later.

Like any government-supported activity, the Erie Canal had unexpected market implications. New England farmers noticed that the influx of cheap western foodstuffs had eroded the prices of their own goods. Kingston, New York, merchant Abraham Hasbrouck recorded in his account books that by 1820, 40 percent of his customers lived outside the Kingston area, including a number of farmers who had gained access to the Kingston market through the Delaware and Hudson Canal and who had started to compete with local farmers.[23] And increasingly states and regions started to compete in efforts to gain federal expenditures for roads and harbor improvements. Internal improvements, such as the Maysville Road, became political cudgels used to bash enemies or precious jewels to reward partisan supporters.

Every region could make a legitimate claim that it had projects that only the government could fund. The Chesapeake and Delaware Canal Company, for example, received almost $500,000 in federal funds by pleading that it could provide strategic and military value for American armed forces. Rivers that traversed state boundaries fell under federal jurisdiction; therefore, underwater obstructions such as trees and rocks that threatened vessels were federal problems. Between 1815 and 1850, of the 736 steamboats lost on the rivers, submerged obstacles accounted for 419 of them (20 percent of the total tonnage). Entrepreneurs could clear the snags (at about $4 per snag), but only by obtaining federal contracts.[24] Government hesitated to raise tolls to cover such costs, instead shunting them off onto taxpayers, consumers, or importers. The difficulties in establishing a coherent policy had long-lasting implications, especially when it came to financing the railroads after the Civil War.

Nevertheless, the experience with the Erie Canal convinced most voters that similar canal projects in their own states, funded by the state government, could vastly improve their lives. Pennsylvania's 394-mile-long Mainline Canal from Philadelphia to Pittsburgh required 174 locks to cross a rise of mountains. Ohio and Indiana constructed elaborate networks of waterways to connect major cities and rivers. The canals certainly lowered freight rates over land transportation, with costs falling by 15 cents a ton-mile on average. Cities along canal routes thrived, as did markets for raw materials in the West.

For all its obvious advantages, the state financing of the canals came at a substantial cost. Typically, states issued bonds for construction projects or placed the "full faith and credit" of the government behind the enterprise. Unfortunately, when the canals failed, they flopped in colossal fashion. The heavy investment in bonds by state governments carried two fundamental dangers. First, it subjected states disproportionately to sudden economic changes that could have caused the value of bonds to plummet. During the Panic of 1837, the value of state-backed canal bonds collapsed, driving many states to the brink of financial ruin. Canal bonds bankrupted Indiana and Pennsylvania and eroded Ohio's credit, not to mention decimating dozens of banks across the United States. Private institutions, however, deserved their fate; they knowingly and deliberately—often enthusiastically—invested in canal bonds. Thus, the second deleterious effect fell on state taxpayers, who had to bear the brunt of debacles involving canals they never saw and could never use. When state-backed bonds went bad, the state had to indemnify the bondholders or repudiate the debt. Planters in upstate Louisiana and rural Mississippi paid costs for New Orleans canal bonds, just as backwoods South Carolina farmers later paid for failed railroads emanating from Charleston. More than 75 percent of canal investment came from public agencies in one form or another—although usually not through taxation—and often foreign investors, particularly British, bore the brunt of the losses when states or companies repudiated their bonds.

Such potential losses, which might be spread across the public as a whole or to foreigners, seemed inconsequential to the commercial groups and politicians advocating canals, who undertook exceptionally ambitious projects, usually with disappointing results, between 1826 and 1840. In 1828, the Chesapeake and Ohio Canal Company began work on a waterway to connect the District of Columbia to the Cumberland River, which it reached only in 1850 after significant cost overruns. A similar project, the James River and Kanawha Canal, never crossed the Appalachians. Ohio had produced a canal system that covered over 800 miles at a cost of $16 million, but the toll revenue never repaid the investment. Indiana's Wabash and Erie Canal, which promised to join Lake Erie on the Ohio side to Evansville, Indiana, was the longest canal in the United States—and one of the worst investments. When investors lost fortunes, occasionally costing individuals their life savings, the public had some sympathy. But when foreigners were involved, no small amount of gloating took place. Many Americans remained oblivious to the damage done to state and local credit, a fact the Confederacy learned years later when it sought financial support abroad, only to be reminded that several of its member states had defaulted on loans in the past.[25]

Specific losses, however, did not diminish the genuine contributions of the canals to society and the economy. As Jeremy Atack and Peter Passell note, overall canals drove down costs of shipping from 20 cents per ton-mile to 2 to 3 cents per ton-mile.[26] Ultimately, the authors concluded, even "a noted financial failure like the Ohio Canal yielded a respectable 10 percent social rate of return."[27]

Steam Power Comes to Ships: Fulton and Vanderbilt

Rivers were a popular and cheap form of shipping goods during the early 1800s. But sailing upstream was extremely time-consuming and expensive, involving the use of keel boats propelled by twenty or more men pushing long poles into the riverbed or flatboats pulled by draft animals on paths to the side. Either way was painfully slow, perhaps explaining why so much folklore evolved related to the American rivers, in that bored keelmen or captains had to tell stories to stay awake. As for pulling flatboats with mules or oxen on paths to the side of the river, clearing a road for animals cost as much as making a primitive wagon road, defeating the purpose of the investment.

Robert Fulton changed all that in 1807 when he demonstrated the first steamship in America as his *Clermont* sailed from New York City up the Hudson River to Albany. Fulton's technical accomplishment with the *Clermont* only accounted for part of his success; the remainder can be attributed to the fact that the "New York legislature gave Fulton the privilege of carrying *all* steamboat traffic in New York [state] for thirty years."[28] Along with his partner, Robert L. Livingston, Fulton created the Mississippi Steamboat Company in 1809 and constructed the *New Orleans*, a side-wheeler vessel for use on western waters. But as occurred with Whitney, Fulton's success merely demonstrated the feasibility of making steam-powered boats, and a host of imitators soon followed. Access to the business was easy, with basic vessels costing as little as $20,000, and returns accrued quickly at a rate of up to 24 percent, according to one study.[29] More than 700 steamboats plied the western rivers by 1850, constituting perhaps the single most important ingredient in the nation's internal trade.

Steam vessels played an even more important role on the Great Lakes, where ships occasionally exceeded 1,000 tons and, in the case of the *City of Buffalo,* displaced a whopping 2,200 tons. Operated by single entrepreneurs, partnerships, and corporations, steam companies dominated transportation in the Great Lakes region; by midcentury, "the tonnage on the Mississippi River and on the Great Lakes exceeded that of all shipping from New York City by over 200 percent."[30]

With ease of access, relatively low technology costs, and open interstate waterways, it was to be expected that an industry as vibrant as steamboating would find itself at the center of constitutional questions. Steamboats, and a new star on the business horizon, Cornelius Vanderbilt, were involved in a key Supreme Court ruling on the monopoly power of charters. Thomas Gibbons, a New Jersey steamboat owner, had hired a young entrepreneur named Cornelius Vanderbilt to challenge the Fulton passenger monopoly between Elizabeth, New Jersey, and New York City in 1817. Technically in violation of the law, and pursued by agents of the Fulton monopoly, Vanderbilt "defied capture as he raced passengers cheaply" between the two sites for sixty days, becoming a "popular figure on the Atlantic as he lowered the fares and eluded the law."[31] The rebellious captain even hoisted a flag over the mast of Gibbons's ship that read, "New Jersey must be free." Although the wheels of justice ground slowly, they finally provided a decision in 1824 in the case of *Gibbons v. Ogden,* in which the Supreme Court ruled that only the federal government, and not the states, could regulate interstate commerce. Citizens of New Jersey, cognizant that the Court had struck a blow for consumers, greeted Commodore Vanderbilt (as they called him) in New Brunswick with cannon salutes; New Yorkers launched steamships of their own—one named for John Marshall, the Chief Justice who had delivered the favorable ruling. Fares plummeted everywhere: The cost of a trip from New York City to Albany fell from $7 to $3 after Gibbons's (and Vanderbilt's) victory.

Vanderbilt pioneered a concept, which infused mass markets almost a century later, called a "loss leader," in which one product is sold cheaply (or even given away) as a means to attract customers, enabling the business to make profits on related goods and services. A staple of the modern motion picture theater's business strategy, tickets to movies are disproportionately reduced in price while soft drinks and other concessions are sold at prices double or triple those of the products elsewhere. Vanderbilt understood the concept of "loss leaders" perfectly. When he moved his steamboat business to New York's Hudson River, he calculated that he could cut the fare to Albany from $3 to ten cents! Eventually, he charged no fare at all, estimating that if he could fill each boat with 100 passengers, he would make a profit if each person ate or drank up to $2 worth of food.

Vanderbilt's two boats, called the "People's Line," competed with the powerful Hudson River Association, which reluctantly admitted that it could not match his prices. The association concluded that it was cheaper to buy out Vanderbilt than to cut costs or increase efficiency, and it offered him a one-time payment of $100,000 plus $5,000 annually to leave the region—the 1800s version of the "golden parachute." Vanderbilt took the deal, and the association quickly boosted its rates back to around $3, still slightly less than before the Commodore ever entered the fray. But Vanderbilt had not only made himself rich, he had lowered costs permanently for all travelers, because every entrepreneurial steamboater on the Hudson soon competed to carry passengers, with each promising a lower fare. All the association gained was a treasury $100,000 smaller.

Of course, Vanderbilt did not disappear. He had watched the rise of another business, that of transatlantic shipping and passenger travel, especially after Congress had started to pay shipper Edward K. Collins to deliver mail across the Atlantic for a subsidy payment of $3 million down and $385,000 per year. In return, Collins promised to outrace the British competition, the Cunard shipping line. Samuel Cunard himself had attained his dominance of the oceans through a subsidy from the British government to run a packet line from Liverpool to Boston. Congress, reacting to concerns over "unfair competition," was certain no individual entrepreneur could defeat the English company without assistance. When the Cunard line added New York City to its destinations in 1848, competing directly with American companies, Collins saw an opportunity to convince Congress to subsidize an American competitor.[32]

The American sailing companies still clung to the beautiful, but suddenly obsolete, "clipper ships." Clipper ships, with their numerous sails, attained remarkable speed in their time, and they facilitated the China tea and porcelain trade. Eventually, though, as steam technology moved from the rivers to the oceans, the clippers found themselves outclassed. Cunard understood the exceptional advantages offered by steam, and when Collins made his first proposal for a subsidized line in 1847, the appearance of the Cunard line ensured that he received a warm reception. Collins formed the United States Mail Steamship Company, commonly called the "Collins Line." He promised to build five steamships that would be the fastest in the world, and indeed his ships beat the English crossing the Atlantic by about a day. But his costs never fell. Using taxpayer money, Collins had no incentive to reduce costs at all, and his expenses doubled from 1847 to 1852! Instead of finding ways to improve his performance, and his ships' efficiencies, Collins "artfully lobbied in Congress for an increase to $858,000 a year" to keep the English on their heels."[33]

Vanderbilt knew Collins's prices were too high, but the Commodore was not immune to the lure of government subsidies. Thus, when Vanderbilt first announced that he could deliver mail for less than Cunard and half the price Collins received, his first goal was to obtain a federal subsidy for himself. He offered to run the Atlantic routes for $15,000 per trip (compared to $33,000 per trip for Collins). Congress, perhaps embarrassed by committing too much, too early, to Collins, could not abandon him easily.

At that point, Vanderbilt took the battle directly to the market, slashing prices on both mail and passenger fares. He cut costs by eliminating insurance, and instead ploughed the money into sturdier ships and hired excellent captains. (In doing so, Vanderbilt also recognized another maxim of business, namely that insurance cannot prevent a loss, only replace some of the lost value.) Vanderbilt's cheaper boats quickly attained greater economies than Collins's bloated fleet, but the Commodore still had to contend with Collins's cushion of subsidies. He complained that it was "utterly impossible for a private individual to stand in competition with a line drawing nearly one million dollars per annum from the national treasury."[34] Yet Vanderbilt did just that.

Rather than reduce his investment, the Commodore put more into the enterprise, spending $600,000 on a new steamship, the *Vanderbilt,* which beat Collins's ship in a race to England. Further embarrassment greeted Collins when two of his ships sank and the replacement vessel he constructed using government funds—a $1 million, 4,000-ton paddle-wheeler called the *Adriatic*—was a phenomenal failure. The most ironic twist of all came after Vanderbilt finally achieved victory over Collins, while simultaneously William Inman in England had driven out the subsidized Cunard line with his own version of Vanderbilt's unsubsidized fleet! Inman had revolutionized steamships by incorporating new screw propellers and iron hulls, and by 1858, "two market entrepreneurs, Vanderbilt and Inman, led America and England in cheap mail and passenger service."[35]

Vanderbilt had one more lesson to teach on the superiority of market forces over government subsidies. He had struggled to gain a share of the burgeoning California mail, freight, and passenger business, but once again he faced two competitors each armed with annual $500,000 federal subsidies. Those lines charged a staggering $600 per passenger from New York to California, via Panama. Vanderbilt ignored Panama and constructed his own river route through Nicaragua, paying the Nicaraguan government $10,000 a year for canal privileges. He then slashed passenger fares to $400 and offered to carry the mail free! Within a year, New York–to–California fares dropped to $150. Typically, rather than compete with Vanderbilt, the established lines begged Congress for a higher subsidy; and when a Nicaraguan revolution resulted in Vanderbilt losing his canal rights, he simply moved to Panama and cut fares again, to $100. Unable to compete with the Commodore, the California companies finally bought him out, at a cost of $672,000, or 75 percent of their (increased) annual subsidy. As might be expected, with Vanderbilt out of the picture, the California steamers raised prices, to $300.

Was Vanderbilt, who almost singlehandedly made steamboat travel affordable for the average customer, lionized as a friend of the consumer? One could hardly tell it by some of the comments of the day. According to one court, Vanderbilt's price cutting was "immoral and in restraint of trade," while the *New York Times* compared him to "those old German Barons who, from their eyries along the Rhine, swooped down upon the commerce of the noble river and wrung tribute from every passenger that floated by."[36] Polemics aside, it is difficult to see how a man who did not even charge fares "wrung tribute" from anyone. But even when he no longer competed directly, the Commodore's influence benefited travelers: The $300 fare charged by the California companies after they raised prices still represented a 50 percent reduction from the pre-Vanderbilt rates.

Birth of the Rail Age

Just as steam technology improved transport by water, it had a revolutionary effect on transportation on land through a relatively new invention, the steam-powered locomotive. In 1825, George Stephenson developed effective locomotives, and in 1830 his *Rocket* made its debut in England, speeding down rails connecting Liverpool and Manchester. The American railroad industry was born in 1828 when a hardware merchant and bank president named Phillip E. Thomas led a group of Baltimore businessmen to obtain a charter for the Baltimore and Ohio Railroad (B&O) to compete directly with the Chesapeake and Ohio Canal. Hardly a technological wonder at first—the company depended on horse-drawn wagons that rode the rails—the B&O received its first steam locomotive that summer. At that time, a New York inventor named Peter Cooper brought his "Tom Thumb" to the line; it promptly lost a race against a horse and left investors to discount the value of steam-powered rail traffic. But steam-powered railroads did not go away. By 1831, several railroads demonstrated steam locomotives, and the B&O adopted steam as its sole means of rail power.

One of the first to show that steam locomotives could be profitable was the South Carolina Canal and Railroad Company, which extended westward from Charleston. In 1830, its locomotive *Best Friend of Charleston* (the first ever built for sale in the United States) lugged its 140 passengers on the first steam locomotive trip in American history. Within a few short years, railroad building reached levels contemporaries referred to as a "fever," a "frenzy," and a "mania." The explosion in railroad building benefited from associated gains in technology, such as when Robert L. Stevens, the president of the Camden and Amboy Railroad in New Jersey, created the familiar "T-rail," a remarkable advance over the existing wooden rails. The new iron T-rails rested on large wooden ties laid across crushed stone roadbeds.[37]

Matthias Baldwin Builds Locomotives

One might expect an iron merchant to create the first successful locomotives in America, but instead a jeweler, Matthias Baldwin, built the best railroad equipment. Baldwin grew up in Philadelphia—a thriving center of railroad technology—and completed an apprenticeship as a jeweler, but he found that career unrewarding, describing his nine self-employed years as the low point in his life. At age thirty, he opened a bookbinding machine-tool business with a partner. Baldwin revolutionized a process used to etch designs onto rolled metal surfaces, and, over time, the Baldwin-Mason partnership needed a larger factory. Searching for a means to power the tools in the workshop, Baldwin tinkered with a steam engine before he gave up and decided he could build his own, better, engine. He soon produced little else but steam engines.

A Philadelphia museum official contacted Baldwin about providing an engine for a model locomotive at the museum, one capable of pulling four passengers. His locomotive attracted such attention that in 1832 the Germantown & Norristown Railroad contracted with him to build a full-sized locomotive. Baldwin worked with existing designs, turning out "Old Ironsides," a steam boiler on a wooden frame that drove wooden wheels. But the railroad, claiming that the locomotive did not meet its performance goals, attempted to cheat Baldwin out of a portion of his $4,000 contract. Baldwin, livid at the railroad's deception, vowed never to build another locomotive again, but he was besieged by railroads demanding locomotives. Within five years, he built ten more locomotives before moving to a new plant, where he turned out more than 1,500 locomotives until his death in 1866. By that time, Baldwin Engine and Locomotive built a variety of engines for export, shipping his first overseas to Cuba in 1838.

Expansion into the new facility had brought substantial debt, however, which coincided with the Panic of 1837. Despite his success and his contracts, Matthias Baldwin was bankrupt. A devout Christian and a teetotaler, though a man of dry humor, Baldwin put his faith into action. He "negotia[ted] with his creditors, convinced them not to seize his property, pledging to pay off the debts—with interest—within three years."[38] As convincing as Baldwin may have been, the creditors no doubt looked with dismay on the prospect of receiving only 25 cents on the dollar if they liquidated his works at that time. In reality, it took him five years, and a "rather gutsy bet."[39] Baldwin, knowing he needed relief from his administrative duties to concentrate on a newer, more powerful locomotive design, brought in another partner, George Huffy (along with a third partner, George Vail, who had helped keep the business afloat with a $20,000 loan), who contributed only his expertise and managerial talent for his one-third interest. In 1839 and 1840, Baldwin created a flexible-beam design that transmitted power to three axles, with the front two capable of pivoting. Armed with a winning design, Baldwin nevertheless found sales slow in the early 1840s, leading him to develop a new sales strategy in which he accepted half his payment in cash upon delivery and the remainder within six months.

By 1850 Baldwin's factory actually consisted of three machine shops supported by a boiler factory, a foundry, and a smith shop, each with its own foreman. As the biographer of the Baldwin business noted, the foremen "oversaw all work in their departments, ensuring that parts were made on time to the required dimensions and coordinating output among the shops. These considerable powers made the foremen the absolute masters of their own departments."[40] Inside the shops, a small army of skilled artisans worked sheet iron and copper, built boilers, made patterns and molds, improved and repaired machines, etched metal, painted, and built the necessary lumber scaffolds. In addition, the firm employed numerous unskilled carriers and "gofers." Up to 400 men could work at one factory alone by 1840, with a force of just over 200 capable of turning out a locomotive in 60 days.

Railroads and American Life

Thanks to productive firms like Baldwin's, by the 1840s America's railroads already were having a profound effect on daily life. For example, service on the Erie Railway linked Orange County, New York's leading dairy county, to New York City, and in 1842 an agent for the railroad, Thomas Selleck, persuaded a local farmer to ship his fresh milk to the city, where it sold out instantly. Shortly, the price of fresh milk brought by rail was lower than that of "swill milk"—milk from cows kept by brewers and distillers in New York, which had been the only source of milk for most people. Swill milk also had been the source of such diseases as tuberculosis, cholera, and milk-borne diseases, contributing to the city's high infant mortality rate, and was virtually eliminated, thanks to fresh milk supplied by the railroad.[41]

Most states had railroads by 1840, while states along the Atlantic seaboard held more than 60 percent of the total rail mileage in the nation. Nevertheless, by the 1840s, the golden age of railroading was at least a decade away. In part, the Panic of 1837, whose effects lasted in some states until 1842, bankrupted several roads and dried up financing of others. As with the canals, foreign investors suffered heavily in the collapse, forcing American railroads to turn to the early capital markets in New York or to the states for financing.[42] Seldom did individuals start railroads alone, although some pioneers, such as William Earl Dodge, played key roles in promoting or founding several railroads. Dodge, for example, who had worked in his father's dry-goods store, then inherited it, left the mercantile business to join with Anson Phelps to start Phelps Dodge, a metal import firm in 1832. In the process of supplying metal products, William Dodge became intimately familiar with railroads and their operations. He promoted the New York & Erie, eventually being named a director; then he founded the Central Railroad Company of New Jersey, ultimately resigning his position as a director because of his disagreement with the railroad's policy of running on Sundays.[43] Dodge's railroad career typified those of dozens of other nineteenth-century entrepreneurs, including John Garrett, Francis Drake, and Collis Huntington, some of whom rose from abject poverty to head powerful railroad corporations. Usually, however, they did so from the outside, starting or expanding their own (or their family's) businesses, investing in railroads, and increasing their interest until they attained a sizable enough position to run the enterprise themselves.

Railroads' high capital demands distinguished them immediately from other forms of business organization, but they differed from other large-scale enterprises such as canals in other aspects. Railroads came into existence much later than canals, when the nation had more relative wealth and thereby could tap more capital for more extensive growth. Unlike canals, they spawned industries—such as iron—almost entirely devoted to filling their specific demands. And, in terms of structure and organization, most railroads were not sole proprietorships, but were corporations chartered by state governments.

Railroads and the Corporate Form

Railroads, of course, were not the first enterprises to use the corporate charter as a form of business organization. Compared to other undertakings, however, railroads used the corporate form far more extensively. The railroads' unusually large capital demands often required them to sell securities to raise funds, which required the corporate form. Moreover, railroads crossed long stretches of land, making geographical oversight by a sole proprietor difficult. Our look at railroads, therefore, must take a brief side excursion into the appearance and refinement of corporate law in the nineteenth century.

Companies had used incorporation as a standard practice since the London Company, but the majority of American businesses in the early 1800s were owned by a single person or a partnership. That changed with the turnpike and canal movements, which introduced many businessmen to the economics, finance, and organization of large-scale enterprises. At their root, corporations imitated "the hierarchical organization structure of armies, governments, and churches."[44] While large size had some drawbacks, particularly what economists call "agency risk," wherein the corporate hierarchy tends to operate an organization for its own benefit at the expense of the corporation's established purposes, the undesirable traits were controlled easily through the sale of shares by dissatisfied stockholders.

Corporations had the other obvious advantages discussed in previous chapters: limited liability, unlimited life, and ease of ownership by small investors. Early corporations, from local hospitals to the Bank of the United States, also had implied monopoly benefits. The corporate charter gave the company rights to do business within certain geographic areas or to offer a certain product or service (such as issuing notes). In the first decades of the 1800s, however, new refinements of corporate powers and responsibilities occurred through four momentous Supreme Court cases.

First, the Supreme Court, under Chief Justice John Marshall, ruled on two cases in 1819. In *Dartmouth College v. Woodward,* Dartmouth College had a charter from pre-Revolutionary times, which represented a contract as stipulated by the Constitution. The Court ruled that subsequent legislatures could not revoke the charter (as New Hampshire had attempted to do) or otherwise abrogate contracts. Justice Joseph Story's concurrence also held that if a state wanted to control a corporation, it merely needed do so in the original charter or reserve the right to alter or amend the charter at a later date.

The second critical case for American business, *Gibbons v. Ogden* (1824), established the authority of the federal government over interstate waterways, having the unintended effect of enhancing competition. A third case also involved the principle of competition, namely *Charles River Bridge v. Warren Bridge* (1837). Chief Justice Roger B. Taney presided over the court, which ruled on a claim of charter violation, thus impinging on the sanctity of contracts. The Charles River Bridge Company assumed that its charter had given it a monopoly over toll traffic across the Charles River. When the Warren Bridge Company attempted to compete, the former firm sued. Ruling in favor of the Warren Bridge Company, the Supreme Court took a giant step away from the pre-Revolutionary notion that a charter implied monopoly power. Only if the charter stated that a monopoly was granted did it delegate such rights, the Court stated.

A fourth case involved the actions of "foreign corporations," or businesses chartered in one state attempting to do business in another. The issue came before the Court in the 1839 case *Bank of Augusta v. Earle,* in which Joseph Earle, a debtor, sought relief by claiming that the creditor, the Bank of Augusta, chartered in Georgia, had no legal authority in Alabama.[45] Appreciating that a ruling against corporations could stifle all interstate trade, the Court ruled that corporations could conduct business under laws of "comity," or mutual expressions of good faith, across state lines unless expressly prohibited by the legislatures of the states in question.

Taken together, those four cases established the framework that allowed entrepreneurs in America to flourish. Sanctity of contracts, the preeminence of competition over monopoly, the presumption that corporations were interstate entities, and the open passage of federal waterways all contributed to business enterprise. Jointly, though, the cases also signaled that the federal government, and not the states, was in charge. Corporations certainly benefited from most, if not all, of the decisions, which meant that railroads, the most numerous of the newly incorporated businesses, stood to gain considerably from their legal positions as corporations. But merely possessing the corporate form and actually obtaining the capital to operate a railroad were two separate issues. The development of commercial and investment banking during the period was fundamentally interwoven into the story of the railroads. Thus, our side excursion requires yet one more stop, nineteenth-century banking.

Like railroads, banks used the charter process often, but under closer observation by state regulators or legislators than the railroads. When necessary, banks incorporated *with* railroads, using the mechanism of banknote issues to finance rail-line construction. By the 1830s, the banking population had exploded, almost-doubling between 1834 and 1840—including three depression years. Because bank operations before the Civil War were so different from today, a few of the basics bear repeating. Any chartered bank could issue money (notes); it backed those notes with a specie reserve of gold and silver coin; and banks were established primarily to provide loans to the directors and other so-called insiders. Banks tended to finance smaller-scale operations and provided merchants and farmers with working capital. Generally, they did not invest in large-scale projects, such as canals or railroads. When they did, banks usually had political support from the state or localities to guarantee the bonds in case of a financial collapse. Gradually, specialists appeared to finance large projects, while commercial banks focused on the business of merchants and farmers.

Periodic panics (1819 and 1837) had led to attempts to make the banking system more sound, yet at the same time relieve the state legislatures of the burdens of issuing charters individually. Yet knowledgeable legislators and bankers alike differed over the best way to accomplish those ends. Part of the difficulty stemmed from the tumultuous history of the Second Bank of the United States (BUS) and the "Bank War" that resulted in its death.

Nicholas Biddle, Andrew Jackson, and the "War" on the BUS

After its recharter in 1816, the Second BUS had been blamed (inaccurately) for the Panic of 1819, but it struggled through to stability by 1823, when the directors brought in a new president, Nicholas Biddle. A Pennsylvania lawyer and former secretary to the U.S. ambassador to France, Biddle found himself managing his wife's estate outside of Philadelphia. He threw himself into farming, experimenting with crops and livestock to improve productivity and publishing some of his research.

Biddle's previous political connections gained him a seat on the board of directors of the Second BUS, and in 1823 Biddle took over the reins of the largest business institution in the nation. Capitalized at $35 million, the BUS dwarfed other enterprises. Biddle took his job seriously and scientifically, and "in many ways [was] the forerunner of the modern business executive."[46] He oversaw the operations of the bank, exerting control over managerial personnel in branches, maintained a steady flow of information from the branch managers, and instituted regular inspections by teams of cashiers sent from the central office to examine the accuracy of records.

Under Biddle, the BUS has been credited with maintaining discipline among the state banks, over which the BUS had no direct control. But, according to some scholars, the BUS restrained the state banks from overissuing notes by posing the threat of "raids." The discipline imposed by the BUS worked when state banks issued notes backed by specie reserves. A bank's notes were exchanged at other banks for specie, whereupon the notes were returned to the source of origination. The BUS, which had branches scattered throughout the Union, acquired the notes of most banks at one point or another during its normal business. It could, if BUS managers suspected that a bank was overissuing notes, stage a "raid" in which the BUS would collect large amounts of the suspected violator's notes and present them in a surprise visit for specie or BUS notes. That threat, in theory, required the state banks to keep either large specie reserves or substantial reserves of BUS notes on hand. In either case, the BUS, acting as an early "central bank," instilled discipline on the entire commercial banking sector.[47]

Most historians accepted this interpretation of the BUS's powers, and they proposed an explanation of the Bank War and the Panic of 1837 as deriving from Jackson's destruction of the bank. Briefly, according to the "traditional" interpretation of events, Biddle blundered by attempting to get Congress to recharter the BUS in 1832—an election year, and four years ahead of the charter's expiration—by reasoning that the politicians could not oppose the recharter of such a popular institution.[48] President Andrew Jackson, who had a personal history of difficulties with banks, judged that he could gain politically from vetoing the bill. Jackson framed the debate as pitting "the elites" and the "moneyed interests" who supported the BUS against the "common man" oppressed by the large, monopoly institution. Although Congress passed the bill, it did not have the necessary two-thirds majority to override Jackson's veto. Jackson then withdrew the government's deposits from the BUS and placed them in state banks controlled by his political friends, giving the banks their nickname "pet banks." With its deposit base shrunken dramatically and a charter certain to expire, the BUS limped through the last years of its life.

Meanwhile, according to the theory, the state banks, sensing that the BUS had lost its ability to discipline them even before the final nails were driven into its coffin, started to issue notes in greater quantities. Not only did this generate inflation by putting additional money in circulation, but many of the notes gravitated to the western regions, where settlers used them to pay for newly purchased land. Jackson attempted to stop the practice of paying for land with paper money by issuing the Specie Circular (1836), mandating that buyers use specie to pay for western land. At roughly the same time, Jackson took the federal government surplus and returned it to the states, but not in proportions they had paid in tariffs. The disruption of the financial markets caused by the massive shifts of government and private funds in all directions, topped by the Specie Circular, sparked the Panic of 1837. According to traditionalists, then, Jackson was responsible both for the prepanic inflation and for the policies that started the worst depression in American history up to that point.[49]

A number of scholars, however, started to question the traditional school as early as 1961, when Richard Timberlake published the first of several articles or books on antebellum banking, and capped by the appearance of Peter Temin's *The Jacksonian Economy* (1969).[50] These works showed that (1) the demise of the BUS had no significant effect on the inflation of the period; (2) the inflation could be traced to silver flows from Mexico to the United States to China to England, which lowered interest rates on loans to companies and projects in the United States; and (3) the depression occurred when the Mexican silver dried up, raising interest rates. Subsequent research refined further the positions of the adversaries, in particular showing that Jackson and the Democrats were opposed not to a national bank per se but rather one controlled by their political enemies, and revealed that in 1829 Jackson himself had enthusiastically embraced a national bank plan designed by his own party members.[51]

Meanwhile, the demand for banks and capital continued unabated, leaving state legislatures looking for ways to relieve themselves of the burdensome task of dealing with petitions for banks while making the banking system *sans* BUS safer, more stable, and more solvent during times of distress. States adopted a number of reforms, including general incorporation laws (called "free banking" laws for banks), primitive deposit guaranty or insurance funds, and clearinghouse arrangements. The "free banking" laws allowed any individual or company to establish a bank after it placed on deposit with the secretary of the state in question a predetermined dollar value of acceptable bonds. Frequently, entrepreneurs used state government bonds or railroad bonds.

Some states had unmitigated disasters with free banking, leading to calls for greater government control over the banking system. But as a number of articles by Federal Reserve Board economists Arthur Rolnick and Warren Weber have shown, the weakness lay in the wording of the laws themselves by permitting bankers to put bonds on deposit whose *par value* (face value) might be higher than their market value. Shady operators quickly identified states with those specific provisions and managed to use the disparity between the market value of the notes they issued, and for which they took in good notes or specie, and the face value of bonds, which they willingly forfeited when they skipped town. States quickly adjusted by inserting market-value clauses into their laws, but the episode gave a bad name to "free banking," which in any event was never "free market banking," but merely a different version of state control over banking via the bond requirements.[52]

The state of New York attempted to curtail bank losses by establishing a type of reserve fund, called the Safety Fund, which resembled modern deposit insurance. In the Safety Fund (established in 1829), each bank in New York City paid an assessment to provide an emergency fund to cover losses to depositors. Proponents of the fund point out that it paid 100 cents on the dollar, but the fund failed to prevent runs during the Panic of 1837, which did not keep advocates of deposit insurance schemes from using it as a successful example for federal deposit insurance in the 1930s. Boston tried a different approach, creating a clearinghouse association in 1852, whereby member banks established a central location for clearing notes and currency. Both the Safety Fund and the clearinghouse associations represented nongovernment, private attempts to organize and streamline antebellum banking based on the assumption that bankers and depositors would behave rationally if they had reliable information. Subsequent studies on financial panics and manias has suggested that indeed the weakest element in the banking system in the nineteenth century was the transmission of information, a weakness the BUS had avoided, as its enthusiasts pointed out.[53]

Banks and Railroads, Reprise

Professionals in the financial system recognized the need for unprecedented new levels of capital, especially by the railroads. By the Civil War, each of the fifty largest railroads had a capitalization more than *ten times* that of the next largest manufacturing company, creating virtually a separate market for railroad securities. States could meet some of the demand through bond sales, issuing more than $90 million in bonds to finance railroad construction between 1845 and 1860. But private investors, not governments, supplied most of the capital required by the railroads in the antebellum period. Securities dealers scoured markets in Europe, while in America prominent bankers formed syndicates, or large groups of investors, to fund railroad building. Men such as Ohio's Alfred Kelley, who had once promoted canals as a means to economic growth, turned to railroad building in the 1840s. But essentially they remained commercial bankers dabbling in investment banking, and to handle the huge financial demands the railroads posed, an entirely separate group of financiers appeared.

Among the most famous of the early investment bankers, George Peabody, a Massachusetts dry-goods merchant, had aided the state of Maryland when it verged on bankruptcy in 1835. Peabody and his partner, Elisha Riggs, sold $8 million in state bonds, saving Maryland from disaster, after which he returned his $200,000 fee to the state. Peabody's career was typical of a new generational path among businessmen, literally inverting the previous patterns. Whereas New England merchants started banks to support their textile, iron, and other businesses, in the 1840s and 1850s bankers themselves started to look at railroads as a source of investment. Peabody, for example, incorporated the Eastern Railroad in 1836, then, convinced his American managers could run the operation, moved to London, where he intended to develop his investment firm to support the railroad.

Another prominent investment house of the era, Drexel & Company, originated in Philadelphia in 1837. Anthony Drexel learned from his banker father and became a full partner in his father's firm in 1847. Within a decade, he had a reputation as the guiding genius of the operation. Drexel concentrated on government bonds and railroad issues, eventually taking as a partner Junius Morgan, whose own career had centered on bonds and stocks. Morgan worked as a partner in J. M. Beebe, Morgan & Co., a Boston dry-goods wholesaler, and in the course of that work he went to London as the company's representative. There, he met Peabody, who by that time needed a younger man to run his business. Morgan joined the Peabody firm, employing Morgan's son, John Pierpont (J. P.) as a secretary in the counting house. Young J. P. Morgan, educated in Switzerland, lived in comfort in London but nevertheless took his duties seriously, "tirelessly copying letters and documents for which neither typewriter, carbon paper, nor copying machine yet existed."[54] But J. P. Morgan did not make his mark on American finance until after the Civil War, even though he returned to America to take a clerkship with Duncan, Sherman & Company. But already firms such as Peabody's, Drexel's, and dozens of others had turned on the financial faucets to domestic industries, especially railroads.

As the available capital flowed into the railroads, track mileage grew steadily, while technology, including standardization of rails and couplers, improved continuously. An entire ancillary industry sprang up to support railroads, including wheel shops, brake and coupler manufacturers, boiler makers, and rail manufacturers. At one time, "railroads absorbed as much as 30 percent of the iron produced in the 1840s."[55]

The lifeline, therefore, between the banks and the railroads extended further into the economy, boosting the already flourishing iron industry. As with textiles, the iron industry reacted to foreign competition by appealing to Congress for protective tariffs against British iron producers. In 1842, Congress responded by placing duties on imported iron. When tariffs ended and protection was greatly reduced, iron production in America *increased*.[56] American iron producers seemed stimulated by the renewed competition, and by 1860 American mills had become fully competitive with the British, in part because the end of protection eliminated the old charcoal smelters and obsolete mills, leaving the newer anthracite smelters in a position to meet the demand for the newer nonrail products.[57]

Thus, by 1850, the transportation revolution had brought within its web aspects of the U.S. economy as diverse as banks and boiler manufacturers, canals and couples, wheels and wheat. Interlacing each of these elements—welding one to the others—was a revolution in communication and information, which made standardized manuals, bond prices, train schedules, and toll costs available to a large segment of the business community.

Communication Networks, National Markets

With vast distances linked by an expanding national network of roads, canals, and railroad tracks, the flow of information accelerated faster than ever, lowering prices for producers and consumers alike. "Information costs," as economists call them, refer to the "costs, to both buyers and sellers, of obtaining accurate and timely information for sound business decisions."[58] Banks, for example, had to hope that their edition of *Dillistin's Bank Note Reporter* was the most recent, or that they had the most recent bond prices if they dealt in bonds. Merchants could gain or lose significant amounts of money if they did not have appropriate information about their markets—a fact not lost on Lewis Tappan and his Mercantile Agency, which in 1841 began to provide early credit information for a fee. Tappan's creation of a centralized source of information on merchants and wholesalers was enhanced by the local opinions and reports of confidential agents, often lawyers whom Tappan contacted to become his correspondents.[59] A rival business, the Cincinnati-based Bradstreet Company, founded eight years after the Mercantile Agency, beat its competitor to the punch, publishing the first credit-rating reference book in 1857. Bradstreet's reports emphasized large cities. Tappan's Mercantile Agency, on the other hand, which concentrated on country businesses, issued its first credit-reporting volume in 1859, thus providing no shortage of credit evaluation and reporting instruments for the business community before the Civil War.

The same year that Tappan had established the Mercantile Agency, a grain broker in Chicago, W. I. Whiting, teamed with a grain-elevator operator named Thomas Richmond to establish criteria for inspecting and grading grain, pork, or beef, further expanding the concept that value was added by information. They founded a club that eventually became the Chicago Board of Trade. Manufacturers counted on the timely delivery of new orders from buyers, or accurate notification about delivery of raw materials; merchants needed reports of creditworthiness; commodities buyers needed systematic and timely data about produce, meat, and grains; and everyone could benefit from intelligence about competitors.[60]

One proven and established source of information transmission, the U.S. Post Office, had been provided for by the Constitution and formed the earliest internal communication network in the nation. The post office, with 18,468 branches by 1850—one for every 1,300 people, reaching across thousands of miles of roads—touched almost every developed area of the United State.[61] A town obtained a post office branch by lobbying Congress, and as branches proliferated, so did the number of letters sent and received. Lacking a post office branch, correspondents frequently shipped their letters with regular transportation companies, such as shipping firms or stagecoaches, known as "common carriers." Steamboats carried mail as early as 1813, and in 1837 the first railroad mail car appeared. In remote areas, people commonly entrusted personal letters that had no business urgency to private individuals traveling in the general direction of the letter's destination. Under those circumstances, a person gave up privacy rights to whatever he had written or would read, for it was generally known that the carriers, while en route, tended to open and read the mail for entertainment. Entrepreneurs like Vanderbilt kept the pressure on subsidized mail carriers to maintain good service and somewhat reasonable prices. The famous postage stamp, introduced in 1847, allowed people to mail letters even when the local post office branch might be closed. Postal charges of three cents for a single letter mailed in 1851 reflected not only lower transportation costs but also the fact that the post office, despite 1850 revenues of $5.5 million, did not pay for itself.

As the number of U.S. Post Office branches increased, and with each branch in charge of several employees, the post office wielded considerable political clout. In the mid-1800s, the position of postmaster general was a political plum next to secretary of state. Richard John, who has written extensively on the post office, found that in 1831 the postal system controlled over 8,700 postmaster jobs alone—over three-fourths of the entire federal civilian workforce and larger than the army.[62] Such patronage explains, in part, the ability of companies receiving federal mail subsidies to repel challenges from private entrepreneurs to the government's monopoly on mail, which, as Federal Express has demonstrated, continues in modern times. Entrepreneurs established "private expresses" in the mid-1830s to wrest business away from Uncle Sam, but Congress responded by lowering the subsidized postal rate to the point that most private entrepreneurs (other than an occasional Vanderbilt) could not sustain the long-term losses needed to compete in regular mail delivery of letters.

A second factor helped explain the determination on the part of Congress to keep the mails in public hands. As John observed, "Since congressional apportionment was based on population and constituents were constantly clamoring for new routes, there existed a built-in bias in favor of expanding the postal network on the basis of population rather than . . . commercial demand."[63] Many of the new routes did not bear more than *1 percent* of their cost. Later, as Congress understood the franking privileges of using public mails, still another incentive was added to defeat private competitors. The surprising thing is not that private competitors lasted only a short time but that, given the structural disincentives, they existed at all.

Proponents of the public mail system point to its benefits, especially in subsidizing the distribution of newspapers: Between 1800 and 1840, the number of newspapers transmitted through the postal system rose from just under 2 million to almost 40 million. According to John, by permitting newspapers to be shipped through the mails at substantially cheaper rates, the government created a national market for information long before a similar market for goods developed. But if newspapers had to pay the same rate as other mails, their transmission costs would have been *700 times* higher.[64] Ironically, since books and larger magazines did not receive the same postal rates, publishing businesses concentrated on the more profitable newspapers and less on books, with newspapers being highly politicized organs of the existing parties. Since partisan political arguments received the "condensed" treatment from the daily or weekly press, which catered to summary discussions of events instead of deep, thoughtful inquiries, the system built in a bias in favor of brief, and often shallow, treatments at the expense of longer and (possibly) deeper intellectual treatments.

Wells Fargo Delivers the Mail

Shipping packages, however, was a much different story than letter delivery. In the late 1830s, a steamboat agent in New York City had started a package express delivery service to Boston, where the receiving agent was a young former shoemaker with a speech impediment, Henry Wells. For several years, Wells had run a chain of speech-therapy schools in central and northern New York, which, despite moderate financial success, had failed to solve Wells's own speech problems. Almost immediately upon the opening of the New York–Boston route, Wells imagined a stage carrier line running westward to Chicago and beyond. He worked through a string of jobs over a ten-year period in which he moved closer to his dream of a transcontinental stage line, in the process associating with William George Fargo. An 1842 encounter with a hotel operator who desperately wanted to feature oysters on his menu provided the motivation for Wells to undertake unusual and difficult deliveries. He realized that some people would pay handsomely for the fastest possible delivery (Wells charged $3 per 100 oysters, an unimaginable sum at the time), and in 1845 he founded a company with Fargo and Daniel Dunning that stretched westward to Cincinnati, Detroit, and Chicago.

Wells's company embodied all that customers expect from a mail or delivery service. He dispatched messengers with simple instructions in the worst weather: "You are expected to get there. That is all."[65] Insisting that public confidence was his company's greatest asset, he wrote "There was one very powerful business rule. It was concentrated in the word—courtesy."[66] The firm's exceptional record—and lower prices than the government—soon opened it to attacks by the federal monopoly, and the central offensive came against the company in upper New York State, where federal agents arrested the express messengers daily. Citizens, who realized the value of Wells's service, posted bail immediately, and for a short time Wells's company carried virtually all the mail that moved between Buffalo and Rochester. For his own part, Wells detested government involvement, arguing, "Government should do little as possible of that which the People can do."[67] Not until 1851, when Congress lowered the postage rates to three cents, did federal rates come into line with those charged by Wells, and he proudly responded to the popular nickname, the "Peoples' Postmaster General."

But Wells had a few more tricks up his sleeve. After associating with John Butterfield, a former competitor, the two divided up the market in a pool. In 1850, Butterfield, Wells, Fargo, and other of their business partners consolidated their delivery services into American Express, capitalized at $150,000. The alliance came apart within two years as Wells and Fargo split with Butterfield over a proposed extension of the route to California, leading to the formation of the famous stage company, Wells Fargo. In 1858 the company's directors formed a second firm, the Overland Mail Company, to run stagecoaches along a southern route through Texas to California, with a northern route running from St. Louis to Salt Lake City, then across the Rockies. Briefly, the company ran the Pony Express mail service, and by 1866 Wells Fargo stagecoaches dominated western land travel.

Telegraphs and the Dawn of Modern Communications

Just as Vanderbilt had forced the steamboat monopolists to lower their prices, Wells forced down the price of mail. An important difference existed, however, between the competitive effects on Vanderbilt's private rivals and Wells's encounters with the government. The U.S. Post Office had to lower prices, and businesses welcomed the lower rates provided by Wells, Vanderbilt, the government or anyone else. Over the long term, however, the decision to free the post office from having to pay its own costs of operations on an annual basis (in essence relieving the government of having to charge a market price for mail delivery) had far-reaching effects for consumers, businesses, and the body politic.

Without the competitive pressure to incorporate the latest technology or cut costs, for example, the post office missed the most significant technological achievement in communications up to that point, the invention of the telegraph by Samuel F. B. Morse. A part-time inventor and professional portrait artist who lived for long periods in England, Morse's artistic career seemingly had peaked when Congress turned down his proposal to paint a fresco in the Capitol building's rotunda in the 1830s. Although still able to sustain himself by painting common portraits, Morse turned his attention to inventing, and in 1832 he met Charles Jackson, who demonstrated electromagnetism to Morse. Applying Jackson's idea to the transmission of concepts, Morse finalized his design in 1837 and applied for a patent soon thereafter, leaving Jackson to complain that Morse stole his ideas. Morse could not interest private businesses in the device, and, turning to government, received a $30,000 appropriation in 1843 to build a short telegraph line. He forged a partnership with his colleague Alfred Vail and started work on the demonstration line connecting Baltimore and Washington, D.C., by wire. Morse "had no talent for business and no idea of how to construct a line . . . lay[ing] the wires underground, inside a pipe along the Baltimore & Ohio right-of-way."[68] Needing further expertise in digging, Morse engaged the services of Ezra Cornell, who had created a machine to dig trenches of exactly the sort Morse envisioned, only to realize that the trenches cost far more than they could afford. The group switched, instead, to overhead wires hung from poles. In May 1844, they connected Washington and Baltimore, quickly displaying the remarkable potential of the new technology.

By that time, the government had eliminated any further funding—just as the technical marvel had started to unfold—and Morse and his associates used their remaining resources to connect New York City with Washington. Neither Morse nor his partners knew how to market the new technology, and they repeatedly sought government support. When that failed, they sold licenses to the telegraph machinery. Using the Morse licenses, other private competitors (including Henry Wells and his associates in Buffalo) entered the market, and the mileage of telegraph lines grew from 40 miles in 1846 to 23,000 by 1852! After understanding both the principle and the potential, other inventors wedged their way onto the scene with new designs or technologies, most notably Royal H. House, a Vermont inventor who patented a telegraph and printer in 1846.

At that point, the most unlikely figure changed the shape of telegraphy. Hiram Sibley, a drifter and handyman who had finally gained some measure of respect as a real estate agent, a banker, then a sheriff in New York, learned about the House patent. In 1849, with a partner, Sibley organized a telegraph company to compete in Albany and Buffalo, then sought to build lines that would unite the numerous pockets of telegraphy around New York and the Old Northwest. He switched to the Morse systems, acquiring rights to new areas for relatively small amounts, including the midwestern rights, which he bought for $50,000. After a struggle with Cornell in 1855, who held most of the remaining Morse patents in the West, Sibley merged his company with Cornell's in a new enterprise called Western Union Telegraph Company.

Businesses already had realized the great value offered by faster information transmission. Regional stock exchanges closed when investors could obtain reports quickly from New York; railroad dispatchers changed schedules and routes to accommodate traffic; and news of all sort moved at lightning speed. The members of the Chicago Board of Trade (CBOT), whom Whiting and Richmond had enlisted to assist in delivering daily reports of market conditions, used the telegraph to report grades and prices to members, and soon the CBOT competed with Wall Street in trading securities—an accomplishment made possible only by the telegraph's capacity to offset New York's advantage as a coastal city.[69]

Interlude: The Pony Express

Extension of the telegraph and railroad virtually destroyed a much more romantic, but less efficient, mode of communication, overland mail via the Pony Express. The brief history of the Pony Express provides a classic case study for understanding job creation and destruction in a free market. Created in January 1860, the Pony Express was the brainchild of William Russell, who had taken advantage of the postmaster general's dissatisfaction with his existing mail service to organize a company based on traditions of Mongol riders in China.[70] He envisioned horsemen covering a 1,966-mile trail from St. Joseph, Missouri, to Sacramento, California, with 119 stations interspersed for riders to change horses. Every 100 miles, the carrier was allowed to rest, but not for long; speed in mail delivery was the key. The company hired predominantly Mormon riders, who had developed good relations with the Utah, Ute, and Shoshone Indians in the territories and who had grown up under such severe conditions that a ride of 100 miles did not seem extraordinary to them.

Russell gave his managers a mere sixty-five days to procure horses, mules, and space in St. Joseph, Carson City, Sacramento, and other locations. The Express attracted some of the most unusual characters in the West, and the arrival of the first mail by Pony Express set off celebrations and parades. When the final riders crossed in October 1861, the company's riders had made 300 runs each way, covering a total of 616,000 miles and carrying almost 35,000 pieces of mail. Then, suddenly, telegraph wires linked the coasts and the Express was made obsolete instantaneously. Dozens of riders awoke to find themselves out of work, unneeded as mail carriers. Yet the total number of jobs in the economy created by the telegraph grew exponentially, as workers had to place poles, string wire, run the telegraph offices, lay track, design and build telegraphs and locomotives, and serve as engineers and conductors on the trains.

The Pony Express represented a classic example of a business made obsolete by technology. As for the employees, the losses in a single area—Pony Express riders—represented a 100 percent "downsizing." Were they helpless victims? Not hardly. Raymond and Mary Settle have traced the history of most of the Pony Express riders.[71] Their stories are inspiring for what they accomplished *after* their layoffs. Don Rising, for example, carried dispatches at the battlefield for the Union army, gaining promotions to assistant wagon master. He eventually moved to New Mexico, where he started a mercantile and hotel business. Harry Roff became an insurance salesman who received promotion after promotion to become Pacific manager of the Home Insurance Company. William Page, Elijah Maxfield, "Happy Tom" Ranahan, Robert "Pony Bob" Haslam, and many others stayed in the general occupation of driving stages or scouting; others (including John Frye, who, along with Johnson Richardson, was one of the first riders to ride the circuit) found work in rodeos, circuses, and on ranches; still others, such as Martin Hogan, found themselves in demand by the railroads. Of the riders that the Settles could find information on, virtually all of them found better jobs when they were "downsized" by the Pony Express—with one exception, a hermit who retreated to a wilderness location! In short, the death of the Pony Express did not make a pauper of anyone, according to remaining records.

Meanwhile, gigantic new businesses, employing far larger numbers of people, arose to take their place. Western Union, the most successful of the new telegraph companies, emerged from the Civil War as a giant—the largest nonrailroad corporation in America, with a $40 million capitalization—and it dominated the market. It controlled virtually all of the telegraphy in the nation and produced electrical equipment, with scores of electricians and mechanics working in its labs. As exciting as was the image of a lone, daring Pony Express rider desperately lashing his horse to deliver the mail on time, compared to the dullness of the relentless click of the telegraph or the steady bounce of the stagecoach on its iron springs, the plain fact was that dullness and steadiness also meant reliability, lower cost, and higher efficiency. Perhaps symbolically, then, the Pony Express was put out to pasture by new, large-scale corporations.

Small Business, Entrepreneurs, and the Antebellum Experience

Emphasizing the rise of large-scale businesses, such as the railroads, canals, telegraph companies, and textile and iron manufacturers, captures the glamour of the era and the heights to which a single entrepreneur could rise, but it also ignores the vast number of small-scale entrepreneurs who made comparatively moderate gains that constituted significant advances for them. While Morse struggled with his telegraph prototype, jewelers in Newark, New Jersey, opened their first independent shops using a wide variety of new, small machines, including circular saws and lathes.[72] At a time when Vanderbilt's efficient steamers were driving Collins's subsidized lines from the oceans, more than 9,600 retail merchants did business in New York City alone.[73] When the male riders of the famous Pony Express were being fired, between 80 and 200 female entrepreneurs in Albany, New York, had established businesses that were successful enough to be listed in the R. G. Dun records for up to twenty years![74]

Entrepreneurship came in all varieties. It emerged from the ranks of manual workers in Poughkeepsie, New York, where up to 20 percent of all the journeymen of various trades opened their own shops during the period 1850–1870.[75] It swelled from mercantile establishments on the western frontiers, where peddlers became general-store owners, then bankers, then mining company owners. It evolved from the laboratories and workshops of inventors like Morse and Fulton, or from the shipping businesses of Fargo and Butterfield, or from the iron forges of Matthias Baldwin. Most of all, entrepreneurship constantly provided new products or services—filling a gap in the market.

One of the most important services needed in the mid-1800s, when buyers and sellers still had to overcome distance and time without the benefit of rapid transit, was that of financial or goods intermediary, or a "middleman." In the South, middlemen known as factors purchased cotton in the interior and sold it in the seacoast cities, in the process developing powerful financial businesses of their own. Factors charged an average of 2–3 percent commission, for which they developed expertise in foreign markets and domestic cotton or other products. They maintained large accounts with the New Orleans, Savannah, and Mobile banks, from which they advanced money to planters and purchased supplies for planters throughout the year. Until banks reached the inland areas of Mississippi, Alabama, and South Carolina, factorage remained one of the most influential and renumerative of businesses. If weather destroyed a cotton crop, driving several planters into debt, the factors who had advanced them money stood liable for their bills. Nevertheless, factors themselves faced extinction as banks extended branches into the southwestern areas, and indeed the presence of factors may have delayed the extension of banking services into areas of the South.[76]

When no factors appeared to serve as an intermediary between planters and buyers, the task fell to general-store owners, who as part of their normal business made purchases that the planters and farmers needed.[77] When necessary, the shop owner accepted payment *in kind*—that is, in produce, livestock, or some other nonmonetary renumeration. The scarcity of paper money and coin so afflicted early Missouri, for example, that citizens paid taxes in "shaven deer skin at three pounds to one dollar," while in California, cowhides circulated so widely they acquired the name "California Bank Notes."[78] Store owners also extended credit, leading many of them into related fields of banking. Once a year or more, the store owners would journey to a large city—New York, Philadelphia, or New Orleans—where they would order goods for the coming season.

Exact data on the number of factors, middlemen, and general-store owners does not exist. Most scholars rely on the records of R. G. Dun, but those reports were incomplete at best, missing thousands of entrepreneurs who started a business, then failed before ever reporting to Dun. The Dun records also miss largely self-sufficient merchants, who did not themselves need a credit-reporting agency or whose own credit was beyond reproach; they also ignored people who dabbled in a business secondary to farming. Most important, though, even those businesses that Dun's surveys captured provided no more than a snap-shot picture of a specific region, taken at one brief moment in time.

A multitude of relatively unknown entrepreneurs walked the American stage from 1830 to 1850, providing people on a daily basis with products and services. Society as a whole felt the benefits of their actions, even if it could not correlate them with specific names. Some, however, achieved such business success or made products of such lasting importance that they became almost synonymous with the product they created or the service they founded.

The name Gail Borden, for example, instantly brings to mind milk. But for most of his life, Borden had nothing to do with milk, although he was born on a New York farm.[79] In fact, Borden's career had touched on almost everything except milk, and he had reached the point in his life when modern Americans plan their retirement. By age fifty-six, Borden had worked as a schoolteacher, surveyor, newspaper editor, real estate salesman, customs collector, and inventor—the job he liked best. Unfortunately, Borden, a kooky "idea man," came up with products or contraptions that hardly seemed practical. He invented a "Terrapin Wagon"—a completely amphibious vehicle with wheels and sails that plunged a group of observers into the Gulf of Mexico. Living in Galveston, Texas, at the time, Borden proposed moving the entire population of the city into a giant ether-cooled refrigerated building that he planned to construct. His flat dehydrated meat biscuit flopped (or bounced, depending on the humidity that day!). But the concept appealed to judges at the 1851 Crystal Palace Exhibition in London, who awarded him a gold medal.

Borden's return voyage to New York from London changed his life—and ours—as a result of a tragic event: Four children died from drinking contaminated milk taken from sick cows on the ship. Determined to improve the safety and quality of milk, Borden applied his experience with the meat biscuit to his extensive knowledge of refrigeration, experimenting with processes that would remove the water from milk to reduce the moisture content, thus enhancing its freshness. While visiting a Shaker colony in New Lebanon, New York, Borden witnessed the use of a vacuum process to condense maple sugar, and he reasoned that he could place milk in vacuum-sealed pans, boil it, and reduce the moisture content with a low level of heat, avoiding a burnt taste. He received a patent in 1856 for a process that took out 75 percent of the water from milk and added sugar as a preservative. Opening a small Connecticut plant, Borden failed and was out of business in a year.

Most successful entrepreneurs, and almost all of the truly great ones, fail several times in their careers, and so it was with Borden. He tried again, this time with better financing (although still capitalized at a relatively low level of $100,000 in 1857), and during the Civil War his infant business took off when the U.S. Army ordered 500 pounds of condensed milk. Six years after his second milk company was founded, he opened a facility in Brewster, New York, that turned out 20,000 quarts of condensed milk *a day!* Only then did Gail Borden retire; but even in retirement he continued to invent, delving into the mysteries of condensing fruit juices or creating instant coffee. But by that time—and for generations thereafter—"Borden" meant milk.

Business on the Eve of Transformation

In many ways, Gail Borden typified the entrepreneur of his age. Mobile and willing to work at different endeavors, he persisted with his true interest until he could achieve success. A northerner, he was inspired by the needs of the markets in the South and West. A failure, he triumphed.

Structurally, the Borden story also reflects the antebellum age. Borden needed investors, but the business remained fundamentally his to oversee and direct. He epitomized the entrepreneur-oriented business, run by the owner-founder. But the sheer size of the nation— its vast geographic expanse and its swelling population—made for mass markets that few individually run businesses could serve. The speed of transactions, made possible by the railroad, steamship, and telegraph, compounded the difficulties faced by a single owner attempting to manage a business. Finally, the financial demands of larger enterprises required investors, and as the shares of ownership passed into the hands of numbers of unrelated people, permanent managers were needed. Fortunately the Bordens, Vanderbilts, Wellses, and other trail-breaking entrepreneurs did not disappear in the new age. Rather, they took on a somewhat different persona—the "captains of industry," or the "vital few," as Jonathan R. T. Hughes called them. As such, they had to control the new corporate structures, with their thousands of employees and facilities stretched across several states. They had the same ambition and vision as the Bordens and Wellses, but the times demanded new skills and approaches. The nation stood on the brink of a revolution in business.

TALES FROM THE CRYPT: ENTREPRENEURS WHO CAME BACK FROM THE DEAD

Daniel Drew: The First Wall Street "Speculator"

IF ONE KEPT SCORE, DANIEL DREW (1797–1879) came back from the dead, financially speaking, more often than Freddy Kreuger or Jason have returned to life in horror-movie sequels. Drew did not have an easy life, despite his early affluence on his father's farm in New York. Relatively uneducated, Drew spoke and dressed like "a hick" most of his life, even when he had money. At the age of fifteen, his father died and Drew had to find work, finally enlisting in the army to fight in the War of 1812. Returning after the war in which he saw no combat, Drew, with his army bonus and a small amount left from his father's estate, began his first career as a cattle drover. He purchased cattle and drove them to New York City butcher shops. Briefly, he interrupted his cattle enterprise to tour with a circus, then returned to the livestock business, buying and selling his own herds.

At the Bowery in New York, he opened an inn at the stockyards, where he kept his own cattle and rented space to other drovers. Drew's cattle drives soon stretched to Pennsylvania, and ultimately to Illinois, where his horse was struck by lightning and killed. Apparently for reasons unrelated to the lightning bolt, Drew abruptly shifted his interest to canals and steamships, where he found himself engaged in a price war with Cornelius Vanderbilt. Drew lost, and the magnitude of his setback would have ruined most entrepreneurs. In

Notes

1. The classic work on this is George Rogers Fink, *The Transportation Revolution, 1815–1860* (New York: Holt Rinehart, 1962). Also see Guy S. Callender, "The Early Transportation and Banking Enterprises of the States in Relation to the Growth of the Corporation," *Quarterly Journal of Economics,* 17 (1902): 111–162; Albert Fishlow, "Internal Transportation," in *American Economic Growth,* Lance Davis, et al., eds. (New York: Harper & Row, 1972), 468–547.

2. Sidney Ratner, James H. Soltow, and Richard Sylla, *The Evolution of the American Economy: Growth, Welfare, and Decision Making,* 2d ed. (New York: Macmillan, 1993), 110.

3. Albert Gallatin, "Reports on Roads and Canals," document no. 250, 10th Congress, 1st session, reprinted in *New American State Papers—Transportation,* vol. 1 (Wilmington, Del.: Scholarly Resources, 1972).

4. *Historical Statistics of the United States—Colonial Times to 1970* (White Plains, N.Y.: Kraus International Publications [U.S. Department of Commerce, Bureau of the Census], 1989), 1114–1115.

5. The theory underlying the entire public/private goods debate is characterized in the seminal article by Ronald Coase, "The Problem of Social Cost," *Journal of Law and Economics,* 3 (1960): 1–44.

the process of his struggle with Vanderbilt, the two men cut prices drastically on the Hudson River, initiating a golden age for river travelers.

In 1839, Drew established his own steamship company, the People's Line, which featured some of the most fantastic luxury liners ever seen on American waterways. His 300-foot-long *Isaac Newton* had berths for 500 passengers. Yet while Drew's business grew, and although he continued to expand by acquiring other steamship companies, he became restless and left steamboating to enter a brokerage business. He lasted ten years with that firm, before he developed an interest in railroads. Again, he encountered Vanderbilt.

Drew's struggles with the Commodore to control the Harlem Railroad drew "Uncle Daniel" into a series of stock manipulations that cost him dearly. In truth, Drew was bankrupt, owing more than $500,000, which Vanderbilt covered and about which he incessantly reminded Drew. Having been defeated twice, Drew abandoned his attempts to get even with Vanderbilt, rebuilding his fortune with still other speculations. Next, he directed his ire at his former business partners, Jim Fisk and Jay Gould, in yet another manipulation that cost him a small fortune.

Hailed as the first Wall Street "speculator," Drew had made and lost several fortunes. His final years were marked with a series of setbacks, and he died penniless in 1879. Drew was a man of remarkable contrasts, described by one biographer as "an astute money manager, suffering repentant sinner, cheat, philanthropist, and bankrupt." Even while he participated in the Erie Railroad, it was remarked that he was both "a good friend of the road and the worst enemy it had as yet known."

Sources: Carol M. Martel, "Daniel Drew," in Schweikart, ed., *Encyclopedia of American Business History and Biography: Banking and Finance to 1913*, 158–162; Clifford I. Browder, *The Money Game in Old New York: Daniel Drew and His Times* (Lexington: University Press of Kentucky, 1986).

6. Bryant and Dethloff, *History of American Business*, 94. Also see John Stover, *Transportation in American History* (Washington: The American Historical Association, 1970) and Nathan Miller, *The Enterprise of a Free People: Aspects of Economic Development in New York State During the Canal Period, 1792–1838* (Ithaca, N.Y.: Cornell University Press, 1962).

7. Ratner, Soltow, and Sylla, *Evolution of the American Economy*, 114.

8. Joseph A. Durrenberger, *Turnpikes: A Study of the Toll Road Movement in the Middle Atlantic States and Maryland* (Valdosta, Ga.: Southern Stationery and Printing Co., 1931). Also see Robert F. Hunter, "The Turnpike Movement in Virginia, 1816–1860," Ph.D. dissertation, Columbia University, 1957; William Hollifield, *Difficulties Made Easy: History of the Turnpikes of Baltimore City and County* (Cockeysville, Md.: Baltimore County Historical Society, 1978); and Roger N. Parks, "The Roads of New England, 1790–1840," Ph.D. dissertation, Michigan State University, 1966.

9. The *Palladium* quoted in Thomas S. Wermuth, "Rural Elites in the Commercial Development of New York: 1780–1840," in William J. Hausman, ed., *Business and Economic History*, 23 (Fall 1994): 71–80 (quotation on 76).

10. Ibid. For a more developed discussion, see Wermuth's dissertation, "To Market, to Market: Yeoman Farmers, Merchant Capitalists and the Transition to Capitalism in

the Hudson River Valley, 1760–1840," Ph.D. dissertation, Binghampton University, 1991.

11. Gunderson, *Wealth Creators,* 63.

12. Daniel B. Klein, "The Voluntary Provision of Public Goods? The Turnpike Companies of Early America," *Economic Inquiry,* 28 (October 1990): 788–812 (quotation on 790); David Beito, "From Privies to Boulevards: The Private Supply of Infrastructure in the United States during the Nineteenth Century," in *Development by Consent: The Voluntary Supply of Public Goods and Services,* ed. Jerry Jenkins and David E. Sisk (San Francisco: Institute for Contemporary Studies, 1993), 23–49; and his unpublished paper, "'A Spirit of Rivalry in Road Building': Toll Roads in the Great Basin, 1852–1890," presented at the Western History Association, 1994. Also see Klein's "Tie-ins and the Market Provision of Collective Goods," *Harvard Journal of Law and Policy* (Spring 1987): 451–474, and his papers with John Majewski, "Private Profit, Public Good, and Engineering Failure: The Plank Roads of New York," working paper 88/3, Institute for Humane Studies, George Mason University, 1988, and "Privatization, Regulation, and Public Repossession: The Turnpike Companies of Early America," working paper, University of California, Irvine, 1988.

13. Christopher T. Baer, Daniel B. Klein, and John Majewski, "From Trunk to Branch: Toll Roads in New York, 1800–1860," ed. Edwin Perkins, in *Essays in Economic and Business History,* 11 (1992): 191–209 (quotation on 196).

14. Douglass C. North, *Growth and Welfare in the American Past* (Englewood Cliffs, N.J.: Prentice-Hall, 1966), 100.

15. David L. Birch, "Who Creates Jobs?" *The Public Interest* (Fall 1981): 3–14; George Gilder, *The Spirit of Enterprise* (New York: Simon & Schuster, 1981), 251.

16. Birch, "Who Creates Jobs?" 7.

17. Blackford and Kerr, *Business Enterprise in American History,* 82.

18. Forest G. Hill, *Roads, Rails and Waterways: The Army Engineers and Early Transportation* (Norman: University of Oklahoma Press, 1957).

19. James Willard Hurst, *Law and the Conditions of Freedom in the Nineteenth Century United States* (Madison: University of Wisconsin Press, 1964).

20. Morton Horowitz, *The Transformation of American Law* (Cambridge, Mass.: Harvard University Press, 1979).

21. Atack and Passell, *A New Economic View of American History,* 150; Carter Goodrich, *Government Promotion of American Canals and Railroads, 1800–1890* (New York: Columbia University Press, 1960); *Canals and American Economic Development* (New York: Columbia University Press, 1961) and his *The Government and the Economy, 1783–1861* (Indianapolis: Bobbs-Merrill, 1967); Ronald E. Shaw, *Erie Water West: A History of the Erie Canal, 1792–1854* (Lexington: University of Kentucky Press, 1966); and Ronald W. Filante, "A Note on the Economic Viability of the Erie Canal, 1825–1860," *Business History Review,* 48 (Spring 1974): 95–102.

22. See B. R. Burg, "DeWitt Clinton," in Schweikart, ed., *Encyclopedia of American Business History and Biography: Banking and Finance to 1913,* 123–130.

23. Wermuth, "To Market, to Market," 224–331.

24. Louis Hunter, *Steamboats on Western Rivers* (Cambridge, Mass.: Harvard University Press, 1949).

25. See Douglas B. Ball, *Financial Failure and Confederate Defeat* (Urbana: University of Illinois Press, 1991).

26. Atack and Passell, *New Economic View of American History*, 150–156.

27. Ibid., 155; Roger Ransom, "Social Returns from Public Transport Investment: A Case Study of the Ohio Canal," *Journal of Political Economy*, 78 (September-October 1970): 1041–1064, and his "Interregional Canals and Economic Specialization in the Antebellum United States," *Explorations in Entrepreneurial History*, 5 (Fall 1967): 12–35.

28. Folsom, *Myth of the Robber Barons*, 2.

29. This is discussed in Pusateri, *History of American Business*, 121–123. For returns on steamboats, see James Mak and Gary M. Walton, "Steamboats and the Great Productivity Surge in River Transportation," *Journal of Economic History*, 32 (1972): 619–640, and their book, *Western River Transportation: The Era of Early Internal Development, 1810–1860* (Baltimore, Md.: Johns Hopkins University Press, 1975); Jeremy Atack, et al., "The Profitability of Steamboating on Western Rivers: 1850," *Business History Review*, 49 (Autumn 1975): 350–354; and Erik Haites and James Mak, "Ohio and Mississippi River Transportation, 1810–1860," *Explorations in Economic History*, 8 (1970): 153–180.

30. Bryant and Dethloff, *American Business History*, 104.

31. Folsom, *Myth of the Robber Barons*, 2.

32. Further material on shipping is taken from John G. B. Hutcins, *The American Maritime Industries and Public Policy, 1789–1914* (Cambridge, Mass.: Harvard University Press, 1941). Biographical material on Collins appears in the *Dictionary of American Biography* (New York: Charles Scribner's Sons, 1958), 2: 305–306.

33. Folsom, *Myth of the Robber Barons*, 7.

34. Quoted in Wheaton J. Lane, *Commodore Vanderbilt: An Epic of the Steam Age* (New York: Alfred A. Knopf, 1942), 148. Also see William E. Bennett, *The Collins Story* (London: R. Hale, 1957).

35. Folsom, *Myth of the Robber Barons*, 10. On the detrimental effects of the shipping subsidies, see Royal Meeker, *History of the Shipping Subsidies* (New York: Macmillan, 1905), 5–11, and Walter T. Dunmore, *Ship Subsidies: An Economic Study of the Policy of Subsidizing Merchant Marines* (Boston: Houghton-Mifflin, 1907), 92–103.

36. Quoted in Lane, *Vanderbilt*, 124, 136.

37. See John F. Stover, *American Railroads* (Chicago: University of Chicago Press, 1961), and his *Iron Road to the West* (New York: Columbia University Press, 1978).

38. James Hipp, "Matthias W. Baldwin," in *The Encyclopedia of American Business History and Biography: Railroads in the Nineteenth Century*, ed. Robert L. Frey (New York: Facts on File, 1988), 17–20 (quotation on 19).

39. John K. Brown, *The Baldwin Locomotive Works, 1831–1915* (Baltimore, Md.: Johns Hopkins University Press, 1995), 10.

40. Brown, *Baldwin Locomotive Works*, 17.

41. Quoted in John Steele Gordon, *The Scarlet Woman of Wall Street* (New York: Weidenfeld & Nicholson, 1988), 101.

42. An interesting aspect of the effects of having different groups capitalize the railroads is presented in John Majewski, "Who Financed the Transportation Revolution? Revional Divergence and Internal Improvements in Antebellum Pennsylvania and Virginia," *Journal of Economic History,* 56 (December 1996): 763–788.

43. Richard Lowitt, "William Earl Dodge," in Frey, ed., *Encyclopedia of American Business History: Railroads in the Nineteenth Century,* 98–104.

44. Nathan Rosenberg and L. E. Birdsell Jr., *How the West Grew Rich: The Economic Transformation of the Industrial World* (New York: Basic Books, 1986 [1985]), 190.

45. *Bank of August v. Joseph B. Earle,* 13 Peters 580 (1839); Eric Monkkonen, "*Bank of Augusta v. Earle:* Corporate Growth v. States' Rights," *Alabama Historical Quarterly* (Summer 1972): 113–130.

46. Edwin J. Perkins, "Nicholas Biddle," in Schweikart, ed., *Encyclopedia of American Business History and Biography: Banking and Finance to 1913,* 51–63.

47. This interpretation appears in Robert V. Remini, *Andrew Jackson and the Bank War* (New York: Norton, 1967), and, to a lesser extent, Thomas Govan, *Nicholas Biddle: Nationalist and Public Banker, 1786–1844* (Chicago: University of Chicago Press, 1959).

48. Traditional interpretations appear in Remini, *Andrew Jackson and the Bank War,* as well as Bray Hammond, *Banks and Politics in America from the Revolution to the Civil War* (Princeton, N.J.: Princeton University Press, 1957); and Arthur Schlesinger Jr., *The Age of Jackson* (Boston: Little, Brown, 1945).

49. Thomas Payne Govan, "The Fundamental Issues of the Bank War," *Pennsylvania Magazine of History and Biography,* 82 (July 1954): 305–315, and his *Nicholas Biddle: Nationalist and Public Banker, 1786–1844* (Chicago: University of Chicago Press, 1959); and Walter Buckingham Smith, *Economic Aspects of the Second Bank of the United States* (Cambridge, Mass.: Harvard University Press, 1953).

50. Richard Timberlake Jr., "The Specie Standard and Central Banking in the United States before 1860," *Journal of Economic History,* 21 (September 1961): 318–341 and his book, *The Origins of Central Banking in the United States* (Cambridge, Mass.: Harvard University Press, 1978); Peter Temin, *The Jacksonian Economy* (New York: W. W. Norton, 1969).

51. These ideas were developed in a series of articles by David Martin, "Bimetallism in the United States before 1850," *Journal of Political Economy,* 76 (May/June 1968): 428–442, and "Metallism, Small Notes, and Jackson's War with the B.U.S.," *Explorations in Economic History,* 11 (Spring 1974): 227–247, while new information on the Jacksonians' positions appeared in Larry Schweikart, "Jacksonian Ideology, Currency Control, and 'Central' Banking: A Reappraisal," *The Historian,* 51 (November 1988): 78–102.

52. The literature on the "Free Banking Era" is extensive, and is reviewed in Schweikart, "U.S. Commercial Banking: A Historiographical Survey." See especially Hugh Rockhoff, *The Free Banking Era: A Reexamination* (New York: Arno Press, 1975), and Arthur J. Ronick and Warren Weber, "New Evidence on the Free Banking Era," *American Economic Review,* 73 (December 1983): 1080–1091, and their "Banking Instability and Regulation in the U.S. Free Banking Era," *Federal Reserve Bank of Minneapolis Quarterly Review* (Fall 1982): 10–19.

53. On the crucial role of information transmission in banking panics, see Charles W. Calomiris and Gary Gorton, "The Origins of Banking Panics: Models, Facts, and

Bank Regulation," in *Financial Markets and Financial Crises,* ed. R. Glenn Hubbard (Chicago: University of Chicago Press, 1991), along with Calomiris and Larry Schweikart, "The Panic of 1857: Origins, Transmission, and Containment," *Journal of Economic History,* 51 (December 1991): 807–834.

54. Albro Martin, "John Pierpont Morgan," in Schweikart, ed., *Encyclopedia of American Business History and Biography: Banking and Finance to 1913,* 325–348 (quotation on 327). The best single source on the Morgan family is Vincent P. Carosso, *The Morgans: Private International Bankers, 1854–1913* (Cambridge, Mass.: Harvard University Press, 1987).

55. Dobson, *History of American Enterprise,* 120. A provocative, but flawed, interpretation of the "spinoffs" of railroads appears in Walt W. Rostow, *The Stages of Economic Growth* 1960, reprint (Cambridge: Cambridge University Press, 1990).

56. Brownlee, *Dynamics of Ascent,* 203.

57. Peter Temin, *Iron and Steel in Nineteenth-Century America: An Economic Inquiry* (Cambridge, Mass.: M.I.T. Press, 1964).

58. Pusateri, *History of American Business,* 134.

59. J. Wilson Newman, *"Dun & Bradstreet" Established in 1841 "For the Promotion and Protection of Trade"* (New York: Newcomen Society, 1956).

60. Gregory J. Millman, *The Vandals' Crown* (New York: Free Press, 1995), 104.

61. See Table 5-4, "Growth of U.S. Postal Services, 1790–1860" in Ratner, Soltow, and Sylla, *Evolution of the American Economy,* 128; Alan R. Pred, *Urban Growth and the Circulation of Information* (Cambridge, Mass.: Harvard University Press, 1973), 80.

62. Richard R. John, *Spreading the News: The American Postal System from Franklin to Morse* (Cambridge, Mass.: Harvard University Press, 1995) and his "Private Mail Delivery in the United States During the Nineteenth Century—A Sketch," William J. Hausman, ed., *Business and Economic History,* 2d series., 15 (1986): 131–143.

63. John, *Spreading the News,* 49.

64. John, *Spreading the News,* ch. 2, passim, and 39 for the 700 percent estimate.

65. Quoted in Robert J. Chandler, "Henry Wells," in *Encyclopedia of American Business History and Biography: Banking and Finance to 1913,* ed. Schweikart, 491–496 (quotation on 493).

66. Chandler, "Henry Wells."

67. Ibid.

68. Sobel and Sicilia, *Entrepreneurs,* 234.

69. Jonathan Lurie, *The Chicago Board of Trade, 1859–1905* (Urbana: University of Illinois Press, 1979).

70. Raymond W. and Mary Lund Settle, *Saddles and Spurs: The Pony Express Saga* (Lincoln: University of Nebraska Press, 1955); Fred Reinfeld, *Pony Express* (Lincoln: University of Nebraska Press, 1966).

71. Raymond and Mary Settle, *Saddles and Spurs,* 94–112.

72. Susan E. Hirsch, "From Artisan to Manufacturer: Industrialization and the Small Producer in Newark, 1830–60," in *Small Business in American Life,* ed. Bruchey, 80–99.

73. Stuart Blumin, "Black Coats to White Collars: Economic Change, Nonmanual Work, and the Social Structure of Industrializing America," in Bruchey, *Small Business in American Life,* 100–121.

74. Susan Ingalls Lewis, "Female Entrepreneurs in Albany, 1840–1885," in William J. Hausman, ed., *Business and Economic History,* 2d series, 21 (1992): 65–73.

75. Clyde and Sally Griffen, "Business and Occupational Mobility in Mid-Nineteenth-Century Poughkeepsie," in *Small Business in American Life,* ed. Bruchey, 122–141.

76. Material on factors appears in Ralph W. Haskins, "Planter and Cotton Factor in the Old South: Some Areas of Friction," in *The Changing Economic Order* ed. Alfred D. Chandler Jr., Stuart Bruchey, and Louis Galambos, (New York: Harcourt, Brace & World, 1968), and the classic by Robert Davis, *The Southern Planter, the Factor, and the Banker* (New Orleans: n.p. 1871). On the role of bankers, see Larry Schweikart, "Antebellum Southern Bankers: Origins and Mobility," in Jeremy Atack, ed., *Business and Economic History,* 14 (1985), 79–103; "Entrepreneurial Aspects of Antebellum Banking," in *American Business History: Case Studies,* ed. Joseph Pusateri and Henry Dethloff (New York: Harlan-Davidson, 1987), 122–138; and "Private Bankers in the Antebellum South," *Southern Studies,* 25 (Summer 1986): 125–134.

77. For the role of the storeowners, see Lewis E. Atherton, "The Pioneer Merchant in Mid-America," *The University of Missouri Studies,* 14 (April 1939); John G. Clark, *The Grain Trade in the Old Northwest* (Urbana: University of Illinois Press, 1966); David Dary, *Entrepreneurs in the Old West* (New York: Knopf, 1986); and John Haeger, "Economic Development of the American West," in *American Frontier and Western Issues: A Historiographical Review,* ed. Roger Nichols (New York: Greenwood Press, 1986).

78. Lewis Davids, "'Fur' Money and Banking in the West," *Journal of the West* (April 1984): 7–10; Lynne Pierson Doti and Larry Schweikart, *California Bankers, 1848–1993* (New York: Guinn Press, 1994), 11.

79. Material for Gail Borden comes from Fucini and Fucini, *Entrepreneurs,* 13–16.

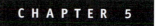

CHAPTER 5

The Rise of Managers, 1850–1880

MORE THAN FIFTY ANXIOUS, PERSPIRING BROKERS PRESSED AROUND THE fountain in the "Gold Room" on Broad Street, next to the New York Stock Exchange, as the caller marched to his position on September 24, 1869. The operator cleared his throat, then shouted "145 for 20,000," a code indicating that he had a bid for 20,000 ounces of gold at $145 an ounce. Instantly the price surged still higher, streaking up to $155 as "operators became reckless, buying or selling without thought of the morrow or consciousness of the present."[1]

The account, a description of "Black Friday," climaxed a struggle called the "Gold Corner," in which Jim Fisk and Jay Gould, two of the most notorious business speculators, attempted to corner the market on gold. Fisk and Gould, acting on "insider" information bought from Abel Corbin, the brother-in-law of President Ulysses S. Grant, had assurances that the government would not sell gold when the price started to rise. Along with other members of their plot, Fisk and Gould had acquired "buy" orders for gold at $135. Under the terms of a buy order, a person places an order to buy a certain quantity of goods in the future. The group was convinced that, absent a huge sell-off in government gold, their buy orders would stimulate gold prices and send them spiraling up well past their purchase price. Indeed, gold climbed to over $160, sending speculators into a frenzy as they attempted to grab what they thought were inflated prices.

While Grant kept the gold in the nation's vaults for a brief time, he finally ordered the Treasury to sell gold, sending the artificially high gold prices plummeting as speculators now sought to get out before prices fell below their entry-level price. Gould, informed that Grant planned the gold sale, escaped with millions of dollars in profits, although a paltry amount compared to what he would have gained if the government had not acted.

This remarkable scene reflected the growing influence of Wall Street and the speed of communications, which made the stakes of such speculations higher than ever by linking investors outside New York to the nation's money capital. And while gold was the object of speculation in this case, other scams usually involved railroads and their bonds. Together, the narrow confines of Wall Street and the vast ribbons of iron rails reaching across America represented the twin poles of a new age—magnetic opposites that at times both attracted and repelled. But they shared a powerful, common link in that they used and institutionalized a new form of corporate form, generally described by historians as a "managerial hierarchy."

Railroads and the Rise of Managerial Hierarchies

Three factors combined to create the virtually new business arrangement in the mid-1800s: the speed of transactions, communications, and travel; the size of companies (including both numbers of employees and capital demands); and the scope of operations, spanning thousands of miles. Simply put, no single owner could any longer expect to maintain tight control over an enterprise that might span three time zones, conduct business in a dozen different states, employ thousands of people, and require millions of dollars of capital every year.

Small shops, employing artisans or family members, still existed and still thrived. Chandlers, silversmiths, tailors, mercantile stores, and other small businesses of almost every conceivable type operated efficiently with owners performing basic management chores. But railroads, with their rapid speed and phenomenal capital demands, ushered in a new era of business structure in which owners—consisting of thousands of stockholders who did not even know each other—delegated responsibility for running the business to professional managers.

Railroads triumphed in short order over canals in moving freight and people, taking advantage of their overwhelming productivity advantages, if for no other reason than they could run year round while canals were shut down for up to five months a year by winter weather. Even the Erie Canal, which reached its peak traffic loads in the mid-1850s, could not compete with railroads. Rails could extend into areas canals could not reach, providing branch lines that could straddle factories or stockyards. Cities that never could have hoped for access to a canal sprang to life with railroad service. Speed differentials between steamboats and railroads widened, with rail travel moving three to four times faster than boats on canals. River travel still possessed elegance and romance, but as discount airlines would prove more than 130 years later, travelers often gladly exchange comfort for time.

By 1860, 30,000 miles of railroad track crossed the United States—an astounding increase of over 20,000 miles in the decade of the 1850s alone—with the Old Northwest experiencing a construction boom unmatched in other regions. Ohio and Illinois ranked first and second in miles of railroad by the start of the Civil War, and almost a dozen roads stretched into Chicago, the dominant departure point for the West. Branch lines connected to larger trunks that wove a quilt of track across the North, while in the South, shorter railroads linked waterways to cities. As one economic historian commented, "By 1860 it was possible to travel from any of the great East Coast ports to Chicago or St. Louis and thence to New Orleans at speeds inconceivable only 30 years earlier."[2]

Many roads used different gauge track, making uninterrupted shipment nearly impossible, especially in the South, where "by 1860 only one connected route carried passengers from the east coast to the Mississippi by way of Richmond and Memphis."[3] Companies established roads in close proximity to each other, often going the same direction and targeting the same markets. To some industry observers, the confusion and competition begged for some structure of control. Three individuals in particular had a dramatic impact on developing such a framework for railroad operations.

Thomson, McCallum, and Fink

Business's transformation into managerial hierarchies did not originate with any one person, but J. Edgar Thomson and Daniel C. McCallum stood out as organizational geniuses in the mid-1800s, while Albert Fink introduced modern accounting methods to business organization. J. Edgar Thomson achieved fame with the Pennsylvania Central Railroad, chartered in 1846 by a group of Philadelphians as a defensive measure against the entrenched B&O Railroad and the Main Line Canal. The president of the Pennsylvania Central, Samuel Merrick, already had notoriety as a successful businessman in a half dozen different ventures, ranging from insurance to ironworks. Merrick recognized that he lacked an understanding of railroads, and to gain such expertise he hired Thomson, a professional engineer from a family with a history of canal and railroad building.

Thomson traveled extensively in England to study the operations of railroads and to analyze English technology on a firsthand basis. He returned to a position with the Georgia Railroad and Banking Company—just one of the many combination bank-railroad businesses popular at the time—extending the line westward to Atlanta; then he took up Merrick on his offer to run the "Pennsy." Thomson quickly demonstrated the difference between himself, a representative of the new professional manager class, and the more traditional employee foremen. Moreover, he directed the railroad without consulting the owners (i.e., the board of directors, who represented them). Expansion of the Penn Central under Thomson occurred rapidly, as the railroad joined Philadelphia to Pittsburgh, then extended onward toward Chicago. By 1852, the board had named him chairman, symbolizing the complete dominance of the professional manager over the positions once held only by actual owners.[4]

In a ten-year span, Thomson took a railroad with less than 250 miles of track, and revenues under $2 million, and turned it into a railroad system with 438 miles of track and $11 million in revenues. Such expansion would not have been possible without developing a *managerial hierarchy*—a pyramidal framework of managers with a top-down authority structure in which *strategic decisions* (long-range, "big picture" decisions) are made by the top levels of management, including the chief operating and chief financial officers, while daily or *operational decisions* reside with mid- and low-level managers.

Thomson was not the first to use that structure, nor the most famous. Daniel C. McCallum, who started his early career with the New York and Erie Railroad, had emerged as the best-known proponent of managerial hierarchies, formulating both a philosophy by which to understand them and a series of rules by which to create and empower them. McCallum became famous, in part, because the editor of the *American Railroad Journal,* Henry Varnum Poor, had featured McCallum in his magazine, touting his efficiency gains. Poor was so impressed with McCallum's distribution of work and authority that he lithographed McCallum's organizational chart and offered it for sale.[5] By the late 1850s, McCallum's new employer, the Pennsylvania Railroad, reflected an entirely new organizational structure, roughly defined by *line and staff* positions that depicted the flow of authority and the basic function of each element of management. At the top was a general superintendent, who carried out the president's strategic decisions by managing the flow of resources to each division. Each division had a division superintendent, who transmitted to the employees the decisions of the top management. (A matured version of this structure appears in Figure 5.1). Broadly speaking, each division had little need to know about anything other than its own operations, and therefore the managers played a critical role in the transmission of information, much like in the days when human telephone operators literally plugged in lines connecting parties across miles of telephone lines. In their role as information transmitters, the managers sorted out those items that each division needed to know from those they did not, evaluating marginal information in between. The system provided remarkable direction at the bottom, because workers did as they were

FIGURE 5-1 *The Centralized Management Structure*

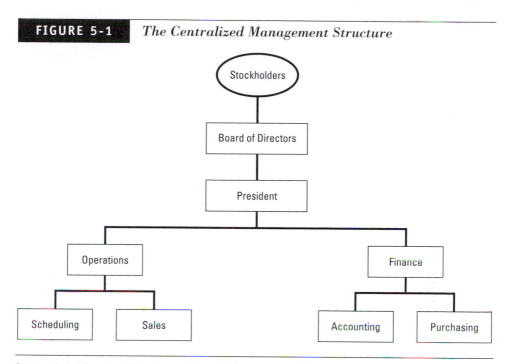

Source: Adapted from Louis Galambos and Joseph C. Pratt, *The Rise of the Corporate Commonwealth: U.S. Business and Public Policy in the Twentieth Century,* p. 8. Copyright © 1988 by Basic Books, Inc. Reprinted by permission of Basic Books, a member of Perseus Books, L.L.

instructed, with little opportunity (given the media of the day and the still local emphasis on news) to see the larger picture.

Prior to leaving the New York and Erie Railroad, McCallum's 1855 *Superintendent's Report* to the stockholders established several principles that the new business organizations adopted:

✦ Division of responsibilities.

✦ Reliable reports on the execution of duties.

✦ Prompt reporting.

✦ Confidential reports, so as not to embarrass officials or reduce their authority.

✦ Authority delegated to officials to permit them to execute their duties.[6]

Within just a few years, McCallum's structure and principles had spread to the other major railroads, which had already started to separate management of operations and finance. The combined functions of those two areas had opened the door to substantial mischief by allowing railroad officials to "create a construction company separate from the railroad's operating company . . . retain[ing] all of the construction company's stock for themselves."[7] Opportunities for shenanigans increased still further if the railroad had a bank as part of its charter, although the demands of note holders on the reserves of the bank provided some measure of discipline. Nevertheless, suffice it to say that early railroaders—and many of the later, unscrupulous ones, such as Jim Fisk and Jay Gould—did not pay adequately for new capital expenditures, refurbishing of equipment, or purchases of new locomotives and rolling stock. Roads deteriorated and became unsafe. Thus, McCallum's structure addressed those problems directly by placing long-term financing under a separate division while dividing operations and scheduling into their own departments. Intracorporate struggles acted as a check on the excesses of any division and tended to reveal any abuses of funds.

A constant, reliable stream of information proved key to the efficient operation of the new bureaucracies, causing the demand for information to generate a revolution in accounting. Indeed, according to Alfred Chandler, whose seminal work *The Visible Hand* won a Pulitzer Prize for history, accounting truly emerged for the first time as a profession, replacing the traditional double-entry bookkeeping.[8] Again, J. Edgar Thomson and the Pennsylvania Railroad pioneered the new accounting practices, which fell into three major categories: financial accounting, capital accounting, and cost accounting. Financial accounting recorded the financial transactions of the railroads and prepared reviews of the company's financial performance. That required far more sophistication than bookkeeping offered. The company had to know how much gross revenue it needed for each part of the road to meet operating costs. Capital accounting involved finding ways to depreciate the equipment, and thus plan for its replacement at future, usually higher, costs. Cost accounting appeared last, as a means to track the performance of individual divisions. Albert Fink, a civil engineer, excelled at applying this new form of accounting. Fink, who worked for the Louisville & Nashville as its general superintendent, derived a carrying cost for one ton per mile of each of his divisions, a feat that required him to determine what percentage of each part of his rolling stock was full at a given time. He also understood that his estimates had to come from actual data from each class of rolling stock—not mere average—which led him to develop elaborate mathematical formulae that he applied to the data.[9]

Achieving profitability from such estimates required the manager to take advantage of *fixed costs*—those costs that remained constant, such as a mortgage on land or a payment on a factory building. Other costs, known as *variable costs,* changed depending on the number of items produced, and included labor costs, raw materials, and expenses related to providing power, light, heat, or water to a factory. By taking advantage of fixed costs through a high volume of

| FIGURE 5-2 | *Economies of Scale* |

THOMSON RAILROAD TIE COMPANY

NUMBER OF UNITS	FIXED COST	FIXED CPU*	VARIABLE COST	VARIABLE CPU	TOTAL COST	TOTAL CPU
30,000	$15,000	.50	$9,000	.30	$24,000	.80
75,000	$15,000	.20	$22,500	.30	$37,500	.50
100,000	$15,000	.15	$30,000	.30	$45,000	.45

*CPU= Cost Per Unit

Source: Adapted from Gerson Antell, *Economics: Institutions and Analysis.* (New York: AMSCO Publications, 1970), p. 87.

production, an entrepreneur or manager could achieve *economies of scale* (see Figure 5.2).

But extracting profits based on economies of scale and using the new forms of accounting demanded a certain amount of planning on the part of railroad owners and managers. That, in turn, required a commitment to making the railroad pay for itself out of its own operations. To many railroaders, the frenetic competition threatened to make it impossible to run a sound business enterprise. As Alfred Chandler observed, "Never before had a very small number of very large enterprises competed for the same business. . . . And never before had competitors been saddled with such high fixed costs."[10] However, many of the well-known railroaders of the mid-1800s had little intention of holding on to a railroad long enough to improve it, let alone see it achieve productivity gains. They bought and held railroads for only one reason: to make quick profits from stock fluctuations. No incidents better illustrated the differences in goals and methods than a series of confrontations between some of the most famous railroaders of the day in what became known as a "Chapter of Erie."

A Chapter of Erie: Drew, Fisk, Gould, and Vanderbilt

Predictably, some railroaders ignored genuine business improvements and efficiency gains, trying instead to gain riches through manipulating the political machinery. The "Erie Wars," a series of clashes between some of the most flamboyant railroaders of the mid-1800s over the Erie Railroad, epitomized the role of "political entrepreneurs."

In 1853, Erastus Corning, an Albany iron business owner, created the New York Central Railroad. Corning was primarily a politician, serving in the state senate and as a congressman. He had manipulated the New York legislature to obtain a law authorizing the consolidation of a group of railroads, including the Erie, the New York Central, and others into a single, giant corporation capitalized at $23 million. Having obtained the incorporation, Corning quickly tapped the company treasury by selling the road $1.09 million worth of his company's iron products.

Corning had obtained and sustained his position only with the help of Cornelius Vanderbilt. The Commodore had a simple philosophy for running a railroad: "1, buy your railroad; 2, stop the stealing that went on under the other man; 3, improve it in every practicable way within a reasonable expenditure; 4, consolidate it with any other road that can be run with it economically; 5, water the stock; 6, make it pay a large dividend."[11] Modern students might be alarmed at item number 5, "watering stock," a term scandalized by writers such as Charles Francis Adams Jr. that referred to increasing the number of shares outstanding without increasing the paid-in capital or reducing the par value—a tactic that seemed to cheat the stockholders or dilute their equity. But with Vanderbilt the term was inapplicable. He held large stock positions in the railroads he ran, and under his management, the stock of his railroads rose rapidly. Without increasing the number of shares, the prices would have skyrocketed. In essence, his policies consisted of paying "lavish stock dividends," or giving shareholders extra stock instead of cash.[12] Vanderbilt recognized what Wall Street has since institutionalized, namely issuing stock whose par value is meaningless and whose market value counts for all.

By that time, Vanderbilt's railroad career crossed that of another legendary Wall Street figure, Daniel Drew. "Uncle Daniel," as he was known on the Street, started his career as a cattle drover and had originated the term "watering stock" when he adopted the practice of stopping his herds for water just outside the point of sale, feeding them salt, then letting the cattle drink their fill to increase their sales weight.[13] By 1853, Drew held substantial stock in the Erie, and even held a seat on the board of directors. Drew had a reputation for speculating in the stock of railroads, relying on his political contacts to affect the value of the road while completely ignoring the company's operational interests. In that way, Drew fit the "political entrepreneur" mold, which brought him into direct conflict with a "market entrepreneur" like Vanderbilt. The two men clashed in a pair of separate incidents, the "Harlem Corner" and the "Erie War."

THE "HARLEM CORNER"   Both Drew and Vanderbilt had interests in the Harlem Railroad in 1857, and in 1864 the railroad sought to extend its line beyond its original charter. Drew, sensing the stock profits associated with the extension, purchased still more shares of the railroad and used his influence with the New York City Common Council to get the extension approved. He then *sold short.* Selling short involves borrowing from a broker shares of stock (say, 100 shares at $1 per share) and selling it immediately (for $100) with the promise to repay the shares of stock at a future date for a price determined at the time of the transaction. Obviously, a "short seller" hopes that stock prices fall before the repayment date. (In this example, assume that the price indeed fell to 50 cents per share by the time the speculator needs to repay the stock. He has sold for $100, then, at a later date, repurchased the same number of shares for $50, repaid the broker, and has a $50 profit.) Short selling can lead to large profits; but the impending delivery of the stock also means that if the price rises after the initial sale, the short seller is in trouble and must acquire stock to meet his future obligations (known, literally, as "covering his shorts").

In the case of the Harlem, Drew first convinced the Common Council to *reject* the extension, causing the price to plummet, then, abruptly (after he sold short and made huge profits) reconsider and approve the extension. Drew would have both his railroad extension and his profits, while the Common Council members and the state legislators—whom Drew had enlisted to sell short along with him—would have nice bonuses courtesy of Uncle Daniel. If all went according to plan, Drew and his insiders would borrow shares of Harlem stock and sell them. When news of the extension rejection reached the street, Harlem shares would plummet, Drew and his friends would buy back in, repay their debts, and keep the profits. At that point, the council would reconsider, forcing prices back up and restoring Drew's original stock holdings to their value.

On the recommendation of Drew, legislators mortgaged their houses to raise cash to purchase the Harlem stock, which started the year at $100 per share, then had soared to $140 by March, when the committee hearing testimony on the franchise extension reported on the bill unfavorably (as Drew expected). Stock prices fell to just over $100, dropping almost 30 percent in a couple of days. Had Drew and his cronies bought short early enough, they would have made huge profits. Instead, most waited for the stock to drop to $50 based on Drew's prediction that it would.

One of the primary losers in the scheme was Vanderbilt, who did not appreciate being the object of manipulation. Nor did he approve of the legislators acting against his interests. After all, he had supported some of them quite well and on occasion had himself enlisted their allegiance. As one observer quipped, "Being a man of honor, [Vanderbilt] expected the Legislature, once paid for, to stay bought."[14] In fact, however, virtually all business owners had to support one party or the other or risk harassment by local officials at the behest of their superiors. Usually, rather than going to government for help, Vanderbilt handled his own challenges, as he did in this case: Along with an ally, John Tobin (who also had suffered stock losses due to Drew's escapade), the two concluded they would teach the speculators a lesson. Using aliases, Tobin and Vanderbilt's agents moved into the market and proceeded to buy thousands of shares with funds from a "war chest" of more than $5 million. By March 30, just four days after the prices had collapsed, they reversed again, rising to $125, then, after a week, to $137. In early April, Vanderbilt's money pushed prices past $175, then to $224 as panicked short sellers themselves had joined in bidding for the scarce shares. Begging for mercy, brokers representing Drew and the legislators asked Vanderbilt what he would do. "Put it to a thousand," he replied. But he was counseled that such a move would spread to other, stable businesses, affecting all of Wall Street. He had, after all, taught a sublime lesson. Vanderbilt agreed to let the legislature off the hook at a price of $285, not only making millions of dollars for himself but "taking those millions out of the hides of people whose misfortunes were entirely self-inflicted."[15] Indeed, Vanderbilt had used the market to discipline a corrupt legislature and to reaffirm one of Wall Street's cardinal truisms: "Bulls make money and bears make money but pigs never make money."

THE "ERIE WAR"   Drew, though temporarily defeated, hungered for revenge. He owed Vanderbilt and his associates more than $1.5 million, and after pleading for mercy—which the Commodore did not show—Drew became defiant. He quickly realized his predicament and apologetically approached the Commodore with a promise that he would support Vanderbilt's interests in the New York Central and would cease his attempts to drive down the stock prices of the Erie Railroad. In return for his *mea culpa,* Drew was allowed to remain on the Erie board.

Among the other members appointed to the Erie board in 1867 were "a batch of nobodies," including Jay Gould and James Fisk Jr.[16] Fisk, better known as "Jubilee Jim," had spent time as an animal keeper in a circus before joining a Boston mercantile firm. He had the great insight to set up an office in Washington, D.C., immediately after the first shots on Fort Sumter, wining and dining congressmen to generate a sea tide of federal contracts. Later, he ran the Union blockade of the Confederacy, and at the end of the war, the prosperous Fisk headed to Wall Street, where he met Jay Gould. Born on the same day as Vanderbilt—May 27—Gould worked as a child on his parents' dairy farm. He found a job as a surveyor, rendering maps of New York, Ohio, and Michigan in a delicate and artistic style. In his spare time he wrote a history of Delaware County, a 450-page book manuscript that burned in a fire at the publishing house. Gould merely started again and reproduced the book from memory. He purchased stock in a small railroad, expanded his equity, and in 1867 found himself on the board of the Erie with Fisk, Drew, and a pair of Vanderbilt's agents.

Individually, the Commodore could control any of them. Together, they made a formidable set of opponents, especially when lodged on the board of the Erie. Vanderbilt wanted the Erie to work with the New York Central and the Pennsylvania to form a pool, and he was not interested in momentary stock speculation. Concluding that he could not control the Erie with surrogates, Vanderbilt set out to purchase the railroad outright, a feat of some undertaking, given the road's $17 million market value and considering that the Commodore had his money tied up in the Harlem, the Hudson Railroad, and the New York Central.

Making matters worse, Drew advanced the Erie $3.4 million in return for 58,000 "phantom" shares. Breaking his vow never to go to court to fix a problem, Vanderbilt pursued legal remedies, and a court enjoined the Erie from accepting Drew's offer of a cash-for-shares exchange. Drew merely ignored the court's order, adding to the chaos. Increasingly, the entire market hung on a word . . . "Erie!"

Not to be left out, Jim Fisk weighed in with Drew, personally overseeing the printing of 50,000 new phantom shares of Erie stock, trying to make it impossible for Vanderbilt to buy control. Nevertheless, Vanderbilt and his allies held nearly 200,000 shares—and Drew, Fisk, and Gould had more than $7 million of Vanderbilt's money. But no sooner had they started to celebrate than the court gave the Commodore the breakthrough order he needed, dispatching sheriffs to bring in the trio for contempt. Unceremoniously, Drew grabbed the first ferry to New Jersey, although Fisk and Gould remained in New York, where they dined blatantly at Delmonico's restaurant (protected by lookouts) before themselves retiring across the Hudson River with Vanderbilt's cash. From New Jersey, they not only defied the Commodore but also Judge George Barnard, who promised to have them arrested if they came into his jurisdiction. To ensure that no one took them back to New York against their will, the triumvirate turned the Taylor Hotel into "Fort Taylor," replete with armed guards and three twelve-pound cannon! They also attempted to convert the Erie into a New Jersey corporation, dragging the state assemblies of New York and New Jersey into the fray.

Realizing they could not win, Fisk and Gould negotiated with Vanderbilt, paying him for his shares and agreeing to remove Drew from the Erie board. Although the Commodore may have taken a small loss, he emerged from the battle essentially unscathed. However, after the settlement he paused to warn friends, "The Erie is going down."[17] It was a prophecy and not a threat, reflecting Vanderbilt's understanding of the approach to railroading held by Gould and Fisk.

Hardly had the ink on the agreement dried than Gould and Fisk made good Vanderbilt's prediction. In 1868, Drew stepped down and Jay Gould took his place as president of the Erie, with Fisk his chief operating officer. The duo promptly drove down the price of the railroad's stock by 35 percent. The Erie had revenues of just over $14 million, but expenses were barely under that, leaving it with a net revenue of $22,000. While the Erie lurched on, Vanderbilt's New York Central epitomized the new efficiency of the professionally run railroad. Between 1867 and 1868, the company's revenues rose only 2.9 percent, but Vanderbilt chopped 13.3 percent from expenses, increasing profits by almost 55 percent, or almost *200 times* that of the Gould-Fisk-run Erie. Even more important, while the Erie had accidents that killed twenty-six and injured seventy-two, all of Vanderbilt's roads *combined* had zero fatalities and only eleven injuries. Accident rates on the Erie led reformers such as Charles Francis Adams Jr. and his brother Henry Adams—great grandsons of the second president of the United States and the grandsons of the sixth president, John Quincy Adams—to publish an exposé called *Chapters of Erie* (1871), which argued for public regulation of railroads.[18]

Partly due to the Erie wars, Wall Street, more than seventy years before the creation of a Securities and Exchange Commission, took it upon itself to reform the sales of securities internally. In November 1868, the NYSE passed a resolution to require public registration of securities traded on the exchange, making it impossible to secretly water stock. After the resolution passed, only the Erie and three other similar companies had not complied. Within a year, even Jay Gould had to adhere to the registration requirement. As John Steele Gordon noted, "Effective self-regulation of the New York stock market would increase greatly in the next few years [and it would be] self-regulation rather than government that would successfully guide Wall Street for the next two generations, as it eclipsed London and grew into the largest financial market on earth."[19] Of course, the NYSE was not perfect in regulating itself, in no small part because each new evolution in financial instruments brought different challenges that the exchange could not anticipate. But there is little reason to suspect that the government could have done better—it completely missed the junk bond revolution in the 1970s and was flummoxed by the appearance of the currency futures market in the 1980s.

The "Erie War" marked Vanderbilt's final epoch. Though appreciating the essential necessity of having new management professionals, with their focus on efficiency gains, Vanderbilt remained a man of an earlier business era. He was the owner who ran his businesses, the individualist who could see strategic issues and attend to minute details, or the entrepreneur/speculator who could manage stock fluctuations and yet still understand the underlying basis of value in rolling stock and track quality.

Nor were Fisk and Gould, for all their notoriety, representative of the new wave of business leaders either. Obsessed with making quick profits from stock manipulations or rapid resale of roads, they had little interest in achieving productivity gains within the railroads themselves. More than Vanderbilt, however, Fisk and Gould characterized the attitude among most of the railroaders of the day in their quest to eliminate competitors, either by driving them out of business or by forming cooperative oligopolies. As early as the 1850s, most railroaders wearied of rate wars and sought stability and security within their established routes. To that end, railroad companies met at large conventions to set "official" rates with which every company would comply, standardizing the classifications of weight and making rates uniform. Senior railroad executives met in 1854 to agree, in J. Edgar Thomson's words, "upon general principles which should govern Railroad Companies competing for the same trade, and preventing ruinous competition."[20] They accepted basic principles of charging on the basis of the value of the transported product, and they arrived at a cooperative rate base. Still, individual railroaders occasionally evaded the agreements by secretly offering "rebates," or refunds for heavy railroad use, and lowered their prices in public when they could.[21] For a time, the roads managed to maintain discipline, with brief exceptions during the Panics of 1857 and 1873, until a new era of competition dawned in the 1880s.

Rate setting, however, generally did not prove as useful in maintaining market share as did the tactic of dividing territory into spheres of influence. In 1870, three major railroads that ran the Chicago-to-Omaha route agreed to split traffic evenly. The "Iowa Pool" was copied elsewhere until the 1880s, when many of the informal arrangements collapsed. Most pools operated as follows: The railroads set prices and contributed a percentage of revenue to a pool. The pool then paid the difference when the traffic could not justify the preset rate and the railroad shipped the freight at the below-rate cost. In addition to rate setting and pooling, railroads tried yet another means of controlling their competition, whereby they purchased large blocks of the shares of competing roads. Owning substantial sums of stock allowed the railroads to put their own directors on a competitor's board, a tactic called *interlocking directorates*. Having the same people on both boards decreased the likelihood of competition. In the case of the New York Central and the Hudson River Railroad, for example, Dean Richmond of the Central served on the board of the Hudson River, and while Vanderbilt was not personally on the Central's board, his hand-picked agents were.

Government and Railroads: The Preliminary Phase

Competition ironically was reduced in another way: by the involvement of state governments and, eventually, the federal government.

With the sole exception of James J. Hill and his Great Northern, most of the major railroads sought assistance from the states or Uncle Sam at one time or another. But the notion that the government had to step in because private entrepreneurs would not meet public demand for railroads has been challenged.[22] By 1860, the public had contributed more than $250 million to railroads—one-quarter of the railroads' total expenditures. Government aid for railroads usually came in the form of loans or bond guarantees from the states. By 1838, states had amassed a total railroad-related debt of over $40 million, with the state of Missouri alone granting nearly $25 million to several rail companies. When not investing directly, states guaranteed the bonds of the railroads, pledging their "full faith and credit" should the roads collapse. States also granted generous charter conditions, including monopoly rights, to railroads, in no small part because they learned that even with the riskiest of railroad ventures, the effects of railroad construction on prop-erty values generated enough growth in property taxes to almost offset losses in worst-case scenarios, and to give the state and communities a windfall in taxation in the event of successful railroad operations.[23]

Prior to the Civil War, the federal government did not involve itself in railroad grants, with the important exception of land given to a group that wanted to build a railroad to the Pacific that would cross the Nebraska Territory. The politics required to obtain land for that road were largely directed by Illinois Senator Stephen A. Douglas. But in the attempt to provide land for the railroad through the creation and settlement of two new territories, Kansas and Nebraska, Douglas set in motion the political events that led to the Civil War.

Both proslave and "free-soil" settlers moved into Kansas in the mid-1850s, leading to violence. Most observers thought that, in time, "free-soilers" would outnumber the proslave immigrants, and the "free-soilers" would vote (under Douglas's concept of "popular sovereignty") to make Kansas and Nebraska free states. In 1857, however, the United States Supreme Court issued a ruling in the *Dred Scott v. Sanford* case saying that neither Congress nor popular votes could prohibit slavery from a territory. The decision sparked an upheaval in the financial markets as the securities of railroad companies with lines running to the West suddenly crashed. Uncertainty over future market conditions had caused a panic—significantly none of the roads that ran north and south were affected—which quickly spread to the New York financial markets in general, where the large banks held significant sums of railroad bonds. In the resulting Panic of 1857, the maturation of new mechanisms of transmitting financial and economic information, which had been occurring over the previous decade, suddenly became visible to many people for the first time. Anxious to prove their ideological points, spokesmen for the North and South both used the panic to argue for the superiority of their respective regions. The economic theorists of the South, for example, concluded that the southern economy had surpassed that of the North, because few southern banks even suspended, let alone failed, while the North experienced a crisis nearly the equal of the Panic of 1837.[24] Northerners, on the other hand, used the same information to suggest that slavery insulated the South from even severe market reactions, and therefore market incentives could not prod slave owners toward emancipation.

Southern polemicists missed important factors that had protected the South in the panic. First, the South had very few roads that touched the West, and therefore had only a small number of companies that were affected by the developments in Kansas. Second, the southern banking system—far more than the northern banking system—had adopted branch banking, making the transmission of financial information much quicker and more reliable. That proved crucial in preventing a panic mentality from developing. Resisting any tendencies toward the creation of larger banking institutions, northern attempts to create a banking structure that retained the inefficient unit banks had only resulted in confusion and chaos during financial distress. A third, and final, factor contributing to the panic involved sudden changes in wheat prices in the North, related to the end of the Crimean War. Once again, the South read the wrong message. With an economy dominated by cotton, Southerners felt no reverberations from the Crimean War in 1857.[25] But it ignored the fact that it had been spared due to its reliance on a crop that was just as vulnerable to its own enemies, as attacks by the boll weevil in the 1920s revealed.

Shaking off the immediate effects of the Panic of 1857, federal intervention in railroad construction expanded dramatically during and after the Civil War, especially in the form of providing land grants. Typically, the government granted land to a railroad in a checkerboard pattern along the right-of-way, giving the company only half the land fronting its railroad. Remaining land stayed in the hands of the government for other uses. The Illinois Central, for example, received several million acres of federal land in 1850, which it sold to settlers to establish farms near the railroad; the Northern Pacific—a transcontinental route—received a whopping 42 million acres. Land grants carried twin benefits, in that the land sales brought revenue, which railroads applied to track and rolling stock, and also established a built-in consumer base for the finished railroad consisting of farmers who needed the railroad to ship products to the East and bring finished goods from urban centers. Accordingly, the land adjacent to railroads proved the most highly prized and brought far higher prices than land further away.

Railroads earned nearly $500 million from land sales. Land-grant railroads transported government freight and mail at reduced rates, which saved the government millions of dollars over the years, exceeding the amount spent on the land grants by the taxpayers. But those savings, and the high social rates of return, came at the expense of private stockholders and bondholders by encouraging redundant, ill-planned, and speculative building. It also required taking large portions of Indian land (for which, in many cases, the U.S. government had to pay reparations decades later). Homesteaders did acquire land that was extremely valuable because of proximity to the railroads. But did settlement occur artificially? Were many areas settled only because of the presence of the railroad line? It is difficult to measure the benefits of the transcontinentals when such considerations are taken into account.

Eager to sing the praises of the railroads (and, indirectly, the efficacy of government assistance), some historians have contended that the subsidies hastened completion of a nationwide rail network, sooner than it might otherwise have occurred, linking the nation with a ribbon of iron rail. Clearly, many businessmen curried favor with the government for grants and prospered as a result—an exercise in "political entrepreneurship," not market success. Measurable benefits indeed resulted, but the industry incurred not only the cost of the grants themselves but also the subsequent cost of reorganizing or rescuing numerous poorly constructed or ineptly managed roads, factors that rarely enter into the equations of economic historians examining the era. More important, however, grants created incentives to build without concern for efficiency or reliability. Subsidies thus encouraged the activities only of people like Fisk and Gould, perhaps discouraging other builders less interested in getting the land than they were in establishing efficient railroad networks. Clearly the government for its own reasons (many of them involving the war) aligned itself with some business interests. But that hardly represented a triumph of market capitalism. It is entirely possible that without the land grants there would have been fewer, but better, railroad systems at roughly the same time. Evidence for this exists in the accomplishments of James J. Hill, America's greatest railroader.

James J. Hill's Great Northern

James J. Hill, born in Canada, supported his widowed mother by working in a grocery store for $4 a month. An accident deprived him of his right eye. Handicapped and poor, Hill hardly seemed destined for wealth and success. Yet while working for a shipping company, Hill learned the transportation business. He wove his expertise with a vision of Minnesota and northern America that included plains filled with farms and cities. Hill completed his entrepreneurial persona with that final essential ingredient, faith. In 1878, he and a group of Canadian investors bought a bankrupt road in St. Paul, Minnesota. That railroad had received federal subsidies and had experienced stock manipulation and deplorable management; its record was so pitiful that critics dubbed it "Hill's Folly" when Hill announced his intention to complete the route. It not only ran profitably upon completion, but the road's success inspired Hill to keep building, turning the enterprise into the Great Northern Railroad.

Extending his railroad across the Northwest, Hill built more slowly than the subsidized roads, knowing he had to pay the cost himself. He therefore chose routes for durability, safety, and efficiency, not scenery. "We want," he observed, "the best possible line, shortest distance, lowest grades and least curvature. . . ."[26] Hill had no land from subsidies, which other roads sold to settlers; instead, Hill had to *pay* settlers to go West, offering $10 each if a settler would farm near his railroad. To ensure that the settlers prospered, Hill imported 7,000 cattle from England and distributed them at no cost to the pioneers along his line. He established his own experimental farms to develop new seeds and livestock, and promoted crop rotation and fertilizers.

Not only did he expand the market for his service, but he understood that lasting profits came from lower operations and maintenance costs. That, coupled with his "obsession" for shorter routes and lower grades, allowed him to catch up to his subsidized rivals in the time it took his company to lay rail, and eventually outrun them. Although moving more slowly at first because of the constant insistence on quality over speed, Hill's roads experienced less "downtime" in which repairs ate up construction time and effort. Whereas Hill's competitor, Henry Villard, who received over 42 million acres of free government land, lavishly laid his tracks along areas of beautiful scenery, Hill chose the safest and most efficient paths. To be fair, Villard catered to tourists, and to an extent he had to place his routes through scenic territories, while Hill built for permanent settlers. Apart from their target market, however, Hill showed superior planning. Inevitably, his shorter routes and lower repair costs saved his road money on every trip. While Hill got his coal from Iowa, Villard had to ship his from Indiana at a cost of $2 a ton more than Hill.

Typically, Villard responded by attempting to use government—not the market—to battle Hill. Congress, which had granted Villard his land in the first place, frequently delayed permits to the Northern Pacific to cross Indian land, even though his rates remained lower than Villard's. Of course, Hill paid for his rights-of-way.

Even with all their supposed advantages, Villard and the other transcontinental owners found themselves in dire straits during the depression of 1893. Only Hill, who had received no money from the public treasury, avoided bankruptcy. The Union Pacific, the Northern Pacific, and the Santa Fe all had to be reorganized. When Hill said, "We have gone along and met their competition," he understated his case.

In retrospect, the subsidies themselves accounted for much of the mismanagement of the roads, in that subsidies were given based on miles completed, not the quality of miles completed or the effectiveness of the road. The incentives of subsidies encouraged overbuilding and constructing circuitous routes aimed at laying as many miles of track as possible. With no concern for terrain, the subsidized roads ran up steep gradients that increased fuel costs or along weak shoulders that contributed to accidents. Villard, for example, built his railroads well ahead of demand, often in rough, empty areas. Everywhere, the subsidies encouraged higher repairs and operating costs, while at the same time fostering a contemptuous attitude toward settlers; after all, the farmers needed the roads, not vice versa. Hill, in contrast, simply could not afford either the costs or the attitudes of the government-backed roads, and as a result he had lower fixed costs than all his competitors and an appreciation for the settlers he needed to make his railroad profitable.

Perhaps more important, the subsidies contributed to a competition for federal favors instead of railroad customers, ushering in an era of corruption unmatched in American history. During the 1860s, a construction company for the Union Pacific (one of the subsidized transcontinental roads) called Credit Mobilier, sold $150 million in bonds, a sum far beyond what the railroad needed for its construction. In 1867, Congress considered an investigation of the company, prompting Credit Mobilier to pay bribes to members of Congress and Vice President Schuyler Colfax in the form of selling them stock well below market price. Five years later, the scandal became public, tainting the already damaged Grant administration and characterizing the period as the "Era of Good Stealings."

Nevertheless, Credit Mobilier has been viewed as illustrating the weakness of "federal institutions to regulate such a crucial business event as the completion of the nation's first transcontinental railroad."[27] One business historian cited "this sort of behavior [as] just one cause for the widespread hostility toward railroads. . . . Protests arose over unfair freight rates, overcapitalization, sloppy or dangerous operating procedures, and monopoly or oligopoly control."[28] Yet neither appraisal is accurate or appropriate. The Union Pacific encountered difficulties not because it was inadequately regulated but because subsidies provided the road and its builders with the wrong incentives. To obtain government land, the Union Pacific built on ice and encroached on Indian lands, while both it and the Central Pacific tried to slow each other by blowing up each other's tracks. And the subsidies had repercussions with consumers, whose complaints may have been directed at "unfair freight rates" or "monopoly control" but for whom the underlying issue involved the sense on the part of taxpayers that they had paid for the railroads and thus were entitled to certain considerations.

Meanwhile, the two subsidized roads worked from opposite directions to meet in the middle. One road, the Union Pacific, stretched from Nebraska westward. General Grenville Dodge, the chief engineer, supervised nearly 10,000 men laying track at breakneck speed. With each new mile laid, the Union Pacific qualified for more land and loans, meaning that "the haste with which the road was built inevitably produced sloppy workmanship. . . ."[29] From the Pacific Coast, the Central Pacific line labored to overcome the more difficult of the two routes, crossing the Sierra Nevada mountains and other ranges. Four of the most powerful individuals in California history, Leland Stanford, Collis P. Huntington, Charles Croker, and Mark Hopkins, controlled the Central Pacific, which imported most of its labor. Chinese workers were prominent among the Central's labor force and were given the most difficult and dangerous work.[30] A contemporary saying—"There is a Chinese buried under every tie"—sadly came close to accuracy, and yet in the famous photograph of the joining of the tracks, a single, lone Chinese is visible. The Central shipped its tools, supplies, and the rails themselves by sea before bringing them overland to the railheads, and by early 1869 both it and the Union Pacific had rails in proximity. They did not wish to connect, however, because their funding would have ended; instead, they surveyed land and built parallel roads. Finally, even Congress had enough, forcing them to join rails.

On May 10, 1869, a simple message was dispatched across the telegraph wires: "Done." Celebrations broke out across America when the public learned that work crews of the Union Pacific and the Central Pacific had driven the famous golden spike at Promontory Point near Ogden, Utah, completing the first transcontinental railroad. (Of course, the spike did not remain—looters would have stolen it and gold would not sustain the beating produced by trains—but it was put on display in California.) Another transcontinental, the Northern Pacific, soon appeared, followed by the Southern Pacific, which resulted from a political negotiation that allowed Rutherford B. Hayes to become president in the Compromise of 1877.[31]

Thus, five transcontinental railroads hauled freight and passengers across the United States, with total track mileage in the nation exceeding 193,000. Nevertheless, a depression in 1893, brought on by attempts to force the U.S. government to buy silver at above-market prices, resulted in the bankruptcy of three of the five transcontinental roads.[32] Hill had written Congress, arguing that "the government should not furnish capital to [those] companies, in addition to their enormous land subsidies, to enable them to conduct their business in competition with enterprises that have received no aid from the public treasury."[33] At the time the other transcontinentals were in forced reorganization, Hill's Great Northern cut costs by 13 percent. Ironically, the government may have discovered that its policies had gone awry. In 1874 Congress passed the Thurman Law requiring the Union Pacific to pay 25 percent of its earnings to the government in return for its $28 million debt. Yet much of that debt stemmed from overblown construction costs, corruption, and poor planning that related directly to the subsidies and government funding.

Perhaps more troublesome to consumers, especially farmers, was the fact that the Union Pacific and the Northern Pacific both charged higher rates than did the Great Northern. In the past, railroads had attempted to divide territory geographically with agreements not to compete in each other's region or to form pools. But the Great Northern offered different challenges to the rate structure. The transcontinentals already had a degree of geographic monopoly, and Hill would not participate in a pool. Concerned that they were losing business to their unsubsidized competitors, the roads (although certainly not all of them) lobbied for rate regulation, which Congress supplied in 1887 with the Interstate Commerce Act.[34] The act made it illegal to give discounts to shippers who dealt in large volumes or mass quantities, essentially outlawing "volume discounts" for railroads. Rather than reducing prices for the smaller shippers—as was the intent—the law required that prices be consistent, so shippers merely raised prices for the shipment of long-haul goods. In addition, the act created a new federal bureaucracy to determine the "fairness" of rates, with the authority to investigate the records of the nation's railroads.

Some have argued that many railroaders wanted federal regulation as a way to formalize their internal price-fixing arrangements. Others, such as historian Albro Martin, have argued that the railroaders hoped to avoid formal rate regulation and instead wanted the government to validate their informal pooling arrangements.[35] Only when the Interstate Commerce Act outlawed pooling did railroaders turn to the market by investigating profitable consolidation of existing roads— something for which Hill had argued.[36] Determining exactly what the railroad managers thought at a given time presents a host of problems, as does establishing a person's motivation for choosing any particular strategy. No doubt some wanted government help, and others believed they could work matters out among themselves. Regardless, while they may have differed over strategy, the major railroad magnates did not hesitate to seek federal help in enforcing prices or in validating the pooling arrangements that they could not maintain through market forces alone.

Competition from the unsubsidized roads continued to drive prices down. During a thirty-year period after the Civil War, the rate for carrying wheat fell by 70 percent (at a time that general prices only dropped 14 percent), and individual roads sliced their fares. The Santa Fe cut its prices 42 percent; the Chicago, Burlington, and Quincy reduced rates 50 percent; and the Northern Pacific, 46 percent. New advances in railroad technology, especially the sleeping and dining car developed by George Pullman and the air brake invented by George Westinghouse, also increased passenger traffic and forced prices down. Westinghouse, only twenty-two years old when he invented the compressed air brake, spent two years attempting to convince railroad officials that his invention would save lives. (Westinghouse made a

---

FIGURE 5-3   *Horizontal and Vertical Combination in the Oil Industry*

Horizontal combination brought together the various firms performing one function such as refining. Vertical combination brought together the enterprises performing different functions in the sequence from acquiring raw materials to selling finished goods or services to consumers.

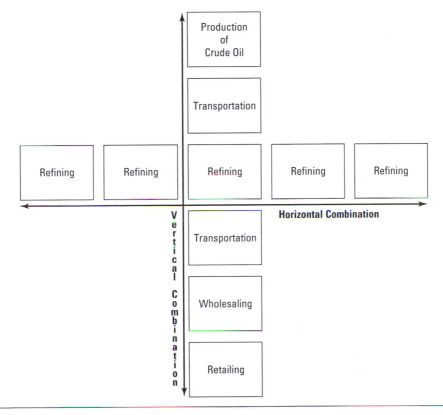

Source: Adapted from Louis Galambos and Joseph C. Pratt, *The Rise of the Corporate Commonwealth: U.S. Business and Public Policy in the Twentieth Century,* p. 8. Copyright © 1988 by Basic Books, Inc. Reprinted by permission of Basic Books, a member of Perseus Books, L.L.

fortune on the air brake but did not quit inventing, beginning work on alternating current [AC] electricity.) But whether because of technology or market pressures, the pooling agreements had failed to work, bringing to an end horizontal combinations. Salaried, professional managers assumed active direction of the major roads, turning them into efficient vertical combinations. The railroads had, through convulsion and confusion, ushered in the "managerial revolution" in business.

Simply establishing line-and-staff organizations did not complete the transition from owner-operated businesses to the new form of business enterprise. That required another step, in which firms vertically *integrated,* that is, moved backward from their original product to obtain control over raw materials or forward to absorb sales and distribution networks (see Figure 5.3). With control established over raw materials, transportation of their product, wholesaling, and retail outlets (as well as, later, marketing and research and development), firms held their fate in their own hands. They did not have to rely on outside teamsters or railroaders for shipping—they had their own transportation networks. Companies established their own warehouses. Thus, at no point did outside businesses threaten to disrupt the flow of goods, therefore the managers could plan for every aspect of the business. Increasingly, the focus shifted from eliminating competitors to stabilizing the flow of production. And, as Andrew Carnegie learned, controlling costs was everything. Firms did not respond to price cuts by competitors as much as they constantly sought productivity gains within themselves. Managers, under whose authority the productivity increases rested, not only justified their existence but were elevated to the pinnacles of business. At that point, when business evolved into vertically integrated, manager-dominated firms, American companies became "big business."

Alfred Chandler's "Visible Hand"

The appearance of "big business," first with the railroads, then expanding to other areas of production, was the most obvious development in American enterprise between 1850 and 1890. Alfred D. Chandler Jr. produced a capstone work analyzing that evolution in 1977, *The Visible Hand,* which embodied major themes he had studied for years and presented in segments in his several other books.[37] Chandler's theory was significant for a number of reasons, not the least of which is that truly "American" historical theories are scarce. Many historians suggest that Frederick Jackson Turner's "Frontier Thesis" (1896) represented the only genuinely new addition to the practice of history, but based on the national and international response to the concepts in *The Visible Hand,* it seems that Chandler has joined Turner as an American original. At some point, the business history of virtually every industrialized nation has been subjected to an analysis based on Chandler's propositions. For these and other reasons, Chandler's central theory demands attention.

Chandler outlined eight general propositions that traced the appearance and dominance of what he called the "visible hand" of management—itself the essence of the managerial revolution of the 1800s. The propositions were:

1. Modern business enterprise replaced small traditional enterprise when administrative coordination permitted greater productivity, lower costs, or higher profits than did the market.

2. The advantages of internalizing the cost-saving activities required the appearance of a "managerial hierarchy," which Chandler argued was "a defining characteristic of the modern business enterprise."[38]

3. Modern business enterprise first appeared in history when the volume of economic activities made administrative coordination more efficient or profitable than market coordination.

4. Once the managerial hierarchy was formed, it became permanent and powerful within a business.

5. The managers became increasingly technical and professional.

6. As business grew in size and complexity, the management of enterprise became separated from ownership.

7. The professional managers favored policies that enhanced long-term stability rather than those that maximized profit.

8. Large enterprise, dominated by managerial hierarchies, expanded from railroads into other major sectors of the economy, thereby altering the structure of those sectors as well.

Cumulatively, the eight propositions described a business culture in which the "most important" enterprises, or "big business" in the Chandler definition, spread from railroads to most other large firms. In doing so, the structure of business enterprise was changed fundamentally, from a "market-directed" culture to a "manager-directed" culture. More broadly, the new managerial firms de-emphasized competition and stressed internal controls for the purpose of increasing efficiency. While Chandler saw capitalism as maturing with the managerial revolution, his theory championed planning and nonmarket forces, fitting well with those (such as John Kenneth Galbraith) who sang the praises of government-business "cooperation." In Chandler's world, at least in its most modern manifestations, there was little room for entrepreneurs who built the businesses. Instead, the key parts were played by nonentrepreneurial managers, and the rise of big business signaled the death of the entrepreneur.

Of course, some managers exhibited entrepreneurial tendencies, as illustrated by J. Edgar Thomson and, later, Charles Schwab or Walter Wriston. Usually, however, when managers acted like entrepreneurs, they *were* entrepreneurs, owning large blocks of stock and having a substantial and immediate financial stake in the companies they ran. However, the confusion regarding the roles of the managers has led many business historians, perhaps in resignation, to treat managers *as* entrepreneurs, even to the point of defining them as such.[39] But to the extent that most managers did not use their own money, they were not, by definition, entrepreneurs. Thus, Chandler's theory seemed to suggest that the days of entrepreneurs had ended, displaced by a professional managerial class.

The "Other" America: Entrepreneurs

At the very time that the managerial hierarchies started to reshape business enterprise, attracting the bulk of public attention with high-profile deals, ever expanding production, and swelling ranks of labor, another sector of business quietly thrived. Entrepreneurs had not disappeared when railroads made professional managers a permanent feature of the business landscape, although occasionally their activities could appear less important because of the small size of most entrepreneurial firms. Indeed, some entrepreneurs just got lost in the shuffle; but others would stand out in any crowd.

Lydia E. Estes, one of twelve children, had received a solid education and held a job as a schoolteacher before she married Isaac Pinkham. Isaac readily took any job, yet never prospered. When the Panic of 1873 hit, the Pinkhams and their five children drifted into abject poverty. Partly out of desperation, then, in 1875 Lydia Pinkham started selling her special vegetable compound for "female complaints" (a nebulous term that referred to any discomfort or injury related to the female anatomy). Giving away the "remedy" at first, Pinkham and her sons found that the compound was extremely popular. They manufactured the remedy as "Lydia E. Pinkham's Vegetable Compound" in their basement. Lydia oversaw actual production, while sons Daniel and William used wages they earned at other jobs to market the compound and procure supplies. Isaac, then in a wheelchair, folded pamphlets. Daniel distributed more than 20,000 "Guide for Women" pamphlets in ten days, whereupon a leading pharmacist started to sell the product. While in Boston, Daniel used his remaining per diem of $60 to place a front-page ad in the *Boston Herald,* and sales went up. Grasping the value of advertising, the Pinkhams dedicated more of their budget to newspaper promotions, even mortgaging their house to buy additional ads.[40]

At age sixty, Lydia Pinkham put her own portrait on the remedy, making it a recognizable trademark. The ad campaign reached billboards, bottles, newspapers, magazines, and streetcar signs, and it turned Lydia Pinkham into a household name. Offered $100,000 for the company, the family declined. In 1881, annual sales surpassed $200,000. After both brothers contracted tuberculosis and died, Lydia Pinkham gave up control over the business to other family members, who maintained it until the 1980s. The product increasingly came under attack from public health officials and from the medical profession as ungrounded in any medical science. It was, ultimately, the product itself, and not the entrepreneurial form of the company, that ended Pinkham's business.

Lydia Pinkham started late in life but never considered herself too old to succeed. And if age proved incapable of stifling the entrepreneurial instinct, neither did bad luck. Heinrich Steinweg, for example, was as unlucky as one person could get. At age eleven, Heinrich's mother and many of his siblings in Germany died fleeing from Napoleon's advancing troops. Years later, Heinrich, along with his father and remaining three brothers, took shelter during a thunderstorm in a hut when lightning struck the building, killing everyone but Heinrich. Left an orphan, Heinrich Steinweg joined the army, where he learned to make musical instruments, including pianos, in his spare time.[41]

Steinweg married and had five sons, who joined him to construct pianos in Germany. When business dropped during the revolution of 1848, Steinweg and his family decided to move to the United States. They arrived in New York in 1850 and realized that the pianos that sold in Germany might not appeal to Americans. Consequently, the Steinwegs all took jobs with different New York piano factories to learn American tastes and technology. Confident they had absorbed all that American piano manufacturers had to offer, the family started the House of Steinway & Sons in 1853, producing a single piano each week. Within twenty years, Steinway pianos had received some of the world's top prizes for musical instruments, bolstering the company's reputation and battling imitators who used similar-sounding names, such as "Steinmay" or "Shumway." Despite the look-alikes, the demand for Steinways reached such proportions that in 1872 the family built Steinway Village in Long Island—a model housing project for employees that included a library, a school, and a free bathhouse. The family retained control, and the pianos maintained their quality over the years, until in 1972 CBS purchased the company.

Steinway pianos achieved a reputation as being among the finest musical instruments in the world because the Steinweg family dedicated themselves to making great pianos. Elisha Otis, on the other hand, took twenty years of repeated business failures to find his calling. Born in 1811 in Vermont, Otis had a building business in Troy, New York; started, operated, and closed a grist mill in Vermont; built fine carriages for seven years until that enterprise dried up; and then labored in Yonkers, New York, as a master mechanic at the Yonkers Bedstead company. His inveterate tinkerer's spirit led him to invent a machine for automatically turning parts of bedsteads much faster than before, which Otis then contracted out along with other labor-saving machines.[42] Seeing an opportunity to create his own business, Otis attempted to manufacture machinery of various types until his water supply was appropriated by the city of Albany. Otis, at age forty, was again in debt and out of work. However, his former Yonkers employer hired him to supervise the construction of a new factory. Otis had considered going to California to search for gold, but unexpectedly, success got in the way.

While studying a problem with the new factory, Otis had to move heavy woodworking equipment to the second floor of the building. He constructed a platform hoist, but, unlike other elevators of the day, he had developed a safety device—a rachet and spring that engaged when the main cable broke, stopping the elevator instantly. As he made plans to leave New York, the burly mechanic was contacted by a furniture business that had experienced an elevator accident and wanted to ensure that it never happened again. Demand for his product encouraged Otis to form the E.G. Otis Company in 1853, ending his intentions to strike it rich in the mountains and streams of California— perhaps too quickly, he no doubt concluded after his early torrent of orders turned to a trickle. Freight elevators were common in New York; but no landlord wanted to risk human passengers in one of the contraptions, and thus the largest market in the city remained closed to Otis's elevators. A true entrepreneur, Otis displayed the faith and vision that had characterized the Pinkhams, the Vanderbilts, the Astors, and others. He did what few other entrepreneurs seldom did: He put his own life at risk based on his faith in his product. He demonstrated his lift at the 1854 American Institute Fair at the Crystal Palace in New York. Standing on the platform (with some boxes and barrels for added weight), Otis was elevated far above the thousands of people watching when he ordered an assistant to chop the cable. The lift plunged instantly, but the safety catches brought it to a sudden stop. Otis bowed deeply and stated loudly, "All safe, gentlemen, all safe."[43]

Having obtained free publicity that would have cost thousands of dollars if he had bought it, Otis expected a new surge in orders. He was mistaken. The next year he sold only fifteen elevators, and the year after that, twenty-seven, all freight lifts. Not until 1857 did Otis make his first passenger elevator sale, to a five-story Manhattan china store—an elevator that still carried passengers in 1984. Otis did not live to see the business he started reach maturity. He died in 1861, leaving his two sons to run the $5,000 company. Like the Steinwegs, the family not only continued the business but improved and expanded it. Charles and Norton Otis invented more than fifty patented technical refinements for elevators, including air brakes (1864) and the introduction of the electrical elevator (1869). Elevators as a product, however, differed substantially from home-remedy medicine and pianos in that they required technical expertise from the sales force to instruct buyers and a qualified repair and support staff. The Otis company provided both, training sales personnel to understand the technical basis of the elevators. In so doing, Otis's company further accelerated the professionalization of business management brought on by the railroads, continuing and spreading the managerial revolution still further.

For residents of multistory buildings, however, elevators were nothing less than blessings. The elevator also made more convenient some of the most famous tourist attractions in the world: Otis elevators carried people to the top of the Washington Monument (1888) and the Eiffel Tower (1899), and returned them safely. When combined with the architectural advances of William Jenney, who in 1885 perfected a method that used an iron frame to support buildings' weight, Otis elevators made possible true skyscrapers.

John Deere had a much less difficult life than Pinkham or Steinweg, and unlike Otis had an immediate demand for his product. He received an education in Middlebury, Vermont, schools. He took a position as an apprentice to a local blacksmith, where he quickly learned the trade. Deere's quality work earned him a reputation with the state's farmers for producing the finest shovels, hoes, and pitchforks. In 1836, anxious over the depressed condition of Vermont's economy, Deere joined other Vermonters relocating to Grand Detour, Illinois. There he established a new forge and held the respected position of "village smithy," when he learned that farmers had difficulty tilling the heavier western soil with their eastern plows. Deere, "working with a discarded sawmill blade," built a prototype of a new plow with a curved shape made of highly polished steel.[44] The new plow immediately gained popularity with local farmers, and by 1846 Deere contracted a Pittsburgh steel company to supply steel, allowing him to mass-produce plows. Within a year, Deere moved his facilities to a better location near the Mississippi River. At his new factory in Moline, Illinois, sales reached 10,000 by 1857.

Deere continued to refine his plows and make other implements. He changed his marketing strategy, growing more sophisticated. Where once he loaded a wagon with plows and visited farms until he had sold them all, he soon developed a network of local dealers who sold the plows on commission. Deere watched his dealers carefully, recording in a book his observations about their personal honesty. Charles Deere, John's son, joined the company in 1858, and as the business grew, John and Charles looked for further ways to improve tilling the soil. In 1874, they devised the first two-wheeled riding plow, in essence heralding the advent of the high-volume farm implements of the late 1800s, during which time the Deere Company also employed a "high-tech" sales and repair force to join the managerial revolution.

When it came to advances in farm equipment, no entrepreneur had a greater impact than Cyrus McCormick, who revolutionized wheat harvesting. Born in Virginia, Cyrus had watched as his father worked unsuccessfully on their Shenandoah farm to develop a mechanical harvester, a design that Cyrus built in modified form in 1831, using a saw-toothed blade to cut the stalks pulled into the cutter by a reel device. By 1834, he had a patentable reaper, then inexplicably turned his attention to other matters for half a decade, flirting with an iron business that failed. Then, in 1840, McCormick improved the design further and made his first sale. He quickly beat back competition from a rival; then, as "one of the first American industrialists to face the necessity of making a major move in order to be closer to his markets," McCormick relocated to Chicago in 1848.[45]

A reaper could harvest 15 acres of wheat in a day, and, while effective on its own, generated extensive productivity gains when combined with other mechanical devices just starting to appear, including binders, steam threshers, and other powered machinery.[46] Even when the reaper did not "pay for itself" initially, farmers often purchased the device with the intention of expanding their wheat crop. The reaper, in essence, changed the way farmers thought about their business.[47]

Not only did McCormick usher in agribusiness, he continued the trend toward vertically integrated companies through his business practices. His factory had the capacity to turn out forty reapers a day, and in 1856 the McCormick company produced 4,000 machines. But the new equipment differed substantially from other mass-produced items of the day in that no one had seen a reaper before—making it an alien piece of technology—and it bore a hefty price tag ($115 in 1850, or the equivalent of well over $100,000 in 1990s money). Evidence in the McCormick archives suggests that neighboring farmers pooled their resources to purchase reapers jointly, and professional thresher companies passed through the farmlands regularly, selling their services to farmers.[48] Nevertheless, to overcome the "purchase anxiety" of customers for the reapers, McCormick enlisted salesmen who learned the operation of the product and could demonstrate it. He offered credit to make it easier to purchase the expensive reapers, requiring only a $35 down payment. By instituting the use of credit, McCormick placed an additional demand upon the dealers, requiring them to judge the creditworthiness of buyers, and, when necessary, to collect on past-due accounts.[49] The dealers, assisted by heavy doses of company advertising from the Chicago office, not only sold the reapers; they had to provide efficient service for the equipment, again, supported by the Chicago administration that ensured delivery of spare parts.

After the Civil War, a new challenger eclipsed the McCormick reaper, but Cyrus McCormick, admitting he was bested in one area, applied himself to the production of wire binders, an associated technology invented by Charles Withington in 1877. McCormick's entry into the market put him into competition with John Deere's Deering Plow Company. The two titans, both born of farmer-entrepreneurs, merged into a single business, the McCormick-Deering International Harvester Company in 1903.[50]

Thanks to McCormick and Deere, rapid advances in agricultural technology generated an abundance of crops that flowed from American farms at levels previously unimagined. The combined effects of mechanization in wheat production, provided by devices such as the reaper, and the westward movement of farmers resulted, according to one estimate, in an astronomical 377 percent increase in labor productivity between 1840 and 1910.[51] Associated with such astounding productivity, northern farms returned profits at an average rate of over 12 percent on every dollar invested.[52] Although the full impact of the mechanical advances and comprehensive settlement of the West was not as clear in the mid- to late 1850s as it would be decades later, many observers already had pointed to vastly different—and, to them, mutually incompatible—economies and business cultures between the North and the South that they traced almost exclusively to slavery. Both the North and South used the economic events of the 1850s to justify their business and labor systems, initiating a debate that touched the very essence of free-market systems.

Sectional Differences: "Free Labor," Business, and Economic Growth

The sectional split had festered since the signing of the Constitution in 1787, which received support from southern delegates only because it would contain no prohibitions against slavery. Delegates at the Constitutional Convention had their most heated debates over those sections of the Constitution involving representation and taxation because they realized that the outcome would affect the direction the nation would take toward slavery. Following a series of compromises, the convention agreed to permit slaves to count as "3/5 of a person" for purposes of representation and taxation, and to place a twenty- year moratorium on any legislation related to the slave trade. Otherwise, slavery went untouched.

In 1808, Congress banned the importation of slaves, but that merely added to the value of slaves already within the United States. By that time, plantation slavery had been thoroughly rooted, making it impossible for minor legislative tinkering to redress the problem. Slavery spread to every southern state, as well as Delaware, Maryland, the District of Columbia, Kentucky, and eventually Missouri, but the economic impact of slavery was suppressed until Whitney invented his cotton gin in 1793. When the cotton gin solved the problem of cleaning the short-staple cotton that grew easily in the rich southern soil and the temperate climate, production increased across the entire lower tier of American states, especially in the land along the Mississippi River Valley. Pulled west by steadily higher yields, the momentum of "King Cotton" showed no evidence of slowing. That, in turn, placed increasing stresses on the American political party system, which had been designed to avoid a confrontation between the sections. After the Missouri Compromise of 1820, each new territorial expansion raised the specter of war; and yet each new expansion, so desperately sought by southerners, increasingly illuminated the political weakness of the South.[53]

When the Republican Party appeared in the 1850s, its opponents labeled it an antislavery party, but some of its major spokesmen, such as Abraham Lincoln, only wanted to limit the extension of slavery into the territories, not prohibit it outright. Lincoln espoused a position known as the "natural limits of slavery," which held that slavery could function only in cash crop plantation settings; that such cotton- and rice producing areas that existed in the South were, through processes of land expiration, moving steadily to the southern and western regions; and thus if trapped within its "natural limits" and lacking new territories to prolong its life, slavery would vanish.[54] Unfortunately for Lincoln and later proponents of the "natural limits" theory, the relentless expansion of the cotton frontier and the introduction of slaves into urban and industrial labor suggests that slavery would not have disappeared on its own.

Business, "Free Soil," and "Free Labor"

Perhaps of more immediate concern to businesses in the 1840s and 1850s, however, were the new arguments for and against slavery from the perspective of labor. Slavery became thoroughly intertwined in the minds of both advocates and opponents of "free labor" (a term used to describe work for wages) with other issues such as the tariff and "free soil." Lincoln assumed a prominent role in the debates, as did leaders of the business and industrial communities, and in many ways they touched on the understanding of entrepreneurship in the 1850s.

The term "free soil" referred to western territories that were threatened by the expansion of slavery. Slaves had traveled with their masters as far as Utah—although not in great numbers—and the potential for slavery in the territories dominated the politics of the era. Many had thought the issue solved when Henry Clay drafted the Missouri Compromise in 1820, which prohibited slavery above the 36 degree 30′ parallel but allowed new territories admitted to the Union as states *below* that line to choose to be free or slave states. New controversies arose with the admission of Texas and the subsequent Mexican War, which made California a state. (California, which lay both above and below the line, brought its own compromise, the Compromise of 1850, that unraveled the earlier Missouri Compromise.) In 1854, the Kansas-Nebraska Act formed two new territories that sought statehood, on the basis of a new doctrine introduced by Sen. Stephen Douglas of Illinois, "popular sovereignty."

Each new controversy heightened the tension over slavery. Northern political economists argued that the extension of slavery directly attacked the foundation of free labor—workers free to select their employment and bargain for their pay. The basis of individual advancement came through hard work, which produced high wages. Many northerners feared that the competition from slave labor would drive down wages paid to free workers. Those concerns increased when wages stagnated or when high unemployment occurred, as in the Panic of 1857. Settlement on western lands, or "free soil," offered an attractive solution. Nevertheless, many northern writers supported high tariffs and "free soil" as a primary means of maintaining wages for "free labor."[55] Some argued purely from the perspective of wages, contending that land would draw away "excess laborers" and thus raise wages.[56] For many advocates of "free soil," the issue transcended wages; available land promised any individual the opportunity to improve his lot in life, and slavery threatened that opportunity. Some theorists, including Lincoln, saw industrial work as a passing phase to farm ownership and running a small business, the ultimate expressions of entrepreneurship. "Free soil," then, embodied the essence of entrepreneurship, even if it was closely linked in the minds of its advocates with wage labor and tariffs.

"Free labor" meant wage labor in the North: the ability to work for the employer of one's own choosing at a wage mutually agreed upon.[57] But at least one well-known southern critic of the industrial system, George Fitzhugh, attacked free labor as "slave labor," arguing that the wages paid in the North provided a living standard worse than that of plantation slaves. A Virginian and an unabashed socialist, Fitzhugh's controversial book *Cannibals All!* revealed exactly how far slavery was from free markets. He contended that the only true freedom came when a person's needs were met, and that only slaves enjoyed such a healthy situation. Northern factory owners "enslaved" their workers with inadequate wages; but plantation owners cared for their slaves' needs conscientiously. Thus, in one of the classic inversions of capitalism, Fitzhugh maintained that "free labor" (i.e., wage labor) in reality meant slave labor, while "slave labor" really constituted free labor! He called for a socialist government that would care for all people, run by a few masters who were enslaved by their obligations. No one was truly free, he contended; we are all "slaves without masters."[58]

Many critics in both the North and South had suggested just the opposite, namely that the South lagged behind the industrial North in providing material well-being for its employees because the system of slave labor was not as productive as free labor. As Nathaniel Banks argued in 1857 before audiences in Boston and New York, slavery was "the foe of all industrial progress and of the highest material prosperity."[59] Likewise, Frank Blair, from an influential family of Missouri and Maryland antislave activists, wrote that "no one from a slave state could pass through 'the splendid farms of Sangamon and Morgan, without permitting an envious sigh to escape him at the evident superiority of free labor.'"[60] But were such assertions true?

Slavery and the "Factory in the Fields"

Plantation agriculture had entrenched itself in southern life and culture since the 1600s. Buoyed by primogeniture, mixed with the chronic labor shortage and the economics of cash-crop production of cotton, rice, or tobacco, the financial logic of using slaves was unchallenged by all but a few southern theorists. Writers such as Hinton Helper urged non-slaveholders to resist the political programs of the slave owners, but for every Helper there were more influential proslave voices such as John C. Calhoun, or more idiosyncratic ones.[61] Of course, almost half of all southerners had no slaves, and "most of the slaves were held by only 12 percent of all slaveowners. . . ."[62]

The economics of slavery were relatively simple. The number of slaves in the United States had risen from 894,000 in 1800 to 3.95 million in 1860, with most of the slaves employed in agriculture. Prime field hands cost $1,800 in 1860, and prices rose steadily because new slaves could not be regularly imported. Regardless of its immediate profitability, slavery was *viable,* meaning that the costs of raising slaves—food, shelter, medical care, and even interest—were less than the prices at which they could be sold, with the differential widening between 1815 and 1860. *Profitability* was a different concept, relating to whether slaves produced more than it cost to purchase and care for them. For a few decades, some debate existed about the profitability of slavery, largely derived from the writings of Ulrich Bonnell Phillips and Charles Sydnor. Phillips and Sydnor both relied on the manuscript plantation records of owners as evidence of income and expenses, and although they arrived at roughly the same conclusion—that slavery was not very profitable—they did so along different erroneous lines.[63] Phillips's problems arose from his reliance on the assessments of the owners themselves, who tended to overstate their expenses or difficulties, particularly in correspondence to family members or friends, and to underestimate their returns. Sydnor, on the other hand, had the correct data but erroneously counted items as expenses that really belonged to other investment categories. When using Sydnor's data correctly, Kenneth Stampp found that slaveholding returned 8.4 percent investment, not counting the increasing value of slaves for resale purposes.[64] In 1958, Alfred Conrad and John Meyer applied modern accounting techniques to plantation records and arrived at a completely different conclusion than that of Phillips and Sydnor: Slavery was profitable in almost all cases, but in the more fertile western lands, returns ran as high as 13 percent.[65]

Subsequent studies have sustained and refined the conclusions of Conrad and Meyer. It was hard *not* to make money with slave labor. Slavery, as a business practice protected by state laws, provided unfair advantages against those employers not using slaves, and thus economic incentives supported and sustained slavery within its sealed environment. While plantation slavery was *primarily* an economic system, the entire structure of slavery demanded social, cultural, and political support. It seems unlikely, then, that slavery could have disappeared by application of market forces alone because it required more than market forces to sustain it. Religion, law, social attitudes, and education all played a part in reinforcing the notion of racial inferiority inherent in black slavery.

Businesses did have substantial incentives to make a transition into manufacturing. One study found, for example, that by 1860 the *lowest* rates of return on industrial capital in southern manufacturing exceeded 22 percent (and the highest, 45 percent).[66] The researchers also found that large-scale manufacturing in the South and West in the pre–Civil War decade greatly resembled the pattern set in the Northeast.[67] However, many southerners knew cotton cultivation well: It held few surprises, and produced regular profits. It would have required exceptionally daring farmer-entrepreneurs to abandon cotton for the unfamiliar enterprise of manufacturing and industry, although clearly many did make exactly that transition. But it also required that individuals resist the social and cultural milieu that encouraged slave-based agriculture, and for many the pressures were too great, even with the promise of returns of 22 percent.[68]

Successful plantations achieved steady profits on the basis of an organizational system for slaves called the "factory in the fields." That term described gang-based slave labor in which a handful of managers—slave drivers and overseers—could control hundreds of slaves picking cotton. Although the rate of exploitation (or expropriation, a term meaning the difference between the amount produced by the slave and the amount consumed by the slave) was a relatively low 12 percent when measured over the entire lifetime of the slave, the exploitation rate during a field hand's prime years reached as high as 65 percent.[69] That exploitation constituted the essential difference between free farmers and slaves. Slaves worked longer hours as well, making it difficult for even the worst planter/businessman to lose money with a slave workforce.[70] In their controversial work *Time on the Cross,* Robert Fogel and Stanley Engerman concluded that southern farms were 35 percent more productive than northern farms, and slave plantations produced even higher efficiencies. In his later solo work, *Without Consent or Contract,* Fogel reiterated that the "technical efficiency of the slave farms, particularly the intermediate and large plantations, accounted for about 90 percent of the southern advantage [over northern farms in the antebellum period]."[71]

The economic efficiency of slavery grated on free marketeers: How could a system so immoral be productive? And why did the returns in manufacturing not erode slavery through market pressures? At the same time, Marxists such as Eugene Genovese struggled to rationalize the plantation South as a "pre-capitalist" culture, recognizing that slavery was incompatible with traditional Marxist theory. Instead, Genovese argued, the southern economy represented a challenge to the capitalist North precisely because it represented a precapitalist culture based on slavery.

One approach is to view each set of questions as flip sides of the same issue. Slavery achieved high levels of productivity because the application of force, which could not exist in free labor situations, led to longer hours, if not measurably harder work. Moreover, the gang system was not tolerable to free laborers but was an efficient

THE ECONOMICS OF BUSINESS

How Important Were Railroads?

ESTABLISHING THE CONTRIBUTIONS OF A PARticular business, or sector of enterprise, for years offered a nettlesome problem. Testimony of contemporaries, manuscripts of owners and managers after their death, and even records of the business itself offered only partial glimpses of the impact of a firm. As the profession of economic history has unfolded, one of the recurring objectives has been to quantify the significance of specific businesses and technologies. One of the first exercises in applying these techniques occurred with the assessments of the savings to society generated by the railroads, where many economic historians, unsatisfied with generalizations about their economic impact, endeavored to arrive at more specific measurements of the difference railroads made. Members of a subgroup, who sought to apply economic data

to historical models using counterfactuals, or "what if" hypotheses, are called "cliometricians." Early cliometricians, such as the economist Robert Fogel, sought to arrive at measurements based on comparisons of existing systems with other systems that did not exist but were historically feasible and imaginable (called a "counterfactual"). Using the cliometric approach, Fogel at first only generated additional controversy about railroads, with most of the challenges involving the methodology used by the cliometricians themselves!

Fogel, who in 1994 won the Nobel Prize for his research, developed estimates of the social savings for railroads based on data for the year 1890. To determine how much "better" railroads were over other systems—say, canals—Fogel had to compare canal data with that of the railroads. Yet the canal era had been over for decades by the time the railroads reached their prime. Fogel concluded that a direct comparison was impossible but that he could still compare canals to railroads by using a U.S. Army Corps of Engineers study that proposed a canal system across the Great Plains. Fogel asked, "What if such a system indeed had been built?" Proceeding as though such a system were feasible, Fogel calculated construction, operation, and maintenance costs for such a canal system, then compared the costs to organization for field workers. Slavery had another fundamental incompatibility with capitalism in that it enslaved consumers. Fifty years after the Civil War, Henry Ford, aware that his employees also constituted potential consumers, instituted the $5 day; in 1918 he made it $6, recognizing that his wages eventually came back to buy Ford cars. No such circle existed in the plantation system because the consumers were captives without capital. So Genovese was correct insofar as his argument applied to the labor system of plantations: Slavery was not capitalistic.

Nor were the returns in manufacturing or other endeavors sufficient to override the profits of slave agriculture because even *relatively* lower rates of return in agriculture concurred with other, less

those of the railroads. He estimated that a savings would have accrued of about 5 percent of GNP in 1890 and concluded that without the railroads, the 1890 GNP of the United States would not have been attained until 1892.

Posing the analysis in the form of a "what if," and using data from a canal system that had never been constructed, only planned, Fogel advanced economic history by taking econometrics, or the application of statistics to test economic models, to cliometrics. Although some criticized the concept, and although it can be carried to absurd limits ("What if Davey Crockett had machine guns at the Alamo?"), Fogel had broken new ground, and others quickly followed. The key to successful use of cliometrics was to apply data to a realistic and possible alternative, not a fantasy.

Using the counterfactual hypothesis, Albert Fishlow used a similar analysis to place the social savings for the year 1859 at 4 percent of GNP. Fishlow argued that Fogel needed to compare data for periods when railroads and canals competed directly. Separately, Fogel and Fishlow arrived at similar conclusions, finding that railways were important to, but not indispensable for, American economic growth in the nineteenth century. Other scholars have challenged or modified the calculations and conclusions of the pioneer cliometricians.

On the other hand, notions such as "backward linkages," or the demands that railroads place on other industries, are, as Jeremy Atack and Peter Passell conclude, "a disappointment to those convinced that the railroad was crucial to nineteenth-century American industrial development." Certainly the expansion of railroads brought unforeseen benefits, and in many ways linked the nation spiritually, socially, and psychologically. As a result, economic historians generally agree on the fact that the railroads were important and that the exact impact of the railroad upon the American economy remains somewhat in doubt. But they also agree that the notion of the railroads' economic "indispensability," once a staple of every American history textbook, rests in peace.

Sources: Robert W. Fogel, *Railroads and American Economic Growth: Essays in Econometric History* (Baltimore, Md.: Johns Hopkins University Press, 1960); Albert Fishlow, *Railroads and the Transformation of the Antebellum Economy* (Cambridge, Mass.: Harvard University Press, 1960); Jeffrey G. Williamson, *Late Nineteenth Century American Development: A General Equilibrium History* (Cambridge: Cambridge University Press, 1974); Paul David, "Transport Innovation and Economic Growth: Professor Fogel on and off the Rails," *Economic History Review*, 32 (1969): 506–525; and the chapter on railroads in Atack and Passell, *New Economic View American History* (quotation on 454).

material returns, including social status among whites, racism against blacks, and the risk involved in entering unfamiliar business ventures. Slavery was comfortable, at least for the masters.

To what extent the entire southern business structure suffered because of slavery's pernicious effects is difficult to estimate. Some elements of the South's economy had actually surpassed in sophistication their counterparts in the North, including aspects of its banking system. The South had high rates of patent registrations and other evidence of technological innovation, although over time the South appeared to drift behind the industrialized North in the ratio of patent registrations.[72] And clearly the South as a region was neither poor nor insulated from market factors. Its manufacturing base, however, lagged behind even the Midwest, it trailed the United States per-capita value-added average in 1860 by a substantial $7, and pockets of deep rural poverty existed.[73] Regardless, when either southern businessmen or northern abolitionists attempted to entice, reason, or cajole plantation owners away from slavery, slave owners cast long-term returns to the winds.

Did that mean that the "market failed" to liberate the slaves? Quite the opposite. As Mark Thornton has argued, "Slavery is demonstrated to have survived in the antebellum South . . . because political forces prevented the typical decay and destruction of slavery experienced elsewhere."[74] Likewise, Jeffrey Hummel, in his *Emancipating Slaves, Enslaving Free Men,* contends that the political setting and legal structure significantly reduced the private costs of slavery—"externalizing" the costs—through a variety of legal and political means.[75] Slaveholders passed statutes that drafted non-slaveholders into slave patrols to catch runaways; they used the criminal justice system to enforce slave codes; and they restricted or prohibited private manumission of slaves. States had laws against educating slaves, prohibiting slaves from testifying in court, and against miscegenation. In dozens of ways, those acts made it impossible for slaves to purchase their own freedom through earnings (which had occurred at increasing rates in the South prior to 1800), to marry a white person, or to acquire any personal property. Those laws existed on top of yet other statutes that restricted the movement of free blacks within the South and against sending abolitionist material through the mails. As Thornton and Hummel show, the costs of those restrictions were substantial, but the slaveholders successfully shifted the expense onto the public at large and, specifically, onto non-slaveholders (who usually were not as wealthy). Thus, southern slaveholders managed to obtain a government subsidy for slavery for over 200 years and cleverly avoided bearing the full costs of slavery themselves.

Unwilling to consider religious or moral repudiations of slavery, the South had only the political structure or the market to correct its

Henry J. Heinz: Fifty (Seven) Ways to Love Your Burger

As A CHILD, HENRY HEINZ WAS SURROUNDED by bricks. He worked in his father's brickyard and even purchased an interest in it from the proceeds of his "other" business, selling a horseradish he bottled. Although he had a knack for business, Heinz at a young age learned the harsh realities of the market when he and his partners drove their pickle company into bankruptcy. When only twenty-five years old, Henry Heinz was arrested twice for fraud related to the bankruptcy—although he was cleared both times—and his reputation was all but destroyed. At that point, most people would have retired to the safe confines of the family brickyard, but not Heinz.

With $3,000 he borrowed from relatives, he again entered the food business. More conservative with his cash, he audaciously marketed his name, emphasizing brand names for bottled and canned goods. One of his best-known products still was pickles, which he used as a marketing tool. At the 1892–1893 Columbian Exposition in Chicago, his remote location made it easy for fairgoers to ignore Heinz's booth. Heinz quickly assessed the problem and had a local printer make thousands of small white cards that offered a free pickle to anyone presenting the card at the Heinz booth. Located on the second floor, the booth suddenly attracted such large crowds that fair officials had to strengthen the supports of the gallery floor. By the time the world's fair ended, Heinz had given away one million pickles but had gained advertising that would have cost far more if he had paid for it directly. Newspapers and magazines further publicized the stunt, to the effect that schoolchildren soon begged for a Heinz pickle lapel pin.

Heinz had turned the corner. He also had a "hook"—something with which to grab the public. In the 1890s, Heinz had seen an ad for a local shoe company that featured "21 Styles of Shoes." The idea of identifying the product with a number led Heinz to create the slogan "57 Varieties," even though he already had more than sixty different kinds of pickles alone. Before long, Heinz's "57 Varieties" graced billboards and railroad cars, making Heinz products a household name without naming a particular product. Heinz, too, had a new name: "the pickle king." He increased his efforts to improve his product and expand advertising. The company built a huge industrial complex in Pittsburgh, a building designed so well that it won architectural awards, and he offered guided tours of the plant. In 1900, Heinz erected a huge billboard that was among the first to use electric lights, run at the then-astronomical price of $90 a night to illuminate.

Yet the "pickle king" never forgot his origins or his God. Deeply religious, Heinz not only closed his business on Sunday but allowed no ads for his products to run in Sunday papers. He served in the World Sunday School Association for most of his life. When he died in 1919, Henry Heinz, who built his kingdom on a pickle, had, in the business sense, come back from the dead.

Source: Fucini and Fucini, *Entrepreneurs,* 102–105.

death spiral. But the plantation owners had dominated the political system, even if their dominance was not as complete in 1861 as it was a century earlier. In the final analysis, only the market or a violent confrontation with the North could have rescued the South. When the slaveholders foisted the costs of the peculiar institution onto the southern citizenry at large, thus politicizing it, no market correction was possible. By rejecting both morality and the market, southern slave owners set themselves and their entire region on a course to war.

Notes

1. James K. Medbury, *Men and Mysteries of Wall Street* (New York: Fields, Osgood & Co., 1870): 264–265, quoted in Dobson, *History of American Enterprise,* 143; and Kenneth D. Acerman, *The Gold Ring: Jim Fisk, Jay Gould and Black Friday, 1869* (New York: Harper Business, 1988).

2. Puth, *American Economic History,* 172.

3. Dobson, *History of American Enterprise,* 111.

4. Sobel and Sicilia, *Entrepreneurs,* 105–112.

5. See the *American Railroad Journal,* 29 (May 3, 1856): 280, as well as Alfred D. Chandler Jr., *Henry Varnum Poor, Business Editor, Analyst and Reformer* (Cambridge, Mass.: Harvard University Press, 1956).

6. *Reports of the President and Superintendent of the New York and Erie Railroad to the Stockholders, for the Year Ending September 30, 1855,* in *The Railroads: Pioneers in Modern Management,* ed. Alfred D. Chandler (New York: Arno Press, 1979), 34–36.

7. Dobson, *History of American Enterprise,* 116.

8. Alfred D. Chandler Jr., *The Visible Hand: The Managerial Revolution in American Business* (Cambridge, Mass.: Belknap Press, 1977), 110–118.

9. Chandler, *Visible Hand,* 116–121. Fink's formulae and tables are reproduced on 119–120.

10. Chandler, *Visible Hand,* 134.

11. Quoted in William A. Croffut, *The Vanderbilts and the Story of Their Fortune* (Chicago: Bedford, Clarke, 1886), 75.

12. Gordon, *Scarlet Woman of Wall Street,* 88.

13. Clifford I. Browder, *The Money Game in Old New York: Daniel Drew and His Times* (Lexington: University Press of Kentucky, 1986).

14. Gordon, *Scarlet Woman of Wall Street,* 90.

15. Gordon, *Scarlet Woman of Wall Street,* 91.

16. *New York Herald,* October 9, 1867.

17. Fowler, *Ten Years in Wall Street,* 506.

18. Charles Francis Adams Jr. and Henry Adams, *Chapters of Erie* (Boston: Osgood, 1871).

19. Gordon, *Scarlet Woman of Wall Street,* 213.

20. Thomson, quoted in Gordon, *Scarlet Woman of Wall Street,* 125.

21. Gordon, *Scarlet Woman of Wall Street,* 126.

22. See John Majewski's study of Pennsylvania and Virginia railroading in "Urban Invest-ment versus Local Enterprise: Railroad Financing in Pennsylvania and Virginia, 1830–1860," ed. William J. Hausman, *Business and Economic History,* 23 (Fall 1994): 92–101.

23. See Jac C. Heckelman and John Joseph Wallis, "Railroads and Property Taxes," *Explorations in Economic History,* 34 (1997): 77–99.

24. Charles Calomiris and Larry Schweikart, "The Panic of 1857: Origins, Transmis-sion, and Containment," *Journal of Economic History,* 51 (December 1991): 807–834. For an opposing view, see James L. Huston, *The Panic of 1857 and the Coming of the Civil War* (Baton Rouge: Louisiana State University Press, 1987).

25. These developments are described in Larry Schweikart, *Banking in the American South from the Age of Jackson to Reconstruction* (Baton Rouge: Louisiana State University Press, 1987).

26. Stewart Holbrook, *James J. Hill: A Great Life in Brief* (New York: Alfred A. Knopf, 1955), 93; Albro Martin, *James J. Hill and the Opening of the Northwest* (New York: Oxford University Press, 1976), 366; and Folsom, *Myth of the Robber Barons,* 26–27.

27. Blackford and Kerr, *Business Enterprise in American History,* 220.

28. Dobson, *History of American Enterprise,* 167.

29. Ibid., 162.

30. On the "big four," see Oscar Lewis, *The Big Four: The Story of Huntington, Stan-ford, Hopkins, and Crocker, and the Building of the Central Pacific* (New York: Alfred A. Knopf, 1938).

31. Don L. Hofsommer, *The Southern Pacific, 1901–1985* (College Station: Texas A&M University Press, 1986); Neil C. Wilson and Frank J. Taylor, *Southern Pacific: The Roaring Story of a Fighting Railroad* (New York: McGraw-Hill, 1952); and James Marshall, *Santa Fe: The Railroad That Built an Empire* (New York: Random House, 1945).

32. On the effects of silver politics on the economy, see Milton Friedman, "The Crime of 1873," *Journal of Political Economy,* 98 (December 1990): 1159–1194.

33. Martin, *Hill,* 410–411.

34. For the differences among railroaders regarding business unanimity on the Inter-state Commerce Act, for example, see Edward A. Purcell Jr., "Ideas and Interests: Businessmen and the Interstate Commerce Act," *Journal of American History,* 54 (December 1967): 561–578.

35. Albro Martin, "The Troubled Subject of Railroad Regulation in the Gilded Age—A Reappraisal," *Journal of American History,* 61 (September 1974): 339–371.

36. Martin, *Hill,* 296–297, 409–410, 537.

37. Among Chandler's numerous books on the railroads and the new forms of business, see especially *Strategy and Structure: Chapters in the History of American Indus-trial Enterprise* (Cambridge, Mass.: M.I.T. Press, 1962).

38. Chandler, *Visible Hand,* 7.

39. See the introductory essay by Henry C. Dethloff and Keith L. Bryant, "Entrepreneurship," in Dethloff and Pusateri, *American Business History: Case Studies,* 4–21, especially "The Manager as Entrepreneur."

40. "Lydia E. Pinkham and Her Vegetable Compound," in Sobel and Sicilia, *Entrepreneurs,* 193–196.

41. "Henry Steinway," in Fucini and Fucini, *Entrepreneurs,* 47–50; Rich K. Lieberman, *Steinway & Sons* (New Haven, Conn.: Yale University Press, 1995).

42. Clinton Woods, *Ideas that Became Big Business* (Baltimore, Md.: Founders, 1959), 33–34.

43. The following discussion is taken from "Elisha G. Otis," in Woods, *Ideas that Became Big Business,* 60–63.

44. Fucini and Fucini, *Entrepreneurs,* 58; Wayne Broehl Jr., *John Deere's Company: A History of Deere and Company and Its Times* (New York: Doubleday, 1984).

45. Robert Sobel, *The Entrepreneurs: Explorations within the American Business Tradition* (New York: Weybright and Talley, 1974), 60.

46. Bryant and Dethloff, *History of American Business,* 83.

47. See the discussion in Paul A. David, "The Mechanization of Reaping in the Ante-Bellum Midwest," in *The Reinterpretation of American Economic History,* ed. Robert W. Fogel and Stanley L. Engerman (New York: Harper & Row, 1971), originally published in *Industrialization in Two Systems,* ed. H. Rosovsky (New York: John Wiley, 1966): 3–28; Robert E. Ankli, "The Coming of the Reaper," in Paul A. Uselding, ed., *Business and Economic History* (1976), 1–24; and the chapter in Atack and Passell, "Northern Agricultural Development Before the Civil War," *A New Economic View of American History,* 274–298.

48. Alan L. Olmstead and Paul W. Rhode, "Beyond the Threshold: An Analysis of the Characteristics and Behavior of Early Reaper Adopters," *Journal of Economic History,* 55 (March 1995): 27–57, and Olmstead's original piece, "The Mechanization of Reaping and Mowing in American Agriculture, 1833–1870," *Journal of Economic History,* 35 (June 1975): 327–352.

49. Pusateri, *History of American Business,* 83.

50. Cyrus McCormick, *The Century of the Reaper* (Boston: Houghton Mifflin, 1931), 89–127. Also see Clarence H. Danof, *Change in Agriculture: The Northern United States, 1820–1870* (Cambridge, Mass.: Harvard University Press, 1969).

51. See William N. Parker and Judith L. V. Klein, "Productivity Growth in Grain Production in the United States, 1840–1860 and 1900–10," in National Bureau of Economic Research, *Output, Employment and Productivity in the United States after 1800,* Studies in Income and Wealth, vol. 30 (New York: Columbia University Press, 1966), 533.

52. Atack and Bateman, *To Their Own Soil,* passim.

53. The best single work on these developments remains David M. Potter, *The Impending Crisis, 1848–1861,* completed and edited by Don E. Fehrenbacher, The New American Nation Series, ed. Henry Steele Commager and Richard Morris (New York: Harper & Row, 1976); but also see the exceptional article by Richard D. Brown, "The Missouri Crisis, Slavery, and the Politics of Jacksonianism," *South Atlantic Quarterly,* 65 (Winter 1966): 55–72.

54. The most famous advocate of the "natural limits" theory, aside from Lincoln, was historian James G. Ramsdell. See his "The Natural Limits of Slavery Expansion," *Mississippi Valley Historical Review,* 16 (1929): 151–171.

55. L. Huston, *The Panic of 1857 and the Coming of the Civil War* discusses the antebellum literature on these issues extensively. See in particular, however, the efforts of the New York Children's Aid Society (*New York Daily Tribune,* October 26, November 11, 1857) and John Commerford of the Land Reform Association (ibid., November 25, 1858, July 21, 1859); George M. Weston, *Southern Slavery Reduces Northern Wages* (Washington, D.C., 1856); and issues of the Washington, D.C. newspaper, *National Era,* including November 12, 1857.

56. See the Salem, Ohio, *Anti-Slavery Bugle,* November 7, 1857. Historians have challenged the idea that western lands have maintained higher wages, including Fred A. Shannon, "A Post Mortem on the Labor-Safety-Valve Theory," *Agricultural History,* 19 (1945): 31–38 and Henry Littlefield, "Has the Safety Valve Come Back to Life?" *Agricultural History,* 38 (1964): 47–49.

57. A thoughtful analysis of these distinctions appears in John Ashworth, *Slavery, Capitalism, and Politics in the Antebellum Republic,* 2 vols., Volume 1: Commerce and Compromise, 1820–1850 (Cambridge: Cambridge University Press, 1995).

58. George Fitzhugh, *Cannibals All! or Slaves Without Masters,* ed. C. Vann Woodward (Cambridge, Mass.: Belknap Press, 1960 [1856]). The best exposition on the relationship between slavery and freedom in Fitzhugh is Robert J. Loewenberg, *Freedom's Despots: The Critique of Abolition* (Durham: Carolina Academic Press, 1986).

59. *The Great Questions of National and State Politics, Speech of Hon. Nathaniel P. Banks . . . ,* quoted in Eric Foner, *Free Soil, Free Labor, Free Men: The Ideology of the Republican Party Before the Civil War* (New York: Oxford, 1995 [1970]), 62.

60. Foner, *Free Soil,* 63.

61. On Calhoun, see Richard Hofstadter, "John C. Calhoun: The Marx of the Master Class," in Sidney Fine and Gerald S. Brown, *The American Past: Conflicting Interpretations of Great Issues,* vol. 1, 3d ed. (London: Macmillan, 1970), 460–479; and on Fitzhugh, see the sources cited in notes above.

62. Puth, *American Economic History,* 192.

63. Ulrich Bonnell Phillips, "The Economic Cost of Slave Holding in the Cotton Belt," *Political Science Quarterly,* 20 (1905): 257–275; Charles Sydnor, *Slavery in Mississippi* (New York: Appleton-Century, 1933).

64. Kenneth Stampp, *The Peculiar Institution* (New York: Knopf, 1956).

65. Alfred Conrad and John Meyer, "The Economics of Slavery in the Antebellum South," *Journal of Political Economy,* 66 (1958): 95–130, esp. Table 9 on 107.

66. Fred Bateman, James Foust, and Thomas Weiss, "Profitability in Southern Manufacturing: Estimates for 6860," *Explorations in Economic History,* 12 (1975): 211–231.

67. Fred Bateman, James D. Foust, and Thomas J. Weiss, "Large-Scale Manufacturing in the South and West, 1850–1860," *Business History Review,* 15 (Spring 1971): 1–17, and papers by Bateman and Weiss alone, "Manufacturing in the Antebellum South," in *Research in Economic History,* vol. 1, ed. Paul Uselding (Greenwich, Conn.: JAI Press, 1976), and "Comparative Regional Development in Antebellum Manufacturing," *Journal of Economic History,* 35 (1975): 182–208.

68. Fred Bateman and Thomas Weiss, "Manufacturing in the Antebellum South," in and their book, *A Deplorable Scarcity,* passim.

69. Richard K. Vedder, "The Slave Exploitation (Expropriation) Rate," *Explorations in Economic History,* 12 (1975): 453–458; and Robert W. Fogel and Stanley L. Engerman, *Time on the Cross: Evidence and Methods* (Boston: Little, Brown, 1974).

70. See the extensive discussion in Atack and Passell, "How the Southern Slave System Worked," *A New Economic View of American History,* 326–354.

71. Robert W. Fogel, *Without Consent or Contract: The Rise and Fall of American Slavery* (New York: W.W. Norton, 1989), 77.

72. David L. Carleton and Peter A. Coclanis, "The Uninventive South? A Quantitative Look at Region and American Inventiveness," *Technology and Cultures,* 36 (April 1995): 302–326. Carleton and Coclanis's study begins at 1870 extends well into the twentieth century, and thus is not indicative of inventiveness in the antebellum period. Nevertheless, it uses regression analysis to suggest that the South was not less inventive because it was *the South* but because it was a "frontier" or "periphery" region of the industrial eastern seaboard. That, in turn, begs the question of *why,* as late as the 1870s, the South was a periphery.

73. Gavin Wright, *Old South, New South: Revolutions in the Southern Economy Since the Civil War* (New York: Basic Books, 1986), Table 2.4 on 27.

74. Mark Thornton, "Slavery, Profitability, and the Market Process," *Review of Austrian Economics,* 7 (1994): 21–47 (quotation on 23).

75. Jeffrey Rogers Hummel, *Emancipating Slaves, Enslaving Free Men: A History of the American Civil War* (Chicago: Open Court, 1996).

CHAPTER 6

Entrepreneurs in the Age of Upheaval, 1850–1880

DAVID KENNEDY ARRIVED IN FINK, TENNESSEE, IN 1842 TO START A dry-goods store. Within a few years, his reputation for solid business practices led to his election to the board of directors of the Fink branch of the powerful Bank of Tennessee, and he eventually resigned to form his own bank, the Bank of Northern Tennessee. He continued to run a prosperous but uneventful business until April 11, 1861. That day, the South Carolina "fire eater" Edmund Ruffin touched off a cannon fuse that opened bombardment on Fort Sumter, igniting at the same time the bloodiest conflict in American history. For the next four years, while war raged, Kennedy's banking business experienced swings as the Confederacy attempted to persuade Kennedy to support the new nation with his bank's gold (he would not) and then as Union troops took Clarksville. As federal troops drew near, Kennedy loaded whatever gold he could carry on his horse and made his way through Mississippi to a point where he could catch a steamer to New Orleans. There, he transferred the bank's assets to safety in an account in England. After the war he withdrew the assets and shipped the specie from England to Tennessee, where he reopened the bank, one of the few in the entire South to survive the war.

Kennedy's difficulties during the Civil War, first in resisting confiscation of the bank's assets by one government and removing them from the grasp of another, underscores the tremendous difficulty in conducting most businesses during time of war. Some historians have contended that war is "good for business"—a theory generally subsumed under the heading "merchants of death," and a broader mythology has developed that wars are sure cures to depressions. While it is true that *some* businesses can prosper during wars, especially arms manufacturers, as a rule businesses dread the disruption of their markets and the human toll that war takes. Companies involved in interregional or international trade suffer particularly extreme hardships in time of war. The stark logic of the incompatibility of most businesses to armed conflict can be seen in the answer to the question, "Would you put a car dealership in downtown Beruit, or a new multiplex cinema in the middle of Sarajevo?" Clearly, entrepreneurs would not—and could not—conduct normal business activities if rocket shells are landing nearby or if land mines threaten customers browsing along a sidewalk.

The Civil War as a Business Stimulant?

The American Civil War exacted such a cost on business. During the conflict, the Republican Congress granted extensive lands to the railroads, enacted the Homestead Act, passed protective tariffs, and established a system of national banks—all seen by most historians as supportive of business. After the war, the destructive effects of the War Between the States left more than half a million men dead and inflicted long-lasting wounds on the southern economy. But for the North (and, on average, the nation as a whole), historians have debated the long-term effects. Some have contended, beginning with influential early works by Charles Beard and Louis Hacker, that the war was a positive development and a turning point for American economic and business growth.[1]

The "Beard-Hacker Thesis" held that the shift of political power to northern business interests from the southern "slaveocracy" ended agrarian resistance to capitalist industrialism. By destroying slavery, the war ended the feudal or "pre-capitalist" labor system. Finally, the wartime demand for goods and services in the North accelerated the nation's economy, despite the costs of the conflict. Beard touted the war as the "Second American Revolution," opening the floodgates for corporate expansion and social equality.

The "turning point" concept offered an attractive interpretation of the Civil War, with only one small problem. It wasn't true. According to the comprehensive analysis of recent research on the effects of the Civil War, Jeremy Atack and Peter Passell conclude that "it is very difficult to identify the Civil War as the turning point in economic growth or industrialization from the historical data."[2] The U.S. economy grew *more slowly* in the decade after the Civil War than in the decade before it; the manufacturing sector especially slowed, falling by 1.8 percent per year. During the 1860s, however—precisely the time that wartime economic expansion should have been at its peak—commodity output *fell* by 2.6 percent.[3]

Clearly, however, national averages would include the ravaged South. What would happen if the analysis could be limited to the "winner"—the North? Growth tests make a somewhat better case for the Beard-Hacker Thesis, although not much. From 1840 to 1860, northern per capita income rose at an annual rate of 1.3 percent, while from 1860 to 1879, the rate was 1.7 percent—an increase, though hardly a "revolution." A central question remains, however: to what extent did the period 1860–1879 merely ride on the coattails of efficiency gains already put in place before 1860? The railroad, the reaper, the steam engine, the telegraph, and dozens of other critical technologies had just moved into the market. Would not that alone have accounted for substantial post-1860 growth?

Indeed, some shocking anomalies exist for the proponents of the Beard-Hacker Thesis, not the least of which is the intriguing fact that boot production *fell* by 13 million pairs from 1855 to 1865! Considering that boots were a staple of any army, shoe and boot manufacturing should have skyrocketed during the war. On the other hand, wool production rose substantially, but that represented a shift away from cotton, which the South had embargoed as a strategic measure, an embargo that failed miserably. Other impacts, including "wage lags" and increased profits, did not occur on a large enough scale to be considered in the "watershed" category.

On the other hand, the Civil War inflicted huge economic costs, the most important of which was the 600,000 Americans killed and 500,000 wounded. In purely sterile, bloodless terms, economists have put a value on those lives of approximately $2 billion, depending upon the method used to calculate a lifetime's economic value.[4] Static approximations, however, provide only estimates of the losses due to the deaths of 600,000 "average" Americans. The problem with such estimates—while they are the best econometricians can offer at present—is that there is no way of knowing how many Andrew Carnegies, Cornelius Vanderbilts, or, for that matter, Abraham Lincolns were among those 600,000 soldiers. In other words, averages provide at best a still photograph of a situation, but they can in no way capture the dynamics of people who may have been in the infant stage of making a fantastic discovery, embarking on a nation-shaping political career, or founding an extraordinary business when the war cut short their lives.

Nor when the cost of the $1.1 to $1.4 billion in destruction of physical property (exclusive of slaves) is calculated can it be estimated how many new factories on the verge of exceptional production gains or new firms on the threshold of gaining remarkable management efficiencies were abruptly ended. Of course, some factories were in the process of decline; others businesses were failing. But the point is that no average or measurement can predict the appearance of an individual genius or business "superstar." Predicting what gains *might* have been made is an impossible task, but the record leaves hints. For example, the southern banking system in some states had achieved a degree of sophistication unseen in the North through widespread branch banking. Tennessee, North and South Carolina, Georgia, and Virginia all had thriving branch-banking systems that virtually evaporated with the Confederate defeat. In turn, that contribution could have been substantial. Had such systems survived intact, and perhaps spread to other, newer southwestern states, such as Oklahoma, Colorado, or even into the Midwest, to Kansas and Nebraska, it is possible that much of the banking collapse of the 1920s and 1930s might have been averted.

Civil War Legislation and Business Growth

Several measures passed by the Republicans during the war did benefit certain sectors of the economy and specific businesses. Tariffs raised revenues and fulfilled the promises of the Republicans to northern interests made before the war. The Homestead Act (1863) sold western government land at the minimum price of $1.25 per acre or at a maximum price determined at an auction. With vast new acreages opening up, and the addition of mechanical devices like the reaper, the man-hours of labor to produce an acre of wheat dropped from thirty-five to twenty between 1840 and 1880; for corn the number dropped from sixty-nine to forty-six. The number of farms rose from 2.6 million in 1870 to 4.5 million by 1890, and continued to rise well into the twentieth century.[5] Farm acreage shot up to 623 million by 1890, from 407 million two decades earlier. While certainly many farmers would have moved west even without the Homestead Act, it nevertheless contributed to the settlement of the Plains states and the extension of the farm belt.

Equally important—and perhaps more so—Congress passed a series of bills from 1862 through 1865 collectively known as the National Bank and Currency Acts. To finance the war, Secretary of the Treasury Salmon P. Chase had chosen to avoid taxation as much as possible, relying instead on bond sales. The National Bank Act provided the mechanism for selling those bonds by establishing a new system of chartering national banks that had to purchase U.S. government securities with a portion of their capital. In return, banks received National Bank notes (i.e., money) for up to 90 percent of the face value of the bonds. Banks then disbursed the banknotes through loans or in exchange for specie. Each national bank had its name inscribed on the notes it received—an extremely valuable source of advertising.

Bank purchases of bonds proved critical to financing the war, but the national banks found themselves in competition with state-chartered banks, and the restrictions placed on national banks, including lending restrictions on real estate and higher capital requirements, made the federal charters less attractive than those offered by individual states. Consequently, Congress passed a 10 percent tax on all state banknotes that drove out of circulation all state and private note issues. Without their note advantages, state banks no longer could compete with the national banks, and the number of national banks grew rapidly, comprising 75 percent of all banks in the United States. As state banknotes quickly disappeared from circulation, the United States found itself with a uniform currency for the first time in its history. Until the national banknotes appeared, for the first few years of the conflict, greenbacks constituted the primary currency. The government declared them *legal tender,* meaning that citizens and merchants had to accept them for payment of debts. With specie payments on banknotes suspended during the war, the greenbacks made up much of the circulating medium in the North until the appearance of the national banknotes, and tended to fluctuate in their gold value based on consumers' assessment of Union war prospects.[6] Greenbacks were not redeemable in specie immediately after the war, but the government, true to its promise, redeemed them in 1879.

As banks moved into the West, they became ingrained in the romantic images of the wild 'n' woolly frontier, usually in the context of bank robberies. Unfortunately for Hollywood, there *were no Western bank robberies* to speak of (see "Challenge Your Perceptions! Were Bank Robberies Common in the 'Wild West'?"). Bank buildings, located in the middle of town, usually with other buildings adjacent, were constructed not only with security in mind but also with an eye toward image. It was critical, for example, for a bank to "look rich." Banks featured the finest cabinetry, ornamentation, and metalwork. In short, banks gained the trust of customers because they appeared solid and safe. The remarkable security of bank buildings constituted half of the visible symbols of safety that bank customers evaluated when they decided to place their money in one bank, with the other being the status and reputation of the banker. Before a merchant could think about entering banking, typically he had to prove himself with years of successful business, usually in a mercantile firm. Bankers had to have personal wealth, most likely as a sign that they could be trusted with the cash of others. And to start a bank, an individual had to provide most of the capital himself, signifying a long-term commitment to the community.[7]

For local economies, the unregulated banking system worked remarkably well. Few banks failed in normal times, and even fewer

unscrupulous characters bilked customers. Instead, bankers reinvested their earnings into mines, railroads, ranches, civic projects,
and local charities. An even more important financial sector, the investment banking sector, had grown during the Civil War, and
brought to the fore a remarkable salesman, Jay Cooke.

Jay Cooke's Bond Sales

Born in Sandusky, Ohio, Jay Cooke grew up in a political family. His
father practiced law, winning several terms in the Ohio legislature before going on to the U.S. House of Representatives. Jay attended local
schools, then Adams Academy, gaining enough skills to clerk in local
stores and keep their books. Eventually, he migrated to Philadelphia,
where he worked for his brother-in-law, William G. Morehead, the
president of a prominent transportation company.

Cooke learned to craft eye-catching newspaper advertisements,
well out of the normal style of such ads in major papers. But only a
year after he joined the Washington Packet & Transportation Company, it failed (just as had a previous business). Rather than become
depressed or consigned to lifelong failure, Cooke instead took stock of
his talents and searched for another job to pay bills until he found his
career interest. While bookkeeping in one occupation, he came to the
attention of exchange broker E. W. Clark, who had a Philadelphia
banking house. Within two years, Cooke's skill at balancing accounts
and reconciling overdrafts of up to $100,000 gained him the opportu-
nity to write business columns for the Philadelphia *Daily Chronicle*.
More important, his tasks at Clark familiarized him with sales of federal securities for the Mexican War, as well as municipal and state
securities issues.

Yet fate was not finished with Cooke. Clark's numerous banking
houses could not withstand the Panic of 1857, and the company dis-
solved into several smaller units owned by the remaining investors.
Cooke, out of a job again, at least had a substantial nest egg from his employment, but he also had several mouths to feed, being married with
five living children (and three more who died in infancy). Again, Cooke
demonstrated his character, settling his obligations stemming from the
panic "so conscientiously that his father and his brother Pitt repri-
manded him for extreme generosity."[8] He spent approximately four
years working with railroad reorganizations, where he learned to price
railroad securities and to evaluate the companies' books. Then, using
money he saved from Clark, just months before Abraham Lincoln was
inaugurated, Jay Cooke & Company opened at the most inauspicious of
times: As the nation drifted toward war, markets soured and the federal
debt soared.

Cooke saw a silver lining around the cloud. Remembering the Mexican War experience, Cooke's company snatched up all the U.S. government bonds it could acquire at a time when other banks refused them. As cannon shells hit Fort Sumter, Cooke's firm obtained $200,000 worth of government securities for resale. Using his newspaper advertising experience, Cooke reasoned that he could market bonds to the general public with patriotic sales pitches. His first chance came with a bond issue in Philadelphia, where he distributed handbills across the state urging the public to come to the aid of the Commonwealth in its "hour of trial" and reminding the patriotic investors of the bonds' 6 percent interest rate! Cooke sold every bond he had, not to mention some he did not have. The loan was oversubscribed, requiring Cooke to purchase still other bonds from the state.

In 1862, Cooke opened a partnership office in Washington, D.C., which provided entry into the Treasury circles. The Union government struggled to sell its 6 percent, $500 million bond issue, and Treasury Secretary Salmon Chase turned to Cooke, naming Cooke's banking house as its special agent for the marketing of securities in 1862. Although he was not the "exclusive agent," Cooke alone aggressively pushed the bonds, engaging 2,500 agents to sell "five/twenties" as they were called (because the government had the option of retiring them in five years, or allowing them to mature in twenty years). Employing posters and handbills to great effect, Cooke also used his staple advertising medium, newspapers, which he enjoined to run favorable stories about the bonds in return for advertising business. He pressed his own writing skills into the service of the Republic, as when he wrote a pamphlet entitled "How to Organize a National Bank Under Secretary Chase's Bill" to promote the National Banking Act of 1863.

Although the national banking system pushed bond sales to new heights, it was Cooke's strategy of involving average American families in bond sales that changed the nature of the market, as more than a million citizens held the securities by 1863. Cooke's firm made little profit on all this activity—an astonishingly low one-sixteenth of a percent! Yet politicians and those newspapers in which he did not advertise carried stories of outlandish returns to the company. His personal commission totaled only $300,000, but his contributions to the Union victory could not be measured. When Chase's successor, William Fessenden, tried to eliminate Cooke (and his commission), the Treasury's agents sold only $133 million of a new issue of bonds, whereupon he contritely begged Cooke to reassume his old duties. In less than six months, Cooke sold $600 million, most of that after Appomattox. By 1865, the Philadelphia house had earned profits of $1.13 million, of which Cooke sent

10 percent to charities. Memorials appropriately remembered the efforts of gallant soldiers who fell in combat, but the man who ensured that they had adequate boots and bullets went largely ignored. No coins celebrated his accomplishments; no statues marked the deeds of the financier of Union victory. Nevertheless, in only three years, Jay Cooke had revolutionized the sales of securities to the American "middle class." It would be another sixty years until Charles Merrill repeated his feat in the sales of stocks to the middle class.

Business and the State in the Union and Confederacy: "Yankee Leviathan"

The activities of the federal government during the Civil War, and the ostensible "states rights" emphasis of the Confederacy, have led many scholars to assume that the Union succeeded in part because it had better planning and federal direction of the war effort. Certainly, the land grants to railroads, the National Bank and Currency Acts, tariffs, income taxes, and the Homestead Act all reflected an activist government role, one not seen prior to 1860.

At the outset of war, the Union had substantial military, material, and economic advantages over the Confederacy. Yet the federal government managed to allow the market to provide the necessary war materiel with a minimum of statist controls. A remarkable study by Richard Bensel comparing Union and Confederate wartime mobilization concluded that "the northern war effort left the industrial and agricultural sectors almost untouched by central state controls and only skimmed the surface of northern labor pools. . . ."[9] Union officials informed businessmen and factory owners of their needs, provided a means to pay, then allowed the business sector to meet the demand. Not only did northern enterprise rise to the occasion, but the response left the federal armies with few shortages.[10] In addition, a mature railroad system, which was in place prior to Fort Sumter, contributed mightily to the comprehensive economic mobilization in the North and in providing military supply.[11]

But the surprising fact of the Civil War was not that the Union did not use statist policies to direct the business community as a whole but that the Confederacy *did*. In the Confederacy, as Bensel points out, "the all-encompassing economic and social controls . . . were in fact so extensive that they call into question standard interpretations of southern opposition to the expansion of federal power in both the antebellum and post-Reconstruction periods."[12] If, however, as has been argued here, the South was not so much a capitalist region as precapitalist, with pockets of market sophistication, then the concept does not appear quite as novel. In fact, a commonsense understanding of the situation puts Civil War mobilization in perspective. When a society has the necessary open-market mechanisms for supplying the military with wartime materials and for financing that expansion, government can simply skim the surface of private enterprise and its productivity. However, when a society lacks an abundance of industrial resources, the state must force production in necessary areas. As a result, the Confederate government—outmatched by the manpower and machine power of the North—rapidly turned to state controls over business enterprise.[13]

Despite its willingness to adopt centralized economic policies, the South faced constant deficiencies of resources throughout the war. Stanley Lebergott has argued that the planters' concern with maintaining their postwar cotton monopoly led them to retain all their slaves in the production of cotton—which was not exported due to the Confederate embargo—and thus kept them from performing war-related tasks such as repairing railroads, building forts, or otherwise doing tasks that kept white soldiers from the front. That "second great army," as Lebergott called it, again reflected the weakness of a precapitalist economy and the natural progression to a command economy on the part of the central government. The government "simply took away the corn, mules, food it needed. . . . It was easiest, if harsh, to take corn and mules from the small farms" run by the wives of soldiers on the battlefields.[14]

The absence of a widespread, thriving industrial sector on the same scale as in the North handicapped the Confederacy, and even as it created arsenals, foundries, and munitions works, southern production of small arms was "woefully deficient," as Secretary of War Judah P. Benjamin noted.[15] Southern businesses did contribute to the war effort in substantial ways—Georgia entrepreneurs Louis and Elias Haiman manufactured swords, then branched out into sidearm production, while private production of salt in Florida occurred despite constant federal raids—but the South lacked a strong manufacturing base, and when the war created a sudden demand by the government, interference from bureaucrats effectively squelched any early burst of capitalism.[16] Moreover, the industrial expansion that did occur depended on a Confederate "military-industrial complex" and relied exclusively on demand provided by government.[17] Perhaps the Confederacy's greatest success came in its improvement of an internal railroad system. Although construction and renovation was uneven and incomplete, the resulting "network of routes cultivated by the Confederacy may have been the rebellion's most lasting geographical and physical legacy."[18]

Emancipation and Enterprise

Lincoln's Emancipation Proclamation, the symbolic expression of Union victory, constituted perhaps the single most significant business-related event of the war. While having no immediate effect—it freed not one slave in the Confederacy, and it did not affect slavery in the border states or territories—the long-term impact of the proclamation changed forever southern enterprise. Some Lincoln critics continue to invoke the "needless war" arguments to contend that slavery would have disappeared due to market forces and that the growth of government in the North over the long term "enslaved free men."[19] Slavery was certainly not on the verge of extinction, and the suggestion that Lincoln provoked the South has been laid to rest by a generation of historians.[20] Ultimately, the only defense of the so-called states' rights position relies on a Calhounian interpretation of the Constitution as a compact of states, not people, which, of all the founders, perhaps only George Mason really accepted. Moreover, the promises to protect life, liberty, and the pursuit of happiness demanded that no individuals could be denied their constitutional rights. Lincoln, therefore, prioritized the protections of liberty inherent in both the Declaration and the Constitution, applying the protections to all. His actions had three dramatic consequences, two of which are well discussed, and a third, which is important to business history, which has not been quite so deeply examined.

First, when emancipation became the "war aim," no longer would any debate exist over the personhood of slaves. In essence, the proclamation symbolically extended the "free labor" umbrella to all workers and made the South itself "free soil." Second, the ex-slaves not only constituted a new labor force—a point beaten to death by historians and economists—but also embodied a huge addition to the nation's consumers, for in the technical sense the slaves had not been consumers in that they had no choice about their consumption. The addition of three million consumers in the United States as a whole would have demanded remarkable changes; but when contained almost exclusively in the southern region, it represented a revolutionary transformation. Third, free slaves, both men and women, often became entrepreneurs themselves, and among the three million souls able to utilize their skills, talents, and ideas for their own purposes, thousands of self-employed business owners would emerge.[21]

Most, of course, began as farmers or sharecroppers, and, based on evidence from North Carolina at least, a surprising number of blacks owned their own land by 1870.[22] Sharecropping arose out of the unique situation in the South after the war in which, previously, "labor was wealth and wealth chiefly labor."[23] It entailed the sharecropper "pay-ing" up to one-third of the cotton grown on the land to the landowner. That arrangement worked well for a society in which blacks had no land or capital, but had labor, and whites had no labor supply but still retained their land. It offered a sense of independence and entrepre-neurship, in that the freedmen could gain personally by increasing pro-duction. However, it had a drawback in that without ownership the freedmen had little incentive to invest in long-term improvements on the land (digging ditches, building fences, and so on), and without the full profits from the crop, the white owners usually did not have the means to improve the land. In the short term, however, the system worked well, and efforts to form cartels by the owners to keep wages down failed. Whites competed for croppers by offering higher shares, allowing the freedmen to keep larger profits and rendering the cartels ineffective.

By 1880, blacks owned a small percentage of the land in the cot-ton South and tenanted approximately 30 percent, sharecropping two-thirds. At the turn of the century, blacks owned 27 percent of the land they worked and rented 36 percent.[24] Freedmen acquired land, although it was a slow process. Still, as Robert Kenzer's study of North Carolina showed, in five counties black ownership of town lots rose from 11 percent in 1875 to almost 19 percent by 1890, despite the fact that cultural attitudes, legal codes, and racism all presented barriers.[25] Free blacks before the war, especially mulattos, had distinct advan-tages over the freedmen. Nevertheless, by 1880, in an economy in which whites owned most available land already and dominated the political structure, blacks already owned 8 percent of the total land in the South. Farming paid well enough that some wage laborers could choose to farm rather than work for a white mill owner, and whites comprised the majority of sharecroppers (60 percent by 1900).[26]

Alabamian Nate Shaw, an illiterate tenant farmer who grew up in a society of ex-slaves, moved from farm to farm, expanding his share and using his mules to haul lumber or do other odd jobs on the side. Despite facing competition from an influx of poor whites, unscrupu-lous landlords who repeatedly attempted to defraud him of his crops, and merchants unwilling to extend credit, Shaw became self-sufficient and eventually became a leader in the Sharecroppers Union. Hauling lumber paid well, but Shaw was determined to become completely in-dependent of others. Even after he joined the Sharecroppers Union and went to prison in a protest against land seizures by sheriffs deputies in the 1930s, the land he had worked to secure remained in the hands of his family.[27]

Andrew Jackson Beard, a slave born in Jefferson County, Ala-bama, owned a farm near Birmingham. Once he tried to sell apples in Montgomery using a team of oxen to pull his wagon, but after the trip took three weeks, he quit farming and constructed a flour mill in Hardwicks, Alabama. Experimenting with plow designs, Beard patented a plow in 1881, then sold it in 1884 for $4,000—a fantastic sum at the time. He continued to refine plow designs; then, with his total savings—approximately $30,000—Beard entered the real estate market. Still, he continued to invent, creating a remarkable rotary steam engine patented in 1892. Early work in railroad yards provided Beard with firsthand exposure to the hazards of hooking railroad cars together. The process was done entirely by hand, requiring a worker to stand between cars and place a metal pin in the coupling devices at the very instant that the cars came together. Fingers, hands, and arms all fell prey to accidents with the metal couplers, and Beard suffered the loss of a leg in a coupler accident, focusing him on a solution. In 1897, he received a patent for the famous "Jenny" coupler, in which the coupling devices secured themselves when bumped together, much like hands shaking. An improved version of the Jenny remains the foundation for the modern automatic coupler, and Beard saved untold hundreds of railroad employees from severe personal injury.[28]

Even before the Civil War, a few slaves had established an entrepreneurial legacy. "Free Frank," the slave of George McWhorter, managed his owner's estate and received permission to hire himself out for the purposes of buying his own freedom. After securing his own emancipation in 1819, along with that of his wife, he engaged in a wide range of business enterprises in Pulaski County, Kentucky. Migrating to Illinois, Frank acquired hundreds of acres of land that he improved, then sold, and founded the town of New Philadelphia, selling lots in the town and continuing to purchase slave children to free them.[29]

Of course, not all the new entrepreneurs in the black community were either freedmen or self-manumitted former slaves. Elijah McCoy, born in Canada where his parents had fled to escape slavery from Kentucky in 1837, had benefited from his father's successful lumber business by going to Scotland for training in mechanical engineering. After becoming a master mechanic and engineer in Edinburgh, McCoy returned to the United States after the Civil War and settled in Ypsilanti, Michigan, where he worked for the Michigan Central Railroad. His skills and technical training qualified him for a position as a fireman—no lowly position but a prestigious job "somewhat equivalent to the co-pilot of an airplane."[30] McCoy surpassed the requirements of his job, using his technical skills to address problems with the locomotives, especially their tendency to overheat. The locomotives needed regular engine oil, but if they stopped frequently, the delays cost the company time and money. McCoy invented a device that lubricated the engine parts while the train was in motion, securing a patent in 1872 and making constant improvements to the design. White workers degraded the devices, calling them "nigger oil cups" at first, but then "they listened carefully when the oilers were installed and he gave instructions on their use."[31] Imitators attempted to sell their own lubricating cups, but McCoy maintained a standard of quality so high that people referred to his parts as "the real McCoy." At age 77, he patented an improved air-brake lubricator, and that same year (1920) he founded the Elijah McCoy Manufacturing Company in Detroit, although he owned little stock, having sold rights to the patents for cash to develop still other inventions.[32]

Overall, black entrepreneurs comprised a substantial portion of the southern business community. No comprehensive study is available, but snapshots tell a great deal. For example, from 1865 to 1879, R.G. Dun & Co.'s credit records for the state of Virginia contained credit information on up to 1,000 enterprises, of which over 220 were operated by blacks (based on notations made in the record books). Despite the fact that southern whites wrote the credit reports sent to Dun, many of the personal evaluations testified to the high character of black entrepreneurs. Although black businesses usually located in towns of higher-than-average black population, the advertising from the businesses indicated that black entrepreneurs had white customers and seldom appealed to strictly black customers. Most of the Virginia black businessmen in one study were in either a mercantile business or a skilled trade, and almost 80 percent were single-owner firms. The owners apparently gained experience in business, because over time the ratio of new firms to failed firms dropped after 1869, and many businesses were considered failed simply because the proprietor died.[33] In fact, when compared against the research of Roger Ransom and Richard Sutch, two Reconstruction economic historians, the Virginia data showed virtually no difference in failure rates between black merchants and white merchants from 1870 to 1875 (which included the panic years). Of black merchants in business in 1870, 71.2 percent survived through 1875, compared to 71 percent the white merchants.[34]

Old South, New South

Many whites, like the freedmen and the yeoman farmers of the antebellum period, remained on the land and struggled to create a "New South." Cotton prices, though falling in the Reconstruction period, remained higher than those of other commodities, making it attractive to farm.[35] Manufacturing, however, marked the New South far more than it had the Old: In 1860, the South had approximately 30,000 manufacturing establishments; by 1870, it had 50,000, then, by 1890 the number rose to 60,000.[36]

Southern entrepreneurs established themselves in traditional industrial enterprises, beginning with railroads, creating a construction boom.[37] In the 1880s alone, southern railroad mileage increased by 108.6 percent, with more than $150 million invested between 1879 and 1881 alone. And not involved with the "iron horse," entrepreneurs of the New South worked with iron. Birmingham, Alabama, emerged as the center of the new iron business, which served the railroads. Milton Hannibal Smith, who headed the Louisville and Nashville (L&N) for half a century, helped direct more than $30 million of railroad money to furnaces and iron ore production. But just as the iron mills depended on the railroads as their primary consumers, the railroads benefited from shipping iron. In 1888 the L&N carried more tonnage in pig iron and minerals than the annual average weight of the entire cotton crop of the nation for the previous fifteen years. Henry De Bardeleben, the son-in-law of the powerful New Englander Daniel Pratt, mobilized a coal and iron empire that included seven blast furnaces, seven coal mines, and 900 coke ovens, as well as quarries and railroads. De Bardeleben bragged that he "wanted to eat up all the craw-fish I could—swallow up all the little fellows," but De Bardeleben soon himself was gobbled up in a series of buyouts that left his business in the hands of J.P. Morgan.[38]

Another road to success in New South businesses came from textiles, where Henry Hammett, George Gray, and Daniel Tompkins rose to the top ranks of enterprise in the late 1800s. Hammett, a North Carolinian, had been born of a yeoman family and worked in a cotton broker's office in his youth. He learned the trade, gaining promotion to business manager, and after a brief fling with railroads (using money inherited from his wife), he founded the Piedmont Manufacturing Company at the peak of the Panic of 1873. The panic almost caused his business to fail, but he pulled through with a loan from a northern machinery manufacturer. By 1890, he had three mills that made better grades of cloth; "his buildings and villages became models for other mills, while his plants served as training schools for future owners and managers."[39]

George Gray, whose father worked in a cotton mill until he died in 1859, found himself helping to support a large family. At age eight, Gray swept factories in twelve-hour shifts for 10 cents a day. He applied a natural mechanical ability to mill machinery, attracting the attention of his supervisors. His expertise gained him repeated promotions until he became mill superintendent. Then, in 1888, he founded the Gastonia Cotton Manufacturing Company at Gastonia, North Carolina.

Within twenty years, he had a dozen plants that featured the most recent technology and hydroelectric power.

Of the three men, only Tompkins was born into affluence. His family's plantation survived the war, and Tompkins went to the University of South Carolina and Rensselaer Polytechnic Institute. Over a nine-year period, he worked at Bethlehem Iron Company, gaining experience in the iron business. He moved to Charlotte, North Carolina, where he eventually established mills and newspapers that emphasized industrialization.

The Managerial Revolution Accelerates

While Hammett, Gray, Tompkins, and other "New South" entrepreneurs moved into the industrial vacuum created by the Civil War, a broader trend encompassed business enterprise in all regions as the managerial revolution accelerated. Originating in the railroads, by the postbellum period the managerial hierarchies spread in particular to firms in four areas: (1) users of continuous-process technology; (2) processors of perishable products; (3) machinery makers who required specialized marketing services; and (4) manufacturers of large-scale, specialized machinery. Starting in the 1880s, mass production met mass distribution in each of these areas as managers embarked on the strategy of *vertical integration*. Whether they did so because "existing markets were unable to sell and distribute products in the volume they were produced," as Alfred Chandler argued, remains a matter of interpretation.[40] For a brief period, production capacity surged ahead of distribution networks; but quickly businesses shifted their focus to sales, marking a traditional ebb and flow of business management strategy. (One could reverse the question and ask whether, prior to the managerial revolution, "existing *producers* were unable to manufacture products in the volume they could be distributed and sold.") Each of the four areas of focus can be closely identified with one or two well-known entrepreneurs.

Continuous Process Technology: James B. Duke

High-volume production machinery permitted managerial change in the first area, that of continuous-process technology. When it appeared, as in the adoption of the Bonsack cigarette machine or mechanized canning and jarring processes for food, hand production virtually overnight became mass production. James B. Duke's American Tobacco Company illustrates not only the rapidity of change but the scope of dominance one company could have. Washington Duke, a former Confederate soldier who had returned to his Durham, North Carolina, farm to find it looted by scavengers, took advantage of the only resource untouched by the vandals—a store of tobacco. With his two sons, James Buchanan and Benjamin, Washington Duke cured and prepared tobacco for sale in packages under the brand name "Pro Bono Publico."[41] Within a decade, Duke's backyard operation became W. Duke, Sons & Co., which competed directly with the major chewing and leaf tobacco manufacturer, Blackwell & Carr and its "Bull Durham" brand. By that time, James Duke, who directed the operations, chose to target another product, rolled tobacco, assisted by a cigarette roller he had helped develop in 1878. The Bonsack machine made packaged cigarettes possible, for a single Bonsack could produce 120,000 cigarettes a day. Since the major markets were in the North, the company established an operation in New York City in 1884, where it advertised heavily. Production soared, well above the capacity of his existing network to sell or distribute the cigarettes and leaving Duke with warehouses of unsold cigarettes.

Duke embarked on a program of developing an extensive sales organization, complete with marketing agreements with wholesalers around the world. He established advertising campaigns, purchased storage and curing facilities, and systematized the flow of cigarettes, to the point that Duke's company grew to be the largest manufacturer in the industry. By 1889, Duke's machines produced over 830 million cigarettes with sales of over $4.5 million. When competitors attempted to compete with Duke on his own grounds of high production and marketing, Duke's advertising costs soared—as did their own. Although they hoped to buy out Duke's business, instead he offered a consolidation: In 1890, the major four cigarette manufacturers merged into the American Tobacco Company, with Duke as president. American Tobacco controlled 90 percent of the market, with products ranging from smoking tobacco and chewing tobacco to cigarettes and tobacco retailing. Duke abhorred inefficiency and constantly emphasized cutting waste. Like other successful entrepreneurs of his day, he left a vast fortune—$100 million—to charities, much of which went to Duke University, which, ironically, created a famous medical school known for its research into lung cancer.

Similar mechanization and processing changes took place in businesses engaged in producing canned or bottled goods. Heinz's pickle company and Campbell's Soup both made use of canning and jarring production lines to turn out millions of items a year. Joseph Campbell, who founded Campbell Preserve Company, packed products under several private labels, including Crescent and Joseph Campbell & Company. Not until the 1890s, however, did the company produce its trademark soup. Dr. John Dorrance, a nephew of Arthur Dorrance, who had run the company after Campbell's retirement in 1893, discovered that for all the products Campbell's offered, it did not make soup. Dorrance, a chemist, devised a process to condense soup so that its ingredients did not separate after canning. Before long, Campbell's offered five varieties of condensed soup. The public, however, "had to be educated to eat soups," Dorrance recalled.[42] Cookbooks omitted soups entirely, and Franco-American and Hutchins both represented strong competitors. But Dorrance had created a high-quality product that the company produced more cheaply than its rivals. With Dorrance's intense advertising campaign, including clear instructions on how to prepare the condensed soup, Campbell's soon stood alone at the top, selling more than 16 million cans by 1904.

Concern for efficiency constituted a dominant theme with all producers using continuous processing. As a result, the use of waste products gave birth to entire new industries that themselves used continuous processing, such as soap and candles, made from animal fat obtained from slaughterhouses. One of the most famous soap manufacturers, Procter & Gamble, involved a partnership between a candle maker and a soap maker from the pork production capital of the nation, Cincinnati.[43] British-born soap maker William C. Procter and his brother-in-law chandler, James Gamble, began processing and selling lard, candles, and soap in 1837. The Civil War brought new contracts for candles and soap for the Union army and made "P&G" a nationally known company. Procter & Gamble used mechanical processes to mix and crush the products used for bar soap, turning out 200,000 cakes of its Ivory soap daily by 1880.

Gamble conceived of the new soap in 1878, charging his chemists to achieve the fineness of luxury soap without using the expensive olive oil that constituted the major ingredient of fine soaps. While working on the new product, an employee ran a mixing machine too long, puffing the soap mixture more than usual so that it floated. That gave Gamble the advertising hook he needed: "It Floats!" The company's analysis of the composition of Ivory showed it contained only .56 percent useless impurities, giving the company its slogan, "99 and 44/100 percent pure."[44] P&G placed itself at the vanguard of the new marketing wave, by 1905 spending $400,000 on advertising. But the company went beyond marketing; in 1886 P&G built its Cincinnati plant, introducing labor programs that others considered radical, including giving workers Saturday afternoons off with pay and in 1887 instituting one of the first profit-sharing plans in the nation.

Semiperishable Packaged Products and Gustavus Swift

The second category in which managerial hierarchies reshaped business was in the production of semiperishable packaged products. In the case of meat, the movement of those products over short distances had relied on ice cakes cut from lakes—the process that made Frederick Tudor the "Ice King"—then carried in crude refrigerator cars to keep meat and milk cold. For shipping over longer distances, however, live animals had to be transported in cars for local slaughter and processing. In the 1870s, Gustavus Swift implemented a more efficient approach. Born in Sandwich, Massachusetts, into a family of twelve, Swift worked at his brother's butcher shop where he "perceived the simplicity of the business" that allowed a butcher to purchase an animal, slaughter it and carve it into cuts, and sell the parts for more than the cost of the whole animal.[45] He soon had his own shops, purchasing local cattle and extending his sales operations to Albany and Buffalo.

Swift recognized that most beef came from the West and was shipped live to eastern markets—a process that embodied substantial waste and inefficiency. Almost two-thirds of an animal was inedible, yet the whole cow was transported thousands of miles. If the cattle could be slaughtered in Chicago, with only the processed meat shipped east, lower freight costs alone would make beef cheaper. Chicago butchers had already experimented with shipping meat in refrigerated cars, so Swift moved to Chicago in 1875, where he purchased a local slaughterhouse and used the strategy of shipping meat hung in cars, relying on cold winter air to keep the meat fresh. But Swift sought a better alternative. In 1877, he hired a refrigeration engineer named Andrew Chase to develop a completely insulated refrigeration car that used ice packed into the roof. The car required Swift to acquire a secure source of ice along the route and to sell the meat immediately once it arrived, or refrigerate it quickly.[46] Using his own shops and storage houses, Swift employed local sales forces to move the dressed meat in refrigerator cars to nearby locations. His shops placed a few select cuts of meats on display—usually the slower-moving cuts—in glass cases. After early resistance, competitors soon followed Swift by building comparable networks of branch houses, including Chicagoan Philip Armour and the Cudahy brothers in Omaha.[47]

Obsessed with efficiency and eliminating waste, Swift introduced overhead conveyors to transport the carcass to each processing station within the slaughterhouse. His focus kept returning to Bubbly Creek, which ran behind one of his yards and into which the effluent from his slaughterhouses ran. Swift continuously examined the water for its fat content and was convinced that any fat in the water meant that too much of the animal carcasses was being discarded. Thus, for economic, and not environmental, motivations, Swift cleaned up the water by finding ways to use virtually all parts of beef and pig carcasses. He developed a series of by-products that included glue, soap, fertilizers, beef extract, and bone products, joining the uses of other parts of the animals—leather shoes, gloves, baseball covers, paint made from blood, and so on—already in place. A century later, the process that Swift started reached almost 100 percent efficiency, but even at the time Swift accurately could boast that "we use all of the hog but the grunt."[48]

Machinery Makers: Isaac Singer's Sewing Machines

Manufacturers started to bypass wholesalers in another area, that of new machines produced in high volume that nevertheless were not especially simple to operate. Such machines not only required a skilled sales force capable of explaining and demonstrating complex products, but also demanded mechanical expertise to service and repair the devices. One example of a device that required special sales training and a qualified repair staff was the sewing machine.

By the 1850s, the sewing machine industry had given birth to several competitors, each with a staff of sales agents and marketing organizations. Agents operated on a small salary and a commission but lacked any means of extending credit to buyers and often personally had little understanding of the machine itself. Isaac M. Singer, an actor in a theatrical troupe that abruptly disbanded in Fredericksburg, Ohio, was the individual who revolutionized the industry. Out of work and nearly broke, Singer found employment at a printer's type factory. There, he invented a type carver, which he hoped to sell to New York and Boston publishers. While in the midst of his unsuccessful sales trip, he observed a sewing machine in a Boston shop and immediately saw opportunities to improve the design. Indeed, as David Hounshell argued, "Singer's changes constituted a new invention," which formed the basis of his company, founded in 1851.[49] A New York lawyer named Edward Clark acquired an interest in the business to manufacture the Singer products. Singer, however, was soon served with a lawsuit by Elias Howe, claiming Singer had replicated the patented needle and lockstitch. Clark fought the suit on behalf of the company for years, until the court ruled that Singer had to pay Howe a substantial royalty. Undaunted, Singer mass-produced the machines with a heavy reliance on hand finishing.

Where Singer *had* modernized, however, was in copying the tactics of a rival to establish branch sales offices, each with a female demonstrator, a sales staff, and a full-time mechanic. Offices provided credit to purchasers, endowing Singer with important advantages over enterprises relying on commission agents. Singer, although not the industry leader at the time, nevertheless dominated the market—Singer and two other competitors controlled three-fourths of the industry's output by 1860—with Wheeler & Wilson manufacturing 85,000 sewing machines a year, and Singer second at 55,000.

After 1860, Singer "moved more aggressively than the other two in replacing regional distributors with branch stores supervised by full-time, salaried regional agents."[50] Clark had convinced Singer of the shortcomings of a commission-oriented staff, which failed to manage inventories, waiting too long before ordering new machines, then telegraphing large orders. Agents delayed transmitting payment to the main office and lacked technical training. Singer turned the business over to Clark in 1863, whereupon Clark expanded and reorganized the marketing operations and extended overseas operations.[51] Singer Sewing Machines built factories around the world, including the largest ever constructed, in Elizabethport, New Jersey (1871). The Kilbowie, Scotland, plant had the capacity to manufacture 10,000 machines a week, whereas less than a decade earlier it had taken thirty-one boys and men in a Glasgow factory to produce thirty units. To prevent delays or other interruptions in work, the company had its own timberlands, iron mill, and railroads.

Other businesses imitated the organizational structure of the sewing machine industry. Cyrus McCormick's reaper company began to employ full-time sales staff and territorial agents who provided repair services and credit. John Deere & Company used its expertise in plows to market other less complex farm implements through their sales organization. Each company constantly looked for opportunities to expand beyond its original product, but into machinery that required similar expertise or production skills.

E. Remington & Sons, for example, had become famous for manufacturing the modern breech-loading rifle. Although the company was well familiar with mass-production manufacturing, producing an astounding 350 barrels a day at each of four furnaces at the hands of only four men, Remington also made use of the contractor system.[52] After the Civil War, the company searched for nonmilitary customers, investigating products to fabricate in its metal-manufacturing facilities. When the company moved into farm implements, it did not employ the McCormick-type sales force, and failed. Likewise, when approached by a former Singer executive to develop a new sewing machine, Remington, despite having a technically superior sewing machine, failed to create the necessary sales force, and failed again. At that point, many people would have, literally, stuck to their guns. Not the Remingtons. An inventor named Christopher Sholes visited the Remingtons in 1873 with his new device, the typewriter. Moving conservatively this time, the Remingtons worked with a firm that had existing networks and finally established a solid business. Unfortunately, when Remington attempted to sell the typewriter overseas, the company approached Singer, which had the best foreign network. Singer refused to market it, requiring Remington to establish its own, expensive organization. That, and the recession in the firearms industry, pushed Remington into bankruptcy in 1886, at which time the typewriter division was sold off as Remington Typewriter.

Heavy Specialized Equipment and George Westinghouse

Just as Andrew Jackson Beard had saved countless railroad workers' limbs and fingers with his Jenny coupler, George Westinghouse saved untold numbers of lives and injuries with his compressed air brake. At the time he approached a group of railroad executives to demonstrate his invention with a test in 1868, Westinghouse was only twenty-two years old. Stopping a train required a large crew of burly brakemen to manipulate heavy brake shoes then in use. During the test, with Westinghouse aboard, a horse unseated its rider onto the rails in the path of Westinghouse's oncoming train. The engineer activated the Westinghouse brake and the onrushing train ground to a halt only four feet from the hapless horseman. At the end of the test, no executive needed any further convincing. Within a year, Westinghouse Air Brake Co. began filling orders for the air brake from its Pittsburgh factory, and by 1873, Westinghouse air brakes appeared on more than 10,000 locomotives and cars.

Not yet thirty years old and a millionaire, Westinghouse went to work every day as if he was a brakeman himself. He never quit inventing. During the 1880s, he started work on alternating electric current (AC), a superior alternative to the direct current (DC) then in use. Whereas AC could travel over longer distances, its high voltage made it more difficult to control. Westinghouse founded Westinghouse Electric Company in 1886 to build the equipment needed to control AC, developing a system of transformers and generators. He proved the reliability and safety of the AC equipment but found himself in competition with the legendary Thomas Edison, whose devices used DC. Edison's company enthusiastically publicized accidents from AC voltage, to the point of conducting experiments in which cats were electrocuted to show its dangers. Newspapers cooperated with stories, whose headlines read "Electric Wire Slaughter," and "Another Lineman Roasted to Death."[53] After the state of New York adopted electrocution (using AC) as its means of capital punishment, Edison officials referred to it as "Westinghousing" the condemned.

Most people who worked with electricity knew better. In 1892, Westinghouse won the contract to provide lighting for the Chicago Columbian Exposition, proving to the world the safety and efficiency of AC power. Over a six-month period, the fair was illuminated nightly with safe AC electricity without a single accident. That was the breakthrough Westinghouse needed, and contracts to provide electricity to homes and businesses flooded Westinghouse Electric. In his mid-60s, Westinghouse retired, confined to a wheelchair. His relentless inventor's spirit still propelled him to create, however, and he spent his last year working on an electric wheelchair.

Large machinery of types other than electric dynamos also demanded specialized sales and technical service, requiring well-trained and skilled technicians. Elisha G. Otis understood that assuaging the public's fears of elevators depended in no small part on his reputation in installation and servicing his elevators, and after his death his sons centralized the administration of the business and oversaw the vertical integration of the company. The family-owned Otis company was, by the late 1890s, a "big business," yet because it, like many others, did not separate ownership from management, it did not fit the Chandler definition of a modern business organization. But the neat, clean separation of management and ownership did not always occur in the emerging corporate giants, as seen in the case studies of Frederick Weyerhaeuser's lumber business.

Frederick Weyerhaeuser, Environmentalist and Lumberman

Driven from Germany at a young age by revolution, Frederick Weyerhaeuser found employment as a day laborer, a "gofer" on construction crews, as a lumber grader, and as a bookkeeper. In 1857, the Illinois lumberyard he managed went bankrupt, putting Weyerhaeuser on the street and out of work. He managed to raise the funds necessary to purchase the bankrupt lumberyard, then, using the wood to barter, Weyerhaeuser worked a number of trades with local farmers. Leasing an idle Rock Island sawmill, he purchased logs and hired a miller to saw them, then used the cut wood to construct houses and other buildings.

Already, Weyerhaeuser had vertically integrated, obtaining raw lumber, owning the processing facility, and selling the final, finished product. Although never a woodcutter himself, Weyerhaeuser filled almost every other position in the company at one time or another, overseeing the production, accounting, sales, and financing. Earnings were solid, but not spectacular—$8,000 for the first year and nine months. When the Civil War brought new demand, Weyerhaeuser joined with his brother-in-law to expand further, taking advantage of the relative dearth of lumberyards and abundant timber in the Midwest.

Weyerhaeuser employed a firm called the Beef Slough Company to collect logs, float them down the Mississippi, and sort them for cutting. But he realized that at any time his supply could be interrupted by management decisions at Beef Slough or by natural impediments to shipping. He therefore started to purchase his own timberland of yellow pine in Wisconsin. Along with other loggers, he formed his own river transportation company. By 1885, the firm processed more than

500 million board feet of lumber.[54] The phenomenal amount of timber that passed through Weyerhaeuser's mills only convinced him further of the need to maintain his own supplies of raw timber, leading him to embark on an ambitious land-acquisition program. He held more than 300,000 acres by 1879, but already focused on the newly developing western territories. In 1891 he moved to St. Paul, Minnesota, residing next door to James J. Hill, whose Great Northern had become a major purchaser of Weyerhaeuser's timber for railroad ties.

Hill already had understood the value of having consumers next to his road; and Weyerhaeuser appreciated his largest customer. By the 1890s, the Great Northern had sold some of its own timberlands to Weyerhaeuser, including 900,000 acres in 1900. The sale required $5.4 million, forcing Weyerhaeuser to put together a large syndicate under the name Weyerhaeuser Timber Company. When he sent inspectors to the lands, however, Weyerhaeuser learned that they were not as rich in virgin timber as he had believed. At about that time—perhaps because of that sudden awareness—Weyerhaeuser started to devote considerable resources to reforestation, soil erosion, and fire prevention.

Then, as today, more net forest lands are lost due to fires (most of them natural, caused by lightning) than are lost due to harvesting. Stephen Pyne's magisterial book on fire, for example, records that in the period 1940–1965, lightning ignited more than 228,000 fires in the United States.[55] The very remoteness of such fires has made them difficult, if not impossible to fight, unlike fires in urban areas, and made the fires phenomenally destructive, often burning more than one million acres of forest![56] Weyerhaeuser recognized the threat nature posed to his empire and fully realized that without trees, he had no business. Certainly he could not contribute to deforestation. Thus he embraced conservation, which as a movement was in its infancy.

The strategy of replacing forests already had started in the timber business, but it included measures far more aggressive than just "not cutting," and already all the major users of lumber and paper products had adopted reforestation measures. International Paper, which owned land since 1898, established its own nurseries, by the 1990s turning out 190 million seedlings a year. As of 1924, International Paper controlled 20 million cords, or four million more than it consumed, and added 800,000 new cords of wood every year through forestry methods already in place.[57] (By the 1990s, International Paper alone planted more than 48 million trees a year—five times more than it harvested—and donated or sold the rest for additional reforestation.) Another producer of paper products, Kimberly-Clark, in 1902 embarked on the first long-term woodlands management program that employed hundreds of professional foresters.[58]

In one sense, Frederick Weyerhaeuser and other lumber producers faced unique problems from other entrepreneurs in that they dealt with a resource that, unreplenished by humans, could have been depleted entirely, especially given the time lag between planting a tree and harvesting it. Cotton growers or textile manufacturers did not face the same resource problem. From another perspective, though, Weyerhaeuser typified several of the major entrepreneurs of the day, for even in the midst of the managerial revolution he maintained control and ownership over his organization. Adopting the structure of managerial hierarchies, he retained the substance of entrepreneurship.

Innovations in Food Processing and Sales

In farming and food sales, entrepreneurs also sought ways to adopt new management methods to family-owned firms. Innovators in agriculture perceived that the days of the small-acreage, limited-crop farm had ended. Successful food-oriented businesses, even if families retained control, had to incorporate elements of the new management structures and extend their markets. A. P. Seabrook, for example, had farmed a relatively small acreage in Bridgeton, New Jersey, in the 1880s—an unlikely prospect for evolving into the world's largest farm.[59] Seabrook specialized in peas, beans, limas, and spinach of such quality that others contacted him about furnishing seed. His vegetables, packed in ice and shipped by rail, reached Philadelphia, New York, and Baltimore. After learning of a Danish process for growing cauliflower using overhanging pipes that sprayed water, the family installed the system and realized a profit of $25,000 on the operation. By the early 1900s, the Seabrook family started to can its own foods and mechanize its farming.

Weyerhaeuser in lumbering, A & P in grocery stores, Seabrook farms, Jack Daniel with his whiskey, and Dr. Welch's juice company—several family businesses had started to make the transition from family-owned firm to modern corporation. None of them, however, better bridged the gap between the traditional structure of an owner-controlled business and the new organizations relying on professional managers than the greatest nineteenth-century entrepreneur of them all, Andrew Carnegie.

Andrew Carnegie and American Steel

Enough chroniclers have told Carnegie's story that all the details need not be repeated here.[60] A Scottish immigrant raised in poverty, Carnegie rose to the pinnacle of American business, becoming the greatest steelmaker in history. Carnegie left Scotland at age thirteen with little formal education, locating in Pittsburgh, where he worked a number of jobs, including one as a bobbin boy. He toiled twelve hours a day for $1.20 a week, and by 1849 had a better position at the O'Reilly Telegraph Company, where his keen memory and ability to translate Morse code without writing it down first made him a valuable employee.

By age sixteen, Carnegie earned more than his father, but his career had only started to develop. His telegraph talents had caught the eye of Thomas Scott, district superintendent of the Pennsylvania Railroad, who hired Carnegie as his personal secretary. In a few years, Carnegie had gained precious experience in two booming industries: steel and railroads. Scott even educated Carnegie on the stock market and loaned him money to purchase Adams Express stock. Several transactions followed, with Carnegie making a small fortune in each. With his available cash, Carnegie invested in the Keystone Bridge Company, where he became a partner. That investment served as the "parent of all the other works," and proved a brilliant choice. Railroads had started to stretch across the nation, and at each valley or river they required a bridge. Thus, as one Carnegie biographer observed, "Carnegie's decision to found a company to build iron bridges put him into the middle of one of the most rapidly changing technologies of the day and at the same time opened spectacular opportunities for achievement."[61]

The short jump from bridge construction to steel manufacturing seemed natural to Carnegie, who had invested in iron forges in 1861 and had organized the Cyclops Iron Company in 1864. Whether in bridge construction or iron production, Carnegie energetically devoted himself to controlling costs. When it came to manufacturing iron, he learned that few of the experienced iron manufacturers even knew their costs, with owners providing tons of raw materials to mills daily without an accurate accounting of the supplies delivered. His accounting systems detailed the expenses of every department, at which point Carnegie reduced costs. But his most significant efforts to control costs involved the then common backward and forward integration. The Cyclops and Union Mills supplied iron plates and beams to Keystone Bridge, and in 1870 he ordered construction of the Lucy blast furnace to provide pig iron to the mills. That furnace turned out record tonnage of iron—642 tons in one week, compared to an industrial average of 350, and 100 tons in a day—and Carnegie's blast furnaces worked so hard that he had to reline the interiors every three years.

Still, American technology lagged behind that of the British, especially after the introduction of a new process designed by Henry Bessemer, who discovered that he could purify hot pig iron of its carbon with a blast of cold air. Bessemer's converter looked like a large, open-topped egg, with air blasted into the molten iron through vents in the bottom. The infusion of oxygen cleared the iron of silicon, and it was not long before steelmasters were able to control the exact content of carbon in the steel through the Bessemer process. Alexander L. Holley of Connecticut, who studied Bessemer's plants in Sheffield, England, returned to America to create his own Bessemer furnace in Troy, New York, in 1864.

Carnegie recognized the technology as the wave of the future and entered into Bessemer steel production in 1866, using imported British equipment. Attracting other investors, Carnegie maintained the controlling interest in a new company, Carnegie, McCandless & Company, with the goal of producing rail steel with the Bessemer process. Always aware of the contributions of experienced and talented employees, Carnegie hired many of the best iron and steel men in the industry, and more than a few came to him because of his reputation. One of the best, "Captain" Bill Jones, proved a superior plant manager. Others, such as Julian Kennedy, constantly improved Carnegie's plant technology, contributing more than 100 patents (of which over fifty found their way into Carnegie's plants during Kennedy's lifetime). Carnegie did not hesitate to employ any technology—homegrown or otherwise, regardless of cost. He hired Alexander Holley to build a mill near Pittsburgh, naming it the J. Edgar Thomson Steel Works—ever with an eye to his chief customer, the railroads.

Carnegie attracted most of his senior managers with shares of ownership, although Bill Jones declined such an offer and instead demanded "one hell of a big raise," which Carnegie paid ($25,000, then a fantastic sum). The Carnegie companies were partnerships, with Andrew Carnegie the majority partner. In an age of corporations, when ownership and management were separated, Carnegie merged the two as never before. All new partners came into the firm under the "Iron Clad Oath," in which they agreed to offer their shares for sale back to the other partners before putting them on the open market. In that way, Carnegie constantly built up his ownership position when partners left or, in some cases, were forced out. Giving the top managers a share of ownership produced unmatched gains in output, although, again, Jones was the exception. After he received his "hell of a big raise," he promised Carnegie that his mills would outproduce the Cambria Iron Works, and they did, turning out 8,000 more tons of steel in 1881 than Cambria.

The partnership business form that Carnegie took allowed him to finance virtually everything internally, providing a constant circle of profits back into the business, to the consternation of some stockholders. Carnegie virtually never paid dividends, and while the stock value soared, the partners received little cash flow other than their salaries. Internal financing gave Carnegie the enviable advantage of having money when no one else did. In depressions, such as the Panic of 1873, he bought when others sold at bargain-basement prices. He eagerly scooped up new mills and equipment from overextended competitors, often obtaining state-of-the-art machinery "on the cheap." And in all of his dealings, Carnegie stayed focused on the bottom line of cutting costs in order to reinvest and expand. Hardheaded at times, Carnegie could be persuaded when confronted with evidence, especially if it showed lower costs.

Those traits made him a ruthless competitor—even more so because, as Jonathan R. T. Hughes observed, "His competitors were considered enemies, not gentlemanly rivals."[62] There was none of the collusion that had befallen the railroads with Carnegie, who sought to bury his challengers, not praise them. When he acquired the Homestead Steel Works, he offered the owners cash or the equivalent stock value in his own company; they foolishly took cash. The only investor who took stock saw his $50,000 stake grow to $8 million in a fifteen-year period. To the dynamic Carnegie, the key was action: act when others would not or could not. The Scotsman "bought in depressions, rebuilt in depressions, restaffed in depressions, then undercut his competitors when business was good."[63] In so doing, Carnegie performed an extraordinary public service, as he forced prices for steel downward until it became a basic metal. He, of course, did not refuse government help when he got it, supporting the steel tariffs of the 1870s, although he claimed that "even if the tariff were off entirely, you [British] couldn't [sell] steel rails west of us."[64]

A conspicuous exception to his obsession with lowering prices involved hiring and retaining expensive labor. Carnegie reasoned that the most expensive labor in a free market was also the most valuable due to its productivity. In this, he was persuaded by Jones, who argued on behalf of an eight-hour day, that "it was entirely out of the question to expect human flesh and blood to labor incessantly for twelve hours."[65] Others, particularly union leaders, often failed to understand Carnegie, or, conversely, understood precisely that his relationships with labor required thoughtful workers willing to bargain individually. That was anathema to union organizers, who fought Carnegie repeatedly over collective bargaining. Carnegie did not mind paying higher wages, as long as individuals negotiated them. Indeed, nowhere in the American labor movement does the fundamental philosophical difference appear more stark between those who believed that individuals were helpless and those who thought that all power emanated from the individual than in the clashes between Carnegie's company and the unions.

By the time the issue came to a head, however, Carnegie had left for Scotland, leaving a man of less lofty ideals, Henry Clay Frick, to preside over one of the worst strikes in American history. Frick was not without his own success story to tell, starting as a clerk in a department store. By age twenty-two, Frick had his own firm, and founded the Henry C. Frick Coke Company in 1871, forging it into one of the most powerful businesses in America and bringing him into Carnegie's orbit. In 1882, to ensure a steady supply of coke for his steel mills, Carnegie had purchased half of Frick's interests, making Frick a Carnegie partner. At that time, Frick, age thirty-three, wielded control over 12,000 coke ovens. A few years later, with no other clear successor in sight, Carnegie made Frick president of the Carnegie companies, reorganized yet again in 1891 as Carnegie Steel Co.

Carnegie already had crossed swords with the Amalgamated Association of Iron and Steel Workers when it won a strike at Homestead in 1889. The new contract came up for renewal in 1892, by which time Carnegie had left the tactical details to Frick, but he advised his president to shut down the plants and let the workers decide to come back. Instead, Frick provoked a fight, turning Homestead into a fortress with armed guards. When the entire workforce went on strike, Frick tried to break it by hiring Pinkerton guards, who were little more than otherwise unemployed riffraff. The Pinkertons, supposing to take the mill under the cover of darkness, arrived from the river to avoid the picket lines; but they were spotted, and a miniature war broke out on the riverbank. After the Pinkertons surrendered, they walked through the town, which had felt the brunt of the labor policies. A crowd turned into a mob, killing several Pinkertons and beating most of them. After that, the union's Advisory Committee, in full control of Homestead, "ran the town with a heavy hand reminiscent of Robespierre's Committee of Public Safety. . . ."[66] The governor called in the state militia to restore order, then Frick reopened the plant with nonunion workers—although union workers were invited back on a prestrike basis, and, after the strikers realized they had lost, they, too, returned to work. Homestead operated as a nonunion plant, with each worker signing an individual agreement with the company. In a statement to the Pennsylvania grand jury related to the case, Chief Justice Edward Paxon of the Pennsylvania Supreme Court reiterated the fundamental rule free markets: "The relation of employer and employee is one of contract merely. Neither party has a right to coerce the other into the making of a contract to which the mind does not assent."[67]

Ironically, both Carnegie and the union emerged as villains, while Frick survived just short of a hero—at least, temporarily. Frick's status derived from an unsuccessful assassination attempt on him during the strike by an anarchist. Alexander Berkman burst into the president's office, shot Frick twice in the neck, then attempted to commit suicide and blow up the room by biting down on a capsule of fulminate of mercury. After the maniac was subdued, Frick sat in his chair while a doctor removed the bullets without anesthesia. Not only did Frick remain at his job that day, but he wrote his mother a letter in which he scarcely mentioned the incident, stating, "Was shot twice today, though not seriously." Meanwhile, editors and labor leaders heaped scorn on Carnegie, who, they argued, could have prevented the episode at Homestead with a word. (Carnegie, of course, had no more control over Frick than did the union.) The Amalgamated suffered a fatal blow to its prestige from the ease with which modern production methods replaced the skilled craftsmen, who learned that mechanization had made the craft unions obsolete. Even Frick, though, ultimately had to pay for his role in Homestead, finding himself pushed to the periphery of Carnegie's business. He still owned his Frick stock, resulting in a bloody battle with Carnegie to exact full payment for his shares. After a suit, Carnegie paid Frick $31 million, then did not speak to him again, except once, in old age, when the Scotsman offered to reconcile. Frick told the intermediary, "Tell Mr. Carnegie I'll meet him in hell."

Carnegie turned his company over to a young genius, Charles Schwab, who had started as a stake driver at the Edgar Thomson plant, rising to the top of the corporate world as the president of Carnegie Steel at the age of thirty-five. Schwab knew how to persuade Carnegie, barraging him with data on savings until he achieved his goal. Schwab continued the Carnegie evolution of integrating the company entirely. Although Carnegie Steel owned its own sources of coke and limestone, it still had to purchase iron ore. That weakness became all too apparent when John D. Rockefeller purchased control over the rich Mesabi, Minnesota, iron-ore range, making Carnegie dependent on him for his raw materials. Carnegie moved quickly, working out a lease arrangement with Rockefeller for the land. He built his own railroad to haul ore from Lake Erie to Pittsburgh, saving the company $1.5 million annually. Next, he acquired a fleet of ore boats that saved an additional $2 million, all the while increasing his capital investment in his main business, steel.

Those improvements, and Carnegie's good sense in attracting talent, made Carnegie Steel the most efficient steel manufacturer in the world. Between 1888 and 1898, the company's capital rose from $20 million to $45 million while its production tripled, rising to two million tons of pig iron a year and 6,000 tons of steel a day. By 1900, Carnegie accounted for one-third of all the steel produced in the United States and had surpassed the British in efficiency.

Called a "robber baron," Carnegie astutely summed up the entrepreneurial realities: Two pounds of iron shipped to Pittsburgh, two pounds of coal (turned into a quarter pound of coke), a half a pound of limestone from the Alleghenies, and a small amount of Virginia manganese ore yielded one pound of steel that sold for a cent. "That's all that need be said about the steel business," he adroitly noted.[68] But that was not all that need be said about Carnegie. He once admitted that his life's goal was to give away $300 million, but he did not do it: He gave away more! His Carnegie Institute of Technology received $27 million, and his retirement fund for teachers netted $10 million. By 1904 alone—about the time he started giving away money "full time"—he already had donated more than $180 million to charities.

Most of that money came from the sale of Carnegie Steel in 1900. For some time, J. P. Morgan had listened to Schwab explain the advantages of streamlining the steel industry. Morgan had reorganized railroads and thought their structure could be brought to steel. Morgan was aware that Carnegie had considered selling the company, flirting briefly with a syndicate involving John W. "Bet-A-Million" Gates of Chicago. Gates, who had founded a thriving barbed-wire business, was known for his outlandish bets, yet the key sale of his life—of barbed wire to a group of San Antonio ranchers—was hardly a gamble in that Gates had challenged the ranchers to bring their steers to town to test a fence made of his wire. Gates, suspecting that no rancher would risk his own cattle, had his own wild-looking (but actually docile) steers run into town, where, promptly, they stopped at the wire and ensured Gates's sale.[69] But the sale with the Gates group fell through, and Morgan talked further with Schwab. The banker asked Schwab to serve as the courier and asked Carnegie to fix a price. Dutifully, Schwab, the president of one of the largest companies on earth but reduced to the capacity of a messenger boy, transmitted Morgan's request to Carnegie on the golf course. Schwab and Carnegie made a few calculations, then Carnegie scratched a figure—$480 million—on a small piece of paper. When Morgan saw it, he said, "I'll take it." The titans finalized the deal aboard Morgan's yacht, the *Corsair,* with Morgan extending his hand to Carnegie, saying "I congratulate you on becoming the richest man in the world."

Although Carnegie's role in his steel company ended, Morgan, true to his vision, reorganized Carnegie Steel into U.S. Steel Corporation, which included Federal Steel, National Tube, American Steel and Wire, American Steel Hoop, American Tin Plate, American Sheet Steel, American Bridge, Shelby Steel, and many other holdings. The final business, capitalized at $1.4 billion, constituted the world's largest corporation. Under Schwab's leadership, the company maintained unprecedented production levels. But under Morgan, Schwab managed a much different steel business than he had under Carnegie. Unlike the Scotsman, Morgan wanted stability instead of innovation and failed to see the elegant simplicity of cost-cutting to obtain market share. Soon, Schwab was gone.

The young executive had not abandoned Carnegie's concepts, however, and using his own private company, Bethlehem Steel, Schwab quickly repeated, and even surpassed, his performance at Carnegie. He selected fifteen young men "right out of the mill and made them my partner," Schwab recalled.[70] Within ten years, the *New York Times* called Bethlehem "possibly the most efficient, profitable self-contained steel plant in the country."[71] The workforce at Bethlehem doubled every five years; U.S. Steel's workforce shrank.

Schwab proved that it was not the size of the company that mattered, nor even its heritage. No company was better grounded to capture the American steel market entirely than U.S. Steel after Morgan finished his consolidation. Instead, U.S. Steel abandoned the vision and faith that had created it. Morgan should have known better; as a banker, he broke new ground constantly, taking unimaginable risks. But as a manager of a steel empire, he lost sight of the soul that gave life to Carnegie's structure, namely the willingness to sacrifice existing plants and systems for the potentially better and cheaper processes. All Morgan had to do was to heed Carnegie's words, "Watch the costs and the profits will take care of themselves."

Big Business, Banking, and J. P. Morgan

It was fitting that Morgan took over for Carnegie, much the way only a Joe DiMaggio could wear the Yankee pinstripes made legendary by Babe Ruth. Morgan personally represented the fusion of the sole-proprietor entrepreneur with the managerial approach of the new integrated industries. He attacked problems aggressively and individually, relying on the help of syndicates but never beholden to them. More than any person, Morgan reorganized businesses with managerial hierarchies, introducing them to stability and conservatism. Yet Morgan's deals themselves epitomized entrepreneurship and risk-taking—the exact opposite characteristics embodied in the managerial revolution.

Raised in a home as luxurious as Carnegie's was bleak, Morgan increasingly focused his career on rescuing distressed railroads. As the price for his support, Morgan insisted on managerial changes. He merged unprofitable lines with sound railroads, underwrote securities to equip roads that lacked internal funding, and corrected abuses in chronically overextended roads such as the B&O. During the process of selling securities for the New York Central, Morgan obtained a seat on the board of directors. From an inside position, Morgan demanded management changes, setting a pattern for Morgan's future dealings. While reorganizing the Reading Railroad, he perfected the "voting trust," giving bankers control over a company until the company met prescribed performance objectives. Not surprisingly, by the late 1800s, railroads came to look like banks with their professional management structures.

Morgan's more important accomplishments, however, involved his contributions to investment banking and, indirectly, the structure of the American banking system itself. By the late 1800s, national and state banks provided the commercial funds and circulation needed for daily economic life. Large investment banks, such as Morgan's, handled the issue of securities for new firms or to recapitalize old ones. When necessary, the syndicates formed by the investment banks could supply even the U.S. government with cash. Thus, while historians have referred to the "dual banking system" of state and national banks, really there were two sets of "dual systems," with one system involving regulatory oversight and control and the other dealing with the types of services and funds provided. Both, however, suffered in the event of a depression or panic.

In 1873, the failure of Jay Cooke's bank triggered runs and a panic. The system lumbered along for two more decades, struggling to provide enough cash in flush times or to contract the money supply in tight periods. With the amount of national banknotes tied to the amount of bonds that the banks had on deposit with the government,

---

TALES FROM THE CRYPT: ENTREPRENEURS WHO CAME BACK FROM THE DEAD

Charles W. Post: The #1 Bran Fan

CHARLES POST PROBABLY THOUGHT HIS LIFE could not get any worse than it was in 1890. That year, at thirty-seven years old—almost a decade older than when George Westinghouse racked up his first million—Post was nearly broke. He had invested in a land development scheme and textile mill in Texas, and his health failed. Stomach disorders and nervous problems, with which he had struggled most of his life, grew worse after his financial collapse. Per-

haps naturally, he also suffered from severe depression. Only on the advice of his relatives did he agree to move his family to Battle Creek, Michigan, in 1891.

Battle Creek was home to the idiosyncratic doctor John Harvey Kellogg, who practiced restorative treatments at the Seventh-Day Adventist Sanitarium. Kellogg, true to the Adventist faith, was a vegetarian and an advocate of "biologic living," or what might today be called holistic treatment. Along with his brother, Will Kellogg, John Harvey Kellogg endorsed hot tub baths, exercise, inspirational talks, and a diet of "natural foods," especially molasses, fruit, and bran.

When Post arrived at the sanitarium, he had virtually no money, even to the point that he had to trade in blankets from his bankrupt mill as a down payment on the medical costs. Unfortunately for both Post and Kellogg, Post's health deteriorated further. His wife, in desperation, withdrew Post and placed him in a Christian Scientist's home for treatment. There, remarkably, he recovered.

By that time, Post was nearly forty and still without a means of employment.

expanding the money supply rapidly proved difficult. Moreover, the seasonal nature of a still strong agricultural sector placed particular demands on certain areas of the country not shared by the large industrial centers. Political shenanigans with silver (the Bland-Allison Act [1878] and the Sherman Silver Purchase Act [1890]) tended to exacerbate the institutional problems with the money supply, ultimately contributing to the Panic of 1893. The overvaluation of silver caused money to flow out of the nation at unprecedented rates, threatening the financial structure of the United States itself.

Into the breach stepped J. P. Morgan. He formed a syndicate with August Belmont & Company and the European bankers, the Rothschild family, to deliver to the Treasury 3.5 million ounces of gold—certainly the largest private "bailout" of the government in history. President Grover Cleveland, however, rued the assistance, deliberately keeping Morgan waiting on at least one occasion. When John Kennedy, himself elected president in 1960, wrote his Pulitzer Prize-winning book

---

He did, however, have something of a reputation as the man who came back from the (nearly) dead. Post used that "hook"—his recovery—as a basis to start his own health sanitarium, La Vita Inn. Meals at La Vita stressed grains and bran, as well as a coffee substitute made of New Orleans molasses, bran (naturally!), and wheat berries. In 1895, he marketed his coffee substitute to retail grocery stores under the brand name "Postum." Did things change for Post? Not hardly. He lost $800 on the product in the first year, and he was still lacking money needed for advertising.

Post's breakthrough came when he persuaded a Chicago advertising firm to lend him money for ads in *Scribner's*, *Harpers Weekly*, and other publications. He had considerable writing skills, which he focused on the dangers of coffee drinking, successfully frightening thousands of consumers into trying his product. Post accused caffeine of causing rheumatism, heart disease, blindness, cowardice, sloth, and stupidity! His ads challenged consumers with questions such as "Is your yellow streak the coffee habit? Does it reduce your working force, kill your energy, push

you into the big crowd of mongrels . . .?" (Fucini and Fucini, 106) Post's tactics worked. Sales of Postum reached $3,000 a month by 1893, but already he had started work on his next product, a cereal of yeast, whole wheat, and malted barley flour, called "Grape Nuts." The cereal was not made from grapes or nuts, but its texture was nutty and the baking process turned the starches into a sugar that tasted like grapes.

Post sold cereal, became a millionaire in a few short years, and founded a cereal empire. He nevertheless probably would have been chagrined to learn that the company that bears his name today markets such healthful products as "Alpha-Bits" and "Cocoa Pebbles," but then he may have been relieved to know that nutritional information is mandated to appear on every box—usually somewhere below the notice of the free decoder ring or the Michael Jordan T-shirt offer!

Sources: Frank Rowsome Jr., *They Laughed When I Sat Down* (New York: McGraw-Hill, 1959); Nettie L. Major, *C. W. Post: The Hour and the Man* (Washington, D.C.: privately published, 1963); and Fucini and Fucini, *Entrepreneurs*.

Profiles in Courage, he praised the politician Cleveland as a hero but ignored the astounding accomplishment of the entrepreneur, Morgan, who had saved the country. As Jonathan Hughes aptly put it, "For a private banker to stem the gold outflow of the United States was a breathtaking feat."[72]

To some, Morgan's assistance represented the worst of the American business system and the weaknesses of a banking system that still required the efforts of one man to set it right. Many saw it as a sign that the nation needed a central bank capable of doing what Morgan did, supplying money in recessionary times. Several monetary reform movements were spawned during the late 1800s, most of them somehow tied to the creation of the American Bankers Association in 1876. The association initially focused on making uniform state banking laws, but at its Baltimore convention in 1894 Alonzo B. Hepburn and Charles C. Homer put into motion a plan that ultimately served as the basis for the Federal Reserve Act, reforming the financial system.

CHALLENGE YOUR PERCEPTIONS!

Were Bank Robberies Common in the "Wild West"?

IN ALMOST ANY HOLLYWOOD WESTERN movie—and certainly most of those produced in the period prior to 1970—a staple scene was the bank robbery. Whether in Texas, Colorado, Arizona, Montana, or some other part of the "wild west," bank robbers, it seems, found "easy pickin's" when it came to banks. Unfortunately for the Hollywood screenplay writers, such scenes were about as common as UFO landings in Central Park.

To understand why there were no successful bank robberies in any of the major towns in Colorado, Wyoming, Montana, the Dakotas, Kansas, Nebraska, Oregon, Washington, Idaho, Nevada, Utah, or New Mexico, and only a pair of robberies in California and Arizona before 1900, it is important to appreciate the location and construction of bank buildings on the frontier. Bankers always placed their buildings in the center of town, where businesses surrounded them. On the frontier, most towns featured "concealed carry" gun laws, so that much of the citizenry was armed. In addition, sheriffs and deputies were nearby. Townspeople noticed new faces immediately, and prepared accordingly. The notion that a band of five or six complete strangers in long coats, who just happened to meander near the bank, would go unnoticed is sheer fantasy. Even if a gang could execute a daring holdup of a bank, the thieves still had to escape through a population in which every armed citizen had a direct monetary interest in stopping the getaway. And a posse would follow in minutes.

Were banks vulnerable in other ways, say, to explosives during the night? Bank

Indeed, no term better captured the thrust of the new business-government relations than "reform." Americans came to view "big business" increasingly as "bad business." Labor unions, social activists, politicians, editors, and others complained about monopolies, the profits earned by "robber barons," and the inordinate power of large corporations over American politics and life. An entire political movement, the Progressive wing of the Republican Party (then later, the Progressive Party itself) stood for reform of all aspects of society, including several aspects of business and the economy.

In some ways, then, Morgan's actions in 1893 marked the temporary end of a relatively brief period in the nation's business history when a small minority of talented individuals completely dominated the scene, improving the lives of everyone in quantum terms. Edison not only provided light: He changed American nightlife and the landscape of the cities. Carnegie not only provided cheap steel: He made buildings, railroads, and ships safer than ever before. Swift did not just

---

walls usually adjoined other buildings, with the vault located on an interior wall. It was possible to blow open a vault, but that did not guarantee access to the safe, which stood inside the vault. Early safes were "ball" safes, in which a large iron ball containing the cash stood atop a large metal box with legs. The box held important documents and nonmonetary valuables. It was almost impossible to blast open a ball safe using the dynamite of that time, because the round shape of the ball diffused the explosive effect and there was no way to affix a charge to the exterior of the safe. If the crooks chose to blow off the ball from the box, they had to figure out how to get a several-hundred-pound iron ball out of town, which at the very least would have required a wagon. In short, the vault and safe alone deterred most crimes. When combined with the banks' location, few bandits wanted to attempt a bank robbery.

A few did occur, including one in Nogales on the Arizona-Mexico border at the turn of the century and a couple in California. In Colorado, the members of Butch Cassidy's gang attempted to use a vial of nitroglycerine to coax a bank president into opening his vault, but the heist failed. Otherwise, bandits discovered it was far easier to rob trains and stagecoaches, as seen in the records of Wells Fargo, whose stages suffered recurring holdup attempts. Not until the 1920s, with the proliferation of automobiles, did bank robberies in the wild west become a reality.

Where, then, did the myth come from? Several raids by the famous James Gang and Quantrill's raiders in the Minnesota-Missouri region contributed to much of the bank robbery myth. Otherwise, like the frequent movie plots involving robberies of Fort Knox, the western bank robbery sprang to life entirely out of the minds of writers.

Sources: Lynne Pierson Doti and Larry Schweikart, *Banking in the American West from the Gold Rush to Deregulation* (Norman: University of Oklahoma Press, 1991) and John and Lillian Theobald, *Wells Fargo in Arizona Territory,* ed. Bert Fireman (Tempe: Arizona Historical Foundation, 1978).

find a more efficient way to produce beef and pork: He improved the dietary habits and health of generations.

Perhaps it was the very fact that not everyone could accomplish those great feats—that a chasm stood between the "vital few" and the average American. Yet, as we have seen, countless numbers of "average Americans" suffered setbacks and financial failures before developing products and services that changed all our lives for the better. But the convergence of large-scale industry, combined with a national market and the elements of mass production and marketing, allowed anyone of exceptional talent to rise to unprecedented levels of success. Right behind them, however, marched an army of professional managers, more conservative by nature, who could not replicate the feats of the "captains of industry." The appearance of the professional managers fit nicely with the new Progressive movement, which reveled in constant, evolutionary reform toward an ill-defined notion of perfection. Progressives not only viewed human control over commerce as superior to that of the market, but also assumed that their own intellect was superior to the collective wisdom of the market.

Notes

1. Charles A. and Mary Beard, *The Rise of American Civilization* (New York: Macmillan, 1927); Louis M. Hacker, *The Triumph of American Capitalism* (New York: Columbia University Press, 1940).

2. Atack and Passell, *A New Economic View of American History,* 363.

3. Robert Gallman, "Commodity Output, 1839–99," in National Bureau of Economic Research, *Trends in the American Economy in the 19th Century,* vol. 24, Series on Income and Wealth (Princeton, N.J.: Princeton, University Press, 1960).

4. Claudia Goldin and Frank Lewis, "The Economic Cost of the American Civil War: Estimates and Implications," *Journal of Economic History,* 35 (June 1975): 304–309. Also see Peter Temin, "The Post-Bellum Recovery of the South and the Cost of the Civil War," *Journal of Economic History,* 26 (December 1976): 898–907.

5. U.S. Department of Commerce, Bureau of the Census, *Bicentennial Statistics* (Washington, D.C.: Government Printing Office, 1976), 407; U.S. Department of Commerce, Bureau of the Census, *Historical Statistics of the United States: Colonial Times to 1970,* 2 vols. (Washington, D.C.: Government Printing Office, 1975), I: 456–5200.

6. See Timothy W. Genion, Harvey S. Rosen, and Kirsten L. Willard, "Messages from 'The Den of Wild Beasts': Greenback Prices as Commentary on the Union's Prospects," *Civil War History,* 41 (December 1995): 313–328.

7. This discussion is developed in Lynne Pierson Doti and Larry Schweikart, *Banking in the American West from the Gold Rush to Deregulation* (Norman: University of Oklahoma Press, 1991).

8. Joseph F. Rishel, "Jay Cooke," in Schweikart, ed., *Encyclopedia of American Business History: Banking and Finance to 1913,* 135–143 (quotation on 137); and the two biographies of Cooke, Henrietta M. Larson, *Jay Cooke: Private Banker* (Cambridge, Mass.: Harvard University Press, 1936), and Ellis Paxson Oberholtzer, *Jay Cooke: Financier of the Civil War,* 2 vols. (Philadelphia: Jacobs, 1907).

9. Richard Bensel, *Yankee Leviathan: The Origins of Central State Authority in America, 1859–1877* (Cambridge: Cambridge University Press, 1990), 94.

10. Bensel, 95.

11. Edward Hagerman, *The American Civil War and the Origins of Modern Warfare: Ideas, Organization, and Field Command* (Bloomington: Indiana University Press, 1988).

12. Bensel, *Yankee Leviathan,* 95.

13. See, for example, Louise B. Hill, *State Socialism in the Confederate States of America* (Charlottesville, Va.: Historical Publishing, 1936) and Raimondo Luraghi "The Civil War and the Modernization of American Society," *Civil War History,* 18 (September 1972): 230–250, as well as Richard E. Beringer, Herman Hattaway, Archer Jones, and William N. Still Jr., *Why the South Lost the Civil War* (Athens: University of Georgia Press, 1986).

14. Stanley Lebergott, *The Americans: An Economic Record* (New York: W.W. Norton, 1984), 243. Also see his "Why the South Lost: Commercial Purpose in the Confederacy, 1861–1865," *Journal of American History,* 70 (June 1983): 58–74, and "Through the Blockade: The Profitability and Extent of Cotton Smuggling, 1861–1865," *Journal of Economic History,* 41 (December 1981): 867–888.

15. Benjamin quoted in Mary A. DeCredico, *Patriotism for Profit: Georgia's Urban Entrepreneurs and the Confederate War Effort* (Chapel Hill: University of North Carolina Press, 1990), 27.

16. Robert A. Taylor, *Rebel Storehouse: Florida in the Confederate Economy* (Tuscaloosa: University of Alabama Press, 1995), 55.

17. Emory M. Thomas, *The Confederate Nation, 1861–1865* (New York: Harper Torchbooks, 1979), 207, 212.

18. Scott Nelson, "The Confederacy Serves the Southern: The Construction of the Southern Railway Network, 1861–65," *Civil War History,* 41 (September 1995): 227–243 (quotation on 243).

19. See Jeffrey Rogers Hummel, *Emancipating Slaves, Enslaving Free Men: A History of the American Civil War* (Chicago: Open Court, 1996).

20. Among the recent literature on this, see James McPherson, *Battle Cry of Freedom: The Civil War Era* (New York: Oxford University Press, 1988) and his *Ordeal by Fire: The Civil War and Reconstruction* 2d ed. (New York: Alfred A. Knopf, 1992) and Roger L. Ransom, *Conflict and Compromise: The Political-Economy of Slavery, Emancipation and the American Civil War* (Cambridge: Cambridge University Press, 1989), plus the numerous interpretations dealt with in the classic by Thomas J. Pressly, *Americans Interpret Their Civil War* (Princeton, N.J.: Princeton University Press, 1954).

21. I have argued this in Larry Schweikart, "Abraham Lincoln and the Growth of Government in the Civil War Era," *Continuity* (Spring 1997): 25–42.

22. Robert C. Kenzer, *Black Economic Success in North Carolina, 1865–1995* (Charlottesville: University Press of Virginia, 1989).

23. Wright, *Old South, New South,* 34.

24. Roger L. Ransom and Richard Sutch, *One Kind of Freedom: The Economic Consequences of Emancipation* (London: Cambridge, 1977), 84, and Puth, *American Economic History,* 334.

25. Kenzer, *Black Economic Success*, 18 (Table 5).

26. Several sources provide excellent discussions of these developments, including Lebergott, *The Americans*, 241–268; Puth, *American Economic History*, 330–339; Gavin Wright, *Old South, New South: Revolutions in the Southern Economy Since the Civil War* (New York: Basic Books, 1986); Joseph Reid, "Sharecropping as an Understandable Market Response: The Postbellum South," *Journal of Economic History*, 33 (March 1973): 106–130; and William Brown and Morgan Reynolds, "Debt Peonage Reexamined," *Journal of Economic History*, 33 (December 1973): 862–871.

27. Theodore Rosengarten, *All God's Dangers: The Life of Nate Shaw* (New York: Alfred A. Knopf, 1974).

28. "Andrew Jackson Beard" in *A Salute to Black Scientists and Inventors*, vol. 2 (Chicago: Empak Enterprises and Richard L. Green n.d.), 6.

29. Juliet E. K. Walker, *Free Frank: A Black Pioneer on the Antebellum Frontier* (Lexington: University Press of Kentucky, 1983).

30. See the letter of Robert W. Cosgrove of the New York Central System Historical Society, *Detroit News*, March 20, 1996.

31. *African Americans: Voices of Triumph* (Alexandria, Va.: Time-Life Books, 1993), 1:32.

32. Burton Folsom, "Real McCoy Showed Depth of Black Enterprise," *Detroit News*, February 28, 1996.

33. Robert C. Kenzer, "The Black Business Community in Post Civil War Virginia," *Southern Studies*, new series, 4 (Fall 1993): 229–252.

34. Kenzer, "Black Business Community," 250, n. 58.

35. Stephen DeCanio, "Cotton Overproduction in the Late 19th Century Agriculture," *Journal of Economic History*, 33 (1973): 608–633 and his "Productivity and Income Distribution in the Postbellum South," ibid., 34 (1974): 422–446; Gavin Wright, "Cotton Competition and the Post Bellum Recovery of the American South," ibid., 34 (1974): 610–635 and his *Old South, New South*, passim; and Robert A. McGuire and Robert Higgs, "Cotton, Corn and Risk in the Nineteenth Century: Another View," *Explorations in Economic History*, 14 (1979): 167–182.

36. Gavin Wright, "The Strange Career of the New Southern Economic History," *Reviews in American History*, 10 (December 1982): 164–180; Donald B. Dodd Wynelle S. Dodd, *Historical Statistics of the South, 1790–1970* (Tuscaloosa: University of Alabama Press, 1973).

37. Henry Hudson, "The Southern Railway & Steamship Association," quoted in C. Vann Woodward, *Origins of the New South* (Baton Rouge: Louisiana State University Press, 1980 [1951]), 122.

38. Quoted in Woodward, *Origins of the New South*, 128.

39. John Samuel Ezell, *The South Since 1865* (New York: Macmillan, 1963), 141.

40. Chandler, *Visible Hand*, 287.

41. Dobson, *History of American Enterprise*, 135.

42. Dorrance quoted in Douglas Collins, *America's Favorite Food: The Story of Campbell Soup Company* (New York: Harry N. Abrams, 1994), 38. See also Alecia Swasy, *Soap Opera: The Inside Story of Procter and Gamble* (New York: Times Books, 1993).

43. Alfred Leif, *"It Floats." The Story of Procter and Gamble* (New York: Holt, Rinehart and Winston, 1958).

44. Sobel and Sicilia, *Entrepreneurs,* 214.

45. Sobel and Sicilia, *Entrepreneurs,* 74; Lewis F. Swift and Arthur Van Vlissington, *The Yankee of the Yards: The Biography of Gustavus Franklin Swift* (New York: A.W. Shaw, 1928).

46. Mary Yeager Kujovich, "The Refrigerator Car and the Growth of the American Dressed Beef Industry," *Business History Review,* 44 (1970): 460–482.

47. "Armour & Company, 1867–1938," in N. S. B. Gras and Henrietta Larson, *Case Book in American Business History* (New York: F.S. Crofts & Co., 1939), 623–643.

48. Sobel and Sicilia, *Entrepreneurs,* 77.

49. David A. Hounshell, *From the American System to Mass Production: The Development of Manufacturing Technology in the United States* (Baltimore, Md.: Johns Hopkins University Press, 1984), 82.

50. Chandler, *Visible Hand,* 303.

51. Andrew B. Jack, "The Channels of Distribution for the Innovation: The Sewing Machine Industry in America," *Explorations in Entrepreneurial History,* 9 (February 1957): 113–141, and Robert B. Davies, "Peacefully Working to Conquer the World: The Singer Manufacturing Company in Foreign Markets, 1854–1889," *Business History Review,* 43 (Autumn 1969): 299–346.

52. Alden Hatch, *Remington Arms: An American History* (New York: Rinehart & Company, 1956), 148.

53. Fucini and Fucini, *Entrepreneurs,* 18.

54. Sobel and Sicilia, *Entrepreneurs,* 62.

55. Stephen J. Pyne, *Fire in America: A Cultural History of Wildland and Rural Fire* (Princeton, N.J.: Princeton University Press, 1982), 11.

56. Pyne, *Fire in America,* 26.

57. An internal history of International Paper provides background on this company. See W. E. Haskell, *The International Paper Company, 1898–1924: Its Origin and Growth in a Quarter of a Century With a Brief Description of the Manufacture of Paper from the Harvesting of Pulpwood to the Finished Roll* (New York: International Paper, 1924), 8–9.

58. Woods, *Ideas,* 110.

59. Ibid., 313–314.

60. The outstanding biography of Carnegie is Joseph Wall, *Andrew Carnegie* (New York: Oxford University Press, 1970), and Carnegie wrote the *Autobiography of Andrew Carnegie* (Boston: Houghton Mifflin, 1920).

61. Stuart Leslie, "Andrew Carnegie," in Pascoff, ed., *Encyclopedia of American Business History and Biography: Iron and Steel in the 19th Century,* 47–71 (quotation on 51).

62. Hughes, "Andrew Carnegie," in *The Vital Few,* 237.

63. Hughes, "Carnegie," in *The Vital Few,* 238.

64. Quoted in Leslie, "Andrew Carnegie," 61.

65. Leslie, "Andrew Carnegie," 65.

66. Charles W. Baird, "Labor Law Reform: Lessons from History," *CATO Journal,* 10 (Spring/Summer 1990): 175–209 (quotation on 190).

67. Paxson, quoted in Baird, "Labor Law Reform," 192.

68. Quoted in Leslie, "Andrew Carnegie," 69.

69. Oliver E. Allen, "Bet-A-Million," *Audacity,* 5 (Fall 1996), 18–31.

70. Quoted in Folsom, *Myth of the Robber Barons,* 70. Much of this material comes from Robert Hessen, *Steel Titan: The Life of Charles M. Schwab* (New York: Oxford University Press, 1975), and Schwab's own *Succeeding With What You Have* (New York: Century, 1917).

71. *New York Times,* April 13, 1915.

72. Hughes, "J. P. Morgan," in *The Vital Few,* 443.

CHAPTER 7

Business under Attack: Populists, Progressives, and the Image of Business, 1870–1920

AN 1889 CARTOON BY J. KEPPLER, CALLED "THE BOSSES OF THE SENATE," showed diminutive senators sitting in their chamber while behind them stood a line of obese figures in top hats with the names "Steel Beam Trust," "Copper Trust," "Sugar Trust," and others emblazoned on their vests. By the turn of the century, many Americans shared the cartoonist's view that huge business combinations controlled their lives, or, at least, their economic lives. Politicians tapped into such fears and hostility and turned them into votes for "reform" and regulation.

The attempts by some individuals to monopolize, the constant search for government favors, and hostile attitudes toward labor all contributed to the Janus-faced image of businessmen in the late 1800s. On one hand, they looked forward, standing for achievement and progress, personally embodying the American dream of "rags to riches." Few people rejected material wealth in the name of higher spiritual or ideological values at the time; and fewer still did not somewhat envy the successful, prosperous individuals, especially if they had earned it rather than inherited it. On the other hand, business looked backward to the mercantilist era when it received monopoly powers through government favors, or even to feudal times when owners treated labor as expendable. Those attitudes led many people to suspect that the "robber barons" had come by their riches unethically or simply illegally, and virtually always at some-one else's expense, whether labor, the farmer, the consumer, or other small businesses. Certainly many people compared the vast wealth and earnings of a Carnegie with those of common wage earners, who toiled for only a fraction of the value of their products. While the public admitted that perhaps some business leaders indeed had gone from rags to riches, the perception developed that more had re-ceived inordinate advantages from government or other members of their social class, inheriting or stealing wealth rather than produc-ing or creating it.

The Myth of Horatio Alger's "Rags to Riches" Stories

Such attitudes were reinforced by a best-selling author of the day, Ho-ratio Alger, whose message over the years has been distorted and mis-understood. Modern Americans associate Alger's name with the phrase "rags to riches," which implies that investment, business talent, and perseverance can take an average soul to a life of abundance. But a self-made man such as Carnegie would never have recognized the ca-reer patterns of the Alger characters. According to popular miscon-ceptions, Alger's heroes represented the downtrodden rising to wealth through hard work and personal achievement through business enter-prise. But Alger, the son of a Unitarian minister and recipient of a qual-ity education, disliked capitalists, and, indeed, the most frequent villain in his stories was a mill owner. While Alger emphasized good morals, good luck was the central element in the success of most of his heroes. Alger associated with Newsboy's Lodging House in New York, where he picked up stories of young boys who had gotten out of poverty. As a part of the middle-class reform effort of the day, Alger ac-cepted "hereditary determinism," in which good blood would tell, and the rich who were mysteriously made paupers somehow were restored during the story.

Usually, Alger's stories involved a young boy who made the (fortu-nate) acquaintance of a wealthy patron, then, through charm, virtue, and some industry, received a legacy from his guardian. *Ragged Dick*, Alger's first book (1868), proved enormously popular, and soon his *Luck and Pluck* (1869), *Tattered Tom* (1871), and other volumes dominated the 1800s version of the best-seller lists. But in Alger sto-ries, seldom did hard work result in riches. Usually characters achieved middle-class status; and heroes seldom advanced through traditional capitalist enterprise but rather through luck and "connec-tions." Thus, while criticized as perpetuating the "rags to riches" myth of American business, Horatio Alger's message was the opposite of the values later associated with him: achievement through capitalism, effort, and working one's way "up the ladder." At best, Alger fashioned a formula for modern capitalism that "could be used by a diverse class of audiences to make sense of, participate in, and even protest against and rectify abuses of modern capitalism."[1] Only after securing his place in literary circles with his novels did Alger write biographies of self-made statesmen, such as Lincoln, but he still eschewed stories of entrepreneurs. Producing more than 110 books—writing as rapidly as a book every two weeks—Alger spent virtually every cent he got, resulting in his own life working out exactly the opposite of his stories, going from riches to rags and dying poor.[2]

Alger made good reading, but most people did not believe that serendipity would transform their lives, any more than modern bored housewives think that reading a "bodice ripper" reflects the likelihood that Fabio will appear at their door in plumber's attire ready for romance. Instead, many Americans saw large business combinations threatening their traditional labor patterns and blocking their route to personal economic growth. The rise of the factory system and the appearance of managerial hierarchies only made more impersonal the already frightening factory work that claimed the labor of so many workers. At the same time, the scope of industrialization translated relatively small per-unit profits into vast sums of wealth for ownership. Astute investors, such as Vanderbilt, Carnegie, and John D. Rockefeller, who created an oil empire at that time, gained millions of dollars by risking capital to own substantial shares of (what turned out to be) successful businesses. Understandably, average American workers seldom saw or considered the risk and investment that originated the businesses or the fact that the returns per unit were tiny, only that the final tally was more wealth than most of them ever could hope to own. From the perspective of publicity, the highest echelon of the business class made matters worse by flaunting their money in the most unimaginable ways.

Lifestyles of the Rich and Famous, 1800s-Style

The tycoons and social elites (although they often were not synonymous) gained notoriety in the late 1800s for their often blatant and outlandish displays of wealth. Their exploits received widespread attention in the press because the wealthy sought and craved public attention at a certain level and the public often secretly envied them, desperately hoping for a peek at how the other half lived. Social columns in urban newspapers reveled in recording the latest balls at immense mansions, with the parties equaling anything modern-day Hollywood can offer with its "A" and "B" guest lists. Surreal stories emanated from Newport, Rhode Island, abodes of the elite, who lit cigars with $100 bills—at a time when most wage earners never received a *weekly* wage of that magnitude—and threw parties where favors included diamond bracelets and pearl necklaces. Delmonico's restaurant in New York, often the scene of similar shenanigans, hosted a dinner for a pet dog; the owner presented the pooch with a diamond necklace worth $15,000. In another display of flagrant wealth, perhaps predating the antics of Dennis Rodman, a millionaire had holes drilled into his teeth to insert rows of diamonds, almost literally displaying a "million-dollar smile."[3] Such behavior seemed obscenely wasteful, affronting and insulting wage laborers, farmers, and small business owners.

The sheer gap in wealth far transcended that seen in modern America (perhaps with the exception of Bill Gates), with the top groups holding 300 to 400 *times* the capital owned by ordinary working people. For many people, however, the houses built by the rich, and in particular, Newport's mansions—"a froth of castles" erected by wealthy business leaders—struck many Americans as beyond the pale.[4] There, servants' quarters contained more square footage than the typical middle-class house, while the mansions themselves had more rooms than some hotels. One of the Vanderbilt's estates, in Ashville, North Carolina, had forty master bedrooms and a dining room so large that it had three fireplaces abreast at the end. Yet many people, while envious, were not surprised at the extravagance; quite the contrary, they understood it and would have done the same had they owned such wealth. After all, most of the "robber barons," having lived in poverty, scarcity, and cramped living quarters, made certain that they had plenty of space, privacy, and possessions once they earned their fortunes.

As ostentatious as those abodes were, it is interesting to note they were established in relatively remote places. Newport was some distance from New York or Boston, and Ashville did not lay on the beaten path. The wealthy built mansions in areas where no crowds could gather to gape; they constructed their "big houses" to impress their fellow millionaires, not the masses. The closest most members of the wealthiest sector of society came to putting on a display for the commoners was in the traditional Easter Parade, when they presented to the public their finest clothing in a genteel march down New York's Fifth Avenue.

A number of critics still thought the "conspicuous consumption" (as Thorstein Veblen called it) too much, leading some to propose "sumptuary legislation" against the rich, which would restrict the amount they could spend on housing or other displays of vanity. Social—and socialist—reformers found themselves aligned with some members of the older business elites, to whom the appearance of the new magnates whose wealth came from industry or finance represented a departure from traditional avenues of economic improvement, such as commerce and agriculture. Witnesses testifying before the Senate in 1885 recalled their youth, when "a man that had a farm worth $1500 or $2000 was considered 'A, No. 1'," yet Carnegie's sale of his steel company gave him a *daily* income of $40,000![5] As a sign that the economic system had failed, many people cited the fact that between 1865 and 1892, the number of millionaires in the nation rose from a handful to more than 4,000. In fact, the number of millionaires reflected the risk inherent in business at any time, but particularly during economic upheavals. Substantial gains always accompany high risk, and the late 1800s proved especially volatile. Rating reports from credit agencies suggested that business failures rose rapidly in the late 1870s, steadied, then got much worse during the depression of the 1890s. Yet business failures—just like business successes—did not represent permanent conditions, and as previous chapters have shown, some of the most famous names in the history of the American economy experienced not one, but several, financial setbacks or bankruptcies.

Business's Image

Outlandish displays of wealth were only one of the reasons that business leaders suffered attacks on their image in the post–Civil War era. Another criticism arose from the perception that the traditional source of economic independence, the family farm, was declining and that the plight of farmers was somehow inversely related to the wealth of the industrialists. The most oft-used target of scorn and blame for farmers was the banker, especially the invisible "big city" bankers who, many people were convinced, pulled the strings that manipulated the political system as well as the economy.

Farmers' complaints tended to address three major issues. First, farm prices had fallen sharply in the decade after Appomattox. Using an index base of 100, prices plunged from an index high of 161 in 1864 to less than half that in 1878. Declining prices reflected the general deflation that occurred in the late 1800s due to international conditions, but most critics focused their rhetoric on federal policies, dwelling on the government's refusal to monetize silver or issue new greenbacks (unbacked by gold). Lower prices for all goods, even those farmers purchased, did not alleviate agrarian distress, they argued, because farmers had signed long-term mortgages on their land whose rates did not change with other falling prices. Thus, farmers saw themselves drifting further behind other enterprises, with the only solution being an inflated money supply that would boost overall prices.[6]

Second, farmers depended heavily, and in some cases almost exclusively, on railroads and grain elevators that stored their grains until the trains arrived. In some cases, a relative monopoly existed, insofar as most areas had only one grain elevator or were close to one railroad. Even when others existed, farmers complained, they were so far away as to make real competition nonexistent. Railroads and the elevators, farmers alleged, then took advantage of their position to levy exorbitant rates.

Finally, although they could not express it in the political arena, farmers had come to the realization that they no longer constituted the majority of the population nor the most important wealth holders. While still praised by politicians and in popular literature, farmers did not dominate politics or the economy the way they had fifty years earlier. Even the Republican Party—the chief advocates of "free soil"— seemed a fading, ghostly ally. As the chasm that separated the image of the farmer from the reality of political and economic power widened, rural Americans expressed their anger and frustration through political organizations and protest movements.

Perceptions often *are* reality, of course, and certainly the cost of farming had climbed regularly in the late nineteenth century, attributable in large part to the rising real price of land and efficient new, but expensive, farm machinery. Farmers occasionally defrayed the cost of buying machinery by forming cooperatives. Mortgages, however, constituted a different problem. Most mortgages were short term—often three years or less—with large balloon payments required at the end of the mortgage period. Rural bankers, obviously, preferred such loans, yet why did borrowers also find them attractive? The loans permitted new borrowers—fresh faces in town—to establish a creditworthy reputation. And despite complaints that the monopoly power of the banks permitted them to charge exorbitant interest rates, "the evidence . . . suggests that the western mortgage industry was immensely competitive."[7] Other evidence contradicts the notion that farmers' mortgages made them susceptible to falling price levels: Short-term mortgages were readjusted in *current* (not constant) dollars every renewal. If prices fell, so did the mortgages after the renewals, usually within three years. Mortgage rates did not reflect a permanent condition. Moreover, farmers knew better than to borrow at levels their crop production could not support, as seen in foreclosure evidence, which showed the "risk of individual foreclosure was quite small," as low as 0.61 percent in Illinois in 1880 and 1.55 percent in Minnesota in 1891.[8]

As for the monopoly profits of railroaders, few lines even managed to maintain their rates, let alone increase them; freight rates fell along with crop prices, and even dropped faster than other prices after 1890.[9] Critics retorted that the issue was less an actual monopoly than arbitrary discrimination, where railroads charged shippers different rates. The criticism might have had validity if farmers had no options, and some monopolies exist for brief times in some areas. Regions in the far West, for example, frequently had only one railroad, and there rate discrimination against local shippers was possible. In the Midwest, however, where the clamor against the railroads reached its acme, few such monopolies survived. Jeffrey Williamson's study of railroad rates in Kansas found little to suggest farmers labored under excessive freight rates.[10] And as one moved toward the Atlantic Coast, between 1870 and 1900 rates fell by two-thirds, hardly suggesting exorbitant rate increases. Overall, as one survey of the literature concludes, "It is difficult to make a strong case for widespread victimization of the farmers."[11]

Still, it would be a mistake either to dismiss the agrarian discontent as simply irrational. Enough farmers joined organizations like the Grange and expressed their frustrations at the ballot box to conclude that many of them truly were struggling. But it would be equally erroneous to assume that farmers universally opposed corporations or other large business firms. Most of them did not hate business or want to socialize America, nor did organizations such as the Grange want to eliminate corporations, only reduce their power. Indeed, as farm historian David Danbom noted, early groups such as the Southern Alliance hoped to substitute fraternal support systems for the intrusive grip of industry.[12] Even the grand master of the National Grange told the Chicago Conference on Trusts in 1899 that the Grange hoped to frame legislation that would not interfere with legitimate enterprises or the development of the resources of the nation.[13] In that vein, the philosophy behind many of the "Granger Laws" regulating railroad rates rested on the premise that unequal or discriminatory rates violated freedom of enterprise and thus denied individual farmers, lumbermen, and merchants opportunities to engage in business activity due to an uneven playing field.[14]

So what do we conclude from the expressions of anger and fear coming from rural America in the late 1800s? Many historians, including perhaps the best analyst of the era, Richard Hofstadter, have observed that while only a minority of farmers experienced general distress, a much larger percentage *thought* times were hard. (A similar phenomena existed in the early 1990s.) In part, "psychic insecurity" in rural America occurred because land had become such a central component of the American dream that it almost represented an entitlement to some, while excesses by the railroads or occasional gouging by elevator operators was especially obvious to shippers. Other forces were also at work. Higher shipping rates drove land prices down relative to yield—but that had the inverse effect of making land more attractive to purchase. In a sense, Hofstadter was right: The real problem involved status and perceptions.

Increasingly, the emphasis, especially after the rise of the Progressives, was on what one *did* or what one *knew,* not who one was. The Jeffersonian notion of reverence for farmers qua farmers gave way to the concept that farmers, like any other part of the workforce, had to serve others with their products. And even farming succumbed to the changes in business organization that demanded professionalization and organizational structure; that was the impetus in part behind the Morrill Act, which sought "to make agriculture a scientific endeavor practiced by educated professionals."[15] Yet farmers were exempted from the constant chorus of criticism about "big business," and instead rural Americans' agrarian protests constituted the first of two major sources of impetus for regulation of business in the late 1800s (with the other being the the Progressive movement), culminating in the rise of the Populist Party.

Organizations of farmers had originated as early as 1867, when Oliver Kelley, a government appointee sent to the South to investigate agricultural conditions, created a secret fraternal society called the National Grange of the Patrons of Husbandry. The Grange swelled to more than 850,000 members by 1875, and was soon followed by similar groups, including the Farmers' Alliance in the 1880s. However, the most important of the farm protest organizations, the Populists, broadened their base by attracting miners and wage earners through their calls for an expanded money supply to alleviate farm credit problems.

The discovery of new silver veins had led to increased production of silver, shifting the ratio of silver ounces it took to buy an ounce of gold from 16:1 to 17:1, presenting an opportunity to inflate the money supply by requiring the government to buy and mint silver coins at the higher (artificial) price. When Congress passed the Coinage Act of 1873 (soon called "the Crime of '73"), it refused to mint the silver dollar, essentially recognizing that the nation had adopted a monometallic standard. Bimetallism, it has been argued, might have benefited the nation by reversing the general deflation.[16] Outraged silverites pressed for new legislation to coin and mint silver, including the Bland-Allison Act (1878), which required the government to buy large quantities of silver, but at market prices, not fixed inflationary prices. Silverite legislation finally passed in the form of the Sherman Silver Purchase Act (1890), with its related economic dislocations solved ultimately only by J. P. Morgan and the repeal of the act. Populist power reached its zenith in the election of 1896, when the Democratic Party nominated William Jennings Bryan of Nebraska for the presidency. Bryan fit the mold of the ideal Populist candidate so well that the Populist Party threw its support behind the Democrats. Bryan gave a stemwinder of a speech at the convention, warning the monied interests that "you shall not crucify mankind upon a cross of gold." The Republican Party, increasingly dominated by its own reform Progressives, rejected the call for "free silver" and offered William McKinley as its nominee and the gold standard as a primary plank in its platform.

McKinley won the election in what political scientists term one of many "watershed" elections in American history insofar as it solidified the Republican base for the next thirty years. More importantly for farmers, McKinley's victory destroyed the Populists as a political movement. Their longest-lasting contribution was an unwitting one: Populism served as the basis for the classic story *The Wonderful Wizard of Oz,* a remarkable tale on several levels, written by a remarkable businessman.

The *Wizard of Oz* as a Parable of Populism

Frank Baum, born into a wealthy New York family, had watched his father skim crude oil off the river that flowed through the fields. Benjamin Baum, Frank's father, established himself as a moving force in the Syracuse region, but young Frank had little interest in the oil business, preferring instead the entertainment and consumption side of capitalism.

As a teenager, Baum loved the theater, writing and producing plays and acting. In the midst of his acting "career," he fastened on merchandising, turning his focus to the sale of an axle grease made of crude oil under the name "Baum's Castorine Company." His wife toured with him, and her family had planted themselves in Aberdeen, South Dakota. By the late 1880s, Baum had established a retail store, Baum's Bazaar, along the lines of the F. W. Woolworth chain he had seen in Utica, New York. Baum honed his already substantial marketing skills in his new business, employing a steady stream of newspaper ads to sell Chinese lanterns, candy, cigarettes, ice cream, and other products. A depression that struck the region destroyed the economy, putting Baum's store out of business. While certainly not broke, Baum, out of work, turned his attention to a newspaper he acquired, writing almost everything in the paper.

That, too, proved short-lived, failing in 1891 because of the continued business blight. This time, Baum *was* broke, losing nearly all of his property. He moved again, to Chicago, arriving there in the midst of the building and sales boom accompanying the Columbian Exhibition. Having failed twice, Frank Baum stood on the threshold of his greatest success. After a brief stint with a newspaper, Baum took a position with a leading crockery and glass wholesaler, and before long he was on the road again. He thrived in the new business, emerging as one of the best salesmen in the company and regaining much of his fortune. Then, tired of the road, Baum hit upon a crucial change in merchandising.

Aware of a strong need on the part of Chicago retailers for show windows, Baum "had a plan, a method, a new display strategy that would show merchants how to move their goods and increase profits."[17] Modern retailers, he surmised, required a new treatment of goods based on new display techniques that could produce drawing power. The window offered the best sales tool of all, and Baum was particularly suited to decorating and presenting merchandise. Baum began publication of *The Show Window*, a heavily illustrated monthly journal replete with drawings and photographs and full of advertising. The journal instructed merchandisers in using lights, display arrangement, mechanical devices, and virtually anything to get consumers to look at the window. He also founded the National Association of Window Trimmers in 1898, which soon claimed 200 members. But Baum's reputation rested in large part on his journal, called by some the "Bible" of merchandise advertising.

Baum's writing skills extended well beyond advertising into children's books, and he published *The Wonderful Wizard of Oz* in 1900. It reflected his South Dakota years and demonstrated his writing skill, deftly weaving a simple story on the surface with a powerful Populist message buried underneath, yet retaining its entertaining quality for both children and adults.[18] In the story, Dorothy, living in Kansas—a hotbed of Populism—is lifted up and transported to Oz in a tornado. After all, the Populists thought of themselves as a whirlwind, disrupting "politics as usual" in Washington. Dorothy lands on the Wicked Witch of the East—an allusion to eastern capitalists—and is instructed by the Good Witch of the North to take the shoes off the deceased hag. Unlike the movie version, which had red slippers, Baum's shoes were silver.

Told to talk to the Wizard of Oz about returning to Kansas, Dorothy starts on her journey, where she encounters several characters symbolic of different elements in society. The Tin Woodsman had been a human lumberjack before the ax flew off and amputated a limb. With a metal ("bionic") arm, the Woodsman worked even faster, and subsequent accidents left him completely metal but extremely efficient, illustrating that, like the industrial workers, the more they adapted to mechanization, the more efficient, but less human, they became. The Woodsman, therefore, only wanted a heart. Next, Dorothy encountered the Scarecrow, who had admirable character traits but needed a brain, and who symbolized farmers. Finally, the party meets the Cowardly Lion, a caricature of all politicians, but most likely William Jennings Bryan, who needed courage, as the Populists thought Bryan weak on several issues. As the group travels the "yellow brick road," the picture of Dorothy's silver shoes on gold bricks paints a clear portrait of the Populist goal of bimetallism. Moreover, the motley group marching on Oz looked remarkably like Coxey's Army, a protest march on Washington led by Jacob Coxey in 1894.

When the group arrived at the Emerald City (ostensibly Washington, which even today virtually runs on greenbacks), they met the Wizard individually. To each character the Wizard appeared in a different form—just as politicians tend to say different things in front of different groups of voters. Each character must perform a task on a journey west, after which each will be granted his or her desire. The party encounters the Wicked Witch of the West, whom Dorothy defeats by dousing her with water: After all, the West's most pressing need was water, and water solves all the region's woes. Upon returning to the Wizard, the Woodsman learns he had a heart the entire time (he is the only one to cry!); the Scarecrow finds he had a brain (he devised a strategy for every emergency); and the Lion had courage in several incidents. The Wizard stands revealed as a little man, impotent and insignificant. Stripped of his office and regalia, he is like anyone else. But he had no way to return Dorothy to Kansas. She returns home only when the Good Witch of the North instructs her to click her heels together three times and say, "There's no place like home," symbolizing the expansion of the money supply by multiplying the silver on top of the gold.

The Wonderful Wizard of Oz saw print after the Populist movement itself was all but defunct. Politically, many of the agrarians in the Populists had moved into the Democratic Party, while many of those concerned with reforming business drifted to the Progressive wing of the Republican Party. Ironically, both the children's book Baum penned and the design concepts he advanced survived much longer than the ideas of the Populist Party about which he wrote.

Corporations under Assault

The prodigal lifestyles of business leaders and complaints by agrarians about railroads, banks, and elevators all contributed to the declining image of business in the late 1800s. Critics of business found yet another ally from a most unexpected source, business itself. Business enterprises had contributed to their own bad "press," from the excesses of the Fisk/Gould variety to criticisms of one business group by another, and of small business versus big. Small business owners continually blamed their problems on large corporations, and big business repeatedly sought protection or other special favors from government in the form of tariffs, land grants, or informal support of private collusive activities that injured smaller firms. (Adam Smith had warned that businessmen seldom even met except to conspire to fix prices.) Business was never monolithic, and even examples of several competitors in a single industry standing together were rare.

Of course, the scale and scope of some businesses had changed remarkably, making them as different from the owner-operated store as the space shuttle is from a Cessna. A single railroad could employ

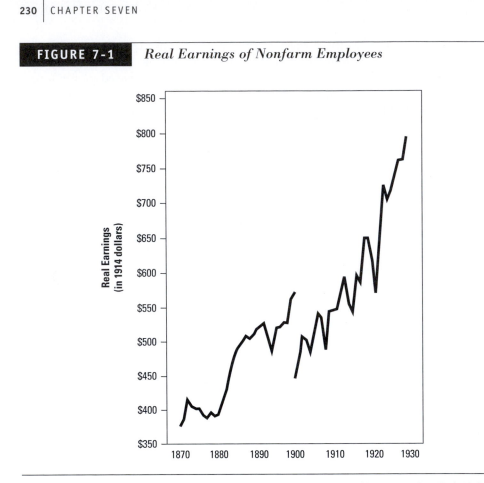

FIGURE 7-1   *Real Earnings of Nonfarm Employees*

Source: Stanley Lebergott, *Manpower in Economic Growth: The American Record Since 1800,* (New York: McGraw-Hill, 1964) p. 524. Copyright © 1964 by the McGraw-Hill Companies. Reprinted by permission of The McGraw-Hill Companies.

up to 36,000 people. As the numbers employed by large corporations in the industrial sector swelled, the damaging effects of depressions increased proportionately. Labor unrest and strikes could disable entire industries and unemploy whole towns; the introduction of new technology no longer threatened just a few artisans but vast numbers of skilled workers.

Increasingly, concerns over the power and wealth of the industrial sector smoldered, then ignited under new reformers known as Progressives. At the same time, an urbanized counterpart of the farmers' distress appeared among the new masses of factory workers. Factories, unlike small owner-operated firms, relied on mass production that fostered impersonal relationships between managers and laborers. Many capitalists viewed workers as another cog in the ma-

FIGURE 7-2				

Indexes of Real Wages for Adult Males in Northeastern Manufacturing by Geographic Area, Urbanization, and Size of Firm, 1820 to 1860

WEIGHTED*	1820	1832	1850	1860	PER ANNUM GROWTH RATE, 1820–1860
Middle Atlantic	100	122–143	159–202	157–188	1.2–1.6
Rural	90	118–139	131–166	166–199	1.6–2.1
Urban	111	150–176	165–209	154–185	0.8–1.3
Major urban	115	—	171–217	151–180	0.7–1.2
Small	81	93–108	129–163	140–168	1.4–1.9
Medium	106	128–151	142–180	163–195	1.1–1.6
Large	110	123–144	171–216	159–190	0.9–1.2
New England	101	131–154	149–188	164–197	1.3–1.7
Rural	95	133–156	143–181	156–187	1.3–1.8
Urban[†]	110	130–153	150–190	165–198	1.2–1.5
Major urban	122	170–200	154–195	182–218	1.0–1.5
Small[‡]	90	125–147	159–201	172–206	1.7–2.2
Medium	99	127–149	152–193	163–195	1.3–1.8
Large	110	133–157	146–185	164–196	1.0–1.5
Total	101	128–150	155–197	159–191	1.2–1.6

*Weighted averages are weighted by number of employees in each group. [†]Urban firms are those located in counties with a city of 10,000 or more; major urban, the same for 25,000 or more. [‡]Small, firms, 1 to 5 workers; medium, 6 to 15; large, 16 or more.

Source: Kenneth L. Sokoloff and Georgia C. Villafor, "The Market for Manufacturing Workers during the Early Industrialization: The American Northeast, 1820 to 1860," in *Strategic Factors in Nineteenth Century American Economic History: A Volume to Honor Robert W. Fogel,* ed. Claudia Goldin and Hugh Rockoff (Chicago: University of Chicago Press, 1992) p. 36.

chinery of industry—a standardized part to be used until worn out, then replaced. The fact that they paid laborers steadily higher wages did not mollify workers' anxieties. After all, real wages rose between 1860 and 1900 at the very time that overall prices were falling; real wages for manufacturing in 1865 hovered at just under $1 a day, then nearly doubled by 1890.[19] With a brief downturn between 1870 and 1880, real nonfarm earnings rose more than 60 percent from 1870 to 1900 (see Figure 7.1). From 1820 to 1860, real wages for adult males in most regions of the country rose over 1 percent per year, then after the Civil War increased "somewhat more rapidly after 1860 than before," at approximately 1.4 percent annually (see Figure 7.2).[20] But whereas factory work may once have represented only a brief phase in a laborer's career, preceding self-employment or farming, by the turn of the century factory work increasingly became a permanent position.

The Psychic Insecurity of Labor

The entire question of whether upward mobility still existed in America thus seemed appropriate. Sociologist C. Wright Mills proclaimed the end of opportunity for individuals to advance as early as 1840, and in 1893, historian Frederick Jackson Turner announced that the frontier was "closed," indicating that the possibility of farm ownership had forever disappeared.[21] Even education did not provide security, with stories abounding of college graduates unable to find advancement.[22] Such attitudes remained in place well into the 1930s, when a study concluded that "about ten per cent of the population produced seventy per cent of the contemporary business leaders and that the businessmen as a class were 112 times more productive than was the class of lowest paid laborers."[23] But not only is the use of such statistics subject to mischief, it was not supported by other evidence. A study of forty Scranton, Pennsylvania, founders and developers in 1880 revealed that "only nine of the forty leaders had even one son, son-in-law, or grandson who forty years later was an officer of even one corporation in Scranton." The fathers and sons, the author concluded, provided a "stunning contrast."[24]

Among prominent American families, one could point to successful offspring who followed in the founders' footsteps, such as William Vanderbilt, who emerged as a renowned railroader in his own right. Vanderbilt understood railroads, and invested in them accordingly. But none of Cornelius's other children did as well as William. In contrast to William Vanderbilt, Conrad Matthiessen, the son of a wealthy sugar-producing family, inherited management of the Glucose Sugar Refining Company, which he mismanaged by paying out high dividends instead of reinvesting in the manufacturing plants. But even Matthiessen worked his way into the business, starting as a production worker at $1.50 a day, then going to college, before gaining a management position. Examples of children who successfully ran the family business, such as Vanderbilt, were the exception, not the rule. It is true that the sons of most successful businessmen achieved a rank in the firm comparable to that of their father or grandfather. But holding a title in a corporation dominated by professional managers is a far cry from founding and creating a powerful enterprise and the wealth associated with it.

Some of the industrial giants, such as Carnegie, left no heirs to the business (explaining in part why he sold his company). With others, such as J. P. Morgan, the family line of exceptional bankers disappeared after his son, J. P. "Jack" Morgan, died. Banking, considered the epitome of the capitalist elite class, proved a remarkably mobile profession, yet one that did not lend itself well to succession. Into the middle of the nineteenth century, bankers almost universally came from the ranks of merchants, peddlers, farmers, or shipping agents, not from banking families.[25] Railroads, on the other hand, for a brief time permitted nepotism because a relative could hide in the bureaucracy, protected by layers of professional managers. As managerial hierarchies spread throughout industry, the sons of the early magnates often had lifetime jobs; but seldom did they run a company; still less did they run it well; and rarely if ever did they exceed the growth curve established by the founder. A survey of railroad managers or owners in the *Encyclopedia of American Business History and Biography* revealed that in the nineteenth and twentieth centuries combined, 171 men achieved the level of manager or above, with 106 listed heirs. Only 61 of the sons achieved the same level or above as their father or grandfather. This is, however, only a stark statistical assessment. More telling might be the number of sons who matched their father's or grandfather's *influence* on the company or the industry, based on the people viewed as worthy of inclusion by the *Encyclopedia's* editors. Based on that criterion, in the nineteenth-century volume, only in two out of thirty-four cases did sons of famous railroaders achieve a position of such influence that they rated a biography in the volume on their own merits, and both were Vanderbilts! The Commodore's son William and grandson Cornelius II both held official positions.

Nor were railroads unique. In the same *Encyclopedia* series for "Iron and Steel in the 19th Century," compiled by different editors, 184 men attained the level of manager or above, with 127 listed heirs, but only 64 of the sons achieved the same level as their father or grandfather. Of those thought worthy of inclusion in the *Encyclopedia,* only one had a son or grandson who was in management before 1900. In banking and the auto industry, the totals were higher for the heirs who achieved the same level as their predecessors, but again, the numbers deemed important enough for inclusion in biographical volumes remained tiny. And the fact that a son inherited the business certainly did not ensure its success; for every James B. Duke, who improved upon his father's enterprise, there were dozens of Remingtons who presided over decline.[26] In an even more modern industry, airlines, of sixteen industry leaders, *none* had a son or grandson who reached a level of prominence in the industry sufficient for selection to the *Encyclopedia.*[27] A survey of the *Encyclopedia* volumes does underscore the fact that the children of the wealthy business classes had an initial advantage, as illustrated by the number of sons of railroaders who worked in management. Nevertheless, it also suggests that those advantages fizzled out in a professional sense fairly quickly, and that by the third generation, few benefited from their grandfathers' positions.

Nevertheless, the specialization of the new managerial hierarchies militated against a rapid rise to riches through the corporate ladder without the benefit of technical and/or professional training and education. Carnegie's promotion of Bill Jones stood out as unique. Usually, the new managerial class consisted of professionals who had training in mechanical engineering, accounting, banking, or other specialized areas. They attempted to separate and segregate themselves further through the establishment of professional journals and societies. Laborers who through hard work within the corporation ended up in the boardroom became rare. Instead, those of meager backgrounds who successfully stormed the corporate gates did so through new ideas that allowed them to form their own firms, in essence sidestepping the corporate ladder in favor of the elevator.

Several studies have disputed the "rags-to-riches myth." Most of those studies, using samples of business leaders or CEOs of large corporations, found few coming from lower-class families or unskilled workers. William Miller, for example, studying more than 200 leaders of early-twentieth-century corporations, found that fewer than 3 percent started as immigrants or American farm boys.[28] Others, such as C. Wright Mills, used biographical entries from the *Dictionary of American Biography* to conclude that business elites virtually always came from money, with fewer than 3 percent coming from working-class families.[29] Herbert Gutman, however, conducted a case study of Paterson, New Jersey; he found that while it was true that people who had started life as workers seldom headed major existing corporations, they started their own businesses in droves. Gutman, recording fantastic upward mobility, concluded that "so many successful manufacturers who had begun as workers walked the streets of the city [between 1830 and 1880] that it is not hard to believe that others less successful or just starting out on the lower rungs . . . could be convinced by personal knowledge that 'hard work' resulted in spectacular material and social improvement."[30] While Carnegie's ascent is remembered by most students of business, forgotten were the dozens of other partners, many of them engineers, who also grew wealthy by contributing small but important technology or physical capital to the Carnegie companies. Indeed, the managerial revolution had brought a new emphasis on education and technical expertise, but often the most stellar career histories frequently belonged to men (and, by the latter part of the nineteenth century, women) of limited education and formal training.

The immediate effect in the late nineteenth century, though, of the stratification between management and labor was to create the impression that upward mobility had slowed. Factory laborers did not see their counterparts who moved on to start new businesses; instead, they saw professional managers directing their activities based on credentials that most of the laborers never hoped to attain. Factory conditions exacerbated the concerns of laborers. Often unsafe, factory work more often was numbing in its mechanization. An early 1900 volume called *Work in America,* written by a task force working for the Department of Health, Education, and Welfare, found that "significant numbers of Americans are dissatisfied with the quality of their working lives. Dull, repetitive, seemingly meaningless tasks are causing discontent among workers at all occupational levels."[31]

More than the nature of work had changed. The composition of the labor force itself added to workers' insecurity and perceived career stagnation of the new industrial system. A growing number of immigrant workers arrived at Ellis Island with "irregular" work habits. Some of those work habits were so "irregular" that "Great Lakes dock workers 'believed that a vessel could not be unloaded unless they had from four to five kegs of beer.'"[32] Moreover, the dramatic shift from rural-oriented, village-centered artisan labor to urban-centered factory work involved more than just the time employees spent on the shop floor. It represented an entire shift of work habits and culture. No longer could workers imbued in the artisan tradition alternate bursts of intense labor and idleness whenever it suited them; the factory demanded regular hours and production. As social historian Herbert Gutman reported, the practice of starting the "real" workweek on Tuesday was widespread, and illustrated by coopers, who used Mondays to sharpen tools, obtain stock, and discuss current events in preparation for the week: "Thus, 'Blue Monday' was something of a tradition with the coopers. . . ."[33]

Some immigrants brought with them a distrust of industrialism, fearing that capitalism fostered dependence and "proletarianism." Their attitudes were reflected in the movements for currency reform, railroad regulation, the rise of trade unions, and in calls for social welfare legislation. But whatever their hesitations about business, overall they understood the opportunities that free enterprise offered. Many immigrant groups coming from southern and eastern Europe, with its depressed economies and oppressive governments, saw in American capitalism great opportunities despite the dangerous factory work, the long hours, and, what for "old stock" Americans might seem low pay (ignoring the fact that their own ancestors had come to North America as low-paid soldiers, landless peasants, or common artisans). From 1891 to 1910, immigrants from Italy, Austria-Hungary, and Russia alone exceeded seven million; and Chinese, especially, came to the United States in large numbers, with husbands working for years to bring their families over at later dates. In 1882, the government enacted restrictions on Chinese immigration, the only group to be so singled out, due to both racism and pressure from labor groups. Overall, the tides of people longing to escape even relatively advanced nations of Europe for the still greater possibility of economic advancement in America brought millions of new citizens into the economy.

Social Critics of Capitalism

Immigrant workers coming from Europe, in particular, left an industrial system that had started to adopt social security, accident insurance, and other social welfare programs, and at the same time had powerful trade unions. Yet, even as millions of laborers abandoned the European systems, American critics of enterprise began to call for exactly those reforms in U.S. industry. Social commentators such as Henry George espoused concepts of wealth redistribution that had originated with Karl Marx twenty to thirty years earlier. Marx's fundamental underlying principle was that all value derived from labor, even the contributions of capital, which represented a type of sunk labor. The "labor definition of value" was not original to Marx; he had lifted it—typically, for Marx, without ever giving credit to anyone else—from Pierre Proudon, Claude Saint-Simon, and, most importantly, English socialist Robert Owen. Indeed, while it is unclear who first created the term "socialism," Owen's newspaper is credited with being the first to use it in print in 1827. According to the theory, labor, and only labor, makes value. All else, including the contributions of natural resources and capital, represents past effort of others.

If it is easy to see the absurdity of such a doctrine, it is equally easy to understand the attraction it had to workers in industrialized countries. Marx at once was both simple and obtuse. His ideas ultimately were reducible to extremely simple concepts, but he hedged and concealed his ideas, even changing them over time, making it difficult to "prove" where he stood on particular issues.[34] Marx argued that, while "vague," it was a fact that "the value of commodities is determined by the labor contained in them."[35] In its most simplistic form, if the concept were true, a person could dig a hole in the Sahara and have created value. Service to others is irrelevant, because it was assumed that any labor served others. The wants and demands of individuals, and their ability to choose for themselves what was valuable, were all considered by Marx to be merely attitudes determined by one's class. But typically Marx clouded the entire discussion by contending that prices themselves were an artifact of the capitalist system and could not be set by governments.[36] Whatever Marx meant—and scholars have penned dozens of volumes trying to explain him (often without quoting him at all!)—by the late nineteenth century in America, "Marxist" ideas had come to be identified primarily with a group of social reformers and a segment of the labor movement that desired radical change in control over the "means of production" (i.e., land and capital).

From that perspective, the value derived directly from labor represented the true value in society, and any profit derived from "only" owning land was targeted as "unearned." Henry George's *Progress and Poverty* (1879) used such an approach to argue for a "single tax" on revenue derived from land. Sales of *Progress and Poverty* topped two million, bringing George substantial "surplus value" in the form of royalties! For all his income, George lived in almost constant debt, existing "in a helter-skelter sort of life—working as a clerk, sailor, printer, and, peddler—searching for gold, sleeping in barns, agitating," even wearing borrowed clothes to his own wedding.[37] George, though one of the first reformers, was certainly neither the last nor the most famous. In 1888, Edward Bellamy published *Looking Backward,* in which the hero falls asleep in 1887 and awakes more than 100 years later to a utopian society in which the government owned all factories and businesses, but Bellamy cloaked it in softer language and a general appeal to nationalism, differing substantially in tone from other works. Henry Lloyd's *Wealth Against Commonwealth* (1894) epitomized the more straightforward hostile attacks, and was described as a "prolonged diatribe against the Standard Oil Company and a call for nationalization of the trusts."[38] As the financial editor for the *Chicago Tribune,* Lloyd had ample opportunity to express his anti-Standard views, and in an article for the *Atlantic Monthly* he described the company as "the greatest, wisest, and meanest monopoly known to history."[39] Attacking Standard Oil and other large corporations proved a popular way to sell magazines and books, but it often represented little more than facades for personal revenge. Lloyd, for example, while denouncing John D. Rockefeller—who had done more to lower the price of kerosene and oil for the American consumer than any other individual alive—was related to an unhappy oil man. Ida Tarbell, whose "History of Standard Oil Company," serialized in *McClure's* (1902) and later published as a book, remains a monument to the new craft of "muckraking," but the author did not publicize the fact that her father was a disgruntled Pennsylvania oil producer and competitor of Rockefeller.[40] But muckracking sold, and magazines such as *Life, Harper's* and *Collier's* all joined the chorus of Standard Oil critics.

Matthew Josephson managed to synthesize the individual attacks on all the large corporations into a single, convenient volume, *The Robber Barons* (1934).[41] While presenting no substantially new charges, the book offered an across-the-board attack on virtually all sectors of business, epitomizing the view that the few had gained at the expense of the many. But it did not reach middle-class Americans the way a more graphic novel, *The Jungle* (1906), by Upton Sinclair, did.[42] Sinclair described the experiences of Jurgis, a Lithuanian immigrant who arrived in Chicago with the dream of working hard in order to own a home. Soon, however, the entire family finds itself laboring twelve hours a day in horrid conditions, including shoveling manure until covered with it from head to toe. The most grotesque scenes involved the meat-packing plants, in which sausage was dyed to conceal rot and disease and where workers routinely fell into meat-cutting machinery without so much as a stop in the line. Jurgis begins to drink, and he and his family fall deeper in debt. With that story, Sinclair hoped to provoke a socialist revolution in the United States, much the way Marx hoped to ignite a communist revolution with *The Communist Manifesto* (1848). Instead of spurring revolution, *The Jungle* stirred Americans to demand government quality control for food and drugs. The result was the Pure Food and Drug Act (1906) and the creation of the Food and Drug Administration.

Nor did tales of the dangers or working conditions in factories dissuade millions of immigrants from pouring into the United States. Where Sinclair and George saw only oppression and evil, people around the world saw opportunity, freedom, and hope. When Tarbell and Lloyd railed against the shackles of capitalism, immigrants all but beat down the doors to get into America. While to most social critics, American business constituted an impediment to "real" progress, to millions of people around the world, American business *was* real progress.

Immigrant Entrepreneurs

One eastern European immigrant couple, Hyman and Rebecca Cohen, had come to the United States in the 1860s to escape the pogroms visited upon Jews in that region of the world. Hyman Cohen made hats and expected to send all of his nine sons to college. One son, Joshua Lionel, enrolled in Peter Cooper Institute, then proceeded to ignore his studies—with the exception of a technical shop class. As a teenager, he developed an electric doorbell, but dropped the idea (probably the first such doorbell) when a teacher convinced him it had no practical value. He next set out to create what he called an "electric flowerpot," which was a tube with a battery at one end and a lightbulb at the other, illuminating a plant inside. Conceived as a decorative device, the flowerpot flopped, although Cohen sold the rights to a restauranteur, Conrad Hubert, who then took out the flowers and sold only the handheld light as the Everready Flashlight. Hubert and Joshua Lionel Cohen became millionaires from the project.

Cohen continued to invent, creating a mine detonator for the U.S. Navy and earning a respectable $12,000. At only twenty-three years of age, Cohen and a friend founded the Lionel Manufacturing

Co., working on their first product, a small, fan-driven wooden railroad car and strip of track for use in display windows. Frank Baum's glass display windows had only started to enjoy widespread use as a sales tool, and the circular wooden train seemed a natural to attract attention. Indeed it did. The first day, the store owner returned to Cohen's office to request six more trains to sell! Only then did Joshua Lionel Cohen realize that he had in his "Lionel Train" a children's toy and not a window display item. He quickly added metal tracks, miniature suspension bridges, and electric-powered cars, advertising his toys through a catalog that by the 1950s was the third most widely distributed catalog behind those of Sears and Montgomery Ward.

By then, Cohen had Americanized his name as Cowen and manufactured not just trains but a childhood rite of passage: Every young boy had to have a Lionel Train (as did the author!). His ads focused on father-son relationships and spurred model railroad building as a hobby for adults. Ultimately, the end of the railroad era and the arrival of the jazzier space age caused the decline of the business, until in 1958 Cowen sold his interest and retired.

It is misleading to suggest, however, that only the downtrodden, politically oppressed, or poor saw opportunity in America. The "land of the free" held out the promise of improvement for people of almost any means or background. A shining example of this was Adolphus Busch, a salesman with a St. Louis brewery, who came from a wealthy family.[43] His father had a brewer's supply company in Germany, making it possible for Adolphus to attend the most prestigious schools. The large Busch family (Adolphus was the youngest of twenty-one children) was neither poor nor oppressed, but Adolphus concluded that his opportunities, even with access to a family business, were better in America. In the depression year of 1857, Busch arrived in the St. Louis and started at the bottom of the ladder, working as a clerk with a wholesale firm. Busch's father died in 1859, leaving him an inheritance that allowed him to go into business selling supplies to local breweries. At that point he met Eberhard Anheuser, who had been the principal creditor to the Bavarian Brewery in St. Louis. Anheuser had struggled, lacking a knowledge of the brewing business and taking as a receiver the assets of a company that scarcely stood out among dozens of German beer makers in the city. When Busch married Anheuser's daughter, he acquired an interest in the brewery and improved the beer's sales.

Busch proved a spectacular salesman, developing a trademark jackknife with the company's logo with a peephole at one end, which revealed to Busch a picture of Busch himself. He also procured beautiful delivery wagons that he drove through the streets with teams of show horses. Flash and glitter, however, only took the mediocre beer so far. Busch had to have a higher quality product for the business to grow. In 1876, a friend brought back a recipe for a new beer that he had tasted in the German village of Budweis. That beer had a natural carbonation from a European brewing process called kraeusening, providing not only an unusually smooth texture but also preserving the flavor over long periods even after bottling. Employing the sales techniques that had served him well with an inferior product, Busch attacked the market with his high-quality "Budweiser" beer, hosting parties for customers in which he introduced his new beer. Trays and posters bearing the Budweiser logo were given out freely, and even 100 years later the Clydesdale horses pulling the beer wagons are familiar symbols of a quality alcoholic beverage.

While already making a fine beer, Busch endeavored to develop a higher quality drink that would appeal to elites—a beer that liquor drinkers might consider in lieu of brandies or wines. He produced a draft-only beer called Michelob in 1896. Since the beer was sold only in draft, Busch had to provide an "infrastructure" to support it, establishing a railroad distribution system that used refrigerated railroad cars and a string of icehouses along rail routes. With products like Budweiser and Michelob, Anheuser-Busch surpassed the national leader, Pabst, in 1901 as the largest beer producer in the United States, with sales of one million barrels annually.

Bootleggers and Teetotalers: Family Businesses in the Corporate Age

Beer production, like other items requiring processing in volume, reached ever increasing levels of efficiency in the late 1900s. Ultimately, successful entrepreneurs had to find ways to mass produce and sell even specialized products such as Budweiser. Nevertheless, amidst a growing number of manager-dominated companies, family firms still survived and thrived. Two such businesses involved competitors, of a sort, to Anheuser-Busch. At age seven, Jack Newton Daniel had started to learn the secrets of distilling fine whiskey from sour mash, and the source of his knowledge, of all people, was a Lutheran minister.[44] When the minister's congregation forced him to abandon his hobby, he offered the business to Jack, then only thirteen years old. Jack Daniel shipped his product from Lincoln County, Tennessee, to Huntsville, Alabama, during the Civil War, selling first to the Confederates then to the Union occupiers. After the war, he moved his still to Lynchburg, Tennessee, where he found a location with particularly sterile water, which Daniel then purified again through a filter of charcoal. Unlike Busch, Daniel had no extensive sales network, but his "Old No. 7" whiskey achieved widespread fame by word of mouth. By 1890, he was the largest sour-mash maker in Tennessee, and a wealthy man. But he never created a management structure to distribute or sell his product; only after he passed his company on to his nephew, Lemeul Motlow, did the business take on the form of a modern corporation.

Jack Daniel had a great deal in common with another entrepreneur, Dr. Thomas Welch. Both were extremely devout and religious men—Daniel a Baptist and Welch a Methodist. Obviously, however, Daniel read the passages in the Bible admonishing men to not be drunk with wine as allowing room for other spirits! Welch, on the other hand, so detested alcoholic beverages that he "cringed at the thought" of using an intoxicant like wine in church communion services.[45] As a dentist, Welch often accepted fruit in lieu of cash for his services, providing him the raw material he needed to search for an alternative "wine" beverage. Nightly he experimented with treating grapes so they would not ferment, which he accomplished by putting the grape juice in pots of boiling water, destroying the yeast particles in the fruit. Having successfully produced a nonalcoholic grape juice, Welch discovered that churches wanted no part of it. Traditional, fermented wine remained a staple of communion. Welch's son, Thomas, envisioned the grape juice as a commercial product. Using a $5,000 loan from his father, Thomas Welch created a production facility, coined the name "Welch's Grape Juice," and, following the lead of the "Pickle King," Henry Heinz, Welch gave out free samples at the Columbian Exposition. More importantly, he gained entrance into broader sectors of society through ads in national magazines, devising clever puzzles and gimmicks for the promotions.

Thomas Welch never lost touch with his father's original goal, promoting temperance, and one of his ads featured a young woman with a glass of grape juice and the caption, "The lips that touch Welch's are all that touch mine." When Prohibition was enacted, the company spent $575,000 a year on advertising that emphasized its nonalcoholic quality, at which time Welch's had started to develop the managerial hierarchies similar to those in place at other food-processing firms.

Mass Production and the Quest for Efficiency

Although some companies, like Jack Daniel and Welch's, straggled behind, a trend clearly was in place whereby large companies achieved higher levels of production and more efficient distribution by changing their control structure to that of a managerial hierarchy. In turn, managerial hierarchies had imposed vertical combinations on most industries. For such operations, labor had to perform different tasks—in different ways, and at a different pace—than ever before in the past. The relaxed, careful artistry of skilled craftsmen in Whitney's musket shop or Baldwin's locomotive works had long since given way to a frenetic, often dehumanizing, pace of laborers assembling machinery, slaughtering animals, pouring chemicals, or shoveling piles of fertilizer. Factory work, even when demanding highly skilled labor, such as the manufacture of steel, still tended to be repetitious, noisy, and, above all, dangerous. Carnegie's best manager, "Captain" Bill Jones, died in a furnace explosion—a fate that claimed hundreds of steel workers a year with less publicity. Coal mines caved in; catwalks collapsed over moving machinery; and fingers, hands, arms, and legs disappeared daily in a blizzard of moving gears and slashing blades.

Labor grudgingly adjusted, and with acceptance came a certain competence, bringing improvement in safety as well as demands that factory owners improve conditions. The most serious complaint for workers was neither hours nor pay, but loss of job autonomy to the bosses. That was epitomized by the shift in practice from each worker bringing his own tools to the appearance of furnished work stations. Individuality vanished even more when managers started to examine the laborers' physical movements to identify wasteful motion and energy.

From management's viewpoint, coordination and control over the activities of its labor force involved more than squeezing out marginal efficiency gains. By 1900, the sheer size of a factory workforce could dwarf the number of employees at a large company fifty years earlier. Plants employed thousands, as in the case of the McCormick factory in Chicago with its 4,000 workers in 1900 and 15,000 employees in 1916.[46] Other plants, such as Ford's Highland Park, Michigan, facility counted more than 33,000 workers. Management, by then obsessed with efficiency gains as a means of providing stability for their companies, saw the direction of labor as crucial to achieving the rule of the "visible hand."

Directing the productivity of labor on such a scale demanded structures and tactics unheard of by a Jack Daniel with his personal sales of whiskey, or to Lydia Pinkham with her family operation. Factory management relied upon discipline, organization, and a steady stream of seamless effort from workers. Yet managers realized that not every employee could produce with the same efficiency or equality of talent. That led a metal manufacturer named Frederick W. Halsey to create "gain-sharing plans," which in essence meant higher pay for higher output, or a rudimentary piecework system. Another metalworks manager, Henry Towne, had presided over the introduction of a system in 1884 that used a contract with the workforce to share any per-unit savings with all employees. Up to 40 percent of the savings that the company received from increased productivity went to line workers, while foremen received smaller shares.[47]

Taylorism and Scientific Management

By the 1880s, most managers had investigated a number of ways to improve the productivity of labor, and certainly many of them were a far cry from the Simon Legree image of a black-clad, mustachioed overseer brandishing a whip on the backs of helpless wage laborers. On the other hand, managers tended to view workers as pieces of machinery to be fine-tuned, not human creations to be encouraged and nurtured to attain greater accomplishments. The classic example of this view of labor was a Midvale Steel Company manager named Frederick W. Taylor, who had introduced a variable wage rate based on individual production, called a "differential piece rate." Taylor's greater fame, however, emerged from a process he called "scientific management," first appearing in "Shop Management," a 1903 article for a professional journal, then later (1915) expanded into his famous book, *The Principles of Scientific Management,* called the "most influential work on management ever published."[48] Taylor's "scientific management" typified the Progressive-era reliance on statistics to evaluate and science to govern a wide range of human activities from criminal justice to municipal planning. He emphasized, for example, time-and-motion studies, in which he used a stopwatch to determine a standard time in which each task in a factory could be performed. Based on that standard time, workers either received higher or lower piece rates according to their output. Contrary to the fears of the workers, Taylor never favored increasing production without a systematic and equal increase in wages. Indeed, the greatest difficulty Taylor faced was in convincing management (which had to be scientifically reorganized as well) that the sum total of productivity improvements would generate more than enough revenue to pay the higher wages.[49]

Monitoring the work of the line laborers, Taylor proposed a system of administration that relied on an elaborate eight-layer structure of clerks and bosses, including a "shop disciplinarian," who reviewed the workers' "virtues and defects" and assisted them in making corrections.[50] An earlier attempt by Taylor to supervise a system of controls using slips filled out by the foremen and workers had proven unworkable, as no one wanted to spend the time to fill out the papers properly. Even under his new scientific system, Taylor's approach tended to lack a clear chain of command, focusing, as one critic of the day said, on the specifics of individual tasks rather than on the production processes of the entire organization. But it still constituted an improvement over most other management systems, and Taylor rapidly became known as a guru whose advice enabled ordinary managers to extract extraordinary production out of their labor forces.

Consequently, other businesses quickly copied Taylor's methods: Remington's typewriter factory created its own "department of productive efficiency," charged with studying all manufacturing methods and labor activities.

Taylor had intense opposition, however. Unions, of course, attempted to block imposition of piecework at every turn. Taylor found management even more difficult than labor, with managers consistently failing to follow the principles he laid out. Congress went so far as to outlaw time study and incentives in 1915 at the crest of the Progressive tide. It was a losing battle. After World War II, U.S. experts introduced Taylorism into Japanese factories, where, without the union and government opposition that existed in America, they took root. While Japanese management methods were widely hailed by the 1970s, works such as *Japan in the Passing Lane* recounted the human cost of some Taylorite methods. Nevertheless, the tension between management in its quest for greater efficiency and higher output, and labor, concerned with personal rights and the desire to be treated as humans instead of machines, has continued not only in Japan but in the United States well into the 1990s.

Even when the structures did not work as well as they should, the size and scope of production required an orderly flow of information, which, in the best systems, went through a series of filters from top management to the line foremen. At each step, managers took what they needed to know and passed on only what the next group needed. Despite the skill and common sense of many of the workers, most had neither the education nor the information to place their work in the context of the firm's larger business strategy, giving managers a key role in information transmission. With far more information available than workers could use, absorb, or apply in the context of their specific tasks, managers served as valuable intermediaries between the strategic decisions at the top and the actual productive process at the bottom.

The role of managers took on added importance after 1890, when new waves of unskilled immigrants reached American shores. Managers assumed that they needed to monitor their workforce more closely, but labor and management alike realized that the new highly technical processing machinery required more than reorganization of the workplace itself. As W. Elliot Brownlee observed, "The bias of technical change and the falling relative price of capital created incentives not only for swift capital formation but also for market improvements in the quality of labor."[51] Accountants in the organizations appreciated the waste and inefficiency of ill- or undertrained labor. Clearly in an era when Gustavus Swift was dipping his finger in the streams behind his slaughterhouses to determine the amount of fat, and therefore the degree of waste from his plants, the potential productivity gains from an educated and skilled workforce did not escape the efficiency-obsessed managers of the late nineteenth century. Thus, business participated in widespread efforts to improve education, whether within public schools or at the new trade schools. Resources devoted to education in the United States doubled between 1860 and 1900, with businesses seeing an opportunity to enlist the contributions of taxpayers in their drive to improve labor efficiency. From that perspective, it certainly worked, in that expenditures for public education rapidly outpaced expenditures for private-sector education. Business also realized—as many critics of American capitalism were quick to point out—that public education provided a convenient introduction to factory-style organization with its structure and its management of tasks according to the clock. Critics rightly maintained that education socialized recent immigrants for the purposes of patriotism and introduced some of them to structured organizational settings. Certainly education served to "Americanize" the foreign-born. English language classes, reading, writing, and basic math all enhanced the value of an immigrant child as a future worker.

Despite the influx of relatively unskilled labor and the difficulties in measuring productivity at the time (Taylor's claims notwithstanding), it appears that wages rose in close proximity to productivity increases (or about 1.3–1.5 percent annually). Perhaps equally important, however, workers enjoyed greater amounts of leisure time, reducing both the workweek and the individual workday. Contrary to Sinclair's depiction of poor Jurgis toiling away for fourteen-plus hours a day, the number of hours worked by the average laborer had *declined steadily* since 1860. A typical workweek consisted of sixty hours as early as the 1880s, but by 1914 had dropped to just over fifty-five hours.[52] And the workweek continued to shrink, in part due to the electrification of factories. As the work hours were reduced, however, business expected increased attendance and attention from its labor force. Gates on factories combined with time clocks to regulate when workers could arrive, leave, or take lunch breaks; companies levied fines or dismissed employees who were chronically absent; and talking or wandering around the workplace without direction could bring disciplinary action.

Labor, naturally, reacted to the increased mechanization and control over workers' lives with dismay. One response, the formation of unions, has received considerable attention and evoked romantic portrayals of labor's pioneer leaders, but prior to 1900 the movement itself remained small and highly concentrated in a few industries. As of 1900, less than 3 percent of the workforce was unionized, and, indeed, until the 1842 Supreme Court decision *Commonwealth v. Hunt*, government treated labor unions as "conspiracies." The general rising wage levels had made it difficult to organize large segments of labor.

After the Civil War, however, labor organizations found new life in mass production, which inadvertently lumped all workers together by wage scales and working hours. Large numbers of workers, suddenly bound together by the factory whistle and, soon, Taylor's stopwatch, had far more in common than had many of the skilled artisans of earlier "factories."

Terence V. Powderly's Knights of Labor, while not the first national union, was the first to claim such a title. Hoping to attract workers of all types, skilled and unskilled, Powderly's organization enlisted over 700,000 by 1886 but it became unwieldy and unfocused, even allowing farmers as members. An incident in 1886 at Chicago's Haymarket Square doomed the Knights of Labor when a protest against the McCormick Reaper Works turned into a riot as a bomb exploded in the crowd, killing ten and injuring dozens. Although anarchists loosely associated with the Knights had called the meeting for their own purposes, a jury nevertheless convicted eight Knights members of murder. The episode ended the Knights as a force and provided a lesson that unions had to screen their members carefully—especially in light of the fact that government at that time was clearly not in their corner—and stay focused on economic issues.[53]

Samuel Gompers Unionizes America

It would be hard to overstate the role of Samuel Gompers in improving the life of American skilled laborers. Gompers, an immigrant like so many other wage earners, arrived in the United States from England less than a month after Pickett's ill-fated charge at Gettysburg. When Gompers disembarked into the streets of New York City, the looting that had accompanied the draft riots had only recently subsided. In England Gompers had worked as a cigarmaker, a trade in which one of the workers usually served as a "reader," providing an oral summary of the important newspapers and magazines of the day to other workers in the quiet shop. Thus, if lacking a formal education, the workers acquired a general knowledge about current events and assessed the opinions prominent in the publications of the day. A natural organizer, Gompers had read Marx, but apparently adopted only a bit of rhetoric needed for his own purposes.[54] Nevertheless, Gompers rejected radicalism in the union and excluded from any role in union policy any intellectuals who were not genuine laborers. He appreciated the crucial role that coordinated effort played in the success of a union, and he intended to eliminate "wildcat" (unauthorized) strikes in his trade union, even if it meant allying with management in the process.

Despite his European background, he did not fear industrialization's effects on labor in the way some radicals did. On the contrary, he wanted laborers to control and master the change, not be controlled by it. By insisting that the unions make good on contracts, even those that left their members at a disadvantage, Gompers ensured that he would gain public support when management reneged on some of its contracts. Gompers appreciated the weaknesses of Powderly's scheme, especially in its goal of uniting skilled and unskilled workers. In a sense, he secured the labor unions for labor, eliminating the rancorous radicals that alienated the public or the pompous intellectuals who had little in common with the rank-and-file. By focusing his efforts on skilled labor only, he gave the union a weapon to fight with, namely the skills of its members. Basing his efforts on an earlier organization called the Federation of Trades, Gompers created a new union to replace the Knights of Labor called the American Federation of Labor (AFL), organized in 1886. Founded at the very time Powderly's Knights reached its apex, the AFL was threatened by the larger Knights but quickly attracted many of the skilled workers from that organization. Gompers did not avoid conflict when necessary, but otherwise he stressed policies that brought labor into the very middle class that previously had distrusted it.[55] The AFL stuck to the "bread and butter" issues of wage increases and shorter workweeks, and sided with the middle class on policy matters such as literacy tests for immigrants. Moreover, Gompers had the philosophy of preparing the union for strikes and using the strike only as a last resort, preferring to wait for victory instead of rushing to defeat. Thanks in large part to Gompers's strategic vision, by 1893 the AFL had over a quarter of a million members.

The union's general compliance with the law gave it a much stronger base of support with the public than the Knights or other rival unions enjoyed. Gompers realized that until the labor movement convinced businesses and voters that it posed no threat to social harmony or economic growth, it would face opposition from each, manifested in frequent applications of state power against labor. In 1877, President Rutherford B. Hayes had used federal troops to break the railroad strike; in 1892, state troops ended the Homestead Strike that had resulted in the defeat of the Pinkertons; and in 1894 President Grover Cleveland used federal soldiers to end the Pullman Strike.

More damaging to the labor movement on a daily basis were the various tools industry used to resist unions, including the "yellow dog" contract (in which a prospective employee had to agree not to join a union as a condition of work), the blacklist (a list of organizers or "troublemakers" circulated to all local employers), the injunction (a court order restricting strike activity), and highly effective harassment techniques available to public officials at all levels, from sheriffs to tax collectors. Business tried to paint labor leaders as nuisances at best, and at worst as anarchists bent on the destruction of the capitalist economy. Certainly most were no such thing. On the other hand, neither were they the saints often portrayed by modern-day Hollywood (*Coal Miner's Daughter* or *Matewan,* for example). Unions did not hesitate to use fists and clubs to keep renegade members and defectors in line, while strikebreakers ("scabs," as they were called)—often little more than hungry unemployed former skilled workers themselves—suffered worse fates at union workers' hands.

Progressive legislation figured prominently in changing the face of the workplace, though not always for the most admirable reasons. The shrinking workweek, for example, "coincided with adoption of laws limiting hours of work for women," in no small measure because male-dominated trade unions championed the legislation to exclude competition from women.[56] But shorter workweeks also stood squarely in the middle of Gompers's approach of identifying achievable, tangible results as opposed to the lofty, often illusory, goals of radicals and socialists. Shorter workweeks enhanced the worker's independence and reduced his actual working time. Organized labor, led by Gompers, joined business in supporting restrictions on immigration and on child labor.[57] Such measures—whatever their motivation—reflected the gradually increasing influence of labor (although union membership still did not exceed 10 percent prior to World War I), and, more important, the willingness of Americans to use the government to redress perceived inequalities in business. Nevertheless, despite the contributions of Gompers and the gains of organized labor, the modest shifts in labor law paled in comparison to the broader and more substantial uses of government power against corporations in the arena of antitrust law, which accelerated under the Progressive movement.

Regulating Industry: From "Sunshine" to Sherman

State and federal regulation brought together the separate streams of protest in the agrarian sector and within industrial labor, merging the conceptual rapids of high idealism from socialists like Bellamy and George with the calmer waters of pragmatism represented by reformers like Charles Francis Adams. While people quickly identified the names of Sinclair, Lloyd, Tarbell, and George, it was Adams who played the more critical role in changing the face of regulation, earning him inclusion as one of four "prophets of regulation" in Thomas McCraw's multiple biography.[58] The public knew Adams from his publication of "Chapter of Erie" in the *North American Review* (1869), among numerous other articles he wrote for that journal. Viewing railroads as having acquired an identity and character unique among all businesses, Adams contended that a lag had occurred between the evolution of the railroad industry and the institutions developed by the public to respond to it. Adams argued for creation of a permanent, apolitical body to regulate large industries such as railroads. Far from resisting the drift toward monopolies in railroads, Adams contended, society should accelerate the tendency, because only when a railroad could handle the largest possible volume could the community obtain the lowest possible price. But Adams recognized that Americans called for more competition, not less, and argued for creation of a permanent commission to investigate more than regulate.

As a result of that publication, Adams won an appointment to the Massachusetts Board of Railroad Commissioners—not the first regulatory agency in America, but the most important. It represented the first incarnation of regulatory bodies. The commission's primary purpose was to disclose and publish important railroad data on safety, rates, and schedules. Once the public had information, Adams maintained, it would regulate industries through the market. Thus, the Massachusetts body was referred to as a "sunshine commission," and laws that required publication of such indicators as banks' deposits, railroad rates, or memberships on boards of directors were called "sunshine laws." Sunshine laws took an elevated view of the consumer, assuming that if the public knew relevant information concerning a bank or railroad, consumers could make their own decisions.

Sunshine commissions did not satisfy the more rabid critics of industry, especially of the railroads. In the 1870s, largely in response to increasing complaints about discrimination against individual shippers and localities from midwestern states, the federal government was petitioned regularly for national regulation and control of railroads. Although a review of aggregate rates has shown no such discrimination, individual cases of discrimination had led to a widespread fear that railroads wielded monopolistic power. The so-called Granger Laws, enacted between 1871 and 1874 in Illinois, Iowa, Minnesota, and Wisconsin, reflected the concern over rate discrimination. The laws used independent regulatory commissions with powers well beyond those of the "sunshine commissions," including the authority to set rates. Small businesses, seeing an opportunity to lower their own rates, also joined the Grangers in their cases, the most famous of which, *Munn v. Illinois,* involved an elevator operator from Chicago. In 1877, the Supreme Court, which had heard eight Granger cases in total, ruled that the states could regulate a business in the "public interest."

Nine years later, the Court further expanded regulatory power over business, although denying it to the states, in the *Wabash, St. Louis, and Pacific Railway Company v. Illinois* case. The case was significant for two reasons. First, it involved an appeal regarding a state ruling that had prohibited a shipper from charging more for a short haul than a slightly longer haul. Of course, modern air travelers know that longer routes frequently cost less to operate than shorter routes, in part due to the fuel costs involved in taking off but also in the expense entailed in stopping to load or unload passengers. Second, not only did the Court rule against the railroads, it also ruled against the states, finding differential rates to be evidence that states could not regulate railroads effectively. Even though no express federal laws on the regulation of interstate commerce existed, the Court held, states did not have the power to regulate interstate commerce.

A new regulatory wave ensued, evolving from sunshine (exposing industry operations and rates to public scrutiny) to actual control. In 1887, Congress acted against rate discrimination by passing the Interstate Commerce Act, prohibiting pooling, outlawing different rates for short hauls and long hauls, and prohibiting discrimination between persons, commodities, or localities. The act established a five-member commission to enforce the law. It was an "ombudsman," as Albro Martin observed: "It was not to usurp the actual rate-making function, but to [relieve] individuals from the indifference, incompetence, and malice which in the real world frequently impede the smooth workings of economic theory."[59] Martin then concluded that the failure of Progressive regulation came when the railroads "were deprived of the freedom to follow *their* own self-interest in a society in which all others retained that right. . . ."[60] By the 1880s, however, the menace of railroad power seemed to grow inordinately through its alliance with other large-scale enterprises, especially steel and another new industry, petroleum. The potential for malicious behavior, critics thought, reached its zenith with the combination of railroads and oil, especially under the control of John D. Rockefeller.

John D. Rockefeller Saves the Whales

Described as a "brooding, cautious, secretive man," who founded the "wisest and meanest monopoly known to history," John D. Rockefeller made plenty of enemies in his lifetime.[61] At the time of Rockefeller's death, one observer quipped that "Hell must now be half full." Forever associated with the concept of "fossil fuels," Rockefeller was hardly a founder of Greenpeace. Nevertheless, he may have done as much to save the whales as anyone who ever lived.

Americans had relied on a number of different fuel sources for their light and power. The advent of steam engines made coal a valuable resource, but people still fueled their stoves and fireplaces in many parts of the nation with wood. Of course, a log is too cumbersome to use in smaller interior lighting fixtures, making it necessary to find a cheap, portable fuel. Candles were popular, and whale oil, though expensive, worked nicely for lamps, giving rise to a large American whaling industry.[62] Although people knew of the existence of crude oil, which some people bottled as medicine, most farmers disliked the black film, plowing around it on their land. A Yale chemistry professor, Benjamin Silliman Jr., had experimented with the oil, in 1855 purifying it into a product called kerosene, which he found an even better illuminant than whale oil. The oil did not seem a practical energy source, because Silliman and his fellow investors would have had to transport small deposits of crude oil from northwest Pennsylvania to the larger urban markets. Silliman's Pennsylvania Rock Oil Company of Connecticut dispatched an unemployed railroad engineer, "Colonel" Edwin Drake, to Titusville, Pennsylvania, to undertake a drilling operation based on principles learned from salt-well drillers, who encountered oil as a by-product. Silliman thought that oil could be pumped out of the ground just as could water, and in 1859 Drake constructed a 30-foot derrick that burrowed 70 feet into the earth. In the face of rampant skepticism, Drake struck oil.

Actually, the process was easier than Drake had made it. He "took nearly two years to drill the sixty-nine feet, the costly and exasperating penalty which his company paid for hiring an amateur."[63] The low cost of entering the oil business—as little as $1,000 purchased the drilling equipment (substantially more than a McCormick reaper, but infinitesimal compared to the cost of starting even a small railroad) and a refinery could be built for as little as $200—combined with the availability of oil land to open the business to almost anyone. Within a year of Drake's demonstration, speculators streamed into the region, "cluttering it with derricks, pies, tanks, and barrels. 'Good news for whales,' concluded one newspaper."[64] So many producers emerged that prices fell too low for anyone to make a profit. Drake himself died in poverty, earning little from his breakthrough. Crude oil prices plummeted from $4 to 35 cents a barrel (42 gallons) in 1862 alone. Yet when the Civil War started, the Union army's demand drove prices up again, to a whopping $13.75 a barrel. According to one report, a blacksmith purchased $200 worth of drilling equipment to drill a well worth $100,000, while yet others lost fortunes just as quickly. One writer observed that "almost everybody you meet has been suddenly enriched or suddenly ruined (perhaps both within a short space of time). . . ."[65] Within a decade, oil production rose to five million barrels, much of it in the form of kerosene, which not only displaced whale oil in homes but also provided new factory fuel and a wide variety of by-products, including tars for paving, lubricating oil, and paraffin for candles.[66]

John D. Rockefeller ended his oil career as the wealthiest man in American history, but he was born into scarcity, the son of a New York peddler and a stay-at-home mother. He recalled at an early age being trained to work, save, and give. He attended a Cleveland high school, and upon graduation immediately started work as an assistant bookkeeper at 50 cents per day. As with Carnegie, Rockefeller's rise to riches began with a low-wage job. All the time he did the books, Rockefeller studied the business for which he worked, absorbing the intricacies of enterprise. Bookkeeping suited him in a sense, because he had a penchant for exacting detail and justice. A business partner noted, "if there was a cent due us, he wanted it. If there was a cent due a customer he wanted the customer to have it."[67] A devout Baptist, Rockefeller made certain that the Lord had His, too, tithing his entire life. Fittingly, and perhaps on the biblical principle "Give and it shall be given unto you," Rockefeller met Samuel Andrews at church, where Andrews related to Rockefeller a new, exciting venture he had invested in, oil drilling. In 1865, Rockefeller joined Andrews in speculative ventures, building a refinery.

Fascinated with oil and kerosene, Rockefeller nevertheless directed most of his energy and talent into an agricultural wholesale products firm, where he worked until 1867. Along with Henry Flagler and Andrews, Rockefeller started a new partnership to drill oil and refine the petroleum, although he quickly emphasized refining over drilling. Employing the same pursuit of efficiency that had characterized Hill in railroads and Swift in meat production, Rockefeller set out to reduce the excessive waste he saw petroleum refining, leading his firm to examine by-product uses; to avoid paying for insurance on refineries by building them to last; to hire his own plumber and to purchase his own timber. Rockefeller saved more than $1.50 per barrel by having his own kilns to dry the wood and wagons to haul it. The Rockefeller, Andrews, and Flagler barrel-production business alone constituted a remarkable demonstration of cost-cutting and mass production. The business soon grew to one of the largest in Cleveland, at which point Rockefeller reorganized, bringing in his brother William and naming the firm Standard Oil Company.

One of the first results of Rockefeller's quest to eliminate waste was that prices fell so low on kerosene that not only did it drive out fuels such as whale oil and coal oil but for a while it kept electricity at bay. Standard Oil hired chemists to find still other uses for the by-products, eventually producing more than 300 different products from a single barrel of oil. But Rockefeller did not ignore increasing production and eliminating waste from the refining process itself, pushing prices still lower. Between 1865 and 1870, kerosene prices dropped 50 percent, even though Rockefeller made a profit. By that time, other refiners failed in droves, but consumers cheered each new drop in the price of fuel, as did the whales, no doubt.

Standard Oil embarked on a program of ambitious expansion, interrupted by a brief attempt to form a pool in 1872. Tom Scott of the

Pennsylvania Railroad had suggested an alliance between the large refiners and the railroads in which they would agree to fix prices. Rockefeller stood to gain from the stable prices and rebates, but in the process antagonized the public—his consumers—with the resulting outcry leading the Pennsylvania legislature to revoke the charter of the price-fixing company Scott designed, which never shipped any oil. Rockefeller abandoned attempts to form pools with others, admitting it was a mistake, and turned his attention to forming the world's most efficient oil company.

Like Carnegie, Rockefeller acquired other oil companies for a pittance, usually buying in depressions. As he purchased or absorbed other businesses, he welcomed their officers and employees, placing several individuals from merged firms in positions of power within the Standard Oil hierarchy. When possible, however, he exchanged Standard Oil shares instead of money, again, like Carnegie, reinvesting the cash in the company. The tactic worked; dozens of other refiners joined him or sold directly to Standard, giving the company 80 percent of the kerosene market by the 1880s. With size came special clout with the railroads. Since Standard shipped far more than anyone else, the company could obtain "rebates," or discounts, from the railroads, which were caught in their own price wars. The rebate became the symbol of unfairness and monopoly control; but in reality it constituted a commonsense response to the fact that some customers used the service so much that the railroad gave them a "volume discount." Virtually any modern American shopper who has purchased an item at a small, boutique grocery store in an urban area and then priced the same product at a large "megastore" understands that all businesses grant, and seek, volume discounts. Rockefeller himself saw the rebates as benefiting the railroads more than Standard Oil.[68] No market justification existed, then or now, for criticizing rebates. Companies as disparate as Blimpie's sub sandwiches and Blockbuster video offer cards that are punched, then used to reward the customer with a free sandwich or rental after all the squares have been punched. Businesses from auto dealers to children's shoes provide rebates in the form of cash back or free products. Not surprisingly, consumers do not complain about rebates they receive.

To some members of the public then, however, and to many of Rockefeller's competitors on the losing end, the rebates represented an unholy alliance of the large railroads and Standard Oil. Phrases such as "ruthless price cutting," "unfair pricing," and "unfair competition" filled the major magazines and ingrained themselves into the American vocabulary. (Again, very seldom have consumers complained about "unfair pricing"; from the consumer's point of view, there can be no such thing, because the lowest possible price is, to the consumer, the *most* fair!) At the very time Standard reached 90 percent of the market, kerosene prices had fallen from 26 cents a gallon to 8 cents, completely in contradiction to traditional scenarios of monopoly pricing. Meanwhile, the tonnage of imported whale products had started a precipitous decline, as prices rose dramatically relative to those of oil.[69] But at no time did Rockefeller have in mind driving all the competitors from the field. Rockefeller's partner Charles Pratt stated, "Competitors we must have, we must have. If we absorb them, be sure it will bring up another."[70]

Whether Rockefeller had such lofty ideals that he wanted to drive from the market those companies who "tarnished the whole trade by selling defective oil," as Burton Folsom suggests, remains subject to scrutiny.[71] But it is clear that Rockefeller had far more on his mind than money. In his 1909 memoirs, Rockefeller wrote, "I know of nothing more despicable and pathetic than a man who devotes all the waking hours of the day to making money for money's sake."[72] It is worth noting again that he contributed 10 percent of his income *throughout his life* to his churches and his religious beliefs—giving away, proportionally, more than most modern charitable organizations can raise in a healthy year—hardly suggesting a money-driven miser who wanted to count his pennies at the end of every night. Instead, Rockefeller wrote in 1885, "Let the good work go on. We must ever remember we are refining oil for the poor man and he must have it cheap and good."[73] He told a partner, "Hope we can continue to hold out with the best illuminator in the world at the *lowest* price."[74]

Standard had organized itself vertically, acquiring supplies of crude oil from Standard-owned fields, building its own tanker fleets, and constructing pipelines, and then integrating forward, establishing systems of licensed dealers and even overseas subsidiaries. Typically, however, one of the most significant gambles required Rockefeller to risk his own capital. In 1885, drillers had found oil in the Lima, Ohio, area, but the oil had a sulphur base that caused it to smell like rotten eggs and making it totally impractical. Producers and customers alike shrank from the Lima oil—all except for Rockefeller, who purchased leases representing more than 40 million barrels of the sulphurous, and useless, oil. Rockefeller was convinced that it could be made fully practical, however, and hired chemists to purify the oil. By that time, even his directors recoiled in horror at the thought of spending another dime in the stink-oil fields. Rockefeller voluntarily offered to personally underwrite whatever was necessary to make the project work, at which point the board concluded that hope must exist for the chairman to exude such confidence. The project ate still more money—by the millions—until finally "one of our German chemists cried 'Eureka!' We . . . at last found ourselves able to clarify the oil."[75]

At that time, whales no longer were at risk; rather, the entire American oil industry was. Russians had drilled for oil in Baku, staking out the finest oil lands in the world and determined to dominate the world's oil markets. Within six years of the Russian oil discoveries, America's share of world production of refined oil fell from 85 percent of the total to 53 percent. The U.S. oil industry found itself on the endangered species list, with Standard at the top. In every way, the Russians had significant advantages over Standard Oil, including a more centralized location, more productive wells (280 barrels per well daily for Baku, compared to 4.5 for American wells), a better quality natural oil, and a closer location to European and Asian markets. European competitors made matters worse by offering a low-grade oil that they labeled "Standard Oil Company," tarring the name of Rockefeller's quality product. Undaunted, Rockefeller built a large fleet of tanker ships, unleashed his chemists to squeeze yet more product out of a barrel of oil through the "cracking" process, and further chopped costs, using less iron in the barrel hoops and removing the waste from coal heaps to fire his refineries. In the ultimate demonstration of efficiency, Rockefeller made fuel out of leftovers, junk, and waste. Despite those gains, Standard had to sell higher quality oil for a lower price—just over five cents a gallon—than the Russians to regain Standard's reputation. In the decade 1882–1891, Standard grabbed more than 60 percent of the world market in oil, prying much of it from Russian hands.

Yet as chairman of one of the richest, most powerful companies in American history, Rockefeller still found time to visit the fields, loading barrels with workers, or carrying shavings at the barrelworks in wheelbarrows, or praising employees. Other oil men considered Rockefeller the equal of Carnegie in hiring and retaining the highest quality employees and managers. Throughout it all, he put God first, praying daily and attending church regularly. Perhaps for that reason, he said of himself, "I was not what might be called a diligent business man," because his work came third, after faith and family.[76] Folsom thus asks a legitimate question about Rockefeller: "How could someone put his career third and wind up with $900 million[?]"[77] Certainly he was not alone: Carnegie had as a lifetime goal to *give away* $300 million; getting it was only a tool for the final activity. As Rockefeller himself said, "Mere money-getting has never been my goal. I had an ambition to build."[78] Indeed, while an exception can always be produced, rare is the successful entrepreneur who says, "My goal was to get rich!"

But Rockefeller even outdid Carnegie when it came to giving. His tithes had increased from $100,000 per year at age forty-five to $1 million annually by age fifty-three—an astounding amount considering that even many modern large churches have *annual* budgets of only $1 million. At eighty years old, Rockefeller gave away $138 million, with his lifetime philanthropies exceeding $550 million, mostly for schools and churches to preach the Gospel.

Rise of the Trust

Rockefeller's personal philanthropy counted for little in the minds of those who thought he and his corporate "robber baron" friends wanted to end all competition. And Rockefeller gave them plenty of ammunition! Rockefeller, convinced that pools would not work (he called them "ropes of sand"), had devised a new form of corporate organization called a "trust." Trusts, the creation of S. C. T. Dodd, one of Rockefeller's lawyers, had a legal history as a fiduciary device used to manage property or the savings of another. Dodd suggested using the mechanism to trade stock in a voting trust, "a technical form of business organization" in which the former owners received trust certificates in exchange for the shares of stock in their own companies.[79] Or, in essence, the smaller businesses turned over control of all of their businesses for a part ownership in the trust. Standard Oil formed its trust in 1879 in Ohio, and three years later some 40 oil companies exchanged their shares for Standard Oil trust shares. Sugar, whiskey, cottonseed oil, linseed oil, tobacco, lead smelting, and other industries all witnessed the formation of trusts by the major producers by the 1880s. However, they soon aroused more hostility than pools or other forms of combinations ever had.

Stuart Bruchey pointed out that "the fatal defect of the trust form of combination was that it was a matter of public record."[80] Suits flooded state courts, arguing that the combinations restrained trade, and in 1892 the Ohio Supreme Court began the final unraveling of the Standard Oil trust. But even before that, the trusts had come under sharp attack at the national level. When Senator John Sherman introduced his antitrust bill in 1890, Congress thought public sentiment against trusts so clear that the combined Senate/House vote was *294 to 1* in favor of the Sherman Antitrust Act. But did that mean that the public despised all the large combinations? Were they all viewed as evil? Perhaps no such sentiments lay behind the Sherman Antitrust Act at all. As Bruchey noted, it was so broadly worded as to be absolutely unenforceable—symbol without substance—and business itself "regarded the Act as impractical, unenforceable, and hence innocuous."[81] Monopoly and monopolistic power, in the form of the trusts, offered an easy target for politicians and a symbol, similar to the Bank of the United States in Jackson's time. The antitrust act allowed Congress to pass a public resolution and take credit for farsighted legislation. Meanwhile, it had "punted" the difficult issue of sorting out which combinations were monopolies to the courts and to future administrations.

Aware that neither state governments nor the federal government would allow trusts to proceed without challenge, many of the corporations turned to yet another form of organization, the holding company. Most states allowed holding companies, wherein one company could hold, own, or control the stock of another, only by special chartering legislation. In 1889, New Jersey liberalized its general incorporation laws to permit holding companies, even if the "held" companies resided in other states. Within a decade, several companies had established themselves in New Jersey, abandoning their trust framework for that of the holding company. Standard Oil, recapitalized in 1899 to $110 million, was one of them. As with many other businesses, Standard changed little but the names on the stock shares; its officers and directors from the "old" Standard continued to administer Standard Oil of New Jersey.

The most publicized holding company, called the Northern Securities Company, had been the creation of J. P. Morgan and James J. Hill. Hill had battled another railroader, Edward H. Harriman of the Northern Pacific Railroad, over the Chicago, Burlington, and Quincy Railroad, which represented a crucial rail link to Chicago. Hill had acquired the Burlington, extending his line from Chicago to the Pacific, essentially shutting Harriman's Northern Pacific out of the route. In 1901, when Harriman tried to acquire a majority share in Hill's Northern Pacific (something Hill had no intention of letting him do), a bidding war for Northern Pacific stock erupted, sending the price of shares up to $1,000 each.

To prevent the railroad stock war from affecting Wall Street, Morgan stepped in to form a holding company that would incorporate both Hill's and Harriman's interests. The Northern Securities Company—again, incorporated New Jersey—was capitalized at $400 million and brought under one umbrella the stock of the Northern Pacific, the Great Northern, and the Burlington. The new president, Theodore Roosevelt, who had succeeded the assassinated William McKinley, was a Progressive who supported federal restraint on the power of business. Roosevelt instructed his attorney general to file a suit against Northern Securities on the grounds that it violated the Sherman Act. In 1904, the Supreme Court ruled against the Northern Securities Company, contending that it constituted a threat to the freedom of commerce, even though it had not engaged in any *behavior* that threatened commerce. The Court had taken antitrust legislation to a new level in which existence alone posed a threat to commerce. Ultimately the Court's action did not restore competition to the midwestern lines, but only eliminated an efficient and sensible consolidation of rail properties, forcing Hill and Harriman to do informally what they would have preferred to do publicly.

Thanks to the Northern Securities Case, Teddy Roosevelt acquired the moniker "Trustbuster." And although Roosevelt started a case against Standard Oil's trust, it was the administration of his successor, the self-admitted Progressive William Howard Taft, who pursued it. Thus, the best known antitrust case of the early 1900s came before the Supreme Court in 1911, at which time the chief justice, Edward White, required Standard Oil to be broken up into more than thirty subsidiaries separated from the parent company (with some of the companies developing into modern-day, Exxon, Sohio, and Chevron). At the same time, however, the Court inserted the "rule of reason" into antitrust jurisprudence. Only combinations that "unreasonably" restrained trade were unlawful, the Court said, opening further the door to business consolidation. Roosevelt himself, three months later, grudgingly recognized "the inevitableness and the necessity of combinations in business."[82] Or, as two modern big-business historians, Louis Galambos and Joseph Pratt, describe the futility of antitrust regulation, "Neither the presidents, the regulatory agencies, nor the courts put forward an effective measure of concentration that could be understood by potential offenders and used as the lynchpin of antitrust policy."[83] They did not state what to some may have been obvious—that no such measure could be devised.

The Merger Wave

Indeed, the antitrust legislation Congress enacted had the exact opposite of what lawmakers intended, in that it helped spark the largest merger wave in American history. After all, the intent was to increase competition and reduce the control large firms had over the marketplace. Between 1895 and 1904, however, the most frenzied period of business combination ever witnessed to that point swept across the American corporate scene.

Thousands of firms disappeared, swallowed up in mergers. On the one hand, business had reached the natural stage at which it became more efficient to have fewer producers rather than more. Inefficient companies were absorbed droves, with more than 2,500 taken over from 1898 to 1902 alone. On the other hand, the ability of the large investment banks to marshal significant amounts of money on short notice meant that they could market securities by, in essence, guaranteeing the success of a stock offering with some of their own funds. An investment bank's confidence alone often ensured the success of a merged company's stock. Naomi Lamoreaux, one of the most widely cited authorities on the merger wave, has argued that it resulted from the confluence of a unique set of historical events, including the maturation of mass-production manufacturing, the unparalleled growth of capital-intensive industries, and the business recovery after the Panic of 1893. Other factors made it possible to develop and market new securities, however, including the expansion of electrical power and

CHALLENGE YOUR PERCEPTIONS!

Are Monopolies Bad?

FROM AN EARLY AGE, MOST AMERICANS ARE taught that monopolies in the free-market system either are morally wrong or a signal of an imperfect market. But is that the case?

Consider the following scenario. An enterprising scientist, working without government funding, finds a vaccine for multiple sclerosis (MS). His cure is so unusual that no other scientists are even close to replicating his approach. He has a "monopoly" on the product—there are no competitors. Is it wrong that he offer his vaccine to the public, even at a "high" price? What if the alternative were that the medicine not be provided to anyone at all? Of course, the United States has patent and copyright laws to protect an idea for a period of time, for exactly this reason: Rewarding individuals who develop a new way of solving problems will encourage people to spend their time finding solutions.

Although not as dramatic as the situation described above, examples of "monopolies" occur daily in capitalist societies. Edwin Land had a "monopoly" on the first instant self-processing (Polaroid) camera; he had the only design for a while. Was the public better off or worse off that he extracted "monopoly profits" from his camera? Clearly, people were better off, because until Land showed up, there was no color camera. What incentive would there be to invent new products if some-

one could copy them instantly and reap the profits? Any individual with a radical idea will have a monopoly, just as any musical group with a special sound—from the Beatles to the Blues Travelers—will have a monopoly. That is why Frank Sinatra, Elvis, and Barbra Streisand could demand fantastic sums of money for performing in the prime of their careers. After all, there was only one Elvis, despite the horde of imitators in Las Vegas!

But even when a company has "control" of a market by owning, say, all the fast-food stands in a particular city, and has a monopoly, is it free to charge what it wants or to provide below-grade service? Not really. If consumers are dissatisfied with the price or the service, they find substitutes. In the case of fast-food, rising prices would prompt people to eat at home more often on the one hand, and, when they did eat out, choose more expensive "sit-down" restaurants whose prices now are close to those of fast food. Any business must compete against not only exactly the same types of firms but against a panoply of related or similar enterprises. Even with so-called inelastic goods—goods that people need, such as gasoline and fresh food—history has shown that consumers are capable of substituting. The "oil crisis" of the early 1970s gave birth to dozens of energy substitution schemes; some worked, some proved impractical, but many of them reduced the demand for oil, bringing the price down. Propane, already used extensively on farms and in rural areas, suddenly was the fuel of choice for school districts and some companies with large fleets of cars. Even the dormant solar-power industry staged a rapid surge even though people learned that, for the most part, solar power cannot provide the convenience or reliability of oil. But the substitution effects were powerful just the same.

Second, having a monopoly at one time certainly does not mean that a firm

Continued

Continued

either will be successful or that it will maintain the monopoly against future competition. Virtually anyone who has played a video game knows the name Nintendo. But that Japanese company was "locked out" of the American market by a company with a virtual monopoly position in the video game industry, Atari. Atari had developed the first real home video game system and dominated the market for a few years. Then it failed utterly. Why? There are a number of reasons (discussed in a later chapter), most of them having to do with poor management planning and the inability to provide consumers with what they wanted. The threat of "future competition" keeps all competitors "in line." Any successful idea is copied, and any company that appears to have a market "locked up" is exactly where its competitors want it—overconfident and inflexible. In our example, if the fast-food monopolist attempts to exploit its market position by raising prices too much or decreasing the quality of service, people who never had any intention of entering the food industry would see the opportunity to undercut the monopolist and still make huge profits. (At the same time, as firm Number 2 plans to enter the market to undercut the monopolist, firm Number 3 already is planning to undercut Number 2, and so on!) Thus, even a company in a monopoly position must keep prices low and service high to block the entrance of future competitors.

That raises the key point regarding monopolies. If the threat of future competition and substitution constrain the monopolist to furnish a quality product at a reasonable cost, how is the public harmed? Pure laissez faire proponents or consumer advocates might argue that the price might come down an extra n percent if competition existed. In reality, however, the processes required to lower prices that extra n percent—start-up costs for businesses and, often forgotten, brand-name loyalty and *habit* for consumers—are market forces themselves. Whether true or not, cigarette manufacturers claim that their advertising is directed at convincing existing smokers to switch brands, and that brand loyalty is fierce. Certainly monopolists extract an additional profit margin from the fact that consumers choose their (higher-priced) known product over a newcomer, as the generic brands have found out in their struggle for market position.

Nevertheless, the legal tradition in America, especially after the rise of the large corporations in the late 1800s, has been to use law and regulation to attack monopolies and to force competition into markets. The most famous example, the Sherman Antitrust Act, specifically targeted one type of organization (the trust), inadvertently encouraging other combinations of business (vertical combinations, for example). Ultimately, the Supreme Court has twisted and turned trying to establish the

telegraph/telephone communications and the relentless expansion of the banking system.

Yet historians often overlook one of the most important elements in such a growth spurt—and the merger wave could be interpreted as a preliminary to the "Roaring '20s," interrupted by World War I—namely, business and consumer confidence. If the Panic of 1893 represented a financial reaction to Congress's ill-advised experiment with the silver standard, then by 1900 the nation had witnessed a period of point at which a monopoly causes harms to society, or when monopolies can exist in "the public interest" (as with utilities) or deserve special exemptions (as in organized major league sports). On occasion, the Court even has been reduced to distinguishing between a "good trust" and a "bad trust."

By the 1980s, a significant body of scholarship had appeared that produced important theoretical and empirical criticisms of two of the major tenets of antitrust doctrine. First, the traditional "barriers to entry" arguments started to crumble when scholars increasingly found government subsidies, support, or other interference in the market as the primary explanation for the very existence of "barriers to entry" in the first place. Second, the concentration doctrine has come under attack for failing to produce any evidence of a long-run relationship between high profits and high concentration levels. Finally, an overall understanding of competition as a process over time, rather than a state of fixed equilibrium, has led to a reevaluation of American antitrust policy. While antitrust laws remain on the books, for the most part, the climate of support for them has changed, and the rationale upon which they rest has been severely challenged.

Moreover, the entire notion that consumers passively accept products from a confined or concentrated market bears reassessment. In the 1980s, for example, the combination of videocassette tapes, cable television, and a new network (FOX)

sharply undercut the once total dominance of the "Big 3" television networks (ABC, CBS, NBC). The networks, which once had a complete oligopoly on the evening news, watched in horror as their viewership plummeted, losing more than 20 percent of their entire market in the 1980s alone. Meanwhile, another medium, once written off for dead, AM radio, provided a serious challenge to networks' control over news content. By 1995, many Americans obtained their news and analysis from "talk radio" rather than the once powerful television media. And political "junkies" favored C-SPAN, which broadcast congressional deliberations and committee hearings live, most of all. The combination of consumers and entrepreneurs proved it could overcome almost any monopoly status enjoyed by a firm or group of businesses.

Sources: James Langefeld and David Scheffman, "Evolution or Revolution: What Is the Future of Antitrust?" *Antitrust Bulletin,* 31 (Summer 1986): 287–299; Robert H. Bork, *The Antitrust Paradox: A Policy at War with Itself* (New York: Basic Books, 1978); Harold Demsetz, "Barriers to Entry," *American Economic Review,* 72 (March 1982): 47–57; Yale Brozen, "Concentration and Profits: Does Concentration Matter?" *Antitrust Bulletin,* 19 (1974): 381–399; Franklin M. Fisher and John L. McGowan, "On the Misuse of Accounting Rates of Return to Infer Monopoly Profits," *American Economic Review,* 73 (March 1983): 82–97; and Dominick T. Armentano, *Antitrust and Monopoly: Anatomy of a Policy Failure,* 2d ed. (New York: Holmes & Meier, 1990 [1982]).

almost unbroken growth. Productivity particularly rose at a rapid clip, but the value added in manufacturing came disproportionately from companies that had achieved high concentration ratios. Thus, it may well be that the merger wave merely *reflected* optimism that the economy would continue to expand. Certainly the higher prices investors paid for merged companies' securities indicated that the investing public had a great deal of confidence in the future of American business.

Ironically then, many Americans may have railed against large combinations while at the same time they provided the very psychological safety net and optimistic encouragement needed to make them successful. And while enacting laws designed to limit the power of business consolidations, the government actually fostered the formation and stability of the most productive and efficient of those combinations.

TALES FROM THE CRYPT: ENTREPRENEURS WHO CAME BACK FROM THE DEAD

Phineas Taylor ("P. T.") Barnum: Living Life as a Circus

KNOWN AS THE MASTER OF HYPE AND A HUCK-ster extraordinaire, Phineas Taylor, or P. T., Barnum was one of those kids everyone went to school with—the type who would set off fire alarms to get out early or hire an airplane to fly over an outdoor assembly while pulling a banner reading "Principal Jones Sucks!" Barnum parlayed an ability to "sell ice to Eskimos," some of which was natural and some of which he honed as a bartender, ticket salesman, and publisher, into a name commonly associated with outrageous claims and unusual attractions. Had he been alive, there is no doubt that Barnum would have sponsored Evil Knievel's failed attempt to jump the Snake River Canyon on a motorcycle, the Bobby Riggs–Billie Jean King tennis match, or the reunion of the Beatles.

Barnum had a long history as a trickster, and had himself experienced well-known practical jokes (including one in which he was almost lynched by a mob, when a friend of Barnum's spread the news that P. T. was an escaped killer). From those pranks, Barnum learned the old adage that even bad publicity is better than no publicity. He managed an attraction at the American Museum in 1835, where he put on display a woman he claimed was 161 years old and a former slave of George Washington's. After a time, interest in the woman dwindled, prodding Barnum to write editorials to the paper under assumed names accusing him of fraud involving the woman. Bad publicity worked its magic, and the crowds returned. Hokum sold, and Barnum did not hesitate to help out Mother Nature with such exhibits as the "Feejee Mermaid," a creature that apparently consisted of a monkey's head and body sewn to a large fish tail; and in cases where the attractions consisted of live animals or people, Barnum took the unusual and made it the unbelievable, increasing the size of the "World's Largest . . ." whatever and reducing the size of the "World's Smallest . . ." through the deft use of exaggerations in advertising.

Not all of Barnum's attractions involved untruth or even oddities. Barnum had great promotional skills and instincts, which he used to make a small fortune in 1850. He outbid other promoters for the rights to produce the first American concert tour of a Swedish singer, Jenny Lind. "The Swedish Nightingale" had a huge following in Europe, but little in America. Barnum put his marketing skills to work, selling out most of Lind's concerts and drumming up a crowd of 30,000 to meet her at the pier.

It was a scene somewhat comparable to a boxing match, in which the public, motivated by fairness, provided the mouthpiece, headgear, and gloves. Then, adopting a different persona, the rubes proceeded to scream at the opponents to pulverize each other. Or, as a popular Russian immigrant comedian Yakov Smirnoff asked in the 1980s, "Is this a great country, or what?"

While he had some success, Barnum still had an inclination to believe the hype of others, leading him to disaster in 1855. A clockmaker, Chauncey Jerome, persuaded Barnum to lend him $110,000 to move his clock company to a tract of land in Connecticut that Barnum had started to develop. The move never took place, but during the protracted financial dealings over the next few months, Barnum found himself bankrupt, losing more than $500,000 in the process.

Ashamed, broke, and outhustled, Barnum rebuilt his fortune through the same techniques he had used to acquire it the first time. He promoted unusual acts, laced with humor and pranks. (In one museum, convinced customers were lingering too long, Barnum placed a large sign reading "TO THE EGRESS"; many people, thinking the "egress" was a bird or animal, walked through a self-locking door to find themselves on the street.) Since the 1860s, however, he had incorporated an increasing number of animal acts. His exhibitions included the only giraffe in America at that time, wild cats, birds, and, of course, his trademark elephant, "Jumbo." After forming a partnership with W. C. Coup, an old circus hand, Barnum studied the possibilities of moving the animal acts rapidly by rail to new locations. Essentially, Barnum sought to take advantage of fixed costs, and, like the railroads, get maximum use of his investment.

The circus proved popular, but even as gate attendance increased, Barnum was hard-pressed to show a profit, especially in the face of strong competitors such as the London Circus, run by James A. Bailey. By 1880, Barnum even leased the circus to various managers, removing himself from direct oversight. Along with his friend, James Hutchinson, Barnum decided that merger offered a better alternative than slow erosion. He suggested a consolidation with Bailey's circus, offering his promotional talents; the result was the forerunner of the business most associated with Barnum today, the Barnum & Bailey Circus. Barnum's circus traveled the world, and President Ulysses Grant even told Barnum that his name was familiar to people who had never heard of President Grant. The television, amusement parks, video games, and zoos have all contributed to the diminishing popularity of circuses on the scale Barnum produced in the 1800s. His own health failed soon after he created his namesake circus. But traveling circuses still remain, while the hype that once characterized them has spread from attractions to products. If alive today, P. T. Barnum would be a consultant for Hollywood movie "trailers" or for the World Federation Wrestling. And loving every minute of it!

Sources: Robert B. Sobel and David Sicilia, *The Entrepreneurs: An American Adventure* (Boston: Houghton Mifflin Company, 1986); Phineas T. Barnum, *Struggles and Triumphs; or, The Life of P. T. Barnum, or, Sixty Years' Recollections* (Buffalo, N.Y.: The Courier Company, 1889); Neil Harris, *Humbug: The Art of P. T. Barnum* (Boston: Little, Brown, 1973); and Irving Wallace, *The Fabulous Showman: The Life and Times of P .T. Barnum* (New York: Alfred A. Knopf 1959).

Notes

1. Carol Nackenoff, *The Fictional Republic: Horatio Alger and American Political Discourse* (New York: Oxford University Press, 1994), 7, 10.

2. "Horatio Alger" in the *Dictionary of American Biography* (New York: Charles Scribner's Sons, 1928), 178–179; Gary Scharnhorst and Jack Bales, *Horatio Alger, Jr.: An Annotated Bibliography of Comment and Criticism* (Metuchen, N.J.: Scarecrow Press, 1981) as well as Scharnorst's *Horatio Alger, Jr.* (Boston: Twayne Publishers, 1980).

3. These stories, and others, are related with glee by Matthew Josephson in his famous critique of American enterprise called *The Robber Barons: The Great American Capitalist, 1861–1901* (New York: Harcourt Brace, 1934), 338 and ch. 14, passim.

4. Edward Chase Kirkland, *Dream and Thought in the Business Community, 1860–1900* (Chicago: Quadrangle, 1964 [1956]), 32.

5. Testimony from the *Report of the Committee [on Education and Labor] of the Senate upon the Relations between Labor and Capital, 1885,* quoted in Kirkland, *Dream and Thought,* 6.

6. An excellent summary of farm attitudes and problems during this period appears in Danbom, *Born in the Country,* ch. 7.

7. Atack and Passell, *New Economic View,* 412.

8. Atack and Passell, *New Economic View,* 414. Also see James Stock, "Real Estate Mortgages, Foreclosures and Midwestern Agrarian Unrest, 1865–1920," *Journal of Economic History* 44(1984): 89–105.

9. Robert Higgs, "Railroad Rates and the Populist Uprising," *Agricultural History,* 44 (1970): 291–297 (esp. chart on 295).

10. Jeffrey Williamson, "The Railroads and Midwestern Development, 1870–1890: A General Equilibrium History," in David Klingaman and Richard Vedder, eds. *Essays in 19th Century Economic History* (Athens: Ohio University Press, 1975), 269–352.

11. Atack and Passell, *New Economic View of American History,* 422.

12. Danbom, *Born in the Country,* 156–157 and ch. 7 passim.

13. Jack Blicksilver, *The Defenders and Defense of Big Business in the United States, 1880–1900* (New York: Garland, 1985), 137.

14. A well-argued exposition of this thesis appears in George H. Miller, *Railroads and the Granger Laws* (Madison: University of Wisconsin Press, 1971).

15. Danbom, *Born in the Country,* 151.

16. Friedman, "Crime of 1873," passim.

17. William Leach, *Land of Desire: Merchants, Power, and the Rise of a New American Culture* (New York: Pantheon, 1993), 59.

18. Henry M. Littlefield, "The Wizard of Oz: Parable on Populism," *American Quarterly,* 16 (Spring 1964): 47–58; Hugh Rockoff, "The 'Wizard of Oz' as a Monetary Allegory," *Journal of Political Economy,* 98 (August 1990): 739–760.

19. Clarence D. Long, *Wages and Earnings in the United States, 1860–1890* (Princeton, N.J.: Princeton University Press, 1960), Table a-10.

20. Atack and Passell, *New Economic View,* 536; Claudia Goldin and Robert Margo, "Wages, Prices, and Labor Markets before the Civil War," in *Strategic Factors in Nineteenth Century American Economic History,* ed. Claudia Goldin and Hugh Rockhoff (Chicago: University of Chicago Press, 1992), Tables 2A.1, 2A.2, and 2A.3.

21. C. Wright Mills, "The American Business Elite: A Collective Portrait," *Journal of Economic History: The Tasks of Economic History,* 5 (December 1945): 20–44.

22. Quoted in Blicksilver, *Defenders and Defense of Big Business,* 60.

23. Frank W. Taussig and Charles S. Joslyn, *American Business Leaders: A Study in Social Origins and Social Stratification,* quoted in Jack Blicksilver, *The Defenders and Defense of Big Business*, 45.

24. Burton Folsom, "Like Fathers, Unlike Sons: The Fall of the Business Elite in Scranton, Pennsylvania, 1880–1920," *Pennsylvania History,* 46 (October 1980): 291–309, quoted in Folsom, *Myth of the Robber Barons,* 57.

25. Lynne Pierson Doti and Larry Schweikart, *Banking in the American West from the Gold Rush to Deregulation* (Norman: University of Oklahoma Press, 1991).

26. Statistics from this section are taken from a survey railroaders in *The Encyclo-pe-dia of American Business History and Biography: Railroads in the Nineteenth Century,* ed. Robert L. Frey (New York: Facts on File, 1988), and *The Encyclope-dia of American Business History and Biography: Railroads in the Twentieth Century,* ed. Keith L. Bryant Jr. (New York: Facts on File, 1988). Special thanks to Elizabeth Koslik, who conducted a detailed tabulation of all of these volumes. Two cautions are in order with the data from these volumes. First, some biographies only noted number of children with-out specifying sex, and some did not note if the men had any children at all. Second, some people were included in the *Encyclopedia* due to the spectacular nature of their failure or illegal activities (Charles Ponzi, for example).

27. William Leary, ed., *The Airline Industry* (New York: Facts on File, 1992).

28. William Miller, "American Historians and the Business Elite," in William Miller, ed., *Men in Business: Essays on the Historical Role of the Entrepreneur* (New York: Harper & Row, 1962), 309–328.

29. C. Wright Mills, "The American Business Elite: A Collective Portrait," in *Power, Politics and People: The Collected Essays of C. Wright Mills,* ed. Irving Horowitz, (New York: Oxford University Press, 1962), 110–139. Also see Reinhard Bendix and Frank W. Howton, "Social Mobility and the American Business Elite," in *Social Mobility in Industrial Society,* eds. Reinhard Bendix and Seymour Martin Lipset, (Berkeley: University of California Press, 1959), 114–143.

30. Herbert Gutman, "The Reality of the Rags-to-Riches 'Myth,'" in Herbert G. Gutman, *Work, Culture and Society in Industrializing America* (New York: Vintage, 1977 [1966]), 211–233 (quotation on 232).

31. Quoted in Seymour Martin Lipset, "The Work Ethic—Then and Now," *Public Interest,* Winter 1990, 61–69 (quotation on 63).

32. Quoted in Herbert G. Gutman, "Work, Culture, and Society in Industrializing America, 1815–1919," *American Historical Review* (June 1973), 531–588 (quotation on 548).

33. Gutman, "Work, Culture, and Society," 559.

34. Anyone attempting to explain Marx in "commonsense" terms faces an almost insurmountable challenge, in that Marx rested any single part of his concept upon all the others, then completely obfuscated matters by creating an idiosyncratic vocabulary ("class struggle," "surplus value of labor," the "dialectic," and so on). Ultimately, the effect is to render explanations of Marxist doctrine, which require simplification, to become even more amorphous. While an explanation, by its very nature, simplifies, efforts to simplify Marx almost always result in charges of rendering the interpretation "simplistic." Two fascinating looks into both the ideas and, more importantly, the personality of Marx appear in Paul Johnson, *Intellectuals* (New York: Harper & Row, 1988), and Frank E. Manuel, *A Requiem for Karl Marx* (Cambridge, Mass.: Harvard University Press, 1995).

35. Karl Marx, *Capital*, 3 vols., vol. 1, introduction by Ernest Mandel, trans. Ben Fowkes (New York: Vintage, 1977 [1867]), vol. 2 (1981), introduction by David Fenbach, III: 203.

36. An excellent analysis of the pitfalls of Marxism—and in some ways an interesting defense of it—can be found in Thomas Sowell's *Marxism: Philosophy and Economics* (New York: Quill/William Morrow, 1985).

37. Daniel Aaron, *Men of Good Hope* (New York: Oxford, 1961), 58.

38. Pusateri, *A History of American Business*, 234. On Bellamy, see Joseph Dorfman, *The Economic Mind in American Civilization*, 5 vols. (New York: Augustus M. Kelley, 1969), 3: 152, and Arthur E. Morgan, *Edward Bellamy* (New York: Columbia University Press, 1944), as well as Bellamy's "What 'Nationalism' Means," *The Contemporary Review*, July 1890.

39. Quoted in Dorfman, *The Economic Mind in American Civilization*, 3: 117.

40. Henry Demarest Lloyd, *Wealth Against Commonwealth* (New York: Harper & Bros., 1894); Ida M. Tarbell, *The History of the Standard Oil Company* (New York: Harper and Row, 1966); Allan Nevins, *Study in Power: John D. Rockefeller*, 2 vols. (New York: Charles Scribner's Sons, 1953).

41. Josephson, *The Robber Barons*.

42. Upton Sinclair, *The Jungle* (1985 [1906]).

43. Material for this section comes from Fucini and Fucini, *Entrepreneurs*, 19–22, and James D. Robertson, *The Great American Beer Book* (Ottawa, Ill.: Caroline House Publishers, 1978).

44. "Jack Newton Daniel" in Fucini and Fucini, *Entrepreneurs*, 8–10.

45. "Dr. Thomas B. Welch," in Fucini and Fucini, *Entrepreneurs*, 69–72.

46. Pusateri, *A History of American Business*, 251.

47. Chandler, *Visible Hand*, 274–275.

48. Frederick W. Taylor, *The Principles of Scientific Management* (New York: Harper & Bros., 1915); historian Spencer Klaw quoted in Oliver E. Allen, "This Great Mental Revolution," *Audacity*, 4 (Summer 1996): 52–61 (quotation on 60).

49. Allen, "The Great Mental Revolution," passim.

50. Chandler, *Visible Hand*, 276.

51. Brownlee, *Dynamics of Ascent*, 277.

52. This discussion draws from Brownlee, *Dynamics of Ascent*, 319–340; Clarence D. Long, *Wages and Earnings in the United States, 1860–1890* (Princeton, N.J.:

Princeton University Press, 1960); Albert Rees, *Real Wages in Manufacturing, 1890–1914* (Princeton, N.J.: Princeton University Press, 1961); Atack and Passell, *New Economic View,* 542–543; Jeremy Atack and Fred Bateman, "How Long Was the Workday in 1880?" *Journal of Economic History,* 52 (March 1992): 129–160; and Robert Whaples, "The Great Decline in the Length of the Workweek," working paper, University of Wisconsin–Milwaukee, 1988.

53. A useful review of labor history can be found in Melvyn Dubofsky, *Industrialism and the American Worker, 1865–1920* (Arlington Heights, Ill.: Harlan Davidson, 1975); and Sidney Lens, *The Labor Wars: From the Molly Maguires to the Sitdowns* (Garden City, N.Y.: Anchor Books, 1975).

54. Harold Livesay, *Samuel Gompers and Organized Labor in America* (Boston: Little, Brown, 1978).

55. Ibid.

56. Claudia Goldin, "Maximum Hours Legislation and Female Employment: A Reassessment," *Journal of Political Economy,* 96 (1988): 189–205, and *Understanding the Gender Gap: An Economic History of American Women* (New York: Oxford University Press, 1990), and her work with Robert Margo, "Wages, Prices, and Labor Markets before the Civil War," in *Strategic Factors in Nineteenth Century American Economic Growth: A Volume to Honor Robert W. Fogel,* ed. Claudia Goldin and Hugh Rockoff (Chicago: University of Chicago Press, 1992), 67–104.

57. A useful review of this era appears in Samuel P. Hays, *The Response to Industrialism, 1885–1914* (Chicago: University of Chicago Press, 1957).

58. Thomas C. McCraw, *Prophets of Regulation* (Cambridge, Mass.: Belknap Press, 1984).

59. Martin, *Enterprise Denied,* 44.

60. Ibid., 359.

61. Tarbell, *The History of the Standard Oil Company,* briefer version, ed. David M. Chalmers (New York: Norton, 1969 [1904]), 27. The quotation is Henry Lloyd's, from his article in the *Atlantic Monthly,* quoted in Dorfman, *Economic Mind,* 3: 117.

62. Margaret S. Creighton, *Rites and Passages: The Experience of American Whaling, 1830–1870* (Cambridge: Cambridge University Press, 1995).

63. Pusateri, *A History of American Business,* 206.

64. Quoted in Folsom, *Myth of the Robber Barons,* 85.

65. J. W. Trowbridge quoted in Allan Nevins, *Study in Power: John D. Rockefeller,* 2 vols. (New York: Charles Scribner's Sons, 1953), 1: 132.

66. On the economic relationship between the falling prices of kerosene and decline of whaling, see Alexander Starbuck, *History of the American Whale Fishery* (Secaucus, N.J.: Castle Books, 1989 [1877]); David Moment, "The Business of Whaling in America in the 1850's," *Business History Review,* 31 (Autumn 1957): 261–291; and Teresa D. Hutchins, "The American Whale Fishery, 1815–1900: An Economic Analysis" (Ph. D. dissertation, University of North Carolina, 1988).

67. Quoted in Folsom, *Myth of the Robber Barons,* 84.

68. John D. Rockefeller, *Random Reminiscences of Men and Events* (New York: Doubleday, Page & Company, 1909), 111.

69. See figures 1 and 2 in David Moment, "The Business of Whaling in America in the 1850s," 283. Admittedly, several factors were involved in rising relative whale prices, including some whaling fleet disasters and the effects of the Civil War.

70. Nevins, *Rockefeller,* 2: 76; 1: 277–279.

71. Folsom, *Myth of the Robber Barons,* 89.

72. Rockefeller, *Random Reminiscences,* 20.

73. Nevins, *Study in Power,* 1: 672.

74. Ibid., 1: 208.

75. Ibid., 2: 29–30.

76. Rockefeller, *Random Reminiscences,* 22.

77. Folsom, *Myth of the Robber Barons,* 94.

78. Nevins, *Study in Power,* 1: 328.

79. Stuart Bruchey, *The Wealth of the Nation: An Economic History of the United States* (New York: Harper & Row, 1988), 124.

80. Ibid., 125.

81. Ibid., 132.

82. George E. Mowry, *The Era of Theodore Roosevelt and the Birth of Modern America* (New York: Harper & Brothers, 1958), 55.

83. Louis Galambos and Joseph C. Pratt, *The Rise of the Corporate Commonwealth: U.S. Business and Public Policy in the Twentieth Century* (New York: Basic Books, 1988), 62.

CHAPTER 8

The Emergence of a Consumer Market: Business from 1900–1920

THE NEW CENTURY BROUGHT FUNDAMENTAL CHANGES IN THE WAY MOST Americans did business. Households left behind self-sufficiency to rely more heavily than ever on the market to supply their daily needs. By the 1920s, transportation had changed from dependence on animals to autos, while food storage and preparation had moved from home canning to supermarkets. Whereas housewives once almost exclusively made dresses and clothing articles for children, now they purchased them through catalogs or at one of the new department stores. The home garden was replaced by the exotic seeds of Burpee; home-brewed beverages gave way to Coca-Cola; local bankers found themselves tied to the national system by the Federal Reserve Board; and Madison Avenue sold a thousand different types of products with methods made famous by P. T. Barnum. Homemade soap was replaced by Lux, the neighborhood barber gave way to Gillette's razor, and the carriage was replaced by Henry Ford's car.

Given the extent of change, it is unlikely that the career of any individual entrepreneur captured the full range of the transition affecting business as a whole in the first decades of the 1900s. After all, individuals in history rarely span the entire spectrum of change in any area of human endeavor. Napoleon's tactics proved unbeatable in 1800 but obsolete by 1815 at Waterloo. The Beatles, once the world's most popular band, found that they could not reproduce their studio sound in concert and stopped touring at the peak of their popularity. Video game maker Atari, with a virtual monopoly on the market, went out of business at the very time a Japanese toymaker, Nintendo, had identified video games as the wave of the future. Still, on occasion an individual's career crosses through momentous transitions and reflects them. Such was the case with Henry Leland.

Henry Leland and the Dawn of the Auto Age

It is odd to think of Detroit, the "Motor City," as a place hostile to unions. But at the turn of the century, one of Detroit's great attractions to entrepreneurs involved the antiunion attitudes in many of the machine shops. That reputation, among other natural advantages, drew Henry Leland to Detroit in the early 1890s. Leland came from a farm family that had gone broke, forcing Henry to take a shoe-factory job at age eleven. Like Rockefeller and Kellogg, Leland had strong religious roots (in his case, Seventh-Day Adventist), and like virtually all entrepreneurs, had a penchant for hard work. Through his church, he found a position as a mechanic on textile machinery, providing him the experience that shaped the remainder of his career.

During the Civil War, Leland went from repairing and maintaining machinery to designing it, making lathes for the production of musket stocks. In 1865, however, Leland was given his pink slip. That merely inconvenienced a person with Leland's skills and talents, but none of the jobs Leland held, including police work, satisfied him. Eventually, he found an opportunity at the Brown & Sharpe Armory in Providence, Rhode Island, a company known for its cutting-edge technology in machine tooling. Leland absorbed everything Joseph Brown could teach him, especially the production of interchangeable parts, working on everything from screws to sewing machines and ultimately heading the sewing-machine division. When not involved in designing new machines, Leland "would conduct Bible readings during lunch time and lecture the workers on theology and morality."[1]

Leland's designs included more than those for factory machines. He created a horse clipper that proved so adaptable that barbers adopted it; by the 1880s Brown & Sharpe turned out more than 300 Leland clippers a day. In 1889, however, Leland took perhaps the biggest risk of his life. Convinced by a traveling salesman that the Detroit area offered exceptional opportunities for machine shops, Leland left Brown & Sharpe to form his own company, Leland, Faulconer & Norton, in 1890. Leland had impressed his former employers so much that they loaned him more than half of his share of the investment in the business. The company quickly achieved success by manufacturing everything from pencil sharpeners to bicycle gears, becoming one of Detroit's leading industrial firms.

At that point, the mass-production technology that had dominated industry in the nineteenth century met the automobile, the innovation that dominated much of the twentieth. An automaker named Ransom E. Olds (later shortened for the popular R.E.O. Speedwagon sportsters) had a demand for three times as many engines as his factory could produce. Olds placed an order with Leland for 2,000 engines, even though Olds had only sold 200 cars up to that point! Leland responded with new tweaks on the Olds design, to the point that the Leland redesign was so superior to the Olds engine that Olds had "to retard the L & F engine so it would idle as roughly as his own."[2] Olds, who had done much to pioneer autos in America, let his stubbornness stand in the way of greater success. When Leland offered a newly designed 10-horsepower engine that was better than the Olds power plant, the automaker rejected it.

Leland found a new buyer, William Murphy, a Detroit lumberman, who had an auto design and needed an engine. The new motorcar, named after the French founder of Detroit, was the Cadillac. Although expensive ($750 for the cheaper "A" version and $900 for the "B"), the Cadillac became the nation's best-selling automobile, gaining a reputation for the highest quality in the industry. According to historians Robert Sobel and David Sicilia, in 1907 three Cadillacs were completely disassembled at a London racetrack with the parts painted red, yellow, and blue, after which a team of judges selected parts at random that were reassembled. Each of the three randomly assembled cars was then driven 500 miles![3]

Leland's authority within the company continued to expand, and he eventually managed the entire auto-production process. By 1906, Cadillac had sold over 4,000 cars, only to see the Panic of 1907 almost drive the company out of business. In 1909, Leland and Murphy sold Cadillac to William C. Durant, who was creating the first "megacar company," General Motors. Leland then organized a new auto company of his own, the Lincoln Motor Company, for which he built "Liberty" engines.

Ironically, Leland, who may have best embodied the new generation of auto entrepreneurs, failed at his next venture, in part because he refused to take advantage of the First World War to make a profit on the Lincoln. (No "merchant of death" was Henry Leland!) Only a few years after the end of World War I, America's two best autos, the Cadillac and the Lincoln, had both been the result of the efforts of Henry Leland. But the short postwar depression all but killed sales of the Lincoln, and Leland offered the company to a rising star in the automotive world, Henry Ford. Although the sale called for Leland to have a managerial position in the Ford company, he soon excused himself, unable to tolerate the imperious Ford. Ford's unmatched role in the American economy will be the subject of a later section, as prior to World War I the industry remained in its earliest infancy, but the appearance of primitive motorcars at the turn of the century heralded a new age in manufacturing for those who perceived it.

New Business Strategies for a New Age

Henry Leland reflected the difficulty nineteenth-century entrepreneurs would have adapting to the twentieth century. Large-scale manufacturing could bring vast profits, but sudden shifts in the market could also mean huge, often insurmountable, losses. The federal government, once all but invisible on the shop floor, had become a presence with labor and antitrust legislation. Perhaps more relevant for many businesses, Uncle Sam also could be a substantial customer. As rails, roads, and telegraphs linked the country, the sheer size of the American economy connected even local and regional firms to other businesses around the nation. Depressions in one sector often spread to others, while the boom-and-bust cycles in manufacturing industries affected a growing number of suppliers, including many entrepreneurial or smaller firms.

As a response to the new environment, large corporations had internalized the need for planning. More important, the managers who were the top decision makers in corporations had come to *believe* in the concept of planning and to see it as a necessity, not an option. The strategic view of managers whose business philosophy emphasized steady— if smaller—profits in return for greater stability tended to make corporations more risk averse and less entrepreneurial. (This is often considered a response to stockholder pressure for consistent profits.) Increasingly, businesses wanted government to enhance economic stability, whether through tariff adjustments or the financial structure, so that their own strategic plans would not be disrupted. Perhaps grudgingly, but often willingly, business accepted regulation as a fair trade- off for government's contributions.

Progressives enjoyed the broad support of the public for most of their legislation. It was easy to show outlandish examples and genuine suffering, even if it represented a fraction of the business or product under scrutiny, while the tiny erosion of each consumer's welfare was all but impossible to publicize. A clear case involved the federal government's expanding powers over food products. Respectable journalists and less-upstanding muckrakers had energized the public to demand health standards for the meat and drug industry. Just as *The Jungle* had outraged the meat-buying public, so, too, did a series of scathing articles in *Collier's* in December 1905 aimed at the pharmaceutical industry. The two businesses seemed naturally to fall under a similar regulatory rubric in which the federal government needed to provide basic inspections and maintain health and safety standards in food and food handling. In 1906, passage of the Pure Food and Drug Act and subsequent Meat Inspection Acts of 1906 and 1907 gave the federal government the authority to inspect meat and ban the sale of tainted, or rotted, meat (providing the famous "USDA Approved" stamp). Likewise, products such as Lydia Pinkham's Vegetable Compound had to acknowledge their drug content—in Pinkham's case, the company had to state that the elixir contained almost 20 percent alcohol, explaining its remarkable ability to ease pain!

Progressive Fervor and "The Real Thing"

Ironically, one of the products that many people assume was affected and changed by the Pure Food and Drug Act, Coca-Cola, had already eliminated cocaine from its recipe two years before passage of the act.[4] Coca-Cola originated with an Atlanta pharmacist named "Doc" John Pemberton and his partner, a Yankee advertiser named Frank Robinson. Pemberton had the inspiration to create a drink to compete with hot coffee or tea, a drink that in the South could be poured over ice or served cold. In 1886, he mixed kola seeds (which had been made available commercially only a few years before) with sugar, caffeine, carmel, citric acid, and a fluid extract of coca leaves, otherwise known as cocaine. Although modern researchers into Coke's past have difficulty establishing the level of cocaine in early mixtures, it had four times as much caffeine as modern Coca-Cola, as well as sugar and the coca extract. Certainly Pemberton had created a drink that promised excitement! Pemberton himself, however, soon fell ill—one biographer suggesting that he had developed a cocaine addiction—and Robinson took over merchandising the product with a remarkable ad campaign, including hundreds of posters, 500 street car signs, and materials for almost every soda fountain operator in the major cities of the South. But as Pemberton's health continued to fade, Robinson found himself with nothing to sell. The partner entrusted with manufacturing the beverage simply had not done his job.

Robinson soon met another local druggist, Asa Griggs Candler, who suffered from frequent headaches. Robinson had touted Coca-Cola to Candler for almost a year before Candler found that the drink alleviated his pain and even helped his indigestion. He took over manufacturing of the product, and, with Robinson, started to look for ways to reduce the cocaine content. By that time, cocaine (which only a few years earlier had been hailed as the wonder drug for all sorts of health woes) had come under a low-level, but growing, attack. The company still had not taken off, and in 1892 a stock offering fizzled. Candler responded with one of the earliest Coke "taste tests," sending letters to people all around the country with tickets to redeem for a free taste of Coca-Cola. In no time, the company had redeemed $50,000 worth of tickets. Pharmaceutical tests showed that the amount of cocaine in the drink at that time was 1/30 of a grain of cocaine, meaning that after many drinks an extremely sensitive person might feel some effects.

Candler was on the horns of a dilemma. The growing clamor for the regulation of drugs could damage his product, but for honesty in advertising and security of his patent and trade name, he thought he needed a slight by-product of the cocoa leaf in the syrup. After several evolutions, Candler arrived at a "secret formula" that so diluted the cocaine that "it seemed unlikely that cocaine (or anything else for that matter) could survive." Coke had eliminated coke, although Candler fought a twenty-year war with the Food and Drug Administration to prove it. The final twist came in 1909–1910 when the government, no longer able to claim that Coke had cocaine in it, initiated a series of charges against the company over the process it used to dilute the cocaine *out*. The leader of the government's case, Dr. Harvey Wiley, was not only a prominent nutritional reformer but, as one might expect, a leading Progressive. He also "repeatedly made statements favoring some companies' products over others," opposing products with glucose but endorsing those containing sucrose.[5] An activist interested in enhancing the prominence of his own bureau, Wiley showed his partisanship when he supported straight whiskey over rectified whiskey, and his efforts to rectify whiskey in favor of "pure" whiskey "had little to do with the public interest . . . [and were] if anything, harmful to the consumer, because he endorsed the more poisonous product."[6]

Whatever Wiley's motivations in the 1911 Coca-Cola trial in Chattanooga, the case bordered on the absurd. By that time, the product contained no cocaine at all, but the government still prosecuted the product as "misbranded" because it *did not* contain cocaine and was "adulterated" by the addition of caffeine! Adopting the proven methods of the muckrakers, the government paraded witnesses "whose testimony was designed to horrify the jury and alarm the public," yet the government's central evidence opened with the incredible revelation that a worker, "doing hard physical labor next to a steaming hot kettle in a factory in the Deep South in the middle of July, was *sweating* (emphasis in original)."[7] Quite appropriately, the government's case collapsed when it could produce no genuine Coca-Cola "fiends." What would modern consumers and culture have lost had the Progressives succeeded in the case of Coke?

Most companies willingly changed their advertising or claims, regardless of personal testimonies, rather than invoke the wrath of the federal government. For the most part, the public supported the government, suspecting that unscrupulous hucksters or murderous meat packers would afflict helpless consumers whenever possible. And certainly neither the fraudulent "snake-oil salesmen" nor the packinghouses described by Sinclair were fictions. Over time, however, the government settled into a role of establishing standards for meat, fixing acceptable levels of foreign objects that an efficient and careful manufacturing process would allow, and separating fraud from advertisers' embellishments. Contrary to the Coke experience, the federal agencies concerned themselves less with product claims—who, after all, really believes that lacing up a pair of Nike sneakers will add 30 inches to a vertical jump?—and more with the presence of harmful contents in ingredients. In general, that standard lasted until the 1960s, when a new wave of Progressives, under the banner of "consumer rights" groups, again tried to shift the burden to producers to prove that products could deliver any and all advantages they claimed.

Progressives also enacted a new wave of antitrust laws designed to enhance competition. In 1911, as a result of long-term cases against the Standard Oil Company and the American Tobacco Company, the Supreme Court enunciated a "rule of reason" that required the government to prove that harms existed and that they had specifically occurred due to a monopolistic condition. Congress responded with the Clayton Act in 1914, which prohibited interlocking directorates and tying clauses, in which a company could require a retailer to handle all of its products in order to sell one or two favored products. The Federal Trade Commission Act of 1914 also established a permanent regulatory body to examine trusts. But the federal government's antitrust lawsuits remained a major weapon, especially as wielded by Teddy Roosevelt and William Howard Taft. Intentions, once again, did not necessarily yield the desired results of competition. Some research suggests just the opposite: George Bittlingmayer's study of antitrust laws and business activity reveals that waves of antitrust filings against large firms coincided with business downturns, and implies that the downturns resulted from the application of such laws.[8]

In the process of enacting the food and drug laws, antitrust legislation, and workplace regulation, the Progressives had changed the makeup of the institutions that enforced those reforms. Gradually, Progressive administrations placed more emphasis on academically trained specialists who moved into government positions, while technical and statistical solutions became more widely accepted by the people who staffed those positions. A program that could be quantified could be planned; and a program that could be planned could be achieved. The process, however, only reflected a trend that already had transformed large-scale American enterprise.

Businesses had incorporated statisticians and accountants in the railroad age, and even by Carnegie's time many corporate leaders came from the ranks of bankers instead of production men. Not surprisingly, then, business and government gradually started to share a "world-view"—not in all things, of course, but in enough that corporate bu-reaucracies and business managerial hierarchies looked similar. In the event of a crisis, their interests could merge rapidly, as occurred during World War I. The fusion of business and government in wartime, how-ever, was made possible only by one last set of Progressive reforms that gave the federal government unprecedented control over the nation's capital: the income tax and a central banking structure.

Progressives at High Tide: Income Taxes and the Federal Reserve

Although Prohibition would be their last and most fatally flawed pro-gram, the Progressives advanced key elements of their economic worldview by enacting new banking legislation and gaining passage of an income tax amendment, both in 1913. Those "reforms" repre-sented the cumulative efforts of the Roosevelt, Taft, and Wilson ad-ministrations, all of which considered themselves "Progressive" in one or another sense of the term. (The relative concept of who was a Pro-gressive reached the absurd point that Roosevelt, in 1912, did not find Taft sufficiently "progressive" to deserve another term as president!) The income tax and the creation of the Federal Reserve System con-tributed heavily to the economic upheavals of the next sixteen years, with income taxes accounting for stagnating Treasury revenues and contributing to the rising postwar debt as well as the 1920–1921 re-cession, and the Federal Reserve system seriously constricting the banking system at key times in 1929–1930.

The Income Tax

An income tax of 3 percent on all incomes over $800 had been enacted in the Civil War and the rates raised twice thereafter. Then, in 1894, Congress passed a 2 percent tax on all incomes of over $4,000. The fol-lowing year, the Supreme Court ruled income taxes unconstitutional. During the Progressive Era, calls for income taxes led to the imposi-tion of a corporate tax of 1 percent on the net income above $5,000 of every corporation. That presented a problem, since a corporation was a legal entity, a fact the Supreme Court circumvented by labeling the tax an "excise" tax rather than an income tax.[9] Income taxes had some appeal in that they could replace the then central method of raising government revenue, the tariff system. At the time, the government was small and federal budgets did not ex-ceed $1 billion, making it possible for tariffs and land sales to provide all the money the government needed. But tariffs, it was argued, unfairly targeted certain regions, and the population paid for tariffs through higher prices on other goods while businesses benefited from the reduced competition. Perhaps more importantly, as economic historian Stanley Lebergott has stated, the substitution of income taxes for tariffs "efficiently conserved legislative energies: Life became simpler for Congress [because] the battle against tariffs had always involved direct, urgent, and threatening lobbies," whereas the income tax "affected only a small group of widely censured individuals. . . ."[10] At the same time, as the historian of American tax policy Elliot Brownlee observed, passage of the income tax amendment involved a cession of power from the legislative to the administrative/executive branch, and shifted the control of taxation from local to national.[11]

Thus, the most important advantage of the income tax that supporters could point to was that it promised to "equalize tax burdens borne by the various classes . . . [and] paid by the wealthier classes."[12] Many Progressives sought an income tax solely as a way to redistribute wealth, which had been the basis for many of the radical writers' tracts in the late 1800s. The income tax had little to do with revenue and everything to do with reform.

But since income taxes were unconstitutional, proponents had to secure a Constitutional amendment, the Sixteenth Amendment, ratified in 1913, to enable Congress to tax incomes. Once again, reformers could gain support for their program only by making it appear to afflict only "the rich." The subsequent tax code featured low rates and generous exemptions. Anyone earning less than $3,000 (and married couples earning less than $4,000) paid no tax, while those earning $20,000 to $50,000 paid only 2 percent. The top rate was 7 percent on incomes over $500,000, leaving most Americans paying no taxes at all or a mere 1 percent, while the entire tax form was contained on a single page (see Figure 8-1, First Income Tax Form, 1913). Carried away with the prospects of an egalitarian utopia made possible by the income tax, one Missouri congressman beamed that passage of the income tax marked "the dawn of a brighter day, with more of sunshine, more of the songs of the birds, more of that sweetest music, the laughter of children well fed, well clothed, well housed . . . good, even-handed, wholesome Democracy shall be triumphant."[13] Just over seven decades later, Stanley Lebergott's conclusion stands as a monumental understatement: "The net contribution of the income tax to inducing equality is not obvious."[14]

Income taxes also promised to increase the powers of the federal government, a prospect not at all unpopular with the Progressives. Minor rate changes—half a percent here, a percent there—could be enacted without a public revolt (and later deducted in hidden form directly from workers' earnings). Crisis situations, however, presented the opportunity to hike the rates at will. Once again, Brownlee summed

FIGURE 8-1 *First Income Tax Form, 1913*

TO BE FILLED IN BY COLLECTOR.

Form 1040.

INCOME TAX.

TO BE FILLED IN BY INTERNAL REVENUE BUREAU.

List No.................................

.................District of...................................

Date received...............................

THE PENALTY
FOR FAILURE TO HAVE THIS RETURN IN
THE HANDS OF THE COLLECTOR OF
INTERNAL REVENUE ON OR BEFORE
MARCH 1 IS $20 TO $1,000.
(SEE INSTRUCTIONS ON PAGE 4.)

File No....................................

Assessment List..............................

Page.................... Line ....

UNITED STATES INTERNAL REVENUE.

RETURN OF ANNUAL NET INCOME OF INDIVIDUALS.

(As provided by Act of Congress, approved October 3, 1913.)

RETURN OF NET INCOME RECEIVED OR ACCRUED DURING THE YEAR ENDED DECEMBER 31, 191___

(FOR THE YEAR 1913, FROM MARCH 1, TO DECEMBER 31.)

Filed by (or for).. of ....
(Full name of individual.)   (Street and No.)

in the City, Town, or Post Office of .... State of ....
(Fill in pages 2 and 3 before making entries below.)

1. Gross Income (see page 2, line 12)... $...

2. General Deductions (see page 3, line 7).. $...

3. Net Income .... $...

Deductions and exemptions allowed in computing income subject to the normal tax of 1 per cent.

4. Dividends and net earnings received or accrued, of corpora-
tions, etc., subject to like tax. (See page 2, line 11) .... $...

5. Amount of income on which the normal tax has been deducted
and withheld at the source. (See page 2, line 9, column A)......

6. Specific exemption of $3,000 or $4,000, as the case may be.
(See Instructions 3 and 19)....................................

Total deductions and exemptions. (Items 4, 5, and 6)............ $...

7. Taxable Income on which the normal tax of 1 per cent is to be calculated. (See Instruction 3)..... $...

8. When the net income shown above on line 3 exceeds $20,000, the additional tax thereon must be calculated as per schedule below:

	INCOME.	TAX.
1 per cent on amount over $20,000 and not exceeding $50,000........ $...........................		$...........................
2 " " 50,000 " " 75,000...........		
3 " " 75,000 " " 100,000...........		
4 " " 100,000 " " 250,000...........		
5 " " 250,000 " " 500,000...........		
6 " " 500,000...........		
Total additional or super tax...........................		$...........................
Total normal tax (1 per cent of amount entered on line 7)...........		$...........................
Total tax liability...........................		$...........................

up the situation well: "By creating instruments of taxation that had acquired an independent legitimacy and were administratively more robust, each crisis opened up new opportunities for proponents of expanded government programs to advance their interests after the emergency was over."[15] Incrementalism and "emergency-ism" constituted the working model of the day. When Congress started preparing for war in 1916, it raised the top rates to 15 percent on incomes of $2 million and doubled the lower rate of 1 percent on incomes of less than $20,000—a minuscule amount by current standards, but evidence of a disconcerting trend. Before long the Wilson administration doubled the lowest rate again and raised the rate on top incomes to a staggering 77 percent, while corporate rates jumped to 18 percent. During the war, Americans paid $7 billion in taxes, while lending the government billions more by purchasing Liberty bonds.

Neither the taxes nor the bonds kept the national debt from ballooning from $1.5 billion in 1916 to $24 billion in 1919. And despite the fact that top rates rose *by a factor of ten,* revenues to the Treasury grew very slowly after 1918. Not surprisingly, by 1921 the number of returns filed by those with incomes of over $300,000 had plummeted, from almost 1,300 to 246, while the net income of those in the top brackets dropped to one-third of the 1916 level. If the Progressives intended to transfer wealth from the rich to the poor, all they had succeeded in doing was to ensure that either there were fewer rich or they had more successfully hidden their resources from the government. In either case, it hurt the workingman; real GNP fell after 1918, and unemployment rose from 1.4 percent in 1918 to 5.2 percent in 1920, a factor partly related to the expansion of labor unions and their ability to drive real earnings for those who had a job up during the war years.[16]

The combination of higher wages, the agricultural depression brought on by renewed European output, and the suddenly expanded labor pool of returning veterans all contributed to the 1920–1921 recession. Still, high taxes played an important role in choking off investment and expansion, as well as sending a clear signal about incentives to achievement. Even Wilson, a professed Progressive, knew that the government was taking too much; he admitted that "in peace times high rates of income and profits taxes discourage energy . . . and produce industrial stagnation," and more than one historian has found strong links between Andrew Mellon's tax cuts and Wilson's positions.[17] Nevertheless, Wilson's successor, James Cox, ran in 1920 on a platform of continuing the high tax rates.

The Federal Reserve System

An equally momentous change occurred in the nation's banking system, where two decades of reform efforts resulted in the Federal

Reserve Act. By 1900, the financial structure of the United States operated on three layers: (1) commercial and investment banks that allocated commercial credit and circulated money, (2) a monetary structure made up of demand deposits and notes issued by national banks, and (3) a gold standard that after 1896 represented the metallic backing for the money in the system. By 1913, each layer had started to display its own problems, beginning with the so-called "dual banking system" of national and state banks.

After the National Bank Act of 1864, only the national banks could issue money (national banknotes), even though banks could get their "license to operate"—their charter—from either the states or the federal government. At the same time, the system had evolved into one that provided two highly distinct types of banking services. One, commercial banking, accepted deposits, made loans, exchanged notes, and increasingly handled checking accounts (known as demand deposits). A second set of services was provided by the investment banks, led by J. P. Morgan, Kuhn, Loeb & Co., and others. Those banks provided financing through securities sales for large-scale industrial undertakings. Some banks, such as Morgan, handled both functions, although legally they could issue notes only if they had a national charter, as did National City Bank of New York.

In states that prohibited branching, hundreds of small "unit banks" appeared, mostly in the North and Midwest farm states. Those areas ignored branch banking that evolved in the South and West. As a result, the banking system was not as integrated as it could have been, making it more difficult to withstand financial crises, especially in the northeastern commercial centers where economic upheavals often struck. Bank panics demanded coordinated responses. By their very nature, panics are irrational and usually required little more than the appearance of stability. In unit-bank systems, however, getting hundreds of banks in rural states such as Kansas to act in concert, especially in an age before telephones and computers, was impossible. Fearful depositors, panicked by the latest rumor, could close a perfectly healthy bank before the system could mount a response. Moreover, the tendency of unit banks to reflect the health of local economic conditions made them highly susceptible to sudden downturns in a particular crop or an unusually cold winter.

Nor could the banking system, lacking competitive note issue, provide sufficient cash to the business or consumer sector. By placing the sole authority to issue new notes in the hands of the national banks (although any bank could "create" money through demand deposits), the system was constrained by the number and the capital of national banks. In essence, the money supply could not grow unless the government created more banks or allowed the existing banks to expand their note issue. That made responding to sudden economic changes extremely difficult, a characteristic that critics of the system called "inelasticity." (Prior to the Civil War, the competitive note issue system really only was limited by the amount of specie reserve in the vaults.)

By 1900, though, the international gold standard itself contributed to a lurking problem. Many nations had "central" banks—large national banks that had the authority to issue notes, handle financial transactions of the government, and make loans to the government. For the international gold standard to work, all nations had to abide by the basic "rules of the game." Gold provided a reserve in each country, allowing, say, England, to issue money (pound sterling notes) based on the amount of gold reserves England held. The money then served as a basis for commercial and business loans by banks, which expanded industrial and agricultural production and generated employment. When England bought more goods from the United States than it sold, a trade deficit occurred that had to be made up in gold. In such an exchange, the United States would gain gold reserves while Britain would lose gold reserves, causing the money supply in England to shrink, in turn causing business to reduce output and employment. At the same time, the increased gold reserves in the United States should have had the reverse effect, increasing the money supply, expanding the number of loans, and increasing employment and output, but also increasing prices. Soon, American goods would be more expensive than British goods, and the United States would import more and export less reversing the process. All things remaining equal, the system would come into balance. Of course, all things did not remain equal—politicians often had incentives to "improve" their nation's economy. On the whole, however, countries did not tinker with the value of their currencies because the gold standard made the real value readily known.

In the years 1900–1912, the international gold standard functioned well, trade deficits at any given time were low, and nations could either adjust their prices, employment, and output or fix their imbalance by adjusting the value of their currency against gold. Like a teeter-totter with two people of approximately equal weight on opposite ends, the system tended to balance in the middle with mild economic swings. However, it behooved any nation that acquired gold through trade surpluses to expand its money supply, while those countries with deficits worried about running out of gold to pay their deficits. Only in that way could its prices rise and the trade cycle balance out—only in that way could the teeter-totter swing back. If a nation constrained the growth of its money supply, it could have serious international repercussions, because other nations could not climb out of their own recessions and, ultimately, would cease to consume products made by the nation having the surpluses. Conversely, the system also punished any nation *not* abandoning the gold standard if all others started to leave, much like a group of people holding a huge cement block, with individuals pulling out on their own. At some point, the last person under the block will be crushed!

ENDING NEW YORK'S "MONEY POWER"   A final problem afflicted the American financial system—one of perceptions and image. As New York replaced Philadelphia as the money center of the nation, other regions started to fear the financial might located in New York City, especially among the largest banks. People used phrases such as the "House of Morgan," the "Money Power," and the "Wall Street banks" to characterize New York's growing financial presence, frequently with the assertion that a "conspiracy" to control the nation's money was directed from within the boardrooms of the city's banks. More often than not, the characterizations involved anti-Semitism, with the phrase "New York banks" simply being a code phrase for "New York Jewish banks." Like most paranoia about conspiracies, this one was groundless. The leading investment bankers, including Morgan and Peabody, had been Protestants, as were most of the men who dominated the large commercial banks, such as James Stillman at National City Bank. Still others were nonpracticing Christians. Far from dominating Wall Street, well until the 1970s, when the investment bank of Drexel Burnham Lambert gained fame for its creation of low-grade securities called "junk bonds," Jewish-owned investment banking houses suffered second-class treatment.

Each new panic, however, resulted in a search for scapegoats. The fact that individuals such as Morgan actually saved the U.S. Treasury on occasion only tended to exaggerate the fears of a "New York money conspiracy," especially during the Populist era. Consequently, when designing any new system, the banking reformers of the late nineteenth century inevitably sought to reduce New York's influence. That concern, along with the efforts to address elasticity, provide a "lender of last resort" for the nation's banks (in place of Morgan), and centralize some of the banking functions in the United States, played a key role in shaping the eventual legislation that became the Federal Reserve Act.[18]

In November 1910, in a setting that could well have been viewed as itself "conspiratorial," five men met in secret on Jekyll Island, Georgia, to design a new financial system for the nation. Frank Vanderlip (of National City Bank), Paul Warburg (a powerful partner in Kuhn, Loeb & Co.), Senator Nelson Aldrich of Rhode Island, Henry Davison (a Morgan partner), and Harvard professor A. Piatt Andrew created a plan that provided the skeleton for the Federal Reserve System. After they presented their plan to Congress, it drifted listlessly, in part because the concept was too centralized, and in part because it failed to address the problem of diminishing the power of New York. It became even more clear in 1912 that any plan had to deal with the issue of New York influence.[19]

If anyone needed any evidence that the "money conspiracy" theorists were correct, the Pujo Committee sought to provide it. In 1912, Louisiana congressman Arsene P. Pujo, using the House's Committee on Banking and Currency to investigate the "Money Trust," called witnesses (including Morgan) and gathered more than 30,000 documents on the concentration of financial power among the nation's largest banks.[20] The committee revealed that through directorships, stock ownership, and holding companies, the concentration of wealth in the country was worse than critics had alleged. George F. Baker, the chairman of First National Bank of New York, for example, held fifty-eight directorships in 1912. But the committee's investigation, spearheaded by Samuel Untermeyer, described as "a wealthy New York corporate lawyer who had become increasingly anti-big-business," tried to redefine "trust" as cooperation by bankers instead of formal consolidation.[21] Untermeyer's questioning of Morgan produced testimony that frustrated critics of the "big banks" and, indeed, of the entire business system. Untermeyer asked Morgan if he favored cooperation over competition. Morgan replied he liked combination, but "I do not object to competition, either. I like a little competition. . . ."[22] At that point Untermeyer, thinking he had Morgan, asked "Is not commercial credit based primarily upon money or property?" to which the banker responded, "No, sir, the first thing is character. . . . Before money or anything else. Money cannot buy it."[23]

The irony of the Pujo hearings was lost on most of the reformers. Through the clearinghouse system the nation's banks had taken important steps to reduce the likelihood and severity of financial disruptions, but the most crucial tool in defusing panics was the cooperation and collaboration of the major banks. In essence, Untermeyer attacked the bankers for *strengthening the system and protecting depositors!* More ironic still, in the 1930s, the Percora investigations "by contrast, effectively blamed the *competitiveness* of the securities industry for the 'evils' that beset the market during the late 1920s."[24]

Nevertheless, the Pujo hearings resulted in sentiment for creation of a central bank, and Congress obliged. Passed in 1913, the Federal Reserve Act created a system of twelve Federal Reserve Banks located across the United States, a majority of them in the South and West. The pressure to diminish the significance of New York was clear from the locations of Reserve Banks in Dallas, Atlanta, San Francisco, and Cleveland. Missouri actually had two reserve banks, one in St. Louis and one in Kansas City! Each bank was a corporation owned by the member commercial banks in its region, who pledged 6 percent of their paid-up capital and surplus each to belong to the system. In return, a member not only received a 6 percent dividend but also could borrow from the reserve bank. A separate board of governors, housed in the Treasury building in Washington, D.C., consisted of representatives from each reserve bank, but had little power. Despite the board in Washington and the decentralized structure, the New York Federal Reserve Bank emerged as the most powerful institution in the system, and Washington deferred to its views more often than not. Run by its talented governor, Benjamin Strong, the New York Fed wielded far more influence than any other bank.[25]

The Fed's role of "lender of last resort" was obvious: It provided a central pool of reserves for emergencies and could shift funds (if necessary) from one district to another. The Fed could also lend money to member banks, using their assets as collateral for the loans. That allowed a basically solvent bank—but one with liquid assets, such as property or business loans—to borrow against that collateral by "rediscounting" it at the Fed. If a bank held a note from a business worth $50,000, it could "sell" that note to the Fed for a charge equal to that of the bank's original discount. As a "banker's bank," the Fed provided psychological as well as monetary stability to the system. The Fed also introduced new paper money, Federal Reserve notes, which replaced the National Bank notes, further federalizing the money supply.

Still, the Fed could not control nonmember banks as well as it could members, and even though the number of national banks nearly doubled between 1900 and 1910, the number of state charters given to banks rose even faster, leaving a growing number of institutions outside the control of the federal government. Most worrisome were some of the extremely large California banks, including A. P. Giannini's Bank of Italy and Joseph Sartori's Los Angeles First Security Bank and Trust. To entice them to join the system, the Treasury Department and the comptroller wanted the owners to convert them to national banks, and to do that, the government had to permit the banks to keep their extensive branch networks. In 1927, Congress passed the McFadden Act, which expanded the branching powers of national banks by permitting national banks to operate branches in states where state laws permitted branching. Moreover, any state bank that joined the national system would be allowed to retain all the branches it had when the law went into effect. Giannini most likely was betrayed by the politicians in this exercise: Congress and the comptroller's office, despite initial signs they might support interstate branching, ultimately rejected it after a huge lobbying campaign from unit bankers, and as of 1996, interstate branching still does not exist. Sartori also brought his Los Angeles First Security Bank and Trust and its 100 branches into the national system.

Great controversy surrounds the strategies of the Fed between 1913 and 1930. Some historians, including Elliott Brownlee, complain that the Fed exercised too little control over credit and "contributed strongly to the [post-WW I] inflation."[26] Others, including economists Milton Friedman and Anna Schwartz, have argued that the Fed's sudden contractions later in the 1920s triggered the Great Depression.[27] Still others, emphasizing the role played by the international gold standard, maintain that the Fed failed to understand or control the effects on the U.S. financial system of the gold standard.[28] Critics of the Fed from the left, including Gerald Epstein and Thomas Ferguson, have sought to show that the Fed erred because it sought to protect bank earnings, while others, such as David Wheelock, have shown that the Fed's policy remained *too* traditional from its World War I experience and therefore did not permit the board of governors to protect bank earnings or take other necessary actions.[29] In fact, most of the views can be squared with the observation that the government consistently failed to enact the appropriate policies. Or, more to the point, the government hardly represented an improvement over the competitive money and "free banking" system that served the country well before the Civil War.

"Over There" Shapes "Over Here"

The Civil War had provided a "practice run" for the mobilization of World War I, although the federal government had gained vast new powers since 1865. Unlike that of the Civil War, however, the mobilization of World War I did not occur when the first shots were fired. European powers drifted into war in the fall of 1914, at which time the United States declared strict neutrality and stated its intention to trade with all belligerents based on international rules of "freedom of the seas." Of course, throughout history only those nations with credible navies had enjoyed genuine freedom of the seas, and while the American navy featured some modern ships, it neither could secure U.S. merchantmen from boarding by the British nor protect them from sinking by German U-boats.

President Woodrow Wilson had hoped to keep the United States neutral in its other dealings as well, but that, too, proved impossible. Britain, as America's largest trading partner, also held millions of dollars in U.S. investments. Exports almost doubled (from 6.1 percent in 1914 to 11.5 percent in 1916), and did not fall to the pre-1915 levels until 1918.[30] As the Allies purchased supplies, they converted pound sterlings and francs into dollars, making the United States a net creditor and shifting the center of international banking from London to New York. Even if the American public could have remained neutral in emotions—an impossibility given the Anglo heritage of a majority of Americans—the economic health of the United States increasingly demanded that the business community support the Allies.

English and French demands for American supplies soon outstripped the credit arrangements the Wilson administration had made. By 1915, Britain and France needed to borrow directly from the American public, or the domestic markets could be plunged into depression. J. P. Morgan's son, "Jack" Morgan, who had taken over the famous firm upon his father's death in 1913, had maintained his bank's connections with England. When Wilson permitted the Allies to sell bonds, J. P. Morgan & Company sold $500 million to U.S. investors through a network of 2,200 banks and over the staunch opposition of Irish and German American groups. Over the course of the war, Americans purchased nearly $1 billion in Allied bonds, while the Morgan firm handled Allied orders for more than $3 billion worth of supplies from the Allies and earned commissions of $30 million.[31] After America joined the war, Morgan even loaned the Coast Guard his father's yacht, the *Corsair,* for use as a submarine chaser.

German U-boat attacks on merchant ships and on the *Lusitania* passenger ship in 1915 signaled that the United States could not remain neutral for long, generating an entirely new set of problems. The last American war, the Spanish-American War in 1898, had revealed serious military (and logistical) deficiencies and, at the same time, powerful advantages. Admiral Dewey's ships far outclassed the obsolete Spanish tubs in firepower, armor, and speed. On land it was a different story. American soldiers faced Spanish adversaries armed with smokeless powder and still used the thirty-year-old Gatling gun as the staple automatic weapon. The Spanish-American War had also highlighted a growing need in the economy to maintain specialized weapons manufacturers. Armor plate for battleships, for example, had only one customer, the U.S. Navy. Producing specialized armor diverted resources from steel that a company could sell to private consumers, and as a result prices for armor plate ran as high as $545 per ton. Most armor plate was produced by Morgan's U.S. Steel, allowing it to charge high prices. The Morgan network expanded further in 1915 when the company acquired Midvale Steel and Remington Arms Company, creating a military "mega-manufacturer."[32]

Merely getting material to the other side of the Atlantic also involved great risk. As the British dedicated their fleet to more direct military purposes, American shippers raised rates accordingly, anywhere from 500 percent to 1,000 percent. The prospect of having one's ships blown up by U-boats caused transportation companies to charge substantially to sail through war zones (virtually everywhere) and, of course, generating accusations by the secretary of the treasury, William Gibbs McAdoo, that the rates were "absurdly high" and representative of an "orgy of profiteering."[33] McAdoo's solution, a state-owned shipping business called the Emergency Fleet Corporation, overcame stiff opposition from numerous groups besides the expected shipping lobby.

Within a year of the corporation's creation in 1917, the government had absolute control of merchant shipping that in any way related to the American war effort. It marked the initial, but not the last, creeping intrusion of government into enterprise that previously was the domain of private capitalists.

Despite McAdoo's contentions, freight rates reflected risk. Certainly in a broader sense, most business historians reject the "merchants of death" thesis as an explanation for America's entry into World War I.[34] Had economic forces constituted the major element in bringing the United States into the European conflict, the war would have been joined in 1915, not April 1917. As W. Elliott Brownlee has pointed out, "The initial choice of Britain as the nation's major trading partner, in 1914, was more a response to military realities . . . than economics."[35] Indeed, no single event or outrage forced the American declaration of war as much as an assortment of deliberate antagonistic actions and idiotic blunders by the Germans, including the resumption of unrestricted submarine warfare (despite Wilson's repeated warnings) and the Zimmerman telegram to Mexico, which urged Mexico to join the Central Powers and declare war on the United States! (The Mexicans politely refused.)

Anticipating the need to mobilize, in 1916 the Army Appropriations Act created the Council for National Defense charged with organizing civilian advisory boards to plan for mobilization. Based on the Civil War experience, planners concluded that it would use existing private companies, not government plants, to supply munitions and arms. The private sector had already responded to the needs of the Allies; physical production had soared after 1914, bringing the U.S. economy almost to full production by 1916. Ford had introduced a four-wheel trailer designed to be pulled by a Model T in 1915, making it possible to use trucks in transport. By 1917, "Truck convoys from Detroit to Baltimore . . . proved that long-distance truck transportation could be feasible. . . ."[36] The actual production of goods proved easier than the distribution of goods and supplies. Government enlisted the aid of hundreds of business and industrial leaders, who served as advisers for a token salary of $1, for tax purposes. Known as the "Dollar-a-Year Men," the business leaders brought expertise but soon found that the more than 5,000 agencies the Wilson administration created diluted their influence. Boards and bureaus overlapped each other, fought over control, and had ill-defined responsibilities, resulting in "economic havoc as the army spent over $14 billion in three years through its inefficient supply system."[37]

When the government put one individual in charge of an operation, as occurred when Bethlehem Steel's Charles Schwab was named the head of the Emergency Fleet Corporation, it got better results. Schwab replaced the "cost-plus" system at the shipyards, where shipyards received a set profit over the cost of building a ship, with a "fixed-price" system in which the builders received a flat fee and had to achieve cost effectiveness to make a profit. When shipbuilders exceeded production, Schwab paid them bonuses, if necessary, out of his own pocket.[38] Visiting the shipyards and giving pep talks to the laborers, Schwab's speeches even won applause from the radical Industrial Workers of the World. He coaxed Rear Admiral Frank Fletcher into awarding medals and flags to overachieving plants. It worked. Under Schwab's direction, within a few months ships were being completed ahead of schedule, representing, in Carnegie's words, "a record of accomplishment that has never been equaled."[39]

For the most part, however, the system did not run so smoothly, even with business leaders involved in management. Not until 1918 did Wilson turn coordination of the war industry over to the War Industries Board (WIB), led by Wall Street investor Bernard Baruch. The WIB mediated between the powerful and conflicting bureaus, moving arms and supplies along to their proper destinations. As Baruch explained, the WIB addressed complex questions: "Should locomotives go to [General] Pershing to carry his army to the front or . . . to Chile to haul nitrates needed to make ammunition . . .? Should precedence be given to destroyers needed to fight the U-boats or to merchant ships . . . being decimated by the German subs?"[40] Although the WIB had powers never before granted a government agency, including the authority to seize and operate plants, Baruch hesitated to use a hammer when he could use a key, choosing instead to unlock resistance by conciliation and persuasion. Business often proved pliable because many business leaders themselves had pursued a more rational system, and government planning fit well with the managerial revolution and its emphasis on stability and statistical controls. Indeed, the military proved more reticent about working with the WIB than did the business sector.

Ultimately, the war effort succeeded, not because the bureaucrats demonstrated any great omnisciece or special talent—although many were quite capable—but because American consumers sacrificed conveniences, workers went without pay hikes, and owners dedicated themselves to ensuring that American troops had all they needed. Certainly the armed forces gave their all: The government drafted 2.8 million men, of which 2 million served in France under General John "Blackjack" Pershing, and of which 116,500 were killed.

Americans at home willingly gave up freedoms to guarantee victory. Laws punishing espionage and sabotage, and censorship over printed matter illustrated the personal freedoms that Americans generously sacrificed. No less important, however, infringements on economic and consumer freedoms touched everyone directly or indirectly. The Food Administration promoted "wheatless" and "meatless" meals;

the U.S. Grain Corporation "effectively fixed the price of wheat"; the Sugar Equalization Board set prices on sugar; and the Food Administration established a price for hogs.[41] Conserving fuel for military needs, the Fuel Administration ultimately diverted gasoline and coal from civilian uses to the war.

A more difficult problem had developed with the railroads. Over the years, the ICC had refused railroads' requests for rate hikes, but by the winter of 1916–1917 the railroad unions, demanding higher wages that the railroads could not pay, had threatened a strike. Regulation had starved the railroads of capital to modernize, and thus when the war placed its demands on the obsolete system, it collapsed, throwing the distribution networks on the East Coast into chaos. At the suggestion of McAdoo, President Wilson took control of the railroads in December 1917, directing them through the newly created U.S. Railroad Commission under the administration of . . . William Gibbs McAdoo! Historian David Kennedy called the takeover "the most drastic mobilization measure of the war," and it had fulfilled the dreams of the Populists.[42] Virtually the entire American railroad industry was operated as a single unit. Imposing both wage hikes for the railroad brotherhoods and smaller rate increases (that the ICC had denied the railroads while in private hands), the government ensured that the dominant industry of the nineteenth century would later depend on government subsidies. The transfer not only guaranteed that the taxpayers would support the railroads but it severely handicapped the railroads' ability to respond to the ultimate postwar threat to its viability, the automobile. Even after 1920, when the government returned control of railroads to private managers, most never regained their flexibility or independence from federal assistance.

War and Business: A Recapitulation

World War I accelerated many of the larger trends evident in American business history. The war had four especially noticeable affects on enterprise in America. First, it brought corporate management and government officials into close, often daily contact with each other. Not only did that familiarize each group with the practices and problems of the other, it opened opportunities for mobility between the two sectors. Managers in business, some of them for the first time, appreciated the security available in government service, while frustrated bureaucrats saw the freedom offered by private enterprise.

Second, the war increased the government's expansion into the private sector dramatically. While many of the wartime controls receded after 1918, government power never returned to its previous level, validating the "ratcheting effect" of crises documented by economist

Robert Higgs.[43] From the perspective of 1918, the intrusiveness of government had diminished significantly by 1920; but from the levels it had stood at in 1913, the scope of federal authority and the expansion of the bureaucracy had grown a great deal.

Third, the infusion of so many businessmen into wartime programs—the "Dollar-A-Year Men"—impressed on them the need for long-term planning on a macro scale and further solidified the position of professional accountants, economists, and other academics in the business sector. After the war, business leaders who had an "entrepreneurial mentality" as opposed to a "managerial mentality," but who had served on the government boards or in federal agencies, came away with a greater affinity for planning and its benefits. No Carnegies were transformed into faceless bureaucrats overnight, but the overall introduction of businessmen into government strengthened the appeal of "scientifically" predicting and planning for business change, then controlling it. As Charles Whiting Baker in his review of government-business relations during the war wrote in 1921, "Doctrines that were deemed ultra-radical thirty years ago . . . are accepted today without question by railway presidents, financiers and captains of industry."[44]

"Political entrepreneurs" of the nineteenth century had disguised their quest for government favors as isolated emergency actions needed to protect the public. After World War I, many businessmen steeped in the Progressive tradition dropped all pretense of claiming a special need and took the position that "government should intervene more actively in the affairs of business (particularly big corporate business) and that the intervention should be ongoing and institutionalized."[45] Certainly not all entrepreneurs bought into this new notion, and many fought tenaciously against it. But from their elite upbringings to their management training to their Progressive worldview, the established managerial hierarchies had much more in common with a government bureaucracy than they did with an entrepreneur or a small, family operation struggling to stay afloat.

Finally, to many, World War I seemed to validate the premises of the Progressive movement, successfully using the income tax, effectively mobilizing the capital markets through the Federal Reserve System, and revitalizing farming through wartime farm programs. Wartime controls had subdued labor with the carrot-and-stick approach of controls and increased wages, while mollifying corporations by legalizing price fixing in certain circumstances.

Is There an Entrepreneur in the House?

By 1920, the activities of government and the collective effort of the war had obscured the impact of entrepreneurs. Carnegie and Morgan had died, leaving behind capable and even entrepreneurial successors in

Charles Schwab and Jack Morgan. But in firm after firm, the expansion-oriented risk-taker tended to be replaced with conservative risk-avoiders—men bent on sustaining a slow momentum of growth without realizing that all momentum slows on its own.

Entrepreneurs hardly disappeared from the mix, however. The decades from 1900 to 1930 produced some of the most famous American businessmen and women in history. Most successful entrepreneurs of the era accepted, rather than resisted, the changes wrought by Progressivism. Recognizing the new social attitudes, the new entrepreneurs tapped into them (as did many of the advertising moguls) or rechanneled the energies of the time into a new wave of individualistic expression (as did Henry Ford). A scant few actually internalized the Progressive doctrines or embraced the collectivist principles that had underlain the writings of Ignatius Donnelly, Upton Sinclair, Jack London, or Edward Bellamy. But the contributions of one who did continue to affect the daily habits of millions of American men and women in the 1990s.

King Gillette's Close Shave

Any entrepreneur who focuses on making broad improvements in society as his main objective will usually fail, while the person who attempts to improve society one product at a time will succeed. This generalization, however, did not apply to King Gillette, who changed not only the look of society but its daily routines.[46]

Gillette intended to become a writer like Sinclair or London. He published a critique of society and the economy in 1894, *The Human Drift,* which attacked the competitiveness and greed in American business. Calling for a "world corporation," Gillette envisioned a society in which everyone would work, all would be cared for, and cooperation would reign. In Gillette's utopia, all people would have to work five years for the cooperative before they could work for themselves. Fortunately for Gillette, no one paid any attention to his book, forcing him to improve people's lives in a more direct fashion. Gillette had made a living as a salesman, representing, among others, the manufacturer of a disposable bottle stopper. The idea of using a product once, then throwing it away, appealed to Gillette, who focused on a disposable razor blade. Introduction of such a product, however, required altering the entire grooming culture.

Shaving was a time-consuming activity in the late 1800s. From lather to steam towel, the process could consume half an hour. Using a straight razor to shave beards required painful practice that could only be inflicted on oneself, and maintenance of the razor itself demanded some attention. Foisting the entire activity off on a paid barber explained the popularity of barbershops in the late 1800s, but when tastes shifted and beards went out of style, daily visits to a barbershop became impractical.

Gillette's remedy was a small, sharpened blade that could be clamped into a handle, with enough of the blade extended to cut the hairs but not so much as to slice flesh. He approached the disposable blade methodically, examining all available products in the field.[47] Experimenting with the designs and achieving the fine tolerances necessary to the razor required more money than Gillette could earn as a salesman. Obtaining $5,000 from friends to form the Gillette Safety Razor Company, he nearly went bankrupt and survived only when a second group of investors poured $60,000 into the enterprise. Not until 1903 did Gillette produce his first razor for sale. With blades cheap enough that customers did not need to sharpen them when they dulled, Gillette had his market. By 1904, the renamed American Safety Razor Company sold over 12 million blades and 90,000 razors, aided by a memorable color ad showing a lathered baby shaving himself to demonstrate the safety of Gillette's device. Downplaying the product's disposability, Gillette emphasized its safety. Gradually, even the most loyal straight-razor customers switched to the convenient disposables, but not before a rift between King Gillette and his primary investor, John Joyce, led to Gillette's sale of his interest in 1910.

Government, however, provided the company's ultimate customer. During World War I, soldiers needed portable shaving products, opening the door for the sale of millions of Gillette razors and ensuring a loyal customer base after 1918. Gillette had improved the lives of almost every adult American male, yet he continued to see himself as a social reformer and writer. His books flopped miserably, even after he had his portrait placed on every blade box in an effort to promote his books. All Gillette accomplished was to permanently associate his own clean-shaven (but mustachioed) image with that of the Gillette razor.

Retail Rules! Stewart, Burpee, Sears, and Ward

King Gillette appreciated the extent to which the mass American consumer market had grown since the late 1800s. His advertising showed that he also knew how to tap it. Certainly he was not the first to have that revelation. Alexander H. Stewart was one of the first large-scale merchants and one of the few entrepreneurs who inherited his "start-up" capital. In 1823 he opened a small shop on Broadway, close to another soon-to-be retail giant, Lord and Taylor. Stewart anticipated Carnegie's later practice of expanding during depressed times. In the Panic of 1837, he acquired $50,000 worth of silk and sold it for a profit of $20,000.[48] He promptly planned to reinvest his earnings into a risky venture, a huge shopping emporium in New York.

Although most contemporaries, including John Wanamaker, thought Stewart foolishly chose the wrong location, the store soon emerged as the locus of Manhattan's retail district. The *New York Herald* called Stewart's the "Marble Palace," and carriages lined up for the grand opening in 1846.[49] More than 1,000 visitors an hour strolled through the magnificent structure, examining the $600,000 worth of merchandise—a virtual cornucopia of products. Stewart's New York department store soon evolved into a large-scale retailing enterprise that used the latest in marketing methods to move huge quantities of merchandise to distributors. By 1870 alone, Stewart distributed $42 million in goods and employed 2,000 people.[50] Stewart extended short-term retail credit, divided his organization into specialized departments, and actively recruited the most talented staff. At one time, Stewart was the nation's largest importer and one of the world's leading retail dry-goods merchants.[51] It became common for retailers in other cities to compare themselves personally with Stewart: Potter Palmer of Chicago was known as the "A. T. Stewart of the West," and John Shillito was called the "A. T. Stewart of Cincinnati."

Like Gillette, Stewart concocted grandiose plans for a utopian community, located at Garden City, New York. But in other ways, Stewart looked nothing like the other business icons of the nineteenth century. When he died, he left nothing to charity; he collected valuable artworks but gave nothing to public museums. To modern thinking, he did not "give back to society"—an astonishing contention considering the products he made available for the first time to thousands of ordinary customers, the breakthroughs he attained in sales and marketing that made millions of people's lives more comfortable, and the employment and wages he paid to thousands of employees over the years. It could be argued that Stewart's customers and employees *were* his charities. The business quickly disintegrated after Stewart's death; he left no heir, and in a bizarre incident, grave robbers dug up his body and held it for ransom (itself an act of questionable mental capacity, given that he had no heirs!).[52] Reports had Stewart's body popping up in a number of locations.

One of Stewart's contemporaries, John Wanamaker, opened his fabulous Philadelphia palace in 1911. Standing twelve stories tall (with three more below ground), Wanamaker's store featured a center court with a 150-foot-high dome resting on exquisite marble arches. Bays opened to the court on seven stories, and from them could be seen the largest organ in the world—one of three in the colossus—allowing Wanamaker to quip "Surely we are well organized."[53]

John Wanamaker sold clothes in Philadelphia, dedicating most of his off hours to the First Independent Church of Philadelphia. Applying his business acumen to religious enterprises, in February 1858 he opened the Bethany Mission in South Philadelphia, bringing to it "the same evangelical drive and conviction that would characterize his retail career."[54] Wanamaker had maintained a sales operation, and with a partner acquired a new clothing store just as the Civil War broke out, providing a burst of orders. Embodying the essence of capitalism, service, Wanamaker insisted that merchants had to serve the public, which he enforced by selling at 10 percent lower than any competitor.

In 1869, Wanamaker opened a New York store, bringing him in direct competition with Stewart. Searching for the finest men's clothing items, Wanamaker traveled to England in 1871, opening him to the potential of a new type of store, a true department store that went beyond even what Stewart offered. He needed a building, which he found at the abandoned freight depot of the Pennsylvania Railroad. That gigantic facility offered the space he needed. After donating the building to a revival for the evangelist Dwight Moody ("the Lord's business first," Wanamaker stated), a mass of workmen descended on the site, turning it into an American version of the Bon Marché in Paris. Opening in 1876, the Grand Depot sported one of the world's largest signs stating "JOHN WANAMAKER." The store was so large that Wanamaker provided a guidebook to give directions and explain policies of the emporium. With over 120 counters and 2,000 clerks on a ground floor that covered three acres, Wanamaker's easily was the most impressive retail store in the nation. Departments rippled out in concentric circles, adding to the visual image of energy and enterprise.

Wanamaker eventually acquired Stewart's company after his death and "resurrection," and although he remained with the Philadelphia store, he dispatched a trusted subordinate to operate the New York business. Fittingly, Wanamaker's acquisition of Stewart's store united the companies that had introduced the department store to America.

Department stores such as Stewart's and Wanamaker's expanded through branches that stretched from the major urban areas to smaller cities, laying the foundation for the true twentieth-century chain stores such as Wal-Mart.[55] But a second market existed outside the major cities, where rural areas depended almost exclusively on local merchants and general stores. Those businesses served critical daily needs but could not offer much choice and seldom carried the latest products. Satisfying that market depended on a newly maturing business, that of the mail-order house. One mail-order pioneer, Washington Atlee Burpee, originated his famous seed empire out of his parents' home. Except Burpee did not start with seeds—he sold purebred birds, including chickens, geese, and pigeons. As a high school student, Burpee already had established himself as such an expert on the breeding of fowl that he wrote articles for poultry trade journals.

Burpee's father, a physician, insisted that his son go to medical school, and he complied, attending the University of Pennsylvania for a year after convincing a wealthy Philadelphian to invest in a poultry business. The firm, W. Atlee Burpee & Company, intended to sell mail-order birds, but a significant factor in maintaining the health of the birds was proper food, leading Burpee to offer several varieties of farm seed in his catalog. Orders rolled in, but not for birds. Everyone wanted the Burpee seeds. In 1880, Burpee shifted the emphasis of his company to seeds, advertising cucumbers, tomatoes, turnips, and other garden foods and a one-time-only price of 25 cents (normally $1 value). He also offered a free sewing machine to anyone wanting to become a Burpee dealer and who sold 300 packages. The response was overwhelming, with each promotional sale bringing more than 400 orders a day to the company. Although Burpee maintained livestock in his catalog, the seeds dominated the advertising, and the Burpee catalog itself, filled with humorous anecdotes and farm stories, soon became a popular reading item on its own. Not content with the success his business already had achieved, Washington Atlee Burpee scoured Europe for new types of vegetables, fruits, or flowers that he could bring to American homes and farms. He "discovered" for American consumers Burpee's Iceberg Lettuce, Golden Bantam Corn, and Bush Lima Beans. After Washington Atlee Burpee's death in 1915, his son David took over the business with great success, even mounting a national campaign to have the American Marigold declared the national flower in 1959.[56]

Other pioneers in the infant catalog business had intentions of providing a wider variety of products than seeds. Aaron Montgomery Ward, a former barrel maker, had switched to retailing at a local general store at age nineteen. That started a career in retailing, in which he gained experience as a traveling salesman before starting his catalog business in 1872 specifically to reach farm communities through the mail. The proliferation of railroads, the rise of express companies, and the appearance of telegraphs and improved postal systems made a mail-order business much more feasible after the Civil War than it had been before. Ward, who had worked for the Marshall Field department store, produced a single-page catalog that featured low prices and an emphasis on customer satisfaction. In 1873, Ward received a contract for the National Grange, opening a massive new market. Aware of the opportunity the Grange contract presented, Ward gave Grange members ten days' grace period on payments and advertised the fact that his was "The Original Grange Supply House." As important as the Grange business, however, Ward benefited from its own guarantee policy that made it clear that the company would accept any returned goods. Over a twenty-year period, Montgomery Ward's business thrived, and he expanded his catalog to feature more than 24,000 items in over 500 pages. Marking Ward's success, the Ward tower rose on the Chicago skyline at the turn of the century, and by 1913 the company had annual sales of $40 million.[57]

Such success naturally caught the attention of competitors, including Richard Sears and Alvah Roebuck, two watch salesmen. Roebuck had gone to work for the Sears Watch Company in 1887, which had a watch and jewelry catalog-sales business. After a brief retirement and "unretirement" by Sears, he returned with a larger stake in the company than he had before. The partners quickly expanded their merchandise to appeal to Ward's customers, although they still emphasized watches, chains, and jewelry. But they also added soap, firearms, and sewing machines. A.C. Roebuck & Company was founded in 1893, and less than fifteen years later had an annual business of $38 million, due in large part to the contributions of Julius Rosenwald as head of the firm in 1895. Sears, Roebuck divided the business into departments that specialized in certain goods, with a separate catalog division charged with marketing the products. Individual warehouse managers handled the inventories at their businesses and placed new orders.[58]

Both the Sears and Ward firms relied on rural consumers and competed primarily with local merchants—the "mom and pop" stores associated with small towns, who energetically resisted the encroachment of foreigners into their markets. Consumers loved the concept of mail order, however, lobbying Congress in 1912 to expand postal service specifically to make it easier to obtain the mail-order catalogs.[59]

The challenge for the mail-order and catalog firms, however, was the demographic shift in America. Since the Civil War, families had left farms in increasing numbers, flocking to urban areas. World War I accelerated that pace with its promise of employment, and Sears found itself with skyrocketing inventory levels after the 1920 recession. In 1924, Julius Rosenwald, who by that time managed the company and who had put up $20 million of his own money to keep the business afloat during the depression, hired a former army quartermaster and participant in the construction of the Panama Canal, Robert E. Wood, to stop the hemorrhaging. Wood urged Rosenwald to de-emphasize the catalog portion of the business and to enter retailing in the larger urban areas. Rosenwald authorized Wood to proceed with his plan, and after four years, 324 Sears and Roebuck stores (with the name eventually shortened to "Sears") appeared in major urban centers. Wood stressed sales of the large electrical appliances such as stoves and refrigerators that were quickly becoming necessities in 1920s households. The company maintained the catalog sales but increasingly carried catalog items in the stores, where customers could purchase them in person.

Even with the services provided by Montgomery Ward and Sears, Roebuck, a gap remained in the retail market. Large urban areas had the major stores, and urban areas had catalog sales, but small cities were not really touched by either source. A new form of retailer, geared toward smaller towns or suburbs, emerged in the form of James Cash ("J. C.") Penney. Originating in Kemmerer, Wyoming, at the end of fifteen years the J.C. Penney Company had 71 outlets with sales of more than $3.5 million. While Sears's management still pondered whether or not to establish its own chain of stores, J. C. Penney had opened more than 500, with the number rising to more than 1,400 stores by the mid-1930s.[60] The company relied on high volume, coordinated and centralized merchandise purchases, centralized accounting, and an obsession with placing stores in prime locations.[61]

Rise of the Supermarkets

The economies of scale offered by centralized purchasing played a key role in the expansion of the chain grocery stores, which represented the earliest supermarkets. In 1859, a New York company exclusively focused on selling tea evolved into the earliest of the supermarket chains. George Gilman and George Hartford had purchased tea in large quantities directly from ships, cutting costs and lowering prices. Within a decade, the Great Atlantic and Pacific Tea Company had several stores, and by 1880 had over 100 locations stretching from St. Paul, Minnesota to Norfolk, Virginia. Known increasingly as A&P, the company handled a variety of beverage and baking products, including coffee, sugar, cocoa, and other traditional grocery items.

A&P hardly resembled a modern grocery store, though, despite its wide variety of products and its policy of allowing customers to "run a tab." John Hartford, George's son, concluded that a practical cash-only business might be more profitable, and the company allowed him to open such a store under the A&P name in 1912. The cash business proved so profitable that A&P created a separate division that established stores at the rate of 50 per week. By 1925, A&P had 14,000 outlets, virtually all of them small operations run by the owner. Consequently, A&P reconsidered its entire approach and eliminated more than 10,000 of its outlets in favor of fewer, but larger, supermarkets. No longer flush with the volume profits provided by the additional 10,000 stores, A&P integrated backward, starting its own food brands, including baked goods, sugars, and coffee, as well as creating salmon canneries, a cheese warehouse, and a laundry service.

Other companies rose to powerful market positions in other regions, such as Kroger and Safeway. Kroger was the creation of Bernard Kroger, a failed Cincinnati farmer and, later, tea peddler.[62] By the 1920s, Safeway had become a powerful competitor, thanks to the efforts of Wall Street securities broker Charles E. Merrill, who had pioneered a new marketing approach to stock sales and invested heavily in Safeway. Well after the turn of the century, grocery stores still had the old-fashioned touch, using stock clerks to take items from the shelves for the customer and box the purchases. Even that tradition faded when a Memphis grocer named Clarence Saunders applied assembly-line techniques to grocery store shopping in 1916 at his Piggly Wiggly store. All items were marked with a price and displayed on shelves. The customer walked down aisles with a basket and pulled them off for checkout by a clerk at the front of the store.

Saunders's strategy only worked when products came in packages that consumers could identify clearly. Packaging already had become an integral part of selling a number of products, especially foods, of which "there has probably never been a product that sold its package more aggressively than Uneeda [biscuits]."[63] Rather than emphasizing the crackers in the box, Nabisco's Uneeda advertising campaign, introduced in 1898, stressed Nabisco's patented "In-Er-Seal" package that kept crackers fresh. Prior to the appearance of packaged products, grocery stores kept goods in bins, filling the customer's request for, say, a pound of flour from an open bin. Unfortunately, any number of foreign objects, including codfish, kerosene, salt, floor sweepings, or even lost earrings could fall into the bins, then into the customer's package. Of course, Nabisco was not the only food processor to use packages. Heinz's vegetables and sauces, Campbell's soups, and many other products were sold in packages by 1900. That practice allowed grocery owners like Saunders to rearrange their stores to feature shelved items instead of large bins.

Taken together, the change in packaging, when merged with the appearance of supermarkets, chain stores, department stores, and mail-order businesses, brought products much closer to the consumer than ever before. That, in turn, severely reduced what once had been a thriving layer in the economy, middlemen. Between 1879 and 1929, the ratio of goods that reached retailers through traditional wholesale networks and those purchased directly from manufacturers fell from 2.4 to 1 to 1.5 to 1. Urbanization accounted for some of the transformation, but other factors contributed mightily. Transportation had improved enough that people could shop in different locations to compare prices, even to the point of traveling to different towns in the same weekend. Electricity made possible better displays in stores, making products more attractive, and, at the same time, lowered their price by reducing the energy component of mass production. Wonders such as the telephone and radio caused a revolution in communications, making it difficult for even rural areas to remain too isolated. Consumer tastes changed as well, symbolized by the acceptance of Gillette's razor, and consumer attitudes were shaped by (although not controlled by) new marketing techniques among advertisers. For the first time, advertising became an industry unto itself.

Hucksterism Becomes Respectable

P. T. Barnum's great strength and great weakness was his constant self-promotion. Until the late 1800s, in many quarters it was considered poor taste for businesses to promote themselves. Aside from the posting of a bank's ownership and hours in a newspaper, for example, early bank advertisements refrained from making any claims about service or even (usually) safety. And while gradually firms and individuals published a simple notice of their existence in newspapers, few companies actively advertised any aspects of their products other than brand names.

Although change did not occur evenly, after the Civil War entrepreneurs began to advertise in the modern sense. The notion that publicizing the benefits of one's products was mere "hucksterism" slowly faded as companies experimented with different ways to attract the public's attention. The free sample—made famous by Heinz at the Chicago World's Fair—worked well enough, but many items were too large or expensive to be given away or tried out prior to purchase. Using a familiar brand name, such as Burpee's seeds or Campbell's soup, also succeeded, but hardly helped the person with a new product or the business trying to sell in a new section of the country. Moreover, after the advent of "sunshine laws," the government required businesses to prepare and make public some information. Why not accentuate the positive elements of that data for the consumers, such as the capital for a bank or the number of departures for a train? Accordingly, advertising "developed from a modest $10 million business in 1865 to a hefty $95 million industry by 1900."[64]

The rise of mass-circulation nineteenth-century newspapers was the direct result of the need by political parties to get their message to the public, and the value of turning news into free advertising was not lost on hucksters such as P. T. Barnum, of course. But by the late 1800s, the audience had become national. With the proliferation of magazines such as *Harper's* or *Atlantic Monthly*, companies could reach every region of the country with their advertising. A sudden burst of women's magazines in the 1870s and 1880s, including *McCall's, Woman's Home Companion, Good Housekeeping,* and *Cosmopolitan,* further expanded the advertising base. None, however, surpassed the *Ladies Home Journal,* which was founded in 1883 and reached a circulation of one million by 1900. So-called block ads touted everything from books to violin bows, with the emphasis on brand names.

Advertising expanded beyond the scope that businesses themselves, or even the journals, could manage on a regular basis. Instead, specialists were needed who could place ads in national magazines and newspapers, write effective ads, and track the appearance of the advertising. Early advertising middlemen acted in much the same way as had land speculators. They purchased blocks of newspaper space, then resold the space in smaller parcels to the advertiser at whatever price the parties could negotiate. Writing the ad, arranging artwork, and overseeing editorial matters remained the concern of only the buyers of the ad parcels. N.W. Ayer & Son, a Philadelphia business founded in 1869, marked a departure from the "speculator" model. Francis Wayland Ayer (the firm was named after his father) and his son Frederick worked for a fixed commission, turning the advertising specialist into a professional. Within twenty years, the company had a fulltime copywriter and had lined up accounts from numerous national businesses, including National Biscuit Company (later Nabisco), Procter & Gamble, Burpee Seeds, and Montgomery Ward.

The professionalization of advertising, replete with editors, artists, writers, and typeset designers, fit into the Progressive preference for having specialists, especially academics, directing society's activities wherever possible. Agencies soon incorporated psychologists to analyze consumers' desires and the impact of pictures or copy on potential customers. But the most prevalent type of advertising remained either publicizing a brand name (hence, quality) or the increasingly popular "reason why" copy, in which the written portion of the ad explained to the consumer why purchasing a particular product would be beneficial. As a historian of advertising explained, "Not charming or amusing or even necessarily pleasing to the eye, a good ad was a rational, unadorned instrument of selling . . . ."[65] Far from trying to appeal to the customer's base instincts, "reason why" copy appealed to the intellect, all the while seeking to "predigest" the content for the consumer. Only later did companies stress the romantic benefits of products, and then in subtle fashion.[66]

J. Walter Thompson, a New Yorker who worked in advertising most of his life, set the stage for much of the "reason why" copy. Thompson was employed in the 1860s by a small Manhattan agency, and over time so many advertising firms had their headquarters in New York on Madison Avenue that the street itself symbolized the profession. He mustered sufficient cash to purchase the business in 1878, changing the target of his advertising strategy to magazines, correctly observing that women, who spent much of family's disposable income, tended to read magazines more than newspapers. In 1896, Thompson incorporated his business as the J. Walter Thompson Company, known in the business simply as JWT. But while the firm became the largest advertising agency in the world by 1916, Thompson himself was spent. He sold the company for $500,000 to a group that included one of his most talented writers, Stanley Resor.

After a short stint with Procter & Gamble's ad agency, Resor worked his way up within the Thompson agency. He perfected "reason why" and started to look for ways to expand the appeal of the ads. Along with his capable coworker and wife, Helen Landsdown, Resor sought to incorporate romantic images with the written copy. Their most famous collaboration—but primarily Helen's concept—became the most famous print ad in history. Developed for Woodbury's Facial Soap, the ad used an Alonzo Kimball painting that showed a man in a tuxedo and a woman in an evening gown embracing, highlighted with the phrase, "A Skin You Love to Touch." A small amount of traditional "reason why" copy was placed at the bottom of the picture, but the emphasis was no longer solely on intellectual appeal. The Woodbury ad led many to credit Helen Resor with the first use of sex appeal in marketing.

In fact, Helen Resor relied on a keen sense of psychology to introduce another advertising technique that soon was an industry standard. She thought that people could be persuaded to purchase products based on the recommendations of others, especially celebrities, giving rise to the testimonial, in which well-known people related their own positive experience with a product. Testimonials worked particularly well, she thought, if the person providing the testimony was in a higher social class than most consumers. To that end, by 1926, Resor had lined up socialites and royalty, doctors and clergy to hawk different products. In addition to the queens of Romania and Spain, Helen and Stanley Resor ultimately ran ads with philosopher John Dewey, George Bernard Shaw, Joan Crawford, and Janet Gaynor. Even today, the testimonial remains an important tool for advertisers.

JWT, in particular, secured inexpensive testimonials from dozens of movie stars at a time when Hollywood had suddenly started to capture the public's attention. The firm's Hollywood representative, Danny Danker, provided a free crate of Lux soap to then unknown actresses in exchange for their promise to endorse the soap if they became stars, allowing JWT to gain the services of Crawford, Gaynor, and Clara Bow for pennies.[67]

Stanley Resor had proved his own worth to the firm in a much less obvious way. Shortly after he took over, Resor eliminated two-thirds of the company's accounts, retaining only the largest and most profitable. He hired exceptionally talented professionals, including John Watson, who introduced the first "blind" taste tests in advertising. Shielding the brand name, Watson asked subjects to taste or use a product, finding that they seldom could tell the difference between their favorite and a competitor's. Unfortunately, Watson's research was misinterpreted to suggest that, in the most simplistic sense, consumers were merely sheep who could be "programmed" to purchase a particular brand. Such tests missed the point—that brand names often achieved their appeal less on a particular single experience but rather on consistent quality or service.[68]

Still, no doubt existed as to the value of effective advertising, and no one worked harder on a product than a competitor of the JWT agency, Lord & Thomas, with its premier executive, Albert Lasker. Lord & Thomas was a Chicago firm founded by Daniel Lord and Ambrose Thomas, a pair of New Englanders who had started their company in 1881 to place advertising for Christian periodicals, Lasker, on the other hand, came from Texas, the son of a reporter. He gained entry into the business through his newspaper knowledge, expecting to stay in Chicago only a short time before moving on to New York to work as a reporter. At Lord & Thomas he found himself in the unceremonious position of sweeping floors and emptying cuspidors. Worse, he acquired a $500 gambling debt, which he repaid with a loan from Thomas, thus requiring that he remain on his job. Before long, Lasker was on the road as a salesman, where he demonstrated an uncanny ability to reel in large accounts.

Most advertisers wrote their own copy, and the agency merely placed the ads. Lasker, however, convinced a company to let him write the ad for a slightly higher fee. His strategy proved so successful that by 1902 Lasker hauled in $10,000 annually, and then, within a few years, $50,000 a year. To Lasker, the only measure of an ad's effectiveness was the number of products it sold, and to that end he originated a department solely focused on evaluating the results of Lord & Thomas's ads. Lasker bought part of the Lord & Thomas Agency and soon directed it. His ability to focus on the bottom line led him to hire unusual employees, such as George Washington Hill of the American Tobacco Company. Hill was a relentless chain-smoker with a four-pack-a-day habit who headed the Lucky Strike cigarette account. As Lasker said of Hill, "I would not call him a rounded man. The only purpose in life to him was to wake up, to eat, and sleep so that he'd have strength to sell more Lucky Strikes."[69] The monomaniacal Hill massaged the Lucky Strike account into $12.3 million in billings in 1929—just under one-third of Lord & Thomas's total billings and the driving force behind the company's return to among the top ad firms in the United States. Just as Helen Resor specifically targeted females as consumers, Lasker sought to turn women into smokers. His campaign phrase "Reach for a Lucky instead of a sweet" used actress Helen Hayes to direct ads at women. Not only did Hill's campaign set off a war with the candy industry but it introduced women to men's vices, with female alcohol use rising in the 1920s along with their increased smoking.

Lux and Lucky Strike showed that a single campaign could make or break an agency, and likewise, companies found products saved from mediocrity by effective campaigns. Lambert Pharmaceutical Company, for example, produced a mouthwash called Listerine, which lumbered along with slow sales until two Chicago copywriters found an obscure medical term for bad breath called "halitosis." Forming a campaign that treated smelly breath as a disease—and not simply a failure to brush one's teeth or eat correct food—suddenly gave Listerine the respect of a medicinal product. Using the phrase, "Even your closest friends won't tell you," the campaign propelled Listerine sales from $100,000 a year to over $4 million.[70]

Not all advertisers took such an amoral approach to the use of truth in advertising. Bruce Barton, who edited a series of magazines and wrote ads on the side, used his writing talents during World War I for the United War Work Campaign, which benefited the Salvation Army, the YMCA, and the YWCA. While in the process of planning those bond campaigns he met Alex Osborn, a Buffalo adman, whose acquaintance translated into an offer to join with Osborn and Roy Durstine in a new agency, Barton, Durstine & Osborn. Like Wanamaker, Bruce Barton planted his business and advertising philosophy on his Christian faith and his knowledge of the Bible. From one passage he concluded that new generations will not remember the things of the old, and that products must be constantly resold to the present generation. The agency located in New York and quickly became the hot agency in town. Sharing the same building with another firm, that of George Batten, the two businesses merged in 1928 to form Batten, Barton, Durstine & Osborn, known as BBD&O.

Even as the work piled up—"We are creating, creating, creating all the time," Barton observed—he reserved time for a major book he had in mind.[71] In 1923, Barton started a revisionist presentation of Jesus Christ, presenting a masculine savior of great compassion but also great humor. Barton stressed that Jesus had all the traits of an advertising executive: persuasiveness combined with the ability to recruit followers and touch each individual with a different message about the same product, topped off with managment skills. When *The Man Nobody Knows* appeared in 1925, it sold 250,000 copies in just over a year.[72] Barton wanted to do more than place Jesus in a contemporary context, however. He sought to elevate all types of work to the level of a religious calling and suggest that capitalism was a moral system as much as an efficient economic system.

By that time, Bruce Barton had become one of the gurus of advertising. Still phrasing marketing slogans in the imagery of religion, Barton argued, "If advertising speaks to a thousand in order to influence one, so does the church." Rejecting the notion that advertising "created" demand, Barton said to a friend in 1926, "We spend our vast advertising appropriations trying to steal each other's customers here in the home market."[73] He also noted that advertising needed to move in a different direction, away from "reason why," observing that "Today there is no more need of advertising the details of automobiles to the American public than there is for advertising the multiplication table."[74]

Barton hoped to aspire to people's better qualities, and no doubt would have been chagrined to see that his predictions about the industry were all too accurate. Over time, the use of subliminal advertising and sex appeal increased, neither of which Bruce Barton would have approved. Nor did Barton share the view that advertising, per se, could sell products people really did not want, and over time a number of marketing studies proved him right.[75] He was not alone in his view that consumers had an inherent sense of value and dignity. Other entrepreneurs, in fields as diverse as autos, communications, electricity, and securities, had recently come to much the same conclusion. Most notable among them was Henry Ford.

Henry Ford and the "People's Car"

If, as some historians claim, the railroads had an unprecedented effect on American economic growth, the arrival of the auto matched and, in most respects, surpassed the contributions of the railroads. Autos fundamentally changed transportation from a collective undertaking, whether in boats or rail cars, to a principally individual experience. Cars represented independence, freeing people not only from the confines of the city but from restrictions imposed by a particular geographic region. Over time, the automobile released people from the tyranny of chronic poor weather, the injustice of local prejudices, and the inequality of restrictive labor markets, opening doors to business opportunity and social mobility. Almost overnight, the auto made real the promise of a truly national market for goods and services.

Charles Duryea had demonstrated a primitive car that utilized a gasoline-powered engine in 1893 and drove an auto from Cleveland to New York in a road test four years later. Others, of course, had also already built cars: Chicago's Columbian Exposition of 1893 displayed six different cars. Still, the auto industry remained small and segmented. By 1900, for example, just over 4,100 cars were sold in America—a tiny fraction of the over 450,000 cars registered in the United States only a decade later.

As business historians Keith Bryant and Henry C. Dethloff observed, "The automobile industry developed under ideal circumstances."[76] America had a high (and rising) per capita income; steel and petroleum, two key ingredients in the success of motorcars, had achieved a level of maturity. The concept was novel enough that autos were virtually unregulated. America possessed both a large, skilled workforce and individual inventors familiar with mass production and factory processes that could be adapted to operations. The auto manufacturers came from the ranks of mechanics and bicycle makers, but a significant percentage (more than one-third) had lived or worked on farms. A study of the auto industry by Burton Klein revealed that of twenty-five well-known pioneers, seven had fathers who were farmers and five others worked in machine shops or manufacturing.[77] That background, a heritage of a "nation of tinkerers," as the United States once was described, enabled sons to learn the basics of technology from fathers. Moreover, the majority of the auto pathbreakers investigated by Klein had only a public school education but knew enough to observe the factory system in operation. And while Duryea had started in Massachusetts, Detroit, Michigan, quickly emerged as the auto center of the nation because of its proximity to water, copper, iron ore, and other natural resources as well as its reputation as a carriage and bicycle manufacturing center.

Henry Ford was illustrative of all those characteristics. He grew up on a Michigan farm, showing a keen mechanical talent. At a job with Westinghouse, Ford worked with steam engines, then in 1891 moved to Detroit, where he joined the Edison Electric Company, giving him the opportunity to work with Thomas Edison. According to some, Ford decided on making a car rather quickly. While at Edison Electric, the story goes, Ford read an article in *The American Machinist* in 1896, detailing the new horseless carriage. It was enough to convince the thirty-three-year-old Ford that he personally could build one. In fact, however, Ford had intermittently labored over auto concepts for years. While at Eagle Iron Works in Detroit, he had repaired an internal combustion engine, but for years had remain convinced that horseless carriages would be powered by steam. In 1893, assisted by his wife, Clara, he assembled a one-cylinder internal combustion engine in his kitchen, and he continued to assemble a car after that time. In 1896, after assembling a four-cycle engine and mounting it on a carriage frame, Ford had his car. The vehicle resembled a large, modern baby stroller without the covering, with the lightweight chassis resting on four bicycle-type wire wheels. Unfortunately, he had constructed the entire vehicle in his woodshed with no consideration for its width. Unable to get it out any other way, he took an ax to the walls.

Since Ford lacked any formal engineering education, his ideas advanced by trial and error. Adaptation, not invention, typified Ford's best work. He recruited other talented mechanics to help him, contracting out ironwork and buying available parts from existing firms. Yet Ford also had developed the engine and wheels himself and always seemed to have the needed mechanical concept when others did not.

Retaining his job at Edison, Ford tested his auto for three years. Then he made his leap of faith. With several reputable Detroit investors, Ford formed the Detroit Automobile Company, only to have it collapse in 1900. He started another company, and in 1901 it, too, failed. Demonstrating the tenacity typical of successful entrepreneurs, Ford started another company in 1903, the Ford Motor Company, with the intention of building every auto exactly alike. But the notion that Ford invented universality in mass production has its skeptics. One associate of Ford, Charles Sorensen, contended that "Henry Ford had no ideas on mass production. He wanted to build a lot of autos . . . [and just] grew into it, like the rest of us."[78] Some took that to mean that Ford did not deserve credit for the Model T or that he had a mechanic's view of the world rather than an entrepreneur's. Some of the impressions of Ford resulted from his own view that there was a virtue in productivity itself.[79] On the contrary, Sorensen insisted, Ford, unable to read blueprints, contributed most of the major ideas, including the use of vanadium steel, the design of the transmission's planetary gears, and the decision to use a detachable head for the block, even though no one knew how to build a head gasket strong enough to withstand the pressure.[80] Moreover, he had the key entrepreneurial characteristics of understanding the consumer at the time and believing his product would meet the needs of others.

Prior to the Model T, Ford built eight models (driving his shareholders to distraction), including the Model N, which he introduced in 1907. The Model N had orders for 100 cars a day. Losing money on heavier cars such as the Model K (a "regular limousine," according to Jonathan Hughes), Ford redirected his efforts to simpler, cheaper autos.[81] Speed was not required—the city of Detroit had a speed limit of eight miles an hour around city hall, and speeders paid fines of up to $100, or two months' wages—but shedding the weight in the heavier lines was. Throughout 1908 and 1909, Ford attempted to eliminate larger cars while concentrating on a new auto that would change history, the Model T. Ford placed all his faith in the new car and instructed his company that he would sell no other model. Furthermore, the Model T would be painted only one color, black. Unveiling the "Tin Lizzie" to the public, Ford advertised it with a statement of his vision: "I will build a motor car for the great multitude . . . . it will be so low in price that no man making a good salary will be unable to own one. . . ."[82] Indeed, at a price of $850, over 12,000 Model Ts sold in twelve months. With each new innovation and product improvement, Ford lowered his price, and with each price drop, Ford sold more cars. By the 1920s he boasted that every time he dropped his price by a dollar he sold 1,000 additional cars.

In 1913, Ford introduced the moving assembly line at the Highland Park facility, perhaps the single most dramatic innovation associated with his career. When the plant reached full capacity in 1916, the continuous-line process had reduced the chassis assembly process from twelve hours to less than two. Giving credit to Ford for the assembly line has proven controversial. Whitney and others had used mass production and standardized parts a century earlier, and Leland had pioneered the technology that improved the ability to manufacture with fine mechanical tolerances. When one of Ford's superintendents arrived at the company from International Harvester, he commented that he found little he hadn't seen at the Deere/McCormick company. Perhaps so, but more than the other visionaries that routinized manufacturing, Ford appreciated the complete interchangeability of parts. His Model T contained 5,000 parts, all standardized. On the other hand, one of Ford's subordinates probably suggested the revolutionary step of moving the assembly line to the worker. But if Ford has received credit where he did not entirely deserve it, his dogged pursuit of turning out cars in the most efficient way possible permitted the constant refinement of the moving assembly line between 1912 and 1914.

All was not harmonious. Ford had perfected a system that brought materials to the workers, which from a management perspective was more efficient. From a labor perspective, especially one steeped in the skilled trades habits of the late 1800s, it was degrading. Worse, managers could speed up the line, placing pressure squarely on the shoulders of workers. At Ford, laborers quit in droves. The turnover reached almost 400 percent prompting Henry Ford to offer higher pay. Contrary to the image Ford promulgated, he did not raise wages out of love for his workers but because he ran out of options to retain them. He also planned to introduce three eight-hour shifts and put out a call for new workers, which brought in so many unemployed that violence broke out at Ford's company gates. The message that others wanted the jobs held by Ford employees came through loud and clear inside the factory, however. But it is doubtful that anxiety over jobs caused the soaring production that ensued after the wage hike.

Whatever his motivation, in 1914, Ford introduced the $5-a-day wage, an amount that represented a truly stratospheric salary to ordinary workers. Only after the wage rate went up did Ford appreciate the fact that one of his employees could purchase a Ford auto on less than a year's salary (and as prices fell and wages continued to rise, on as little as a month's salary). At that point it became apparent that he was ensuring his own sales through his wages. And, to see that workers did not squander their wages on unnecessary products (presumably, cars from rivals!), the company created a "Sociology Department" that policed the lives of employees. Company inspectors visited workers in their homes and interviewed neighbors.

In 1916, Ford lowered the Model T price to $345, causing sales to soar to more than 734,000 units, a number that comprised almost half of all the cars sold in the United States. The price cut—the single greatest leap of faith that Ford had to take—produced an inevitable feedback loop. Falling prices allowed more people to buy Fords; then, as more people bought Fords, the company could lower its profit margin per unit and still make money, with the result being still lower prices for the customer. Yet cost never drove Ford's strategy. His principles of operations stressed the primacy of service over profit. Certainly, he admitted, "well-conducted business enterprise cannot fail to return a profit," but that profit he noted, "must and inevitably will come as a reward for good service."[83]

Ford certainly had his human failings, some of them severe. A bigoted anti-Semite, he referred to Bernard Baruch as a "Jew of Super Power" and disgracefully published the *Dearborn Independent* that initiated a campaign against American Jews in 1920, running such editorials as "The International Jew, the World's Problem." A 1922 *New York Times* article describing Adolf Hitler's headquarters in Munich reported pictures of Ford and a translation of Ford's book present. Ford's ignorance of world affairs and pigheaded refusal to see any event in less than the most simplistic terms was renowned, although occasionally misrepresented. "History is bunk," Ford was quoted as saying, although as David Kyvig and Myron Marty have shown, he in fact spent millions of dollars collecting and preserving historical artifacts and thought "nearby history" was indeed important.[84] In other circumstances, Ford's "do-good" internationalism led him to finance a "Peace Ship" in 1915 to take himself and other peace cranks to Europe to instruct the kaiser to call off the war, oblivious to the boiling cauldron of issues that had caused World War I. Bamboozled into making a speech to the inmates at Sing Sing prison, Ford inserted his foot firmly in his mouth: "Boys, I'm glad to see you here."[85]

Whatever his lack of vision in international affairs or limited understanding of even American politics—he could not even name the causes of the Revolutionary War when he ran for the U.S. Senate—Ford knew cars and car buyers. Early in his career, especially, he had a fundamental appreciation for what a mobile America needed, and he supplied it. Only later, after other auto manufacturers had caught, then passed Ford, did he lose touch with consumers. As with many entrepreneurs, Ford failed to know when to change, sticking to his original vision long after its time had gone. Eventually, Ford's family had to force him out to save the company he built.

Durant, Sloan, and General Motors

As with any business enterprise, when Ford Motors stopped meeting the needs of Americans, its dominance of the market tailed off. A new company, built out of the Buick Motor Company, had emerged under the leadership of William Durant. Mass-producing cars for ordinary citizens was a necessity for a successful automaker in the early 1900s. But Durant, a Flint carriage maker, recognized that sooner or later people would tire of a single model in a single color. He sought instead to tap into the varieties offered by several companies, bringing them together in a single corporate entity that could sell different models to cover different tastes and price ranges.

Durant brought together Buick, Cadillac, Oldsmobile, Oakland, and six other auto companies, plus truck makers and parts manufacturers, to form General Motors (GM) in 1908. Expansion was both Durant's lasting contribution and his fatal corporate flaw; the company's growth lacked direction and strategy. No sooner had he created his empire than auto sales dipped, nearly driving the new company into bankruptcy. Only Durant's ability to convince Wall Street bankers to lend him $13 million saved GM, but the bankers wanted control. They immediately liquidated unprofitable parts of Durant's conglomeration and named a team of managers, including Charles Nash, the head of Buick. Nash's replacement at Buick, Walter Chrysler, eventually left GM to rejuvenate the Maxwell Motor Company, renaming it Chrysler in the 1920s. The bankers and the management team continued to increase auto production but fell behind the prodigious output at rival Ford. GM's market share was halved.

Meanwhile, Durant had approached Louis Chevrolet, a race-car driver, to develop a new, inexpensive car line as an independent company to compete with the Model T. Chevrolet became disaffected, quitting the firm in 1913. Thus, Chevrolet and Buick had founded key elements in the future General Motors line yet had disassociated themselves from the largest automaker in history. Durant, on the other hand, used his stake in Chevrolet and the profits it produced to acquire shares of GM stock until, in 1916, he gained back control of General Motors and handed the bankers their walking papers. A key ally in Durant's revival, Pierre S. Du Pont, came from the famous chemical family that produced explosives, dyes, and paints. The Du Pont family had received huge profits from wartime production but recognized that peacetime might bring a substantial reduction in business, so they looked for other investment opportunities. By the end of the war, the family held almost 30 percent of GM. Nevertheless, Pierre Du Pont managed his family's chemical business, leaving the auto company to Durant. Characteristically, Durant pursued growth at GM.

He laid the groundwork for his new corporate structure in 1916 by converting the General Motors Company (chartered in New Jersey) into General Motors Corporation (with a Delaware charter). Then, between 1918 and 1920, Durant added Chevrolet to GM, as well as Fisher Body, Delco, and other parts and accessories firms. Again, however, Durant's great weakness surfaced. His inability to plan, structure, or rationalize the corporation's growth meant that each division produced and invested without consideration of the whole. Buick might invest in new plants when the greatest need was at Chevrolet. Divisions independently ordered inventory, which the shocked head office had to pay for—often without approving the orders in the first place. And when divisions had cash, they did not necessarily turn it over to Durant's office, meaning that although "General Motors" as a whole was solvent, parts of General Motors were flush while others struggled. Durant's inability to control the divisions led to another near disaster: In 1920 GM had to borrow $83 million from the banks. In desperation, Durant personally had borrowed $30 million that he used to buy GM stock to maintain the price. Forced out a second and final time, Durant turned control of the company over to Pierre Du Pont, who resigned from his family's business and assumed GM's presidency.

Du Pont relied on Alfred P. Sloan Jr., an MIT graduate, an "engineering and managerial genius," and the president of Hyatt Roller Bearing at the time it had merged with Durant's GM. Sloan understood the deficiencies of Durant's helter-skelter system. As a remedy, he prepared a study of the organization that he submitted to Durant, who shelved it. After Du Pont took over, the study was revived and its proposals adopted in 1920. Over the next four years, GM management restructured the company along a rational division system that reported to the head office. Management clearly delineated the distinctions between the different divisions' products, making certain that each division had its own market niche and price. Moreover, the divisions were autonomous to the extent that each contained its own general manager, engineering, production, and marketing, yet all supervised by group vice presidents who headed one of four related groups of products: accessories, affiliated businesses, export products, and the centerpiece of GM, the car and truck division.

Top management divided authority between the executive and finance committees, strengthened by modern statistical controls. The central office received production reports from the divisions and sales reports from the dealers, which then were assessed to establish a statistical estimate of return on investment. GM's new "decentralized" management structure, which resembled that of the Du Pont company, featured a reliance on economists and statistical specialists. In many ways, the reorganization of General Motors marked the high tide of the managerial revolution started more than sixty years earlier. Though not all large corporations switched to decentralized managerial hierarchies, most accepted the need for professional managers to run the companies, even if they did not decentralize management. As a symbol of the entrepreneur with the ability to manage a large company, only Henry Ford seemed to emerge unscathed. But even he would ride a roller coaster in the next twenty years as entrepreneurs went from the victors of World War I to once again being the villains.

Notes

1. Sobel and Sicilia, *Entrepreneurs,* 166. This section relies heavily on the account of Sobel and Sicilia, as well as that of Winifred C. Leland and Minnie Dubbs Millbrook, *Master of Precision* (Detroit, Mich.; Wayne State University Press, 1966) and Hounshell's *From the American System to Mass Production.*

2. Sobel and Sicilia, *Entrepreneurs,* 168.

3. Ibid., 170.

4. Frederick Allen, *Secret Formula* (New York: Harper Business, 1994), 28–66.

5. Jack High and Clayton A. Coppin, "Wiley and the Whiskey Industry: Strategic Behavior in the Passaage of the Pure Food Act," *Business History Review,* 62 (Summer 1988): 286–309 (quotation on 294).

6. Ibid., 307.

7. Allen, *Secret Formula,* 58–59. See also Mark Pendergrast, *For God, Country and Coca-Cola: The Unauthorized History of the Great American Soft Drink and the Company That Makes It* (New York: Collier, 1993).

8. George Bittlingmayer, "Antitrust and Business Activity: The First Quarter Century," *Business History Review,* 70 (Autumn 1996): 363–401.

9. W. Elliot Brownlee, *Federal Taxation in America: A Short History* (Cambridge: Cambridge University Press and the Woodrow Wilson Center Press, 1996), and his edited volume, *Funding the Modern American State, 1941–1945: The Rise and Fall of the Era of Easy Finance* (Cambridge: Cambridge University Press and Woodrow Wilson Center, 1996).

10. Lebergott, *The Americans: An Economic Record,* 407.

11. Brownlee, *Federal Taxation in America,* 3–8.

12. Gerald Eggert, "Richard Olney and the Income Tax," *Mississippi Valley Historical Review* (June 1961), 24–25.

13. Quoted in Lebergott, *The Americans,* 407–408, originally taken from Edwin Seligman, *The Income Tax* (New York: The Macmillan Company, 1911), 420.

14. Lebergott, *The Americans,* 408. Equally as telling as Lebergott's understatement is the subtitle of Elliot Brownlee's edited volume, "The Rise and Fall of the Era of Easy Finance"—easy because it was hidden. As might be predicted, some have complained that the tax system's failure was that it did not go far enough. In *Dimensions of Law in the Service of Order: Origins of the Federal Income Tax, 1861–1913* (New York: Oxford University Press, 1993), Robert Stanley argues that

the tax was a means of social control, symbolic but not truly redistributive. The Progressives—really "conservatives" in Stanley's view—forged a consensus to enact minor taxation as a means to enlist the support of lower classes for long-term domestic tranquility. In reality, however, the heaviest burdens after the income tax soared to new rate levels in the post-World War II period have been carried by the lowest-income class of workers, who have found themselves unable to avoid taxes with clever investments or shelters, escape it by relocating in other areas of the world, or, often, to even pay it. By the 1990s, the average American worked almost *half a year just to pay the federal income taxes*—a far cry from the singing birds and sunshine envisioned by the congressman.

15. Brownlee, *Federal Taxation in America,* 7.

16. See the chart data presented in Ratner, Solow, and Sylla, *Evolution of the American Economy,* 418.

17. Wilson quoted in Folsom, *Myth of the Robber Barons,* 107–108; Andrew Mellon, *Taxation: The People's Business* (New York: Macmillan, 1924), 129; and Lawrence L. Murray, "Bureaucracy and Bi-Partisanship in Taxation: The Mellon Plan Revisited," *Business History Review,* 52 (Summer 1978): 200–225.

18. On the nineteenth-century monetary reformers, see the essays on Amasa Walker, Davis Rich Dewey, A. Barton Hepburn, and others in ed. Larry Schweikart, *The Encyclopedia of American Business History and Biography: Banking and Finance to 1913,* (New York: Facts on File, 1990).

19. An analysis of the reform movements leading up to the Jekyll Island meeting are documented in several of the individual biographies in Larry Schweikart, ed., *The Encyclopedia of American Business History and Biography: Banking and Finance to 1913,* and its follow-up volume, *Banking and Finance, 1913–1989,* especially the essays on John Pierpont Morgan, Frank Vanderlip, Nelson Aldrich, George F. Baker, and others. An excellent technical assessment of the reformer's efforts on the banking system can be found in Eugene N. White, *Regulation and Reform of the American Banking System, 1900–1929* (Princeton, N. J.: Princeton University Press, 1983); James Livingston, *Origins of the Federal Reserve System: Money, Class, and Corporate Capitalism* (Ithaca, N.Y.: Cornell University Press, 1986); and Richard Timberlake, Jr., *The Origins of Central Banking in the United States* (Cambridge, Mass.: Harvard University Press, 1978).

20. Henry C. Dethloff, "Arsene P. Pujo," in Schweikart, ed., *Encyclopedia of American Business History and Biography: Banking and Finance to 1913,* 397–398.

21. Vincent P. Carosso, *The Morgans: Private International Bankers, 1854–1913* (Cambridge, Mass.: Harvard University Press, 1987). A brief, but adroit summary of Morgan appears in Albro Martin, "John Pierpont Morgan," in *Encyclopedia of American Business History and Biography: Banking and Finance to 1913,* Larry Schweikart, ed., 325–348 (quotation on 347).

22. Morgan and Untermeyer quoted in Vincent P. Carosso, *The Morgans: Private International Bankers, 1854–1913* (Cambridge, Mass.: Harvard University Press, 1987), 632–633.

23. Carosso, *The Morgans,* 633.

24. Charles W. Calomiris and Carolos D. Ramirez, "The Role of Financial Relationships in the History of American Corporate Finance," *Journal of Applied Corporate Finance,* 9 (Summer 1996): 52–72 (quotation on 65).

25. See Ross M. Robertson, *History of the American Economy,* 3d ed. (New York:

Harcourt Brace Jovanovich, 1973 [1955]), 466–492.

26. Brownlee, *Dynamics of Ascent*, 379.

27. Milton Friedman and Anna J. Schwartz, *A Monetary History of the United States, 1863–1960* (Princeton, N.J.: Princeton University Press, 1963).

28. Fed ineptness is cited as a problem in Barry Eichengreen, *Golden Fetters: The Gold Standard and the Great Depression, 1919–1932* (New York: Oxford University Press, 1992), although Eichengreen is careful to point out that no central bank successfully dealt with the gold standard, and thus blames the inflexibility of gold more than the government.

29. See the discussion of these various views in Larry Schweikart, "U.S. Commercial Banking: A Histiriographical Survey," *Business History Review,* 65 (Autumn 1991): 606–661.

30. U.S. Bureau of the Census, *Historical Statistics of the United States: Colonial Times to Present* (Washington, D.C.: Government Printing Office, 1975), 884, 887.

31. Dobson, *History of American Enterprise,* 216; Steven Wheeler, "John Pierpont Morgan, Jr.," in *The Encyclopedia of American Business History and Biography: Banking and Finance, 1913–1989,* Larry Schweikart, ed. (New York: Facts on File, 1990), 316–321; and John Douglas Forbes Jr., *J. P. Morgan, Jr. 1867–1943* (Charlottesville: University of Virginia Press, 1981).

32. Johannes R. Lischka, "Armor Plate: Nickel and Steel, Monopoly and Profit," in *War, Business, and American Society: Historical Perspectives on the Military-Industrial Complex,* Benjamin Franklin Cooling, ed. (Port Washington, N.Y.: Kennikat Press, 1977), 43–58. Lischka concludes that monopoly profits did exist, but they were retained by the corporations for new plant expenditures and to bring the par value and paper value of the companies together, removing the large amounts of paper value that had been injected to create the corporations in the first place. Or, in other words, the monopoly profits only covered the risk taken by the entrepreneurs that made it possible for American ships to have armored plate at all!

33. William Gibbs McAdoo, *Crowded Years* (Boston: Houghton Mifflin, 1931), 296–297, 304–309.

34. Anne Trotter, "Development of the Merchants-of-Death Theory," in Cooling, ed., *War, Business, and American Society,* 93–104.

35. Brownlee, *Dynamics of Ascent,* 369.

36. Bryant and Dethloff, *History of American Business,* 143.

37. Ibid., 290.

38. No biography of Schwab exceeds Robert Hessen's *Steel Titan: The Life of Charles M. Schwab* (New York: Oxford University Press, 1975), with his discussion of Schwab's war activities on 236–244.

39. Carnegie quoted in Hessen, *Schwab,* 244.

40. Bernard Baruch, *Baruch: The Public Years* (New York: Holt, Rinehart & Winston, 1960), quoted in Ratner, Soltow, and Sylla, *Evolution of the American Economy,* 411.

41. Ratner, Solow, and Sylla, *Evolution of the American Economy,* 411.

42. David M. Kennedy, *Over Here: The First World War and American Society* (New

York: Oxford University Press, 1980), 253; K. Austin Kerr, *American Railroad Politics, 1914–1920: Rates, Wages, and Efficiency* (Pittsburgh: University of Pittsburgh Press, 1968); and Martin, *Enterprise Denied.*

43. Robert Higgs, *Crisis and Leviathan: Critical Episodes in the Growth of American Government* (New York: Oxford University Press, 1987).

44. Charles Whiting Baker, *Government Control and Operation of Industry in Great Britain and the United States During the World War* (New York: Oxford University Press, 1921), 3.

45. Higgs, *Crisis and Leviathan,* 115.

46. Sobel and Sicilia, *Entrepreneurs,* 16–20, and Russel B. Adams Jr., *King C. Gillette: The Man and His Wonderful Shaving Device* (Boston: Little, Brown, 1978).

47. Adams, *King C. Gillette,* 23.

48. Sobel and Sicilia, *Entrepreneurs,* 204.

49. Harry E. Resseguie, "A.T. Stewart's Marble Palace—the Cradle of the Department Store," *New York Historical Society,* 48 (April 1964): 131–162.

50. Bryant and Dethloff, *History of American Business,* 322–323.

51. See Harry E. Resseguie, "Alexander Turney Stewart and the Development of the Department Store, 1823–1876," *Business History Review,* 39 (Autumn 1965): 301–322, and his "The Decline and Fall of the Commercial Empire of A. T. Stewart," ibid., 36 (Fall 1962): 255–286. An excellent source for the story of most of the major retail giants is Robert Hendrickson, *The Grand Emporiums* (New York: Stein and Day, 1979).

52. Sobel and Sicilia, *Entrepreneurs,* 208.

53. Maury Klein, "The Gospel of Wanamaker," *Audacity,* 4 (Summer 1996): 26–39 (quotation on 27).

54. Klein, "Gospel of Wanamaker," 28.

55. Godfrey M. Lebhar, *Chain Stores in America, 1859–1962* (New York: Chain Store Publishing Corp., 1963), and Tom Mahoney, *The Great Merchants* (New York: Harper Brothers, 1955).

56. Fucini and Fucini, "Washington Atlee Burpee," in *Entrepreneurs,* 5–8; Ken Kraft, *Garden to Order* (Garden City, N.Y.: Doubleday & Co., 1963).

57. Sobel and Sicilia, *Entrepreneurs,* 209–211.

58. Boris Emmett and John E. Jeuck, *Catalogues and Counters: A History of Sears, Roebuck and Company* (Chicago: University of Chicago Press, 1950).

59. Bryant and Dethloff, *History of American Business,* 325.

60. See Lebhar, *Chain Stores in America.*

61. Norman Beasley, *Main Street Merchant: The Story of the J.C. Penney Company* (New York: Whittlesey House, 1948). For the story of a similar store, F. W. Woolworth, see John K. Winkler, *Five and Ten: The Fabulous Life of F.W. Woolworth* (New York: Robert M. McBride & Co., 1940).

62. George Laycock, *The Kroger Story: A Century of Innovation* (Cincinnati, Ohio: The Kroger Company, 1983).

63. Thomas Hine, "The Packaging Made the Product . . . and Remade the American

Grocery Store," *Audacity* (Summer 1995): 28–31 (quotation on 28).

64. Bryant and Dethloff, *History of American Business,* 186.

65. Stephen Fox, *The Mirror Makers: A History of American Advertising and Its Creators* (New York: Vintage, 1985 [1984]), 50. See also Merle Curti's discussion of the way advertisers' views of the "nature of man" changed over time in his "The Changing Concept of 'Human Nature' in the Literature of American Adver-tising," *Business History Review,* 41 (Winter 1967): 335–357.

66. Roland Marchand, *Advertising the American Dream: Making Way for Modernity, 1920–1940* (Berkeley: University of California Press, 1985).

67. Sobel and Sicilia, *Entrepreneurs,* 217–221.

68. In taste tests of Coke and Pepsi, two close rivals, the author not only can always identify the two but usually can pick Diet Coke from Diet Pepsi and even differentiate a caffeine-free Coke or Pepsi from the "real thing."

69. Fox, *Mirror Makers,* 115.

70. Marchand, *Advertising the American Dream,* 18–19.

71. Fox, *Mirror Makers,* 106.

72. Bruce Barton, *The Man Nobody Knows* (New York: Bobbs-Merrill, 1925). A modern version of the book, using terminology tailored to the 1990s, is Laurie Beth Jones, *Jesus, CEO: Using Ancient Wisdom for Visionary Leadership* (New York: Hyperion, 1992).

73. Fox, *Mirror Makers,* 108.

74. Ibid., 109.

75. Joseph Turow, *Breaking Up America: Advertisers and the New Media World* (Chicago: University of Chicago Press, 1997), and the review of this book in *Atlantic Monthly* (June 1997, 113–120) by Randall Rothenberg.

76. Bryant and Dethloff, *History of American Business,* 134.

77. Burton Klein, *Dynamic Economics* (Cambridge, Mass.: Harvard University Press, 1977), Table 3.

78. Sobel and Sicilia, *Entrepreneurs,* 172.

79. See "Henry Ford" in Jonathan R. T. Hughes, *The Vital Few,* expanded ed., 274–356.

80. Ibid., 274–355.

81. Ibid., 290.

82. Ford quoted in Hughes, *Vital Few,* 292.

83. Ford quoted in Sobel and Sicilia, *Entrepreneurs,* 174.

84. David E. Kyvig and Myron A. Marty, *Nearby History: Exploring the Past Around You* (Nashville, Tenn.: American Association for State and Local History, 1982), 1–2.

85. These, and other Fordisms, are detailed in Hughes, *Vital Few,* 306–323, and in Harold Livesay, *American Made: Men Who Shaped the American Economy* (Boston: Little, Brown, 1979), 159–182; as well as his major biographers,

Allen Nevins and F. E. Hill in their three-volume work, *Ford: The Times, the Man, the Company* (New York: Scribner's, 1954); *Ford: Expansion and Challenge, 1915–1933* (New York: Scribner's, 1957); *Ford: Decline and Rebirth, 1933–1962* (New York: Scribner's, 1963). A much more critical work, Keith Sward, *The Legend of Henry Ford* (New York: Rinehart, 1948), and a "court biography" that appears in W. A. Simonds, *Henry Ford* (Los Angeles: F. Clymer, 1946), provide different perspectives.

CHAPTER 9

Deliverance and Despair, 1920–1939

WAR HAD BEEN GOOD TO GOODYEAR. THE TIRE AND RUBBER COMPANY thrived during the conflict, with its sales in 1918 surpassing $130 million. Its market share, contested only by the Ford supplier Firestone, topped 60 percent of the American auto market, and its holdings included cotton and rubber plantations from Arizona to Indonesia, while its products included rubber products and blimps. Yet for all its bright prospects, Goodyear Tire and Rubber was in trouble.

Seeking to ensure a consistent supply of cotton and rubber—the company used 4,000 tons of rubber and 1,500 tons of cotton a month—Goodyear's president, Frank A Seiberling, disregarded the potential downturn brought by peace in Europe and continued to expand his facilities. Within one year, tire and rubber sales crashed, dropping from $732 million to $349 million. Goodyear held nearly $36 million in its inventories of rubber and cotton. More dangerously, the company also traded in rubber and cotton futures using Goodyear stock as collateral. In May 1919, Seiberling's reach exceeded his grasp when he borrowed even more extensively to finance a new factory in California.

Suddenly, car sales plummeted. Overnight, like a gambler needing a big hit to rescue him from a gambling debt, Goodyear had to pay up. With only $19 million in cash and $24 million in immediate materials costs alone, the company was desperate. In its desperation, it may have launched the first era of junk bonds.[1]

No reputable Wall Street bank responded to Seiberling's frantic calls for help. In April 1920, Goodyear's losses reached $18 million, yet the company needed $50 million more. Into the void stepped

Clarence Dillon. A Harvard graduate and son of an immigrant father, Dillon had ditched his European name, Lapowski, in favor of his mother's name, Dillon. He found work at William A. Read & Company, a banking firm, then worked under Bernard Baruch in World War I. After the war, he masterminded several underwritings totaling almost $198 million, claiming at one point that he had brought in 85 percent of his firm's business. After Seiberling's lawyer put him in touch with Dillon, the banker saw a remarkable opportunity. He could succeed where no one else could, and if he failed, no one could damn him. After all, no other bank would even attempt the daunting task of saving Goodyear.

Dillon devised two new high-yield bonds, sweetened with a variety of stock options and preferences. Although technically different from the junk bonds that Michael Milken would create in the 1970s—which capitalized companies with virtually *no* assets—Dillon's high-yield bonds made use of extremely leveraged assets to support a new infusion of money. Goodyear recovered, and within two years had liquid assets of $24 million. But the star of the show was not Goodyear or even Dillon (who battled the company in court for years over fees and commissions), but Wall Street itself, which had emerged as the epicenter of a boom known as the "Roaring '20s." Virtually every one of the high-growth businesses in America during the decade, including autos, electric utilities, radios, and consumer goods, sought to enlist the capital of investors through the investment banks in New York, and they responded. They succeeded so well that the market crash of 1929 in some fundamental sense caused the subsequent Great Depression. Some even argued that the prosperity of the 1920s never existed at all. The boom economy, so the view went, was a fantasy—a myth, an illusion. Or was it?

English historian Paul Johnson, analyzing the history of the modern world from distant shores, has stated flatly, "The view that the 1920s was a drunken spree destructive of civilized values can be substantiated only by the systematic distortion or denial of the historical record."[2] Some distortion has been pure ideology. Some has derived from guilt, as there is no shortage of moralistic commentators who assume that all pleasure must be accompanied by pain. Parties, after all, must be "paid for."

Occasionally, however, the misperceptions have resulted from the tendency to approach the 1920s as a unified whole, essentially treating the decade as "making" the technology and the economy, rather than vice versa. Instead, prosperity of the 1920s resulted from the simultaneous maturation of a number of technologies, capitalized by innovative and aggressive capitalization efforts from Wall Street, all energized by the tax cuts proposed by Secretary of the Treasury Andrew Mellon and incubated in the warm, supportive attitudes of the

Coolidge administration. Stretching over the decade like an umbrella, the optimism of average Americans galvanized the market.

To appreciate the dramatic transformation of entire sectors of the economy, it is useful to examine the growth of a few of them individually, then analyze how they acted interdependently. In the next few sections, therefore, it is important to recognize that none of the technologies discussed was invented in the 1920s, or even had its major growth spurt primarily during that decade. Rather, the focus is on how their maturation combined with that of other industries or business sectors to start feedback loops that reinforced each other's expansion. Perhaps the best place to begin is with Alexander Graham Bell and the telephone.

Bell Telephone and the Communications Explosion

When we last left Western Union, its telegraph lines covered America, transmitting messages over thousands of miles and intertwining every sector of the economy. It had replaced the infinitely slower—and, in its time, equally revolutionary—Pony Express, and by 1879, "Western Union had insinuated itself into the very fabric of American enterprise and seemed destined for years of triumph."[3] The company should have suspected that new technology would allow others to challenge its position, but Western Union's management did not have the historical evidence that future generations of businessmen would have, namely, that the established leader in an area is usually *unlikely* to pioneer the next major breakthrough. Telegraph communication did not develop out of the steamship packet mail business or out of the newspapers, just as 120 years later "e-mail" communications and cellular telephones did not come from the phone companies. The quasi-monopoly position of Western Union also illustrates how consumers benefit from what appears to be a company's attempt to gain control of a market. Not only had telegraph rates fallen precipitously during the competition of the 1860s, as Western Union sought dominance, but the rates remained low long after the major competitors had vanished because both consumers and other potential competitors knew what rates the market could achieve. That threat of "future competition," or the potential for entrepreneurs who otherwise would not engage in a business except for the high profits collected by a monopolist, kept Western Union's rates in line.

Communication changed dramatically in 1876, however, when Alexander Graham Bell, a Boston teacher of the deaf, invented the first telephone, or "harmonic telegraph," as he called it. Bell's device had company, for on the same day as Bell filed his patent, Elisha Gray challenged the patent, claiming to himself have invented a telephonic transmitter. But Bell had the support of Gardner Hubbard, a lawyer with extensive investments and a man familiar with the telegraph. Hubbard immediately saw the potential for revolutionizing the telegraph business. The two men, along with Thomas Sanders, a Haverhill leather merchant, and Bell's lab partner, Thomas Watson, organized the Bell Telephone Company in 1877.[4]

Bell was always more the inventor than the businessman, and he kept to his laboratory while Hubbard handled marketing. Hubbard's first commercial foray involved leasing telephones. Early telephones lacked exchanges and consisted of little more than two-way connections, much like a walkie-talkie. Understanding the voices required all but an interpreter to filter out the oppressive crackling sounds, unless, of course, one had the voice of an operatic tenor.[5] The phones themselves were heavy wooden boxes that sent human speech over a grounded iron telegraph wire through the use of electrical impulses. The partners needed a company that had established lines, and that meant dealing with Western Union. While the new technology might seem a "natural" to the telegraph giant, Western Union's president, William Orton, called the phone a "toy" and rejected Bell's offer to sell the rights to the telephone for $100,000. With that dismissal of the telephone, Western Union once again demonstrated how difficult it is for the leading company in a field to appreciate and embrace radical new technology.

Even Bell's own people did not fully understand the potential of the new technology, touting it as an improved telegraph. Bell himself envisioned telephone offices, where people would go to place calls, much like a stock brokerage house. The first customer, a Boston banker, reported satisfaction, and within a year the company had leased more than 5,000 of its devices at a rate of $40 a year for businesses and $20 a year for residential leases. Commercial leases brought in more than $50,000 in six months. Hubbard, tapping his former railroad connections, recruited a small army of licensing agents who controlled specific geographic areas—the forerunners of the modern "Baby Bells"—and who leased the phones, installed the hardware, strung wires, and collected rents. Early agents included wealthy investors or merchants who themselves had well-established community roots. All of this rested, however, on a somewhat remarkable and flimsy foundation: the Bell patent. The technology itself was so basic that "any competent electrician could easily have copied [it]," which Bell hoped to use to his advantage. After all, he reasoned, no one could copy the telephone without violating the Bell patents, in theory giving the Bell Company a monopoly over telephones for years.

Bell's nightmare, that Western Union would realize the threat to its market, became a reality in 1878 when Western Union dusted off one of Elisha Gray's old patents. In essence, Western Union had been sitting on a telephone of its own for over a year. Terrified of an all-out competitive battle with the industry leader, Bell desperately sought a negotiated settlement with Western Union, hoping to split the market. Again, Western Union rebuffed Bell's offers. The telegraph company had offices in all the major towns, a sprawling system of wires, and a network of potential agents, all of which could be mobilized rapidly to create a long-distance telephone system. A technological breakthrough in 1878 brought such a system closer to reality, when a Connecticut Bell licensee created a switchboard, allowing any one subscriber to contact any other subscriber in the system. By that time, Bell had seen the possibilities, telling investors that "it was now possible to envision a telecommunications system in which 'cables of telephone wires could be laid underground or suspended over head communicating by branch wires with private dwellings, country houses, shops [etc.],'" opening the possibility of worldwide voice communication.[6]

By the late 1870s, both the ill-capitalized Bell and the well-endowed Western Union had improved their respective technologies with new transmitters; both had expanded their systems; but Western Union alone had gained the key cities of Chicago and New York. Bell instituted patent infringement suits against Western Union, which hardly slowed the telegraph company but which served to persuade Bell licensees to remain loyal. Bell's offensive netted more than 30,000 new phone licensees within a year. Still, Western Union would win over the long haul unless Bell developed a new strategy.

When Hubbard united Bell and New England Telephone in 1879 to form National Bell Telephone, he brought in an extraordinary manager, Theodore N. Vail, whose experience in management (like that of most others) came from the railroads. Hubbard then turned the presidency over to William H. Forbes, one of the new investors in the $850,000 company, and with Hubbard's departure, both of the original Bell founders had essentially been pushed out of the telephone business. Invention and entrepreneurship had given way to professional management. Although Vail and Forbes thoroughly restructured the company, creating a foundation of telephone manufacturers, solidifying their control over the licensees, and aggressively expanding the company's patent claims, Bell still toiled away at a considerable disadvantage to Western Union.

At that point, two events changed the shape of the telecommunications industry forever. First, the patent attorneys advising Western Union concluded that Alexander Graham Bell's claim to be the inventor of the telephone was indeed valid. At a minimum, Western Union looked at paying perhaps millions of dollars in back licensing fees. The second event, however, involved the railroad magnate Jay Gould, who had battled Cornelius Vanderbilt, the father of Western Union's primary investor, William Vanderbilt, over railroads for years. Gould, seeking to weaken Vanderbilt's railroad business, attacked him in the communications arena by forming a competitor to Western Union, American Union Telegraph Company. Gould had failed once before to mount a challenge to Western Union's power, but the possibility of combining his own lines and offices with the Bell phones suddenly made Gould a significant threat. Overnight, Western Union reconsidered the Bell offers to settle or consolidate. In 1879, the resulting compromise had Western Union "sell its 56,000 telephones in 26 cities to Bell and grant [Bell] control over the competing telephone patents until 1894, in return for 20 percent of Bell's licensing fees."[7] Further, the National Bell Telephone Company would provide telephone service only—which was local in nature—while Western Union would retain rights to long-distance communications. That limited the Bell exchanges to a fifteen-mile radius of any central office and constricted communications to "personal" calls only; business communications, stock market quotations, and sale messages were to be the domain of Western Union.

Some observers thought Vail had inherited all the problems of the local exchanges with none of the benefits of the long-distance service. Western Union, on the other hand, mistakenly thought the new market would involve primarily business communications. Moreover, the prevailing opinion was that the telephone technology was limited. It could not handle prolonged conversations; it could not replace business mail; and the transmitters were too weak to permit voices to be sent more than a few miles. But even as the ink dried on the agreement, improvements made it possible to send voice messages more than forty miles. Vail, meanwhile, seeing the potential to link the exchanges without violating the letter of the long-distance agreement, won a key point in the final negotiations to develop telephone business *between* exchanges, virtually opening up long-distance transmission in fifteen-mile segments. Vail completed his coup by reorganizing and recapitalizing the company as American Bell Telephone in 1882 and acquiring Western Electric, Western Union's equipment manufacturer. Then, in 1885, at a point when Western Union was no longer powerful enough to resist, the newly formed subsidiary of American Bell, American Telephone and Telegraph (AT&T), opened the door for the company to move into long-distance communication.

Although it might not have been clear to all observers at the time, Bell had achieved utter domination over Western Union and claimed the bulk of the communications market. Some historians, including George Smith, argue that Western Union had acted on a rational corporate strategy when it concluded its deal with Vail.[8] Instead, however, one could conclude that market dominance itself imposes blinders on the potential for new technology. Companies achieve a certain corporate comfort level—a competence with their technology or product—

and almost any breakthrough presents (on the surface) far more problems than solutions. Pressing into unknown waters requires resources that must be diverted from the company's existing area of expertise. Moreover, like any sports team, a good management structure recruits to fill specialized needs related to the technology or product in question. One can hardly fault the telegraph people at Western Union for seeking engineers who specialized in wire transmission and ignoring those whose strength lay in other types of transmitting devices, just as a century later managers of telephone companies would fail to see the potential for transmission of two-way messages by air instead of wire. Indeed, one of the problems with the managerial revolution was that the rationality of the system often worked against its long-term evolution, because pathbreaking ideas rarely seem rational at first.

Vail, meanwhile, came into conflict with the Boston investors. He had a more ambitious expansion plan for the company than they had, and he hoped to replace Forbes as president. But in 1887, when it became clear that the Forbes group would choose another, Vail resigned. At the same time, the Bell patents expired and a swarm of independents entered the market, encouraged by public perceptions that the Bell system had profited unreasonably from its monopoly. Once again, Bell needed cash to reorganize, which it acquired in part by abandoning the restrictive Massachusetts corporation laws and placing the company under AT&T as the new parent. Further financial erosion caused the Bostoners to sell to a J. P. Morgan-led syndicate. Morgan wanted Vail back as the president.

With Morgan's money and Vail's talent, AT&T gradually bought out the independents, improved its own service, and lowered rates. Vail also acquired 30 percent of Western Union in 1909, an acquisition that evoked only howls of protest from the trustbusters. Vail hoped to maintain the company's monopoly status—and shut out future competitors—by embracing a "regulated monopoly" overseen by the federal government. He even shrewdly called for public commissions charged with reviewing AT&T's activities.[9] Company officials held talks with the Wilson administration, resulting in a deal that left AT&T in a position of overwhelming dominance in the telephone business. Although Vail had to unload his Western Union shares, refrain from purchasing other independents (except with the blessing of the ICC), and permit existing independents to connect with Bell System lines, Vail had traded the prospect of an absolute telephone monopoly in the future for three-quarters of the market in 1920, all with the approval and support of Uncle Sam.

In the short term, however, the AT&T empire linked the nation as the telegraph never had. Already by 1912, there were more than 9 million phones in the nation, with over 3.5 million from non-AT&T providers.[10] Vail argued that only large-scale standardization could deliver lower costs to the public, which, of course, was exactly what the larger railroads had claimed fifty years earlier in attempting to limit competition from smaller companies. To an extent, however, AT&T surpassed the railroads as an innovative company because Theodore Vail recognized the value of new products and processes. The company itself had a bureau of research and information that produced the electronic repeater, which, as Louis Galambos suggests, "was clearly formative, not adaptive, innovation."[11] Through the licensing agreements, Vail "taxed" the Bell operating companies for a research and development fund. AT&T represented possibly the best-operated quasi-monopoly in American history.

After 1910, telephones were destined to increase in popularity, regardless of the skills of the telephone companies to market or improve them. A consumer revolution that already had started with dry-goods purchases in department stores now expanded to include small appliances. Moreover, telephones symbolized the new thirst for physical and spatial independence put in motion by the car. Sheer numbers revealed the telephone's popularity.

In 1920, there were 61 telephones per 1,000 city dwellers, and by 1928, there were 92 per 1,000, becoming a standard feature in middle-class housing. The telephone contributed to the feedback loops of the 1920s by making it easier for individuals to place orders with brokers, to maintain contact with businesses and markets, and to conduct enterprise over an ever-expanding area. Telephones, combined with another item commonly found in typical houses, the radio, further enhanced communication. Not surprisingly, a telephone company, AT&T, joined with other firms with electronics interests to establish a patent pool and frame cross-licensing agreements to manufacture radios after World War I. By the "Roaring '20s," the telephone represented a key part in the communications explosion that enhanced overall prosperity.

I Love My Radio

Guglielmo Marconi had conducted radio broadcasts across the Atlantic in 1901, and the introduction of a functional vacuum tube in 1906 made feasible the broadcasting of words, and not merely signals, to the general public on a practical basis. Still, radios were not widely employed, even at sea, until the tragic sinking of the *Titanic* in 1912, which revealed two critical uses of the radio. First, ships at sea had not maintained constant open radio frequencies, often lacking a full-time radio operator. While the crew of the *Titanic* frantically signaled for help, the calls arrived at unattended receivers at ships that conceivably were within range of assistance. Second, the radio signals originally sent from the mortally wounded ship had reached the news desks in New York; but only the *New York Times*, guessing that the first report of a collision with an iceberg, and the subsequent absence of reports, meant that the *Titanic* had sunk, printed the reporters' suppositions without corroborating evidence. As happened, they guessed right. The *Titanic* indeed sank, and the *New York Times* gained an unprecedented respect for gathering "news." Moreover, an eighteen-year-old marine operator of American Marconi, David Sarnoff, gained fame as the man who had received the transmissions of the *Titanic* disaster in New York.

Ships soon used full-time radio crews, with Marconi Wireless receiving a contract to handle maritime radio service for American ships in 1916. Then, after war broke out, the U.S. Navy took over the company in the interest of national security. American Marconi was controlled by British investors, and the prospect of turning such critical technology back over to foreign control—regardless of the recent wartime alliance—generated opposition in the Department of War. The government decided, instead, to allow an American company to assume the assets. In 1919, a group of telegraph and telephone companies, including AT&T, Westinghouse, and General Electric, formed a consortium to assume the assets of American Marconi. The new company, Radio Corporation of America (RCA), had as its first chairman Owen Young, but the most important influence on the actual management of the business was Sarnoff, who had advanced to the position of commercial manager of American Marconi.[12] Years earlier, Sarnoff had rhapsodized about the possibilities of music transmission by wireless, sent to every home.

Sarnoff's vision became possible after a Westinghouse scientist had discovered "broadcasting," which sent signals out over airwaves for whoever wanted to pick them up (as opposed to "narrow casting," or two-way wireless communication). For a small sum, a consumer could purchase a radio and potentially have access to a wide variety of music or information going out over the airwaves. Thus, the initial impetus for supporting radio broadcasting stations came from the indirect profits gained by RCA through the manufacture of radio sets and broadcast equipment. Westinghouse applied for the first license to operate a radio station in 1920—KDKA in Pittsburgh. KDKA's first broadcast, to an estimated 500 listeners on November 2, was the election returns showing that Harding had won the presidency.[13] A year later, WJZ in Newark, New Jersey, broadcast the World Series (actually, reannounced it by relay from the Polo Grounds), gaining as much attention as KDKA had.

By 1922, more than 200 stations had licenses (distributed by the Department of Commerce) to broadcast over the airwaves. Radio-equipment manufacturers supported the expansion of radio broadcasting, endowing it permanently with its indirect funding character.

As the price of radios fell, and as more and more homes acquired radios, broadcasters ran paid commercial advertisements. By 1922, radio advertising sales topped $60 million, and two years later exceeded $350 million. In 1926, AT&T rented wire connections that linked several stations, including WEAF, forming the first radio networks, but the creation of radio station groups under both RCA and AT&T produced concern about a "radio trust." Rather than fight that battle, AT&T sold its systems to RCA, which reformed the enterprise under the leadership of David Sarnoff as the National Broadcasting Company (NBC).[14]

Sarnoff always saw opportunities to tie in related technologies to his radio company, although he was not always successful in obtaining them. After Warner Brothers released *The Jazz Singer* in 1927 as the world's first "talkie" motion picture, Sarnoff purchased patents to the technology from General Electric and forayed into film production with Joseph Kennedy. A year later, RCA had a stake in the Radio-Keith-Orpheum (RKO) theater chain, which utilized RCA sound equipment. With Westinghouse and General Electric, RCA obtained the Victor phonograph company, renaming it RCA Victor, pushing RCA into phonograph sales and recordings. Shortly after the Great Depression had started, the government filed an antitrust suit against RCA, General Electric, Westinghouse, and other members of the so-called Radio Trust, prompting the major investors in RCA to divest their holdings in the company, which made RCA completely independent for the first time. By that time, the government had created a Federal Radio Commission to assign frequencies to stations, ensure a better geographical distribution of broadcasting stations, and to limit power output. Until 1929, however, the future of radio looked bright, especially as the number of radios in the hands of consumers soared from 60,000 in 1922 to more than 7.5 million in 1928. Radio's popularity coincided with Madison Avenue's growing influence and with advertisers' quest to wield every tool they could to sell products. Advertisers quickly learned also that another burgeoning industry could assist in selling products: movies.

Motion Pictures, Max Factor, and Madison Avenue

Actors and actresses, as well as many rock musicians nowadays, have the czar of Russia to thank for their wonderful theatrical makeup. The czar's oppressive policies drove out a talented Polish makeup artist with a Russian opera company, Max Factor, who arrived in the United States in 1904.[15] He established a wig and makeup booth at the St. Louis World's Fair, accumulating the cash the family needed to move to Los Angeles, which had started to evolve as the motion picture capital of America.

Factor's little cosmetics shop featured wigs and toupees, as well as hair dyes and traditional makeup. In 1914, however, his business suddenly took off when Henry Walthall, a silent screen actor, appeared in a movie using Factor's new makeup. Traditionally, stage actors had used stick greasepaint, which went on too unevenly and was too noticeable for the close-up shots of movies. Factor experimented with a cream greasepaint that could be applied in a thin film. Although the breakthrough with Walthall changed his business, Factor developed a more revolutionary makeup in 1928, the Panchromatic film makeup, followed by the famous "Pan-Cake" makeup for technicolor movies in 1937. Already, though, he had capitalized on his fame by marketing his cosmetics nationally beginning in 1927.

Factor developed a sensational reputation with actresses, who came to him for advice on nails, hair, and other aspects of stage appearance. A number of stars, such as Gloria Swanson, Mary Pickford, Clara Bow, and Joan Crawford, received personal attention from the guru of greasepaint. His exaggerated colors and bleaches turned the ordinary into the exceptional, in the process making Jean Harlow into a "platinum blonde." Besieged by beauty "wannabes," Factor created a $600,000 cosmetics factory, opened with a bevy of Hollywood starlets who found entire rooms named after them: the "Blonde Room" for Jean Harlow, the "Brunette Room" for Claudette Colbert, and so on.

Makeup comprised only a small part of the rapidly growing motion picture business. What had started as moving pictures for small "nickelodeons" in the early 1900s had become an entirely independent industry by the 1920s. A group of inventors, led by Thomas Edison, formed the Motion Picture Patents Company in 1908 to collect royalties from anyone using the moving picture process. In 1917, the Supreme Court, responding to the complaints of independent producers who claimed that process did not constitute content, ruled against the patents company and opened movies to anyone capable of making them. Paramount Pictures, which contained a powerful distribution company, had started to produce its own movies, signing the famous Cecil B. DeMille as a director. Paramount soon found itself in competition with another production and distribution firm, Metro-Goldwyn-Mayer, headed by Louis B. Mayer and utilizing the extensive chain of theaters belonging to a partner, Marcus Loew. The new business included the Goldywn Picture Corporation, started by the famous Samuel Goldwyn, who had left to start an independent production company. Other powerful competitors included the Warner brothers (Harry, Jack, Sam, and Albert) and Columbia. Those giants battled over control of distribution, whereby they could produce, distribute, and exhibit their own films.

Ensuring distribution to theaters required presales, which in turn demanded that the companies turn out "formula" movies. To that end, motion picture companies hired directors, actors, and actresses on long-term, exclusive contracts, under the likes of which aspiring young actors like John Wayne would make dozens of highly forgettable pictures on their way to film immortality.[16] Resisting the star system, Mary Pickford, Douglas Fairbanks, Charlie Chaplin, and director D. W. Griffith founded a company called United Artists to ensure that movie artists retained control over their products. Unlike other full-scale integrated companies, however, United Artists only produced films, relying on other companies to distribute and market them. Typical movies had soared in cost, with *Birth of a Nation* (1915) costing $100,000, then escalating to $6 million for *Ben Hur* a decade later.

Still, the industry remained relatively small ($5 million in assets) as late as 1925, until Warner Brothers worked with Western Electric and AT&T to create a talking motion picture, *The Jazz Singer,* which completely revolutionized the industry. Al Jolson's lines, "Wait a minute, wait a minute . . . You ain't heard nothin' yet" became literally prophetic. Overnight, leading men with less than appealing voices and leading ladies who fumbled their lines found themselves replaced by actors and actresses who could speak as well as appear to emote. And, overnight the industry's popularity soared. The number of recording machines in Hollywood increased by one hundred in one year. By 1927, the industry produced 400 to 500 feature films a year, plus a variety of short subjects, and by 1929, the motion picture companies held net assets of more than $160 million.[17] Construction of theaters, therefore, played an important role in the business; palaces such as the Capitol Theater in New York seated 5,300, while the renowned Grauman's Chinese Theater in Hollywood captured the architectural style of the Orient. Huge Wurlitzer organs provided a musical background before the advent of the talkies, while Willis Carrier's new air-conditioning systems were first used on a large scale in New York movie theaters in the 1920s.[18]

Oddly enough, the Great Depression cemented the position of the industry because it remained one of the few cheap modes of escape remaining to people, although most of the eight major studios lost money during the early 1930s. As in other businesses, though, the New Deal attitudes and impediments to entrepreneurship resulted in the "majors" securing more of the market; by 1939, the eight major studios controlled 76 percent of the feature films.[19] Weekly attendance fell from 80 million in 1930 to 50 million by 1932. By that time, the movie stars themselves had been enlisted to sell products for Madison Avenue, exemplified by the Helen Resor's soap commercials that in turn went out over the radio waves. Movies also provided a gentle incentive for consumption, showing people in all parts of the nation the latest and most luxurious goods, creating a demand for products yet unseen in other parts of the nation. But they also reinforced the public perception that business was somehow responsible for the Great Depression, especially in the gangster film genre. There, the gangster protagonists "are confined to acquiring wealth and power . . . [and] are the only ones who understand the system and how to succeed within it. . . . In these films, gangsterism can be seen as supercapitalism."[20] An exception to that pessimistic view came from an unknown cartoonist, Walt Disney, who introduced the world to a whistling mouse in *Steamboat Willie* (1928).

During the 1920s, both motion pictures and radio became industries unto themselves. Both had intertwined themselves thoroughly with Madison Avenue. Whereas radio sold products directly, motion pictures advertised a higher standard of living, generating a generic demand that Madison Avenue filled through specific radio ads. But there the similarity stopped. Unlike movies, the real-time effect of radio made it a part of daily business. Radio reports increasingly relayed critical economic information to investors and traveling salesmen. The radio and the telephone enlarged the information network geometrically, and as they became common items, the ability to transact business over long distances, and even from one's home, accelerated another trend that began in 1920—a rising stock market that seemed to head perpetually higher.

Running with the Bulls

Some of the purchases (though certainly not the majority) were facilitated through the growing use of *margin buying,* wherein brokers accepted a "down payment" of 10 to 15 percent minimum and advanced a customer the balance to purchase a stock. If, for example, someone wanted to buy a $100 stock and had a solid relationship with the broker, $10 would acquire the stock and the rest would be advanced on margin. When the remainder was due, it was referred to as a "margin call." Why did brokers act so generously? The answer was simple: The market had not gone down for years, and had not even dipped for some stocks. It was, in gambling terminology, "a lock."[21] Margin buying rose from $1 billion in 1920 to $8 billion in 1929, leading one wag to quip that people were borrowing not only on the future but also on the hereafter.

Contrary to assertions about the market in the 1920s, however, margin buying acted as a lubricant, not a stimulant. People bought stocks because they represented profitable investments, not because credit was available. (The most generous credit terms in the world could not sell, say, a Yugo!) Led by utilities and industrials, productivity growth brought higher profits and stock prices throughout the 1920s. Using an index of common stock prices with 1900=100, the index topped 130 in 1922, 140 in 1924, and 320 in 1928. At the time of the crash in 1929, stock prices hit their then-record high of 423 on the index.[22] Individual corporate stock prices reflected the general trends, with the purchase of a few thousand dollars' worth of the right stock netting hundreds of thousands of dollars in half a decade. Stocks refused to go down. RCA, for example, which never paid a dividend, went from $85 a share to $289 in 1928 alone, while General Motors common stock worth $25,000 in 1921 was valued at $1 million in 1929. Again, however, substance backed up the stock values. Total assets of the largest 200 enterprises doubled, while individual companies, such as RCA, experienced phenomenal success. General Motors hummed along in 1929, producing profits of $200 million a year. A line worker at GM could own part of the auto giant for which he toiled. For a few dollars a month, an insurance salesman could become a partner with the Morgans.

The knock, of course, was that "average Americans" did not hold stock, only the wealthy. Statistical analysis suggests a different picture, though. Two major changes in the makeup of the investment community indeed had occurred: More people were holding, and trading in, stocks, and they constituted more of a social and economic cross section than ever before. In 1900, extrapolating from a study of stockholder lists of railroads, economic historian Stanley Lebergott estimated that 15 percent of American families owned stock. Most of those families, based on the availability of stock and its share costs, were in the upper class. By 1929, 28 percent of American families held securities, indicating that, obviously, groups other than the wealthy purchased securities. Some analysts, including Lebergott, express skepticism that ownership was spread to a substantially wider segment of the public. Evidence of specific issues, however, confirms that it was. For example, one "analysis of those buying fifty shares or more in one of the largest utility stock issues of the 1920s shows that the largest groups were (in order): housekeepers, clerks, factory workers, merchants, chauffeurs and drivers, electricians, mechanics and foremen."[23] Metal workers held more stock than doctors, and machinists more than lawyers. Dressmakers, on a six-to-one ratio, held more stock than bankers. Nor did people borrow excessively to speculate in the stock market. A recent study of the Federal Reserve Board's activities concluded that while consumer debt as a percent of income had increased, that debt in itself did not produce harmful effects, but rather the Fed's perception that the debt would produce ill effects in the future that led the Board of Governors to strangle the money supply.[24]

Another indicator that common people could, and did, purchase stocks appeared in the subtle shift in advertising and marketing securities that occurred in the decade. No individual did more than Charles E. Merrill to convince middle-class investors to pick up their phone and place an order to purchase the stock of capital-hungry companies.

Charles Merrill: Selling Stock in America

College may provide many people with the training they need in their careers, but for Charles E. Merrill, dropping out of Amherst College in 1906 opened doors to occupations he had never considered. He went to work as an editor of a Florida newspaper, gaining a keen insight into the motivations of the public. He played minor league baseball, which emphasized teamwork and dedication to a goal. At a textile plant, he obtained "the equivalent of a university course . . . in credit, finance, cost accounting, and administration. . . ."[25] Moreover, the textile job put Merrill in contact with Edward Lynch, a soda equipment salesman. In 1909, Merrill got a job with a brokerage house on Wall Street, where in time he headed a newly created bond department. In 1911, Merrill wrote an article for *Leslie's Illustrated Weekly* called "Mr. Average Investor," in which he emphasized a close personal relationship between the investor and securities adviser. He also perceived that profits could be made by meeting the securities needs of thousands of small investors as well as a handful of rich ones.

Merrill brought in Lynch in 1915, and the two fashioned a plan to sell bonds through direct-mail solicitations that consisted of informative circulars instead of the advertisements of the securities that bordered on fraud. Gradually, Merrill had invented a new type of securities market oriented to the ordinary person of limited means.

Merrill Lynch, as the firm became known, underwrote securities for several chain stores, including McCrory and Kresge, gaining a reputation on Wall Street for specializing in chain-store offerings. War interrupted Merrill's business career. He served with the Army Air Corps as a flight instructor. The war also taught Merrill an important lesson about investment. He watched Americans purchase U.S. war bonds on a regular basis, suggesting that the basis existed for selling securities to a broad panoply of middle-class investors.

After the war, Merrill Lynch continued to underwrite chain stores, acquiring in the process controlling interest in Safeway Stores. Assuming a management role in Safeway, Merrill forged a merger between that company and another chain his firm had dealt with, MacMarr Stores. The resulting Safeway company had 4,000 outlets and was the third largest in the United States. Although he did not serve as chief executive officer, Merrill held enough shares that he could decide who held that position, and he played a key role in developing advertising campaigns for the chain.

Management of Safeway further reinforced Merrill's interest in mass-market, high-volume business. Yet he never abandoned his most fundamental principle, namely, that investors deserved the truth. Anticipating the great crash, Merrill Lynch sent a letter to all the firm's clients in March 1928 urging them to quietly liquidate their securities and get out of debt. Nevertheless, the straightforward approach of Merrill Lynch did not keep the firm from being tarred with the broad brush that colored other brokerage houses after 1929. Merrill rebuilt the firm's image and emerged from the Great Depression and World War II with a renewed commitment to reestablishing the securities markets as a place for sound investment by the growing middle class.

"Feast of Belshazzar" or the "Full Dinner Pail"? The 1920s Assessed

Charles Merrill had helped extend investment opportunities that previously only the wealthy and connected had enjoyed to people of all income groups. Yet while he may have deepened the investment boom, he neither created it nor fueled it. Americans could see for themselves the prosperity and optimism that surrounded them. In retrospect, a few economic Jeremiahs invoked biblical images of destruction after the Great Crash, falsely reasoning that the growth of the 1920s *produced* a speculative fervor. Edmund Wilson likened the decade to a "drunken fiesta," while F. Scott Fitzgerald sneered that Americans had engaged in the "greatest, gaudiest spree in history."[26] Even conservative writers, including Paul Johnson, have argued that the new investment mechanisms and margin buying "provided additional superstructure of almost pure speculation. . . ."[27] Reality was much different, and most people knew it. The stock market boom was an indicator of genuine expansion, but also was a critical lubricant, bringing together the funds of millions of investors to fuel the production of autos, plate glass, gasoline, irons, vacuum cleaners, radios, telephones, and other goods.

Referring to the "consumer-durables revolution" of the 1920s, Stuart Bruchey has recorded estimates that showed that by 1928 27 million American homes had 15 million irons, 6.8 million vacuum cleaners, 5 million washing machines, 4.5 million toasters, and 750,000 electric refrigerators.[28] Auto registration rose from 9.3 million to 23 million between 1921 and 1929 alone, while auto production soared 255 percent during the decade. Cars were important because they facilitated production of—and purchases of—a vast multitude of other products. Tires, glass, paint, metal, cement, lumber, steel, cotton, leather—all were needed to make the finished automobile or the factories that produced it. Thus, auto production generated a boom in rubber, cotton, construction, gasoline refining, and other industries directly tied to serving the auto. Car owners needed roads and other peripherals, including good tires, gasoline, and spare parts. A highway construction frenzy began, with initial private highways appearing. Soon, however, politicians raced to fill the public's demand for "cheap" roads by sending a flurry of state bond financing that went through Wall Street. As more people drove cars, auto stocks' value rose to new heights, prompting still more interest in auto securities. The auto companies used the cash that flooded in to further electrify their operations, expand facilities, and thus gain greater economies of scale, lowering prices. Lower prices enticed more people to buy cars, and the cycle started again.

It should start to become obvious, now, how the telephone and stock market facilitated the rapid expansion of autos; how the phenomenal boom in electrical power generation (almost 300 percent between 1899 and 1929) in turn acted as a multiplier for mass production, as well as for providing a direct source of energy for the refrigerators, radios, fans, heaters, and dozens of other consumer appliances that appeared in American homes. The feedback loop accelerated even faster, though. With electricity one could use a radio to obtain the latest news, and based on that news, make certain financial decisions, some of which might require the instantaneous communication offered by the telephone. Electricity, however, actually played a much more expansive role than was reflected in the sheer number of new electrical items, for the *efficiency* of electric power generation rose at unprecedented rates. In 1899, electrical motors accounted for 5 percent of the installed horsepower in the United States, but by 1929 electricity generated 80 percent of the installed horsepower. More important, whereas steam belt-driven machines transferred only a small fraction of the horsepower they produced, electric motors increased the amount of deliverable horsepower by as much as 60 percent.

But the loops also ran in reverse; anyone could see that electricity was a growth industry. Utilities stocks thus emerged as among the most prized of Wall Street securities. With each new offering, utilities companies could open new plants and generate more power, causing prices to fall. With each fall in prices, more homes and businesses could afford electricity, leading to increased profits at the utilities company and, completing the circle, causing utilities stocks to rise even higher.

At each point, investment in a growing industry, *even state-originated investment through bond issues,* further contributed to the efficiencies and expansion of the financial sector. In 1918 state expenditures on highway construction reached $70 million, but by the time stock prices had finished falling in 1930, state highway construction expenditures had grown to $750 million. More often than not, Wall Street houses played some role in the "capital deepening" that occurred in the economy. And it was not just investment banks but commercial banks as well that prospered. Finance companies had been started to provide direct installment credit for smaller items, and installment loans more than doubled, from $1.3 billion to $3 billion between 1925 and 1929. The finance companies had to do something with their swelling deposits. Likewise, the correspondent banks around America (except for those in depressed agricultural areas) had excess reserves that they dumped in big-city banking institutions, providing yet another pool of capital. Unlike a snowball rolling in a single direction, however, the growth of the 1920s more resembled a huge pond ripple, spreading wealth geometrically in almost all directions simultaneously.

Small Business and Entrepreneurs in the Roaring '20s

Because the expansion involved fitting together large, previously unrelated sectors, growth tended to occur predominantly through existing businesses. At least one study suggests that failure rates among small business manufacturers were "notoriously high," and another specific study of Minnesota cities reported more than 62 percent of the firms in the study closed between 1926 and 1930.[29] Yet the same study of manufacturers found that total business firms in the United States rose from 1.7 million in 1919 to 3.02 million in 1929. Small business had taken advantage of new service industries, as well as new openings in radio broadcasting and motion pictures, to move away from manufacturing.

While the number of corporations rose by more than 150,000 over that same period, few memorable entrepreneurs outside the areas of advertising, motion pictures, and radio during the 1920s readily come to mind as in other decades in the nation's business history. Some exceptions existed. Hallmark Cards, which grew from Joyce Hall's little door-to-door postcard sales into a string of card stores that ran from Missouri to New York and employed 120 people manufacturing cards, had established itself by the 1920s. Hallmark recovered from a near fatal factory fire in 1915, at which time Hall rebuilt the company.

Firms like Hallmark demonstrated the hypothesis of Harold Vatter that the 1920s was "a poor decade for new, small manufacturing enterprises, but a decade of expansion in the size of both small and other-sized established manufacturing firms."[30] Total plant numbers did not increase as rapidly as one might expect in such a boom; but the number of corporate manufacturing firms rose from 67,000 to 92,000 during the decade, and the output per establishment rose by more than one-third between 1919 and 1929. But the evidence that noncorporate enterprise "must have suffered a high mortality rate" is not as obvious as some argue, because the new technologies and products entailed new levels of service, and service businesses were not counted among manufacturing firms.[31] Nevertheless, it may well be that the Roaring '20s did not represent a high tide of entrepreneurial new businesses so much as a vast expansion of already established small and midlevel businesses. Whatever the source, a wide expanse of the American public achieved a higher standard of living as never before in history.

Home construction, for example, soared. Starting in 1920, the United States embarked on its longest building boom in history, with more than 11 million families acquiring homes by mid-decade.[32] (Again, the role of the auto cannot be overstated in allowing homeowners to live farther from their place of employment.) More than three-fourths of all urban and nonfarm households had electric service by 1930, contributing to the boom in household appliances. And not just homes reflected the new affluence, but people's entire way of life. One-time luxuries, such as air travel, filtered into the middle class at astonishing speed. Between 1928 and 1930 alone, air passengers increased almost tenfold; then, by 1945, increased again by a factor of 20!

Such affluence, across such a wide spectrum of the population, only could have been possible if the income growth of most Americans actually improved. Indeed it did. Using a 1933–38 economic indicator index of 100, the nation had gone from 58 in 1921 to 110 in 1929, marking an increase in real per capita income from $522 to $716. The rising tide of affluence allowed people to save and invest as never before, acquiring life insurance—policies passed the 100 million mark in 1920—savings accounts, and securities. Moreover, indices of such growth actually *understated* the improvement in the average worker's condition, because tax rates fell from 1920 to 1928, allowing people to retain even more of their earnings. Economists such as John Kenneth Galbraith and Peter Temin have argued that underconsumption caused the Great Depression. But the evidence hardly suggested that consumers lacked either incomes or the desire to purchase goods: In 1921, the consumers' share of GNP was $54 billion, and only a decade later it had risen to $73 billion, representing an increase of an additional 5 percent of GNP, even while prices on consumer goods fell by 14 basis points during the 1920s. (Just for comparison, recall that Robert Fogel rejected the notion that railroads were "indispensable" when they accounted for 5 percent of GNP, let alone a 5 percent per decade *increase* in GNP!)

While in no way causing the boom, government set the tone for the decade, in essence telling people that their efforts mattered and that their wealth was their own. Uncle Sam then proved it by allowing them to keep more of the fruits of their labor. We can see the statistical results, but perhaps more important were the hidden benefits of government's attitudes. Businesses were no longer treated as outlaws or renegades to be brought to justice.

Warren Harding (R-OH) began the transformation in 1920 by insisting that the nation return to normality (not "normalcy," as the reporters misquoted him), and campaigned on the promise to return United States tax rates to their prewar levels. By giving Harding 60 percent of the vote (the largest majority recorded to that point since Washington) and by handing the Republicans control of the Senate and House, the nation expected the president to make good on his promise. He quickly announced his cabinet, made up of "a cross-section of successful America: a car manufacturer, two bankers, a hotel director, a farm-journal editor, an international lawyer, a rancher, an engineer, and only two professional politicians."[33] The most important of his appointees, insofar as it affected American entrepreneurs and working families, was Andrew Mellon, a sixty-five-year-old millionaire of so few words as to make "Silent Cal" Coolidge appear verbose.

Mellon had taken the train to meet Harding at his home in Marion, Ohio, only to encounter a line of local job seekers. Waiting his turn, despite the fact that the President-elect had requested the meeting, Mellon finally shook hands with Harding and proceeded to explain why he should not be the secretary of the Treasury. Harding had exactly what he wanted: a man with enough wealth that he was not for sale and one who did not want the job. For Mellon, heading Treasury required him to leave his safe corporate position at the head of a banking and oil empire to test his theory that the rich had avoided an increasing amount of taxes as tax rates steadily had risen. It represented the first official test of what later came to be called "supply-side economics."

Andrew Mellon Slashes the National Debt (and Helps the Taxpayer!)

Upon assuming office, Mellon suspected that for years the rising tax rates had made it consistently more advantageous for the wealthy to shelter their income rather than invest it and pay taxes on profits. In 1921 he started to analyze the tax rates and resulting revenues systematically. He found that between 1917 and 1921, the number of returns filed by people earning over $300,000 had plummeted fourfold. Net income of those earning above $300,000 likewise had fallen from $731 million in 1917 to $153 million in 1921 (see Figure 9.1). Yet anyone could see that there were more "rich people" in America than ever before. What was happening?

Mellon surmised that wealthy investors had shifted their money into tax-exempt bonds issued by cities and states. At some point, municipal bonds paying a low interest rate returned a higher net amount because of the tax savings. According to Mellon's estimates, by 1923

FIGURE 9-1	*The Decline of Taxable Incomes over $300,000 from 1916 to 1921*			

	NUMBER OF RETURNS		NET INCOME	
YEAR	ALL CLASSES	INCOMES OVER $300,000	ALL CLASSES	INCOMES OVER $300,000
1916	437,036	1,296	$ 6,298,577,620	$992,972,986
1917	3,472,890	1,015	13,652,383,207	731,372,153
1918	4,425,114	627	15,924,639,355	401,107,868
1919	5,332,760	679	19,859,491,448	440,011,589
1920	7,259,944	395	23,735,629,183	246,354,585
1921	6,662,176	246	19,577,212,528	153,534,305

Source: From Andrew Mellon, *Taxation: The People's Business.* (New York: Macmillan, 1924). Copyright © 1924 by Macmillan Press. Permission granted by Burton Folsom.

Americans held $12 billion in tax-exempt bonds, representing an amount equal to half the national debt. Cities built baseball stadiums, recreation centers, and parks while American businesses suffered from capital anemia. Moreover, Mellon, thanks to his family background as oil drillers, knew how risky many corporate investments were. Government bonds, however, presented safe places for capital.

The trick, he realized, lay in making industrial investment profitable, which required tax cuts. He found opposition among those of all ideological stripes against tax-cutting: Progressives had long favored a growing government and rising tax rates as a way of promoting economic equality, while conservative budget balancers worried that lower tax rates would produce less government revenue, hence, a larger national debt. Both groups were wrong about the effect of lower taxes. Mellon intuitively understood a phenomena that fifty years later would be called the "Laffer Curve," a proposition so simple and unshakeable that most critics do not attempt to debate its merits, only its effective rate (see Figure 9.2). According to the creator of the Laffer Curve, Arthur Laffer, there are two tax rates any government can have that will produce no revenue at all. If there is a tax rate of zero, the government collects no taxes. If, however, the tax rate is 100 percent, the government will not collect taxes either, because no one will work to pay his entire income in taxes. Human nature dictated that when government confiscates too much of people's earnings, they will find ways around the tax code legally or, ultimately, refuse to abide by the law. Laffer's simple premise was that *at some point* a government can generate greater revenues by lowering rates. He did not establish at what point that transpired, but argued that the effect looked like a curve, with tax revenues rising with tax-rate increases to a certain point, then declining after that point. A tax rate of 95 percent might bring in far less revenue, then, than a rate of half, or even one-third, that rate.

In 1921, of course, Mellon could not know of the Laffer Curve, which appeared in the 1970s. But Mellon understood human nature and predicted that at rates above 25 percent rich people put their investments in nontaxable shelters or even consumed more rather than pay taxes.[34] Although it took repeated efforts to convince Harding—but fewer to convince Coolidge, easily the most favorable president for entrepreneurs in the nation's history—Mellon proposed his plan to Congress. It consisted of four points and marked a policy stance as momentous as that taken 140 years earlier by Hamilton. First, he urged Congress to cut the top income tax rate from 73 percent to 25 percent. Second, he insisted that taxes on lower incomes had to be chopped as well. People making over $4,000 per year paid 8 percent, and those making under $4,000 paid 4 percent. Mellon wanted to cut those rates to 6 percent and 3 percent, with an eye toward lowering the rates still further at a later date. Related to the lower-class rate reductions, he sought a tax credit of 25 percent on earned income so as to further reduce the burden on working-class taxpayers. Progressives, perhaps showing their true colors, resisted any rate reduction on any groups: Robert LaFollette, the leader of the Progressives in Congress, wanted taxes to start at incomes of $1,000, and as governor of Wisconsin he had supported a state tax on those making as little as $800. Mellon's third proposal was a reduction in the federal estate tax, which he saw as properly the domain of the states, with high estate taxes encouragimg the creation of tax shelters. Finally, Mellon pressed for efficiencies in government, cutting staff in the Treasury Department at the pace of one a day, every day, in the 1920s.[35]

Reductions did not come easy. From 1921 to 1923, Mellon battled the Progressives on taxes, gaining a substantial reduction in large income rates (to 46 percent) but losing on corporation taxes (raised by 1 percent). The Progressives agreed to the politically popular decrease on lower rates below $8,000, but Mellon found himself running in mud. Then Harding died, leaving Coolidge president, whereupon the new chief executive concurred completely with Mellon's plan to lower top rates to ease the burden on lower groups.[36] Throughout it all, Mellon anticipated that some of the new revenue growth that he expected would result from the lower rates would be used to reduce the national debt.

By the time the final incremental reductions fell into place, the top bracket of taxpayers paid almost 50 percent more than before the cut, while those in the lowest brackets paid, on average, between 40 and 70 percent less. A recent study by Gene Smiley and Richard H. Keehn

| FIGURE 9-2 | *The Laffer Curve* |

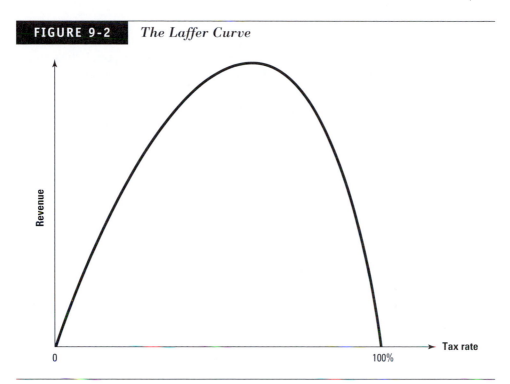

Source: From Peter M. Gutmann, "Taxes and the Supply of National Output," in Bruce Bartlett and Timothy P. Roth, *The Supply-Side Solution*. (Chatham, N.J.: Chatham House, 1982), pp. 265–268, chart on p.142. Copyright © 1982 by Chatham House Publishers. Reprinted by permission of Chatham House Publishers.

concluded that the lower rates ended tax avoidance by a considerable extent.[37] Just as important, Mellon increased revenues to the U.S. Treasury so much that the United States paid off one-third of its national debt—not deficit, but total debt—in less than eight years![38] Given the misplaced emphasis on the national debt in the 1990s, certainly any modern politician who equaled Mellon's feat would be enshrined next to the Lincoln Memorial.

No one living or dead can refute the fantastic increases in wealth during the decade nor the role Mellon played in facilitating it. Consequently, critics have focused almost exclusively on the distribution of wealth in the 1920s—a line of attack that is akin to complaining that although all the dinner guests had eaten their fill, some managed to get extra dessert! Nevertheless, the reasoning, supported in studies such as Charles Holt's, suggests that most of the income gains in the decade went to the top 5 percent.[39] Adjusting the factors used to measure income gains could produce outcomes different from Holt's, but, for a moment, assuming Holt's analysis to be true, it still could be meaningless as far as explaining the practical effects on people. In all capitalist economies, a direct correlation exists between wealth (and thus, capital gains) and age. Few "income inequality" studies address the fact that older people tend to be wealthier than younger people just starting their careers. A simple adjustment for age disparities almost miraculously evaporates large inequalities in wealth. Equally distorting is the inclusion of the entire population in measurements, when recent immigrants usually arrive in the United States with no wealth at all; consider all the Steinways and Carnegies who arrived penniless. When one adjusts for age and residence time in the United States, substantial inequities all but disappear.[40] The best assessment of Mellon's policies in the 1920s, perhaps, was a one-question test candidate Jimmy Carter offered the public in 1976 (and which candidate Ronald Reagan turned against him in 1980): "Are you better off now than you were four years ago?" In 1925, or 1926, or 1927, or even well into 1929, most Americans would have shouted, "YES."

Again, however, the falling national debt did not cause the prosperity but rather reflected it. Keeping more of their earnings than at any time since 1916, entrepreneurs launched new firms at a frenzied pace, soaking up the labor pool, until in 1926 the unemployment rate reached an astonishing *1 percent*—perhaps the only time unemployment fell as low in the history of the American peacetime economy. The index of manufacturing production rose from 15 in 1920 to 23 by 1929, yet the annual earnings of employees rose by one-third and the number of hours worked in manufacturing fell by 5 percent. With little to complain about, workers ignored the unions; the AFL's membership dropped from 4 million in 1920 to 2.7 million in 1929, and overall union membership shrank slightly faster.[41] Union leaders complained that the affluence and luxury produced by the economy had made their role superfluous.

Government's role in the boom consisted of more than cutting taxes and providing rhetorical encouragement. The Harding and Coolidge administrations avoided any foreign entanglements, with the resulting decade of peace debunking the later cold war notion that it took expenditures for the "military-industrial complex" to keep the economy afloat. The administrations' business policies were not perfect, and Coolidge and Mellon in particular tended to support tariffs. While ultimately a tariff—Smoot-Hawley—would contribute heavily to the Great Depression, nevertheless, when Coolidge left office the United States stood as the world's economic power. As a share of world production in 1929, America held 34.4 percent, compared to Britain and Germany, each with a little over 10 percent.

Coolidge had good reason to say that "No Congress . . . ever assembled, on surveying the state of the Union, has met with a more pleasing prospect. . . . The country can regard the present with satisfaction and anticipate the future with optimism."[42] Modern Americans might laugh at such a statement less than a year before the Great Crash, if not for the fact that authorities as varied as historian Charles Beard and writer Walter Lippmann echoed them in other works. *The Nation* published a three-month series on the permanent state of prosperity, with discussions of the pockets of people not yet enjoying its benefits. Ironically, the opening article coincided with the sharpest drop in stock prices in the history of the New York Stock Exchange. Coolidge, it appears, anticipated a recession, and he intuitively appreciated the fact that despite his austere approach to federal spending, which remained virtually flat during his tenure, the government's growth had placed undue pressures on the economy. He despised his successor, a "forgotten Progressive" Republican named Herbert Hoover, who had wielded federal power as head of the Food Administration during World War I, then as secretary of commerce in the Harding-Coolidge administrations.[43] Steeped in his wartime experience with crisis, Hoover employed the government willingly to solve the nation's problems, especially in the agricultural sector, where he personally stepped in to craft the 1929 Agricultural Marketing Act. Far from being a laissez faire capitalist, Hoover more closely resembled the corporatists that had gained power in Europe, envisioning a mutual cooperation between business, labor, and the government. He rejected fascism and overt statism, seeing himself as a free society's alternative to Italy's Mussolini. Most important, he embodied the managerial revolution's maxim that efficiency could be attained through planning and that a scientific and rational approach to the economy would yield beneficial results. As Hoover quickly found out, planning proved a thoroughly inadequate shield against irrational panic. Nor did planning help when it relied on constructs that put into motion some of the problems management was expected to solve. Indeed, planners had struggled for a decade with solutions to the recession in the farming sector, with little to show for it.

The Farm Fiasco

Farmers had produced at record levels during World War I. Slogans such as "Plow to the Fence for National Defense!" and "If You Can't Fight, Farm" reiterated the critical role food played in the conflict. Government guarantees gave farmers profit levels usually associated with the greedy railroad monopolists. Well into the war effort, the Wilson administration had guaranteed farm prices, and, as late as June 1920, the price of land reflected the new incentives. Whereas land values rose less than 5 percent a year from 1870 to 1915, suddenly, over the next five years, values gained over 11 percent a year. Seeing an opportunity to make unprecedented profits, farmers borrowed as never before on land. American wheat farmers had the price of their product pegged by Congress at $2.26 a bushel, when Australian farmers received only 98 cents a bushel. As might be expected, the United States "was sitting on a mountain of surplus wheat. . . ."[44]

Then, reality hit agriculture like a twister. As European and Australian farmers returned to the fields, prices plummeted, but the interest rates on the mortgages held fast. Yet even at their peak in 1927, the bankruptcy rate for farmers (1.8 per 100) was still below that of all businesses. Large corporations had suffered from the speculation of the agricultural boom and bust, too. National City Bank, speculating on high sugar prices, had opened sixteen branches in Cuba in 1919, then paid for it heavily when world sugar prices plunged.[45] By most statistical measures, farm values remained high; farm income had risen, making the 1920s "moderately prosperous" for agriculture.[46] But comparing farm to nonfarm income, a formula developed by the USDA's Bureau of Agricultural Economics called "parity," farm lobbyists argued that farmers were falling behind. Like all other businesses, farmers, through the Grange and the Populist movement, had sought special favors for agriculture from the government. By the 1920s, farmers possessed one of the most powerful lobbies in Washington, and after World War I they supported import tariffs with increasing enthusiasm.

Beginning in the 1920s, farmers opened a new campaign to gain federal export subsidies. The McNary-Haugen bill, named after Senator Charles McNary of Oregon and Representative Gilbert Haugen of Iowa, attempted to boost farm income. McNary-Haugen contained the contributions of George N. Peek, a former John Deere executive and head of Moline Plow Company who worked under Bernard Baruch in the war. Peek and his associate, Hugh Johnson, sought to fix domestic prices for farm products based on a "parity" relationship between farm and industrial goods using a price structure indexed to 1909–1913 prices. It encouraged "dumping" the surplus—which it did nothing to alleviate—at world market prices. Sensibly, Coolidge vetoed the measure twice, acting on the advice of his secretary of commerce, Herbert Hoover. As W. Elliot Brownlee notes, Hoover understood "a serious, probably fatal flaw in the McNary-Haugen proposals: the omission of production controls, specifically the production that farmers could achieve."[47] Moreover, "parity" never existed except in the minds of the planners, any more than a natural relationship between computer prices and hula hoops ever existed. When it came to agriculture, though, even the promarket Coolidge abandoned his better judgment, arguing that government must encourage orderly and centralized marketing" and supporting federal funding of marketing coops.[48] The real dilemma for farmers, and the one they refused to confront, was simple.

On the one hand, there were still too many farms, producing too much, to be profitable, especially when considering the strong increase in Canadian and Russian grain exports. Limiting the analysis to the United States alone, it took only half the nation's farmers to produce 90 percent of the agricultural output. The remainder constituted self-sufficient family organizations more than actors in a capitalist market, especially in pockets of Appalachia and northern Wisconsin. On the other hand, there were too few farmers to force through pro-farm legislation with veto-proof majorities. Ultimately, farmers never mustered a great deal of support from the large urban areas. As Stanley Lebergott has observed, "Most farmers were up against a basic fact by 1920–21: Americans were reasonably well-fed."[49] The public used its surplus to buy luxuries such as cars, not more food.

Autos, of course, had helped improve farm productivity by greatly expanding market points and permitting greater mobility on the farms themselves. Productivity rose from a 1909 index of 100 to a 1929 index of 110, with the labor hours per unit of virtually every farm product falling from 1915 to 1930. Much of that productivity growth occurred due to the mechanization of agriculture. Farmers purchased more than a million tractors in the 1920s. The Fordson, a small, gasoline-powered tractor introduced in 1917, had started the application of auto technology to the farm, followed by the International Harvester row-crop tractor, with its width-adjustable rear wheels that allowed a farmer to plant, cultivate, and harvest row crops. Allis-Chalmers introduced a rubber-tire tractor in 1929 that permitted farm vehicles to move on public roads for the first time, while the rubber tires gave the machine improved traction. But these advances produced surpluses, resulting in a surge in supply that forced prices down 25 percent from the wartime high. The value of farm land and buildings collapsed by more than 50 percent in a six-year span.[50]

Adding to the woes in the prairies and mountain areas, the unpredictable weather slammed different regions, each in their turn. Wyoming, for example, had record cold winters in the mid-1920s, destroying cattle herds and making unheated businesses so cold the ledger books froze shut.[51] The crash in wool prices all but destroyed the sheep industry in Nevada, and yet, ironically, a *rise* in cotton prices had sparked a surge in cotton production in the South that contributed to a worldwide cotton glut, eventually causing that sector to collapse. Cotton swung wildly from a high of 42 cents a pound to 9 cents. Droughts in the Great Plains served only as harbingers to much worse conditions in the 1930s. A boll weevil invasion helped destroy southern cotton production.

Yet agricultural policy damaged the farm recovery more seriously than the weather. The government emphasized cutting production, urging farmers in the South to destroy every third row of cotton.

(Farm politicians sarcastically suggested a better strategy would be to destroy every third member of the Farm Board.)[52] By subsidizing crops through federal irrigation projects, the government only lowered prices. Potatoes produced on federal irrigation projects cost potato farmers overall $15 million, reducing the price four cents per spud. Preaching to farmers to limit production, the federal government gobbled up wheat at 18 to 20 cents above world prices, sending a clear signal to grow more.

The fantastic productivity achieved by farmers—to their detriment—was repeated in a number of farm-related businesses, again, with reverberations to the farm itself. Cheese, for example, had constituted a relatively small part of Americans' use of dairy products until the early 1900s, when James Lewis Kraft, a grocery clerk, reasoned that he could sell more of the product if it were less perishable.[53] Typically, stores kept a huge wheel of cheddar cheese on a counter protected by a large glass jar, with the grocer slicing off a wedge at a time (and in the process leaving the exposed part open to spoilage). Worse, in hot temperatures, the cheese separated into butterfats and solids that reeked with an unmistakable odor. Kraft concluded that the product would maintain its freshness if he packed it in smaller glass jars or tinfoil packages. Still, the cheese was susceptible to spoilage, leaving Kraft to continue working on his problem. In 1916, he patented a blending and pasteurizing process that extended the shelf life, even in warm climates. The U.S. Army, needing lightweight packaged foods that troops could carry into battle, purchased six million pounds from Kraft in 1917.

Further experimentation yielded the tinfoil-wrapped five-pound cheese brick that then went into a wooden box for sale. Within a month after developing the foil wrap, Kraft's factory processed 15,000 blocks of cheese daily. By 1923, Kraft saw sales reach $22 million, and in 1928, Kraft merged with a rival, Phoenix Cheese Co., acquiring its famous trademarked product, Philadelphia Cream Cheese (which was always produced in New York City!). At the time of the stock market crash, Kraft produced 40 percent of the cheese consumed in America. James Kraft, like Jack Daniel and Thomas Welch, was a religious man, serving as a Baptist deacon and supporter of the Northern Baptist Theological Seminary. As Kraft became a household name, his contributions to extending the shelf life of dairy products ironically allowed Americans to waste less cheese than ever before, bringing prices down despite higher overall cheese consumption.

In general, crop prices remained low because production remained too high. Government plans, such as McNary-Haugenism and Hoover's schemes, attempted to control production voluntarily, and modern critics have faulted President Hoover for failing to impose a statist solution of production controls on farmers.[54] Yet even proagrarian voices admit that opportunities for improvement outside of farming existed if farmers wanted to move, and an unwillingness to abandon agriculture—for whatever reasons—led many to remain on the land far longer than was economically feasible. One of the most damaging developments for farmers was the deflation of the early 1930s, which made farm mortgages vastly more expensive in real dollars, adding to the desperation in the farm belt. Still, had agriculture remained an isolated depressed part of the economy, the problems may have straightened themselves out after enough farmers left the business to make the occupation profitable again. Instead, as the agricultural swamp deepened, it started to drag in another victim, the banking sector.

Banks in Crisis

Banks in agricultural states suffered horrendous losses even in the prosperous 1920s. Farm problems themselves decreased bank portfolio balances, needless to say. Yet structurally, the banking systems of almost all of the farm states had adopted a particularly weak method of attempting to ensure stability, deposit insurance. Later heralded as the savior of the banks in the New Deal, deposit insurance in fact promulgated widespread *instability* in states that adopted it.[55] Studies by Charles Calomiris, for example, comparing deposit-insurance with non-deposit-insurance states revealed that banks in states with mandatory deposit insurance were more likely to fail than those in states with only voluntary deposit insurance or no deposit insurance. States with branch banking proved the most stable and solvent of all. Meanwhile, anecdotal evidence from legitimate bankers and unscrupulous swindlers suggests that the notion that the depositors "were covered" tended to encourage more reckless use of bank investments.[56]

No structure or system, no matter how well designed, could mitigate some of the more severe problems of banking in the agriculture sector. South Carolina, for example, averaged a suspension rate for banks double the national average from 1920 to 1936, and the bottom five states in bank suspensions included only one nonagricultural state (Michigan). South Carolina's case was especially interesting and, by all measures, unusual, because of all the states that experienced high failure rates in the 1920s, only South Carolina allowed branch banking, but even branching could not save that state's banks from the decline in the agricultural sector. Banks in agricultural states could run, but they could not hide. With that exception, however, the other disasters afflicting banks during the 1920s almost exclusively struck states that prohibited branching, even if they allowed chain banking, in which a single owner held several banks but the assets and operations of each remained independent. One chain bank, therefore, could not help out another easily.

The most notorious chain bank failure, in Nevada, again resulted from falling farm-sector prices—this time the plummeting wool price. George Wingfield had built a banking empire in Nevada by financing sheep and mines. The cantankerous banker, determined to beef up security in his chain of banks, had instructed all banks to keep a shotgun handy, "for instant use in the bank," and distributed weapons and shells to every office in his system, for which he later billed the cashiers![57] Wingfield operated a chain of banks, which meant that although he owned a majority of stock in many banks, the institutions could not shuffle or commingle their funds. Even intrastate branch banking might not have saved Wingfield's chain, because it was heavily committed to the state's sheep growers. Yet contrary to the images of evil bankers anxious to throw helpless farmers off their lands, Wingfield continued to carry the sheep ranchers long after it was commercially prudent. When finally his chain had to be closed, Wingfield still had not abandoned the ranchers.[58]

Banks in other states suffered from completely unrelated, and often unpredictable, shifts not entirely related in any general sense to the health of the economy. In Florida, for example, a bust followed a boom in the early 1920s because tourist attitudes abruptly changed, plunging Florida's banks into a depression.[59] Whether sheep or sunbathers, trouble in a variety of unrelated business sectors steadily chiseled away against the banking industry, awaiting only a sudden shock to crack the edifice permanently.

The Crash and the Great Depression

Had A. P. Giannini not accepted the turn-of-the-century offer of a small savings and loan to serve on its board, Joseph Francis Sartori easily would have been remembered as the greatest banker in California history. Like the football all-pro who labors in the shadow of a Hall of Famer, Sartori carved an empire for himself out of the southern California financial landscape, crafting laws that still shape banking in the Golden State and directing one of the most important banking groups in America. More conservative than Giannini, Sartori embraced branch banking slowly, coming to dominate Los Angeles. In January 1928 he warned his fellow bankers that a major recession lay ahead.[60] Other members of the California banking community disagreed. The economy was sound, they argued. Sartori continued to prophesy trouble ahead, but few paid any attention to his warnings.

On October 15, 1929, stock prices, which had fluctuated for a month, turned down for good. Not until October 24, "Black Thursday," did the real dives begin, and by the following week, on "Black Tuesday," October 29, 16 million shares traded hands as stock prices plummeted. Even the "blue chip" industrials saw their values tumble, with General Electric, U.S. Steel, and AT&T prices dropping anywhere from 17 to 47 points in a day. Volume overwhelmed the technology, causing the stock tickers to run more than an hour and a half behind, further inflaming the panic. In less than a month—by November 13—the stock index stood at 224, down from 452 only weeks before. The bad news was that it had just started: By 1932 the index bottomed out at 58! U.S. Steel shares, once selling for over $260, could be acquired for $22, and mighty General Motors, which had boasted profits in the hundreds of millions just months earlier, saw its stock collapse to $8.

What caused the crash? Most economic historians subscribe to the view that multiple factors coalesced to drive down confidence, including falling industrial production and a restrictive Federal Reserve policy that began in 1928 but had just started to affect business by mid-1929.[61] To those factors, others have added irrational panic and the aforementioned "speculative bubble."[62] No specific event explains the collapse of the market. Rather, several factors were at work. First, manufacturing indices already had turned down in mid-1928, and it is likely that investors concluded by late 1929 that those indicators were not going to revive. The timing, in that case, may be entirely coincidental, and could have happened earlier, or later.

One factor that does seem to shift perceptions, however, was the movement through Congress of the Smoot-Hawley Tariff. For decades, historians and economists in general have dismissed the effects of the Tariff, which increased rates already enacted under the Fordney-McCumber Tariff, by about 20% on average—but much higher on some specific goods. Obviously, the passage of the Tariff in 1930 makes it an unlikely candidate to shape perceptions in late 1929. Or was it? Jude Wanniski raised the argument again in 1978 with his book, *The Way the World Works,* arguing that uncertainties over the effects of the tariff may have triggered the stock market sell off.[63] Murray Rothbard noted that "the stock market broke sharply on the day that Hoover agreed to sign the Smoot-Hawley Bill. . . ."[64] Dismissed by "mainstream" economists as a "pop" writer, Wanniski's theory was given little attention by the academy. But in the 1990s, a new generation of scholars interested in trade revisited Wanniski's views, with Robert Archibald and David Feldman finding that the politics of the Tariff generated significant business uncertainty, and that the uncertainty began in 1928 (when manufacturing turned down) and grew worse in late 1929.[65] Uncertainty involved both uneasiness over domestic price increases (and a possible decline in sales) and foreign retaliation. If companies believed that the Tariff would pass, and if they therefore expected hard times in 1930, it stands to reason that among other precautions they would take, firms would increase liquidity by selling off some of their own stock. Such sales alone could have sent dangerous signals to "average" investors, which then could have sparked the general panic.

Were businesses right to expect problems associated with Smoot-Hawley? Hadn't business interests lobbied for many of the duties that Congress tacked on to the original bill? Business had indeed favored tariffs for decades; but favoring something in general and assessing its impact in specific are completely different, much the way people "support" seat-belt laws, yet often do not wear a seat belt personally. It becomes easier to discover the source of industry's unease from hindsight. Douglas Irwin has produced several studies in which he finds that the Tariff reduced imports by 4–8% in nominal terms, but when deflationary effects are factored in—and it seems that almost everyone in the country except the Federal Reserve understood that some degree of deflation had set in by late 1929—the real decline in trade attributable to Smoot-Hawley accounts for one-quarter of the 40% decline in imports after 1930.[66]

Other economists have challenged the impact of Smoot-Hawley by pointing out that the total trade of the United States represented only a small share of output. How, then, could changes in trade, no matter how dramatic, affect the entire economy? Mario Crucini and James Kahn have addressed this by showing that changes in trade had a ripple effect throughout the economy, and that the tariff war alone could have reduced the U.S. GNP by 2% in the 1930s. Moreover, "had such tariffs been introduced in any other time period they could have brought about a recession all by themselves. . . ."[67] In addition, Crucini has found that, once again, the Fed played a critical role in its deflationary policy, in that monetary policy's influence on prices made the real impact of the Tariff far more devastating than originally appeared.[68] Thus, we are left with some fairly obvious conclusions: (1) the Smoot-Hawley Tariff had important disruptive effects; (2) few people knew exactly what form those disruptive effects would take; and (3) unknown to anyone at the time, the Fed made the harmful effects even worse through its policy of deflation. The only link that seems to remain for further research is how much the perceptions of impending chaos affected securities sales prior to the Great Crash.

When combined with other factors, such as monetary policy mistakes, the tariff bill easily could have added to the instability. In September, the Bank of England had raised its interest rates, making it more difficult to sell American goods in England. Then, the Fed, which had already raised interest rates trying to rein in the stock market, suggested it might hike rates a second time. Overnight, millionaires found themselves reduced to paupers, although it is a myth that brokers jumped from their offices to the cement below on Wall Street.

Yet the crash also turned many individuals of modest means into millionaires. Joseph P. Kennedy, father of the later-assassinated

American president, substantially increased the fortune he acquired running rum during Prohibition by purchasing legitimate companies at rock-bottom prices. Unfortunately, most average investors, who had aspired to own a piece of corporate America, had their savings wiped out.

Unscrupulous sorts, who plied their trades in great numbers in the 1920s, also contributed to the crash by undercutting public confidence. Other businessmen, trying to save their companies, were caught up in after-the-fact accounting changes that made it appear they had "jimmied" the books. Samuel Insull, of Midwestern Utilities, for example, was accused of shifting assets back and forth among his own holding companies, allowing each in turn to post additional assets prior to the release of stock reports, sending the price of his holdings skyrocketing before the crash. But a far different picture of Insull's activities appears in the scholarly analysis of Forrest McDonald, who argued that Insull's companies were more stable than most others and that Insull had tried to save his business.[69] Yet for every Florida real-estate salesman who dealt in swampland, other legitimate businessmen found themselves accused of horrendous crimes in the search for villains after 1929. Bankers, or "banksters" as investigators called them, came under intense scrutiny.

In the 1930s, congressional committees and investigators hauled numerous securities brokers and bankers, such as National City Bank chairman Charles E. Mitchell, before them with allegations of misconduct and fraud. Mitchell, the "scapegoat of the crash," unfairly received the appellation as the man "more responsible than all the others put together for the excesses that have resulted in this economic disaster."[70] Yet when the Senate Banking Committee, spearheaded by its counsel, Ferdinand Pecora, investigated Mitchell in the early 1930s (with the government indicting him for tax evasion soon thereafter), it could produce no evidence sufficient for a conviction in a criminal court. Acquitted in 1933 on one set of charges, the Internal Revenue Service filed a new set of charges that Mitchell finally settled out of court. Thomas Huertas, in his minibiography of Mitchell, argued that Mitchell had invested National City Bank's funds wisely based on estimates of returns he had at the time, and that when matters turned sour, he threw the bulk of his personal fortune into the battle to stabilize the investments.[71] In more general terms, as has been observed, the Pecora investigation complained that banks had competed *too much*, whereas just twenty years earlier the Pujo hearings had charged that banks competed too little!

In retrospect, scholars have found that most of the claims about the "weaknesses" once thought to have caused the crash played little if any role. Two theories, in particular, seem to have been discredited. One view, packaged cleverly by John Kenneth Galbraith in *The Great Crash*, held that the 1920s prosperity really only consisted of a speculative bubble driven by the stock market.[72] As has been shown extensively, the 1920s economy had unprecedented real growth by almost any measure. But even specific tests of the "bubble" thesis in recent publications have failed to find any meaningful speculative component. Peter Temin, Charles Kindleberger, Gerald Dwyer, and Gary Santoni have all found no evidence of a bubble or have shown that "common stock yields and price-earnings ratios . . . did not suggest that stock prices were bid up unrealistically high in the late twenties."[73] Or, as economic historians Jeremy Atack and Peter Passell put it, until the second quarter of 1928, "stock prices rose more or less in line with rising dividends. . . ."[74] A different approach, comparing the observed price with the *expected* price, however, suggests that lenders and brokers, using their margin rates as a measure, may have thought that stock prices had been bid too high. Of those who have detected such a bubble, Bradford De Long and Andre Shleifer have accounted for an overvaluing of as much as 30 percent in composite stock price indices.[75] However, an index does not capture the dynamic of individual stocks any more than placing Michael Jordan on any given NBA team would increase the team's scoring average by more than a few points. For the individual involved (just as for any team fortunate enough to have Jordan), the change can be revolutionary. Speculation exists in any financial endeavor, but it appears that most investors had stock values pegged about right: Stock prices recovered in November and continued back through April of 1930, suggesting that the crash actually sent stock prices too low.[76]

A second misperception was that the large banks, which had affiliates that dealt in securities, had contributed to the instability and had risked depositors' dollars in their flighty schemes. Eugene White, conducting a study of those banks with "securities affiliates" (brokerage houses) and those without, found that exactly the reverse was true: Banks that *had* affiliates were more likely to remain solvent and less likely to fail than banks that did not.[77]

The Banking Panic Spreads

Yet perceptions count for a great deal. Even if the Wall Street crash had no direct ties to the banks' troubles, and even if most people did not know the difference between an investment bank and a commercial bank, what happened during October in the stock market gave the impression that the nation's financial structure was weak. Another virtually invisible enemy to the banking system, the erosion of the nation's gold base, further undercut stability.

By 1930, a banking crisis was in full swing. The Bank of United States—no relation to the Biddle BUS—failed in New York in December of that year, while a few months earlier the troubles of a Nashville investment house, Caldwell and Company, dominated newspapers in the South. Whether any single failure "spread" the contagion of panic is doubtful, but the overall impact of bank failures, which accelerated in 1930 (and which geographically affected virtually the entire United States) generated a climate of concern.[78] People, perhaps gradually at first, then more rapidly, went to their local institutions to withdraw deposits. As people pulled their money out of banks, banks grew weaker, leading more people to pull out their deposits. Whatever started the cycle, the Fed proved unable or unwilling to break it.[79] Instead, private bankers' clearinghouses responded remarkably well, and in some cases might have prevailed if the monetary authorities had provided more strategic liquidity assistance, as, for example, in Chicago.[80] But the Fed did not act, and the destruction of money rippled throughout the system as the money supply declined by one-third.

President Herbert Hoover, a Progressive with a proclivity for bureaucratic solutions, had no qualms about using the government to attack the problems America faced. He slashed immigration, thus reducing the flow of free labor and entrepreneurship. European immigration plummeted 90 percent, just as the totalitarian dictators grasped power and drove the best and the brightest from their borders. Hoover's subsidies to shipbuilding produced a glut at the same time his tariffs choked off trade in the products those ships might carry. His solution to the banking difficulties, such as the Reconstruction Finance Corporation (RFC), offered taxpayer-financed loans to struggling banks and businesses. As with many government programs, however, the cure only made the disease worse. Recipients of RFC loans had to be listed in newspapers, which made people doubt further the solvency of any bank listed as an RFC borrower. Concern over an RFC loan actually had the perverse effect of making the recipient weaker, adding still to the growing crisis. RFC loans carried their own problems, including short terms and a relatively high interest rate for their purported purpose. They also seemed to foster a dependence by the recipients, dulling the firm's ability to make competitive decisions.

Hoover also tried a tax cut—not a "supply-side" cut that would have encouraged businesses to invest but a 1929 consumption-oriented across-the-board 1 percent cut that disappeared instantly and increased deficits. Surprisingly to many, Hoover ran larger deficits to GNP than did Roosevelt. He could not control the Fed, however, and when President-elect Roosevelt indicated he might abandon the gold standard, gold flowed out of the country at an even faster pace. Never fully convinced of the benefits of tax cuts, Hoover abruptly reversed course and imposed a huge tax hike—the worst in peacetime history— sending the top rates to 63 percent. Business and investors responded predictably, pulling their money out of the productive sector at astounding rates. In addition, the federal government imposed a two-cent tax on bank checks (equal to about $30 per check in modern terms) in June 1932, and that contributed to the monetary contraction. Economists have estimated that the check tax accounted for as much as a 12 percent decline in the money stock.[81]

The nation thought Roosevelt could do better, and certainly business thought he could hardly be worse than Hoover. A study of business expectations from 1929 to 1939 shows that, based on orders, anticipated employment, and other indicators, business prepared itself for a strong recovery after 1932.[82] (That was fully in keeping with the unceasing torrent of comments by business leaders that the economy was sound, or that recovery was "just around the corner.") Roosevelt had his opportunity. He had already promised a "new deal for the American people" in his 1932 nomination acceptance speech. Unknown to the voters, at a time when the nation needed confidence in the economic system more than anything else, FDR had deliberately refused to announce any support of Hoover's programs, even when he agreed with them entirely, for political advantage. Thus, before he initiated a single policy to save the United States from the Great Depression, Roosevelt had already ensured its extension.

In his last months in office, Hoover presided over a nation in turmoil, and, worse, an international economic debacle that in many ways needed a healthy American economy as a stabilizer. The United States had an average unemployment of 25 percent and, in some states, the rate nearly doubled that. Both the agricultural and financial sectors had collapsed, with more than 9,000 banks failing since 1928 and farmers, unable to obtain prices for their goods that offset costs, allowed entire wheat, apple, and other crops to rot rather than harvest them.

Traditionally, a lower interest rate would stimulate investment. But by 1932, even interest rates of as low as 1 percent did not spur borrowing, as a shroud of pessimism hung over the nation. More than a million people wandered about, representing the nation's first truly homeless group. In 1931 railroads, counting transients that they eventually had to kick off their trains, tallied more than 186,000 who spent at least one night riding the rails. Soup kitchens and "Hoovervilles" marred the urban landscapes, while an army of unemployed veterans who camped in Washington, seeking early bonus payments, were driven out at gunpoint by soldiers. The Soviet Union, sensing a huge propaganda victory, advertised for 6,000 skilled workers and received applications from 100,000.[83]

The auto industry, of course, collapsed as people attempted to stretch the lives of their existing cars. Production plummeted from 4.3 million cars in 1929 to 1.5 million in 1933. Over half the assembly-line workers in Detroit were idle, and without incomes, they ceased to pay taxes, causing midwestern cities' finances to nosedive into the red.[84] Indeed, the whole economy resembled a car, but a V-8 running on two or three cylinders because the ignition wires to the others had been pulled out. Fundamentally, nothing was wrong with the "car," but reality said that supply and demand within the economy were not making contact. Monetarists added that, since the money supply fell so drastically, people could not make the connections; the money just didn't exist.

"Do Not Pass GO": Charles Darrow Invents Monopoly

One of the millions of unemployed in 1933, a heating equipment salesman from Germantown, Pennsylvania, had taken odd jobs where he could find them. In between, Charles Darrow invented such useless items as a new bridge scorepad and a contraption that combined a ball and bat. All the time, Darrow thought about success, wealth, and property. If he couldn't have the real thing, at least he could pretend with his little game, "Monopoly."[85]

Darrow used his memories from Atlantic City, New Jersey, which he and his wife had visited on vacation. His game consisted of a board, dice, and, most important of all, "property" that the players could acquire. The deeds carried the names of Atlantic City streets (Boardwalk and Park Place being the most expensive), and the railroads were American legends: the Pennsylvania, the B&O, and the Reading. Unlike other board games, however, where players attempted to gain an objective, in Monopoly they just went around the board, collecting property, paying rent, until finally one player had everything and the others were broke. The game encouraged trades, purchases, improvement of one's property, and even included elements of fortune with cards called "Chance" and "Community Chest."

Meanwhile, the game makers George and Charles Parker, known as "Parker Bros." (with "brothers" never spelled out) had, like other game manufacturers, languished since 1929. Although it still had one popular game, Mahjongg, Parker Bros. struggled, and the opportunity to sell a new game like Monopoly seemed a natural. Instead, when Darrow met with company executives, hoping to sell them the rights to the game, they found it too complicated and unstructured for their customers. Darrow had to sell the product on his own, placing games store by store. The game caught on in Philadelphia, where Wanamaker's placed an order for 5,000 sets. Darrow did not have the capacity to make 5,000 Monopoly games, and again Parker Bros. entered the picture. In 1935, Darrow sold the rights to Monopoly to Parker Bros., which suddenly was swamped with orders. Within a few months, the company produced 20,000 games a week and still had orders for more. By 1936, orders topped 800,000. The game not only captured the unfilled desires of the depression, but after World War II sales continued to grow as people more realistically envisioned themselves "wheeler-dealers."

Aside from a few isolated businesses—Parker Bros., some of the movie studios, the radio industry—hope for getting out of the crisis was dim. If life was Monopoly, then Hoover seemed the cruel landlord. It is ironic, then, to realize he had started more public works, including the Hoover Dam and the San Francisco Bay Bridge, than any administration in history. His RFC threw loans at the sinking economy to the tune of $1.6 billion in cash and $2.3 billion in credits in 1932 alone, and, true to his big-government tendencies, his 1932 Revenue Act saddled Americans with the largest peacetime tax increase in history. Like Roosevelt would do, Hoover increasingly employed militaristic rhetoric to describe the government's activities, comparing the depression to a war, policies to battles that needed winning. Seeking the politically popular approach, Hoover sided with debtors by broadening bankruptcy laws, further weakening the distressed banks.

Some pockets of enterprise endured. In those retail sectors best able to lower their prices, business did not suffer nearly as much as in industry. Movies, and the more unsavory entertainments such as striptease shows, continued to draw. (James Thurber reported that strippers were making as much as $475 a week in 1932!).[86] And only a month after Hoover was evicted from the White House, Prohibition ended and the liquor industry—which had gone underground—came into the light of prosperity. For incoming president Franklin Roosevelt, any success story, even those based on strippers and booze, offered welcome news.

The New Deal

Roosevelt realized that he had a short time to convince the country that things could change. He first tackled the banking crisis, closing the banks in March 1933 by presidential order. The "bank holiday" shut down the banks, pending federal investigations and a certification that they were healthy. With the Banking Act of 1933, the Federal Deposit Insurance Corporation (FDIC) was created to restore confidence in the banks, in the process generating a myth that it saved the banking system. Business historian Joseph Pusateri wrote, for example, that "no single legislative step did more to restore calm and reduce the likelihood of further panics."[87] On this, recent evidence is extremely strong: It did no such thing. Economic historians have isolated Roosevelt's order taking the United States off the gold standard as perhaps the single most important act contributing to the end of the banking crisis. Once the gold reserves of the Fed were off-limits to foreigners, runs on the dollar abroad ended, allowing the banking system's liquidity to build up again.[88] But the rising asset value of banks due to other unrelated factors also enhanced their resurrection.

Politicians have never let evidence stand in the way of legislation, however, especially if the onus is on them to "do something." In 1933, they did: The Banking Act also separated commercial banking from investment banking, under the wrongheaded reasoning that the commercial banks' involvement in securities trades made the institutions unnecessarily weak. Again, Eugene White has shown that banks with securities affiliates were *less* likely to fail than banks without such affiliates. Further centralization of authority over the banking system occurred in 1935, when the Banking Act of that year granted new powers to the Federal Reserve Board of Governors, weakening the regional buffers that the system's founders deliberately had created to reduce the power of New York. But whereas the Progressive founders of the Fed wanted a decentralized system, New York only yielded to an even more powerful Washington. Finally, a system similar to the structure governing banks was established to oversee the savings and loan associations, with a Federal Savings and Loan Insurance Corporation formed in 1934. Not until the 1970s did the weaknesses of the system, especially the distortions and moral hazards caused by deposit insurance, appear in full bloom.

To revive the manufacturing sector and stabilize production and employment, FDR employed a different tactic, seeking to enlist big business in his program. As previously seen, business was receptive, although uneasy, when FDR introduced the National Industrial Recovery Act of 1933. That act established the National Recovery Administration (NRA) to regulate, under the auspices of a government-business "partnership," prices, competition, output, wages, and virtually all other functions of a free economy. The NRA, headed by Hugh S. Johnson (from the War Industries Board in World War I) drafted codes of fair competition, in essence cartelizing existing firms and closing out newly forming businesses. Of course, most businesses did not mind that aspect of the NRA. Another element, though, which guaranteed labor's right to collective bargaining, antagonized big business as well as small.

Social critics, of course, have argued that Roosevelt merely cemented a union between big business and the government. As one historian lamented, "The New Deal did not significantly challenge business's privileged position in politics or the private economy and simply recast the fundamental inequity between employer and employee around their organized . . . interests."[89] Some suggest that leftists and the "brains trust" pushed FDR toward a more antibusiness stance as the depression dragged on. It is clear that as war approached, FDR cleaned out many of the antibusiness New Dealers. Others suggest that Roosevelt's policies so thoroughly erased private confidence in property rights that "private investment [in the 1930s] remained at depths never plumbed in any other decade. . . ."[90] Roosevelt had always antagonized Main Street entrepreneurs, but increasingly his heavy-handed prolabor position and the attacks on the few productive elements that remained alienated some of his early corporate support.

To revive the agricultural sector, the New Deal provided the Commodity Credit Corporation (CCC) in 1933 to offer loans to farmers who participated in acreage limitations enacted by the Agricultural Adjustment Administration (AAA). Yet farmers could limit acreage on one type of crop, receive a federal payment, and produce another crop for which they had not signed a rental agreement with the government. Other market distortions rapidly surfaced: Farmers learned to plant more on their allowable acreage; landlords who received government checks purchased tractors and evicted sharecroppers. Food prices rose, but the distortions in the market more than offset any gains. Prices never got high enough to keep many farmers solvent, and consumers—already struggling—paid more for food. The federal deficit got worse, and what few taxpayers there were shouldered a still greater burden. Although the Supreme Court declared the Agricultural Adjustment Act unconstitutional in 1936, Congress finessed the ruling by passing the Soil Conservation Act (1936) and a second AAA (1938) that survived court challenges. In 1935, the administration admitted that the farm recovery program "had ironically created many victims of its own" by creating the Resettlement Administration to resettle dispossessed farmers and displaced tenants.[91]

Efforts to create jobs included the Civilian Conservation Corps (CCC), the Public Works Administration (PWA), the Works Progress Administration, and the National Youth Administration. All emphasized returning the nation's laborers to work at government expense. Business paid for those programs only indirectly. Of much more immediate effect on the nation's enterprise was the Fair Labor Standards Act and the Wagner Act, both of which had the effect of shifting government's support from business, where it had been in the 1920s, to labor. The Fair Labor Standards Act, better known as the "minimum wage law," established minimum wages business could pay and maximum hours labor could work without overtime. At least one study of the law has shown that virtually all of the unemployment in the late 1930s was correlated to higher wages.[92] Firms could, for example, employ ten people at $1 an hour, or five people at $2 an hour, but not ten people at $2 an hour. The number of hours worked screeched to a halt as businesses could only afford to pay a certain amount, regardless of how it was divided up among the labor force (see Figures 9.3 and 9.4). A similar estimate for unemployment related to the National Industrial Recovery Act suggests that "the Depression would have been completely over (less than 5 percent unemployment) by 1936 [without the NIRA]."[93] Astoundingly, the counterfactual developed by Richard Vedder and Lowell Galloway, which shows that most of the unemployment would have been squeezed out before World War II, did not include the effects of the minimum wage laws, which by themselves drove down employment.[94] In short, the New Deal's adverse impact on unemployment alone should qualify it as a disaster rather than endow it with the

FIGURE 9-3   *Real Wage Index over Time, October 1929–June 1936*

Source: From Stephen J. DeCanio, *Expectation and Business Confidence During the Great Depression,* in Barry M. Siegel, ed., *Money in Crisis: The Federal Reserve, The Economy and Monetary Reform.* (Cambridge, Mass.: Ballinger, Pacific Research Institute, 1984), pp. 157–175. Reprinted with permission of the Pacific Research Institute for Public Policy.

heroic status it has since attained. And still other antibusiness regulations poured forth. The Wagner Act, called the National Labor Relations Act, established the National Labor Relations Board to mediate labor disputes with management. However, it required both sides to bargain in "good faith," and courts frequently ruled against management's definition of "good faith" to the extent that companies soon regarded the law as antibusiness.

Depending on how one interprets the statistics, the unemployment rate fell from 25 percent nationally in 1932 to 15 percent in 1936, before rising again in 1938.[95] Michael Darby, classifying those working for the government as "employed," reduced the rate to about 9 percent in 1938, and he even pushes it further to suggest that if not for the recession in 1937–1938, the unemployment rate would have reached the "natural" level of 5 percent. But this is a definition game: Using that criterion, a person with two broken legs is "as good as new" because crutches can provide some of the legs' same functions. Using such an approach to employment policy, as many would no doubt approve,

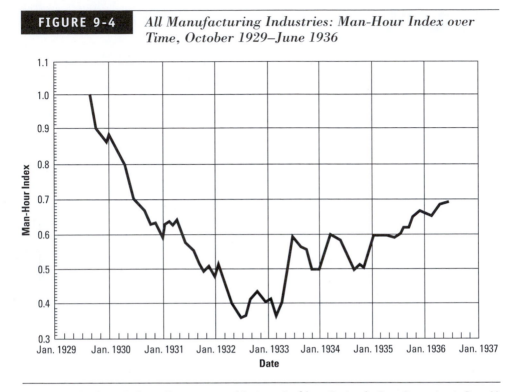

FIGURE 9-4   *All Manufacturing Industries: Man-Hour Index over Time, October 1929–June 1936*

Source: From Stephen J. DeCanio, *Expectations and Business Confidence During the Great Depression,* in Barry M. Siegel, ed. *Money in Crisis: The Federal Reserve, The Economy and Monetary Reform.* (Cambridge, Mass.: Ballinger, Pacific Research Institute, 1984), pp. 157–175. Reprinted with permission of the Pacific Research Institute for Public Policy.

there is no reason not to take the next step and have the government force people to work if unemployment itself is defined as an emergency condition.[96] But if the models developed by Stephen DeCanio and Vedder and Galloway are at all reasonable, then the likelihood is that the economy would have returned to the "natural" level of employment without the distortionary influences of the New Deal anyway.

Using more realistic comparisons—how much the country recovered compared to its previously healthy condition of 1929—we see a vastly different picture. Based on the trend in real GNP from 1921 to 1929, the actual GNP in 1938 was barely *two-thirds* of where it should have been. Worse, if one accepts the arguments of DeCanio, Higgs, and others that the New Deal policies themselves were responsible for the recession of 1938, one cannot excuse the 1937–1938 recession as due to extraneous forces. Finally, there is no reason to assume that a "natural" level of unemployment exists at all, for during the 1920s the nation's unemployment rate dipped to 1.5 percent. (A partisan might ask, "Why is the Coolidge record not the model?") Certainly from that perspective, it could be argued that, even at its best, unemployment under the New Deal was *ten times* higher than under Coolidge's administration. Then the effects of taxation must be added; the rate on top incomes went from the already severe 79 percent to 91 percent under FDR, followed by the hidden but damaging withholding of taxes in the 1940s, wherein two-thirds of Americans were paying income taxes (again, originally intended only for "the rich"). Quietly, however, as revealed in the *Historical Statistics of the United States,* FDR shifted the tax burden, in almost perfectly inverse proportion, from the wealthiest groups to the middle and lower classes by imposition of excise taxes, all the while maintaining rates on the top levels of 79 percent and higher.[97] Both investment and consumption were punished, with many convinced that private property rights were going to come under greater attack in the future. Pulling such a yoke, no economy could have recovered without a noneconomic shock.

Understanding the New Deal's effect on the economy and business also requires an analytical framework that recognizes that the programs were enacted over two presidential terms and under substantially different influences within the administration. Whether after 1934 Roosevelt adopted a substantially different approach to policy and a more hostile attitude to business, as some have suggested, may reflect only the presence of different people in New Deal positions; or it could result from FDR finally settling the financial markets enough to undertake changes that he knew would have generated panic a year earlier. Liberals excuse the New Deal's failures by contending that it did not go far enough, or make deep enough social changes, or spend enough money.[98] Modern economists of a generally liberal bent write favorably of the intent of the New Deal programs but caution restraint so as not to damage the "golden goose" of wealth production.[99] Still others, sensing perhaps that they have lost the quantitative argument, retreat to the position that FDR had to pass substantial reform to defuse social unrest and restore confidence in democracy.

Little evidence exists to suggest that Roosevelt secretly admired businessmen or wanted to see them succeed. Certainly those whom he appointed or associated with despised capitalism. Rexford G. Tugwell, for example, FDR's assistant secretary of agriculture, flatly stated that "redistribution of our essential wealth, the land, is the clearest mandate our society has received from . . . the present depression."[100] He also praised Soviet dictator Joseph Stalin, after the communist government had systematically starved to death millions of peasants, for operating agriculture "in the public interest rather than for profits."[101] Hugh Johnson puffed that if businessmen refused to observe his "voluntary" codes, "They'll get a sock right on the nose."[102] Supreme Court Justice Felix Frankfurter wrote in 1931, "Nothing I believe sustains the present system more than the pervasive worship of success and the touching faith we have in financial and business messiahs. . . . I believe it to be profoundly important to *undermine* that belief. . . . Undermine confidence in their greatness and you have gone a long way towards removing some basic obstructions" to the real social problems of the day.[103] Frankfurter's statement falls nothing short of astounding; at a time when Americans needed successes as role models—when any display of confidence in any sector of business would have helped—he merrily looked forward to the destruction of the economy to solve the serious issues in America!

Even Roosevelt himself did not hesitate to blame business when it suited him. In 1936, Roosevelt said that he hoped he would be known after his second administration as the master of "organized money." He charged that the 1937 recession, correlated highly with the minimum wage laws he supported, was instead the result of a "strike of capital," and he singled out the "economic royalists" and "privileged princes . . . thirsting for power" as the villains for the era. Some business leaders, in hopes of deflecting criticism, jumped on the anticapitalist bandwagon. Charles Abbot, of the American Institute of Steel Construction, called the business policies of the Roaring '20s "Irresponsible, ill-informed, stubborn and non-co-operative individualism."[104] Even *Business Week* magazine joined the chorus calling for government action, under the title, "Do You Believe in Lazie Fairies?"[105]

A few sectors of the economy survived and even prospered in the context of the times. Despite the consolidation of the motion picture industry, many movie companies expanded their operations. A new type of grocery store that catered to mass sales and featured lower prices, the "supermarket," first took hold in the depression when King Cullen opened his first store in Jamaica, New York, in 1930. Proclaiming himself the "World's Greatest Price Wrecker," Cullen's—and other supermarkets such as Big Bear—boomed during the 1930s, posting revenues as high as $6 million a year.[106]

Most entrepreneurs, however, shuddered at the collectivism around them. They reacted as one might expect: They simply withdrew from the economy. Under a cobweb of regulation, hidden taxes in the form of minimum wages, and the atmosphere of mistrust, individual business leaders started to resemble the characters in Ayn Rand's classic *Atlas Shrugged,* where a small group of brilliant inventors and determined industrialists gradually drop out of their ever oppressive society. Finally one of them asks, "What happens when Atlas shrugs?" What in reality happens to societies in which the "vital few" no longer find it rewarding to invest and struggle—to hold up the ordinary? Or to take risks? Or to fail? The latter days of the New Deal suggest that Roosevelt was on the verge of finding out. It took the demonic menace of Nazi Germany and the Empire of Japan to persuade industrialists to again commit themselves.

The New Deal: A Fifty-Year View

Roosevelt's program of reform along quasi-socialist lines represented an approach to recovery, but it was only one path. Another was not tried—a radical political program directed at free-market, pro-enterprise reforms, elimination of tariffs, reduction of taxes, and curbing the power of the Fed to affect financial markets. The distinction between Hoover and FDR is unwarranted. Certainly Hoover showed himself as great an enemy to entrepreneurship as Roosevelt. Furthermore, the economic debate, by nature of the evidence, has tended to focus on what Roosevelt accomplished in the recovery from 1933 and seldom assesses the impact of the New Deal *forward* to look at its impact on post–World War II business.

Merely using the recovery affects of the 1930s as a measure, economist Gene Smiley, summarizing the economic literature, concluded that "though the analytical work necessary to provide quantitative estimates of the retarding effects of the entire New Deal on the recovery . . . has not been undertaken . . . it seems likely that this retardation was substantial."[107] Many elements of long-term structural damage done by the New Deal did not start to affect the American economy seriously until the 1970s, and by the 1990s, virtually every New Deal initiative had produced a disaster or a time bomb. Farm subsidies had seriously damaged American agriculture, idling as much as 78 million acres of farmland in 1988, until finally, in 1995, the Republican-led Congress finally ended most of the New Deal agricultural policies—too late for millions of consumers who had paid higher prices at the store for sixty years or thousands of farmers routinely priced out of world markets.[108] Social Security, enacted solely as a retirement supplement, had grown in such perverse ways that no respected official or private analysis of the program posits any hope for the system to survive the "baby boom" retirements without complete restructuring. Even the most optimistic prognostications have it bankrupt in thirty years.[109] As we will see, deposit insurance played a key role in the collapse of the savings and loan industry, while American commercial banking has suffered lower growth rates because of New Deal restrictions.[110] With very few exceptions, the scholarly literature has concluded that minimum wages and the stifling effects of tax policy have had a negative effect on employment, especially on minority employment. Taking a long-term view of the costs of the New Deal programs that usually evade economists' shorter-term, multivariate studies, and looking beyond merely the recovery in the 1930s, the New Deal was nothing short of a dead weight on the enterprise of America—an "IV drip," dispensing a dulling, but temporarily soothing, narcotic.[111]

Did Business Failures Cause the Great Depression?

HISTORIANS AND ECONOMISTS HAVE MADE excellent careers out of adding new information and analyses to the debate over causes of the Great Depression. Early blame for the economic debacle fell on business. In part, that was to be expected in that the government, through the Coolidge and Harding administrations, had identified closely with business interests and practices. And, when it came time to lay off employees, business was clearly visible handing out the infamous pink slips. Yet the exact failures of business remained somewhat clouded, apart from the banking industry and Wall Street, which came under congressional investigation and suffered much of the ire of lawmakers. What did cause the depression? Are we any closer now to understanding the problems than were those who endured the hardships?

The famous British economist John Maynard Keynes, in his *General Theory of Employment, Interest and Money* (1936), suggested that an excess of saving dried up consumption. His view, characterized as "demand-side" economics because it placed the impetus of moving the economy with consumers as a group, required an outside stimulus to provide consumers with money to purchase goods. In England, that meant that the British government put thousands of laborers to work in government shipyards and in building houses.

Keynes's interpretation also provided academic support for policies already enacted in America under the Roosevelt administration, as Franklin Roosevelt's "brain trust" advisers had studied elements of Keynes's theories in academic papers long before publication of his finished book. Keynes implicitly blamed business for the worldwide recession and saw government as the savior. While the question of whether Franklin Roosevelt's New Deal significantly reversed the recessionary forces is still open, the economy did not collapse altogether under Roosevelt, lending credence to the notion that government spending stabilized American capitalism.

A much different approach, which already had started to formalize in a critique of Federal Reserve policies in the 1920s, was fleshed out in the 1930s and 1950s in a number of works generally referred to as the "Austrian School." Originating with Ludwig von Mises and Friedrich A. Hayek, and supported by numerous studies in the 1970s and 1980s, the Austrian interpretation blamed the Great Depression in America on dislocations caused by flawed Federal Reserve policy. The Fed, Austrians argued, permitted too much credit, allowing the stock market to swell with speculation and distorting prices. Prices, therefore, did not reflect accurately the shift in the late 1920s from consumption to investment, and when businesses finally did discover that their investments were unprofitable, the Fed maintained an expanded money supply to support labor, which, Austrians argued, should have been liquidated. Indeed, one of the major Austrian points that has stood is the high cost of labor after 1929. At that point, government intervention, first by Hoover, then by Roosevelt, artificially propped up the wage rate, causing businesses to lay off still more workers.

Ironically, another school attacked the Fed, but for exactly the opposite reason: that it failed to expand the money supply enough. In their seminal 1963 work, *A Monetary History of the United States,* Milton Friedman and Anna Schwartz led a new group of economists known as the "Chicago School," or monetarists. Monetarists emphasized the role of money in economies. In the case of the Great Depression, they argued that federal monetary policies, most notably fatal errors at the Federal Reserve Board, turned a cyclical recession into a national disaster. Not only did Friedman and Schwartz reject the notion that the depression was business's fault, they argued that the government bore most of the blame for its incompetent interference. (It is interesting to note, however, that Friedman and Schwartz did not entertain a view that the economy could have functioned *without* a Federal Reserve System only that the Fed could have done its job better, whereas the Austrians complain that it was impossible for the Fed to function in place of markets.)

Primarily the debate pitted only the Keynesians and monetarists against each other, with the Austrians relegated to a backseat, until the 1970s. At that time, several restatements of earlier positions, with new looks at the data, emerged, led by Peter Temin's 1976 book, *Did Monetary Forces Cause the Great Depression?* and Murray Rothbard's *America's Great Depression* (1972). Temin supported the Keynesian view, although he admitted that it explained only one-third of the total fall in consumption, opening the door for others to address the other two-thirds of economic decline. Rothbard, writing from the perspective of the Austrian school, disagreed with Friedman in that he thought the Fed intervened too soon and should have allowed conditions to worsen so as to squeeze the excess out of the system. He also reinforced the view that government policies, such as the Smoot-Hawley tariff and public works programs, only choked

off opportunities for reviving the economy through exports or private investment.

In the 1980s and 1990s, though, a new generation of scholars sought a middle ground between the Keynesians and the monetarists, incorporating both streams of interpretation, and attempted to fill in the gaps with new explanations. A series of studies on the gold standard resulted, with the most notable being a book by Barry Eichengreen, *Golden Fetters* (1992), that traced the economic decline to international disruptions caused by nations abandoning the gold standard. Ultimately, Eichengreen contended, the United States remained the only nation on the gold standard, causing a gold outflow and a banking crisis. Even Eichengreen, however, included both lagging demand and poor Federal Reserve policy as contributors to the severity of the crisis.

As of 1997, the amalgamated explanation suggests that each group has made important contributions and that no clear explanation has appeared. The unwillingness to maintain a flexible currency that competed against other currencies—even when pegged to gold—proved a mortal error. Moreover, the weight of the scholarship, including Temin's own *Lessons from the Great Depression,* while reviving the consumption argument, still relies on other factors to complete the demand-side explanation. More important, as Elliot Brownlee points out, the problems cited by the underconsumption school more appropriately described the period 1898–1914. On the other hand, the monetarists' position that the Fed's failure to support the Bank of United States has suffered significant damage; but the other monetarist points involving the decline of the money supply have sustained criticism well. Little has emerged to suggest that the government agencies acted wisely, including studies on the harmful effects of the Reconstruction Finance Corporation, whose loans may have

Continued

THE ECONOMICS OF BUSINESS

Continued

ensured a company's collapse due to the public perception that any company getting such help was in trouble (as Richard Keehn and Gene Smiley point out). The Keynesian/Temin position may have identified underconsumption in some areas, yet it does not jibe with the substantial work showing that the stock market did not absorb the excess in reckless speculation. Or, more to the point, people had to put their money somewhere if they did not put it in autos or houses, and it did not all go to the stock market for speculation. If one melds the three strands together, it suggests that at best government policies made the existing economic situation in the early part of the depression worse; and at worst the Fed's mistakes may have plunged the nation into the Great Depression. Most remarkable of all, almost none blame the depression on the "failures of business."

Sources: Barry Eichengreen, *Golden Fetters* (New York: Oxford University Press, 1992);

John Maynard Keynes, *The General Theory of Employment, Interest and Money* (New York: Harcourt Brace, 1936); Milton Friedman and Anna J. Schwartz, *A Monetary History of the United States, 1867–1960* (Princeton, N.J.: Princeton University Press, 1963); Peter Temin, *Did Monetary Forces Cause the Great Depression?* (New York: W.W. Norton, 1976), and his *Lessons from the Great Depression* (Cambridge, Mass.: MIT Press, 1989); Richard H. Keehn and Gene Smiley, "U.S. Bank Failures, 1932–1933: A Provisional Analysis," *Essays in Business and Economic History: Selected Papers from the Business and Economic Historical Society Meetings, 1987,* 6 (1988): 136–156; Jude Wanniski, *The Way the World Works* (New York: Touchstone, 1978); and W. Elliott Brownlee, *Dynamics of Ascent,* 2d. ed (New York: Alfred A. Knopf, 1979), ch. 15. Historiographical summaries of the various views, showing the inability of any single "school" to explain the depression, appear in Jeremy Atack and Peter Passell, *A New Economic View of American History from Colonial Times to 1940,* 2d ed. (New York: Norton, 1994); Gene Smiley, *The American Economy in the Twentieth Century* (Cincinnati, Ohio: South-Western Publishing Co., 1994), and, specifically to banking, Larry Schweikart, "U.S. Commercial Banking: A Historiographical Overview," *Business History Review,* 65 (Autumn 1991): 606–661.

Notes

1. Robert Sobel, "The Junk That Saved Goodyear," *Audacity,* 4 (Summer 1996): 6–17, and his *Dangerous Dreamers: Financial Innovators from Charles Merrill to Michael Milken* (New York: Wiley, 1993).

2. Paul Johnson, *Modern Times: A History of the World from the Twenties to the Eighties* (New York: Harper Colophon, 1983), 223.

3. George David Smith, "Forfeiting the Future," *Audacity,* 4 (Spring 1996): 25–39 (quotation on 25).

4. George David Smith, *The Anatomy of a Business Strategy: Bell, Western Electric, and the Origins of the American Telephone Industry* (Baltimore, Md.: Johns Hopkins University Press, 1985); Robert W. Garnet, *The Telephones Enterprise: The Evolution of the Bell System's Horizontal Structure, 1876–1909* (Baltimore, Md.: Johns Hopkins University Press, 1985). Other discussions of Bell and his telephone appear in Robert V. Burce, *Bell: Alexander Graham Bell and the Conquest of Solitude* (Boston: Little, Brown, 1973), and John Brooks, *Telephone: The First Hundred Years* (New York: Harper & Row, 1975).

5. Smith, "Forfeiting the Future," 26.

6. Bell quoted in Smith, "Forfeiting the Future," 28.

7. Sobel and Sicilia, *Entrepreneurs,* 248.

8. Smith, *Anatomy of Business Strategy,* 121–138 and passim.

9. See the discussion of this in Pusateri, *History of American Business,* 214–215.

10. Garnet, *The Telephone Enterprise,* 162.

11. Louis Galambos, "Theodore N. Vail and the Role of Innovation in the Modern Bell System," *Business History Review,* 66 (Spring 1992): 95–126 (quotation on 107).

12. Pusateri, *History of American Business,* 270.

13. Erik Barnouw, *A Tower in Babel: A History of Broadcasting in the United States, vol. I, to 1933* (New York: Oxford University Press, 1950), 68–69. Also see Elliot N. Sivowitch, "A Technological Survey of Broadcasting's 'Pre-History,' 1876–1920," *Journal of Broadcasting,* 15 (Winter 1970–1971): 1–20.

14. Sobel and Sicilia, "David Sarnoff: The Entrepreneur as Dreamer," *Entrepreneurs,* 253–263.

15. Fucini and Fucini, "Max Factor," in *Entrepreneurs,* 131–133; Sterling G. Slappey, comp., *Pioneers of American Business* (New York: Grossett & Dunlap, 1970), 162–167.

16. For an insightful look at the studio system and its affect on a Hollywood icon, see James S. Olsen and Randy Roberts, *John Wayne: American* (New York: Free Press, 1995). An investigation of the origins of the American movie industry appear in David Robinson, *From Peep Show to Palace: The Birth of American Film* (New York: Columbia University Press, 1996).

17. Dobson, *History of American Enterprise,* 264–265; Jack C. Ellis, *A History of Film,* 2d ed. (Englewood Cliffs, N.J.: Prentice-Hall, 1985), ch. 9.

18. Much of the material for this section comes from Ellis, *A History of Film,* ch. 8.

19. Ellis, *History of Film,* 180. See also Tino Valio, *Grand Design: Hollywood as a Modern Business Enterprise, 1930–1939,* vol. 5, in Charles Harpole, ed., *History of the American Cinema* (Berkeley: University of California Press, 1995), for the decline in the business during the depression.

20. Ellis, *History of Film,* 189.

21. Gene Smiley and Richard H. Keehn, "Margin Purchases, Brokers' Loans, and the Bull Market of the Twenties," *Business and Economic History,* 17 (1988):129–142.

22. See Lebergott, *The Americans,* Table 33.6, "The Stock Market: 1900 to the Crash of 1929," 442.

23. Robert Sklar, ed., *The Plastic Age, 1917–1930* (New York: George Braziller, 1970), 93.

24. Paul Kubik, "Federal Reserve Policy During the Great Depression: The Impact of Interwar Attitudes Regarding Consumption and Consumer Credit," *Journal of Economic Issues,* 30 (September 1996): 829–842.

25. Edwin J. Perkins, "Charles E. Merrill," in Schweikart, ed., *Encyclopedia of American Business History and Biography: Banking and Finance, 1913–1989,* 284, as well as Sobel's discussion in *Dangerous Dreamers,* 23–36.

26. Both Wilson and Fitzgerald quoted in Johnson, *Modern Times* (1983), 222.

27. Johnson, *Modern Times* (1983), 239.

28. Bruchey, *Wealth of the Nation,* 144.

29. Harold G. Vatter, "The Position of Small Business in the Structure of American Manufacturing, 1870–1970," in Bruchey, *Small Business in American Life,* 142–168.

30. Vatter, "Position of Small Business," in Bruchey, *Small Business in American Life,* 150.

31. Vatter, "Position of Small Business," quotation on 151.

32. Indeed, there is an argument that housing overinvestment perpetrated the Great Depression, with one interesting theory holding the demographic changes led to a sharp decline in construction, bringing on the recession. Of course, by now, the student should expect that another scholar argued exactly the opposite—that the recession *caused* the demographic changes resulting in housing decline! For this debate, see Bert G. Hickman, *Growth and Stability of the Postwar Economy* (Washington, D.C.: The Brookings Institution, 1960) and his "What Became of the Building Cycle?" in *Nations and Households in Economic Growth: Essays in Honor of Moses Abramovitz,* eds. Paul David and Melvin Reder (New York: Academic Press, 1973); Ben Bloch, Rendig Fels, and Marshall McMahon, "Housing Surplus in the 1920's?" *Explorations in Economic History,* 8 (Spring 1971): 259–284; Lloyd J. Mercer, and W. Douglas Morgan, "Housing Surplus in the 1920's? Another Evaluation," ibid., 10 (Spring 1973): 295–304; and Clarence L. Barber, "On the Origins of the Great Depression," *Southern Economic Journal,* 44 (January 1978): 432–456.

33. Johnson, *Modern Times* (1983), 216.

34. Andrew Mellon, *Taxation: The People's Business* (New York: Macmillan, 1924, 9, 16–17, 79–81, 96–97, and his "Taxing Energy and Initiative," *The Independent,* 112 (March 29, 1924): 168.

35. Gene Smiley and Richard H. Keehn, "Federal Personal Income Tax Policy in the 1920s," *Journal of Economic History,* 55 (June 1995): 285–303.

36. The description of Hoover is by Joan Hoff Wilson, *Herbert Hoover: Forgotten Progressive* (Boston: Little, Brown, 1975).

37. Keehn and Smiley, "Federal Personal Income Tax Policy," passim.

38. David Beito, "Andrew Mellon," in ed. Schweikart, *Encyclopedia of American Business History and Biography; Banking and Finance, 1913–1989,* 267–282; and ed., Dwight R. Lee, *Taxation and the Deficit Economy: Fiscal Policy and Capital Formation in the United States* (San Francisco: Pacific Research Institute for Public Policy, 1986).

39. Charles Holt, "Who Benefited from the Prosperity of the Twenties?" *Explorations in Economic History,* 14 (July 1977): 277–289.

40. Both Thomas Sowell and Charles Murray have, in contexts other than the Great Crash, demonstrated what James Scanlon calls "The Perils of Provocative Statistics. (*The Public Interest,* 102 [Winter 1991] 3–14)." See the numerous Sowell works mentioned in "Challenge Your Perceptions" in Chapter 11 and Murray's *Losing Ground: American Social Policy, 1950–1980* (New York: Basic Books, 1984), as well as his "How to Lie With Statistics," *National Review,* 28 February 1986: 39–41.

41. Ratner, Soltow, and Sylla, *Evolution of the American Economy,* Tables 18–7 through 18–10 on 444–445.

42. Donald McCoy, *Calvin Coolidge: The Quiet President* (New York: Macmillan, 1967), 392.

43. An excellent source on Coolidge, and one that explains why modern views of this great president have become so distorted, is Thomas B. Silver, *Coolidge and the Historians* (Durham: Carolina Academic Press, 1982).

44. James Bovard, *The Farm Fiasco* (San Francisco: Institute for Contemporary Studies, 1989), 13.

45. Lebergott, *The Americans,* 439.

46. Joseph S. Davis, *On Agricultural Policy* (Palo Alto, Calif.: Stanford University, 1938), 435; H. Thomas Johnson, *Agricultural Depression in the 1920s* (New York: Garland, 1985 [1961]), 213.

47. Brownlee, *Dynamics of Ascent,* 397.

48. Coolidge quoted in Murray Rothbard, *America's Great Depression* (Princeton, N.J.: D. Van Nostrand Co., 1963), 202.

49. Lebergott, *The Americans,* 439.

50. Smiley, *American Economy in the Twentieth Century,* 37 (fig. 3.1).

51. See L. Milton Woods, *Sometimes the Books Froze: Wyoming's Economy and Its Banks* (Boulder, Colo.: Boulder Associated University Press, 1985).

52. Bovard, *Farm Fiasco,* 22.

53. Fucini and Fucini, "James Lewis Kraft," *Entrepreneurs,* 111–113; Arthur W. Baum, "Man with a Horse and Wagon," *Saturday Evening Post,* 17 February 1945: 14–15.

54. Danbom, *Born in the Country,* 203.

55. Charles Calomiris has pioneered the work in deposit insurance effects. His articles include "Is Deposit Insurance Necessary? A Historical Perspective," *Journal of Economic History,* 50 (June 1990): 283–296; "Deposit Insurance: Lessons from the Record," *Economic Perspectives* (Chicago: Federal Reserve Bank of Chicago), 13 (May/June 1989): 10–30; and an antebellum comparison of systems in Calomiris and Schweikart, "Panic of 1857." Also see V. V. Chari, "Banking Without Deposit Insurance or Bank Panics: Lessons from a Model of the U.S. National Banking System," *Federal Reserve Bank of Minneapolis Quarterly Review,* 13 (Summer 1989): 3–19; David Glasner, *Free Banking and Monetary Reform* (New York: Oxford University Press, 1989).

56. See Carol Martel and Larry Schweikart, "Arizona Banking and the Collapse of Lincoln Thrift," *Arizona and the West,* 28 (Fall 1986):246–263, and Gerald P. O'Driscoll Jr., "Bank Failures: The Deposit Insurance Connection," *Contemporary Policy Issues,* 6 (April 1988): 1–12.

57. Secretary for George Wingfield to [cashier], Virginia City Bank, July 27, 1925, box 115, folder "1925," George Wingfield Papers, Nevada Historical Society, Reno.

58. Larry Schweikart, "George Wingfield and Nevada Banking, 1920–1933: Another Look," *Nevada Historical Society Quarterly,* 35 (Fall 1992): 162–176.

59. See William Frazer and John J. Guthrie Jr., *The Florida Land Boom: Speculation, Money, and the Banks* (Westport, Conn.: Quorum Books, 1995). This book seriously damages an earlier book on Florida's banks blaming bankers and "insiders." See Raymond Vickers, *Panic in Paradise: Florida's Banking Crash of 1926* (Tuscaloosa: University of Alabama Press, 1994).

60. Lynne Pierson Doti and Larry Schweikart, *California Bankers, 1848–1993* (Needham Heights, Mass.: Guinn/Simon & Schuster, 1994), 92–94.

61. A review of these factors appears in Atack and Passell, *A New Economic View of American History,* 606–607.

62. Charles Kindleberger, *The World in Depression, 1929–1939,* rev. ed., (Berkeley: University of California Press, 1986).

63. Jude Wanniski, *The Way the World Works: How Economies Fail—And Succeed* (New York: Basic Books, 1978).

64. Murray N. Rothbard, *America's Great Depression* (New Jersey: D. VanNostrand Company, 1963), 215. Alan Meltzer, in "Monetary and Other Explanations for the Start of the Great Depression," *Journal of Monetary Economics,* 2 (November 1976): 455–471, touched on the Tariff, but viewed it as a contributor to the Great Depression.

65. Robert B. Archibald and David H. Feldman, "Investment During the Great Depression: Uncertainty and the Role of the Smoot-Hawley Tariff," *Southern Economic Journal,* 64 (1998): 4, 857–879.

66. Douglas A. Irwin, "The Smoot-Hawley Tariff: A Quantitative Assessment," *Review of Economics and Statistics,* 80 (May 1998): 326–334; "Changes in U.S. Tariffs: The Role of Import Prices and Commercial Policies," *American Economic Review,* 88 (September 1998): 1015–1026; and "From Smoot-Hawley to Reciprocal Trade Agreements: Changing the Course of U.S. Trade Policy in the 1930s," in Michael D. Bordo, Claudia Goldin, and Eugene N. White, *The Defining Moment: The Great Depression and the American Economy in the Twentieth Century* (Chicago: University of Chicago Press, 1998), 325–352. See also Barry Eichengreen, "The Political Economy of the Smoot-Hawley Tariff," in *Research in Economic History,* vol. 12 ed. Roger L. Ransom (Greenwich, Conn.: JAI Press, 1989), 1–43.

67. Mario J. Crucini and James Kahn, "Tarifs and Aggregate Economic Activity: Lessons from the Great Depression," *Journal of Monetary Economics,* 38 (1996): 427–467 (quotation on 458).

68. Mario J. Crucini, "Sources of Variation in Real Tariff Rates: The United States, 1900–1940," *American Economic Review,* 84 (June 1994): 732–743.

69. Forrest McDonald, *Insull* (Chicago: University of Chicago Press, 1962).

70. Thomas F. Huertas, "Charles E. Mitchell," in Schweikart, *Encyclopedia of American Business History and Biography: Banking and Finance, 1913–1989,* 305–314 (quotation on 305).

71. Huertas, "Charles F. Mitchell," 310–311.

72. John Kenneth Galbraith, *The Great Crash* (Boston: Houghton Mifflin, 1955).

73. Smiley, *American Economy in the Twentieth Century,* 105; Peter Temin, *Did Monetary Forces Cause the Great Depression?* (New York: W.W. Norton, 1976), 42–45; Kindleberger, *World in Depression,* ch. 5; Gary Santoni and Gerald Dwyer, "Bubbles vs. Fundamentals: New Evidence from the Great Bull Markets," in *Crises and Panics: The Lessons of History,* ed. Eugene White (Homewood, Ill.: Dow Jones/Irwin, 1990), 188–210.

74. Atack and Passell, *New Economic View of American History,* 606.

75. Eugene White, "The Stock Market Boom and Crash of 1929 Revisited," *Journal of Economic Perspectives,* 4 (Spring 1990): 67–83, and his "When the Ticker Ran Late: The Stock Market Boom and Crash of 1929," in *Crashes and Panics* ed., White (Homewood, Ill.: Dow Jones/Irwin, 1990); J. Bradford De Long and Andre Shleifer, "The Stock Market Bubble of 1929: Evidence from Closed-end Mutual Funds," *Journal of Economic History,* 51 (September 1991): 675–700.

76. Further information on expectations appears in Peter Rappoport and Eugene N. White, "Was the Crash of 1929 Expected?" *American Economic Review,* 84 (March 1994): 271–281.

77. Eugene N. White, *The Regulation and Reform of the American Banking System, 1900–1929* (Princeton, N.J.: Princeton University Press, 1983).

78. The information on this is extensive. See particularly Elmus Wicker, "A Reconsideration of the Causes of the Banking Panic of 1930," *Journal of Economic History,* 40 (September 1980): 571–583; Joseph L. Lucia, "The Failure of the Bank of the

United States: A Reappraisal," *Explorations in Economic History,* 22 (October 1985): 402–416; Milton Friedman and Anna J. Schwartz, "The Failure of the Bank of the United States: A Reappraisal: A Reply," ibid., 23 (April 1986): 199–204; and Eugene White, "A Reinterpretation of the Banking Crisis of 1930," *Journal of Economic History,* 44 (March 1984): 119–138; as well as the discussions of sources provided in "Challenge Your Perceptions."

79. Several scholars have debated the "mind-set" of the Fed in the 1920s and early 1930s (see Smiley, *American Economy in the Twentieth Century,* ch. 6, for a thorough discussion of each). One interesting view, that the Fed was "captured" by the bankers, contends that the Fed sought to maintain its gold position, thus tried to prop up bond prices. By so doing, the authors argue, the Fed did not undertake open-market purchases sufficient to revive the economy. If true, however, this view provides a deadly critique of allowing government agencies to control the money supply at all, especially if the regulators can be captured so easily, and hardly bolsters the authors' underlying presumption that "big government" is benign! (See Gerald Epstein and Thomas Ferguson, "Monetary Policy, Loan Liquidation, and Industrial Conflict: The Federal Reserve and Open Market Operations of 1932," *Journal of Economic History,* 44 [December 1984]: 957–984, as well as the critique by Philip R. P. Coelho and G. J. Santoni, "Regulatory Capture and the Monetary Contraction of 1932: A Comment on Epstein and Ferguson," ibid., 51 [March 1991]: 182–189).

80. Charles W. Calomiris and Joseph R. Mason, "Contagion and Bank Failures During the Great Depression: The June 1932 Chicago Banking Panic," *American Economic Review,* 87 (December 1997): 863–883.

81. William D. Lastrapes and George Selgin, "The Check Tax: Fiscal Folly and the Great Monetary Contraction," *Journal of Economic History,* 57 (December 1997): 859–878.

82. Stephen J. DeCanio, "Expectations and Business Confidence during the Great Depression," in Barry N. Siegel, ed., *Money in Crisis: The Federal Reserve, the Economy, and Monetary Reform* (San Francisco: The Pacific Institute, 1984).

83. Smiley, *American Economy in the Twentieth Century,* 20.

84. *Giant Enterprise: Ford, General Motors, and the Automobile Industry,* ed. Alfred D. Chandler Jr. (New York: Harcourt, Brace, and World, 1964), 3; Lester V. Chandler, *America's Greatest Depression, 1929–1941* (New York: Harper and Row, 1970), ch. 3; and *The Great Depression* ed. David A. Shannon (Englewood Cliffs, N.J.: Prentice-Hall, 1960).

85. Sobel and Sicilia, *Entrepreneurs,* 28–31.

86. Reported in Johnson, *Modern Times* (1980), 247.

87. Pusateri, *History of American Business,* 2d ed., 288.

88. Many of the more recent sources in "Challenge Your Perceptions" support this analysis, especially Eichengreen and Temin, as well as aforementioned articles by Chari, Calomiris, O'Driscoll, plus another article by Calomiris and Gary Gorton, "The Origins of Banking Panics: Models, Facts, and Bank Regulation," in *Financial Markets and Financial Crises,* ed. R. Glenn Hubbard (Chicago: University of Chicago Press, 1991), as well as Douglas Diamond and Philip Dybvig, "Bank Runs, Deposit Insurance, and Liquidity," *Journal of Political Economy,* 91 (June 1983): 401–418.

89. Colin Gordon, *New Deals: Business, Labor, and Politics in America, 1920–1935* (Cambridge: Cambridge University Press, 1994), 303.

90. Robert Higgs, "Regime Uncertainty: Why the Great Depression Lasted So Long and Why Prosperity Resumed After the War," *Independent Review,* 1 (Spring 1997): 561–590 (quotation on 567).

91. Danbom, *Born in the Country,* 217

92. DeCanio, "Expectations and Business Confidence."

93. Richard Vedder and Lowell Galloway, *Out of Work: Unemployment and Government in Twentieth-Century America* (New York: Holmes & Maier, 1993), 142.

94. Ibid., 142.

95. Michael Darby, "Three and a Half Million U.S. Employees Have Been Mislaid: Or, an Explanation of Unemployment, 1934–41," *Journal of Political Economy,* 84 (February 1976): 1–16.

96. Darby, "Three and a Half Million U.S. Employees Have Been Mislaid," 8.

97. *Historical Statistics of the United States,* 1107 (Table Y 358–373). 88

98. Cary Brown, for example, remains a classic study that suggests that FDR did not do enough. See his "Fiscal Policy in the Thirties: A Reappraisal," *American Economic Review,* 46 (December 1956): 857–879; as well as FDR apologist, Arthur M. Schlesinger Jr., *The Age of Roosevelt,* 3 vols. (Boston: Houghton Mifflin, 1964).

99. The conclusions reached by Atack and Passell, *New Economic View of American History,* ch. 22, reflect this attitude.

100. Tugwell quoted in Bovar, *Farm Fiasco,* 28.

101. Bovard, *Farm Fiasco,* 28.

102. Johnson quoted in Paul Johnson, *Modern Times* (1980), 256.

103. Frankfurter quoted in Arthur Ekirch, *Ideologies and Utopias and the Impact of the New Deal on American Thought* (Chicago: University of Chicago Press, 1969), 27–28.

104. Abbot quoted in Johnson, *Modern Times,* 249.

105. Charles Abba, "Do You Believe in Lazie Fairies?" *Business Week,* 24 June 1931.

106. David B. Sicilia, "Supermarket Sweep," *Audacity,* 5 (Spring 1997):10–19.

107. Smiley, *American Economy in the Twentieth Century,* 136.

108. Bovard, *Farm Fiasco,* 26.

109. The best authority on Social Security is Peter J. Ferrara, *Social Security: Averting the Crisis* (San Francisco: The CATO Institute, 1982), but for a more recent, and highly detailed, analysis of the Social Security Administration and its projected shortfalls, see Peter G. Peterson and Neil Howe, *On Borrowed Time: How the Growth in Entitlement Spending Threatens America's Future* (San Francisco: Institute for Contemporary Studies Press, 1988), esp. ch. 3. Neither the reality of Social Security's pending bankruptcy, nor its inherent injustice to current taxpayers and recipients, seems to bother apologists for the welfare state, however. See Blanche D. Coll, *Safety Net: Welfare and Social Security, 1929–1979* (Brunswick, N.J.: Rutgers University Press, 1995).

110. See, for example, Randall S. Kroszner and Raghuram G. Rajan, "Is the Glass-Steagall Act Justified? A Study of the U.S. Experience with Universal Banking Before 1933," *American Economic Review,* 84 (September 1994):810–832.

111. The view that the government should be examined more for sins of commission, rather than sins of omission, during the depression, can be seen in George Selgin, "The Great Depression: An International Disaster of Perverse Economic Policies," *Southern Economic Journal,* 55 (January 1999): 653–656.

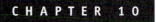

CHAPTER 10

From Villains to Victors: Business in War and Postwar America, 1940–1960

FREQUENTLY, FOREIGN OBSERVERS UNDERSTAND AMERICA BETTER THAN Americans. Certainly the young French aristocrat Alexis de Tocqueville proved uncanny with his predictions and unerring in his analysis of American culture and politics. In the case of World War II, historians have long maintained that the exceptional skill of American fighting men won the war, only to be challenged by Europeanists who claim that the overwhelming might of the Soviet infantry was the decisive factor. Still another group suggests that the superior technology of the United States—culminating in the atomic bomb—made the difference.

British historian Paul Johnson offers a much more straightforward assessment: "The real engine of Allied victory was the American economy."[1] After only a year of hostilities, industrial productivity in the United States exceeded that of Germany, Japan, and Italy combined. Johnson concluded that the "astonishing acceleration was made possible by the essential dynamism and flexibility of the American system, wedded to a national purpose which served the same galvanizing role as the optimism of the Twenties."[2] The war, he observed, "acted as a boom market, encouraging American entrepreneurial skills to fling her seemingly limitless resources of material and manpower into a bottomless pool of consumption."[3]

371

American entrepreneurs proved as adept at fueling the "engine of democracy" as they had in building railroads and starting banks. From traditional entrepreneurs like Henry Kaiser to eccentric innovators like Howard Hughes, from boat builders like Andrew Jackson Higgins to dreamers like Preston Tucker, business leaders in the United States, looking forward from the systematic harassment of the New Deal, did not shrug. They picked up the globe and carried it, emerging from the war with two-thirds of the world's economic production and markets. Not only did they win the war, American businessmen then turned around and rebuilt the devastated economies of their former enemies, ensuring that the defeated nations soon would become their chief competitors.

War, Total War, and the Lessons of World War I

Despite its title as the "Great War," World War I was not a total war effort for the United States. No American cities suffered attack, and at no time was the entire population mobilized to the point that everyone served either at the front or in a factory. Yet the First World War represented a new departure in productivity of military goods and in their lethality. Casualties in a single day exceeded one million at the Battle of the Somme (1916), and by the 1940s the explosives delivered on Nazi Germany alone dwarfed the amount used in previous wars. The Second World War, coming after the New Deal, already had many elements of centralized economic planning in place.

Total war, as World War II would be, demanded cooperation between government and industry to maintain production of war supplies adequate for the country's needs. The nation looked to its World War I experience as a partial guide for the new conflict. After all, while the nation had relied on private contractors for most of its war production, the government had introduced centralized ship designs and built large shipyards that operated alongside private shipbuilders Electric Boat and Newport News.

Government management during World War I, in the form of the WIB, dramatically expanded the scope of federal control over daily economic life, affecting clothing items as well as food and fuel. Entrepreneurs chafed at the intrusion into their businesses, with U.S. Steel's chairman, Elbert Gary, suggesting that the government, through the WIB, had attempted to nationalize steel during the war.[4] During wartime, central planning was essential; but it also required the full cooperation and commitment of business and entrepreneurs as well as consumer sacrifices by a *willing* public. World War I implied that, if left to their own devices, business could manufacture the weapons of war as efficiently and cost-effectively as any government-owned plant if provided production goals by the government. There-fore in the interwar years, the government adopted a policy of identi-fying industries, and even specific companies, that it might need in a military emergency.

Wings! The Airplane Age of Juan Trippe and Howard Hughes

In the case of the aircraft industry, from 1919 to 1929 the peacetime uses of airplanes (predominantly through the airlines) did not produce sufficient profits to maintain several aircraft suppliers. American air-craft companies had produced 14,000 planes in 1918 to fill $365 mil-lion in contracts, but profit margins were small, and government dictated the number and types of aircraft built, making it difficult if not impossible for aircraft firms to look ahead to peacetime. In 1920, the entire industry had only $5 million in capital and received no di-rect support from the government, surviving instead on actual orders. Several mergers swallowed up weaker companies, leaving only four major airframe builders and two engine companies by 1939.[5]

To the extent that the aircraft industry received any help from government, it came from mail contracts, with some of the largest go-ing to Pan American Airlines at the behest of the U.S. Navy. Juan Trippe, who created Pan Am in the 1920s and pioneered the use of fly-ing boats, provided the government with detailed maps and identified areas that might become new landing fields. Trippe's Boeing-built "China Clipper" flying boats routinized flights between San Francisco and Hong Kong, and even flew directly to England by 1938.[6] Well into the 1960s, Trippe's airline profited from government connections, keeping abreast of air force contracts with Boeing and Pratt & Whitney to make decisions about upgrading its fleet. But it also proved Pan Am's eventual undoing, because its reliance on the government left the airline uncompetitive in a deregulated world and often reduced incen-tives to invest in new technology. Mail contracts subsidized some ele-ments of operations, but they hardly provided the necessary capital for radical and innovative new designs. As one observer commented, "Trippe's company had lived by the state and died by the state."[7]

New aircraft innovations had started to appear, transforming the in-dustry. In the mid-1930s, Donald Douglas, who had a small manufac-turing company in Santa Monica, California, met with TWA vice president Jack Frye to finalize specifications for a new twin-engine air-craft, called the DC-3, that provided unprecedented passenger comfort with improved operating capabilities. According to C. R. Smith, presi-dent of American Airlines, the DC-3 was "the first airplane in the world that could make money just by hauling passengers."[8] The advances in aircraft design usually came from barnstorming pilots, backyard mechanics, and wealthy eccentrics such as Howard Hughes.

In the late 1920s, Hughes already had made a movie about flying called *Hell's Angels.* Having inherited his father's tool business (which was founded on the unique Hughes drill bit), Howard Hughes spent half a million dollars to create a private air force consisting of vintage World War I–era airplanes for the movie. Flying one of the aircraft himself, Hughes crashed, suffering severe brain and spinal injuries. He recovered in the near term but lived with lasting injuries. Despite the crash, Hughes was-more hooked than ever on flight.

The depression had grounded Hughes Tool Company, and Howard did his share to siphon off funds with his extravagant playboy lifestyle. Yet when confronted with the desperate plight of the company, Hughes restructured his debt, sold some of the company's stock, and renegotiated the contracts of the talented top executives to ensure their services for several years by giving them raises. He then dispatched his top executive to Houston to oversee operations, expanded the research staff, and started, for the first time in his life, to study the reports sent to him from Texas.

Hughes continued flying, working undercover as a baggage handler to get into American Airlines' pilot-in-training program, where, after handling luggage for eight hours a day, he plopped into the copilot's seat for his flying lessons. Ultimately, someone recognized him as Howard Hughes, and his secret life as an airline pilot ended. By that time, flying had captured the American imagination; in 1927, Charles Lindbergh crossed the Atlantic, returning to a fantastic ticker-tape parade in New York City. Hughes studied flight and practiced ceaselessly, learning to fly "almost every type of aircraft in existence, from ocean-going amphibian seaplanes to the roaring Fokkers."[9] In 1932, he assembled a team to build the fastest airplane in the world. Fabricated in secret and shrouded by a canvas cover, the H-1 *Silver Bullet,* built at a cost of $120,000 and tested in wind tunnels at Cal Tech, launched Hughes Aircraft when it was unveiled in 1935. Hughes posted a world speed record of 351 miles per hour, smashing the existing record held by a French pilot. Then, typically for Hughes, the engine lost power and the plane nearly crashed. Hughes climbed out, unhurt, into a beet field, to announce he could get the aircraft to 365 miles per hour.

With each flight, Hughes added to the technological base of the American aircraft industry. Although still viewed as an amateur by some, Hughes continued to plow his fortune into developing better, faster, and more fuel-efficient aircraft, setting a world record by flying a Lockheed *Lodestar* around the globe in three days, 19 hours, and 17 minutes. Lost in the public celebration was the fact that Hughes and his chief adviser had resurrected the Hughes Tool Company, which had made possible the funding of Hughes's exploits. The company posted profits of $6 million in 1935, $9 million in 1936, and $13 million in 1937, with new bits coming in a steady stream from the expanded research-and-development team Hughes had empowered. He also had assembled a team of aviation specialists in a 1,300-acre facility in Culver City, where, anticipating the demands of the coming war, they experimented with inexpensive wooden airplanes.

In 1939–1940, Hughes bought shares of Trans World Airlines (TWA), assuming hands-on management. Applying his aviation secrets and practical experience, he developed a strategic plan for the airline that doubled TWA's income in 1940. Passenger ridership rose 57 percent from 1939 to 1941, but Hughes had an even grander plan to create a fleet of superliners capable of carrying sixty or more passengers. When he asked Lockheed to submit a bid, deemed by Hughes to be too high for TWA, he instructed the Lockheed president to build them and send the bill to Hughes Tool. The resulting airplane, the *Constellation*, set an industry standard for size, comfort, and range.

The war did not bring the prosperity to Hughes Aircraft that its founder had anticipated. Hughes aircraft and tool plants manufactured machine-gun chute feeders for B-17 bombers (which, ironically, utilized ball turrets produced by another maverick entrepreneur, Preston Tucker) as well as wing panels for trainer aircraft. Hughes Tool also provided manufactured parts for bombers and gun barrels for the U.S. Army. But Hughes hoped to develop unique wooden aircraft for the military, without any interest from the government. He poured millions of his own money into prototypes, including a wooden spy plane, the XF-11, which was canceled before testing. But he did not land a major aircraft contract until he signed a cooperative deal with Henry Kaiser to build a flying boat for the U.S. Navy in 1942.

Hughes's task was gargantuan; no one ever had constructed a 200-ton airplane, let alone an aircraft that size built out of wood! His designers intended to bond skin and structural parts together in layers of wood using waterproof glues. The project proved to be beyond the capabilities of the Hughes-Kaiser companies within the time allocated (and, we should note, of any company since). The *Hercules* (derided as the "Spruce Goose") was not complete when the government canceled its contract. Infuriated at the *Hercules* cancellation, Hughes undertook an ill-advised test flight of the XF-11, which he flew longer than the test plan allowed. The XF-11 malfunctioned, then plummeted down, giving Hughes enough time to steer the plane over the Los Angeles Country Club, landing on the ninth hole in a blazing end-over-end crash. Nearly dead, Hughes was rescued, and after a desperate hospital stay he again cheated death. And, again, he flew.

The U.S. Senate had launched an investigation into Hughes and other "war profiteers" and required the eccentric Hughes, who reviled contact with strangers, to testify in person. Outraged, Hughes took advantage of a recess in the hearings to return to California in one last attempt to prove that the government had not wasted its money. With the Spruce Goose finally assembled in October 1947, Hughes climbed into the pilot's seat. After taxiing around the bay, he opened the throttles of all eight engines—much to the surprise of his copilot—and the *Hercules* lifted off, flying for about a mile. Hughes had proved that the airplane could be built and that it flew.[10]

Although the cumulative effects of the crashes accentuated Hughes's eccentricities, turning him into a virtual hermit and ending his personal contributions to the aircraft industry, Howard Hughes had shown that entrepreneurial progress came in all forms. Hughes's contributions to aviation, most clearly seen in the continued operations of TWA, affected the entire aircraft industry and helped give the United States its dominant lead in combat aviation by the end of World War II. On the other hand, Hughes lacked the same focus as other, more successful, entrepreneurs such as Henry Kaiser. In fact, he never fulfilled a single aircraft contract over which he had direct control. Years later, when Hughes Aircraft had a stellar reputation for building satellites and missiles, the company met its obligations and delivered hardware primarily because Hughes left it alone. The fact that Hughes, along with Preston Tucker and Andrew Jackson Higgins, came under investigation after the war for "profiteering" or other alleged infractions indicated the morass that even the most capable entrepreneur found himself in when dealing with military contracts.

Military Contracts and Contractors

Other than a few ammunition plants and some shipyards, the government usually contracted with private firms for specific weapons. Even in the case of shipyards, the government relied on private companies for management, as with the Todd Works. Government contracted with companies on the following basis: If the design was well developed and not unusual, companies generally signed "fixed price" contracts in which they agreed to supply the government a certain number of items at a fixed cost. A company had to estimate accurately its costs to ensure a reasonable profit. If manufacturers had to develop a new design or use untested or revolutionary technology, they preferred "cost-plus" contracts that paid a specified profit percentage above the cost of making the weapon.

In such a system, where private contractors provide weapons for the government, it was to be expected that critics would level charges that business received excessive profits from wars. Such notions furthered the conspiracy theories that "big business" supported wars, ignoring evidence accepted by most historians that business interests have *opposed* most foreign interventions.

Occasionally, the government ignored cost completely, depending on the need. While that did not necessarily generate high-cost weapons, it did free entrepreneurs to focus solely on production, both in quality and numbers. Such a situation faced the United States in 1939–1940, when, having ignored military needs for more than a decade, America hustled to build ships and planes. But the demand for American materials started long before bombs fell on Pearl Harbor. Adolf Hitler's Nazi Germany swept into Poland in its blitzkrieg in 1939 as the French and British watched helplessly, followed by a similar Soviet invasion from the East just a short time later. France and England proved incapable of stopping the German advance, and France herself fell in a matter of weeks to the Wermacht in 1940. Within months, England stood alone against Hitler, and the Battle of Britain, in which Germany sought to control the skies as a prelude to an amphibious invasion of England, raged during the autumn of that year.

To his great credit, Roosevelt recognized the plight of Britain before many in the United States. He received $37 billion from Congress to rebuild the defense establishment and pushed through a "Lend-Lease" bill in which America leased fifty overage destroyers long-term to eight British bases across the globe. But the mood of the United States remained highly isolationist—by the late 1930s, surveys showed 80 percent of Americans wanted the United States completely out of Asia—and celebrities as well known as Charles Lindbergh lobbied to keep America out of the European conflict.

After Pearl Harbor, American production geared up. Military expenditures rose from $1.7 billion to $22.9 billion by the end of 1942, pouring $8.6 billion into armaments alone.[11] While putting over 12 million men in uniform by 1945, the U.S. economy produced more than 297,000 planes, 86,000 tanks, 193,000 artillery pieces, and two million trucks, and, almost as an aside, created the largest navy in the world, with over 8,800 ships and 87,000 landing craft. After a year, tank output reached 24,000 and aircraft production topped 45,000, representing one of the most rapid buildups in history, altering the balance of war virtually overnight. The staggering productivity of the American economy tends to get swamped in sheer numbers, but it is worth noting that by 1942 the United States produced as much as Germany, Japan, and Italy *put together*, then two years later produced *twice as much* as the Axis powers. Even before December 7, 1941, the United States "produced more steel, aluminum, oil and motor vehicles than all the other major states together," and by 1943 turned out almost as many aircraft as Germany, Italy, Britain, and the USSR combined.[12] The Ford company alone outproduced Italy in army equipment during the war!

The astounding gains—shipbuilding productivity increased 25 percent a year—were due more to the pent-up entrepreneurship driven underground during the depression by regulation and taxation than they were to state planning. To appreciate the limitations of planning, the experience of Germany herself provides adequate evidence. German production surpassed that of the Soviet Union in 1941, turning out four times as much steel, and by 1943, the Germans outproduced the USSR by 22 million tons of steel. But as Richard Overy points out in *Why the Allies Won,* "The new German empire failed to make the most of its economic advantages."[13] The Soviet military machine eventually dwarfed that of the Axis in the number of tanks produced, suggesting that Soviet collectivist planners were better than the Nazi collectivist planners, but the Russians had the liberty of focusing exclusively on certain types of weapons, especially guns and tanks, because they received fantastic amounts of aid, especially in the form of trucks and other military goods. Overy observes that "the United States motorized not only its own army but the Red Army too . . . [supplying] over half a million vehicles" including the critical jeeps and light trucks that provided mobile infantry support to the tanks.[14] (Britain and America also provided 20,900 armored vehicles, of which 12,365 were tanks.) In addition, America shipped 380,000 field telephones and almost a million miles of telephone cable that gave the USSR a crucial tactical advantage in communications, all of which was made possible by the victory at sea, itself decided by America's vast resources.[15]

Air power dominated the war. Although Hitler had to abandon Operation Sea Lion because of the defeat at the Battle of Britain, the critical destruction of the Luftwaffe came from American bombers laying down blankets of fire. Likewise, the war in the Pacific turned first on air strikes from U.S. carriers, then on the long-range B-29 missions that devastated Japan even before the atomic bombs.[16]

Above all, America (with substantial British help) provided the technological edge that prevented Germany from gaining dominance in the air. Radar, sonar, medicinal advances in sulfa drugs, new ship designs, and, of course, the atomic bomb not only hastened the end of the war but, in reverse, denied Germany the time it needed to develop and deploy such weapons. Had the Soviets faced the entire array of Axis power alone, prolonging the war, it was not implausible that Germany could have developed and deployed atomic weapons—possibly mated to the V-2 rockets they did manufacture. No number of tank or infantry divisions would have mattered in that case.[17]

Given the flood of targeted support to the USSR, it is difficult to credit the Red Army with a pivotal role in the destruction of the Axis powers. The Soviets indeed crushed German ground resistance in the East, but the Red air force gained superiority in the air using American and English component designs, and its freedom of action was brought on in part by the storm of bombs falling on German and Italian cities that reduced Axis production. Although estimates of the effectiveness of the bombing campaign are widely debated, bombing may have reduced German aircraft production by over 30 percent and of tanks by over 35 percent. Moreover, planes that otherwise could have thinned the ranks of Soviet armor had to be diverted to protecting the skies over the Fatherland. But everywhere, American productivity led to astonishing results that had a direct relationship to the battlefield. The damaged aircraft carrier *Yorktown,* thought put out of action by the Japanese at Coral Sea, was repaired in forty-eight hours—normally a three-month job—by 1,200 Pearl Harbor technicians, returning to action in time to deliver the fatal dive-bomber and torpedo strikes that sank the Japanese fleet at Midway. At Guadalcanal, American construction battalions ("Fighting Seabees"), using Case and Deere tractors and caterpillars, cleared an airfield in a few days, whereas the Empire of Japan had taken more than a month using hand tools.

Tanks rolled off U.S. assembly lines in five hours' total construction time; those same lines had been idle or turning out civilian cars just years earlier. Aircraft carriers, the centerpiece of modern navies, emerged from Ingalls and Newport News in fifteen months. It took only fourteen months to build the gigantic Pentagon with its 16 miles of corridors and 600,000 feet of office space.[18] Yet despite the prolific weapons programs, the most important items the United States supplied during the first years of the war, cargo freighters called "Liberty Ships," were produced even faster. The government needed to look no further than a pair of individualist entrepreneurs, Henry Kaiser and Andrew Jackson Higgins, to find shipbuilders extraordinaire.

Henry Kaiser and Andrew Jackson Higgins Build Ships

Called by historian Paul Johnson the epitome of the American "capitalist folk hero," Henry J. Kaiser had built large-scale projects prior to the war, including (with John McCone and Henry Morrison) the Hoover, Bonneville, Grand Coulee, and Shasta dams, as well as San Francisco's Golden Gate Bridge. He had created the first integrated steel mill in the West as well as a huge cement plant for his projects.[19]

Roosevelt placed Kaiser in charge of shipyards in California and the Pacific Northwest, instructing him to turn out ships, regardless of cost. Before he could do that, Kaiser surmised that he needed a larger workforce than California and the Northwest could provide. He placed ads in large papers around the nation, luring workers westward. Knowing they needed housing, Kaiser embarked on the largest prefabricated home construction projects ever undertaken. With a workforce in place, Kaiser started to build Liberty ships, cutting construction time at first from 355 days to 108 days. In some cases he directly changed ship welding or construction techniques, while in others he expanded the workforce or found ways to allow laborers to work "smarter."

Eventually, the mass-production methods reached a zenith when the Liberty ship *Robert E. Peary* was fabricated in less than five days! Kaiser yards turned out everything from cargo ships to aircraft carriers, with the yards' final tally of more than 1,400 ships. As a matter of perspective, during the 1980s, when President Ronald Reagan announced he wanted to "rebuild" America's defenses, he and Secretary of the Navy John Lehman announced that they had a goal of *600 total* ships, meaning that Kaiser's factories put almost 2.5 times as many ships in the water in four years as the United States had in its inventory at the climax of the cold war.

The government had learned during World War I that it needed experienced private managerial teams to run its contracts. That, in turn, meant giving additional resources to those such as Kaiser who produced—an ironic twist in that New Deal bureaucrats, like Harold Ickes, had "systematically harassed" Kaiser in the 1930s.[20] Of course, this was serious now. This was war.

Criticism of Kaiser developed after the war as well. Complaining that Kaiser was not a model of free enterprise, historian John Blum argued that the government "supplied [Kaiser's] capital, furnished his market, and guaranteed his solvency on the cost-plus formula—and so spared him the need for cost efficiency . . . and came close to guaranteeing his profits."[21] Historian Bruce Catton echoed similar sentiments in his *War Lords of Washington* (1948).[22] Those charges ignored a few obvious facts, the most glaring of which was that Kaiser was successful where others, receiving far more government support, failed. German, Italian, and Japanese businessmen, bound by socialistic governments and anticapitalist ideologies, were thoroughly outperformed, while Soviet manufacturers (lacking any free enterprise at all) were essentially driven by the lash and subsidized extensively through aid from people such as Kaiser![23] Critics also overlook the fact that after the war, Kaiser, when his profits were not "guaranteed," did not hesitate to risk his fortune on an entirely new enterprise, automobiles. He bought aluminum plants in Washington, Louisiana, and West Virginia, and his steel mill in California stood its ground with eastern companies. Not only had he created the first "prefab" housing, but he introduced employee health-care facilities, "the forerunner of modern health maintenance organization systems."[24] After the war, he moved to Hawaii, credited by his biographer, Mark Foster, as the "*malihini,* or newcomer, who exerted the greatest force in changing [Hawaii's tourist industry]."[25]

Henry Kaiser, a true "market entrepreneur," played the game under whatever rules existed. During the years 1941–1945, Uncle Sam wanted weapons and wanted them fast. Kaiser merely satisfied his customer, as did another capitalist pioneer of the age, Andrew Jackson Higgins. Born in landlocked Nebraska, Higgins had a "lackluster" high school career, then worked in the lumber business in Alabama, then settled in New Orleans where he graduated from slower sailing craft to speedboats.[26] Like Howard Hughes, Higgins loved speed, building racing boats that set records for the New Orleans–St. Louis course before branching into pleasure craft in the early 1930s, expanding his business in the teeth of the Great Depression. Neither speedboats nor pleasure craft made Higgins so valuable to the war effort, however. Instead, responding to a demand for shallow-draft fishing vessels for the bayous and narrow channels of south Louisiana, Higgins developed the "Spoonbill" bow that enabled his boats to run full speed onto sandbars or riverbanks.

Prior to World War II, the U.S. Marine Corps had shown an interest in the Higgins boats as amphibious warfare vessels. With the inclusion of a ramp that dropped forward onto a beach, allowing troops to charge off in rapid order, the LCPs (landing craft personnel) and LCMs (landing craft, medium) gave the navy and marines exactly what they needed for amphibious operations. In 1941, Higgins Industries had $10 million in sales and $3 million in profits, placing Higgins on a plane equal to that of Kaiser. His success had not come without personal hardship. As John Heitmann, a Higgins biographer, described Higgins's situation, "Twice bankrupt and once forced to sell his wife's jewelry, Higgins, who owned nearly seventy percent [of the stock] could boast of being one of the wealthiest men living in the Deep South."[27] Seeing himself as an underdog, locked in competition with huge shipbuilders such as Ingalls and Newport News, Higgins never wallowed in pity. He once said that he did not "wait for opportunity to knock. I sent out a welcoming committee to drag the old harlot in."[28]

Higgins' "welcoming committee" went out to find postwar business well before the conflict ended. Envisioning a peacetime market for pleasure craft and prefabricated wooden houses, Higgins encountered a raft of problems after 1945, including labor troubles. He closed Higgins Industries in 1945 rather than give in to union power. Opening a new corporation, he next ran into the Securities and Exchange Commission, which charged him with stock manipulation, much as fellow entrepreneur and ball-turret manufacturer Preston Tucker was charged and later cleared. The business floundered, and, facing bankruptcy, was sold to a New York shipbuilding firm in 1959.

Detractors lamented that Kaiser, Higgins, and other large-scale producers received contracts at the expense of smaller companies. One study, for example, found that between 1940 and 1944, half of all contracts went to the top thirty-three corporations, and profits for smaller businesses fell from 26 percent to 19 percent between 1939 and 1944.[29] Numbers such as those obscure rather than enlighten. Small business, by nature, depended heavily on one individual or a handful of partners. Military service claimed thousands of such small business owners, who gladly put on their country's uniform to fight, in the process condemning their business to a temporary state of suspended animation, or, in the case of their own death, extinction. Even in a partnership, the loss of an active partner to enlistment or the draft ended hundreds of small enterprises. Large corporations would neither die with the loss of an officer, nor were they likely to suffer if even a large percentage of the male employees went off to war. Instead, they hired women, and more than eight million "Rosie the Riveters" joined the labor force.[30]

A second fact of life for new entrepreneurs and small businesses, high taxes, served as a death knell. The Revenue Act of 1942 raised the excess profits tax from 60 percent to 90 percent, making it virtually impossible to grow rapidly by reinvesting profits. Although high taxation partly accomplished one of its objectives—lessening the postwar debt by financing 40 percent of federal revenue from 1940 to mid-1944—tax rates on individuals rose to intolerable levels (94 percent on "the rich") and exemptions fell. What followed was a sort of reverse "merchants of death" as entrepreneurs were penalized for supporting the war with new ideas or products. More onerous, the Internal Revenue Service, beginning in 1943 (again with the cover of war to insulate it from criticism) enacted a pay-as-you-go system, today known as "withholding," to replace the one-time payment. By making taxes convenient and hidden, the government ensured that it could raise them with much less opposition in the future.[31] But perhaps the most crushing blow for entrepreneurs came when the government hiked the tax rate on the bottom bracket from 4.4 percent in 1940 to 23 percent in 1945, an increase of over 400 percent! Under such burdens, only the largest and most secure businesses could survive.[32]

American Wartime Production in Retrospect

The absolute dominance of the American economy during the war had two additional results. First, it seriously damaged the notion that the New Deal had "rescued" or "saved" private enterprise from the excesses of capitalism. War had motivated business to unimagined productive levels. Why, then, had the New Deal not energized entrepreneurs? Perhaps, some thought, the business system had not needed "saving" after all. Such considerations played a key role in allowing the United States to return to a less regulated and nonsocialized environment after 1945, in sharp contrast to Britain and the European nations.

Second, America's economic power translated directly into increasingly deadly technology—culminating, of course, with the atomic bomb—that the enemy could not match. That was true of Japan as early as 1942 when Gen. Douglas MacArthur's troops at Guadalcanal achieved a 16-to-1 casualty ratio. At Kwajalein, the ratio reached nearly twice that, or 32 to 1. On the tactical level, such overwhelming productivity as American industry could provide led to almost comical matchups. During the Normandy invasion, the Allies put 11,000 planes in the skies over the English Channel; Germany responded with two. Hitler, of course, ignored reality long before the Red Army arrived at his bunker. By then, even *der Fuehrer,* in his madness, knew that Allied aircraft could vaporize entire cities, as they did Hamburg in 1943, leaving almost 40 percent of the population dead. He also knew, based on the failures of German scientists to produce an atomic bomb, that the Allies could not be far from one themselves.

Although Britain led the United States in early design work for the atomic bomb, once again the American drive to produce the weapon, regardless of cost, soon superseded the effort in England. Dubbed the "Manhattan Project," the ultrasecret research program married European physics theory to Yankee resources and "entrepreneurial adventurism."[33] Roosevelt ultimately authorized $5 billion for the project, which he placed under Gen. Leslie Groves, who in turn enlisted the best scientists, then ruled them with a mixture of threats and encouragement. Groves acquired any resource the Manhattan Project required, and, in the course of work, the team created the first fully automated factory, the first plant operated by remote control, and the first sterile industrial process (which laid the foundation for all subsequent work in computer chip manufacturing). Estimates have put the "compression factor," that is, the time under normal peacetime circumstances needed to accomplish the same work, at seven. The Manhattan Project developed the bomb in four years, while it should have taken thirty.

A final explanation for why the war experience allowed the recovery of industry when the New Deal did not lies in the attitude of government toward entrepreneurs. In the case of war, the nation knew it needed its business leaders and restored to them the power and prestige Ickes, Tugwell, and other New Dealers stripped away. By renewing business confidence in private property rights, the war accomplished what FDR could not.

Government and Management of Business

Aware of the need to squeeze the most out of the private sector that he had assaulted for almost a decade, Roosevelt realized he had to provide incentives to business. The government permitted accelerated amortization of plant expansion, for example, and frequently used the more profitable "cost-plus" contracts. Antitrust prosecutions abruptly ended. To the extent that he could, though, FDR remained a central planner, and he sought to manage the wartime buildup through a jungle of bureaus and panels. Prewar planning had been "mismanaged, confused, and marked by political expediency."[34] One FDR-appointed board, charged with preparing a mobilization plan, failed miserably when Roosevelt refused to appoint a chairman, causing the public to refer to the commission members as the "Headless Horsemen."[35]

Ultimately, the Reconstruction Finance Corporation under Jesse Jones emerged as the most powerful of the prewar bodies. Jones himself later admitted that the RFC wielded "perhaps the broadest powers ever conferred upon a single government agency."[36] Jones's vast powers still proved inadequate to organize all the wartime agencies into a coherent force, and in 1942 yet another body was created, the War Production Board (WPB), headed by Donald Nelson, a Sears and Roebuck executive. The WPB entirely ended production of some consumer goods, such as autos, but the WPB lacked the power granted Baruch's WIB during the First World War. Instead, Roosevelt created even *another* layer of management, the Office of War Mobilization (renamed the Office of War Mobilization and Reconversion in 1944) under the "assistant president" James F. "Jimmy" Burns. The resulting maze of bureaucratic structures, dominated by a struggle for succession to the presidency, meant that "the Roosevelt administration . . . did a poor job in coordinating the economic side of the war effort. . . ."[37] Fortunately, the offices only supervised the production of the Higginses and Kaisers, with occasional suggestions as to what they should build. Some have credited the government with eliminating the risk for entrepreneurs, for example, by owning most of the plant capacity for manufacturing weapons and large-scale tools. Those facilities were virtually unwanted after the war, testifying to their uselessness in building peacetime consumer goods. Auto dreamer Preston Tucker acquired the largest aircraft plant in the world for almost nothing from the government to manufacture his revolutionary "Tucker Torpedoes," providing him with more space than an automaker twice his size could use. Nor was he an exception; many facilities were given away for a song. Far from providing business with state-of-the art factories, the government had thrown up the structure for a wonderfully efficient war machine that was totally unrelated to peacetime needs.

World War II did not vindicate Keynesianism, as Jonathan Hughes suggested, and it was not government spending per se that stirred American business out of the Great Depression.[38] As Robert Higgs has shown, if one examines personal consumption expenditures, properly deflated for the effects of price controls, real consumption fell after 1941 and did not recover until 1945, not growing significantly until the postwar period.[39] It was not a simple equation, "government money in, production up," but rather a crisis situation that prompted American entrepreneurs to plunge themselves and their resources ruthlessly into the cause of defeating the totalitarian powers. It also spurred millions of Americans to sacrifice, both in consumption and in extended work hours, to defeat Hitler, Tojo, and Mussolini. (Of course, it goes without saying that vast numbers of soldiers, sailors, and airmen made the ultimate sacrifice.) As Higgs concludes, "It is difficult to understand how working harder, longer, more inconveniently and dangerously in return for a diminished flow of consumer goods comports with the description that 'economically speaking, Americans never had it so good.'"[40] The Nazi threat, not the Keynesian promise, spurred the most astounding military buildup in history. While huge amounts of resources were employed in defeating the Axis powers, as the authors of a study on unemployment in this period concluded, "The World War II era is less of an economic success story than is often portrayed."[41] They calculated the growth rate during the war years at a good, but not exceptional, 4 percent but cautioned that the price deflators were subject to dispute. Further, they argued that if more realistic deflators are used, real wages may have even *fallen* during the "Keynesian expansion."

Instead of producing a recovery through government demand, the war endowed American business with a level of credibility that had collapsed on Black Thursday, restoring the nation's entrepreneurs in the public esteem that disappeared during the depression. Wartime production was the best public relations campaign the American business sector could have mounted, creating a momentum that swept it into the preeminent position in the world after the conflict.

American Business Dominates the World

Once the ink on the surrender documents dried, the war officially ended. But a serious conflict remained: The Soviet Union was a powerful enemy, the governments of many European countries teetered on the brink of collapse, and the Communist parties in almost every nation saw in the wartime destruction potential for radical political change. The United States had to ensure that the victory gained on the battlefields and in the factories was not lost at the ballot box.

At that point, American business again stepped in to flex the sinews of democracy. The U.S. GNP in 1950 reached $284 billion, almost triple the level of 1940 ($100 billion). More important, the U.S. share of world industrial production reached almost 45 percent in 1953, and the U.S. share of world trade steadied at over 15 percent (see Figure 10.1). Europe and Japan had few factories capable of producing domestic goods, such as automobiles or radios. That gave American business a market of captive consumers. Moreover, the United States entered the postwar period with the

| FIGURE 10-1 | *U.S. Economic Power in the Twentieth Century* |

	1913	1928	1938	1948	1953	1958	1963	1968	1971	1973	1978	1980	1985
U.S. share of world industrial production:													
Bairoch	32.0	39.3	31.4		44.7		35.1			33.0		31.5	
Rostow	36.0	42.0	32.0				32.0	34.0		33.0			
U.S. share of world trade:													
Rostow	11	14	10	16		14	11			13		12.5	14.5

Source: From Henry R. Nau, *The Myth of America's Decline: Leading the World Economy into the 1990s,* p. 63. Copyright © 1992 by Oxford University Press, Inc. Reprinted by permission.

most efficient industrial machine in the world, making it the world's leading supplier. Business saw the potential of that situation readily.

Trade with Europe and Japan required that they have money and, ultimately, some productive capacity to generate their own wealth. The Marshall Plan (1947) offered $12.5 billion in direct aid to more than a dozen democratic nations in Europe, specifically to short-circuit communist disaffection with the governments there. American banks generously supplied loans, bought European government and industrial bonds, and otherwise facilitated an economic revival. Fortunately, Europe and Japan recognized their predicament, and set to restoring their economies with clench-jawed determination and Yankee capital. Historians have referred to the results as either a "European Miracle" or written of the "European Lazarus."[42]

Loans provided a way for foreigners to obtain dollars to buy American products until such time as they could sell their own goods for dollars. But foreigners also "bought American" when possible, and U.S. businesses responded by producing high-quality goods that were superior to those made in other places in the world. "American made" constituted a trademark of excellence; whether in autos, electronics, or clothes, American dominance was clearly visible. U.S. auto manufacturers made nine million cars in 1955, more than four times as many as Germany, France, Italy, Germany, and Canada put together![43] The "car culture" not only affected Americans, who owned more autos than the rest of the world put together, but it placed a final ironic epitaph on the Nazi gravestone, mocking Hitler's promise that the Germans would have a "people's car," with the resulting U.S. freeway system dwarfing the vaunted *autobahnen.* Despised by intellectuals as the epitome of crass consumerism, cars offered independence that the

Europeans envied, proving even to be effective weapons in the cold war. When John Ford's movie *The Grapes of Wrath* was shown in the Soviet Union in hopes of depicting the plight of American migrant laborers, Soviet authorities were dismayed to find that Russian viewers "were impressed by a country where even some of the most abject of poor people wore shoes and owned cars."[44] Ford and GM especially competed to satiate the foreign demand for American cars; but the car companies were hardly alone. Increased overseas trade and investment pushed U.S. firms into the international arena as never before.

International Trade, Multinational Corporations

Foreign investment by American entrepreneurs dated back to the nineteenth century, with the construction of a railroad in the Panama Canal region. Vanderbilt and others, of course, had established facilities in Central America, and I. M. Singer's sewing machine plant in Glasgow, Scotland, constituted one of the first "offshore" production facilities owned by Americans. Singer's sales abroad made up half of all the company's sales by 1874. Western Electric followed, building a manufacturing plant in Belgium in 1882, while Edison, Standard Oil, Eastman Kodak, and American Tobacco all established American-owned foreign sources of distribution.[45]

For almost a century, America had been a debtor nation. Indeed, the periods of its most rapid growth—in the 1830s and 1850s, for example—were characterized by extremely high foreign investment, mostly British. World War I changed the situation, making New York the world's money center and the United States a creditor nation. Paradoxically, some managers sought to invest abroad out of fear. They had accepted the view, somewhat inherent in the managerial hierarchies, that domestic markets were exhausted and that Americans could buy no more appliances, steel, or clothes. That message, preached early in the century by communist dictator Vladimir Lenin in his *Imperialism: The Highest Stage of Capitalism,* reached sympathetic ears in The United States, where the depressions of the 1890s and 1907 intensified the belief that American markets were saturated.[46] Quite the contrary, there may have been a glut of "bads," as George Gilder calls them, but there was no glut of "goods." Incredible new technologies had just been invented, including the auto, the radio, and electric devices, awaiting only the infusion of new capital and the maturation of related technologies to bring them to consumers.

Others looked to the substantial potential of foreign markets, particularly the Far East with its sea of people. Unfortunately, lost on many business leaders was a sense of the culture of the area and the backward nature of the markets.[47] Many nations in the Far East remained kingdoms or despotic tyrannies, with little reverence for contracts or concern for human rights. They routinely broke agreements, jailed business personnel, or disrupted markets with brutal repression of local populations who found themselves on the wrong side of a power struggle. In the strategic picture, China, Indochina, Thailand, Burma, and other nations represented the objects of balance-of-power politics among the Western industrialized countries, leading foreigners to attempt to control them and further confusing and destroying market incentives. Even in Latin America, where American investment reached $7 billion in 1929, many companies wanted to gain access to new sources of raw materials, not create new armies of consumers, rendering Lenin's analysis inaccurate again. As a result, trade remained overwhelmingly among the industrial nations themselves.

After World War II, however, interest in foreign markets revived. As the Europeans and Japanese became genuine competitors, American business moved to establish a permanent presence abroad.[48] Often, the multinational corporation, jointly owned by Americans and foreign investors or which one corporation with producing branches or subsidiaries in more than one country, proved the only acceptable solution as many nations resisted penetration by U.S. firms. Beginning in the 1950s, led by the petroleum companies' investments in the Middle East and Asia, multinational expansion accelerated. Then, in the period 1960–1980, they exploded, with the value of American direct investment overseas rising from $32 billion to $227 billion (and surging to almost $2 trillion by the late 1980s).[49] Of course, business welcomed government assistance, benefiting from agencies such as the Agency for International Development to extend loans to firms investing in foreign countries; the United States Import-Export Bank, which facilitated transfers of funds; and the International Bank for Reconstruction and Development and the Inter-American Development Bank, both of which encouraged multinational expansion.

Multinationals solved the problem of access to foreign markets only by raising a new concern, that of accountability to national interest. During World War II, for example, the German company of I.G. Farben had taken advantage of its corporate arrangement with Standard Oil to acquire industrial technologies deemed critical to national security, raising the spectre of American business arming our enemies.[50] Export controls by government have limited the sales of key technologies to foreign nations, especially during the cold war, when the Soviets attempted to purchase important computer equipment. By that time, the fear among some that U.S. firms had "sold out" to multinational interests had become almost a paranoia. Inspired by presidential candidate Ross Perot's warning that the 1993 North American Free Trade Agreement (or NAFTA) would result in the "pitter patter of little feet crossing the Rio Grande" to move American production to Mexico for cheaper labor, Americans grew concerned that foreign nations either competed unfairly with low labor costs or, conversely, were "buying into America" with their capital investments. The other concern, more conspiratorial and sinister, held that American companies sacrificed their patriotism on the altar of money, submitting themselves to some secret international body. Foreign affiliates held assets in U.S. companies of almost $260 billion in 1986, suggesting to some that American companies might owe allegiance to foreign governments instead of the United States. One alarmist commission reported in the early 1980s that multinational corporations controlled between a quarter and a third of all world industrial production, while other authors warned that multinationals would "transcend the nation-state" and operate "planetary enterprise."[51] But even a critic of multinationals such as Robert Heilbroner admits that the power of nation-states is not likely to be diminished by multinationals, if for no other reason than that a corporation cannot inculcate a "spirit of sacrifice necessary both for good purposes, such as development, and for . . . war."[52]

Common sense dictates, however, that Pepsico would not ship all of its products from the United States; instead it produces Pepsi-Cola in hundreds of plants and in more than one hundred nations.[53] The product—and profits—were American, but the production facility and labor often resided in another country. Consequently, most of the top 100 U.S. corporations had facilities in at least six other countries by the 1980s, just as BMW, Toyota, Honda, Sony, and dozens of other foreign companies have facilities in the United States. Indeed, the irony of the criticisms is inescapable; in 1968, Jean Jacques Servan-Schreiber, in *The American Challenge,* terrified Europeans that they faced *American* economic domination if they did not resist with activist government policies. Multinational production also contributed to the misconception that the United States had increasingly imported more foreign products in the 1970s and 1980s. For example, by the 1980s, 20 percent of U.S. imports were goods produced by American firms with manufacturing or assembly facilities located on foreign soil, meaning that Americans were "importing" their own production.[54] Still other confusion arises over the definition of exports; in 1985, for example, U.S. companies sold $80 billion worth of goods not counted as "exports" because they were produced by American plants located in other countries. Typically, however, fears remain, especially about the role of international finance (usually a code term for "Jewish bankers"), and those hostile to the market continue to press for "new safeguards into the world of unrestrained international finance" as a way of preventing "destabilization" of Third World economies.[55] Of course, the new international finance that developed between 1960 and 1996 more appropriately prevented *governments* from inflating, devaluing, or destabilizing currencies—a point most critics of international finance certainly knew.

A more important assessment of multinationals comes, again, through the application of the theories of Alfred Chandler, where it was argued that multinationals represented merely the logical extension of the managerial revolution into foreign markets. The international experience with multinationals resembled that of America, although with important distinctions.[56] That view had merit when applied to Singer Sewing Machines or Standard Oil but seems badly out of touch with the international market of the 1990s, when faxes and modems connect individual firms around the globe through a network of cable and satellites. If anything, further globalization of the world economy will reduce, rather than enhance, the role of multinationals.

Business, Building, and Babies

War's capital demands required that the government restrain consumer spending from 1942 to 1945. Price controls eased just as waves of servicemen returned home to marry and start families. With bulging bank accounts and new children on the way, postwar families needed new housing and purchased homes at an unprecedented pace. Banks used federally insured loans from the Veterans Administration (VA) and the Federal Housing Administration (FHA) programs to accommodate millions of new and first-time home owners. In 1948, approximately 18 million Americans owned their homes, and within five years 25 million were homeowners. The situation stood in stark contrast to the dark days of the depression and "Hoovervilles."

Housing contractors benefited from two shifts that took place almost simultaneously. First, in most cities, middle-class families started to move to the "suburbs"—outlying residential communities developed out of farmland. Suburbs had sprang up as mass-production techniques, such as those used by Henry Kaiser, were adapted to the postwar housing shortage. Suburban living also benefited from the other "big-ticket" item most families purchased after the war, the auto. Auto sales soared after 1946, giving unprecedented mobility to families and allowing them to live farther from the workplace.

At that point, great bankers joined with dynamic builders, and the cityscape bloomed. The most famous suburb, Levittown, New York, near Long Island, was adding a new home every fifteen minutes by 1950. But the real crucible where builders and bankers forged an alliance that had implications for the entire nation was in the West, particularly California and Arizona. California home building had advanced as the Bank of America, under A. P. Giannini's son, Mario, used FHA/VA loans at record levels, providing builder Paul Trousdale enough money to construct two houses a day, seven days a week. During one stretch, Trousdale had 300 houses under construction each day. By 1948 alone, the Bank of America had $600 million in housing loans outstanding, and during the 1950s the bank supplied San Francisco builder Henry Doelger, who began with a credit line of $110,000 in 1936, with more than $75 million to put up tracts in Los Angeles.[57]

As early as 1951, California was linked to 23 percent of all FHA/VA mortgage loans bought nationally, and, per capita, and yet almost any one California bank's efforts was surpassed by Valley National Bank in Arizona.[58] Even a tiny insurance agency, the A.B. Robbs Agencies, got in on the action by originating FHA/VA loans using northeastern insurance money. Between 1947 and 1950, the small company acquired the accounts of nine eastern investors, who purchased more than $12 million in FHA/VA mortgages. By 1953, the company had twenty eastern investors and $30 million worth of home mortgages, supporting the phenomenal growth of Phoenix, which by 1958 ranked eleventh in the nation in new home construction.[59]

The growth of cities such as Phoenix, Los Angeles, Albuquerque, El Paso, San Diego, Tampa, Orlando, Dallas, and Houston characterized a geographical relocation from the "Rust Belt" to the "Sun Belt." It had started during the war as contractors and military personnel relocated to open areas for security purposes. As an increasing number of people were exposed to the natural beauty and generally pleasant climate of these areas, they returned after the war or when they retired, sparking yet more opportunity for entrepreneurs to provide goods and services. Open spaces around most of the Sun Belt cities offered room for expansion. In the West in particular, the uninhabited areas provided essential space to develop and test military weapons, aircraft, and cars, and the dry climates of southern California, Arizona, and parts of Texas and New Mexico attracted electronics manufacturers and, later, computer chip makers.

Quickly, a major demographic shift occurred in which the American population moved from north to south and from east to west, bringing with it the relocations of major enterprises—or at least the establishment of large, regional subsidiaries. State governments contributed to the new, hospitable climate for business through a number of specific policies, including lower taxes, construction of state-of-the-art airports, and "right-to-work" laws that eliminated union pressure and lowered wage costs to businesses. Yet labor did not suffer, because the cost of living was cheaper and taxes were lower than in the unionized Rust Belt states. Over a thirty-year period, Lockheed, Motorola, Delta Airlines, Disney, Martin-Marietta, McDonnell Douglas, Boeing, Hewlett-Packard, Garrett, Dole Foods, Rockwell, and many others either expanded or relocated to the Sun Belt, and they needed housing for their employees. Business quickly formed "booster groups" to encourage further growth in the Sun Belt.

The population shift not only meant that more builders and developers appeared in the West and South than ever before but signaled a fundamental transformation of American business. Electronics, computers, biomedical instruments, financial services, and defense-related businesses all started to boom. With important exceptions in Massachusetts and parts of New York, most of the new growth occurred in the West and South, although some structural changes remained hidden because autos, steel, coal, and the traditional chemical industries still dominated the Dow Jones average and still commanded much of the world market. But the shift was readily apparent in the growth of the banking systems of states like California, North Carolina, Georgia, Arizona, and, to a lesser extent, Texas and Oklahoma, where the financial sector outpaced banking growth in the Midwest and North. Whereas in previous eras businesses may have had to obtain credit from New York or Chicago, by the late 1950s and early 1960s they could get loans from the Bank of America, Texas Commerce, Security Pacific, or powerful southern regional giants.[60]

New houses reflected the need for more family space as well as simple mobility to new locations, because families themselves were growing. In 1947, a record 3.8 million babies were born—hence the famous "baby boom" generation—and birth levels continued to rise until 1953. Between 1950 and 1960, the U.S. population, including immigrants, rose from 150 million to 179 million. By 1958, kids fifteen years and under made up almost one-third of the population; toy sales that year exceeded $1 billion and diaper services swelled into a $50 million business. Children were the objects not only of parental love but of parental consumption, and they, themselves, consumed. Frank Gerber's baby-food company took off during the boom years under the leadership of his son, Dan. Running a small canning company with his father, Dan had a firsthand encounter with straining baby food in the 1920s when he had to delay a social engagement to prepare peas. The company had first introduced canned baby food in the late 1920s, offering its products for free to mothers and their children who would test them. Achieving national sales with an ad in *Good Housekeeping,* the company had gained stability in the 1930s. But in the late 1940s it took off. In 1948, the company sold two million cans of baby food a day, marketing its product with a charcoal sketch of a baby's head. Capturing the look of innocence, the "Gerber baby" has since found its way into most American households. The company introduced chemical additives to its product to make the taste more appealing and to preserve it on grocery shelves, and by the end of the 1950s, the very product of baby food was associated with a single name, Gerber.[61]

War also introduced thousands of women to the workforce, and while many returned to homes to raise their children, mothers looked for part-time jobs to help fill the days as the kids got older. Russell

Kelly had the perfect position for them. Kelly, who had served as a fiscal management analyst in the Army Quartermaster Corps, had created a centralized system to speed up typing, duplicating, and addressing business correspondence among Detroit firms. He brought the work to his office until an emergency call in 1946 from an accountant looking for a typist gave Kelly a new idea: hiring skilled, temporary workers out to businesses from a central location. He recruited at churches and PTAs, training older women who found themselves discriminated against because of their age. The employees were known as "Kelly Girls" for decades. By the 1970s, Kelly Services had grown into the largest provider of temporary services in the United States.[62]

Unprecedented Travel Opportunities Spawn New Businesses

Faced with a postwar slump (temporarily alleviated by Korean War military orders), the aviation industry aimed at new business from family and corporate travelers. Airline companies such as Eastern, American, and TWA offered "coach" class tickets to compete with railroads. Passengers could fly most anywhere in the country for a few hundred dollars—still a substantial sum, but significantly cheaper than ever before. Pan Am's Juan Trippe observed that for the first time ordinary people could afford air travel, and airplanes opened up the same vistas in the late 1950s that trains had a century earlier. Boardings doubled between 1951 and 1958, to 38 million, and on a single day in 1954 New York City played host to the first air "traffic jam" when 300 airliners stacked up in holding patterns above the Big Apple, delaying 45,000 passengers.[63]

Flights became faster and routes expanded to new locations. In 1953, TWA offered the first nonstop air service from New York to California. TWA and Pan Am raced to offer the first nonstop Atlantic flights, with Pan Am the victor. Trippe's company introduced the first true transatlantic airliner, built by Douglas Aircraft (the DC-7) in 1957, surpassing the Lockheed-built *Lodestar* as the most advanced passenger aircraft. Thanks to the DC-7, Pan Am could compete with TWA, which had provided transatlantic flights with only a single refueling stop since the early 1950s and introducing travelers to a new physical and mental malady called "jet lag."

When people could not fly, at least they could travel in their cars. Approximately 40 million cars transited the nation's 1.6 million miles of surfaced highways by 1950. Some 60 percent of the households owned a car, and the "Big Three" (Ford, General Motors, and Chrysler) dominated the market. A handful of smaller competitors struggled to stay in business, including Nash, Hudson, Studebaker, and Willys-Overland, and a new entrant, Kaiser-Frazer, experienced strong sales growth. Nevertheless, Ford and GM posted healthy profits; both automakers produced their 50 millionth vehicle in the 1950s, and GM controlled more than 50 percent of the market. Chevrolet alone offered 46 models, 32 different engines, and more than 400 accessories by 1960. Chrysler, meanwhile, lagged behind Ford and GM because it had the most substantial reconversion to do after the war. Ford had made trucks—and still did—but Chrysler had made tanks, which had no postwar demand. Yet Chrysler retained a position well above the smaller competitors, making it appear on the surface that the Big Three were impenetrable.

Henry Kaiser's attempt to crack into the auto market illustrated that even the extreme concentration in the industry by the late 1940s could not keep out new entrants. Founded in 1945 by Kaiser and partner Joseph Frazer, the Kaiser-Frazer Company consistently lost money despite increasing sales. It had a good product, but, as Kaiser later admitted, his company was terribly undercapitalized from the start. Initial stock offerings received a warm welcome on Wall Street, raising $16 million, but all things are relative. Kaiser needed $320 million to make a dent in the auto market. Within five years, despite consistently rising sales, the company recorded a $34 million loss. The end came in 1950 when Kaiser-Frazer introduced the "Henry J," a compact car priced at $2,000, aimed at the frugal, middle-class buyer. Instead, American customers chose a new European product, Germany's Volkswagen, and Kaiser ended production of the "Henry J" in 1954. Kaiser-Frazer ceased all auto production in the United States in 1955, by all accounts having entered the business more than $2 billion short of the necessary "ante."[64] On the other hand, Kaiser had proved that, sufficiently capitalized, a new auto company could have a future and that, contrary to depiction in the Francis Ford Coppola's film *Tucker: The Man and His Dream,* no "Detroit conspiracy" kept entrepreneurs out of the industry. Quite the contrary, Kaiser showed that managerial talent made up for a myriad of other weaknesses, suggesting that Tucker was more dreamer than businessman.

Kemmons Wilson and Holiday Inns

Autos meant mobility, allowing Americans to use their newfound freedom of movement for pleasure as well as business. Like other travelers, Kemmons Wilson, a Tennessee architect-builder, frequently stayed with his family in one of the numerous motels across the nation. He always had the same complaints. Rooms were dirty, there was not enough space for kids, and children were charged the same as adults.

Wilson decided to open his own motel chain, but not before he had in mind the ideal dimensions, conveniences, and facilities he wanted for himself in a motel. After traveling across country with his wife and family, staying every night somewhere different to take notes, Wilson had his composite motel firmly in mind. He designed the optimal room for a family of four and decided that kids would stay free at his motel. In 1954, Wilson opened the first Holiday Inn.

Common sense dictated that each motel have the same features but did not have to be identical. So while the 280 green-and-gold inns, with more than 30,000 rooms, that were scattered across 35 states by 1962 all conformed to Wilson's original design specifications, each also maintained certain idiosyncratic touches that made it special. The Alexandria, Minnesota, Holiday Inn featured a bar shaped like a Viking ship and a pool area enclosed under the trademarked "Holodome" that allowed residents to swim in any weather—an especially useful characteristic in the frozen North. At Las Cruces, New Mexico, the Holiday Inn featured a restaurant area designed as an enclosed miniature city skyline of old Mesilla (the original Mexican pueblo where Las Cruces now stands). Wilson, appearing on a television talk show in the 1970s dedicated to "self-made men," pointed out that he never sought to get rich. All he wanted was to provide Americans a place where a family could get a "good night's sleep" at no extra cost for children.[65]

The widespread availability of autos and airplane travel, placed within the budget of ordinary people, not only opened up the vast new motel business but improved transportation of all manufactured products and made delivery of everything from mail to mussels and peas to porcelain more rapid, hence cheaper. Detroit automakers and hotel magnates across the country celebrated when Congress passed the National Highway Act in 1958 to construct vast new eight-lane interstate "freeways" across the United States. Just as the railroad subsidies had accelerated the dominance of trains, so the Highway Act ensured the triumph of passenger cars and freight trucking, completing the victory already under way in the auto industry. Already, however, the increased—and increasingly rapid—highway travel, along with the appearance of suburbs, had facilitated the phenomenal rise of one of the best-known chains in American business history.

Ray Kroc and McDonald's

A fifty-two-year-old paper cup salesman seems an unlikely candidate to start the largest fast-food empire in the world. Perhaps more surprising, Ray Kroc had just quit his sales job to focus on a new device, a multiple-milkshake mixer, throwing aside any security he had built in his former position. But paper cups had led him to the milkshake mixer, and the mixer took him from Chicago to the McDonald brothers' store in San Bernadino, California.

Kroc had heard of Mac and Dick McDonald's drive-in that assembled fries, hamburgers, and beverages on a mass-production basis, and in 1954 he traveled to California to observe the operation in person. In his autobiography *Grinding It Out,* he later said, that "I felt like some latter-day Newton who'd just had an Idaho potato caromed off his skull."[66] Kroc admired the simplicity of the procedures that allowed the McDonald brothers to concentrate on quality. He "was carried away by the thought of McDonald's drive-ins proliferating like rabbits, with eight Multi mixers in each one."[67] Working out a franchise agreement with the brothers, Kroc envisioned a network of drive-ins, with each building like the original (including the famous golden arches) and the name, McDonald's, on all of them. It took a year to open his first location in Des Plaines, Illinois, which Kroc perceptively saw as a prototype of many other stores; therefore, he repeatedly refined the design to eliminate problems. During that time, Kroc continued to sell Multi mixers, working, in essence, two full-time jobs. The key, as he saw it, was to maintain the quality he had witnessed in California, and he paid strict attention to the tiniest details—litter in the parking lot, or turning on the sign at exactly dusk. As Kroc said, "Perfection is very difficult to achieve, and perfection was what I wanted in McDonald's. Everything else was secondary for me."[68]

Ray Kroc carefully tailored a family image: no jukeboxes, no pay phones, no vending machines. (Only in the 1990s did stores provide local newspapers for browsing during breakfast.) After more than a year, the first location started to operate as Kroc hoped. He then expanded with three franchises in California, where he could show potential leasees and landlords the successful San Bernadino drive-in still ran by the McDonald brothers. By 1956, Kroc opened eight stores in eight months, moving back to the Midwest with some of his new locations. After five years, McDonald's had 200 restaurants; by 1963, it opened more than 100 per year. Kroc established a training facility, called "Hamburger University," that put employees through the rigors of making every product served at McDonald's. Hamburger U., though, soon took on the task of training McDonald's owners and primary operators.

Meanwhile, McDonald's had purchased millions of potatoes, which it stored to achieve the special McDonald's flavor. That storage cost a great deal of money and was inefficient. One major supplier, J. R. Simplot of Idaho, had sold potatoes to the original McDonald brothers, and while Kroc took over the business and made it grow, Simplot experimented with an easier way of storing spuds. He had managed to freeze-dry both onions and potatoes and suggested the concept to Kroc, who agreed to try frozen french fries at a few stores. On the

basis of a handshake, Simplot invested in a facility capable of producing 39,000 pounds of french fries an hour. By 1960, Simplot produced 170 million pounds of frozen french fries, selling approximately
40 percent of them to McDonald's.[69]

Motown and Disneyland, Entertainment Meccas

If McDonald's represented the postwar approach to fast food for the average citizen, rock 'n' roll and rhythm and blues captured the new musical tastes as music became big business. At the same time, the
burgeoning entertainment industry offered opportunities in areas that
had scarcely been exploited in the past. Two of the most original entertainment companies launched in the 1950s, Motown Records and
Disneyland, in odd ways reflected the continued impact of the auto, illustrated the entrepreneurial opportunities that awaited in the field of
entertainment that made allowances for mobility and travel.

Detroit assembly-line worker Berry Gordy Jr. aspired to write
songs. He had even opened a jazz-oriented record store in 1955—an
enterprise that failed but that provided Gordy with experience in
record retailing. Along with his sister and a friend, Gordy wrote a song
recorded by Jackie Wilson, who soon returned to the autoworker for
another ditty. Gordy penned "Lonely Teardrops," and his connection
to Wilson led him to an up-and-coming group called Smokey Robinson
and the Miracles. Gordy virtually stole them from under the nose of
another studio, paid their recording costs, and leased their record to
nationally distributed labels.

Under a number of different labels and organizations, Gordy continued to record, produce, and publish songs by a variety of black Detroit and northern Indiana acts. Using $800 that he borrowed from his
family, in 1959 he formed Tamla Records, which recorded the Temp-
tations and Mary Wells along with his current bands, such as the Miracles. Although some of the acts never achieved notoriety, many of the
songs—often written by Gordy—became classics: "Do You Love Me?
(Now That I Can Dance)" and "Money," for example. They all featured
a common sound, with the drums brought to the fore on as strong a
plane as the vocals, driving the beat like a Detroit diesel. Gordy reorganized Tamla in 1960 as Motown Records, taking his name from the
auto industry that he had worked in for so long. The sound seemed to
fit the city.[70]

With U.S. record sales reaching $600 million in 1960, Gordy had
entered the market at the right time. Motown had some of the hottest
groups in the nation, and, despite the fact that all the Motown acts
were black in a nation where many stations refused to play black

artists, Motown dominated the charts. Early Motown stars included the Supremes ("Where Did Our Love Go?" and "You Keep Me Hangin' On"), the Four Tops ("I Can't Help Myself" and "Baby, I Need Your Lovin'"), and the Jackson Five ("ABC," "I'll Be There," "Never Can Say Goodbye"). The Motown songs became such an integral part of American culture that dozens of television and radio commercials in the 1990s continue to use the familiar tunes with new variations of lyrics to sell products. Almost without thinking, people sang along to the catchy melodies.

Gordy developed a formula that did for music what Ray Kroc had done for hamburgers, applying an assembly-line approach to record production. All groups had access to staff songwriters, choreographers, and etiquette coaches. He knew that although he had to keep the core black audience, real growth could occur only if he tapped into the other 88 percent of the listening and record-buying market. Groups had to look good and dance even better; they were instructed on public speaking for interviews, ditching black inner-city dialect in favor of proper English, and they had to maintain, at least in public, proper manners. Most of all, they had to stick to the formula. That meant that Gordy did not want groups writing their own material—an issue that finally drove Michael Jackson and the Jackson Five to a new record label. Finally, Gordy realized (but certainly did not publicize to his artists) one fact about recording profits, namely, that while the popularity went to the performers, the profits went to the producers and owners of the songs.

One of Gordy's most successful songwriting teams, Eddie Holland, Lamont Dozier, and Brian Holland (known as Holland-Dozier-Holland), transformed the traditional twelve-bar blues and thirty-two-bar ballads into new, short strains that repeated the "hook" or catch phrase in two- or eight-bar repeats. The Supremes, in particular, knocked out hit after hit in the 1960s using the Holland-Dozier-Holland recipe. Gordy had perceived a maxim of the new radio industry—if the listener can't sing the tune the second time around, it won't be a hit. And since the typical "play time" of a song on the radio lasted only two minutes, the Holland-Dozier-Holland formula did not have time to get old before the song ended, leaving the listeners clamoring for more.

By 1972, *Black Enterprise* magazine recognized Motown as the top black-owned business in America. Although Motown eventually lost most of its top artists over the control issues that drove Jackson away, it set the example for black- and other minority-owned businesses. Appealing to whites, Gordy proved that business is not a "race thing" but a "money thing." Moreover, except for A&M Records, no other company has survived as Motown did simply by expanding from a string of hits.

As unlikely as an auto-line worker was to develop a major record company, it was perhaps even more unlikely that a cartoon artist whose claim to fame was a stick-figure mouse would establish the standard for interactive entertainment, theme-park operations, and crowd control. Walt Disney (1901–1966) had gained a reputation as a cartoon genius for his *Steamboat Willie* talking cartoon in 1928. He moved from cartoon shorts to animated full-length features with *Snow White and the Seven Dwarfs* in 1934, defying the naysayers who claimed no one would pay for a full-length cartoon, especially at the height of the Great Depression! Instead, with the success of *Snow White,* Disney added 750 employees to his studios.

"Walt," as everyone referred to Walter Elias Disney, always considered himself a child trapped in an adult's body. He loved amusement parks, yet found most of them dirty and disorganized, with rides frequently broken. Disney nurtured a vision of an amusement park that would be immaculately clean, with well-mannered staff, and a source of optimism, patriotism, and good, clean "family" fun. Unable to convince his brother, Roy, who handled the studio's finances, to support the project, Walt cashed in his life insurance policy in 1952 and created WED Enterprises to fund his dream, "Disneyland." He located the theme park in an orange grove near Anaheim, California. Although studies he commissioned had estimated the costs at $11 million, Disney had to pour $17 million into the park before it opened. In an incredible act of faith, Disney had staked his last penny on Disneyland.

Construction began on the 160-acre park behind 25-foot-high embankments to shield it from public view. During construction, Disney convinced the American Broadcasting Company (ABC) to air a weekly show from the park for which ABC paid $500,000 and guaranteed $4.5 million more. In addition, ABC purchased one-third of Disneyland stock (kept separate from WED, which owned one-third; Disney personally owned 17 percent).

On July 17, 1955, Disneyland opened with national television coverage. The cameras recorded a steady stream of disasters. Water fountains were in short supply on the hot day because of a plumbers strike. Twice as many people showed up than were expected. Fess Parker, the star of Disney's television show "Davy Crockett," rode in on horseback just in time for the sprinkler system to malfunction and drench him. The full-scale replica riverboat *Mark Twain* nearly capsized because of the overcrowding, and the lagoons dried up in the boiling sun. "A nightmare," one called the opening. "A giant cash register, clicking and clanging."[71] For Walt, the setbacks were only minor irritants. He certainly did not abandon his dream and instead fixed the problems, while continuing to envision newer, and better, attractions. Disneyland set the standard by which future parks were judged. It had an ordered, sequenced layout of attractions that complemented each other;

a single entrance; wide, leisurely walkways; extensive landscaping; attractions unique to Disney; and, most of all, unmatched cleanliness. Walt constantly sought to transfer the ideas from his motion pictures and cartoons to live attractions and tied marketing of his movies to his parks. Disneyland pioneered new types of crowd control, where constant movement and video or audio entertainment in line made the waiting time (occasionally an hour or more for some rides) seem shorter. Even at the most popular rides, waiting became "watching." His techniques became the industry standard at Sea World, Six Flags, Universal Studios, and any number of other parks oriented toward the public. Custodians groomed the grounds every few minutes, and every night an army of tailors, seamstresses, painters, and safety inspectors descended on the park for massive refurbishing. At the end of ten years, Disneyland had grown from twenty-two attractions to forty-seven, and almost 50 million people had passed through Snow White's Castle, including Soviet premier Nikita Khrushchev.

Long after Walt's death, the vision lived on, with new parks planned and attractions gaining in sophistication. In the 1990s, a single ride, the "Indiana Jones Ride" at Disneyland in California, cost as much as Walt had budgeted for the entire original park. Every aspect of the park suggested fantasy. Buildings were deliberately undersized. Tiny lights glistened from plants to add sparkle. Nightly fireworks celebrated the end of the day's festivities.

But despite Disneyland's success, Walt had become frustrated with the location in Orange County. He failed to control the surrounding commercial properties, which spawned a raft of seedy, cheap motels and restaurants not owned by Disney and not controlled by the company. Walt thus secretly started to buy Florida property in the Orlando area for a new project, Walt Disney World. Opened in 1971, Walt Disney World was built with an eye toward correcting all the problems of Disneyland. It was larger (and had much more room to expand), with the park itself sitting on a tiny section of the surrounding 28,000 acres Walt had secured for other parks, hotels, camp sites, and shopping centers. In 1982, EPCOT Center opened on some of the adjacent acreage to the Orlando property, while Tokyo Disneyland took the Disney touch abroad. France's Euro Disneyland followed in 1992, although with much less success than the other parks. Invading Universal Studios movie-studio theme park monopoly, Disney opened the Disney-MGM park in Orlando, all the while updating and improving each of the existing facilities with new attractions.

After Walt's death, the company languished until a new management team, headed by Michael Eisner, revitalized it. Eisner put life back into the Disney-animated full-length cartoons with megahits like *The Little Mermaid, Beauty and the Beast, The Lion King,* and *Aladdin,* but then the studios turned out a series of average animated works that attempted to appeal to "politically correct" crowds, and, by the standards of *The Lion King,* many of the subsequent features were flops. But Eisner had more success with the theme parks, realizing that modern "hip" teenagers, who had significant chunks of cash to spend, would no longer be interested in cartoon mice and ducks. If Disney characters did not translate into rides, Eisner reasoned, he would have to "Disneyfy" existing non-Disney characters. With special marketing arrangements, George Lucas was retained to design and construct a simulator ride based on his colossal hit, *Star Wars,* called Star Tours. Later, Lucas and director Steven Spielberg collaborated on the design of the "Indiana Jones" ride. Disney obtained rights to the highly popular Muppets from master puppeteer Jim Henson.

But it was Walt Disney, not George Lucas, who showed what could happen when a vision of fantasy was joined to mechanical reality. Walt did not live to see most of the robotics and simulator rides available to later engineers, but he certainly would have been the first to say, "That's great. But where can we go from here?"

Birth of the "Electronic Baby-Sitter"

Both Barry Gordy's Motown and Walt Disney's theme parks owed much of their success to the electronics media—Motown, obviously, because the proliferation of radios and cheaper phonographs made possible widespread access to the music, and Disneyland because the key to its advertising was its contract with ABC television. In different ways, radio and television, the new electronics media giants, dominated American culture in the 1950s.

During World War II the government prohibited construction of new radio broadcasting stations, but once the FCC permitted new applications, radio blossomed, with the number of stations rising from just over 900 in 1945 to more than 3,000 by 1948. Two-thirds were traditional AM stations, which were joined by 1,000 FM stations. The National Broadcasting Company (NBC) and the Columbia Broadcasting System (CBS) dominated the airwaves in the early 1940s, with 160 and 107 affiliates, respectively. Programming had expanded to include children's shows, musicals, comedy, mysteries (even early "terror radio"), adventures, news, and the traditional "soap opera" (so named because of the soap companies that advertised on the programs).[72] The two major broadcasters battled for advertisers and listeners, with CBS making itself into a powerful competitor to David Sarnoff's NBC thanks to the efforts of William S. Paley.

Paley, fresh out of college, had worked at his father's cigar company until he noticed the exceptional response that a radio ad for the company's cigars had elicited. On the eve of the Great Crash, Paley had mustered $450,000 to invest in the Columbia Phonograph Broadcasting System, renaming it as CBS and taking over as its president. He expanded it in the teeth of the Great Depression, multiplying the number of affiliates by a factor of six and, equally important, keeping the business profitable.

CBS grew in popularity because Paley attracted a stable of radio personalities, stealing them, if necessary, from NBC. He signed Bing Crosby, Jack Benny, Kate Smith, and newsman Edward R. Murrow. As the CBS personalities became famous, Paley pressured the affiliates to provide them with permanent time slots, gaining control over programming, which in turn allowed him to market the slots to advertisers. His strategy also shifted power from independent producers and affiliates to the national broadcaster, creating a "master/slave" relationship wherein the "locals" (as the affiliates were called) meekly received what the national source sent out.

Radio, which had gained great credibility as the only "instantaneous" source of news during the war, found itself atop the mass communications market, peering down smugly at newspapers, which it had displaced. The industry scarcely noticed the determined, fledgling technology that was climbing that mountain from the back side, television.

A television transmission had taken place at the New York World's Fair in 1927, but unlike radio, television suffered during the depression years. War needs limited the availability of electronic parts, further stifling development, although RCA opened a studio in 1944. By 1946, more than a million sets in some twenty cities received signals generated by more than thirty broadcasting stations. Modern television programming began in 1947, with *The Howdy Doody Show, Kraft Television Theater,* and *Texaco Star Theater.*[73] (Those expressing disdain for the so-called new corporate sponsorship of events such as bowl games and tennis matches might note the titles of some of the first regular television shows!) NBC, again, dominated the early activity, with stations in New York, Philadelphia, and Washington linked by a cable. The drawback was capital, with a citywide broadcast network requiring hundreds of thousands of dollars to set up. Yet the potential was so enormous that investors willingly put up the phenomenal capital required to develop the technology and the networks, confident they could recoup their costs from advertisers. Evidence rolled in rather quickly: In 1952, Hasbro Toys, perceptive to the large number of children watching television, ran the first TV ad for a toy, Mr. Potato Head. Television still trailed radio in generating advertising dollars until 1954. Belatedly, radio realized that it had a genuine competitor.

Television use spread like wildfire, with more than half of U.S. homes sporting a TV in the mid-1950s. The tiny black-and-white circular tubes of the early years had given way to larger screens, with a Sears Silvertone television selling for less than $150 in 1950. Government had attempted to increase competition by allowing stations to broadcast on ultrahigh frequencies (UHF) as well as very high frequencies (VHF, or the receiver in most television sets). Falling prices and expanded programming added to television's popularity, but the real breakthrough came with the introduction of color technology. CBS and NBC/RCA had tried to gain control of the television industry for years with no clear winner. In 1946, however, William Paley's CBS introduced a color television set. It had a severe disadvantage in that it could receive *only* color, and most programming was in black and white. William Paley's counterpart at NBC, David Sarnoff, had instructed his technicians to develop a set that could receive both, called a "compatible" set. Astoundingly, the FCC endorsed the narrow technology of CBS, ruling that the CBS system should be the industry standard. RCA refused to buckle, and in 1953 the National Television System Committee, a group of experts from the entire spectrum of the broadcast industry, sided with RCA. Embarrassed by the industry insiders, the FCC retreated and in 1953 accepted the recommendation that the RCA color system serve as the standard.

When the first sets went on sale in 1954, they cost between $900 and $1,300, or almost five times the cost of a black-and-white unit and one-fourth of a typical household's annual income. To attract viewers, NBC and CBS introduced a new type of program, the "color spectacular," which emphasized color and featured famous stars. Ironically, one of the best-known color shows of the era, the Disney show (which had several names, eventually and appropriately called the *Wonderful World of Color*), was broadcast on the upstart network, ABC.[74] Later derided as an "electronic baby-sitter," and, worse, the "boob tube," television at first drew families together as they tuned in, with an entire generation growing up with Milton Berle, Lucille Ball, Red Skelton, the Lone Ranger, Superman, and, late in the 1950s, a host of cookie-cutter westerns that taught clear moral lessons. In virtually all cases, however, the values emphasized were positive: honesty, loyalty, religious faith, family, and, for the most part, industry and enterprise. Seldom were businesses portrayed as the villains—unless, on occasion, a land grabber in a western had to be dispatched by James Arness in *Gunsmoke*. Quite the contrary. Television reinforced the message, already internalized by most Americans, that the economic freedoms that had been defended during the war had made the United States the most powerful nation on earth.

A natural progression occurred, wherein large radio chains attempted to move into television broadcasting. Before long, radio found itself under siege, losing listeners to the new visual medium, which, by 1960, had more than 500 television stations across the nation. Radio, of course, did not die. It found renewal by concentrating on local markets and emphasizing music over most other types of programming. The widespread appeal of rock-and-roll music among teenagers and of country music in large parts of the South and West kept AM radio healthy, although clearly subordinate to television. Further, radio was enhanced by the development of the transistor in the early 1950s. Motorola Corporation, one of the leaders in transistor devices, led the move out of vacuum-tube technology, again demonstrating that the private sector was well ahead of government, where the Defense Department still subsidized vacuum tubes.

American Business at High Tide

Children of a later generation would learn about the 1950s through yet another television show. The 1970s situation comedy *Happy Days* presented the weekly theme that the 1950s were, well, happy days. After Korea, the United States was not involved in a shooting war for almost a decade. The economy was steady and occasionally spectacular, and new products continued to pour onto the shelves of American stores at an unprecedented rate.

TALES FROM THE CRYPT: ENTREPRENEURS WHO CAME BACK FROM THE DEAD

Emmett J. Culligan: "Hey Culligan Man"

AT AGE TWENTY-EIGHT, A LANDOWNER WITH property valued at more than $200,000, Emmett Culligan, was on top of the world. He had a reputation as a shrewd business negotiator, farmer, and land developer. Then a recession struck, knocking the price of Culligan's land to almost nothing. Bankrupt, Culligan had to leave California, where he had just settled in 1919, and

return to frozen St. Paul, Minnesota, to live with his mother.

Unwilling to wallow in pity or despair, Culligan happened upon an old friend who sold a water-filter device that removed hard minerals from water by using a natural greensand called zeolite. Culligan borrowed a bag of the sand, experimented with it in a coffee can he had perforated, and used tap water to wash diapers. Immediately he determined that his future was in water treatment.

Culligan began by selling products for his friend's company, then started his own firm in St. Paul in 1924. Difficulties still battered Culligan, with a nasty patent suit costing him over $40,000. Although he won the battle—the case, in this instance—he lost the war; with little money left, his company died during the Great Crash. Gold Dust Culligan Company overnight became dustbin Culligan. Twelve years had ensued since his last fortune disappeared, and, again, Culligan was broke. He moved again, this time to Illinois to take a job with a minerals company. He continued,

Businessmen—still mostly men—had regained their predepression position as heroes, and if books hinted that they achieved out of obedience to a mindless routine (as in William Whyte's *The Organization Man*) or accused advertisers of selling the public products they really "didn't want" (as in Vance Packard's *The Hidden Persuaders*), for the most part American business would have agreed that the 1950s were indeed happy days.[75]

American enterprise reached something of a high tide in 1959. U.S.-made autos and steel dominated the world, and the entertainment sector had come of age with a vibrant motion picture industry and a fledgling color television broadcast technology. Less visible, but in the long run just as important, a new recording revolution had started, thanks to a white boy out of Tupelo, Mississippi, who sang black music. Within fifteen years, his songs, and those of hundreds of other artists, black and white, would constitute the most copied and emulated music in history.

Unseen by many business leaders, however, were a number of warning signs those new trends carried with them. Steel and autos, safely

---

however, to ponder the main problem of his now defunct business, namely, how to bring down the cost of the $200–$400 water softener.

The difficulty was in selling the product. What if he could lease it, selling, in essence, a water treatment service? Basing his business on the telephone company's practices, Culligan would install the machines at no charge for a monthly user's fee. He then launched his new enterprise at a time most experts would deem disastrous, in 1936, during the peak of the Great Depression. He had only $50 and a small bank loan, taking out a lease on space in a Northbrook, Illinois, blacksmith shop. He made conditioning machines out of spare parts and used water tanks from junkyards; he saved on electricity by using a converted auto engine to run his machinery. When he started to market his product, he stressed that the customer could cancel the service at any time with no further obligation. He had over half a million subscribers on the eve of World War II.

But the 1950s consumers were different from those of the 1930s. In the past, Culligan had hired salesmen to go into homes to demonstrate the products, much like the famous vacuum-cleaner salesmen and the "Fuller Brush Men." The door-to-door salesman was viewed as a nuisance in the new suburban environment, however, and Culligan struggled to find a way to get inside people's homes for the critical demonstrations. In 1959, a Los Angeles ad company came up with a new advertising campaign, with a woman yelling, "Hey Culligan Man." The promotions worked, reviving at-home sales and providing the water-softener company with a well-known image. By the early 1960s, Culligan sales had doubled, and Emmett Culligan retired—for once, not forced out by unpleasant circumstances.

Sources: Fucini and Fucini, *Entrepreneurs*, 99–101; Emmett Culligan, "Softeners Rented," *Business Week*, 28 (December 1946), 21; and G. Hamilton, "Hey Zeolite Man," *Northbrook* (Illinois) *Star*, 26 (February 1976), 30–31.

insulated from foreign competition, lulled other industries into complacency. Meanwhile, the appearance of mass-media television outlets gave rise to a new generation of Progressives, as members of the new reform elites proved as active as their predecessors of the late 1800s. They created the first consumer movement, gave birth to environmentalism, and used the legal system to generate the first substantial "class action" lawsuits in history. Although it was not readily apparent to anyone involved in free enterprise, the 1960s and 1970s would be far less hospitable to business than were the "happy days" of the 1950s.

Notes

1. Johnson, *Modern Times,* 401–402.

2. Ibid.

3. Ibid., 402.

4. Gary quoted in Edward Robb Ellis, *Echoes of Distant Thunder: Life in the United States, 1914–1918* (New York: Coward, McCann, & Geohagan, 1978), 381. See also the discussion in Pusateri, *History of American Business,* 310–311.

5. John B. Rae, "Financial Problems of the American Aircraft Industry, 1906–1940," *Business History Review,* 39 (Spring 1965): 99–114.

6. Robert Daley, *An American Saga: Juan Trippe and His Pan American Empire* (New York: Random House, 1980).

7. T. A. Heppenheimer, "The Only Way to Fly," *Audacity* (Spring 1995): 16–27 (quotation on 27).

8. "The DC-3 Opens a New Era of Commercial Air Travel," in Frank McGill, ed., *Great Events in History: Business and Commerce Series,* 5 vols. (Pasadena, Calif.: Salem Press, 1994), II: 752–757 (quotation on 753).

9. Peter Harry Brown and Pat. H. Broeske, *Howard Hughes: The Untold Story* (New York: Dutton, 1996), 93.

10. Donald L. Bartlett and James B. Steele, *Empire: The Life, Legend, and Madness of Howard Hughes* (New York: W.W. Norton, 1979), 105–160.

11. Ratner, Soltow, and Sylla, *Evolution of the American Economy,* 494–496.

12. Richard Overy, *Why the Allies Won* (New York: W.W. Norton, 1995), 190; Len Deighton, *Blood, Tears, and Folly: An Objective Look at World War II* (New York: Harper Perrinnial, 1993), Table 5 on 411.

13. Overy, *Why the Allies Won,* 182.

14. S. J. Zaloga and J. Grandsen, *Soviet Tanks and Combat Vehicles of World War II* (London: Arms and Armor Press, 1984), 128 and 206; Overy, *Why the Allies Won,* 214. Zaloga and Grandsen note that Lend-Lease shipments amounted to 20 percent of all armored vehicles made in the USSR during the war, but that they accounted for 16 percent of all tanks, 12 percent of self-propelled guns, and 100 percent of personnel carriers and jeeps! (206) The only way the Soviet Union could dedicate almost 18 percent of its annual steel production to tanks was that it could divert critical production *from* self-propelled guns and transports, not to mention aircraft parts and shipping to bring in all those weapons and parts—all of which the United States provided.

15. Deighton, *Blood, Tears, and Folly,* 108.

16. See, for example, Kenneth P. Werrell, *Blankets of Fire: U.S. Bombers over Japan During World War II* (Washington, D.C.: Smithsonian Institution Press, 1996).

17. For some of the developments in this regard, see Dennis Piszkiwicz, *The Nazi Rocketeers: Dreams of Space and Crimes of War* (Westpoint, Conn.: Praeger, 1995).

18. Johnson, *Modern Times* (1980), 402.

19. Mark S. Foster, *Henry J. Kaiser: Builder in the Modern American West* (Austin: University of Texas Press, 1989).

20. Johnson, *Modern Times,* (1980), 402; Mark S. Foster, "Giant of the West: Henry J. Kaiser and Regional Industrialization," *Business History Review,* 59 (Spring 1985): 1–23.

21. John Morton Blum, *V Was for Victory: Politics and American Culture During World War II* (New York: Harcourt Brace, 1948), 115.

22. Bruce Catton, *The War Lords of Washington* (New York: Harcourt, Brace, Jovanovich, 1976).

23. Overy, *Why the Allies Won,* 2–4 and chapter 6, passim, makes these points.

24. Pusateri, *History of American Business,* 319.

25. Foster, *Henry J. Kaiser,* 254.

26. John A. Heitmann, "The Man Who Won the War: Andrew Jackson Higgins," *Louisiana History,* 34 (1993): 35–40 (quotation on 36). Also see his "Demagogue and Industrialist," *Gulf Coast Historical Review,* 5 (1990): 152–162.

27. Heitmann, "The Man Who Won the War," 40.

28. Heitmann, "The Man Who Won the War," 42; Higgins Industries, *History in a Hurry: The Story of Higgins of New Orleans* (New Orleans: Higgins Industries, 1945), 42.

29. Bruchey, *Wealth of the Nation,* 181.

30. U.S. Census Bureau, *The Statistical History of the United States* (New York: Basic Books, 1976), 132, Series D–29–41; Bruchey, *Wealth of the Nation,* 182.

31. Higgs, *Crisis and Leviathan,* 230.

32. Nevertheless, small business survived, and of course whenever feasible, tried to use the federal government for its own purposes. See Johnathan J. Bean, *Beyond the Broker State: Federal Policies Toward Small Business, 1936–1961* (Chapel Hill: University of North Carolina Press, 1996).

33. Johnson, *Modern Times* (1980), 408; Gary Cross and Rick Szostak, *Technology and American Society: A History* (Englewood Cliffs, N.J.: Prentice-Hall, 1995), 280–283.

34. Sobel, *Age of Giant Corporations,* 3d ed., 158.

35. Ibid., 156.

36. Jesse H. Jones, *Fifty Billion Dollars: My Thirteen Years with the RFC* (New York: Macmillan, 1951), 9.

37. Sobel, *Age of Giant Corporations,* 162.

38. Hughes, *American Economic History,* 483.

39. Robert Higgs, "Wartime Prosperity? A Reassessment of the U.S. Economy in the 1940s," *Journal of Economic History,* 52 (March 1992): 41–62.

40. Higgs, "Wartime Prosperity?" 53.

41. Vedder and Galloway, *Out of Work,* 157.

42. Thomas A. Bailey and David M. Kennedy, *The American Pageant,* 10th ed. (Lexington, Mass.: D.C. Heath and Company, 1994), 893; Johnson, Modern Times (1980), ch. 17.

43. Rae, *American Automobile Industry,* 174.

44. Peter Duignan and L. H. Gann, *The Rebirth of the West: The Americanization of the Democratic World, 1945–1958* (Lanham, Md.: Rowman & Littlefield, 1992), 110.

45. Bryant and Dethloff, *History of American Business,* 341–343; Mira Wilkins, *The Emergence of Multinational Enterprise: American Business Abroad from the Colonial Era to 1914* (Cambridge, Mass.: Harvard University Press, 1970), 201–202.

46. V. I. Lenin, "Imperialism, The Highest Stage of Capitalism," trans. Yuri Sdobnikov in George Hanna, ed., *Collected Works* (Moscow: Progress Publishers, 1964), 22: 265–269, 298–300.

47. H. Wayne Morgan, *Unity and Culture: The United States, 1877–1900* (Baltimore, Md.: Penguin Books, 1971), 138.

48. See Mira Wilkins, *The Maturing Multinational Enterprise: American Business Abroad from 1914 to 1970* (Cambridge, Mass.: Harvard University Press, 1970), 201–202.

49. Bryant and Dethloff, *American Business History,* 352;

50. Joseph Borkin, *The Crime and Punishment of I.G. Farben* (New York: Free Press, 1978).

51. The Brandt Commission, *Common Crisis North-South: Cooperation for World Recovery* (Cambridge, Mass.: MIT Press, 1983). Also see Richard J. Barnet and Ronald E. Muller, *Global Reach: The Power of the Multinational Corporations* (New York: Simon and Schuster, 1974), 14–16. See also Leonard Glynn, "Multinationals in the World of Nations," in *The Multinational Enterprise in Transition,* ed. Phillip D. Brub, et al. (Princeton, N.J.: Darwin Press, 1986), and Phillip H. Trezise, "Some Policy Implications of the Multinational Corporation," *Department of State Bulletin,* May 24, 1971.

52. Robert L. Heilbroner, *The Making of Economic Society: Revised for the 1990s,* 8th ed. (Englewood Cliffs, N.J.: Prentice-Hall), 18.

53. Heilbroner, *Making of Economic Society,* 184.

54. Kenichi Ohmae, "No Manufacturing Exodus," *The Wall Street Journal,* April 25, 1988.

55. Heilbroner, *Making of Economic Society,* 189.

56. Alfred D. Chandler Jr. and Herman Daems, *Managerial Hierarchies: Comparative Perspectives on the Rise of the Modern Industrial Enterprise* (Cambridge, Mass.: Harvard University Press, 1980).

57. Doti and Schweikart, *Banking in the American West,* 160–161; and their "Financing the Post-War Housing Boom in Phoenix and Los Angeles, 1945–1960," *Pacific Historical Review,* 58 (May 1989): 173–194; and Carl Abbot, "The Suburban Sunbelt," *Journal of Urban History,* 13 (May 1987): 275–301.

58. Doti and Schweikart, "Financing the Post-War Housing Boom," 178; Larry Schweikart, *A History of Banking in Arizona* (Tucson: University of Arizona Press, 1982), ch. 6, passim.

59. Larry Schweikart, *That Quality Image: The History of Continental Bank* (Tappan, N.Y.: Custombook, 1987), 8–10.

60. Doti and Schweikart, *Banking in the American West,* ch. 5; Walter Buenger and Joseph Pratt, *But Also Good Business: Texas Commerce Banks and the Financing of Houston, Texas, 1886–1986* (College Station: Texas A&M University Press, 1986). Extensive work exists on individual banks in the Sun Belt, although no historical overview of banking in the South or Texas after the Civil War has been published.

61. Fucini and Fucini, "Dan Gerber," *Entrepreneurs,* 66–69.

62. Sterling G. Slappey, comp., *Pioneers of American Business* (New York: Grosset & Dunlap, 1973 [1970]), 140–144.

63. Larry Schweikart, "Business and the Economy," in *American Decades: The 1950s,* ed. Richard Layman (New York: Gale, 1994), 87; Carl Solbert, *Conquest of the Skies: A History of Commercial Aviation in America* (Boston: Little, Brown, 1979).

64. Several sources deal with Kaiser's run at the Big Three, including David Halberstam, *The Reckoning* (New York: Avon Paperbacks, 1987 [1986]); Mark S. Foster, "Henry J. Kaiser," in *The Automobile Industry* (New York: Facts on File, 1989), 224–230; and James J. Flink, *The Car Culture* (Cambridge, Mass.: MIT Press, 1975).

65. Kemmons Wilson, *The Holiday Inn Story* (New York: Newcomen Society, 1968).

66. Ray Kroc and Robert Anderson, *Grinding It Out: The Making of McDonald's* (Chicago: Contemporary Books, 1977), 66.

67. Ibid., 67.

68. Ibid., 75.

69. George Gilder, *Recapturing the Spirit of Enterprise* (San Francisco: CS Press, 1992), ch. 2.

70. "Berry Gordy Jr., the Gordy Family, and the Motown Record Corp." in David Bianco, *Heat Wave: The Motown Fact Book* (Ann Arbor, Mich.: Pierian Press, 1988); Steve Chapple and Reebee Garofalo, *Rock 'n' Roll Is Here to Pay* (Chicago: Nelson-Hall, 1977); Arnold Shaw, *Black Popular Music in America* (New York: Shirmer Books, 1986); and Randy Taraborelli, *Michael Jackson: The Magic and the Madness* (New York: L. Birch, 1991).

71. Quoted in Larry Schweikart, "Disneyland Opens," in *Great Events in History: Business and Economics* (Santa Monica, Calif.: Salem Press, 1994), 1058–1063 (quotation on 1059); Bob Thomas, *Walt Disney: An American Original* (New York: Simon and Schuster, 1976); Randy Bright, *Disneyland: Inside Story* (New York: Abrams, 1987).

72. Bryant and Dethloff, *History of American Business,* 195.

73. "The 1939 World's Fair Introduces Regular U.S. Television," in McGill, ed., *Great Events in History: Business and Commerce Series,* II: 803–808. See also Albert Abramson, *The History of Television, 1880–1941* (Jefferson, N.C.: McFarland, 1987).

74. Erik Barnouw, *Tube of Plenty,* 2d revised ed. (New York: Oxford University Press, 1990); William Boddy, *Fifties Television: The Industry and Its Critics* (Urbana and Chicago: University of Illinois Press, 1990).

75. William H. Whyte Jr., *The Organization Man* (New York: Simon & Schuster, 1955); Vance Packard, *The Hidden Persuaders* (New York: Packet [1957]). Also see Sloan Wilson, *The Man in the Grey Flannel Suit* (New York: Simon & Shuster, 1955).

CHAPTER 11

Business's Winter of Discontent, 1960–1979

JUST TWO WEEKS AFTER JOHN F. KENNEDY DEFEATED RICHARD NIXON FOR the presidency of the United States, Ford Motor Company announced the end of its ill-fated model, the Edsel. The automaker lost $350 million on the car, named after Henry's son Edsel Ford, who had died in 1943. During Edsel's life, Henry had berated and humiliated the boy endlessly. Perhaps, then, it was fitting that the car bearing Edsel's name returned to haunt the company.

A much more dangerous ghost patrolled the halls at Ford. Robert Strange McNamara, a vice president of the car and truck division, was appointed the new Ford president in 1960, bringing with him a reputation as a "numbers man" who was clever with statistics but who did not understand production or manufacturing. McNamara had not personally backed the Edsel itself, but he developed and encouraged the economic models that prompted the company to develop it. No matter: McNamara's significance to business lay in his personal embodiment of a powerful new trend that swept American business in the late 1960s, in which "finance men" and "numbers men" finally achieved superiority within corporations over "production guys."

Autos and the Apex of Managerial Capitalism

Managerial hierarchies, introduced into the corporate structure almost a century earlier, infused almost every major industry by the 1960s. Automobile companies enthusiastically embraced managerial hierarchies and went further than other industries in allowing division chiefs outside of manufacturing to have access and control of the businesses. McNamara's ascension at Ford, though short-lived, heralded the promotion of the finance divisions in many American corporations. For the most part, the new leaders from finance or accounting had little appreciation for cars—what made them work, why customers liked them, and, most important, why people bought them. Worse, by 1960 many of the accountants and finance gurus had inverted the original intent of having finance and accounting departments in the first place.

Early railroads had embraced planning because of their exceedingly high capital demands and because they had to prepare for the obsolescence of track and rolling stock. In the nineteenth century, finance and accounting executives *came* from entrepreneurial backgrounds. Many worked on the railroads or in the steel business, and they appreciated the role of planning to facilitate growth and investment, not to impede it. Railroads viewed finance divisions as the place from which to manage investments properly.

Professionalization of management in the late 1800s produced an unintended consequence in the early twentieth century, however. As managers became educated specifically for investments and accounting, they no longer had time—nor, usually, the desire—to "work their way up" through the business. Many of them disdained physical labor and manufacturing. As David Halberstam pointed out in his comprehensive study of Ford and Nissan, *The Reckoning,* the separation from production and manufacturing alienated the other divisions, which came to view the "front office" as opposing necessary innovation and investment. When carried too far, as at Ford, the alienation spread to the individual plants, where "the name of the game was Screw Detroit."[1] Buffeted by ever increasing directives from Detroit, managers soon learned that, since the only thing that mattered to headquarters was numbers, the managers produced numbers. They "learned to cheat Detroit as best they could in order to preserve the integrity of their own operation," Halberstam recorded, and "did this with admirable cunning." For example, they manipulated test instruments to yield appropriate results, losing the essential quality that the test was to measure. They increased production—in a devious way that the union failed to detect—by narrowing the space on the conveyor belt by three inches, thus moving more items down the belt. They then simply stored the additional production "for a rainy day when Detroit came down with some impossible production quota that they otherwise could not handle." Managers quietly referred to the reserves as "the kitty." And when the front office expressed its displeasure with plants reporting leftover parts (which, in theory, could not happen because of the planning and statistical controls by executives such as McNamara), the managers "dumped thousands and thousand of useless parts into the nearby Delaware River," making the numbers demanded by the front office match.[2]

Detroit's lack of innovation—a characteristic certainly not confined to Ford—took its most visible form in style, which changed in only minor ways but generally featured an increasing use of chrome. Cars consistently got longer and heavier. In the 1960s, Ford president Lee Iacocca helped introduce the popular Mustang as a sports car. A decade later, it had grown by several inches and more than 1,000 pounds, in the process losing all semblance of a sports auto. That trend would not have been quite so damaging if Japanese automakers had not captured the compact car market in the United States with their fuel-efficient, front-wheel-drive cars. At the time, however, Detroit's front management, well-staffed with "finance men," downplayed the Japanese challenge and ignored the pleas of the production staff.

The accession of the finance and accounting divisions had a second influence on management at the major automakers. Publicly owned corporations had an obligation to their stockholders to make a profit and pay dividends on a somewhat regular basis. Increasingly, the pressure to maintain stock prices, some critics argued, prodded management to adopt short-term profit horizons over longer term interests. Other observers suggested just the opposite: that the pressure on stocks forced major corporations to perform and made them accountable to a broad segment of the market beyond the sales during a particular model year.

Chandler's managerial hierarchies featured a balance between the divisions in the first eighty or so years following the managerial revolution. But by the 1960s, that balance no longer existed. Halberstam, among others, argued that the finance divisions gained control at precisely the same time that securities markets demanded short-term performance, thus locking the auto industry into a downward spiral of shortsightedness and lack of quality.

Consumers, Environmentalists, and Activists

In 1964, a Harvard-educated lawyer named Ralph Nader signed a $2,000 contract with a publisher to produce a book on auto safety, which he delivered a year later under the title *Unsafe At Any Speed*.[3] A friend later described Nader as having "the classic zealot's world view, paranoid and honorless, and his vision of the ideal society—regulations for all contingencies of life, warning labels on every French fry, and a citizenry on hair-trigger alert for violations of its personal space."[4] Nader had taken on Ford's main competitor, General Motors, arguing that its Corvair compact tended to roll easily. At the time, few bothered to read Nader's book, and virtually no one bothered to check his facts;

FIGURE 11-1	Ballooning Bureaucracies of Congress		
	1970	1979	% CHANGE
House and Senate personal staffs	6,833	10,679	55%
Committee staffs	1,337	3,547	165%
Congressional research	332	847	155%
Library of Congress	3,848	5,390	40%
General Accounting Office (GAO)	4,704	5,303	13%
Total direct staff supporting Congress*	10,273	17,229	68%

*Includes congressional research and 30 percent of GAO. Does not include officers of Congress and housekeeping.

Sources: American Enterprise Institute; U.S. Bureau of the Budget; GAO; Library of Congress. From Warren Brookes, *The Economy in Mind.* (New York: Universe, 1982), p. 112. Copyright © 1982 by The Manhattan Institute for Policy Research. Reprinted by permission.

instead, GM executives panicked and launched a personal investigation into Nader that backfired, and the company had to pay $425,000 in damages to the unknown writer.

Years later, independent tests of the Corvair showed that it behaved no worse than any other similar-sized car on the road, but by then Nader had gone on to other crusades, and the auto industry had the reputation of sacrificing safety for profits. Meanwhile, business found itself confronted by a burgeoning health and safety lobby. Ironically, at a time when more Americans lived longer than they had at any time in history, a tide of graduates poured off college campuses full of reformist zeal. As Michael Fumento noted in *Science Under Seige*, a new phenomena soon characterized the environmentalist and consumer movement, in which people who had suffered an accident or disabling disease identified a product or industry that seemed to have a relationship as the "cause" of the problem or injury. Thus, he observed, the "victim as expert" pointed media attention to a source of harm that had yet to be tested scientifically, let alone proven dangerous.[5] (A well-known case is that of football player Lyle Alzado, who declared that his brain cancer was "caused" by taking anabolic steroids, a claim repeated as fact in *Sports Illustrated,* despite the fact that no link has ever been established between steroids and brain cancer.)

To its discredit, businesses frequently attacked the critics personally rather than providing the public with new, and better, research for its own claims. Some of the activists made important points—Rachel Carson's *Silent Spring* addressed the dangers of DDT transmission into the food chain, for example—but by the time the activists' intentions evolved into law, they had serious consequences for business and industry that many did not expect or want. By 1979, for example, total

FIGURE 11-2	*Regulatory-Litigatory Explosion, 1950–79*				
	1950	1960	1970	1978	% CHANGE 1960–70
Pages in the Federal Register	10,286	11,687	20,032	61,283	424%
U.S. District Court civil cases	47,600	59,300	87,300	138,800	134%
U.S. Appeals Court civil cases	1,922	2,322	7,001	11,162	381%
U.S.	708	788	2,167	3,928	398%
Private	1,114	1,534	4,834	7,234	372%
Lawyers	228,000	286,000	356,000	436,000	52%

Sources: U.S. Statistical Abstract; Federal Register. From Warren Brookes, *The Economy in Mind.* (New York: Universe Books, 1982), p. 111. Copyright © 1982 by The Manhattan Institute for Policy Research. Reprinted by permission.

costs of regulation to U.S. business exceeded $100 billion *a year.* A cornucopia of environmental, health, and consumer laws imposed mountains of paperwork on businesses, attended by armies of regulators, and met on the field of battle by industry's own hired guns, lawyers. An entirely new division of the managerial hierarchy equal to the finance and accounting groups took its place as legal divisions appeared in most major companies. But whereas common sense, not to mention the costs of retaining expensive attorneys, had limited the number of lawsuits, the appearance of Nader's "class action" suits not only told people they were "victims" but provided a way to pay for their litigation at virtually no personal cost. The resulting explosion in the legal field—both defending and prosecuting corporations—made law a growth industry itself. By 1980, America had four times as many lawyers per capita as West Germany and twenty times as many as Japan. The litigitory/regulatory boom was reflected (or caused, depending on the analyst) by ballooning federal staffs. Both the House and Senate staffs increased 55 percent during the 1970s; committee staffs exploded by 165 percent and congressional research rose by 15 percent (see Figure 11.1). Meanwhile, the numbers of regulations churned out by federal bureaucracies, and the often trivial use of the court system to settle any product liability problem or consumer complaint, produced an explosion of paperwork and court cases (see Figure 11.2).

Frequently, various regulations had contradictory requirements. The National Traffic Motor Vehicle Safety Act (1966) established a new agency that imposed safety standards on automakers, such as seat belts, impact-absorbing steering columns, dual brake systems, and padded dashboards. In 1975, Congress, acting under the mistaken notion that the world was running out of oil, also passed the Energy Policy and Conservation Act, mandating that car companies achieve an average fuel efficiency of 27.5 miles per gallon by 1985. Little note was made of the fact that the weight the first act added—however small—detracted from gains made in the second! Perhaps the most paradoxical outcome of the entire era was the decline of the "muscle cars," such as Pontiac GTOs, Dodge Chargers, and Chevrolet Chevelles, which critics took to mean that America had moved to less individualistic tastes in autos. Some even hoped that it signaled the advent of greater popularity for mass production. Instead, twenty-five years later, virtually all of the "tricks" that the "muscle car" racers had used to improve performance and lighten their cars for competition had moved into mainstream consumer autos, including fuel injection, turbo- and superchargers, ultralight plastic bodies, and advanced suspensions.

It would be erroneous, however, to blame federal regulations or the consumer movement for Detroit's ills, which instead were largely self-inflicted. From 1968 until the early 1980s, management at the Big Three (again, increasingly dominated by the "numbers men") ignored possible responses to the consumer and environmental movements that might have assuaged some as to business's intent, and instead provoked even more scrutiny from Washington. Rather than undertaking substantial design changes and rethinking the traditional front-wheel-drive V-8 engines, Detroit sought temporary solutions or pursued paths of least resistance. The Big Three chose to use a catalytic converter to reduce emissions, which brought a switch to unleaded gasoline, which, in turn, reduced engine performance. Car companies made no significant headway improving gas mileage until the oil crisis of 1973, and well into the 1970s automakers struggled with poor designs, including the Ford Pinto (which provided late-night comedians with an endless stream of gags because of fuel tanks that were susceptible to explosions when struck from the rear), the Chevrolet Vega (whose aluminum engine heads warped after a year of use), and the American Motors Gremlin (an aptly named auto, to say the least).

Catalytic converters did reduce air pollution in the short run, which certainly was no longer an option after passage of a string of antipollution laws. In 1965, the Motor Vehicle Air Pollution Act, followed by the Clean Air Act (1970), made national standards in line with those already in place in California, where "smog" (smoke and fog) constituted a significant health threat. Antipollution legislation virtually wiped out emissions from new autos, and by the 1980s, most vehicle air pollution came from older cars lacking smog-control equipment. However, improved safety and pollution controls came at a significant cost to consumers and the industry. According to one study, environmental regulation enacted prior to 1990, not counting the Clean Air Act, have reduced the national product by 2.6 percent, or about $150 billion. (A fascinating comparison is to note that the American Revolution had resulted in part from the Navigation Acts, the sum total of which over more than 100 years cost the colonies only about 3 percent of the national income.) Other researchers think that the 2.6 percent estimate is at least half too low, a claim which, if true, would yield $300 billion, or "about half of the combined federal, state, and local expenditures on education."[6]

Yet well into the 1990s environmental laws remained popular with the public, mostly because the benefits were visible to the naked eye while the cost of regulations remained largely hidden, passed on to consumers in higher prices, unemployment, and lower productivity.[7] In 1975 alone, 177 proposed "new rules appeared, as did 2,865 proposed amendments to existing rules, 309 new final rules, and 7,305 final rule amendments for a total of 10,656 new and proposed rules and amendments, most of which applied to nearly all firms."[8] Free-market advocates contended that a property-rights approach to pollution would allocate resources more effectively and more clearly distinguish genuine polluters from innocent victims. But the concept of property rights in such areas is not easily understood by a public conditioned since the New Deal to expect government to solve problems. Moreover, while it is a much more effective solution to overall pollution, the property-rights model faces the difficult "public relations" task of noting that some pollution will continue to exist, only that the polluters will pay for it. Instituting a more free-market approach would mobilize the bureaucracies, which, hostile to change institutionally, would resist any reform, even if it cleaned the atmosphere or improved emissions. As one study concluded, "There is strong resistance to considering alternative and sometimes truly innovative approaches" because of the risk-averse, rigid, and inflexible bureaucracy.[9]

As a result of environmental regulations, consumer safety requirements, and its own shortcomings, U.S. industry started to sag in the late 1960s, although profits remained high. Productivity, however, the compass point of good management, started to reflect the oppressive burdens. The American economy, particularly industrial production, slipped into a virtual coma by 1980, with scant life signs. Especially after the effective date of the new regulations, manufacturing productivity slowed, growing by only 27 percent in the period 1967 to 1977, compared to 70 percent for Germany and 107 percent for Japan. If, however, we start the trend line from 1975, when the most burdensome of the new "social" regulations went into effect, U.S. manufacturing actually declined. Of course, capital gains tax laws and unrelenting inflation after 1968 played a role, but even without the pernicious effects of poor tax policies and rising prices, it has been estimated that the regulations placed a burden of 1.4 percent per annum on growth across all industries.

Japan, Inc.

Despite clear evidence that Detroit's problems lay within the car companies themselves, and, to a lesser extent, Washington, many within the auto industry, from labor to management, saw a different culprit: foreign competition, specifically Japan. In the early 1970s, Nissan, Toyota, and Honda had made substantial inroads into the automobile market. Nissan captured the small pickup market in the mid-1960s, while the Honda Civic, introduced in 1973, held its own against American compacts. By 1980, Japan produced 11 million cars, or almost twice as many units as U.S. auto companies, sending many of them to American shores as exports. That represented a drastic change from 20 years earlier, when Japan made only half a million vehicles, and an almost complete inversion of 1950, when U.S. auto producers commanded 80 percent of the world market.

Lobbyists in the auto industry, as well as steel, textiles, electronics, and other businesses, claimed that the Japanese had an "unfair advantage" in that their Ministry of International Trade and Industry (MITI) subsidized many Japanese corporations. Yankee manufacturers, it was argued, needed protection from that unfair competition, and sectors of American industry, appropriately selected by the government, should receive subsidies. MITI, however, had unsuccessfully attempted to force its own automakers to combine, inadvertently giving them their competitive ferociousness; and MITI did everything in its power to discourage a new motorcycle manufacturer and former lawn-mower designer, Sochiro Honda, from entering the auto business at all. Such realities did not diminish the myth of MITI, to the point that by the 1980s many analysts of the American economy spoke in hushed, reverential tones when describing Japanese "industrial policy" or "planned economies." It was as if they developed amnesia, suddenly forgetting that American ships and planes had flattened the last Japanese planned economy and conveniently ignoring all the times that MITI backed the losing horse.

At the time, however, auto executives and labor leaders were more interested in complaining about Japanese advantages than in learning from their productive policies. "Japan, Inc.," the bogeyman frequently used by industry to explain its own shortcomings, had little to do with Detroit's problems. Instead, the auto industry only had to look at its own executives, designers, and labor leaders to find its weaknesses.

U.S. automakers, for example, had missed the small-car market completely. First, they ignored the huge popularity of a German car, the Volkswagen Beetle, and of a host of British small imports in the late 1950s, capturing 10 percent of the market by 1960. Detroit built enough Mustangs and Camaros to regain some ground, but when those models themselves started to grow larger, as they inevitably did in Detroit, they no longer were small or compact cars. Further market deterioration continued into the 1970s, when American designers held firm to their rear-wheel drives and larger engines. As one author noted, "Ads stressed the comfort of choices of engines and trim packages that automated foreign factories could not match. This avoidance strategy did nothing to prevent the steady encroachment of imports."[10]

The Steel Industry Follows Detroit's Lead

Had only the auto industry fallen prey to shortsighted management and gluttonous wage hikes, the overall impact on the economy might not have been significant. Autos, however, had always maintained a symbiotic relationship with steel (much as had the railroads), and the industries' management practices tended to mirror each other. Just as autos, after World War II, had total domination of the domestic market and virtual control of much of the world market, American steel companies claimed 60 percent of the world output of crude steel.

Even more rapidly than with autos, however, the U.S. steel industry saw its international power whittled away, dropping to 20 percent by the late 1970s and retiring plant capacity in a nonrecession period for the first time since Carnegie. United States Steel, Carnegie's old company, had struggled with competitors such as Schwab's Bethlehem Steel, Republic, and National, all of whom had expanded aggressively. Prior to the Great Depression, U.S. Steel had entered into an era of "benign restraint" under Elbert H. Gary; then the company found it difficult to convert from heavy iron and rail products to the items then in demand, sheet steel and strip steel.[11] After the war, a new merger movement allowed Jones & Laughlin and Inland Steel to expand their markets. Smaller producers fell by the wayside, with the resulting mergers leaving the industry in a position to be more competitive.[12]

Unfortunately for steel, both the nature of the market and the resolve and ability of international competitors had changed. Across the board, steel makers failed to adapt to rigorous Japanese competition, despite revitalizing their plants with a substantial infusion of revenue in the 1950s. Improvements were evolutionary, not revolutionary; only one new plant was built between 1950 and 1970, a Betheleham Steel facility in Indiana. Nowhere did one see the "creative destruction" practiced by Carnegie; instead, the changes eliminated problems of flow within the mills without making substantial capital investments. While productivity rose temporarily, increasing by 50 percent by 1960, overall output of American steel barely moved between 1948 and 1982. Leading steelmen, like Armco's William Verity, sought to diversify their companies out of steel.[13] Meanwhile, foreign competitors increased their production by 700 million net tons, reflecting the missing long-term transformation to new technology. And, in addition to foreign products, steel had to compete with aluminum, fiberglass, plastics, ceramics, and concrete in buildings. Steel's descent also related directly to the hard times in the auto industry and, by the 1970s, to the new federal fuel efficiency regulations requiring cars to be lighter, thus encouraging the automakers to use less steel. Labor unions contributed to the decline, forcing the cost of labor to more than six times that of comparable foreign workers.

By the mid-1960s, spiraling wages, shifting demand, poor management vision, and sharply lower profits led to the expected calls from unions and industry alike for protection from "unfair" foreign competition. In 1968, government obliged with the Voluntary Restraint Agreements to reduce steel imports; but that only whetted the industry's appetite for protective measures, and in the mid-1970s, while the Japanese were attaining labor costs only 70 percent that of the Americans, U.S. companies raised charges of "dumping" by foreign competitors.[14] Appealing to government for relief on the grounds that the "unfairness" came from Japan's subsidies to steel had excellent lobbying value on Capitol Hill but little basis in fact.

During the time that American steel producers drifted into a collusory oligarchy, Japan gave birth to more than fifty-three integrated steel firms, many of them ultramodern and staffed by managers newly trained in American and European methods. Japanese steel was not merely cheap, it was good. Japan had fourteen of the world's largest modern blast furnaces by 1978, while the United States had none, and the seaport location of Japanese plants lowered costs by making it cheap for them to burn low-cost coal delivered to their door by freighters. That year, Japan exported 40 million metric tons—7.5 million to America—whereas U.S. firms exported only 3 million metric tons.[15] Japanese assets in steel plants increased 23 percent from 1966 to 1972, compared to a meager 4 percent increase among the American producers, in part because U.S. executives continued to return almost twice as much to investors. Meanwhile, the "voluntary" restraints failed to deter U.S. consumers of foreign steel products, and Washington, to its credit, refused to go any further. Ultimately, the message to American steel was very Carnegie-like: "Modernize, get competitive, or die."

Bretton Woods, International Finance, and Inflation

Part of steel's problem, especially when it came to the cost of equipment, capital, and labor, came from the inflationary burst of the late

1960s and early 1970s that had its origins in the reshaped international financial structure created after the Second World War. That structure, appropriately enough, was forged at a hotel resort near a New Hampshire promontory called Mount Deception. Fittingly enough, the "town" of Bretton Woods was no village at all. Instead it "was an invention of a hotel promotor of the Gilded Age," and, as "a village without people, a paperwork village," it arguably was "the perfect kind of village in which to smash the champagne bottle across the bow of a new ship of economic state."[16]

Some 700 representatives from more than forty nations descended on the Mount Washington Hotel in 1944, ostensibly to plan the international monetary structure in a rational and cooperative way. Instead, as one Wall Street writer observed, it set off "a scramble among representatives trying to grab as much money as they could."[17] The actual plan, crafted by Harry White of the Treasury Department, had circulated since 1941. It involved creation of an international bank, to which each nation would contribute currency. Each nation would establish a fixed value for its currency and maintain that value through short-term borrowing at the bank when disruptions threatened the stability of its money. During the early discussions, John Maynard Keynes submitted numerous alternatives, requiring only the United States to contribute gold as a reserve, which would then serve as the basis for loans to nations with weaker currencies. Keynes actually sought to fine the United States if its currency became too sound! (That represented a deliberate attempt to avoid the deflation of the late 1920s, which he had thought deflated the global monetary supply.)

Keynes played an influential role at Bretton Woods, instilling in it the bloodless, technocratic worldview that stressed equilibrium models and intellectual dominance of the world's economic structure. According to his most recent biographer, Keynes saw himself as "part of the 'clerisy'—a secular priesthood, setting standards of value and behavior," and who, despite his personal disdain for people, showed "a surprising confidence in the effectiveness of human agency for giving theory a perfect tough in practice."[18] He and White did not get along. In a pre-Bretton Woods meeting about the plan, in which Keynes agreed with White's major points but insisted on rewriting it, White's subordinate asked Keynes why he wanted to redraft the document. "Because your plan is written in Cherokee," Keynes replied.[19]

What emerged from the jealousy and backbiting of the participants was a political accommodation that, while paying lip service to the position of Great Britain, rested upon the shoulders of the United States. It represented a world system created by a tight cadre of economists who had infinite certitude about their ability to plan the economic world better than consumers and producers. Three major institutions resulted: the International Monetary Fund (IMF), the World Bank, and the General Agreement on Tariffs and Trade (GATT).

The IMF intended to meld classical free-trade principles with the socialist/New Deal vision of full employment, and to provide an elastic international money supply with the rigid stability of gold. Nations paid into the IMF treasury subscriptions that comprised 25 percent gold and 75 percent the members' own currency. Ultimately, the reserve was $8.8 billion, with just under one-half coming from the United States, with nations permitted to borrow from the fund based on a quota. In theory, if a nation's domestic policies caused its currency to depreciate, it could borrow from the fund to generate deficit spending without depreciating the currency. Members could manipulate currency values somewhat, but the IMF had to approve changes. The IMF was the financial guts of the operation, with the World Bank created primarily as a lending institution to underdeveloped Third World countries. Congressional approval was sealed only by emphasizing the free-trade aspects embodied in the GATT proposals and by assuring legislators that U.S. aid to Europe would be minimal, on the one hand, and, on the other, that without the system another war was possible.

Whatever sound principles the plan may have contained, the world proved far messier than the technocrats had anticipated. The Soviet Union, of course, never fulfilled its obligations. More important, however, the condition of Europe had deteriorated much further than thought, and in 1947 U.S. Secretary of State George C. Marshall proposed his massive assistance program for the democracies in Europe. Between 1948 and 1952, the United States gave outright grants of $11.6 billion and loans of $1.8 billion to Europe, managed and administered by a swarm of U.S. advisers who helped the democracies get back on their feet. Ironically, the advisers encouraged the Europeans to enact protectionist trade measures as a way of reducing their need for dollars, the international unit of account. Perhaps to the consternation of some of the British representatives at Bretton Woods, the United States had become the world's central banker. With authority went responsibility. So long as America kept her books balanced and did not generate inflation, the system could work, even though individual nations "fell off the wagon" by devaluating from time to time. Still, in the long run they had to settle accounts in the monetary and currency arena, where they had to measure up to the dollar.

Their efforts resulted in a no-win situation called "Triffin's Dilemma" in honor of economist Robert Triffin, who identified the phenomena in 1960. For the world to have economic growth, Triffin posited, the United States had to run deficits, thereby expanding its money supply, while simultaneously converting dollars into gold, which grew more difficult with each new dollar printed. Between 1957 and 1970, gold reserves in the United States fell from almost $23 billion to barely $11 billion, plummeting 7 percent in 1970 alone. The ball of twine was unwinding. When the gold supply dropped below $10 billion, President Richard Nixon halted the redemption of dollars by foreign central banks in gold, then devalued the dollar, to no avail. Devalued again in 1973, when the economy entered a period bordering on "hyperinflation," the dollar crisis started to threaten America's financial stability. Nixon severed the dollar's link with gold in March 1973, instituting a floating exchange rate—an international form of competitive money—and ending the Bretton Woods system. Most assessments of Bretton Woods assume the dominant position of the United States in the international economy. But it was unrealistic to think that the United States could, or should, control 60 percent of world trade. It was downright naive to believe that the American economy could continue to pay for the New Deal programs, firmly ensconced by the 1960s and expanding incessantly.

Added to those pressures, the cold war generated its own spending requirements. Although the government could reduce the size of the standing army and the number of ships at sea, for example, military and strategic planners knew that they could never again rely on a World War II-style defense buildup to rescue the nation from a catastrophe. Increasingly complex weapons required longer design periods and construction times, and the need to keep military contractors available for emergencies meant that the government had to subsidize them in peacetime. Hence the birth of the "military-industrial complex."

The "Military-Industrial Complex"

President Dwight Eisenhower, the first general since Ulysses Grant to win the presidency, probably never thought that one of the most memorable phrases of his presidency would come from his 1961 farewell address. Yet in that speech, after urging the nation to provide for a permanent defense industry, he warned about the power and influence of a "military-industrial complex."[20] As quotable as Ike's phrase was, it misrepresented the facts concerning the relationship he identified. For more than a century, defense contractors had lobbied the federal government for arms contracts. Eli Whitney, of course, got his start with musket contracts. Some early companies, such as Samuel Colt's arms factories, depended heavily—if not exclusively—on government (or foreign government) purchases to stay in business. Others, such as some of the large steel companies, benefited substantially from government contracts for ship hulls. The fundamental change in the relationship between government and industry occurred after World War I, when weapons technology advanced so significantly that new, large items, such as ships, required long "lead times" to produce.

During World War II, when cost was no issue, American manufacturing was capable of truly phenomenal feats. But the production of a tank in five hours or an aircraft carrier in fifteen months was achieved at *peak* production levels, with all the learning skills and machinery in place. No nation could keep that type of production effort in peacetime, nor survive the drain on the private-sector economy, as the Soviet Union eventually discovered. Consequently, a postwar industry demobilized at the same time that the level of sophistication of weapons increased, increasing the lead time between the date the government placed an order for an item and the day the contractor delivered it.

Three trends, then, tended to define the "military-industrial complex." First, the government realized that in the event of a modern war it could not expect instantaneous production of weapons. That posed an insurmountable obstacle for the defense of Europe through the North Atlantic Treaty Organization (NATO), the alliance that existed to prevent the USSR from expanding further into Western Europe, because most strategists expected that a sudden Soviet offensive would reach its decisive point in a matter of weeks. Any hope that the United States might have of stopping an invasion into Western Europe would evaporate before U.S. factories could produce or deliver a single weapon. Thus, America was committed to maintaining a full-time production capacity of the most necessary weapons and the rapid start-up capability for new items.

As a result, the U.S. government frequently found itself asking if a particular contractor needed to be supported in order to maintain national security. On occasions, companies "bet the farm" on their government contracts and, in turn, came to the point that they totally depended on Uncle Sam for survival. Grumman Aircraft, for example, arrived at that point in the 1980s, when the government's decision not to renew the famous "Top Gun" F-14 Tomcat fighter virtually put the aircraft operation out of business. Other companies, such as Lockheed and McDonnell Douglas, struggled to maintain a strong component of civilian sales to offset the vicissitudes of government contracting. But Lockheed still almost went bankrupt in 1971 after it lost $200 million on the C-5A transport and failed to sell the L-1011 Tri-Star in sufficient numbers to the airlines. The government concluded that it needed Lockheed, which had produced the exceptional F-104 aircraft, and bailed out the contractor with loan guarantees. In other cases, the government assumed large shares of contractor losses, as in the case of the *Los Angeles*-class submarines built by Electric Boat in the 1970s, even when the losses may have resulted from contractor mismanagement. The government realized that the resulting bankruptcy would cripple the nation's ability to produce certain weapons.

A second trend related to direct government bailouts and/or subsidies involved a high level of concentration among defense contractors. Douglas merged with McDonnell Aircraft, and numerous missile and electronics manufacturers were absorbed by larger corporations. When not combining directly with other defense contractors, companies sought to diversify or merge into nondefense businesses. North American Aircraft merged with Rockwell-Standard, a machine manufacturer; and Martin Aircraft merged with Marietta Corporation, a cement producer. The trend toward consolidation in aircraft and shipping illustrated the falling number of units ordered by the government. Purchases of military aircraft fell from over 5,000 units in 1956 to 2,700 units in 1969. Compared to the U.S. Navy in World War II, which exceeded 1,400 warships, the United States had a goal in the 1980s of putting 600 ships to sea. Fewer units drove up per-unit cost, even after taking advantage of learning curves and new technology. Less room existed for several competitors in each area.[21]

Those factors contributed to a third trend: The declining numbers of weapons required that the weapons the nation did buy had to be as advanced technologically and as capable as possible. "More bang for the buck" became the slogan in the halls of Congress, driving the military to high-tech weaponry and having the perverse feedback-loop effect of making each unit still more expensive. Attempts to break the cycle resulted in absolute failure. The Northrup Corporation, for example, developed entirely with its own funds a "low-tech" but highly capable fighter prototype called the F-20 "Tigershark," which cost a fraction of the state-of-the-art F-15s and F-16s that the air force purchased. Northrup found that the air force would not purchase the fighter because it was not as capable as existing planes, while Northrup could not sell the Tigershark abroad because no foreign nation would purchase any until the United States had some in its inventory!

"Technology-push" thus built into the system a highly undesirable feature: When the service ordered a weapon, the contractor proposed a design. But by the time the government actually approved the design, enough time had passed to necessitate further design improvements. Those improvements drove up cost, and, under fixed-price contracts, destroyed any profits the contractors might receive. Services, then, routinely presented contractors with a steady stream of changes, which then extended the time between the issue of a contract and the product's final delivery. Contractors responded by filing claims for change orders against the government, generating massive legal fees on both sides. The Trident submarine program of the 1970s illustrates each of the three trends discussed above, making it a useful subject for a case study of the "military-industrial complex."

Electric Boat Company and the Trident Submarine

Threats to the balance of power from the Soviet Union's intercontinental ballistic missiles (ICBMs) persuaded Washington in the late 1960s to make the U.S. deterrent force of nuclear missiles more survivable. The

Pentagon undertook a series of detailed studies that concluded that survivability required that more of the nation's ballistic missiles be located on submarines at sea. Those studies also yielded a new submarine design that eventually became known as the Trident with the then-current ballistic missile submarine builder, Electric Boat (EB), the likely contractor. Only one other shipbuilder, Newport News in Virginia, even had facilities capable of constructing submarines, but Newport News had never built the large ballistic missile boats. EB started the process, then, as a "sole source" contractor.[22]

By the time the government signed its first Trident contract in 1974, the shipbuilder had a general design but only 15 percent of the navy's final designs. Under strong pressure from Vice Adm. Hyman Rickover, the so-called father of the nuclear navy, EB had submitted a fixed-price contract proposal for the first three Trident submarines. Rickover, who strongly supported the new system, assured EB and navy officials that the Trident was routine shipbuilding. In fact, it was a completely new system with some downright revolutionary features. It was substantially larger than any other American submarine (580 feet long and 42 feet in diameter) and contained new missiles and a new nuclear power plant, as well as updated sonar and torpedoes. From the outset, therefore, EB rejected a fixed-price contract for the work to the point that the company even refused to bid on the job. But the navy needed a sub and quietly assured EB that the government would reimburse the company for any losses.

EB reluctantly submitted a bid, the exact amount of which remained a controversy for years. The navy built in a "cost-type [contract] with a ceiling," or, as one critic described it, a "marvelously inventive rubber document."[23] EB calculated the cost of the program for *seven ships* at $1.793 billion, or $256 million per hull, not counting missiles or reactors. That figure depended on EB receiving authorization for all seven ships at one time for planning purposes and in order to achieve economies of scale in purchasing raw materials. Instead, EB got funding for only some of the ships and an initial outlay from the navy of $285 million, or enough to cover one ship and a cushion for changes in the design. Under such circumstances, however, the numbers EB submitted were not accurate—as the navy well knew—and had to be recalculated for four boats. That drove the cost immediately to $300 million a copy, without changes in the design. In the process, EB invested $450 million in revolutionary Swiss welding machines.

Trident reflected issues other than cost overruns. EB experienced difficulties that manufacturers of autos, aircraft, or other large or high-tech items faced, and certainly one with which Eli Whitney had struggled. Once the company had the government contract, it needed to recruit a large workforce. Such a rapid buildup in some cases led to hiring of unqualified workers, spawning quality-control issues. At one point, the U.S. Navy claimed that the shipbuilder used below-grade steel and had inadequate welds. A highly visible public dispute ensued in which EB claimed that it had indeed erroneously used a below-grade steel and corrected the problem but that the navy's 35,000 design changes had caused the welding problems. EB had been unable to double-check all of the welds with X rays as a result of the torrent of changes.

The solution to the controversy illustrated the many pressures on government-business relationships in the military sector. EB could not lose the sizable government contracts, or it would go bankrupt. The navy could not lose its Trident program and the EB contribution to the attack submarine program, or it would lose years while it found another contractor capable of recapturing the progress EB made on the Trident. The Soviet navy, building submarines at breakneck speed, would not politely wait while America became competitive. Finally, if the navy wanted to keep prices down, it needed EB alive as a competitor in the submarine program. Consequently, the navy and EB agreed to split the costs of fixing the steel and welding problems.

That agreement raised again the question of the program's cost, but the relevant lessons for all weapons contracts were clear. Ill-defined force numbers in the Trident program (seven versus four ships) and uncertain design changes could alter the cost of a program dramatically without any "gouging" by the contractor. In 1981, when the U.S.S. *Ohio* went into the water as the lead vessel of the Trident class, it cost $1.2 billion, or almost $1 billion "over budget." But was it over budget? What was the budget for—one ship, four ships, or seven? When was the budget to take effect? EB argued that the budget reflected a lump-sum, upfront payout for seven vessels, while the navy bought fewer ships at first (although ultimately purchasing eighteen units). Who, then, was more accurate: Critics who claim the boat was "over budget," or defenders who say that, given the changes made by the navy over a seven-year period, amounting to $65 million, and allowable contract escalation for inflation ($1 billion), the *Ohio* actually came in under budget?

Ever vigilant for juicy stories, however, the media carried tales of the military purchasing a $450 hammer and a $1,200 toilet seat without providing any explanation of the incredible system of warranties and contractual safeguards that the Pentagon demanded on such products. Nor was it mentioned that, far from a routine toilet seat, the unit in question was a complete plastic toilet form-fitting cover so that an airplane could fly inverted without losing the liquids in the toilet. Jacques Gansler, in an insightful article called "How the Pentagon Buys Fruitcake," traced the circuitous methods by which the Pentagon— and virtually all other government agencies—award contracts and procure products, to the point that a purchase of fruitcake required the government to specify the exact number of cherries or weight of nuts in a single slice![24]

On the grounds of effectiveness and performance, the Trident proved a wise investment. Tridents represented remarkable feats of shipbuilding virtuosity. EB invested $450 million in welding technology that used giant columns to weld steel in a continuous circle for the hull. Since the welding stands varied in diameter, they could weld hulls for the Tridents and for the much smaller *Los Angeles*-class subs with a minimum of adjustments. The circular welding permitted EB to fabricate huge sections of the sub hull, affixed to rails, then adjoin sections in a moving assembly-line process. As the finished boat emerged from the fabrication buildings to the dock, it looked like it was "growing" onto the dock. In that manner, EB could mass produce submarines of different sizes and hull diameters. Finally, by fabricating hull sections, workers could install equipment in each section before adjoining it to the next—a far cry from the days when the entire sub skeleton had to be welded, then plated over with steel, then reopened by a hole cut in the top of the hull to drop in the necessary equipment.

In a host of at-sea performance tests, the Trident subs exceeded expectations. But perhaps the most significant aspect of the Trident system was that it was never used in war. Material available now from the former Soviet Union and from American sources suggests that the Soviets had to pour billions of dollars worth of funds into improvements in their sonar equipment—and even then did not develop the capability to track the Tridents. That diversion of funds placed a further drag on the Soviet economy, which came apart in the early 1990s. Or, in the most simplistic sense, the Trident helped end the cold war without firing a shot.

Defense Defies the "Whiz Kid" Robert McNamara

Unfortunately, the quest for greater cost-effectiveness in weapons often produced results exactly the opposite of those intended by Pentagon "reformers." During the 1960s, for example, Secretary of Defense Robert McNamara (the same man who had presided over the decline of Ford's manufacturing capability) insisted on combining the needs of different services for an aircraft into a single design. The air force and the navy both needed a new fighter, but each had unique requirements. Air force fighter aircraft placed a premium on high-end speed, range, and lower weight. Navy aircraft needed greater thrust at low speeds for launching from aircraft carriers and a heavier, sturdier undercarriage, but compromised by accepting lower speeds. McNamara, convinced that a single airplane could fulfill both service roles, pushed through a design called the Tactical Fighter Experimental (TFX), and the two final bidders were Boeing and General Dynamics.[25]

General Dynamics won the contract, but after the navy added its demands to the aircraft, it needed another engine, variable geometry (moveable) wings, and much less maneuverability. After adding the technology to meet the navy's requirements, the fighter was so heavy that it was no longer a fighter. The navy abandoned the project altogether, while the air force salvaged something out of the potential disaster by turning the inadequate fighter into a fairly successful fighter-bomber, the F-111, which saw action in Vietnam, Libya, and the Gulf War. But the entire episode showed that defense often defies the reformist "whiz kid" mentality. In the world of weapons, where lives literally are at stake, cost and performance are not equals. An expansive system that performs well easily pays for itself many times over, but the sacrifice of performance for cost can both reduce performance and increase costs. Ask Robert McNamara.

Keynesians argued that defense spending buoyed the American economy by generating a peacetime boom. That argument had some merit in that the type of spending for military contracts had much greater potential to act as economic *multipliers* (that is, in expanding the economy through new spending and investment) than did other federal spending. Personnel at defense contractors, for example, tended to have higher-than-average incomes and enhanced the market for more expensive homes, cars, and other goods, compared to, say, welfare recipients. Few, if any, studies have directly compared the economic effects of a dollar spent to build a B-1 with that spent on, say, a farm subsidy or highway repair. Critics contend that a dollar spent on a missile is wasted in one economic sense because the missile really cannot be used (except in war). Or, as they contend, the "sunk investment" (in the case of submarines, literally) is permanently lost, short of a conflict. That, of course, begs the entire point of defense spending, which is to avoid and prevent conflicts. The Duke of Wellington, although not intending it, made a comment on economics as well as human life when he said, "The only thing worse than a battle won is a battle lost." Adam Smith appreciated the absolute necessity of providing a defense structure: It returns to our discussion about the sanctity of contracts requiring a mediator.

Deficits, Oil, and Inflation

To restate the central point, business's winter of discontent started in the 1960s in spite of superficial economic growth, and the problems involved falling productivity, government regulation, and inflation. That inflation had its origins less in the "military-industrial complex" than in the domestic deficits that forced the burial of Bretton Woods. For some historians and economists, however, the notion that the cold war and the defense establishment contributed to rising inflation became a matter of faith. Historian Paul Kennedy, for example, in *The Rise and Fall of the Great Powers,* attempted to draw similarities between the American experience and that of other "empires," maintaining that the burdens of supporting the free world militarily had come home to roost in the U.S. economy.[26] Kennedy's historical parallels left much to be desired. Spain, which warrants an entire chapter in his book, was the epitome of a mercantilist nation, not a capitalist one. More important for the purposes of economic analysis, the idea that defense spending caused falling productivity or inflation has no grounds in the data; defense spending, except for a brief period during the Vietnam War, had fallen consistently since the Korean conflict. In 1960, for example, federal spending on defense as a percentage of GNP stood at 9.5 percent. By 1970, it had dropped to 8.3 percent, and by 1980 it had been cut almost in half, to 5 percent.

With the credible operations of Bretton Woods depending on the United States, the federal government had an obligation to keep the budget in balance. In the mid-1950s, however, federal deficits started to appear, and after Eisenhower achieved a near-balanced budget in 1960, a condition of almost permanent deficits took root. Meanwhile, government expenditures as a share of GNP started to rise in the 1950s, growing from about 20 percent of GNP in 1950 to almost 35 percent of GNP in 1975.[27]

Pressures caused by U.S. budget deficits drove the Europeans to create a currency outside the framework of the IMF and somewhat independent of anticipated fluctuations in the dollar that the Europeans thought those deficits would produce. The "Eurodollar," as this currency was called, virtually erupted during the 1960s, despite President Kennedy's ineffectual attempt to control it. Indeed, the Eurodollar market, according to Citibank's Walter Wriston, was "fathered by controls" and, facilitated by the new electronic communications technology that made it possible to move money, created a financial black market outside the authority of the world's leaders.[28] Taking over the international monetary system, the new currency traders imposed on the parliaments and congresses of the world a restraint they never achieved on their own. Governments soon found that the markets rendered an instantaneous verdict on any policy decision, immune to political arm-twisting or local pork-barrel favors.

The inflation that gave birth to the Eurodollar market had crept into the system almost unnoticed due to the low price of oil. From 1953 to 1969, oil prices fell in relative terms; then, from 1963 to 1969, oil prices dropped in absolute terms. Government policies often kept domestic prices lower than world prices, erecting disincentives to drill in the United States and creating incentives to import. By 1960, America had become a net importer of oil, despite rich domestic fields.

Middle East oil, up to that point, had remained under the control of seven large firms, often called the "Seven Sisters": Jersey Standard (now, Exxon), Socony (Mobil), Standard Oil of California (Chevron), Texaco, Gulf, British Petroleum (BP), and Royal Dutch/Shell (Shell). Britain had emerged from World War II with the premier position in the region, producing 80 percent of the oil, while the major American presence came through a joint venture between Standard of California and Texaco called ARAMCO (for Arabian-American Oil Company). In 1960, the Arab states and other non-Arab oil producers, including Iran and Venezuela, met to wrest control of their natural resource from foreigners. Representatives established the Organization of Petroleum Exporting Countries (OPEC). Eventually numbering thirteen nations, OPEC bargained for higher royalties in the 1960s, finally gaining enough clout to obtain higher profits through the threat of withholding oil. The largest producer, Saudi Arabia, led by Sheikh Ahmed Yamani, had used the growing Western dependence on oil to force the oil companies to relinquish a share of ownership. After the Arab-Israeli War in 1973, the Arab countries started to view OPEC as a diplomatic weapon to be wielded against Israel's allies, especially the United States. Urged on by the radical members, especially Libya and Iraq, OPEC not only announced a price increase of 70 percent but curtailed exports to America by 80 percent.

Normally, demand would fall as prices soared. But the U.S. government, concerned that the American oil companies might gain "windfall profits," placed ceilings on prices that companies could charge. The ceilings ensured that oil would be artificially cheap, with predictable results. Filling stations ran out of gas; motorists drove for miles (burning scarce fuel) to top off their tanks; cars stacked up around gas stations, curving completely around city blocks; and fistfights (and worse) developed as people tried to cut in line. Even with the price ceilings, gas cost more than it had, prompting consumers to charge that "Big Oil," and not the Arabs, had used the crisis to squeeze profits from oppressed consumers. Even some scholars implied that the oil companies got rich from the episode or that it represented "a massive and immediate transfer of funds from oil consumers to oil producers."[29] If that was the case, however, the oil producers were not the American companies but the Arab states that retained the profits, and in any event U.S consumers paid far less than they would have if the government had not established the ceilings. On the other hand the distribution would have been far more efficient, the lines nonexistent, had the price of oil been reflected accurately. The real tragedy did not involve American motorists paying a slightly higher price at the pump but the fantastic damage done to developing economies that relied on oil for their tractors and factories. Thousands, perhaps millions, starved as a result of OPEC's "oil weapon," as Third World incomes plummeted, dropping below their 1970 level—the first such reversal of the modern era.

Domestic oil production had soared because of a number of successive oil strikes in the post-Rockefeller years. The most significant of the early strikes occurred in Beaumont, Texas (at a place called Spindletop) in 1901.[30] As oil gushed out of Spindletop, production in Texas far surpassed any ever seen in Pennsylvania. Anthony Lucas, who brought in the Spindletop gusher, gathered a cadre of backers from the Mellon Bank in Pittsburgh, forming Gulf Oil, and soon a second syndicate's drilling operations appeared in the area. Texas Company (Texaco) and Gulf presented new challengers to the traditional oil companies, spurred on by the automobile craze, and in their efforts to outproduce each other, crude oil prices dropped to ten cents a barrel. Oil-producing states, seeing their tax revenues plummet, sought to ration or otherwise restrict output, even begging the federal government for help. FDR's New Deal administration, of course, did not hesitate to impose controls on oil shipments across state lines. Restrictions effectively threw up barriers to domestic production, and, not surprisingly, foreign imports increased. By the time of the 1973 oil crisis, with its $50-a-barrel prices, the nation suddenly searched frantically for the domestic producers earlier administrations had regulated and harrassed. Oil's impact on domestic inflation—already ratcheting upwards—threatened to push it into double digits. (It has gone almost completely unnoticed that gasoline taxes began a sharp rise in the 1970s, and that by 1996 almost *half* of the cost of a gallon of gas is taxes, making gas only slightly higher now than twenty-five years ago, adjusting for taxes. After adjusting for inflation, it is cheaper.)

Nor were the oil shocks over. In 1979, Shiite Muslims backing the Ayatollah Khomeini in Iran overthrew the shah's government there, sparking a second round of steep price hikes. Led by the new Muslim clerisy, Iran joined the OPEC hard-liners of Iraq, Libya, and Algeria to reduce production and boost prices to punish the "pro-Zionist" West. While it is true that per-barrel profits for the oil companies rose as the price of a barrel of crude went up, overall consumption of imports fell. It was hardly a "windfall" for the oil companies: Estimates put the net income of Exxon, Gulf, Mobil, Chevron, and Texaco at $3.6 billion in 1970 and $14.5 billion in 1980. But that ignores the hyperinflation that accompanied such prices—often 10 percent a year—and the simultaneous demand that domestic producers find new sources of oil in the United States, then pay steep taxes for the "privilege" of drilling, then suffer attacks from environmentalists and pay millions in lawsuits for destroying habitats. Small wonder that companies drilled only when assured of substantial enough profits to offset all these disadvantages.

Computers and the Birth of the Microcosm

Beset by rising energy expenses, inflation, government regulation, and soaring labor costs, business productivity dropped. Investment in research and development (R & D), which had risen over 64 percent from 1960 to 1970, fell to an increase of only 12 percent during the next decade. Worse, basic research, which had grown an astounding 120 percent in the 1960s, crashed, dropping to barely 7 percent despite an increase in the federal government's share of research.

Amidst all the troubles facing American business in the 1960s and 1970s, a quiet revolution had occurred, offering more promise of transforming society than the auto and the airplane put together. The computer generated what industry analyst George Gilder called a "quantum revolution," geometrically expanding the dimensions of enterprise and productivity. Of course, it did not occur instantly.

The concept for a computer had existed since the nineteenth century, when Charles Babbage designed a card-punch, steam-powered machine. World War II brought renewed investment in the technology, resulting in ENIAC (Electronic Numerical Integrator and Computer), which used vacuum-tube technology. The Bureau of the Census saw the potential in an ENIAC-type machine for working the census numbers, and contacted J. Presper Eckert and John Mauchly, the two men who had built ENIAC. After World War II, Mauchly and Eckert designed a new computer, called UNIVAC (Universal Automatic Computer) for the government, only to discover that production cost far more than they could afford. Remington Rand Corporation, an office-equipment manufacturer, stepped in to purchase the company and produce the UNIVAC for the Census Bureau, delivering the first in 1951. Despite its apparent dominant position in the field, Remington Rand soon found itself in stiff competition with Thomas Watson's International Business Machines (IBM). Watson had emerged as a top executive of National Cash Register (NCR), then under the direction of John Patterson, who had pioneered a strategy of giving salesmen specific territories within which to sell the company's products and rewarding them with performance bonuses.

After World War II, Watson prepared his son, Tom Watson Jr., to run IBM, and in 1952 the elder Watson passed the baton to a new generation. The younger Watson saw computing equipment as the wave of the future, leading IBM to deliver its own large computer in 1953. IBM surged to first place in the market, controlling more than 60 percent of the computer business in the mid-1960s, even though its product was never better than its competitors'. Rather, IBM emphasized sales and marketing, practicing the time-tested methods that had served Singer Sewing Machines, International Harvester, and Otis Elevators well.

Even by the late 1950s, however, it was becoming clear that vacuum tubes represented a major hurdle in reducing the size and, thus, the cost of computers. Switches were the key—they were, as George Gilder explains, "the substance of the artificial mind."[31] Thus, the invention of the transistor was not only the first step in the creation of the new technology but the origin of an entire revolution as deep as the commercial revolution that swept Europe centuries ago. On July 1, 1948, William Shockley announced that his employer, Bell Laboratories, had sponsored the successful achievement. Shockley had provided the crucial cost-effective switch that the computers required.

Bell Labs found that its transistors did not work well in high heat, which made the discovery relatively useless for military purposes. Consequently, while the most important technology of the twentieth century unfolded, the Department of Defense unimaginatively funneled huge amounts of money into vacuum tubes. In that context, if the Pentagon illustrated America's "industrial policy," it can well be stated that the United States succeeded in spite of a national industrial policy, not because of one. Still, to make the transistor truly effective required peripheral and supporting technological discoveries. At that point, in 1952—just as Watson introduced IBM's large machine—a small electronics firm in Dallas called Texas Instruments (TI) made the next breakthrough. TI engineers reasoned that by using silicon, with its ability to sustain temperatures of 1,200 degrees Celsius, they could eliminate heat as a problem for the transistor. After more than 1,000 attempts to manufacture a silicon transistor, TI researchers succeeded.

As often happens in such discoveries, the researchers had tried to solve only a specific, narrow problem, but when the company actually started manufacturing silicon semiconductors, it found that silicon dioxide was "both electrically and chemically inert and thus could both protect and insulate the devices of near-micron dimensions that would appear in the next two decades."[32] TI prepared to mass produce silicon transistors in 1954. Bolstered by the instantaneous success of silicon transistors, TI's revenues rose from $24 million in that year to $232 million six years later, growing at a rate of 200 percent a year. Even so, a more significant leap still lay ahead, when silicon transistors could be packed tightly together on a single chip, insulated by their own oxide. When that occured in 1971, not TI but another small company, Intel, managed to put an entire computer on a single silicon chip, called a microprocessor. Another irony associated with the microprocessor was that Intel's first customer, Busicom, had not foreseen the potential for the microprocessor, but the entrepreneurs at Intel decided to give the customer more than he/she asked for. A heated competition to pack more, and faster, microprocessors together ensued, giving birth to the next era of computers, dominated by the personal computer, or PC.

Once the industry had the capability to compress several miniature computers, in the form of microprocessors, on a single chip, an exponential growth in computational power followed. In sharp contrast to almost all other previous industries, the computer technology held that power was gained as the chips got smaller. That represented a fundamental change in the way progress had taken place over history: Virtually every other machine got more powerful only by getting larger, symbolized, ironically, by the internal combustion engines powering the "muscle cars" at the very time the PC was invented.

Intel also created the first usable PC. A California company formed in 1968 by Gordon Moore and Carver Mead, Intel produced its computer on a chip in only three years. That proved a watershed event because the basic raw material of the silicon was sand, which no one could claim was in short supply. But if Intel pioneered the chip and the PC, it took yet another small start-up company to make PCs popular.

At that point, one might have expected the leader in the computing field, IBM, to have brought personal computers to the vast market of consumers. But IBM continued to focus on larger machines, completely missing the real revolution. Instead, a pair of California college dropouts, Steve Jobs and Steve Wozniak, ushered in the PC age.[33] They assembled a small computer called the Apple in Jobs's garage in 1976, which they introduced and sold without a monitor or keyboard for $666.[34] In part, its success relied on the fact that it offered on-board read-only memory (ROM), and orders quickly reached into the hundreds. The Apple and its successor machine, the Apple II, generated tremendous publicity, bringing Jobs and Wozniak considerable financial support in the newly ascending section of northern California called "Silicon Valley." Bank of America provided a loan to further capitalize Apple. In 1977, Jobs and Wozniak launched Apple Computer, Inc., and within two years the company had a stratospheric sales total of more than $118 million, turning Jobs and Wozniak into computer gurus and gaining them reputations as wizards of technology. The company joined the *Fortune 500* companies in less time than any in history.[35] But it also had significant marketing problems, not the least of which originated in the scheme to reap profits from peripheral product sales that would surpass those of the computer itself. In the long run, that encouraged the company to try to retain its technology rather than share it so as to make it an industry standard.

Nevertheless, Jobs and Wozniak had taken a technology of government and big business—perhaps the ultimate depersonalized machinery—and humanized it, putting power in the hands of the people in the most immediate sense of the term. The revolution over which they presided was nothing short of spectacular. In 1960, the United States had about 10,000 computers in operation, but thirty years later, there was one computer for every 2.6 people. Still, one last ingredient was necessary to link the technology to most average people. Computers were still machines—and in some senses extremely complex machines. They required a highly specialized language to operate, a secret code that nonspecialists had to learn to communicate commands to the electronic "brains." Since it was crucial to keep the technology small, languages in vogue in the early 1970s required too much capacity for personal computers undergoing testing at that time.

A Seattle "wonk" attending Harvard, Bill Gates, had read about a personal computer in a 1974 issue of *Popular Mechanics*. Gates's personal background differed sharply from that of many other entrepreneurs. He lived a comfortable life as the son of a well-to-do attorney and obviously had access to a top-flight education. He and former high school classmate, Paul Allen, had become absorbed with computers at a time when other teenagers were dating or playing sports. While still a junior, Gates started a business that made computer data analysis devices for the metal boxes on highways that recorded traffic. They made $20,000 before the federal government started to offer traffic analysis free of charge. At Harvard, Gates developed legendary work habits, putting in thirty-six straight hours before a short sleep, then returning to work. He also played computer games, such as "space wars," where he better learned the "mind" of computers.[36]

When he and Allen discovered that the computer in the magazine still had problems with a language, they immediately contacted the company to suggest that they could solve the problem. In 1975 they boarded a plane to Albuquerque, where they went to a small office in a strip mall with their software program, a refinement of the popular BASIC program. To everyone's surprise, the software responded the first time it received a command. Gates and Allen moved to Albuquerque, working as software engineers, but they quickly formed their own company, Microsoft, developing software that tailored BASIC to specific computers.

Inherent in the new technology and software was a partial rejection of the "hacker ethic," which encouraged a free flow of information to fellow hackers—with the emphasis on "free." For Gates, the obvious problem was, "How do you get your money back after investing it?"[37] Instead, software development was aided by a series of court decisions that upheld intellectual property rights. At first, however, piracy of the BASIC language actually benefited Gates by incorporating the Microsoft product into thousands of machines—some of it purchased, some of it stolen. The net effect, like that of spreading rock and roll throughout the Soviet Union through bootleg records and CDs, was to expand consumption of the overall product, and in the case of Gates, to align users with Microsoft software to the extent that it became the industry standard.

In 1976, Microsoft gained the accounts of General Electric and National Cash Register, giving the company $100,000 in revenues. After moving to Seattle, Gates's programmers developed other popular languages for computers, including FORTRAN, COBOL, and Pascal. Microsoft grew from a small company into a software giant. But when IBM asked Microsoft to develop a disk for its new personal computer, Microsoft found a local company's product, which it purchased for $50,000. The name of the program, refined by Microsoft for IBM, was DOS, and virtually all computers used it by the 1990s. One writer likened the development of DOS to the early days of railroads, when trains ran on different gauge rails: DOS put all the computers—more than 80 million of them by 1990—on the same "rails." Eventually, Gates's interface language included a mouse-controlled icon-oriented program called Windows, which pushed Microsoft's revenues over the $1 billion mark. Only 15 years after he started, Bill Gates, then in his mid-30s, became the youngest billionaire in American history (reaching a wealth level in real dollars equal to that of Andrew Carnegie).

Airlines: From Despair to Deregulation

Computers and rising fuel prices had simultaneous and polar opposite effects on the growing airline industry in the 1970s. The introduction of transistors meant better radios, which in turn meant improved air-to-air and air-to-ground communications. That translated into better safety and rising traveler confidence. Defense spending had spinoff effects, providing the private sector with better radars, aircraft design, avionics, and, as military pilots became civilians, more capable pilots. Over the long run, quality improvements brought lower costs, but those were often difficult to see as fuel costs rose early in the decade.

Four major airlines had received government support through mail contracts: United, American, Eastern, and TWA. By 1977, those, and the major independent national carriers (Delta and Continental), plus a number of small regional services, such as Piedmont, Ozark, Air Florida, Texas International, Pacific Southwest, and others, flew 187 billion passenger miles in more than 2,400 aircraft and employed over 300,000 people. The ten major airlines flew to 430 cities. Unfortunately, competition was directed more toward gaining federal postal route awards than it was toward cost-efficient operations and reasonable fares. As a result, a "strikingly mixed coalition" had started to lobby for deregulation, including "academic economists, Naderite consumerists, liberal Democrats, and conservative Republicans."[38] Congressional hearings produced testimony that the airlines had lost money and had to be protected against "cutthroat competition," but little was made of the fact that the competition had originated in struggles for federal money, not passengers.[39] Economist Alfred Kahn, who had joined the Civil Aeronautics Board (CAB) in 1977, knew well the academic literature that showed that the airline cartel had resulted from CAB policies, which had prohibited new certifications for routes, closing the door to competitors. He concluded that the system had to change.

Meanwhile, Southwest Airlines had shown that it could fly full airplanes at low fares and still make a profit. As Congress held hearings about deregulation, the vested carriers lodged their complaints, with Delta the most vocal. Ironically, Delta had portrayed itself in public as the champion of the free market; but behind closed doors, the company fought to keep regulation in place. Unionized airline employees also enjoyed the higher pay brought by the cartel. It was also ironic that Kahn, who saw himself as a fan of the New Deal, had to bring competition to an overregulated regime in stark contrast to the New Deal policies that had put the cartel in place. Kahn began with a "Peanuts" fare, which allowed airlines to discount nonpeak routes or flights (with the name coming from Southwest Airlines). American Airlines adopted a "super saver," and the other majors soon followed. Deregulation had started, and the trickle became a flood. By 1978, more than half of all fares were subject to discounts.

By the late 1980s, the results of deregulation had emerged with clarity. More passengers than ever traveled on more airlines than ever, as passenger enplanements rose from 225 million in 1977 to 432 million in 1992. Predictably, in a time of sharp competition, the profits of the airlines fell. Overall operating revenues rose by almost $34 billion, but operating expenses jumped by $36 billion, forcing several of the large carriers, including TWA, Braniff, Continental, and Eastern, to declare Chapter 11 bankruptcy. Some failed, or came out as small regional lines instead of national carriers. Piedmont and U.S. Air merged, while many smaller companies, including Pacific Southwest Airlines, went out of business. In contrast, another new airline, America West, grew so fast it overexpanded, and it also had to declare bankruptcy. Eventually America West emerged from Chapter 11 healthier than ever, but critics of the bankruptcy statutes questioned the basic fairness of such laws that protected one competitor from market forces during reorganization only to allow the company to reenter the market when it regained strength. Southwest Airlines, meanwhile, continued to make low fares and efficiency the standard for all to match. Delta, American, and United, while not as profitable as the smaller Southwest, remain generally healthy. A study in April 1997 by Zachs Investment Research showed that almost all of the major airlines reported improved earnings and booming passenger traffic; in 1997 eight of the ten major airlines boosted per-share earnings by increasing their loads and cutting costs.[40] Not only had deregulation not driven out competitors, there were *more, healthy* airlines than ever before.

More important for travelers, the criticism made during deregulation that airline safety would suffer as a result of less regulation has not been borne out. In the early 1990s, the industry went one year with only one major accident and another year with no airline-related fatalities of any sort.[41] The peace was shattered, however, in May 1996 with the crash of a so-called cut-rate airline in Florida, ValuJet. Soon thereafter, a rash of airline mechanical problems were identified, most likely due to the sudden high level of attention devoted to aircraft in the wake of the ValuJet accident. ValuJet appeared to call into question the entire low-fare concept, and as one industry consultant observed, "The larger carriers are probably jubilant about [ValuJet's shutdown]."[42] When the government shut down ValuJet in June 1996, the stocks of the other airlines climbed. Upon further investigation, evidence surfaced that federal regulators actually had permitted the airline to operate despite finding several mechanical glitches that would have grounded other carriers. Far from reflecting badly on the airline industry, the incident exposed weaknesses in the government's regulatory oversight process rather than the safety of airlines themselves. Indeed, the cut-rate carriers, especially Southwest, sport sparkling safety records. Overall, air travel in America has been safer than ever since deregulation.

Airlines were involved indirectly in another, unplanned, deregulation of the market. In the early 1960s, a Yale junior named Fred Smith wrote a term paper on the deficiencies of the mail system, particularly those related to long-distance air freight.[43] He deplored the lack of control or accountability for packages, handled almost exclusively by Flying Tiger or Emery Air Freight, both of which had solidified their oligopolistic positions under government regulation. Smith had a love of flying, and after serving two tours of duty in Vietnam, he used a small stake he had from a restaurant his father had sold to purchase an interest in Arkansas Aviation Sales, which Smith turned into a used-car lot for airplanes. He netted a profit of a quarter of a million dollars in a few years. Smith still toyed with the idea of competing in the air freight business, though. He realized that his two largest competitors each had revenues of $100 million but thought that dissatisfaction with their service might be high.

Commissioning two consulting firms to conduct surveys of the carriers' clients, Smith learned what he already knew. Deliveries were erratic, packages got lost, and overall satisfaction was low. Moreover, more than three-quarters of the shipments originated outside the largest twenty-five markets, especially new research and manufacturing complexes located in more remote industrial parks. Smith observed that since most commercial airlines were not flying between 10:00 P.M. and 8:00 A.M., a window of airport operations was open in which he could conduct takeoffs and landings without concern about air traffic.

It took almost all the capital he and his family had (nearly $8 million) in start-up costs, but Smith gained the confidence of investors, who contributed another $40 million, then brought on board a few banks, bringing the total capital to $90 million. That represented the "largest single venture-capital start-up in American business history."[44] Federal Express, incorporated in 1971, purchased thirty-three French Dassault executive jets that were the largest aircraft he could get without meeting Civil Aeronautics Board requirements for freight haulers. Smith had investigated United Parcel Service (UPS), which itself had intruded into the monopoly of the U.S. Post Office, and observed that the 75-pound limit standardized package sizes and eased loading and unloading. More important, Smith adopted a "hub-and-spoke" operation that sent all packages to a central location in Memphis, then moved them to their final destinations from there, keeping close track of them at all times. Federal Express saw itself as a freight service with 500-mph delivery trucks, catering to electronics, medical, and computer firms that needed rapid service. The company's jets featured bright orange and purple paint, and the company had a rock-solid guarantee of delivering any package to the areas it serviced in twenty-four hours.

The early years posed a challenge, causing Smith to have to sell his own personal jet to meet a payroll and to use winnings from a blackjack game to pay bills. Employees helped, too, leaving personal jewelry as deposit for company gas and hiding the jets when sheriffs came to repossess them. But at that point, the good fortune of the other airlines, now in the process of deregulating, rubbed off on Smith. With so many new passengers flying, the major airlines lacked sufficient aircraft. They willingly sacrificed their parcel service, which Federal Express gobbled up. In 1974, UPS had a strike that took it out of the market for a time, and rival REA Express went out of business. Although throughout 1975 Federal Express continued in the red, by 1976 it reported net income of $8 million on revenues of $109 million. After deregulation, Federal Express moved into larger aircraft. It also by that time had shipped, under the guise of "FedEx Letters," mail that in previous years would have been shipped by the U.S. Post Office. Technically in violation of legislative intent, Federal Express had the market on its side. The post office had developed a reputation for lost mail, slow delivery, and inefficiency. Federal Express, or "FedEx," finally pushed the U.S. Postal Service to compete with its own forty-eight-hour delivery promise, and when the post office was reorganized to pay its own way, the competitive fires of FedEx and other private carriers had shaped the federal postal service into an efficient operation.

Once again, however, the market had outperformed government-sanctioned monopolies. And once Washington had experience deregulating, the government found that it could free several industries besides the airlines. The most prominent was trucking, where

| FIGURE 11-3 | Percentage Share of Intercity Freight Ton-Miles Regulated by the Federal Government, 1950–1990 |

YEAR	TOTAL	RAIL	TRUCK	AIR	OIL PIPE	WATER
1950	62	100	38	100	81	20
1960	58	100	37	100	79	20
1970	59	100	41	100	85	13
1980	55	100	44	0	84	8
1990	31	26	28	0	84	8

Source: From Paul Teske, Samuel Best, and Michael Mintrom, *Deregulating Freight Transportation: Delivering the Goods* (Washington, D.C.: AEI Press 1995). Copyright © 1995 by The American Enterprise Institute. Reprinted with the permission of The American Enterprise Institute for Policy Research, Washington, D.C.

haulers faced intricate restrictions on what they could haul, when, and where. William Childs has chronicled the rise and regulation of the trucking industry, noting that by the 1930s it had become a direct competitor of the railroads.[45] In the late 1970s, the Carter administration undertook a partial deregulation of the trucking industry, with noteworthy results. Trucking freight rates have fallen by 30 to 50 percent since deregulation.[46] From a peak in 1950, in which 62 percent of all truck, air, water, and pipe freight was regulated, by 1990 only 31 percent of all freight was regulated, with the highest percentage in trucking (see Figure 11.3).[47] A recent study of freight deregulation thus found that "deregulation emerged as the common cure to the differing problems of the freight transportation industry," and overall concluded that the various deregulation initiatives were "great successes, exceeding the most optimistic expectations."[48]

Still, in the late 1990s a web of regulations still existed, some of them bizarre. One of the least visible but insidious freight regulations that remains is the "filed-rate doctrine" that presumes that all rates—even those mutually agreed to by shipper and trucker—are unfair unless filed with the ICC. That absurd practice, which one writer called "a deification of government filing cabinets," was generally thought by virtually all shippers to have been repealed with the rest of the freight regulations, but it was not, and as rates kept dropping through market forces to 40 percent below those filed with the ICC, many shippers went bankrupt.[49] Then, in the late 1980s, the ICC, realizing it still had the "filed-rate doctrine" on the books, started to accost the bankrupt trucking companies' former customers for *retroactive* rates on the grounds that the *truckers* had failed to file rates with the ICC! That amounted to a bankrupt airline going back to the customers and saying, "You know that Super Saver fare to Florida we gave you back in 1977? Now you owe us another $900." IBM, for example, received a bill for $60 million from the bankruptcy of a single trucking company. As of 1998, the legislation permitting retroactive billings had not been repealed, providing yet another example of how, in its drive to impose "fair" rates on truckers, the government has fostered fantastic injustices.

Deregulation of the S&L Industry

If airlines and trucking prospered from deregulation, the savings and loan (S&L) industry seemed to offer evidence that deregulation could have disastrous consequences.[50] The real story of the S&L debacle, however, was much more complex and in many ways vindicated the concept of deregulation.

S&L associations had existed as the "junior partner" of the banking industry for generations. Formed to pool capital for home mortgage lending, S&Ls borrowed at one rate and loaned long term at a higher rate. During the New Deal, legislation prohibited S&Ls from providing checking accounts (demand deposits) but rewarded them by allowing them to lend on real estate, primarily home mortgages, and to pay slightly higher interest rates on deposits than could banks. Over time, S&Ls found that they experienced short periods of "disintermediation," in which rising interest rates drove up the cost of deposits above that which the S&Ls received on their long-term—basically fixed—mortgage loans. Those periods lasted only for short times, and in general the S&L industry "found that making money could almost be taken for granted."[51]

The inflation of the 1970s put the S&Ls in a serious position, however. As interest rates rose, the disintermediation effects threatened to erode the capital base of the S&Ls. They had to raise cash, and fast. Regulators first allowed S&Ls to offer jumbo CDs (certificates of deposit), which paid higher rates on deposits of $100,000 or more, and in 1978, dropped the level to $10,000. The interest paid on traditional deposits, however, remained unchanged until the Depository Institutions Deregulatory and Monetary Control Act of 1980 (DIDMCA, pronounced "did mac"). Not only did DIDMCA deregulate the rates S&Ls could charge on loans and those paid on deposits, but it allowed S&Ls to engage in activities associated with commercial banks, such as consumer loans, credit cards, and checking accounts. Locked into mortgage loans that stretched over a fifteen- to thirty-year period, the S&Ls had to find new loans that were repaid over a much shorter time. Such loans carried more risk. By 1982, the new powers of S&Ls could not overturn a ten-year decline in the industry's profitability, and even after the government allowed S&Ls to offer variable-rate mortgages, the existing mortgages could not be made retroactive. In a single year, 1981–1982, S&Ls lost $12 billion.

Another component of the S&Ls' problems stemmed from the presence of deposit insurance. S&L owners had faced growing pressures to find profitable outlets. The more profitable, of course, the riskier the investment, but even conscientious S&L executives could rationalize that drastic measures were needed, and that, after all, the depositors were "covered" by the FSLIC. Economists call this phenomena "moral hazard," in which compensation for a loss, such as fire insurance, creates incentives to have more losses, even through illegal activities such as arson. The moral hazard of deposit insurance encouraged S&L owners— certainly not all, or perhaps even most, but a significant number— to take unusual and extraordinary risks with their institutions because the depositors, whom they would in a free market have to compensate, were "protected" by the government. Consequently, many owners and managers tended to invest in new property-development projects, oil drilling, and, later in the 1980s, junk bonds.[52] One especially preferred scheme, the land flip, involved one S&L owner acquiring land and then selling it to friends or other S&L owners, inflating its value, repeating the process until the "flip" could be unloaded on an unsuspecting third party. The crash of oil prices in the late 1970s and early 1980s, however, send land values plummeting, wiping out any hope of profiting through land flips. Some critics wanted to blame junk bonds for the disaster, and certainly a few S&Ls invested heavily in low-grade securities. But portfolio analysis showed that the S&Ls' weaknesses had more to do with property investment than with junk bonds.

After a brief and illusory recovery in the mid-1980s, the industry collapsed. The FSLIC closed its doors after accumulating losses of $100 billion between 1984 and 1989. Western and southwestern states led the way in troubled firms, with Texas alone having 90 insolvent S&Ls. From 1960 to 1989, the number of S&Ls dwindled from 6,000 to 2,934, and many of the survivors hovered at death's door. Worse, political favoritism appeared to be involved in the regulatory process, as revealed when the California-based Lincoln Savings and Loan investigation showed that five U.S. senators (four Democrats and one Republican) had met privately with the chairman of the Federal Home Loan Bank Board to persuade him to intervene in the investigation. Political favoritism by the S&Ls, especially in Texas, favored the party generally opposed to deregulation (the Democrats) far more than the party in favor of deregulation (the Republicans). It should have been a signal that deregulation itself was not an issue in the S&L collapse when no political party sought to assail deregulation in the political campaigns of the 1980s.

Critics who see deregulation at the root of the S&L problems do not have a great deal of support in the recent evidence. One study, for example, concludes that "the *economic* deregulation of the S&L

(thrift) industry in the early 1980s was basically sensible, but it had been delayed for far too long . . . [and was] embraced only when the industry was in dire financial straits" (emphasis in original).[53] By the time deregulation was accepted, the incentives for moral hazard misbehavior had reached their peak, and the economic deregulation needed an invigorated effort to enforce the safety and soundness regulations on the books. Instead, in an effort to keep the S&Ls alive, the government allowed them to reduce their capitalization, making them weaker.[54] That occurred in part because of public perceptions that thrifts were small, trustworthy local firms whose executives were immune to moral hazard incentives—a view that industry lobbyists perpetuated. When sudden and dramatic losses struck in the early 1980s, the political power of the thrifts grew so intense that legislators wanted to give them quick relief, without examining the different effects of economic regulation as opposed to enforcing accounting standards. Just as Herbert Hoover's RFC loans unintentionally weakened the banking system in the 1930s, government "help" in the S&L crisis only made matters worse. The presence of deposit insurance provided the final bit of regulatory cover that executives needed to engage in the most risky behavior, knowing their depositors were covered in the event of a disaster.

Government "reforms" contributed to the fiasco in other ways. For example, although little noticed in the crisis, the Tax Reform Act of 1986—in an attempt to "soak the rich" and "eliminate loopholes"— had lengthened the depreciation period of real estate and limited the ability of investors to shelter other investments that could offset real estate losses, which contributed to a crash in the real estate market in the Southwest and oil-patch states. Real estate developers suffered huge losses, and the S&Ls had plunged heavily into real estate in the early 1980s because of its previous skyrocketing values. Suddenly, they had on their hands assets worth 10 percent of their original cost. In another perverse regulatory effect, FIRREA forced thrifts to liquidate their junk-bond portfolios, whether they had profitable potential or not. Sparking a government induced junk-bond crash, FIRREA demolished much of the S&Ls' asset base. When the Resolution Trust Corporation (RTC) took over the failed S&Ls, it "became the country's largest owner of junk bonds" (with a $5–6 billion portfolio).[55] Having bought into the notion that junk was, well, junk, the RTC sold immediately, flooding the market with another $1.6 billion in bonds and sending prices plummeting again. But junk was not junk, and the bonds soon returned to higher values. Had the RTC only held the S&Ls' junk bond assets one more year, it could have sold them for $640 million more—recouping more than 10 percent of the total bailout cost (and actually probably much more).

Contrary, then, to much of the reporting in the popular press, the S&L crisis was the result not of deregulation but of a number of

FIGURE 11-4	*Price Reduction Following Deregulation (in 1995 dollars)*			
	REAL PRICE REDUCTION AFTER			ANNUAL CONSUMER
INDUSTRY	2 YEARS	5 YEARS	10 YEARS	BENEFITS (IN BILLIONS)
Natural gas	10–38%	23–45%	27–57%	not available
Long distance telecom	5–16%	23–41%	40–47%	$5.0
Airlines	13%	12%	29%	$19.4
Trucking	not available	3–17%	28–56%	$19.6
Railroads	4%	20%	44%	$9.1

Source: From Robert Crandall and Jerry Ellig, *Economic Deregulation and Customer Choice: Lessons for the Electric Industry.* (Fairfax, Va.: George Mason University, Center for Market Processes, 1997), p. 2. Copyright © 1997 by the Center for Market Processes (recently renamed the Mercatus Center). Reprinted by permission.

factors, not the least of which was the influence of government on real estate values, moral hazard incentives, and bond asset values. Quietly, in the 1990s, the S&L "debt" disappeared in large part as real estate values and oil prices returned and as junk bonds achieved their predicted values, automatically raising the asset value of the S&Ls held or controlled by the government. Deregulation in one area had to be coupled with commonsense government policies in others, including low taxes, elimination of moral hazards (i.e., the promise of government bailouts), and enforcement of accounting regulations then in place.

Economically, though, the deregulation of airlines and trucking had benefited a vast number of consumers, and even with the S&L problems, the legacy of deregulation was unmistakable: Natural gas prices fell almost 40 percent in the first two years after its deregulation, and had dropped by almost 60 percent after ten years. Long-distance telecommunications saved consumers more than $5 billion (1995 dollars) in a decade; and airline deregulation had saved consumers almost $20 billion (see Figure 11.4). The "common man" was the true beneficiary of deregulation.[56]

Even such nonmarket areas of life, such as religion, were affected by the economics of deregulation. According to one study on the impact of deregulation on television broadcasting, the availability of licenses to open bidding generated a revival of religion. It worked like this: Since the 1950s, FCC regulations required television stations to grant programming time to religious groups free as part of their "public service" component. Since the stations received no revenue from this programming, and since there was more demand than could be handled—but no accompanying rise in revenues—the stations offered the broadcasts to their friends, the mainline, well-established local

Text continued on p. 448

Are Statistics Reliable?

BUSINESSES AND ECONOMISTS MAKE GREAT use of statistics. To some extent, many corporations plan their entire activities based on statistical predictions or exotic formulae of production coefficients. Some managers, such as Robert McNamara during his tenure at Ford, so adeptly wielded numbers in meetings that virtually no one could oppose them. Millions of investors every day employ statistics to make decisions about their portfolios. Thus, it is important to know the answer to the question, "Are statistics reliable?"

A glib answer, of course, is "yes and no," or "it depends." Like any number a statistic represents only a single data point or set of data. Comparing unlike sets of data, or including vast ranges of numbers to arrive at a median, or midpoint, an expert can produce conclusions that have little relation to reality. And the student is urged to examine closely all presentations of data in *this* book to analyze the context within which the statistics are placed. It should be noted, for example, that whenever possible monetary units measured over time are expressed in *real* dollars. "Real" makes the value of a dollar—its purchasing power—constant over time by adjusting for inflation or deflation. Otherwise, a nation could be portrayed as "rich" because it had turned on the printing presses that night, while another might be seen as "poor," even though it has money that is literally as good as gold.

Likewise, it would be meaningless to discuss wages in the 1930s without an appreciation of what a dollar in that decade bought. Larger sets of statistics about growth, deficits, and debt also need to be stated as a relationship to the whole, usually expressed as GNP. If you owe $1,000 on your Visa card, is that a great deal or not? No one knows without knowing you and your earnings and net worth. In the case of a nation, what it "earns" is its GNP.

Likewise, in traditional measurements of inflation, prices are depicted in a "mountain range" chart that fluctuates from peaks to valleys. But an alternative approach, developed by Sheila Hopkins, Henry Phelps-Brown, and David Warsh, has suggested that the entire concept of inflation, as most people traditionally employ it, does not capture the increasing sophistication of goods and services. What on the surface appears to be inflation, for example, is an expansion of consumable goods. A new market-basket-of-goods approach might reveal, for example, that the textile in a traditional "market-basket" analysis of, say, the 1200s would include only canvas; but by 1950 canvas was not even considered a suitable textile, and wool yarn would supplement printer's cloth. Or, where in the year 1500 a "market-basket" drink would be $4\frac{1}{2}$ bushels of malt, in 1950 the same component of the basket would include $2\frac{1}{2}$ bushels of malt, $2\frac{1}{4}$ pounds of hops, 5 pounds of sugar, and $4\frac{1}{2}$ pounds tea. Americans have experience a similar "sophisticating effect" on housing technology. In the 1950s, a typical single-family house did not include air conditioning, an enclosed garage, a washer-dryer hookup, a dishwasher, or, in some cases, a refrigerator. Have housing costs "inflated," or have they merely reflected improved value, additional "standard" items, and better all-around quality? Warsh concludes that what economists have been calling "inflation" really is complexity and sophistication of goods. According to Warsh, the inflationary burst of the 1970s and 1980s reflects the capitalization of the information revolution.

Statisticians frequently employ three terms in public writing—"means," "medians," and "modes"—that have apparently similar, but in reality much different, connotations. An arithmetic mean is arrived at by dividing the sum of a series of numbers by the number of quantities in the set. The mean of the following series—2, 2, 3, 3, 6, and 6—equals 4. A median is the middle value in a series, with half the observations falling below and half above the median. In the series 2, 2, 3, 4, 12, 14, and 16, the median would be 4. A mode refers to the number in a series appearing most frequently. The mode of 1, 2, 2, 3, 3, 4, 4, 4, 4, 19, and 100 is 4. Consider these differences in describing a "typical business." By typical, is it meant "average-sized" business? If so, what do you mean by "average"? Do you want to show the type of business that appears most commonly? If so, use the mode. For example, in America, of the three types of business organizations (sole proprietorship, partnership, and corporation), the mode best captures the most frequently used organization, the sole proprietorship. But if you want to gain an idea of the size of businesses, perhaps the mean or median would be more appropriate. Note, however, that a mean can be dramatically raised or lowered by one exceptional observation at either end. In a town with fifty small businesses of $10,000 capitalization each ($500,000), a single large firm of $2 million can make the mean business appear far better capitalized than most in the town are.

Finally, use of trend lines in presenting data can be abused to show what the researcher wishes to show. For example, if examining unemployment trends, one could depict a stunning success in "creating jobs" merely by starting the trend at the peak of the Great Depression or, for that matter, any recession. It is usually helpful to examine data using several different trend lines to obtain a more accurate picture of reality.

Abuse of statistics allows the government to manipulate "official" definitions of such problems as poverty, and to change them at will. Indeed, it is possible to *define* poverty out of existence (say, by lowering the level of poverty to those making less than a dollar a year) or to inflate the number of people "in distress" by raising poverty levels substantially or not counting transfers, such as food stamps, Aid to Families with Dependent Children, and noncash income. Typically, official definitions of poverty do not take into account all noncash income or assistance. In the 1980s, a family of four with an income of $11,000 qualified for the poverty level, even though the total of available benefits exceeded $14,000 a year. In other words, the family "in poverty" had cash and benefits of $25,000, or an amount *above* the average national family income at that time. Likewise, the numbers associated with AIDS have made some dramatic jumps on the surface in the late 1980s, but far from describing a rampant epidemic, the numbers reflect changes in the definition of AIDS that includes other symptoms—the total number of people who are sick with a disease has not changed, only the classification of the sickness. With such opportunities for mischief with numbers, the attentive student will take care to examine not only the statistics themselves but the assumptions and motivations behind them.

Sources: James Scanlon, "The Perils of Provocative Statistics," *Public Interest,* 102 (Winter 1991): 3–14; Mark Skousen, *Economics On Trial* (New York: Irwin, 1991); Thomas Sowell, *Race and Economics* (New York: David McKay, 1975); *Knowledge and Decisions* (New York: Basic Books, 1980), and his *Markets and Minorities* (New York: Basic Books, 1981); Charles Murray, "How to Lie with Statistics," *National Review,* February 28, 1986: 29–41; and David Warsh, *The Idea of Economic Complexity* (New York: Viking Press, 1984).

churches, which could broadcast late at night. With the markets restricted, new or growing denominations (especially minority ministries) were kept off the air. In the 1970s, however, the FCC revised
its regulations under pressure from the National Religious Broadcasters Association, opening up the licenses to the highest bidders. In less
than a decade, the mainline churches lost almost all of their broadcast
share while newer ministries of the so-called fundamentalist and Pen-
tecostal denominations dominated the airwaves, having "honed their
skills at the fringes of the industry. . . ."[57] According to the authors of
a study of deregulation in the religious broadcast industry, the new
competition caused interest in religion to grow; as "the number of religious broadcasters rose sharply, religious viewership increased" and
the indicators of the "religiousness" of the United States rose dramatically.[58] This was particularly relevant to the notion that competition
improves almost any endeavor, as the authors noted that the increased
competition among religious groups in the United States (with church
attendance rates of more than 40 percent) generated a far higher level
of interest in religion than in nations with state-endorsed "monopoly"
churches, such as Sweden, where less than 10 percent of the population attended church regularly.

Signs of Spring

One of the most important components that American business had
lacked for a decade was faith—the faith that its investments would not
be taxed away or eaten by inflation and that federal regulations would
not discourage invention, innovation, and risk-taking. Without faith
on the part of business, capital for new projects had stayed in tax-free
bonds, while the wealth of the rich went to purchase private art col-
lections or to hold gold as a hedge against inflation. Even middle-class
entrepreneurs struggled to protect themselves by trading houses, taking advantage of federal home mortgage loans and the spiraling inflation that pushed home prices up and neglecting critical investment in
small businesses. It was increasingly clear that capitalists would not
take risks in an atmosphere that punished them for doing so.

At the same time, the public had to have faith that the future
would be brighter if they were to purchase large-ticket items. It did not
help when the president of the United States, Jimmy Carter, said that
the United States suffered from a "malaise" or when pipsqueak foreign
dictators took Americans hostages and destroyed U.S. property with
impunity. The National Chamber of Commerce recognized the dire
straits into which the nation's enterprise had fallen with its 1980 slogan, "Let's Rebuild America," indicating American business had fallen
into disrepair.[59]

Deregulation helped dispel the gloom, marking an attitudinal change and signaling the end to the government's more than decade-long involvement in a number of markets. Equally important, the election of Ronald Reagan as president in 1980 sent a message to consumers and producers that enterprise again would be encouraged and celebrated. He sought to curb government spending and reduce regulation still further; he intended to cut taxes, both on individuals and on capital gains—the lifeblood of business; and he announced that he would restore American military strength through an ambitious program of military expansion so as to end threats abroad to U.S. life and property. Much to the annoyance of Reagan's critics, his program ignited the economy by restoring the critical element of faith. Reagan had a clear vision of where he wanted the nation to go, giving consumers and businesses alike a course by which they could plan their futures.

Fittingly, Reagan's election coincided with the technological achievement of the era, the personal computer and appearance of the software industry, which had not begun to tap its potential. As deregulation freed individuals in the legal and regulatory arena, the computer freed them from a system of business structures. But the next quantum leaps in technology awaited the maturation of other, apparently unrelated, electronics media and the expansion of the telephone industry in the realm of technology and of tax cuts in the realm of politics.

During the long winter of discontent endured by American business, the arrival of the computer marked a bud of spring—a turning point, symbolizing the transition from a world of steel and material resources to the universe of ideas and exponential growth. A new version of an industrial revolution was under way, often miscategorized as an "information revolution." The true impact of computer technology, which even by the 1990s had not really been experienced, was to multiply productivity and enhance individual power, turning upside down the tyranny of the physical over the mental and the material over the spiritual. That revolution, paradoxically, had its first impact in the very industries it soon would replace, steel and autos.

Notes

1. David Halberstam, *The Reckoning*, 218.

2. All quotations from Halberstam, *The Reckoning*, 218–219.

3. Ralph Nader, *Unsafe at Any Speed* (New York: Grossman, 1965).

4. Michael Kinsley, writing in 1985 in the *Washington Post*, quoted in Halberstam, *The Reckoning*, 501.

5. Michael Fumento, *Science Under Seige: Balancing Technology and the Environment* (New York: William Morrow, 1993).

6. Robert Crandall, *Why Is the Cost of Environmental Regulation So High?* (St. Louis: Center for the Study of American Business, Washington University, February 1992), 3.

7. Peter Asch, *Consumer Safety Regulation: Putting a Price on Life and Limb* (New York: Oxford University Press, 1988).

8. Smiley, *American Economy in the Twentieth Century,* 381.

9. William Lilley III and James C. Miller II, "The New 'Social' Regulation," *The Public Interest,* 47 (Spring 1977): 49–61 (quotation on 56).

10. Dobson, *History of American Business,* 326.

11. Pusateri, *History of American Business,* 2d ed., 326–328 (quotation on 327).

12. Sobel, *Age of Giant Corporations,* 191.

13. Interviews with C. William Verity, February, 1998, and Larry Schweikart, *Marriage of Steel: The Life and Times of William and Peggy Verity,* unpublished manuscript.

14. See Hans G. Mueller, "The Steel Industry," in *The Internationalization of the American Economy, The Annals of the American Academy of Political and Social Science,* eds. J. Michael Finger and Thomas D. Willett, 460 (March, 1982), 73–82; Robert E. Baldwin, Barry Eichengreen, and Hans van der Den, "U.S. Antidumping Policies: The Case of Steel," in *The Structure and Evolution of Recent U.S. Trade Policy,* eds. Anne O. Kreuger, (Chicago: University of Chicago Press for National Bureau of Economic Research, 1984), 67–103.

15. This discussion draws on Blackford and Kerr, *Business Enterprise in American History,* 430–431.

16. Gregory J. Millman, *The Vandals' Crown: How Rebel Currency Traders Overthrew the World's Central Banks* (New York: Free Press, 1995), 54.

17. Ibid., 56.

18. Robert Skidelsky, *John Maynard Keynes,* vol. I: *Hopes Betrayed: 1883–1920* (New York: Viking, 1986), and vol. II: *The Economist as Savior: 1920–1937* (New York: Penguin, 1994), quotations on 8 and 234.

19. Stanley W. Black, *A Levite Among the Priests: Edward M. Berstein and the Origins of the Bretton Woods System* (Boulder, Colo.: Westview Press, 1991), 39.

20. James L. Clayton, ed., *The Economic Impact of the Cold War* (New York: Harcourt, Brace, & World, 1970), 242–243.

21. These issues are discussed in two books by Jacques S. Gansler, *The Defense Industry* (Cambridge, Mass.: MIT Press, 1980), and *Affording Defense* (Cambridge, Mass.: MIT Press, 1989).

22. D. Douglas Dalgleish and Larry Schweikart, *Trident* (Carbondale: Southern Illinois University Press, 1984).

23. Quoted in Dalgleish and Schweikart, *Trident,* 68.

24. Jacques S. Gansler, "How the Pentagon Buys Fruitcake," *Air Force Magazine,* June 1989, 94–97.

25. Robert B. Coulam, *Illusions of Choice: The F-111 and the Problems of Weapons Acquisition Reform* (Princeton, N.J.: Princeton University Press, 1977); and Jacob Goodwin, *Brotherhood of Arms: General Dynamics and the Business of Defending America* (New York: Times Books, 1985).

26. Paul Kennedy, *The Rise and Fall of the Great Powers: Economic Change and Military Conflict from 1500 to 2000* (New York: Random House, 1987).

27. Smiley presents a detailed analysis of the different components of deficits in his *American Economy in the Twentieth Century,* Figures 15.2–15.9, on 358–365.

28. Wriston quoted in Johnson, *Modern Times* (1980), 664.

29. E. Anthony Copp, *Regulating Competition in Oil: Government Intervention in the U.S. Refining Industry, 1948–1975* (College Station: Texas A&M University Press, 1976), 192.

30. An excellent history of the oil industry and the effects of government regulations appears in Robert L. Bradley Jr., *Oil, Gas and Government: The U.S. Experience,* Vol. 1 (Lanham, Md.: Rowman & Littlefield, 1996).

31. George Gilder, *Microcosm: the Quantum Revolution in Economics and Technology* (New York: Simon and Schuster, 1989), 48.

32. Ibid., 68.

33. Michael Moritz, *The Little Kingdom: The Private Story of Apple Computer* (New York: William Morrow and Co., 1984).

34. "Jobs and Wozniak Found Apple Computer," *Great Events in History II: Business and Commerce Series,* 1611–1615.

35. Pusateri, *History of American Business,* 353.

36. James Wallace and Jim Erickson, *Hard Drive: Bill Gates and the Making of the Microsoft Empire* (New York: Wiley, 1992), and Stephen Manes and Paul Andrews, *Gates: How Microsoft's Mogul Reinvented an Industry and Made Himself the Richest Man in America* (New York: Doubleday, 1993). Also see Steven Levy, *Hackers: Heroes of the Computer Revolution* (Garden City, N.Y.: Anchor Press/Doubleday, 1984), and Robert X. Cringeley, *Accidental Empires: How the Boys of Silicon Valley Make Their Millions* (Reading, Mass.: Addison-Wesley, 1992), which makes the absurd argument that the creations of Gates, Jobs, and other computer geniuses were accidents.

37. William T. Youngs, "Bill Gates and Microsoft," in Youngs, ed., *American Realities: Historical Episodes,* vol. 2, *From Reconstruction to the Present,* 3d ed., (New York: HarperCollins, 1993), 285.

38. Rush Loving Jr., "The Pros and Cons of Airline Deregulation," *Fortune,* August 1977, 209–217, quoted in McCraw, *Prophets of Regulation,* 268.

39. President of the Air Transport Association testifying in 1977, quoted in McCraw, *Prophets of Regulation,* 263.

40. David Field, "Big Airlines Pack in Passengers, Profit" *USA Today,* April 1, 1997.

41. Larry Schweikart, interview with Tanya Wagner, Federal Aviation Administration, July 5, 1995.

42. Jeff Mangum, "ValuJet Woes May Benefit Major Airlines," *USA Today,* June 19, 1996.

43. On Federal Express, see Robert A. Sigafoos, *Absolutely Positively Overnight!* (New York: New American Library, 1984,).

44. Sobel and Sicilia, *Entrepreneurs,* 46.

45. William Childs, *Trucking and the Public Interest: The Emergence of Federal Regulation, 1914–1940* (Knoxville: University of Tennessee Press, 1985).

46. Robert Samuelson, "The Joy of Deregulation," *Newsweek,* February 3, 1997, 39.

47. Paul Teske, Samuel Best, and Michael Mintrom, *Deregulating Freight Transportation: Delivering the Goods* (Washington, D.C.: AEI Press, 1995), 8.

48. Ibid., 206.

49. James Bovard, "The Great Truck Robbery," *The Wall Street Journal,* November 3, 1993.

50. Several sources blame deregulation for the industry's woes: Paul Pitzer and Robert Deitz, *Other People's Money: The Inside Story of the S&L Mess* (New York: Simon and Schuster, 1989); James Ring Adams, *The Big Fix: Inside the S&L Scandal: How an Unholy Alliance of Politics and Money Destroyed America's Banking System* (New York: John Wiley & Sons, 1990); and Stephen Pizzo, Mary Fricker, and Paul Muolo, *Inside Job: The Looting of America's Savings and Loans* (New York: McGraw-Hill, 1989).

51. Anthony Chan, "The Savings and Loan Crisis," in Schweikart, ed., *Encyclopedia of American Business History and Biography: Banking and Finance, 1913–1989,* 378–382 (quotation on 378).

52. George Benston and George Kaufman, "Understanding the Savings and Loan Debate," *The Public Interest,* no. 99 (Spring 1990): 79–95; Edward Kane, "FIRREA: Financial Malpractice," *Durrell Journal of Money and Banking,* 2 (May 1990): 2–10, specifically deal with the FSLIC, but for deposit insurance in general, see Gerald P. O'Driscoll, "Bank Failures: The Deposit Insurance Connection," *Contemporary Policy Issues,* 6 (April 1988): 1–12; George Benston, "Federal Regulation of Banking: Analysis and Policy Recommendations," *Journal of Bank Research,* 13 (Spring 1983): 93–112; Douglas Diamond and Philip Dybvig, "Bank Runs, Deposit Insurance and Liquidity," *Journal of Political Economy,* 91 (June 1983): 401–418; Catherine England and John Palffy, *Replacing the FDIC: Private Insurance and Bank Deposits* (Washington, D.C.: 1982), backgrounder #229; Eugene Short and Gerald O'Driscoll, "Deposit Insurance and Financial Stability," *Business Forum,* Summer 1983, 10–13; John Kareken and Neil Wallace, "Deposit Insurance and Bank Regulation: A Partial-Equilibrium Exposition," *Journal of Business,* 51 (July 1978): 413–438. On deposit insurance, see Charles W. Calomiris and Eugene N. White, "The Origins of Federal Deposit Insurance," in *The Regulated Economy: a Historical Approach to Political Economy* ed. Claudia Goldin and Gary D. Liebecap, (Chicago: University of Chicago Press, 1994), 145–188.

53. Lawrence J. White, "A Cautionary Tale of Deregulation Gone Awry: The S&L Debacle," *Southern Economic Journal,* 59(January 1993): 496–514.

54. Lawrence J. White, *The S&L Debacle: Public Policy Lessons for Bank and Thrift Regulation* (New York: Oxford University Press, 1991). White notes that both the S&L and banking industries opposed elimination of Regulation Q, which provided each with protections against competition. That opposition in itself should have suggested that it was not in consumers' best interests to maintain Regulation Q.

55. Glenn Yago, "The Regulatory Reign of Terror," *The Wall Street Journal,* March 4, 1992.

56. A good overview of deregulation in several industries appears in Goldin and Liebecap, eds. *The Regulated Economy,* with essays on several areas of deregulation.

57. Laurence R. Iannaccone, Roger Finke, and Rodney Stark, "Deregulating Religion: The Economics of Church and State," *Economic Inquiry,* 35 (April 1997): 350–364 (quotation on 361).

58. Ibid., 361.

59. Interviews with C. William Verity, President, National Chamber of Commerce (1980–81), February 1998.

CHAPTER 12

Business in Renaissance, 1980–1995

WHEN THE CONGENIAL, SILVER-HAIRED MAN IN THE BASEBALL CAP TOOK the makeshift stage at one of hundreds of the Wal-Mart discount stores around the country, he hardly looked like a billionaire. "Whoooooooooo," he yelled. "Whooooooooooo," the crowd—all Wal-Mart employees— shouted back. "Pig. Sooey. Razorbacks!" he concluded with a whoop. What was the ruckus? It was just Sam Walton, founder of the largest chain of retail stores in the nation, talking to his employees. Just a little chat between him and the "associates," as he called them.

Sam Walton was one of the "rich who got richer" in the 1980s. He did so by expanding his chain from 200 stores to 1,600. He did so by creating 212,000 *new* jobs in the 1980s alone. And he did so by lowering prices for consumers on a panoply of retail goods.[1] Hardly the image of a miser counting his money by candlelight, Sam Walton got richer by improving the lives of millions of people and hiring elderly or handicapped "greeters" to do little more than say hello at the front door. Yet many in the media and academia concentrated only on the perception that Wal-Mart destroyed downtown areas or "mom-and-pop stores."

Such a "spin" on the real success of Wal-Mart is not surprising. In a decade of revival for entrepreneurs, business staged a hidden, almost secret, renaissance. While Walton and a few other businessmen such as Lee Iacocca received media attention (Walton avoided it; Iacocca encouraged it), on the whole, the entrepreneurs behind the economy and the boom itself went unreported. News stories covering the economy actually diminished as the economy improved throughout the

1980s, leading economist Warren Brookes to describe the decade's growth as the "Silent Boom."[2] Indeed, never in history has such a period of economic growth gone so uncelebrated in the popular media.

In part, however, the untold story reflected the nature of the growth itself: Millions of individual entrepreneurs and thousands of small businesses fueled the explosion. The most vibrant new sector, information technology (comprising computers, software, programming, telephones, fax machines, and the like), stood out in only a few large companies such as Xerox and IBM. Yet it was exactly in that sector that individual entrepreneurs drove the revolution, inventing and developing new technologies. Start-up companies, unburdened with the trappings of managerial hierarchies under which the large corporations staggered, revived several industries, while executives in the traditional big-business sector "downsized" and eliminated layers of management and bureaucracy. And no industry more sharply contrasted the old-style managerial hierarchies in distress with the new wave of thin management layers than steel, where a revival occurred.

Steel Reborn

Continuing a trend that had appeared in the 1960s, "big steel," that is, the largest steel corporations, continued to lose market share into the mid-1980s. U.S. Steel led the way, but deep problems beset all American steel companies. Steelmakers had fallen behind their foreign rivals in investment and paid far more for labor. From 1974 to 1986, steelmaking jobs fell by more than 337,000, and between 1982 and 1987, the industry eliminated 50 million tons annually—more than 30 percent—of its raw steelmaking capacity.[3] One-fourth of the industry went bankrupt, and 75 percent of all steelworkers in America lost their jobs in the crash.

Numerous problems afflicted the steel companies, not the least of which was a worldwide shift in demand. Auto manufacturers, especially, had ceased to use steel in many parts of the manufacturing process, substituting newer, lighter plastics and composites. Consequently, all the major steelmaking nations lost output—not just the United States—with total output of Western nations dropping from 494 million metric tons in 1974 to 368 million tons in 1986. Did "the collapse of the American steel industry [represent] one of the great industrial failures of modern times," as one labor historian put it?[4] Richard Preston, in his recent biography of Nucor Steel, assessed the situation thusly: "[In the 1950s] there was a smell of frying brakes, a wheel hopped the track, and Big Steel toppled over like a freight train and went into a crawling, elaborate wreck that dragged on for thirty years. . . . The steel industry became the *world* steel industry, but the Americans didn't notice."[5]

What happened? Friend and foe of business all agree on this point: The management of the largest steel companies—the same types of people who had sent Detroit into a free fall—failed utterly to invest in the future. Just as Ford's Robert McNamara resisted his production managers, who wanted to install modernized, but expensive, paint ovens large enough for vans, steel managers resisted radical modernization. The one thing steel managers never understood "was how to invest money shrewdly in manufacturing technology, and . . . they were never able to inspire the hot metal workers to do much of anything except to go out on strike."[6] Many business-school graduates never even walked the mills or appreciated the process of turning molten iron ore into steel. Management alone was not to blame, however. Even prolabor historians, such as John Hoerr, admit that unions repeatedly crippled the industry with strikes and outrageous demands. Unionized steel workers received $20 an hour (plus benefits) in the United States, while their competitors worked for $3 an hour in Korea. Government policies played a role, too, as inflation took its toll on profits and regulations placed a further drag on productivity.

Ultimately, however, management had to assume most of the blame. Consequently, even when "Big Steel" turned the corner in 1987, a year in which the six largest domestic producers earned $1 billion and managed to increase prices, the major companies still had to scramble to regain technological momentum. By that time, U.S. steel production was exceeded only by that of the Soviet Union and Japan as individual nations, although the United States remained behind the total production of the European Community. By 1993, however, American steel trailed only the Japanese and comprised over 11 percent of the world market (97 million tons, out of 814 million tons produced in the world).

A clear example of how far the large American steel companies had come—and how far they still had to go—could be seen in the case of United States Steel. The company founded by Andrew Carnegie as Carnegie Steel and incorporated by J. P. Morgan as U.S. Steel adopted a new name in 1986, USX Corporation, with the "X" referring to the company's New York Stock Exchange symbol. USX, symptomatic of other struggling manufacturing companies, had tried to solve its problems through diversification into nonsteel businesses, acquiring Marathon Oil in 1982 and Texas Oil & Gas in 1986. What once was U.S. Steel by that time was more than two-thirds nonsteel business.

Much of the revival of USX could be credited to Thomas Graham, the president, who saved U.S. Steel from bankruptcy in 1983. "We tore three layers of management out of this company after I became president," he proudly noted. When "Lee Iacocca goes on TV and says, 'We're offering a seven-year warranty on the body of every Chrysler car,' nobody credits the American steel industry. That's American steel in that Chrysler car [that] doesn't rust, and that's why Lee Iacocca can make his guarantees."[7] By that time, USX accounted for approximately 11 percent of the steel produced in America.

By the 1990s, USX remained the leading U.S. steelmaker in volume and total earnings. Even in its successful retrenchment, however, instead of recapturing the glory of the Carnegie years, USX tried to insulate itself from failure in the steel business through diversification out of steel. But fear of failure never stopped Carnegie, who always had faith that if he incorporated the newest technology—even at an initial loss—productivity gains would outstrip costs. "Creative destruction" was a way of life at the early Carnegie mills, but modem corporations avoided risk, especially when it meant radical new technology such as the electric minimill.

New Steel, Nucor

In 1965, a small multiproduct manufacturing company called Nuclear Corporation came to a point in its history similar to USX's in 1983. One of the company's chief subsidiaries, Vulcraft Corporation, made roof joists of steel bar for shopping-center roofs, but it also had an air-conditioning-duct business. Its stock hit 11 cents a share, and the company had invested in several long-shot technologies. The board of directors needed to take drastic action, so it brought in a division chief, Ken Iverson, as the new president. Iverson concluded that Nucor needed to get into the steelmaking business to supply Vulcraft with its own steel. However, Iverson's vision went beyond filling a niche, as he already had started thinking of competing with foreign countries' steel companies. "They were the ones we really targeted," he recalled.[8]

Nucor could not afford to build its own blast furnace for smelting iron ore (at a cost of $200 million), pushing Iverson to an alternative steelmaking process that used an electric arc furnace. For raw material, Nucor melted junk metal, which was abundant in America. Iverson wanted to leapfrog the American steel industry, not just catch up. In 1969, Nucor melted its first heap of steel at a minimill in Darlington, South Carolina, using an entirely nonunion workforce. By 1980, Iverson had opened Nucor's fourth minimill, at the same time taking over much of the joist business that the major steelmakers were leaving in force. Nucor's earnings reached $42 million by 1980. Iverson increasingly resembled Carnegie; convinced that the Darlington mill, built only nine years earlier, was decrepit, he had it torn apart and rebuilt.

"Big Steel" looked on the electric arc process with skepticism. Experts from the traditional companies thought that it was impossible to make steel profitably the way Nucor did. But other new competitors thought otherwise, so much so that by 1980 a dozen minimill competitors were putting pressure on Nucor. Hurricane Industries, Border

Steel, Bayou Steel, Florida Steel, and many others hunted Nucor the way Nucor had hunted USX. In the process, the minimills fulfilled Iverson's vision by killing the importation of foreign bar steel into the United States. Iverson had hit the target.

Companies such as Nucor paid wages equal to unionized steel-workers' pay, but with a major difference. In the minimills, bonuses for production played a far more important part in the total wage—more than half in the case of Nucor. All Iverson had to do to keep unions away from Nucor was to tell employees the harsh statistics: There were once 450,000 steelworkers in the United States, but in the 1980s there were only 130,000, and that massive unemployment occurred at the height of union power. Like many of the minimills, Nucor gave the employees stock at regular intervals. With one exception, Nucor never laid off any employees, and in that one event, the Nucor front office overruled a manager who had fired 40 employees, then fired the manager himself. As for bureaucracy, Nucor operated out of a rented office the size of a group dental practice, and, as of 1988, had twenty-two manufacturing plants, with a ratio of 0.8 corporate front-office people per factory!

By 1988, Nucor stock hit $40 a share and the company produced two million tons of steel from junk melted with electricity. At a net profit of a penny a pound, Nucor earned $50 million a year net profits. Yet Iverson continually looked for new technology. In 1989 Nucor opened a new plant in Crawfordsville, Indiana, that featured the world's first continuous steelmaking machine, the Compact Strip Production Facility—a machine 1,177 feet long that would produce hot-band steel used in truck frames and water tanks and then "cold-roll" some of the same steel into paper-thin sheets for computer parts, filing cabinets, and auto fenders. The company specifically located the plant in the Rust Belt because, as Iverson reasoned, the Rust Belt had scrap. Crawfordsville represented a desktop steel mill, capable of unimagined labor-efficiency gains. Whereas the most efficient traditional steel facilities, such as USX's Gary plant, required three to four man-hours to manufacture a ton of hot-band (not finished) steel, the Crawfordsville facility used only .6 man-hours to produce a ton of virtually finished steel. That represented a level of efficiency approximately *five times* better than the best Japanese plants. Success with the Crawfordsville design allowed Nucor to open a similar plant in Hickman, Arkansas, in 1993. That year, Nucor stock passed the $50-a-share mark, and Nucor stood in fourth place among all U.S. steel companies.[9]

Meanwhile, Nucor's old nemisis, Tom Graham at USX, had moved on to head a minimill of his own, AK Steel near Dayton, Ohio, in 1992. Graham, as he had at USX, worked another miracle. He turned AK around. Although he cut the workforce by 3,000, from 9,000, Graham restored the company to respectability. Operating profitability, which had dropped to -$70 per ton of steel, rose to +$70—double the industry average—and AK had a goal of reaching $100. Long known as Armco—the American Rolling Mill Company—the company had been formed at the turn of the century to meet the demands of new firms in Ohio's Miami Valley. Although the company did not have access to a river or raw materials, Armco's founder, George Verity, thought that customer demand would overcome those disadvantages, and he was proved right.[10] Like other large steelmakers, Armco expanded into several non-steel-related businesses in the 1970s, under the rationale that the then-current trends of environmental regulation and price controls would doom any company whose profit center was steel. Armco's chairman, C. William Verity, expressed his awareness that the company had to dramatically shrink its workforce, but the nature of Armco—long developed as a "family" enterprise that had a paternalistic attitude toward employees—made it difficult to act more rapidly.[11] Ultimately, as Verity noted, Graham took the brunt of criticism for making changes that needed to be made. As one wag noted, "If you have a frog to swallow, better swallow it whole." In retrospect, Verity pointed out, Graham's approach proved much less damaging, both to those laid off and to the company, than the "slow death" that had plagued Armco prior to Graham's arrival.

Following the force reductions, AK regained its competitiveness. It did not have the same type of mill as Nucor, but comparisons to the company that had attained an operating profitability of $56 per ton were inevitable. Still, using a nonunion workforce, by 1995 AK Steel cut the man-hours required to make a ton of steel from six to three under Graham.[12] Unlike Nucor, however, AK had developed a reputation for plant accidents, with enough of it warranted to provoke federal investigations in the mid-1990s. The union made certain to publicize any mishap as an excuse to tout union advantages.

OPEC, Oil, and Honor

Between 1980 and 1995, most productivity improvements in American business had come from strategic decisions by management. But other factors assisted in the revival of American business, not the least of which was the abundance of relatively cheap energy. Yet the decade of the 1980s did not start with inexpensive oil.

From its dominant position in the 1970s, OPEC managed to demand, and receive, high prices. Immediately after the Iranian takeover of the U.S. embassy in 1979, spot prices for oil ranged upwards of $50 a barrel. Most OPEC members charged $28 a barrel, although Saudi Arabia maintained a slightly lower price. *Foreign Affairs*, the prestigious journal of international diplomacy, captured the bleak mood heralded by the prices in an article titled "Oil and the Decline of the West."[13]

But it was OPEC, not the oil-consuming nations, that was in trouble. Attempting to take advantage of the temporary market distortions, many OPEC members pushed the price well above $30 a barrel—three times above what it had been a year and a half earlier. Sheik Yamani, the Saudi oil minister, appreciated that the strategy would backfire: "They're too greedy, they're too greedy. They'll pay for it," he told a friend.[14] High prices in the 1970s had made new exploration profitable, and fresh discoveries of oil in Alaska, Mexico, and the North Sea contributed to a 28 percent increase in production by non-OPEC countries between 1978 and 1985. Meanwhile, consumers and industry—often terrified by predictions that the current stock of oil would only last thirty years, or that pollution had gotten worse—shifted away from petroleum products. During the first half of the 1980s, Americans lowered their use of oil as a percentage of total energy consumed by 4 percent, making an astute prophet of Yamani.

Prices started falling, dropping to below $20 a barrel by mid-decade. American oil companies suffered along with OPEC, especially in the Southwest, where more than 300,000 jobs disappeared in a five-year period as refineries closed and investment in new exploration dropped by two-thirds. But America could diversify, and while individuals paid a tremendous price for government restrictions on drilling and the tax-code disincentives to exploration, the economies of Texas, Louisiana, Colorado, California, and Oklahoma eventually bounced back.

OPEC did not get off so lightly, for its ability to set and maintain prices were sharply curbed by another development. On March 30, 1983, the New York Mercantile Exchange (Nymex) introduced trading in crude oil futures. No longer could a group of Arab ministers, meeting in a remote location, decide what to charge for oil. Instead, the price was established instantaneously on the open market. Perhaps symbolically, trading was benchmarked with West Texas Intermediate, a crude that could be easily purchased and sold, ending the temporary identification of oil prices with Arab light petroleum.

American oil companies, though, struggled through the "boom and bust" cycles of the 1970s and early 1980s. Several oil companies had become targets of takeover bids, even while prices rose. T. Boone Pickens Jr., who had formed Petroleum Exploration Co. of Amarillo, Texas, with just $2,500 in cash in 1955, came to embody the new "corporate raider" who epitomized the takeover fever that swept through all American business in the 1980s. Pickens reorganized his oil company into Mesa Petroleum in 1964 and emphasized exploration and drilling.

Under Pickens, Mesa had made several attempts to acquire other oil companies. In the 1970s, Mesa stalked Cities Service Co. but lost it to Occidental Petroleum, making a profit of $31 million in the process when share prices rose in the attempt. Another bid resulted in General American Oil, the target, fleeing to the arms of Phillips Petroleum, leaving Mesa with a $43 million profit, again made possible by higher stock prices caused by the takeover.

By the mid-1980s Mesa had committed $300 million to an exploration program. Unable to recapture the investment in exploration quickly enough, Pickens identified another way of raising money. He observed that Gulf Oil, once the company of the Mellon family, labored under an inefficient bureaucratic structure and, according to one of Gulf's directors, "six years of no decision" from the board.[15] Gulf's stock sold for barely one-third of the company's appraised value. Pickens's stock purchases in 1984 left Mesa with 13 percent of the shares, but once again a third company intervened. In that case, it was Standard Oil of California, which subsumed Gulf into its operations, generating a $760 million profit in the process. More important, in Pickens's mind, Gulf stockholders made a profit of $6.5 billion, while Gulf's operating capital nearly doubled.

Pickens got his operating capital, and the inept management at Gulf gave way to better leadership from Chevron. Pickens, like many other corporate raiders, argued that the managerial hierarchies that dominated American business in the 1970s and 1980s had lost touch. In essence, they contended, owners (the stockholders) were consistently taking losses on their stock value because management had insulated itself, becoming unaccountable.

A classic case of mismanagement involved the company started by J. Paul Getty, Getty Oil. Gordon Getty, the heir to Getty Oil and owner of 40 percent of the corporation, had noticed that the stock had remained far below the level that its assets should have demanded. From 1980 until 1982, Getty Oil stock dropped from $110 to $50, indicating what Gordon Getty characterized as "sorry performance" by the management of the company.[16]

Getty explored the possibility of selling the company on his own, with Pennzoil emerging as the most significant suitor. Ultimately, the Getty board met with Pennzoil representatives and, depending on the source, agreed on a sale or agreed on a sale *price.* Immediately thereafter, Texaco, learning that Getty Oil was "in play," met with Gordon and made its own, significantly higher, offer, which Getty accepted. Getty Oil, then, had been sold twice, once to Pennzoil and once to Texaco. Pennzoil sued for $15 billion in damages, claiming that Texaco knowingly and wrongfully interfered in its "handshake" contract. After a year of court battles, the final verdict of the Houston jury—that Texaco had interfered—was upheld. But the jury's incredible damages, which came to more than $11 billion, would have driven Texaco into bankruptcy. Subsequent courts reduced the amount somewhat, but ultimately only the prospect of Texaco folding completely paved the way for negotiations. Pennzoil received $3 billion from Texaco in a settlement. The Houston jurors had been swayed by the simple concept of honor, and the most important factual event in the minds of the jurors was the handshake agreement between the Getty board and the Pennzoil negotiators. After the verdict, one juror suggested that the trial sent a morality message to business: "We won't tolerate this sort of thing in corporate America. The idea that 'anything goes' is dead."[17]

On the whole, the oil industry faced a deepening recession in the late 1980s as prices plummeted and gas stations engaged in price wars. Conversely, American consumers prospered, reaping a portion of the $50 billion transfer from OPEC to the consuming countries. Of course, the production of oil, as long as it remained substantially in the Middle East, was subject to fluctuations based on political instability. Iran and Iraq fought a seven-year war over largely religious and political differences. Then, not long after that conflict ended, Iraq's dictator, Saddam Hussein, invaded Kuwait for purely profit motives: control of the Kuwaiti and, possibly, Saudi oil fields.

A mutual suicide pact between two of the Middle East's major troublemakers, as the Iran-Iraq war illustrated, did not threaten American businesses or consumers. On the other hand, an Iraqi invasion of Kuwait—with the potential for Iraq to bring Saudi Arabia, Bahrain, and other countries in thrall—manifested a threat to the free flow of oil at market prices. In the hands of one megalomaniacal individual, such as Saddam, it could seriously damage the Western economies. President George Bush, in concert with British Prime Minister Margaret Thatcher, organized a remarkable multinational rescue mission that for the first time in history placed Saudi, Egyptian, French, Syrian, British, American, Turkish, and Kuwaiti troops under unified command, not to mention that Japan, Russia, and Israel all joined the effort either by contributing cash (Japan) or by directly refraining from involvement (Israel and Russia). Within a few months, Kuwait was liberated and the threat contained.

At the same time, the Soviet Union imploded and its bloc of communist satellites, no longer restrained in their orbit by the Red Armies, spun wildly away. The downward effect on oil prices, which had started years earlier, reflected the desperation of the Soviet— then, Russian—government to acquire cash. Thus, by 1999, typical pump prices for a gallon of unleaded gas in the midwestern United States dipped below $1, or about double the price of gas in 1970. However, adjusting for taxes, which accounted for almost 50 cents a gallon, and the effects of inflation (some of which could be blamed on oil price increases), the resource that was supposed to have run out by the year 2000 was more abundant than at any time in American history.

Lee Iacocca and the American Auto Comeback

Oil-related pressures reinvigorated Detroit the same way they had dev-astated the automakers a decade earlier. The auto industry's inability to make small, fuel-efficient cars in the 1970s had allowed imports to enter the U.S. market successfully. Imports as a share of the American auto market rose, surging above 25 percent late in the decade.

Some companies went out of business or were absorbed in such a way as to disappear. American Motors, for example, which only a decade earlier had made inroads into the "muscle car" market, virtu-ally lost its identity when French automaker Renault acquired 48 per-cent of AMC and designed its own compact, Le Car (and Chrysler purchased AMC-Jeep in 1987, mainly for the Jeep business).

The most serious problem, however, existed at Chrysler, where in 1978 the company announced its largest operational losses in his-tory. At that time, the fired president of Ford Motor Company, Lido Anthony "Lee" Iacocca, had just been named the new president of Chrysler. A native Pennsylvanian, Iacocca joined Ford in the late 1940s, playing a much debated role in the creation of a sporty com-pact called the Mustang, which came out in 1964. Possibly because of his working-class background, Iacocca did not get along with the company scion, Henry Ford II, who fired the feisty Italian in 1978. Iacocca since has referred to Ford as "that evil man," and Ford re-portedly fired Iacocca with the blunt comment, "Sometimes you just don't like somebody."[18]

Whatever the reasons, Iacocca moved to chaotic Chrysler. Under-taking a massive top-to-bottom purge of the executive structure—firing thirty-three of thirty-five vice presidents—Iacocca insisted that the company focus on quality to compete with the Japanese.[19] Largely because of his ruthlessness, Iacocca received most of the credit, when the company eventually turned around, even though some analysts suggested that he merely arrived in time to take advantage of a com-pany that had already taken steps to restore itself. Regardless of the extent of Iacocca's contribution, few deny he played a key part in the restoration of Chrysler. His greatest feat, however, was the successful acquisition of federal loan guarantees of $1.5 billion in 1980, provid-ing the company with the capital it needed to retool. Considerable op-position existed in Congress and the public, but ultimately Chrysler was the only U.S. manufacturer of heavy tanks; and thus, Chrysler could make the case that it needed the bailout for national security reasons. Iacocca also tried to portray himself as a market entrepre-neur and claimed to have taken federal funds only as a last resort. Like most entrepreneurs, however—recall how Vanderbilt's first option was to get government contracts—Iacocca embraced government aid when he concluded it represented his only hope.[20] In the end, Iacocca was as much a political entrepreneur as Jim Fisk.

Nevertheless, Chrysler made good. It repaid its federally guaranteed loans and produced a new line of restyled front-wheel-drive cars, recapturing some of its American market share. Convinced that he could sell the product better than an actor, Iacocca went before the cameras to film a series of highly successful commercials. Overnight, Iacocca went from auto executive to media personality. Iacocca restored the public's trust in Chrysler, and after the company had been indicted for selling autos driven by Chrysler executives as new, Iacocca filmed a commercial in which he asked, "Did we screw up? You bet we did. . . . [Chrysler's actions] went beyond dumb and reached all the way out to stupid."[21] By the time he published his autobiography in 1984, Iacocca was held in greater esteem by the public than any business figure since the 1920s.[22]

Chrysler's comeback did not end with Iacocca. The company had one more fit of problems in the late 1980s before introducing a successful line of cars in the 1990s led by the Neon, the minivan, the Jeep Cherokee, the "LH" sedan bodies, the Dodge Ram, and the hot Viper. From 1991 to 1993, Chrysler received the market's approval when its stock leaped from $9.75 per share to $57 per share. The "New" Chrysler Corporation had turned the corner on manufacturing quality and cost control. It had designed into its manufacturing plan, for the first time ever, sales in Japan by building the Neon to compete specifically in Japan with right-side steering wheels and standardized comforts for Asian drivers. Meanwhile, Chrysler had responded to the Japanese challenge on productivity; its Bramale factory in Ontario built midsize sedans in just over twenty labor hours, better than any plant in the world except Tahara in Japan, which had much higher automation costs. But Chrysler also tapped into the spirit of American motoring, introducing in the 1990s the two-passenger convertible sports-racing car, the Viper. Priced initially at $65,000 (and by 1997 soaring up to as much as $100,000 for slightly customized versions), the Viper brought back memories of the Ford Cobra and the Chevy Corvette in their early days. Dodge also marketed the Shadow, a pricy two-seater that looked like the customized Excalibur cars. With baby-boomer males reaching their 40s, such cars fit both the tastes and wallets of more than a few.

GM, "Roger and Me"

While Chrysler apparently had turned its business around, General Motors encountered a few more potholes in the road. GM's problems were all the more surprising given the heights from which it had fallen.

At one time in the 1970s, GM sold one out of every two cars purchased in America, in the process generating hefty profits. In an ambitious move, the company plowed the capital back into renovation and new designs of its entire line of cars, all produced in modernized and roboticized factories. GM thought it was on the top of the mountain, when in reality it was on the edge of a cliff.

The company experienced some plain bad luck: Counting on gas prices to rise, they fell, reviving the "muscle car" mania that had swept the U.S. market ten years earlier. Most of the new models were not only ugly but bulky looking and frequently underpowered. GM diversified in moves that may have made sense "on paper" but contributed little to the company's ability to make better cars, absorbing, for example, Howard Hughes' aircraft company for $5.1 billion to take advantage of the 1980s defense buildup.

GM also relived the mistakes made by McNamara and the Whiz Kids at Ford: When the company decided to emphasize robots, "The robot count quickly became the most important manufacturing statistic in the company."[23] GM, of course, was not alone when it pleaded with Washington to do something about the strong dollar—Lee Iacocca said that if the dollar fell by just 25 percent, the "playing field" would be even. The international finance ministers pushed the yen up and the dollar down, but instead of lowering prices to take advantage of the temporary Japanese higher-cost vehicles, Detroit raised its own prices.

Seeking to learn Japanese methods, GM entered into a joint venture with Toyota to build a Chevrolet Nova that resembled a Toyota Corolla. The New United Motor Manufacturing, Inc. (NUMMI) factory at Fremont, California, was widely hailed as a wonderful experiment in worker-management relations and "*kaizen*"-style management. NUMMI proved a resounding success, posting high returns on investment and attaining unmatched customer satisfaction. In fact, under GM's quality rating, a 145 score was perfect. NUMMI cars consistently received above 140 and often attained perfection.

GM, however, ran into trouble when it attempted to apply the Fremont lessons to other plants. Myrmidon managers not trained intimately in the "Secret," as they referred to Toyota's system, simply did not understand that there was no secret. Instead, Toyota demanded rigid quality control throughout the process—not simply tossing aside broken parts after they *came through* the assembly process—and allowed workers to stop the line to fix a malfunction or design error immediately. Indeed, GM soon faced an entirely unexpected problem associated with the NUMMI Novas it sold: They did not return for repairs! That caused inventory problems, as the company's dealers found themselves with millions of spare parts on hand.

GM eventually, and occasionally with great anguish, managed to apply the "Fremont lesson," even as the Japanese opened their own factories in America. Honda built a plant in Marysville, Ohio, in November 1982, partly to get around 1981 import quotas imposed on the Japanese by Washington. Between Marysville and Fremont, the U.S. auto industry learned that "American workers could build quality automobiles, thus stripped away Detroit's excuses [not to do so]."[24] In that context, the Japanese re-created the American auto industry. Nevertheless, by the mid-1980s things looked bleak for Detroit, even with Iacocca's miracle at Chrysler.

GM had made important changes and had invested almost $40 billion in robots over a ten-year period, but despite the NUMMI miracle, the company's market share dropped to 40 percent. Roger Smith, the nine-year chairman and CEO of General Motors, received much of the blame for the near-death of "the General," as insiders called GM. Designers kept turning out luxury cars that looked like economy cars, while management poured billions of dollars into inefficient factories. To his credit, Smith did approve the Saturn Division, a small-car division—and the first new division added to GM since Alfred Sloan—that was designed from the ground up based on Japanese principles to compete with imports and that was built entirely in Tennessee. Although sales were eventually good for Saturn, its slim profit margin really made it a "loss leader" to attract small-car buyers back to the company. Further, Saturn's good gas mileage helped offset higher gas usage by Cadillacs and other full-sized cars for federal regulatory purposes. By 1996, the jury was still out as to whether Saturn could recapture the more than $3.5 billion Smith poured into the project, and in 1995 a labor rift—which Saturn was supposed to avoid—had developed.[25]

But Saturn was not scheduled to come on-line for years, and GM had immediate problems for which Smith deserved much of the blame. Ross Perot, who headed the huge GM Electronic Data Systems division (EDS) acquired by Smith in 1984, was GM's largest individual stockholder. Perot, referred to as a "hand grenade with a crewcut," immediately saw that GM's bureaucracy was far too big and that the company had neglected labor relations too long. Perot delivered lectures to Smith and the board about how GM needed to "'feed the troops before it feeds the generals," and that executives had to suffer along with the line workers. Perot received a chilly reception.

Relations between Perot and Smith grew so strained that GM bought out Perot for $700 million, fearing that the Texan might attempt a takeover of the world's largest corporation. (In 1995, however, Smith may have had the last laugh, as GM prepared to unload EDS for $10 billion, or four times what the automaker paid for the company.)[26] Smith had made one bad decision after another, closing plant after plant and ridiculed in a movie, *Roger and Me,* in which he would not visit Flint, Michigan, a town destroyed by the closing of the GM plant there. By 1992, even after Smith was replaced by Robert Stempel, GM reported a staggering loss of $4.5 billion. Its factories featured automated parts delivery trucks that cost more than people and were less reliable; its models included pointy-nosed APV minivans that cost as much as competitors' models but held less and were difficult to drive; and its management still had not "gotten it." GM was, as Stempel said in a mixed metaphor, a "kamikaze . . . going down like a rock."[27] Later that year, the GM board directors gave Stempel the boot, and finally the auto giant had a leader, Jack Smith, who had experience with Japanese methods, and, more to the point, with international competition. Jack Smith announced his first goal was to lose "merely" $100 million in the fourth quarter of 1993. Incredibly, that represented a phenomenal yearlong reversal from the $4.5 billion loss Stempel had reported. Smith hit his goal, and GM a year later was back to making money. In February 1994, GM reported that it had turned an annual profit of $427 million—the first profit since 1989.

Ford, likewise, went through a tough bout in the 1980s but began its turnaround with its radical new, aerodynamically shaped Thunderbird and Taurus models—the latter eventually emerging as the best-selling car in America. Copying Japanese methods that actually originated with W. Edwards Deming in the United States, Ford introduced quality circles to involve all employees and instill "continuous quality" processes. Later, Henry Ford's company, in a difficult internal struggle, concluded it had to have a Mustang—and a new one, at that. As one Ford manager told his boss, he could go to remote rural areas in the South and ask what a Jaguar was (Ford had just purchased the British automaker, Jaguar) and might hear that it's a cat. But if asked what a Mustang was, he would hear it was a Ford. That parable apparently convinced Ford's management to aggressively pursue a new, and ultimately successful, Mustang design.

A totally unexpected development in the auto industry that worked in favor of American manufacturers was the arrival of a "truck culture." Popularized by country and western music, trucks emerged as *the* boom market of the 1990s. In 1995, drivers in sixteen states bought more trucks than cars, and trucks accounted for more than 41 percent of new-vehicle registrations in 1994. GM, which lost money on cars in North America, made a profit on its trucks. Truck popularity was based on more than a sudden interest in pickups: Trucks had lower prices because Washington placed no quotas on Japanese trucks, which caused U.S. truck prices to fall; new safety standards (such as air bags and sidewalls) for autos did not apply to trucks; and new luxury models of trucks made them comfortable. The popularity of trucks was with young people and housewives as a second family car. Meanwhile, the minivan (which appeared in significant numbers in 1984) grew more popular.[28]

Yet even as the minivan, or the larger category of "sport utility vehicles" (SUVs), caught on, environmentalist groups launched a counteroffensive claiming that, among other things, SUVs were "too safe." The larger size and heavier weight of the SUVs meant that, statistically, a person riding in an SUV who had an accident was less likely to die or suffer injury. What under other circumstances would be considered great news for the consumer—that particular cars were especially safe!—was turned on its head by the Sierra Club, which complained that SUVs put drivers of non-SUVs at risk. By 1999, the attack on SUVs was clearly under way on a wide range of fronts, with Vice President Al Gore criticizing the suburban lifestyle and with lawsuits against minivan makers alleging that they tended to roll more easily than other cars. In an almost absurd stroke of irony, the assault on the automobile had come full circle, back to Ralph Nader's unfounded insinuations about the Corvair, that it tended to roll.

At the same time, Japan's auto industry started to sag. Nissan and Mazda, two of Japan's "Big Five" automakers, went into the red. In 1993, Nissan even closed a Japanese factory, a once unthinkable act. The advertising campaign for Nissan's 1997 models did not even show a new car, only the old Datsun 2000, driven by clay-animation "Ken and Barbie"-doll figures. All the Japanese automakers suffered. Car sales in Japan fell 4 percent in 1992, then another 8 percent in 1993, and in 1991 Honda quietly cut 25,000 cars from its production schedule for the U.S. market. Nobuhiko Kawamoto, Sochiro Honda's successor, had the unpleasant task of informing Honda's founder—a bicycle manufacturer who bucked MITI to build autos the Japanese government refused to support—that for the first time in history Japanese dealers would have to offer discounts to sell cars.

Meanwhile, by 1993, U.S. automakers had completely overhauled their structures and productivity. At the NUMMI factory, workers hit alarms that played the Beatles' "Hey Jude" to remind everyone "don't make it bad." The line stopped at the behest of the worker—once an impossibility in an American factory—until the problem was solved. NUMMI's Corollas averaged a mere .65 defects per car, and GM warranty payouts overall fell 42 percent from 1989 to 1993. But the most difficult part of the restructuring was the dramatic reduction in labor forces. As factories improved, it took increasingly fewer workers to make a car. GM's payroll once accounted for almost 600,000 American workers. By 1993 it was below 250,000. To its credit, the post-Roger Smith/Stempel management team exercised any and all options to maintain the loyalty of the UAW employees, including handing out layoff pay to more than 8,300 idled workers in certain plants while hiring temporary labor at other locations to keep up with demand.

That year represented the first time ever that Detroit had leaders at all three major auto companies who had international experience, who recognized the real foreign challenge was to provide quality cars, and who had "horizons that extended beyond the Bloomfield Hills [Michigan] Country Club."[29] At the annual 1994 Preview Night over the preceding decade analysts would disparage American styles and Japanese observers would smirk at the quality of Detroit's products. In 1994, though, the reaction of a Toyota executive aptly summed up the revitalization of the American auto industry: "Serious competition. Serious competition."

Business and the Environment

Environmental regulations, as well as mileage and safety regulations, continued to shape the design of American autos and determine to some extent their profitability. Overall, environmental issues reached a peak in the early 1980s, and after that public attitudes grew less supportive of radical efforts to stop growth. American businesses, however, continued to pay a price.

Air pollution, while still serious in some urban areas, started to abate. By almost any measurable data, pollutants from autos and industry in the air fell steadily from 1978 to 1987. Lead particulates, one of the major targets of the catalytic converter, almost disappeared, falling from 128 million metric tons emitted annually in 1978 to 8 million metric tons in 1987; ozone pollutants fell by 4 million metric tons and carbon monoxide plunged by 16 million metric tons over the same period.[30] Cancer rates had fallen, life expectancy had risen by more than six years for males and females since 1950, and the predictions of environmental disaster had proved completely wrong. Most important, "no-growth" theories had been shown to be anti-environment, with the more prosperous market economies in the world also having the cleanest environments, and there was a clear link between capitalism and cleanliness and socialism and pollution, as the Eastern European nations revealed after the fall of communism.[31]

By the 1980s, though, regulation had proved a costly and inefficient way to gain results, with spending on environmental protection growing from 1.5 percent of GNP in 1979 to 2.6 percent by 1996. Even environmentalists started to admit that a major component missing in the approach was one of cost: Air and water essentially were free to polluters. Consequently, government looked to developing incentives for companies not to pollute, and, more important, to "privatize" pollution so that a bargaining process occurred between the polluters and the receptors of pollution. Companies were allowed to buy, sell, or trade "market pollution permits," initiating a process that put a cost on environmental damage. Under the gradually emerging structure, government had a role in the process of registering pollutants and identifying the sources of pollution, but the actual method of cleanup was left to companies based on their available "permits."[32]

Of course, some businesses stood to benefit from the cleanup effort as well. Environmental repair became a multibillion-dollar business. By 1989, businesses engaged in making equipment to abate or control pollution or in cleaning up oil spills and other damage constituted an $11 billion industry. Phillip Rooney, president of WMX Technologies, a holding company for cleanup firms, noted, "Regulation has been very, very good for business."[33] Work related to the environment accounted for 70,000 private and public companies employing more than one million people. Total revenues for the "environmental industry" to which Rooney referred was $130 billion, and not surprisingly companies such as Rooney's were found in the top contributors to environmental groups, donating an estimated $375,000 to the Audubon Society alone. Yet when discussions of corporate lobbying take place, the environmental industry is seldom mentioned. As Rooney explained, every time environmental regulations got tougher, his company had to hire more people and made more profits.

But for most companies, more was lost than gained by the imposition of unreasonable regulations on growth. With the exception of some of the "cleanup" businesses, virtually every business or industry had started to clash with environmental regulations by 1990: Timber companies encountered protected habitats of the spotted owl; oil drillers met with opposition over new offshore rigs; and thousands of projects were held up due to the EPA's strict regulations on preserving "wetlands." As reports of more absurd restrictions started to reach the public, a growing reaction from consumers as well as business set in.

Regulations and Business

It was not just the environment, however. Businesses were subjected to a blizzard of federal regulations that one author called a "legacy to nightclub comics." Among the rulings by federal agencies, suits heard before courts, or extreme examples of regulatory "overkill":

✦ Simply "annoying" a kangaroo rat could cost as much as $100,000 and a year in jail. Shining a flashlight on the animal was considered annoying.

✦ The FDA demanded that a small herring smokehouse that, in a twenty-year period, had produced 54 million fillets without a single case of reported food poisoning, install $75,000 worth of new equipment. The business closed instead.

✦ A striptease bar in Los Angeles, the Odd Ball Cabaret, had to install a wheelchair ramp into its shower stall used in shows because the lack of a ramp discriminated against strippers who needed a wheelchair.

✦ Burger King was sued by a deaf woman who claimed that the drive-through windows discriminated against deaf people.

✦ A farmer who ran over kangaroo rats with his tractor while plowing his field was descended upon by more than two dozen federal agents in helicopters.

✦ Citicorp Credit Services was sued by a woman whose body odor was so bad that co-workers testified in court that her smell made them sick; one manager claimed he could smell her at a distance of 35 feet.

✦ Obesity, alcoholism, and drug addiction were designated "protected" disabilities by the Equal Employment Opportunity Commission. Likewise, businesses found they faced federal investigation when they attempted to fire employees who had serious mental problems and were violently dangerous to other employees and customers.

Businesses found such rulings distressing and costly. By 1995, federal agencies alone added 200 pages of new rulings and regulations per day in the *Federal Register.* The cost to businesses numbered in the billions of dollars per year, passed on to consumers in higher prices or reflected in lower productivity by American firms.[34] Regulatory costs ate up as much as 10 percent of the GDP per year in the 1990s, much of it comprised of paperwork. Individuals seldom noticed the hidden cost of regulations, but by 1996 federal regulatory mandates alone cost each American household $6,083.[35]

The area that threatened to put individuals and government regulations on a collision course, however, was health care. Pharmeceutical companies, whose long-term profitability rested on the development of new drugs, were hamstrung by the federal government, especially the FDA, to the extent that although they routinely discovered new medicines, those medicines were kept off the shelves by a torrent of regulations. As Robert Higgs glumly commented, "We have here a paradox, a government agency created and maintained to protect the public health, yet one whose actual operations have the opposite effect, causing enormous harm to the public health—not to speak of its other pernicious effects, including a far-reaching suppression of liberty."[36] All individuals needing medical treatment, and particularly those who could benefit from the rapid development of new cures, such as AIDS patients, paid the price for this overregulation. So did the health-care industry.[37] Other regulations routinely reduced medical services or made them more expensive; in states that prohibit advertising by optometrists, eyeglasses are more expensive; and in states with restrictions on paradentals, there are fewer dental assistants, keeping the prices of dental work (for routine teeth cleaning, for example) higher.

Pharmaceutical companies especially have suffered government's wrath. Targeted as villains during the health-care scare of 1993–94, drug companies actually have increased R and D on new drugs, but the time needed for them from the FDA approval rose from a few years in the 1960s to six years in the 1970s to more than eight years and rising in the 1990s. Worse still, in its efforts to protect the public from excessive claims of bodybuilding-type muscle enhancement drugs, FDA director David Kessler attempted to insert language into legislation that would have required patients to obtain a doctor's prescription to *purchase vitamin C and nonmedicinal herbal drugs, including some teas!* A groundswell of opposition killed the legislation, but it indicated the almost unlimited powers over the market, not to mention people's lives, that the FDA could wield. The FDA, meanwhile, moved on to attack the tobacco companies and teen smoking—in the midst of a new heroin and cocaine epidemic among teenagers.

The Devastation of the Defense Industry

At the end of the 1970s, continued aggression by the Soviet Union in Afghanistan and by its proxies in Angola and Nicaragua, combined with its astounding buildup of heavy "silo-buster" SS-18 and SS-19 missiles, forced the United States to increase defense spending. Military expenditures as a percent of GNP had fallen from a Vietnam-era high of just under 10 percent in 1972 to 5 percent in 1980. That decline accelerated a long-term drop after World War II in which defense spending dropped from almost 14 percent of GNP in 1952.

Part of the decline came as a result of retrenchment after the Vietnam War, but other cutbacks had occurred as a result of treaty limitations and administration policy decisions. For example, the Carter administration canceled the B-1 bomber, shelved the MX missile, and terminated work on the anti–ballistic missile system. Defense contractors struggled to maintain industrial readiness and qualified workforces in the face of steadily diminishing contracts. They sought to rely less on Pentagon business, but most had a difficult time converting to civilian work. At General Dynamics (GD) top management in the late 1970s expressed an objective to expand its civilian work "as a hedge against the fluctuations of the defense market."[38] Yet by 1985 GD had a *larger* share of its sales (88 percent) dedicated to defense.

Defense contractors, who built mainly weapons, had a difficult task in trying to develop a new civilian product. Consider Lockheed, with its L-1011 civilian jet. The company had to reserve extensive resources for the project yet had no other civilian aircraft on the market upon which the company could depend if the L-1011 flopped. A modest success, it did not achieve the same market share as the McDonnell Douglas DC-10 or Boeing 747. Boeing, on the other hand, had several jets on the market. Despite considerable investment in the 747, the company could still rely on its 737, and then newer 757 and 767 jets to compete if the 747 did not meet its goals.

McDonnell Douglas Aircraft Company (MD) typified the efforts of military and civilian aerospace companies to diversify in the cold war period. When McDonnell and Douglas merged in 1967, aircraft manufacturers employed 850,000 workers. Although the merged company— by 1992 the largest defense contractor in the world—had no trouble winning military contracts, it did have trouble staying profitable. In 1989, as MD neared the number one position as recipient of defense business, the company announced layoffs of 17,000 personnel, and its return on assets was the lowest of any major aerospace contractor except for General Dynamics. In 1990, the company forced 5,000 mid-level managers to resign their titles and to compete for half that number of jobs. The company had the highest debt-to-equity ratio of all the major defense contractors. Over the subsequent two years, the company doubled its profits to $423 million but still searched for ways to move into civilian and commercial work. There, it met powerful foreign competition, especially from the European Airbus consortium that offered a challenge to the MD-80 aircraft on which MD had placed its hopes for new sales.

As a whole, however, the defense industry witnessed sharp cutbacks; while the nominal defense budget appeared to rise—from $81 billion in 1970 to $296 billion in 1990—in real terms, as a share of GNP, defense spending actually *fell* by 4 percent during that period. It is accurate to suggest, as one analyst does, that on the whole the post-cold war drawdown was relatively mild compared to other postwar decreases in the so-called military-industrial complex.[39] But the drawdown had especially harmful effects on some regions more than others, just as the buildup had favored some parts of the country over others. California and Texas, havens for the aerospace firms, were particularly hard hit.

Companies lost crucial contracts that represented the majority of their business, as in the case of Grumman, whose production of the popular F-14 Tomcat fighter was almost ended in the late 1980s in favor of the new AX. As matters developed, the navy canceled the AX and Grumman hung on. General Dynamics showed a $639 million loss in 1990 and had the worst return on equity of any of the nine major aerospace contractors. GD attempted to move out of aerospace by selling its fighter production program, mostly focused on the F-16 Fighting Falcon, to Lockheed Corporation. And Lockheed, which had $9 billion in sales, had a recent success in the production of the famous F-117

Stealth fighter, effectively used in the Gulf War. In March 1995, Lockheed and Martin-Marietta announced a merger, with the new company called Lockheed Martin. Lockheed absorbed the General Dynamics fighter production facility, but otherwise the company intended to lay off 35,000 employees over a five-year period.[40] Only Boeing, with its $30 billion in sales and its twenty-year backlog in orders, was immune to the defense reductions.

By 1990, most of the major airframe and propulsion contractors had concluded that they had to form consortia or teams to survive. On the one hand, that improved the chances of the companies surviving, but on the other hand it defeated the intent of the competitive bid contracts. Nevertheless, the armed forces and the contractors concluded that they had to embrace the consortium concept to maintain the defense industrial base. In the case of the Advanced Tactical Fighter (ATF), a Lockheed-led team won the competition over a rival multi-company team; and in the case of the National Aerospace Plane—since canceled—a five-company team of MD, GD, Rockwell, Rocketdyne, and Pratt & Whitney received a contract to build an 18,000-mile-per-hour aircraft. The Light Helicopter Experimental (LHX) team of Boeing and Sikorsky, plus the team of Allison and Garrett, which was producing an engine, suggested that consortia were the wave of the future in defense contracting. Critics correctly argued that such an approach was not in keeping with "free market" competitiveness; the fact is that the defense sector has never been fully competitive, and research has shown that occasionally attempts to introduce competitiveness into the process have produced more costly weapons.[41]

In the case of the navy, with its aircraft carriers and submarines, only two major shipyards could build nuclear submarines. That placed substantial pressure on both the navy to keep its yards happy and on the yards, which had to perform well enough to ensure a steady flow of contracts. If either contractor faced a lull in contract awards, it could mean sudden death for either of the two major shipbuilders, Electric Boat or Newport News. Consequently, the navy stepped lightly in its claims of misconduct or unacceptable contract performance. While the government had to insist on acceptable contract performance, it also understood that to attack one or the other risked eliminating one-half of the nation's ship construction capability.[42] On the other hand, the influence of arms manufacturers has most likely been overstated. One study of the U.S. strategic bomber program since World War II found that in all but two of the post–World War II bomber programs, industry lobbying had little impact on the decision to purchase the aircraft.[43] While the "military-industrial complex" remained a target for critics of business, a more subtle antibusiness culture surfaced in the media during the late 1960s and intensified during the 1970s and 1980s.

A Clash of Cultures: Media vs. Business Elites

Business's image, especially when depicted through television or motion pictures, had grown consistently darker. Increasingly, business was portrayed as the enemy of the environment and consumer safety, and entrepreneurs were characterized as greedy or inept. By the 1970s, most of the print and mainstream television outlets had adopted a hostile view of industry and capitalists.

In 1981, Linda Lichter, Robert Lichter, and Stanley Rothman of the Media Institute studied eight weeks of prime-time television programming, including dramas, situation comedies, and adventure shows from the 1979–80 and 1980–81 television seasons. The study found that of the 226 businessmen portrayed on television, more than 60 percent were portrayed as criminals. Of those businessmen who were not engaged in illegal activities, the remainder were shown as incompetents or fools. In short, as the study concluded, television portrayed business people almost universally as "crooks, con-men or clowns."[44] Moreover, the further "up the ladder" an executive had moved, the more likely the media depicted him as a "bad guy"—74 percent were portrayed negatively. When a character was a "good guy" in the business world, he or she was extremely unorthodox or unusual, or, in other words, not a "real" businessman or woman. Consider Shirley, the heroine of *One in a Million,* a former cab driver who "inherits" a large corporation. The plots pitted Shirley, who as chief executive officer still lived with her parents and socialized with her cabbie friends, against a pompous, rigid snob of an executive: a typical "establishment" businessman. Or consider Jonathan Hart in *Hart to Hart.* Robert Wagner played Hart, a millionaire who did good deeds and solved crimes. But the show dealt almost exclusively with Hart's role as a private investigator, and there was no mention of how he made a living.

Defenders of the media contended that the media itself was a business and only reacted to public tastes. But later work on the motion picture industry by Michael Medved has challenged that view. Medved found that while motion pictures that were rated G enjoyed excellent box office performance, movie makers opted whenever possible for material that was PG-13 or even R.[45] In the area of religion, for example, television shows virtually never portrayed characters attending church, despite surveys that showed a large majority of Americans attended church regularly. Medved contended that the media—both television and motion pictures—whatever their profit orientation, nevertheless willingly absorbed certain market losses to appeal to elites. And television "news" programs were even worse, with documented cases of so-called exposés in which producers faked tests on pickup trucks (to get them to explode), infiltrated grocery stores with "undercover" employees to persuade genuine employees to engage in unsafe food-handling practices, and flatly made up characters, events, and places for stories that fit their worldview. In the 1990s alone, several leading news organizations, including the *Boston Globe,* the *Cincinnati Inquirer,* the *Washington Post,* and Cable News Network (CNN) all issued embarrassing retractions about falsified stories, usually involving business.

Movies were less kind to business than television. Corporate killers were behind every assassination (except for those few carried out by the CIA), every act of pollution (Steven Seagal's *On Deadly Ground* or Charlie Sheen's *The Arrival,* where even alien invaders find they can manipulate businesses to pollute!), or every assault on the animal kingdom (any *Free Willie* movie). Corporate creeps in film have tried to conceal remarkable breakthroughs in fuel efficiency (*The Formula* with George C. Scott), steal billions of dollars through computer fraud (*Hackers, Weekend at Bernie's*), cheat at small-town sporting events (*Diggstown*), endanger entire space operations by protecting alien killing machines (*Alien, Aliens*), or deliberately encourage unsafe ship operations (*Titanic*). Executives—usually men, but not always—are heartless, cruel, and stupid (as with Dabney Coleman in *Nine to Five*), while entrepreneurs are so busy making money they have no room for people (Eddie Murphy's female boss in *Boomerang* or the entrepreneur in *Waiting to Exhale*). Wherever "corporate types" are involved, no possible good can occur, as shown in *Twister* or *Contact,* where the scientists who have corporate sponsors are depicted as incapable of making a contribution to science for that reason. Even when Francis Ford Coppola made a movie celebrating an entrepreneur, *Tucker: the Man and His Dream,* he chose a subject who employed only a handful of people and who was unable to make a single marketable product or ever turn a profit, all the while portraying the evil auto companies as the villains at a time when they employed thousands and gave millions the freedom of cheap transportation.

A recent analysis of media elites by Stanley Rothman and Robert Lichter studied 240 journalists at America's most influential media institutions, such as the *New York Times,* the *Washington Post,* the *Wall Street Journal, Time, Newsweek,* and the major television networks, and 216 executives in management of major corporations. Rothman and Lichter concluded that the media elite "grew up at some distance from the social and cultural traditions of small town 'middle America,'" and that on attitudinal questions were strongly antibusiness. Almost one-half thought the government should guarantee a job to everyone who wanted to work. Perhaps most tellingly, when asked "Who should rule?" the media elites chose themselves![46] The divisions were deep between the two groups: When presented with hypothetical scenarios, media elites much more frequently than business elites interpreted situations in such a way as to suggest hostility to authority and economic success.

Not only did the media resent business, but a second group looked disparagingly at the new entrepreneurs. Displaced upper classes—the "patrician rich" of yesteryear, or what Gilder called "the declining rich"—saw the surging business class as a threat to their once secure social position.[47] Like Sam Walton, many of the members of the new entrepreneurial wave came from distinctly nonelite areas such as Bentonville, Arkansas; Boise, Idaho; Phoenix, Arizona; or Charlotte, North Carolina. Unlike the wealthy political families, such as the Rockefellers and Kennedys, the new rich, like Ken Iverson, were accessible by a single telephone call, working in a nondescript office with one secretary. They frequented Burger King and the Waffle House on Main Street more often than they did Spago's in Beverly Hills or the Four Seasons in New York City; drove pickups and Chevy Camaros rather than Rolls-Royces and Ferraris; and vacationed at Disney World or Las Vegas instead of the Hamptons or Nassau.

As they rose, through video rental businesses like Blockbuster, computer-language companies like Microsoft, or hamburger chains like McDonald's, the new entrepreneurs embraced risks—which the "declining rich" avoided. Instead, the declining rich chose to work in law, politics, universities, or the nonprofit sector as they struggled to maintain their families' declining fortunes. Consider the Kennedys, whose wealth for decades was cemented by Joseph P. Kennedy's willingness to plunge into the stock market at its lowest point, but whose siblings and grandchildren have abdicated the business sector in favor of law and politics, eschewing the difficult path to re-create the patriarch's financial success. In 1995, the family sold one of the last vestiges of its privileged position—the Palm Beach mansion—and even the Rockefellers, unable to sustain their manorial estates, turned some of them over to the National Trust for Historic Preservation.

A third source of antipathy toward business resided in government. By nature, many who enter public service, especially many bureaucrats, do so because of the security and, in some cases, the power it provides. From the relative safety of government agencies, public servants tend to lose touch with the risks and responsibilities faced by entrepreneurs on a daily basis, especially if they are employed by the federal government in Washington. On the contrary, bureaucrats, often with good intentions, assume that regulations can force employers and employees to act in certain ways, and they seldom seem to deduce that costs levied on business owners (whether through "mandatory" insurance, minimum wages, or regulations) will not usually be borne by the entrepreneur, but passed on to consumers, stockholders, and employees.

Finally, college students increasingly pursued careers in law, medicine, or university teaching, disdaining real entrepreneurship as "tasteless" or less enabling. Business school enrollments, while continuing to increase, often reflected the opportunity to obtain jobs in midlevel management. Few students display an interest in creating their own company or marketing their own product. Meanwhile, public officials call for "voluntary" national service, implying that starting and running a business that employs people and generates tax revenues is somehow not "worthy" of encouragement. Thus, entrepreneurs in American culture have been ignored—if they were lucky—or criticized directly as the cause of a variety of social ills but seldom praised for generating wealth. Bill Gates, we are reminded, must "give back" to society, as if the jobs, wealth created, and taxes paid alone were not enough return! Even the sudden burst of entrepreneurship courses that appeared in the curricula of business schools did not portray entrepreneurs in an appropriate way, because they often give the impression that entrepreneurship was merely a technique to be learned rather than a need perceived, a demand filled, or a vision lived.

Small Businesses, Growing Businesses

If most entrepreneurs did not come from the "established classes," where did they come from? Obviously, they had not disappeared. Indeed, the quickest way to wealth in America remained business. Even more important, entrepreneurship remained virtually the only path to riches open to ordinary citizens who were minorities. The 1996 *Forbes 400,* for example, featured twenty-three immigrants and sixty women, with women falling off the list rapidly as the "old wealth" disappeared (such as Mary Malone, an inheritor of the Campbell Soup fortune) and new, truly entrepreneurial females with their own wealth, such as Oprah Winfrey, replaced them.[48] But while many entrepreneurs saw their efforts result in phenomenal growth, as with Bill Gates or Sam Walton, most business start-ups remained small.

The revival of small business, declared dead as an independent force by John Kenneth Galbraith in his 1971 book *The New Industrial State,* more than offset the decline in employment by the large corporations. Between 1974 and 1984, for example, employment in *Fortune*'s 500 largest companies fell by 1.5 million while net employment in small business, under a variety of definitions, rose. In the 1980s, the phenomenon of small business employment growth accelerated, as the United States created 20 million new jobs, over three-fifths of them generated by independent small businesses with under 500 employees. Record-level start-ups, which had accelerated during the 1980s, allowed 9.5 percent of the workforce to be their own bosses. As early as 1981, Governor Richard Lamm of Colorado announced that "there is a tidal wave behind me. Its name is small business. Any politician who does not look over his shoulder at that wave will be a politician out of a job."[49]

Even the statistics, however, presented an inaccurate picture of the extent of small business's influence on the economy. As one authority on small business pointed out, "Hundreds [of the 3,000 largest corporations] are in reality large small businesses still run by their founders or family heirs."[50] Consider our earlier example of Sam Walton and his family business: Is Wal-Mart a "big business" run as a "small business," or vice versa? More to the point, the goal of small business is to grow, and if successful, *any* small business will grow into a big business. Those lamenting the demise of "mom-and-pop" stores in downtown areas miss the essential dynamism at work in which mom and pop become Sam Waltons through growth and talent.

As small firms grow, they become attractive targets for acquisition by larger companies. During the 1970s, for example, 2,000 to 5,000 publicly announced mergers with a value of more than $500,000 occurred, of which 95 percent involved small companies.[51] Growth among small firms also led to an explosion of incorporations. Small business drove a corporate expansion of 20 percent a year, totaling more than 650,000 new incorporations since the mid-1980s. Although all of those were not true businesses—some were simply tax dodges or were created for other legal purposes—corporate and noncorporate start-ups represented $70 billion in new business investments per year. At the same time, businesses also fail, and 400,000 corporations end their operations every year, although most terminations represent the retirement of the principal owner.

Static assessments of the American economy, using supply-demand curves, failed to capture the revolution in productivity that small business had sparked. Between 1974 and 1984, the U.S. economy grew by 20 million net new jobs, and at the same time accepted 12 million immigrants. Meanwhile, the European Economic Community (now the European Union, or EU) generated no—zero—net new jobs during the decade. The U.S. rate also exceeded Japan's new job growth by a factor of three. American manufacturing held firm at 48 percent, but Europe lost 10 percent of its manufacturing jobs. Since most of that U.S. job growth came from small business, which counted large numbers of immigrants, the numbers were skewed further as Taiwanese, Koreans, Vietnamese, Mexicans, Cubans, and people from scores of other nations surged into the United States creating restaurants, laundries, computer stores, video outlets, software businesses, and grocery stores. Usually, they capitalized their stores with savings and the labor of their families, much of which went unreported in the national wealth and income statistics, but nevertheless was real. In the flight from the Castro regime in the 1960s, over 200,000 Cubans arrived in Florida in less than two years. Doctors, architects, and lawyers escaped to work as busboys or dishwashers in America, while less educated laborers took what they could get. By 1987, the busboys and waitresses had created more than 25,000 Cuban-owned businesses in Dade County alone. A typical entrepreneur, Jose Pinero, peddled secondhand records until he could afford to refurbish a small shop. His record store, called Ultra, catered to Latin customers with the most recent imports. Soon he had expanded his Ultra stores into new shopping malls, and he built a warehouse that imported from throughout the Caribbean and Latin America.[52]

But the Cuban, Vietnamese, and West Indian immigration that generated the new boom was nothing new in American history. Consider Nathan Handwerker and Ida Greenwald, two Polish immigrants who worked in Coney Island restaurants. A pair of singing waiters named Jimmy Durante and Eddie Cantor suggested that the couple—who wed in 1913—start their own frankfurter stand. Using their $300 life savings, Nathan and Ida used a secret spice recipe to fashion a tasty hot dog that became the company's trademark and to establish Nathan's in 1916. Seventy-five years later, Nathan's was one of the best-known hot dog businesses in the United States.

Nathan's illustrated the first reality of most new businesses: They did not originate with a bank loan or government support. And, like most other businesses, Nathan's embodied two other significant realities. First, small business had to use labor, but since family labor is not recognized in official ways (such as Social Security, FICA, and so on), the wealth those businesses generated often went unreported or underreported. Nevertheless, of those statistics we do have, since World War II, families with zero assets based on traditional accounting measurements have generated billions of dollars in net value when measured in other ways. Consider entrepreneurs such as Michael Zabian, a Lebanese from Lee, Massachusetts, who toiled to bring produce from farm areas of Massachusetts and Connecticut to the Lee area, eventually parlaying that labor-intensive business into a network of clothing, office, and retail stores; or Jerry Colangelo, an Italian from the Chicago streets who ran a sports clothing business until he got an opportunity to work with the Chicago Bulls, only to work his way into the position of general manager, then owner, of the Phoenix Suns basketball team and Arizona Diamondbacks baseball team. These men typified the process of scaling the heights of achievement with virtually nothing.[53] In each case, labor capitalized the business.

Colangelo worked selling sweatshirts for a small Illinois firm, then spent two years with the Chicago Bulls, where he demonstrated such promise that the newly christened Phoenix Suns basketball team named him general manager in 1968, making him the youngest GM in the league. As Colangelo recalled, "I arrived in Phoenix with seven suitcases, three kids, no furniture, no car, and a couple of hundred bucks in my pocket."[54] Colangelo put in twelve-hour days, negotiated contracts, oversaw public relations, and even coached the team for one very successful season, eventually bringing his son into the organization. Critics rightly maintained that he foisted some of the costs of the 19,000-seat America West Arena ($110 million) and the new Bank One Ballpark for the Diamondbacks (with the domed stadium costing more than an open stadium, $300 million) onto the taxpayers of Phoenix. He also managed to come up with more than $63 million for the former facility and $66 million for the latter on his own. Providing the city with professional basketball, baseball, and, in 1996, hockey, when the Winnipeg Jets, (renamed the Coyotes) moved to town, would have been sufficient return to the community. But Colangelo did more, bailing out the troubled Phoenix Symphony Orchestra with a $400,000 telephone fund-raiser. He routinely hired former players in executive positions in the Suns/America West organization, including Connie Hawkins, Dick Van Arsdale, and Alvan Adams, and once made good on a new contract offer of $40 million to Danny Manning even after the forward blew out his knee in midseason.

Many entrepreneurs, and some of their family members, have been labeled "workaholics." Lebanese businesses were open, on average, 16 to 18 hours a day, while a study of Koreans in Atlanta showed that they worked an average of sixty hours a week in their stores.[55] The owner's personal presence on the scene ensured quality control and business relations that half a dozen hired employees might not provide. More important, hard work is absolutely critical to economic improvement. Studies from the Institute on Poverty based on work-effort levels outside the home have concluded that to improve in one's economic class, a person must work harder than those already in it. By the 1980s, the poor in America—by the same index—worked less, for fewer hours a week, even after correcting the data for age, education, and other credentials, than previous groups in poverty.[56] Indeed the National Bureau of Economic Research found that the presence of programs such as AFDC (Aid to Families with Dependent Children, frequently generalized as "welfare") drove down labor-force participation. One NBER study found that labor participation would increase forty-seven hours a month for husbands and thirty-two hours a month for wives without such programs. The unfortunate conclusion of the government's own study was that welfare recipients "cannot find entry-level employment that pays much better than the government subsidies to nonemployment" after considering the effect of taxes and work-related expenses.[57]

A second reality of new or growing businesses, also involving families, stands in sharp contrast to common perceptions. It is still widely believed that the only route to business success comes through inheriting assets. As seen in our numerous case studies throughout this book—Nathan's is an example—virtually none of the truly successful entrepreneurs received any substantial inheritance. But studies of male supermillionaires—unlike women, who often are inheritors—revealed that by 1978 only one-third had inherited a significant portion of their money; in the second tier ($2 million net worth, [1979 dollars]), 71 percent reported no inherited assets at all. Moreover, in 1996, one in nine members of the *Forbes 400* were new to the list, and since 1990, 238 new members had displaced an equal number of others. As *Forbes* itself commented, "Forget old money. Forget silver spoons. Great fortunes are being created almost monthly in the U.S. today by young entrepreneurs who hadn't a dime when we created this list 14 years ago."[58]

A recent, extensive study of more than 1,100 millionaires by Thomas Stanley and William Danko, fittingly called *The Millionaire Next Door,* found that *"Eighty percent of America's millionaires are first-generation rich"* (emphasis in original).[59] More impressive, over half of America's millionaires never received a penny in inheritance, while fewer than 20 percent inherited even 10 percent of their wealth, living, in disproportionate numbers to less wealthy earners, below their means. Most never paid more than $30,000 for an auto (and nearly one-third drove cars two years old or older), or never bought a suit of clothes that cost more than $300! Such frugality allowed them to plow more capital back into their businesses.

Starting with no inheritance, using money borrowed from family or friends, and working extensive hours, all made for a difficult life for most entrepreneurs, at least in the beginning of their enterprise. Sacrifices were made, and perhaps such sacrifices should guarantee success. But they never have: Two-thirds of all new businesses in America fail within five years. Many entrepreneurs who failed once, or even twice, never quit. Thomas Edison tried more than 2,000 experiments before he got his lightbulb to work, and writer Louis L'Amour, author of more than 100 western novels with 200 million copies in print, received 350 rejections before his first publication. Radio personality/entrepreneur Rush Limbaugh declared bankruptcy and was fired three times before creating the most popular radio talk show in history. Indeed, failure and destitution often provide the crucial prod to motivate an individual to success. Actor Sylvester Stallone, with the screenplay for *Rocky* in his hands, lived in an apartment without electricity until he could sell his story with himself as the lead. Forest Mars, after one bankruptcy, failed in two other ventures. He then entered the candy market, making a fortune in the process. That stubborn refusal to quit marked the careers of some of the most famous success stories in America, business or otherwise: Elvis Presley was fired from the Grand Ole Opry after one performance, and Lucille Ball was told by the instructor of her drama school, "Try any other profession. Any other."

To an entrepreneur, failure was never final, risk-taking was essential. Jerry Jones worked in his parents' Little Rock, Arkansas, grocery store, went to the University of Arkansas on a football scholarship, and sold anything and everything, including buying student football game tickets for $1 and reselling them for $20. After college, he started working in the oil fields, investing in drilling operations and taking chances no one else would take. He focused on areas where others had failed, hitting on thirty-three of thirty-four wells. In 1989, he purchased the Dallas Cowboys for $140 million, when experts said the franchise was worth only $120 million. By 1998, as the most valuable sports franchise in the world, the Cowboys were valued at over $200 million. Through it all, he worked hard, maintaining twenty-hour days on occasion, but he could relax from time to time by looking at the three Super Bowl trophies Dallas had collected under his ownership.[60]

If hard work was critical, inherited wealth often stood as an impediment to business success. The only part of Howard Hughes's empire that flourished was the aircraft and tool division, which Hughes perceptively declined to touch. Otherwise, he squandered his inheritance on movies that almost never made a profit, radio stations that languished, hotels that crumbled, and a jungle of corporate bureaus that fed Hughes's ego and concealed his codeine addiction. Scores of other wealthy scions who inherited had similar, if not quite as dreadful, stories as did Hughes. Gordon Getty was more interested in playing music than in finding oil. Neither Walt Disney's daughter or son-in-law, Ron Miller, could maintain the Disney studios or theme parks with any imagination.[61]

Business, and particularly small business, not only represented the major avenue to achievement by the owners, but it constituted a source of employment for millions of workers and was the single most significant employer of minorities. Four-fifths of minorities by 1980 held jobs in small companies. Because small firms tended to be more labor intensive and experienced more rapid net increases in capital value than the giants, they hired workers in ever expanding numbers. Most important, however, small businesses often gave workers their first jobs, providing crucial training in "real-life" employment that teaches employees—usually young people—to arrive on time, well groomed, and to take on tasks that are not immediately pointed out to them. Often derided as "minimum wage, dead end" jobs, in fact small business positions ensure success in more long-term, career-oriented jobs. Nor were critics correct in arguing that there was any particular surge in part-time jobs, especially by those who had other options.

FIGURE 12-1   *Part-Time Employment: All Workers*

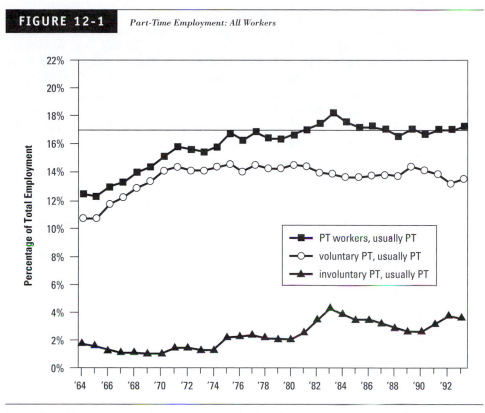

Source: From Alec R. Levenson, "New Evidence on the Growth in Part-Time Employment," *Jobs & Capital.* (Santa Monica, Calif.: The Milken Institute), 3 (Fall 1994): 7–8, chart on p. 8. Reprinted by permission of the Milken Institute.

A 1994 study showed that "there has not been a huge increase in part-time employment throughout the 1980s and early 1990s" and that the number of involuntary part-time workers (i.e., those forced into part-time labor due to hard economic conditions) actually *fell* between 1982 and 1992 (see Figure 12.1).[62]

Fast-food franchises, which in the strict sense are part of big business but to franchisees are the epitome of small business, play a particularly vital role in job training. McDonald's, astoundingly, has given employment to one out of fifteen first-time job seekers in recent years! Approximately 75 percent of McDonald's owners are franchisees, but virtually all of them can look not only at Ray Kroc but at other employees who made good. Michael Quinlan, president and CEO of McDonald's, began as a mailroom clerk with the company; Fred Turner, chairman of the board in 1989, was a door-to-door salesman who started as a "burger flipper" at age twenty-three; Ed Rensi, president of McDonald's USA, dropped out of Ohio State to hustle fries; and more than 50 percent of the store managers started behind the counter.[63] Women made up half of the store managers nationally (at an average salary of $28,000) and McDonald's was the largest employer of black youth in the United States. A 1984 survey by the National Institute for Work reported that minorities made greater skill gains than other groups at fast-food restaurants, illustrated by the fact that *Black Enterprise* magazine ranked McDonald's as one of the fifty best places for blacks to work, with blacks accounting for 17 percent of the management force.[64]

As significant as was the creation of new businesses and jobs in restaurants, laundries, auto shops, landscaping, artistic design, and a host of other businesses, it paled by comparison to the dynamic entrepreneurial upheaval of the 1980s in the computer industry, most of which considered itself "small business." In the mid-1980s, the personal computer (PC) reached a watershed point when some 100 PCs, wired together, beat a Cray supercomputer in a game of chess. That demonstration heralded the arrival of PCs that contained all the computing capabilities of machines once available only to the Pentagon and the largest corporations in America. It also reflected the fact that the computer industry would have the most wide-ranging effects on all business operations and productivity of any device since the steam engine.

Computers, Fiber Optics, and Junk Bonds

A remarkable symbiotic relationship developed in the 1980s between the telephone and computer industries. Devices called modems allowed personal computers to be connected, through phone lines, to other computers and databases. For all practical purposes, an individual with a modem (invented at Bell Labs in 1958) and enough expertise (aided by the right passwords) could gain access to any database in the world. Immense prospects for individuals who wanted liberation from the workplace allowing workers to literally "phone in" certain types of work from their homes or off-site offices. But that scratched the surface of the real revolution. A more complete understanding of the phenomenal, truly revolutionary changes that overtook American business in the 1980s and 1990s requires a historical foundation in several industries. Perhaps the best place to start is with telephones.

At the high tide of deregulation for most industries, the Justice Department brought an antitrust suit against AT&T in 1974, charging that the company had monopolized telecommunications markets. The new round of charges had developed out of the appearance of MCI Communications, a microwave communications firm under the leadership of William McGowen, and his constant prompting of the Justice

Department to end the Bell monopoly. It also had roots in a corporate shift in economic theory that "applauded vertical, not horizontal, integration."[65] The assistant attorney-general wanted a divestiture that indeed produced unsubsidized competition; he wanted the unregulated portions of the business separated from the regulated, protected elements. In 1982, AT&T signed a consent decree to divest itself of its regional Bell systems, and subsequently the regional corporations, known as "Baby Bells," split off into independent entities.[66] Ameritech, headquartered in Chicago, took most of the Midwest; Bell Atlantic in Philadelphia had the region of New Jersey, Pennsylvania, Delaware, Maryland, and Virginia; Bell South in Atlanta had the remaining southern region; Nynex was the New York City region's headquarters with coverage of New York and New England; Pacific Telesis (San Francisco) covered California and Nevada; Southwestern Bell, out of St. Louis, took Arkansas, Texas, Oklahoma, Kansas, and Missouri; and U.S. West provided service for the remainder of the Southwest and Plains states from Englewood, Colorado. Under the new agreement, a division of territory occurred in which the Baby Bells could provide local service but had to stay out of long-distance telephone operations. More important, perhaps, they were prohibited from manufacturing telephone equipment. A new creation, AT&T Network Systems, took the place of Western Electric to supply equipment. AT&T also created other subsidiary systems to handle new high-technology markets.[67]

Breaking up Bell involved many of the same arguments used against the railroads. Important rate differences existed between long-distance service and local service, with the former subsidizing the latter. After the breakup, costs had to be recovered from the service offered.[68] That forced AT&T to regain its competitiveness; the company had become "bovine: the great all-American cash cow to be milked and massaged," dispensing a reliable flow of dividends in its protected environment.[69] Despite the fact that the transistor and the laser both had been invented at Bell Labs, the company had not invested aggressively or embraced new technology. That was especially true in the case of fiber optics, to which the Labs had also contributed. FCC rules had added to AT&T's lethargy, making the company depreciate telephone equipment over periods as long as fifty years. Moreover, AT&T had made use of a system in which wires were cheap and switches were expensive. Consequently, the system composed a top-down pyramid in which wires ran from every household to switches at a central office that served up to 15,000 phones. Where operators once plugged patch cords into switchboards at central offices, followed by the appearance of magnetically controlled switches, by the 1980s they had been replaced by expensive computers.

Meanwhile, as technological issues resolved themselves, the breakup brought down long-distance charges steeply, often by as much as 30 percent. The long-distance market grew highly competitive, especially since the mid-1970s, when regulators allowed companies such as MCI to connect through Bell's local systems. Despite the competition, AT&T had the consumer-friendly "1+area code" service.[70] After the breakup, telephone users selected one of several long-distance services on an individual, citywide basis. A free-for-all of price strategies, heavy advertising, and even telemarketing by the phone companies themselves ensued, causing prices to plummet but temporarily antagonizing customers to all phone companies.

As the telephone drama played out, computers and communications seemed a natural fit. International Telephone and Telegraph (ITT) attempted to enter the computer market by acquiring Dayton, Ohio-based NCR. But in 1995, after a few years of trying to fit the computer company into the communications business, ITT announced one of the largest corporate breakups ever, splitting off the computer division and the entertainment division that owned the Sheraton hotel chain, Caesar's World casino, and the New York Knicks basketball team.

ITT's failure notwithstanding, meshing the new Internet and computer technology with a telephone infrastructure still offered vast possibilities—the forging of a "telecosm," a melding of the computer revolution to communications. It promised nothing short of a fundamental reordering of the communications structure. Most obviously, plummeting chip prices made computers themselves simultaneously more powerful yet less expensive. The most important economic fact of life was that the price of computer chips had fallen from $7 in 1956 to one ten-thousandth of a cent in the 1980s, pulling prices of PCs down and resulting in the installation of 50 million PCs (half the world's total) in American homes and worksites. Prices fell so fast that within seven years, any computer function would expand in power by a factor of 10, while costs would fall by more than 10 times. That reordering of the communications world made the old Bell system of many wires and few switches obsolete. Suddenly, it made more sense to have fewer wires and more switches, because simultaneously the fiber-optic revolution made wire capable of carrying higher levels of information than copper wire. In such a structure, the "intelligence" of the system would move from large, centralized locations to homes and offices through switching systems in phones and computer faxes.

Fiber-optic silicon-glass wire became available by 1978. Glass proved immune to corrosion and lightning and had all the reliability and durability of copper. But AT&T expressed reluctance to move into the new glass wire, with good reason. As the industry leader, it had a global base of copper wire and microwave systems. It took a new company, with everything to gain and little to lose, to embrace the new technology. The opportunity came from the consent decree that had opened the door for MCI to move into the market. William McGowan, MCI's president, recognized the possibilities for fiber-optic telecommunications, especially since his company had used microwave technology. The network of fiber-optic wires would cost upwards of $3 billion, well above what MCI, with its $230 million in revenues, could raise. But the savior of the American telecommunications industry had arrived in the form of an unorthodox bond broker from Drexel Burnham Lambert, Michael Milken.

During the 1970s, Milken had refined—although everyone agrees he did not invent—the high-yield, high-risk securities called "junk bonds." Traditional Wall Street investment banks had ranked, or graded, the bonds of businesses, with AAA being the best. Most companies, and certainly the vast majority of new, rapidly rising firms, could not obtain a AAA rating, while numerous corporations, and more than a few nations, on the verge of collapse still had AAA ratings on their bonds. Milken made an "end-run" around the system, offering new, ungraded securities for companies unable to obtain investment support from the traditional investment banks. Of course, Charles Merrill had begun his career selling junk bonds, and the notion that junk bonds were inherently fragile or weak was, in the words of management guru Tom Peters, "baloney . . . . [J]unk bond financed companies are creating jobs at four times the average rate for the economy as a whole . . . [and] have a third greater productivity, 50 percent greater growth in sales and about three times faster growth in capital spending."[71] Michael Jensen correctly noted that, junk bonds meant the "eclipse" of the public corporation by taking capital out of the hands of Wall Street elites and democratizing it, while Glenn Yago credited junk bonds with nothing short of restructuring corporate America.[72]

Milken saw junk bonds as the currency of fast-rising companies whose bond ratings had not caught up to them. In MCI, Milken perceived that the company had an ocean of "uncapitalized capital" and concluded that McGowan could make a public offering of $1 billion for his new fiber-optic system—at the time, the largest public offering in history. When Milken had completed the bond issue, he raised $2 billion for MCI, which ordered more than 62,000 miles of Corning glass fiber wire. Corning, for its part, thus cemented the worldwide lead in technology it had pursued for almost two decades. But the story still was not complete. It required expansion in two other technological areas to reach full potential.

Cable Television and Cellular Phones

Phone companies of course were not the only businesses to employ glass wire. Cable television companies had originated in "community antenna television" in 1949, when enterprising small-town business-men would erect large antennae atop nearby mountains or tall build-ings to receive signals sent from distant cities and pass them on to home televisions of system subscribers who paid for the service. Dur-ing the 1960s, cable television moved into many of the country's major cities but did not achieve any real profits until the 1970s. The turning point came in 1975 when a subsidiary of Time, Inc., initiated the first national, satellite-delivered programming service. Local cable-system operators promised subscribers a channel of commercial-free, recent motion pictures and other entertainment features under the name Home Box Office (HBO). When more "premium" channels replicated HBO's innovation, cable television offered an attractive alternative to conven-tional network program fare. By the mid-1980s, more than 40 percent of American television homes received cable; by the 1990s, almost 2 mil-lion new homes were wired with cable every year.

Cable television, plus the appearance of a fourth major broadcast network, FOX, in 1986, accelerated the decline of network television. Where once the three national networks (NBC, CBS, and ABC) con-trolled 90 percent of the share of viewers in the evening prime-time hours, since the mid-1980s that number dropped to roughly 70 per-cent. The appearance of unfiltered coverage of Congress by C-SPAN, the Home Shopping Market, and hundreds of niche programs, includ-ing religious, sports, history, and science shows, suggested that the de-cline in the share of television programming commanded by the networks would continue, if not accelerate.

Cable was regulated, deregulated, then regulated again. Cable al-ready was challenged by newly emerging High Definition Television (HDTV), with its potential to improve the clarity of an image by five times, but the format approved by the FCC for HDTV was not com-patible with standard cable lines.[73] Thus, at a critical point, the in-credibly rapid development of the "telecosm" threatened to come to a screeching halt due to regulations. On the one hand, AT&T was pro-hibited from taking fiber networks to individual locations, and on the other, the Baby Bells, a substantial pool of capital and technology, were prohibited from manufacturing telecommunications equipment or to provide new services that would send fiber to homes and offices. And the cable-television monopolies, which *had* the authority to lay the cable, did not install compatible cable.[74]

All this was complicated further by a historical inversion in the technical means of transmitting television signals and telephone messages. Television and radio signals went out over "the air," which is a term for the frequencies between hundreds of thousands and mil-lions of hertz. Higher frequencies were used for direct-broadcast satellite transmission. But from the origins of broadcasting at the net-works, the nature of the transmission was a top-down, "master-slave" architecture in which the "brains" at the broadcast centers originated programs received at the televisions, or "dumb" terminals. That led to simple televisions and intricate broadcast systems.

With the arrival of highly intelligent home-based PCs, however, television technology suddenly had the potential to manipulate signals, replaying them, zooming in or out, storing, and even editing pictures, essentially bypassing the VCR. Data for such a system had to be digital, bypassing the airwaves in favor of cable. Digital signals had an advantage over traditional television analog signals in that they could be stored and manipulated without degradation. When combined with the carrying capacity of fiber-optic wires, the basics existed to transmit television directly to PCs through fiber-optic cable. More important, the technology completely reversed the "top-down, master-slave" relationship into a system with the brains at the bottom—in the PCs—and the programming sent through telephone lines. In such an event, televisions could become telecomputers, capable of altering and interacting with information as well as simply receiving it.

The final component of the telecosm involved the appearance of cellular phones, which did not use wire at all, but, like television and radio, used air to carry transmissions. Ironically, then, "while television service is moving increasingly from air to wire, telephone service is shifting increasingly from wire to the air."[75] (It is therefore erroneous to argue, as does Peter Temin, that the technology shift represented some sort of temporary opportunity; while he correctly points to the emphasis on fiber-optic cables, he mistakenly assumes that the *product* carried by those cables will remain the same, rather than, as Gilder argues, "flip-flopping" with the traditional television product.)[76] As if to complete the circle, McCaw Cellular, which created Cellular One, the largest national cellular system, was funded with junk bonds. Cellular phones by the 1990s had started to digitize, making their acoustics better than copper-wire telephones. In 1994, the cellular phone industry claimed revenues of $14.2 billion with 25 million customers, at a growth of 50 percent per year. McCaw, since purchased by ITT, remained the leader in a more technical industry measurement of usage, population share (or "pops," in the industry vernacular).

The vibrance of cellular systems relied in large part on the steadily falling prices of the switches, making cellular phones competitive in price with plug-in telephones. A typical local phone company bill for standard home service averaged approximately $55 a month for standard service (four phones), while two cellular phones in cars cost an average of $75 a month. Within five years, the cost of the cellular phones easily could fall below that of plug-in phones, providing (generally) more convenient use. George Gilder, the prescient observer of the industry, predicted that when the prices converge, the "Baby Bells will then have to lay fiber to the home, with all its amenities, merely to keep their existing position in the industry."[77] By the mid-1990s, however, the Baby Bells were prohibited from buying equipment from

AT&T, thus from competing effectively in telecommunications. New deregulation of the cable industry emerged from Congress in 1997, ending those prohibitions and offering hope that the telecosm indeed would become a reality, although the "war" between satellite/microwave television transmission and cable transmission had only heated up. Moreover, the once ominous threat of Japanese competition, wherein Japan spent $120 billion to run fiber lines to homes by the year 2000, shriveled with the collapse of the Asian financial markets in the mid-1990s.

American Computers Dominate the Market

Driving the entire revolution, the computer was, and remains, essentially American. U.S. computer industries in 1995 held a worldwide market share of 70 percent, and, more important, American entrepreneurs formed a widespread network of innovation, invention, and capital. More than 20,000 computer firms conducted business in the United States, including 14,000 software companies, 800 digital processing companies, and 1,000 companies in the field of multimedia programming. Still, as history suggests, even such dominance did not dampen the desire of some "political entrepreneurs" to seek government protection for the computer industry.

In 1986, dynamic random access memory chips (DRAMs), which constituted the key data storage device in a computer, glutted the Japanese home market. Japanese manufacturers dumped their chips on the American market in desperation. U.S. computer industry officials lobbied Washington, which cajoled the Japanese into signing the 1986 Semiconductor Trade Agreement to limit exports. But the law of unintended consequences quickly applied itself. Shortages of DRAM chips appeared in almost all American computer models, leading several U.S. companies to delay the introduction of new models or withdraw them from the market altogether. Ironically, the U.S. restrictions on the Japanese bailed out Japan's semiconductor industry at a time that it was flagging.

Japan's inability to break into the worldwide computer market failed even though for two decades MITI had targeted information systems in its industrial policies. Throughout the 1980s, the United States continued to extend its already substantial lead, especially in software. By 1988, according to a study by Lydia Arossa, American software production was five times greater than that of the Japanese.[78] Still better news related to the U.S. global lead in hardware, which remained two-thirds larger than that of Japan's without any significant loss of market share since 1982. Part of the difficulty with the numbers, which occasionally show the Japanese gaining at alarming rates in microchips, is that they ignore IBM, which will not market its chips to other companies. It also underestimates the growth of firms such as Intel, which was the fastest growing big firm in the industry. And at the time that the large firms begged for protection—ostensibly from foreign competitors—they really looked over their shoulders at the ninety-nine new semiconductor start-ups between 1983 and 1988, constituting the fastest-growing new generation of semiconductor firms in history. At the end of the decade, the United States held an astounding 80 percent of the market for hard disk drive systems, and the number of computer scientists had increased tenfold since 1980.[79]

Once again, junk bonds were responsible for the rapid acceleration of the computer industry, thanks to the limitations of traditional financial markets. Between 1986 and 1990, junk bonds financed 80 percent of the industry's expansion, and the share financed by junk bonds could only continue to grow as long as advances in chip technology moved faster than the staid Wall Street investment firms could assess their positions and give their seal of approval. The chip sales of small firms such as Microchip, a Chandler, Arizona-based firm, whose chip sales skyrocketed in the 1990s. Microchip's stock rose from $18 per share to $38 per share, split three-for-two, then starting again in the low $20s, rose again to $41 per share by 1995. Microchip, which invested $75 million in new production facilities, was not even listed on the New York Stock Exchange, nor were thousands of other high-tech computer and energy firms that generated the bulk of the nation's growth in the 1980s and 1990s.

Led by companies such as Microchip and Intel, American chip manufacturers outproduced the Japanese by almost $6 billion when adjusted for exchange rate fluctuations. Perhaps most telling was the commanding lead that the United States enjoyed in software. In 1987 America accounted for $23.6 billion worth of software, an amount that represented more than half of the world's software market and a ratio of market share that was increasing.

The role of entrepreneurial companies should not obscure the resurgence of the industry giant, IBM, which lost hardware sales from 1990 to 1993, taking an $8 billion loss. IBM had a reputation as a cutthroat company, and CEO Louis Gerstner was known for starting meetings with his managers by flashing a photo of Microsoft's Bill Gates on the wall and announcing, "This man wakes up hating you!"[80] But whereas some see "Big Blue" as a looming, threatening figure on the American computer scene, the company has struggled to stay competitive. Its total revenue fell to below $64 billion in 1993, and its research and development dropped by half over a four-year period. Gerstner, and IBM, knew they were in trouble from the newer, more agile companies like Microsoft, which had a $5.2 billion business in personal computer software—a marketplace in which IBM barely ranked. Although Gerstner sliced his workforce some 25 percent, by 1994 IBM still had not reached its profit levels of 1990. When IBM did start to recover, however, it was precisely *because* of the competition from Bill Gates, Steven Jobs, and other entrepreneurs. To make inroads into the PC software market, in the summer of 1995 IBM launched a $3.5 billion hostile takeover bid for the Cambridge, Massachusetts-based Lotus Development Corporation, the third-largest software maker in the world.

Doomsayers, such as MIT's Charles Ferguson, have warned for years that the U.S. computer market would collapse, done in by the Japanese. Instead, American entrepreneurial companies have extended their lead in many cases.[81] In 1985, eleven of the top fifteen computer companies in the world were American, including the top four (IBM, Digital Equipment, Sperry, and Burroughs). The second-place company, Digital Equipment, surpassed the top *two* foreign competitors *combined*. Meanwhile, Japan, at the urging of MITI, had embarked on a "fifth-generation" computer project that swallowed billions of dollars with no substantial impact. By most accounts, the American garage-sized computer shops remained ahead of all other competitors even in artificial intelligence. And the U.S. computer companies were the fastest growing businesses in history. Chips & Technologies, for example, founded in 1985, was a specialized chip designer for IBM-clone computers. It allowed "knockoff" IBM copies to achieve the same computing power with a fraction of the chips, enabling Tandy, PCs Limited, and other U.S. companies to use their clone computers to regain market share over IBM. Chips & Technologies had a sales-per-employee of $650,000—four times the level of most companies. Its customers, such as Compaq, prospered as well, with Compaq the industry leader in the 1980s. Meanwhile, industry dynamos such as Intel rattled out a string of chips that drove processing power up *1,000 percent in less than seven years.*

Indeed, by the 1990s, even the optimists had underestimated American computer-industry growth. Industry estimates placed the increase in the number of PCs at 33 percent. New software and chips made quantum leaps in processing power, with the Intel Pentium chip alone featured in 60 percent of the new systems, and by 1996 more than 80 percent of the systems contained the Pentium chip, significantly upgrading their capabilities, even as new chips came on-line that ran at 1,000 megahertz (MHz), or *quadruple* the speed of the (up to that point) newest Pentium. Domestic penetration of PCs grew at a rate of 40 percent a year, while the price of a bit of semiconductor memory over a thirty-year period had plummeted 68 percent a year![82] Meanwhile, the Japanese were nowhere to be found in the forecast of growth in the computer market. Andrew Grove, CEO of Intel, acknowledged: "In the mid-1980s, people like me were fearing that Japanese companies would take over the U.S. personal computer market . . . . Today, I find them a surprisingly inefficient force."[83]

Revolution in the Air

American success stories soon appeared even in industries long associated with Japanese domination. Radios and televisions, once the proud domain of RCA and GE, Philco and Magnavox, had yielded their markets to the Japanese invasion in the 1960s. Yet many aspects of the radio and television business illustrated the axiom that it is not the saddle that carries the rider but the horse.

Stereo sound enhanced FM radio transmission in the 1960s, leading to a gradual shift away from the popular AM. Traditionally, AM stations played "top 40" songs of no more than two and a half minutes in length (because program executives thought that was all the attention span teenagers, the most numerous listeners to AM, had). By the late 1960s, however, FM started to embody the "counterculture," playing music of styles and lengths that AM programmers would not. Groups unable to get their music on mainstream radio, including Janis Joplin, Jimi Hendrix, Cream, Grateful Dead, and, later, Pink Floyd, Alan Parsons, and Yes, prospered on FM. At the peak of student unrest and discontent over the Vietnam War, FM stations were viewed by many radicals as the "voice of the people." (Contrary to popular myth, however, the rock music industry lagged well behind the radical movement in opposing the war, and the recording industry did not produce, nor did stations play, any significant number of antiwar songs until long after the popular tide turned to the point that the war no longer was as well supported by the general public as it was from 1964 to 1966, when the number one song was "The Ballad of the Green Berets.")[84]

Television continued as the dominant medium in the United States. The most significant development in television technology in the 1960–1980 period, the arrival of the videocassette recorder (VCR), contained significant lessons for small entrepreneurs and large companies as well as implications for "industrial policy." The triumph of the VCR, and, ultimately, of one format of VCR, was not a forgone conclusion. Like other inventions, it had to establish itself against strong competition.

Videotape had existed since 1956, when a group of American engineers at Ampex succeeded in putting images and sound to magnetic tape. At the end of their two-minute demonstration, the group of observers "suddenly leaped to their feet and started shouting and hand clapping."[85] Ampex led the field for a short time but failed to advance the technology from the seven-inch reels of half-inch tape that could record an hour's worth of programming. Early bulky, heavy, versions of the machine required an operator to wind the tape through the reel to start the process. And even though American producers experienced stiff competition from Sony and other Japanese companies, early models introduced in 1966 sold for more than $1,000, finding markets mostly in schools or other educational settings.

A Japanese company, Sony, finally applied the audiotape cassette concept to videotape, developing two formats, a superior Beta and an inferior VHS. In 1974, Sony introduced a videocassette machine called the Betamax, allowing competitors to make VHS machines. Lighter than existing units, Betamax was not cheap. (The so-called "home" unit cost almost $1,300.) Betamax had a recording capacity of one hour, but despite its high cost and limited recording time, the Sony unit had exceptional name recognition. It was marketed for one purpose, recording programs for viewing at a different time. A popular Sony commercial showed a frustrated baseball fan trying to watch two games on different channels at one time, clicking back to a channel just in time to hear the commentator shout, "A triple play! You've just seen a triple play! You don't see *those* very often." Sony chairman Akio Morita coined a phrase that captured the lure of the Betamax when he noted it could "time shift."

Nevertheless, another technology seemed to have the edge in the race to produce a machine capable of playing prerecorded movies, which both Sony and the American companies thought to be the real moneymaking market. A promising concept, developed by RCA, was the videodisc player. In 1965, seeing that the color television industry had topped $3 billion, RCA hoped to capitalized on the popularity of the medium by tapping into the existing phonographic record technology with video "records." Using a format familiar to consumers, RCA hoped to overcome the inherent weakness of the videodisc, namely that it could not record new material, only play prerecorded discs. In addition to familiarity, however, RCA's videodisc offered a clearer picture than tape.[86]

VideoDisc, as RCA dubbed its technology, debuted in 1981 at a cost of $500 per player and $15-25 per disc. While expensive compared to modern VCRs, in 1981 the VideoDisc represented a savings of almost $500 over leading videocassette machines. RCA projected that by 1990 the videodisc business could reach $7 billion and comprise 30–50 percent of the company's entire sales. Those estimates not only proved wrong, but the videodisc was an unmitigated disaster. Sales did reach 550,000, but the total loss to RCA by 1986 exceeded $580 million. Worse, late introduction of the technology meant that dealers had expertise in VCR technology when the new videodisc technology arrived, and therefore dealers had an incentive to "sell what they knew." But the real death knell for RCA's machine occurred when VideoDisc buyers started to return them in exchange for VCRs. RCA totally misread the market for movie rentals and never appreciated the notion that people often rented films as a way of getting information before purchasing a movie.

Meanwhile, Sony, which had the early lead in VCRs, soon came under strong competitive pressure from another VCR manufacturer, JVC (Victor Company of Japan), which the American Victor company had created as a foreign subsidiary to sell U.S. goods in Japan. JVC, using different technical approaches (including more recording "heads"), achieved a two-hour recording capability by using the VIIS cassette, which was one-third larger than the paperback-book-sized Beta. JVC recognized that American movies, and certainly sporting events, lasted longer than one hour.

At that point, a race developed to see which company, JVC or Sony, could enlist the largest number of production companies. Sony lined up Toshiba, Sanyo, and Zenith, while JVC had Hitachi, Mitsubishi, and Sharp. Japan's organ of industrial policy, MITI, was faced with an even competition and could not step in and mandate a format for all Japanese companies under such circumstances—which could have saddled Japan with the less useful Beta format while the world went to the JVC format (called "VHS") if MITI had made the wrong call. By 1977, RCA announced that it would sell Mashushita machines, which used the VHS format, and a bandwagon effect occurred.[87] With each new announcement in Japan of a manufacturer adopting VHS, others had an incentive to jump; and other strong evidence of VHS-format sales in the United States by 1979 showed that the tide had turned. Beta lost, and by the 1980s, Sony ceased producing Beta-format tapes and machines altogether. It was a similar, although certainly not identical, dynamic to the triumph of PC computers over Macintosh computers during roughly the same period.

Japanese "industrial policy," to the extent that it had encouraged the VCR makers of both formats, apparently had an accomplishment worth celebrating. The victory, however, was minor given the stakes: Americans produced and distributed virtually all of the programming. Americans did not watch Japanese movies or use Oriental stars or music in the production of the movies that formed the basis of the burgeoning rental business. Just as in radio and stereo, where Japanese companies made the electronic conduit through which the product came, the music, the information, the programming, movies, specials, and sports events were virtually 100 percent American. Later, in desperation, the Japanese acquired large American entertainment empires in an attempt to control the product, only to witness the explosion of smaller, independent film and recording companies that did not use the major companies for distribution or sales.

Meanwhile, enterprising entrepreneurs started to notice that newly released videocassette-format movies did not have any prohibitions against rentals. Stores renting the Hollywood-made videos sprang up, with dealers going through a process of learning which titles rented well and which did not. Moreover, dealers themselves heard from customers which were the good movies, regardless of the reviews, and acquired films accordingly. Not surprisingly, some of the most popular films were those difficult to obtain—old "classics" and pornography. When larger chains appeared, such as Blockbuster, they concluded that the family audience was more profitable and abolished X-rated movies from their shelves.

Video stores embodied the essence of the entrepreneurial spirit by keeping long hours, and most could not have survived without the proprietors' willingness to work without pay. By 1989, annual VCR sales exceeded one million, making the risk worth the effort. Hollywood, for its part, saw an opportunity to repackage movies, licensing them for rental. Only one last barrier stood in the way of total saturation of the market for rented films, and it had little to do with rented movies themselves. Universal had sued Sony for copyright infringements, arguing that any use of recording movies from television violated copyright laws. It was a case fraught with danger for Hollywood, despite the fact that the suit came from a movie studio. The rental market, and hence, movie revenues, had started to depend on home viewers and the expansion of VCRs. Any barrier to consumers getting full use of the VCR technology threatened to reduce sales. By demanding its rightful return on intellectual property in the near term, Hollywood stood to lose a much larger market in the long term. In 1984, the Supreme Court decided for Sony (and, ironically, for Hollywood). If a person recorded a movie for personal viewing, but not for sale, it was no infringement on copyrights and thus was legal. That constituted the last hurdle to almost universal use of VCRs. Advertisers still had to deal with "zapping," wherein viewers fast-forwarded the tape through the commercials, but no technology effectively removed commercials from a timed-taping process.

Ultimately, no industry fared better from the development of the VCR than the motion picture industry, despite its concerns about the loss of "intellectual property" due to taping. Consumers soon realized that the networks still only offered a limited number of programs at set times; that the movies that did appear on television were old; and that programs were interrupted with commercials and/or edited, which detracted from the original product. Consequently, an entire movie sales business appeared, with companies such as Sun Coast Video providing hundreds of videocassette movies that had recently appeared in theaters, as well as classics, rock videos, documentaries, and exercise tapes. Even more recently, "Web"-based videocassette companies exploded onto the scene. The expansion of VCRs had created an unforseen demand (certainly unforseen in the movie industry) for movies—not to be viewed in theaters, but in homes. By the 1990s the phrase, "I'll watch that when it comes out on video" represented a common market judgment on movies as well as a testament to the real product of the development of the VCR. And, contrary to the dire predictions of the motion picture industry, theater admissions were up. After a brief dip in the mid-1980s, admissions soared to all-time highs in the early 1990s, while theater grosses hit a record $5.1 billion in 1993. Astoundingly, in 1998, the blockbuster motion picture *Titanic* portended to become the first billion-dollar movie, having eclipsed the $530 million mark before even getting to videotape. So much for the VCR killing the theater business!

Meanwhile, with each new acquisition by a large competitor or foreign company, artists in film and music gravitated increasingly to smaller, unaffiliated labels, and such new, burgeoning industries as Christian music that were developing completely outside the entire structure of the media giants. For radio and much of the mainstream music industry, the story was much the same. Although Japanese companies dominated most of the electronics industry, the usefulness of electronic products depended entirely on American musicians and performers, using American agents and playing at concerts worldwide. Perhaps in a final irony, the musical instrument industry itself had seen Japanese and Korean companies enter markets long dominated by U.S. manufacturers, such as Ludwig and Rogers drums, Ampeg and Fender amplifiers, and Wurlitzer pianos. Increasingly, Tama and Yamaha carved out large niches in synthesizers and drums, although by the 1990s American guitarists still demanded Gibson and Fender guitars almost exclusively, while Harley Peavy's Mississippi amplifier company still provided popular amplifiers. Still, the trend was the same. Hardware only constituted a small part of the value of the total product, while American-created, -designed, and -produced "software"—whether music or videos—represented the most significant component.

Nor did the "revolution in the air" end. New surprises were in store in the 1980s, for radio especially. Television and newspapers had dominated news coverage by the 1980s, but increasingly Americans told pollsters that they believed less and less of what the major media figures said and wrote. People simply no longer trusted the major media outlets as sources for news, and worse, often thought that politicians did not listen to the constituents at home. At that point, AM radio made a remarkable U-turn to overtake FM radio by tuning in to the listeners—embarking on "talk radio" formats that encouraged listeners to call in and discuss issues with hosts. Usually, the talk was political, and the dominant voice in the industry was a former low-level marketing employee of the Kansas City Royals who had been fired eleven times from deejay positions. Rush Limbaugh decided his fate rested in his own hands, creating a talk-show format that eschewed guests and used callers as a way to set up Limbaugh's discussions of issues of interest to him. Those issues happened to be of interest to listeners as well. Starting in a local Sacramento, California, station, Limbaugh moved to New York where he flattened another axiom of AM radio, namely, that AM stations were local. Not to Limbaugh, who produced the first three-hour political national talk show in history. In no time, Limbaugh had 660 stations (out of 1,130 total by 1995 that had a talk format), generating $30 million for his syndicator.[88] The real revolution, though, involved

Limbaugh's impact on the traditional newspapers and television news, whose readership and viewership dropped after talk radio expanded. Indeed, the "Big Three" television news broadcasts have steadily lost market share since the revival of AM radio. For a medium considered dead by its more "hip" competitor, FM, and by its other media foes, especially television, AM radio had come back from the grave, stronger than ever.

Americans and Their Entertainments

With computers dominating every other aspect of modern life, it is hardly surprising that they have become a staple of games. The home-electronic game industry (not counting PCs upon which people who are "working" play solitaire or "minesweeper") by 1995 had grown into a $6 billion industry in America. Once again, it proved ironic that the Japanese were most closely identified with an industry dominated by Americans.

Nintendo of Japan transformed itself into one of the world's most powerful companies, surpassing Toyota in profitability, stock performance, and market penetration. The game manufacturer paid higher dividends than almost any other company traded on the Tokyo Stock Exchange between 1988 and 1992.[89] Games easily outsold movies (by $400 million in 1993), and Nintendo seemed to be at the top of the industry. Before it could get complacent, however, another Japanese company, SEGA, vaulted ahead of it with newer technology and the wildly popular—and violent—"Mortal Kombat" game. A seesaw battle erupted between Nintendo, which introduced its 8-bit NES in 1985, followed by SEGA Genesis with its 16-bit system, to which Nintendo responded with its own 16-bit Super Nintendo Entertainment System in 1991. In May 1995, Sega upped the ante again with the 32-bit Saturn system and was joined by Sony's state-of-the-art Playstation. Then in late 1996, Nintendo introduced its new "Nintendo 64," pushing the boundaries closer toward three-dimensional gaming.

Protectionists and doomsayers predicted that the Japanese would control the market. Yet at the very time the Japanese companies that produced the game machines dominated the market, American computer firms increasingly developed not only the games but also the computer simulations in the movies upon which many games were based. Silicon Graphics, a $1 billion California-based company, utilized state-of-the-art computers to create digitized special-effects dinosaurs in *Jurassic Park* and the incredible melting T-1000 in *Terminator 2*, while other American companies provided the astounding special effects for *Titanic*. Silicon Graphics signed a deal with Nintendo in 1994 to provide a 64-bit microprocessor, considered imperative for the game giant to stay even with its competition.

Competition among the major game manufacturers put more than 30 million game machines in the hands of American consumers, with SEGA and Nintendo roughly splitting the $6 billion market. In the 1990s, Japanese companies Panasonic and Atari entered the 64-bit fray with their 3DO and Jaguar systems, which flopped. But the Japanese quickly realized that Americans had vastly different tastes than did their own consumers. For example, Americans wanted sports games that focused on basketball and, especially, football. SEGA and Nintendo quickly located American design and production teams, then opened development offices in the United States. American arcade designers, including the popular Midway group out of Chicago, emerged as powerful design forces. Although the Japanese controlled 90 percent of the game machine market, the pattern that first appeared in computers resurfaced as American software and development companies soon captured more than 50 percent of the market, and by 1995 controlled as much as 60 percent by developing the software at lower cost.[90] Moreover, as digitization merged with motion pictures in the games, American film stars, such as Dennis Hopper and Tia Carrere, started to appear in compact-disc games, while big-name Hollywood producers, such as George Lucas, assisted in producing games, such as the "Star Wars" series. That promised even further domination of the game/software market by American companies and entertainers.[91] And none of those developments touched on the entirely separate game industry developed for PCs, a market almost as large as the SEGA/Nintendo business—virtually all of it developed domestically, including Blizzard's wildly successful "StarCraft" game, which sold $30 million in 1998 alone.

The connection between games, computers, and money was even more pronounced in gambling, where Las Vegas, Reno, and Lake Tahoe, the traditional bastions of the gaming industry, were challenged by several newcomers: Atlantic City, which legalized casino gambling in 1976 amidst promises of prosperity for the city (that failed to materialize) and a host of casinos on Indian reservations (legalized in 1987 by the Supreme Court). Cities and states also got into the act. In April 1989, Iowa passed a bill allowing gambling on casino boats traveling the Mississippi; Chicago planned a $2 billion gambling zone; and Minnesota, by 1993, had more casinos than did New Jersey, including Atlantic City. Computers and slot machines seemed to have a great deal in common, but gambling had its own psychology and economics that differed from the computer-game mentality.

A better approach to uniting innocent games and the higher-stakes gambling products appeared in Steve Wynn's hotels in Las Vegas, the Mirage and Treasure Island, which featured Disney-style rides, attractions, and family shows. Within five years, the Excalibur, the Luxor, and the MGM Hotel all copied the Wynn concept with a family orientation. The Luxor even sported a kids-oriented state-of-the-art arcade with rows of "virtual racers," dozens of arcade machines, and even two full-size flight simulators, while MGM and Circus-Circus featured their own indoor amusement parks.[92] A merger of Disney and Nintendo, if not the actual companies, then the conceptual essence, promised "virtual vacations" in the future.

Not all games involved computers, of course, and nothing had received more of the attention and time of consumers than exercise and fitness. Health clubs, fitness books, tapes, diets—all absorbed Americans' cash at ever-growing rates, with sporting goods' sales exceeding $45 billion in 1991. Ballys, famous for its casinos in Las Vegas and Atlantic City, had the largest health and fitness chain in the United States. In rapidly growing areas in the Sun Belt, where fitness constituted a quasi-religious pursuit, gyms could be found in virtually every strip mall or on any corner. Personal training and bodybuilding, once considered activities only for the narcisstic, became commonplace, while physical therapy was routinely covered by insurance companies as a source of rehabilitation. Specialized sports channels, such as ESPN, filled up to eight daytime hours with workout shows, while the raucous Susan Powter made a fortune on an even newer phenomena, the "infomercial"—a paid, half-hour commercial that appeared to be a regular television program. Powter, an overweight divorcee with small children, made up her mind to get herself in shape, in the process creating a persona and sales technique that made her a millionaire.

Susan Powter epitomized a new trend in direct, media-related sales that originated in 1985 when Lowell W. "Bud" Paxson created the Home Shopping Network (HSN).[93] Paxon had run a small radio station in Dunedin, Florida, and had taken some merchandise in lieu of cash, which he then attempted to sell over the radio at prices far below regular retail prices. The response convinced him to add a daily segment to his show in which he described products and took orders after the broadcast. In 1982, he premiered a cable television show that sold "everything from $2 household items to expensive cruise vacations," generating more than 190,000 orders a month.[94] Paxon had the evidence he needed to go national, launching the Home Shopping Network on a twenty-four-hour-a-day basis, employing ten hosts, each working a shift of two to three hours. A host would offer one item at a time, employing a persuasive sales pitch, with each item limited to a short interval (usually ten minutes). Viewers called a toll-free telephone number to purchase the item. After eight months, Home Shopping Network generated more than $63 million in revenues and almost $7 million in profits. Paxon's HSN stock shot up from its opening price of $18 to $42 a share. Naturally, competitors such as QVC quickly appeared.[95] But Paxon had broken the trail, paving the way for direct sales of everything from "Ab Blasters" to fishing reels and from jewelry to home gyms, in the process drawing in self-made entrepreneurs like

Powter but also presenting as guests well-known personalities such as Victoria Principal, Ivana Trump, and soap-opera queen Susan Lucci.

Entertainment itself had become a substantial industry. By 1993, motion picture industry gross admissions passed the $5 billion mark, while employment in the movie industry exceeded 400,000 that year. Hollywood—which by the 1990s included small motion picture companies located far from California—released 431 new pictures in 1993, or 14 more than the previous year. Music, too, had become "big business," with more than 900 million units sold, including compact discs, cassettes, and music videos. Since 1982, sales had risen more than 50 percent. Whether for minority filmmakers, who have produced well-regarded and profitable movies on minuscule budgets, or for rock 'n' roll millionaires, many of whom lived in abject poverty while "making it," entrepreneurial opportunity in entertainment was stronger than ever.

The strength of the American entertainment industry had important implications for the computer business as well. Increasingly, the most valuable element in a computer system is the information on the CD-ROM or floppy discs; and increasingly entertainment (including games and music) had moved to CD disc format. American entertainers have long dominated foreign movie and music markets, spanning the careers of Jerry Lewis to Huey Lewis and Madonna to Merle Haggard. Thus, the trend reinforced America's lead in the value-added element of computer technology by dominating the product *on* the discs.

The Service Economy, or the "Serviceable" Economy

For the most part, Powter, Wynn, and other entrepreneurs of the 1980s and early 1990s operated in the service sector—they did not manufacture much, or, at least, their product (a book, video, or even a tie) had far more value added as a service than in the actual manufacturing. As the '80s ended, the perception existed that America had become a "service" economy. Typically, that implied lower wages and brought to mind images of McDonald's employees stacking fries and flipping burgers. Of course, service employees included accountants, nurses, lawyers, doctors, financial analysts, top-executives, middle-management, professors, and those in hundreds of other job classifications that were light-years removed from flipping burgers in terms of skills or education needed.

Contrary to popular belief—and claims of labor unions—service jobs on average paid well above the average annual salary in the United States, approaching $26,000 by the late 1980s, an amount far beyond the minimum wages usually associated with services. But because services are viewed as "personal," many economists and sociologists have

FIGURE 12-2   *A $60 CD: Where the Money Goes*

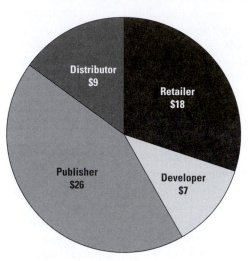

Distributor
$9

Retailer
$18

Publisher
$26

Developer
$7

Source: Adapted from *Electronic Gaming Monthly,* May 1996. (Lombard, Ill.: Ziff-Davis Publishing) All rights reserved. Adaptation reprinted by permission of Ziff-Davis Publishers.

contended that they cannot be made productive. As a result, the United States, with its "service economy," is doomed, in their view, to become a second-class country to the manufacturing nations.[96] Ironically, one of the books making this argument, called *Manufacturing Matters,* provides a superb example of why we should conclude that manufacturing does not matter. As George Gilder points out, the manufacturing costs of a $30 book are, at most $2: Most of the value—and cost—in the book come from services, including writing, editing, layout, art, and marketing. Or consider a compact disc, which costs pennies to manufacture. Most of the value lies in whatever is *on* the disc, whether information or music or a $60 video game (see Figure 12.2).

During the 1980s and 1990s, the trick for American service businesses that wanted to grow was to find a way to reduce paperwork so that they could concentrate on products. Simply writing a three-page proposal to write a history of the U.S. Air Force Museum for the USAF required "boilerplate" forms more than two inches thick, including forms identifying the bidder as a small business, a minority, and other stipulations completely unrelated to either cost or ability to perform the contract. As a result, it takes more than eight hours to prepare all the forms needed to file a proposal, which itself was written and edited in less than an hour! Such paperwork burdens mean that despite "small business set-asides" intended to help entrepreneurs gain federal contracts, government policies make it difficult for small businesses to deal consistently or effectively with the bureaucracy, especially with government bureaucracies.

Office work soon threatened to swamp entrepreneurs with oceans of paperwork. A typical executive finds stacks of "internal" mail in the mailbox, most of it unrelated to the actual production function. Middle managers in small firms suddenly discovered that the computers meant to free them from paperwork now transmit screenfuls of electronic mail ("e-mail") or spew out computer-generated messages that are more time-consuming than meetings. As Arno Penzias observed, "Today millions of well-dressed, deskbound humans still earn a living by 'running errands' between machines—getting a fax, marking it up, typing a draft, making copies, filing some, routing others—just to keep the information moving."[97]

Only recently have American service businesses seriously grappled with productivity. Taco Bell and Burger King have icon cash registers that either spell out or show a picture of the item ordered, so that employees can hit a single button and put the order up on a screen immediately over the food-preparation area. The single-button system also keeps track of inventory—Wal-Mart and Toys "R" Us use scanners with the same function—and reduces errors due to poor communication. Smaller inventories meant less storage costs and permitted a better understanding of what consumers wanted. However, such advances also contained the seeds of destruction; icon and "touch" cash registers reflected the negative fact that most managers no longer think their employees can handle simple math needed to make change or ring up the proper charge, and to that extent the icon system has perpetuated the "dumbing down" of industry by lowering standards. Moreover, the icon systems discouraged traditional business skills—serving the public with custom orders or personal attention, delivering more than required, or simply keeping an agile mathematical mind. To a certain degree, then, the icon-based systems have lowered productivity, even though they offer the potential for important productivity increases in areas of ordering and inventory.

But disadvantages notwithstanding, from hospitals to legal offices, an ever rising stream of new equipment has provided ways to improve the productivity of the service sector. These include: cathode-ray tubes; screen technologies; solid-state memories; data storage discs; CD-ROMs; modems; printers; digitizers; copy machines that enlarge, reduce, collate and staple; ultralight phone headsets; speaker phones; and, of course, computers in a blinding array of sizes, shapes, functions, and capabilities. Paperwork has not been eliminated, and in some areas it has grown worse. But increasingly, service companies have sought to shed the impediments to actual service productivity, with only universities and the government sector slow to get the message of eliminating bureaucracies and paperwork.

Beauty Queen: Mary Kay Ash and the Pink Cadillac

DIVORCED, WITH THREE CHILDREN, LACKING any job training and possessing only a high-school education, Mary Kay Ash would have been an ideal character for a movie like the *First Wives' Club.* She supported her family selling cleaning supplies, making in-home demonstrations. Working for another firm, a direct sales organization, Ash by the late 1950s had attained a more than respectable position and salary of $25,000 a year. She was ambitious, which proved a temporary curse when the company grew concerned about her internal power base, leading to a clash and her resignation.

Mary Kay Ash took with her a decade's worth of experience and knowledge of the direct sales industry, and in 1963 decided to launch her own company, "Beauty by Mary Kay," in Dallas. Joined by her son, Richard Rogers, Ash targeted a part of the market that the largest competitor, Avon, had ignored, skin care. Simple door-to-door sales no longer worked, however, so Ash developed the concept of the "party"—a two-hour in-home beauty show in the residences of women who agreed to act as hostesses. The Mary Kay representatives provided a clinic on makeup, then per-

formed personalized makeup lessons on the participants. Ash realized that the key to successful sales of any good product is the sales force, causing her to explore new and unconventional motivational techniques. She still handed out bonuses and monetary prizes and made certain that talented people moved up the organizational chain. Within three years, the company had sales of $800,000, then, by 1972, volume totaled $18 million.

Suddenly the growth stopped, and reversed. The company could have continued on a path to collapse had Ash not analyzed the problem correctly. She and Rogers found that the cash bonuses had fallen well behind inflation and that a sales director earned no more in real dollars in the late 1970s than almost a decade earlier. In addition to the cash bonuses, Ash added special incentives, awarding pink Buick Regals to salespersons (mostly women) who met a certain volume, and then kicking in an extra $300-a-month bonus to the commissions. Shortly, the sales directors' salary had almost doubled in real terms. Soon, Ash increased the incentives by upgrading from pink Buicks to pink Cadillacs. Recruiting her sales consultants from the ranks of suburban housewives, Mary Kay Cosmetics had more than 120,000 employees in the late 1980s, all of whom could compete for mink coats, diamonds, resort vacations, and other luxuries. The pink Cadillac became much more than a song by Bruce Springsteen—it became, literally, a "cosmetic" symbol of success.

Source: "Mary Kay Ash," in Fucini and Fucini, *Entrepreneurs;* Mary Kay Ash, *Mary Kay* (New York: Harper & Row, 1981); Robert L. Shook, *The Entrepreneurs* (New York: Harper & Row, 1980); and P. Rosenfield, "The Beautiful Make-Up of Mary Kay," *Saturday Evening Post,* October 1981, 58–63.

The Usual Suspects

Entering the 1990s, American business had witnessed a remarkable renaissance. Several factors had coalesced, including the arrival of numerous complementary technologies, the deregulation of a wide range of key industries in transportation, communications, and finance, and a national optimism that shook entrepreneurs out of a decade of doldrums. Major industries, such as autos and steel, had staged unexpected comebacks, while entirely new markets had appeared. The information explosion, due largely to advances in telecommunications and computers, had the dual effect of pressing decision making within organizations downward, reducing the efficiency of—and necessity for—many midlevel management positions, and heralding an unprecedented expansion in the potential productivity of an individual, unshackled from the burdens of geography and time.

Nevertheless, when assessing the business advances of the 1980s, it is easy to ascribe too much credit to technology itself and not enough to the usual suspects, the entrepreneurs who had the vision and faith to develop and use that technology. Although history suggests that "someone would come up with the idea or product" had a specific individual not done so, it is hard to fathom the appearance of cellular phones and fiber optics without the financial genius of Michael Milken or the relentless attacks of MCI's McGowan; or the revolution in retail sales without the discipline Sam Walton imposed; or the direct sales of or the breakthroughs in steel manufacturing brought by Ken Iverson; or most of the modern personal computer market without the contributions of Steve Jobs, Steve Wozniak, Andrew Grove, and Bill Gates. If the charges were "inciting a business revolution," it would not take a police lineup to spot the perpetrators!

Notes

1. Sam Walton with John Huey, *Sam Walton: Made in America—My Story* (New York: Doubleday, 1992); Sandra S. Vance and Roy V. Scott, "Sam Walton and Wal-Mart Stores: The Remaking of Modern America," in *American Vistas, 1877 to the Present* ed. Leonard Dinnerstein and Kenneth Jackson, (New York: Oxford, 1995), 359–380.

2. Warren Brookes, "The Silent Boom," *The American Spectator,* August 1988, 16–19, which contained elements of his article, "The Media vs. the Economy," taken from the *Detroit News,* December 29, 1988.

3. John P. Hoerr, *And the Wolf Finally Came: The Decline of the American Steel Industry* (Pittsburgh: University of Pittsburgh Press, 1988), 606–607.

4. Ibid., 606.

5. Richard Preston, *American Steel* (New York: Prentice–Hall, 1991), 80.

6. Ibid., 80–81.

7. Ibid., 45–46.

8. Ibid., 74.

9. Larry Schweikart, interview with Ken Iverson, June 8, 1995.

10. Armco's story appears in Christy Borth, *True Steel* (Dayton, Ohio: Central Printing Company, 1978 [1941]), and in interviews with C. William Verity Jr. for the author's unpublished manuscript with Jean Lail, *Marriage of Steel: The Life and Times of William and Peggy Verity*.

11. Interviews with C. William Verity Jr., January and February, 1998.

12. Larry Schweikart, interview with Alan McCoy, AK Steel, June 20, 1995.

13. Walter Levy, "Oil and the Decline of the West," *Foreign Affairs,* Summer 1980: 999–1015.

14. Yamani quoted in Yergin, *The Prize,* 705.

15. Yergin, *The Prize,* 735.

16. Thomas Petzinger Jr., *Oil and Honor: The Texaco-Pennzoil Wars, Inside the $11 Billion Battle for Getty Oil* (New York: G.P. Putnam's Sons, 1987), 90.

17. Ibid., 409.

18. Paul Ingrassia and Joseph B. White, *Comeback: The Fall and Rise of the American Automobile Industry* (New York: Simon & Schuster, 1994), 65.

19. Lee Iacocca, "Iacocca: An Autobiography," *N 96 Newsweek,* October 8, 1984, 62.

20. Ibid., "Iacocca," 62.

21. John Bussey, "Lee Iacocca Calls Odometer Policy Dumb," *The Wall Street Journal,* July 2, 1987.

22. Lee Iaccoca with William Novak, *Iacocca: A Biography* (New York: Bantam, 1984).

23. Ingrassia and White, *Comeback,* 33.

24. Ibid., 13.

25. Joe Sherman, *In the Rings of Saturn* (New York: Oxford, 1994); Micheline Maynard, "Labor-Management Link in Peril," *USA Today,* July 17, 1995.

26. Allan Sloan, "Roger Smith's Revenge," *Newsweek,* August 28, 1995.

27. Igrassia and White, *Comeback,* 293.

28. Alex Taylor III, "Trucks Roar; Station Wagons Roll," *Fortune,* July 10, 1995, 26.

29. Ingrassia and White, *Comeback,* 462.

30. U.S. Environmental Protection Agency, *National Air Quality and Emissions Trends Report* (1987), cited in Ben Wattenberg, *The First Universal Nation* (New York: Free Press, 1991), 146.

31. See Joseph L. Bast, Peter J. Hill, and Richard Rue, *Eco-Sanity: A Common-Sense Guide to Environmentalism* (Lanham, Md.: Madison Books, 1995); *Rational Readings on Environmental Concerns* ed. Jay H. Lehr, (New York: Van Nostrand Reinhold, 1992); and Edith Ephron, *The Apocalyptics: Cancer and the Big Lie* (New York: Simon and Schuster, 1984).

32. Terry L. Anderson and Donald R. Leal, *Free Market Environmentalism* (Boulder, Colo.: Westview Press, 1991).

33. Quoted in Wallace Kaufman, *No Turning Back: Dismantling the Fantasies of Environmental Thinking* (New York: Basic Books, 1994), 83.

34. For these and other outrageous suits brought through federal regulations, see James Bovard, "The Lame Game," *The American Spectator,* July 1995, 30–33, and his *Lost Rights: The Destruction of American Liberty* (New York: St. Martins, 1994).

35. Thomas D. Hopkins, "A Guide to the Regulatory Landscape," *Jobs & Capital,* 4 (Fall 1995): 28–31.

36. Robert Higgs, ed., *Hazardous to Our Health? FDA Regulation of Health Care Products* (Oakland, Calif.: The Independent Institute, 1995), 1.

37. For some of the problems associated with the AIDs drug AZT, see Willis Emmons and Ashok Nimgade, "Burroughs Wellcome and AZT (A)," Harvard Business School case study #9-792-004-9 (1992) in *Leadership, Strategy, and Stakeholder Management,* ed. Deborah J. Bickford, James Van Vleck, and John G. Fenic, (New York: McGraw-Hill Custom College Series, 1996), 238–257.

38. Jacob Goodwin, *Brotherhood of Arms: General Dynamics and the Business of Defending America* (New York: Times Books, 1985), 242.

39. See John D. Morrocco, "Defense Conversion Panel Urges Dramatic Changes," *Aviation Week and Space Technology,* 138 (January 25, 1993): 64–65, which provides a comparison of defense drawdowns.

40. "Defense Job Cuts," *USA Today,* June 26, 1995.

41. Several analysts have tackled this issue, including Gansler, *Affording Defense* (Cambridge, Mass.: MIT Press, 1989) and his "International Arms Collaboration," unpublished paper presented at Harvard University, November 8, 1989; Fens Osler Hampson, *Unguided Missiles: How America Buys Its Weapons* (New York: W.W. Norton, 1989); and Thomas McNaugher, *New Weapons, Old Politics: America's Military Procurement Muddle* (Washington D.C.: Brookings Institution, 1989).

42. These issues are discussed at length in Dalgliesh and Schweikart, *Trident.*

43. Michael E. Brown, *Flying Blind: The Politics of the U.S. Strategic Bomber Program* (Cornell University Press, 1992), 307–309. A much different scenario emerged as the cold war reached its apex, and afterward, when the need to maintain the "defense industrial base" required the government to make procurement calculations as much on the basis of keeping contractors available for emergencies as for the immediate need for an aircraft or ship. See Larry Schweikart, *The National Aerospace Plane and the Quest for an Orbital Jet, vol. 3. The Hypersonic Revolution,* Richard D. Hallion, ed., (Washington, D.C.: United States Air Force, 1998).

44. *Crooks, Con-men and Clowns* ed. Leonard Theberge, (Washington, D.C.: Media Institute, 1981); Linda S. Lichter, S. Robert Lichter, and Stanley Rothman, "How Show Business Shows Business," *Public Opinion,* 5 (October/November 1982): 10–12.

45. Michael Medved, *Hollywood vs. America* (New York: HarperCollins, 1992).

46. S. Robert Lichter and Stanley Rothman, "Media and Business Elites," *Public Opinion,* 4 (October/November 1981): 42–60, and their "Personality, Ideology and World View: A Comparison of Media and Business Elites," *British Journal of Political Science,* 15 (1984): 29–49.

47. Gilder, *Wealth and Poverty,* 101.

48. Ann Marsh, "Meet the Class of 1996," *Forbes 400* (October 14, 1996): 100–295.

49. Lamm cited in Arthur Levitt Jr., "In Praise of Small Business," *New York Times Magazine,* December 6, 1981.

50. Steven Solomon, *Small Business USA: The Role of Small Companies in Sparking America's Economic Transformation* (New York: Crown, 1986), 23.

51. Council of Economic Advisers, *Economic Report of the President, February 1985* (Washington, D.C.: U.S. Government Printing Office, 1985), 193.

52. See Gilder, *Recapturing the Spirit of Enterprise,* ch. 6.

53. Material on Zabian is from Gilder, *Wealth and Poverty,* 53–54; material on Colangelo is from an unpublished history of the Phoenix Suns basketball team by Larry Schweikart and interviews with Colangelo.

54. Richard Alm, "Suns' Owner Jerry Colangelo has Made Phoenix Big-League," (January 23, 1996) internet article from the *Dallas Morning News.*

55. Pyong Gap Min, *Ethnic Business Enterprise: Korean Small Business in Atlanta* (New York: Center for Migration Studies, 1988), 82; Alixa Naff, "Lebanese Immigration Into the United States: 1880 to the Present," in Albert Hourani and Nadim Shehadi, *The Lebanese in the World: A Century of Emigration* (London: Taurus & Co., 1992), 148. Also see Thomas Sowell, *Race and Culture: A World View* (New York: Basic Books, 1994).

56. Irwin Garfinkle and Robert Haveman, with the assistance of David Betson, U.S. Department of Health, Education and Welfare, *Earnings Capacity, Poverty, and Inequality,* Institute for Research on Poverty Monograph Series (New York: Academic Press, 1977).

57. Allan Reynolds, "The Ominous Decline in Work Incentives," *Jobs & Capital* 3 (Fall 1994): 9–17 (quotation on 13); Hilary Hoynes, "Welfare Transfers in Two-Parent Families: Labor Supply and Welfare Participation under AFDC-UP," NBER Working Paper, #4407, July 1993.

58. Ann Marsh, "Meet the Class of 1996," *Forbes 400,* October 14, 1996, 100–295 (quotation on 100).

59. Thomas J. Stanley and William D. Danko, *The Millionaire Next Door: The Surprising Secrets of America's Wealthy* (Atlanta, Georgia: Longstreet Press, 1996), 3.

60. "What Makes Jerry Jones Run?" January 25, 1996, Prodigy internet/AP online, in author's possession. See also Jim Dent, *King of the Cowboys* (Holbrook, Mass.: Adams Publishing, 1995).

61. Burton Folsom's study of the Scrantons in Pennsylvania (*Urban Capitalists* [Baltimore, Md.: Johns Hopkins University Press, 1981]), supports this argument.

62. Alec R. Levenson, "New Evidence on the Growth in Part-Time Employment," *Jobs & Capital,* 3 (Fall 1994): 7–8.

63. Ben Wildavsky, "McJobs," *Policy Review,* Summer 1989, 30–37.

64. *Black Enterprise,* February 1988.

65. Peter Temin with Louis Galambos, *The Fall of the Bell System: A Study in Prices and Politics* (New York: Cambridge University Press, 1987), 346.

66. See Alan Stone, *Wrong Number: The Breakup of AT&T* (New York: Basic Books, 1989), and Theodore P. Kovaleff, "For Whom Did the Bell Toll: A Review of Recent Treatment of the American Telephone and Telegraph Divestiture," *The Antitrust Bulletin,* 34 (Spring 1989): 437–450.

67. "AT&T Agrees to Be Broken Up as Part of an Antitrust Settlement," *Great Events in History II: Business and Commerce,* V: 1821–1825.

68. Temin, *Fall of the Bell System,* ch. 2 and 7.

69. George Gilder, *Life After Television: the Coming Transformation of Media and American Life* (Knoxville, Tenn.: Whittle Direct Books, 1990), 60.

70. Pusateri, *History of American Business,* 337.

71. Tom Peters, "A Sampling of Popular Misconceptions," *Washington Times,* September 8, 1988.

72. Michael Jensen, "Eclipse of the Public Corporation," *Harvard Business Review* (Sept.-Oct. 1989): 61–74, and Glenn Yago, *Junk Bonds: How High Yield Securities Restructured Corporate America* (New York: Oxford University Press, 1991).

73. Often overlooked in the discussions of HDTV were the costs to rewire the network system, estimated between $4 million to $40 million per station, requiring the replacement of all current broadcasting equipment. Jack Shandle, "Just How Much Will HDTV Conversion Cost?" *Electronics,* June 1990, 66–67.

74. Gilder, *Life After Television,* 69–72.

75. Ibid., 71.

76. See Temin, *Fall of the Bell System,* 347, as well as Peter W. Huber, *The Geodesic Network,* report prepared for the Department of Justice on Competition in the Telephone Industry, 1987. Astoundingly, Temin cites the structural rigidity of AT&T as an argument for government protection through regulation, contending that the plants were used over an unusually long period of time. This is precisely the point: Carnegie would have been appalled that AT&T was not forced by competition into improving its durable investments. And to maintain that falling phone service costs represented a great contribution by AT&T in its protected state ignores the technology and expanding markets that allowed the giant to reap considerable profits at steadily smaller percentages. Temin, with his use of counterfactuals, above all should recognize that costs might have fallen further and faster had a competitive environment been permitted. Nor is it likely that over the long run consumers will be bothered by the fact that telephones no longer last "forever" or that the utility takes responsibility for the whole network (362). Consumers no longer expect autos to last for 100,000 miles, because the loss of durability came at the gain of phenomenal comfort, vastly improved safety, much improved performance and handling, and lower fuel costs. (A tractor will last "forever," as many rural fields testify today.) The proliferation and acceptance of cellular phones, just in the years since Temin has written, make many of his points obsolete.

77. Ibid., 72.

78. Gilder, "How the Computer Companies Lost Their Memories," *Forbes,* June 13, 1988, 79–84.

79. Gilder, "Freedom and the High Tech Revolution," *Imprimis,* November 1990, Hillsdale College series; Joseph S. Nye Jr., "America's Information Edge," *Foreign Affairs,* March-April, 1996, 20–36.

80. James Coates, "New IBM Chief Clears for Battle," *Dayton Daily News,* June 25, 1995; Richard Thomas DeLamarter, *Big Blue: IBM's Use and Abuse of Power* (New York: Dodd, Mead, & Co., 1986).

81. See Charles Ferguson, "International Competition, Strategic Behavior, and Government Policy in Information Technology Industries," Ph.D. dissertation, MIT, 1988.

82. Not only was this manuscript prepared on a word processor, but this reference was taken from a wire story carried on Prodigy, an online news service, June 12, 1995, entitled "Study: New Trends Driving the PC Market."

83. Grove quoted in Karl Zinsmeister, "MITI Mouse: Japan's Industrial Policy Doesn't Work," *Policy Review,* Spring 1993, 28–35 (quotation on 31).

84. Kenneth J. Bindas and Craig Houston, "'Takin' Care of Business': Rock Music, Vietnam, and the Protest Myth," *Historian,* November 1989, 1–23 (quotation on 16).

85. James Lardner, *Fast Forward: Hollywood, the Japanese, and the Onslaught of the VCR* (New York: W.W. Norton, 1987), 59.

86. Margaret B. Graham, *RCA and the VideoDisc: the Business of Research* (Cambridge: Cambridge University Press, 1986).

87. Michael Cusumano, Yiorgos Mylonadis, and Richard S. Rosenbloom, "Strategic Maneuvering and Mass-Market Dynamics: The Triumph of VHS over Beta," *Business History Review,* 66 (Spring 1992): 51–94.

88. "Everybody's Talkin' At Us," *Business Week,* May 22, 1995, 104–105, 108.

89. David Sheff, *Game Over: How Nintendo Conquered the World* (New York: Vintage Books, 1994 [1993]), 5.

90. Interview with Ed Semrad, editor-in-chief of *Electronic Gaming Monthly,* June 28, 1995.

91. See "Video Game Timeline," *Electronic Gaming Monthly,* January 1988, 112–137, as well as other EGM issues that have provided a running history of the industry.

92. David Johnston, *Temples of Chance: How America, Inc. Bought Out Murder Inc. to Win Control of the Casino Business* (New York: Doubleday, 1992); Larry Schweikart, "Atlantic City Legalizes Casino Gambling," in *Great Events from History II: Business and Commerce Series, IV, 1927–1980* ed. Frank N. Magill, (Pasadena, Calif.: Salem Press, 1994), 1600–1605.

93. "Cable Shopping Channel Woos Viewers Via Direct Response," *Direct Marketing,* 48 (June 1985): 76–149.

94. "Home Shopping Service Is Offered on Cable Television," *Great Events in History II: Business and Commerce,* V:1909–1914 (quotation on 1909).

95. Holly Klokis, "Cable TV: A Retail Alternative?" *Chain Store Age Executive,* 62 (August 1986): 11–14; Judann Dagnoli, "Home Shopping Gets Push from Cable Systems," *Advertising Age,* 57 (June 9, 1986): 64; Lawrence Strauss, *Electronic Marketing: Emerging TV and Computer Channels for Interactive Technologies* (White Plains, N.Y.: Knowledge Industry, 1983); and Mark Ivey and Patrick Houston, "Don't Touch That Dial—You Might Miss a Bargain," *Business Week,* June 2, 1986, 35–36.

96. Among the authors arguing this point, to one degree or another, are Ira Magaziner and Robert B. Reich, *Minding America's Business: The Decline and Rise of the American Economy* (New York: Harcourt, Brace Jovanovich, 1982); Clyde Prestowitz Jr., *Trading Places: How We Allowed Japan to Take the Lead* (New York: Basic Books, 1988); Lester Thurow, *The Zero-Sum Society* (New York: Basic Books, 1980); and Stephen Cohen and John Zysman, *Manufacturing Matters: The Myth of the Post-Industrial Society* (New York: Basic Books, 1987).

97. Penzias, *Harmony,* 50.

CHAPTER 13

Neural Networks and New Markets: The 1990s and the Twenty-First Century

INEXORABLY THE MICROCOSM AND THE TELECOSM BOUND TOGETHER American information and entertainment systems. Just as relentlessly, the entrepreneurial affairs of individuals and the financial/political affairs of nations were bound together in neural networks of fiber optics, faxes, and computers.[1] Size no longer mattered in the same ways it once had. Individuals, on the other hand, had unparalleled levels of creativity and capability at their fingertips. That did not mean, necessarily, that every company or firm used computers well—or even used them at all. Instead, it suggested that entrepreneurs had more of an opportunity than ever before to reach untapped markets, thanks to the incredible advances in communications and transportation that the late twentieth century provided.

By the mid-1990s, the landscape of American entrepreneurship reflected the new diversity of industry, extending far from steel, autos, oil, or banks. Consider some of the "Entrepreneurs Across America" celebrated by *Entrepreneur* magazine:

✦ Andrew Schlessinger's Library Video Company, Bala Cynwyd, Pennsylvania, started with $25,000, distributed more than 6,000 educational video titles to schools and libraries. Sales in 1994: $12 million.

✦ Marian and Bill Sullivan's Sullivan Inc., Sioux Falls, South Dakota, began with $13,500 in 1968 importing a variety of goods, but mostly floral decor. Sales in 1994: $16.8 million.

✦ Mark Juarez's Tender Loving Things, Oakland, California, began with $22,000 to develop accupressure massagers sold in 3,500 locations. Sales in 1994: $10.6 million.

✦ Lillian Lincoln's Centennial One, Inc., Landover, Maryland, started with only $4,000, allowed Lincoln—the first black woman to receive an MBA from Harvard—to leave a highly paid executive job to start her own janitorial firm. By 1995, she had 700 employees. Sales in 1994: $9.8 million.

✦ Eddie Flores and Kwock Yum Kam, L&L Drive-Inn in Honolulu, Hawaii, started with $22,000 serving "plate lunches" of rice and main dishes, to establish 20 locations. Sales in 1994: $10 million.

✦ John Solomon Sandridge, LuvLife Collectables, parlayed a $2,000 start-up cost in paint and materials to become the "black Norman Rockwell," painting nostalgic Coca-Cola-type scenes of black America that are sold largely through J.C. Penney. Sales in 1994: $1.2 million.

✦ Beth Stewart's Denver Transit Advertising, Denver, Colorado, had a "negligible" start-up cost to sell ad space measuring the entire surface of city busses, such as giant hamburgers or pictures of hot-air balloons. Sales in 1994: $2.2 million.

✦ Jim Partlowe's Well-Bred Boxer, Chattanooga, Tennessee, specialized in sales of boxer shorts, including glow-in-the-dark designs, after starting in 1988 with $10,000. Sales in 1994: $6 million.

Given the vast range of individual entrepreneurs, typical in the American economy, and the wide variety of products they make or services they provide, perhaps it is worth revisiting the essence of entrepreneurship.

Reprise: Who Are Entrepreneurs?

It should be obvious by now that any capsule definition of an entrepreneur must fail. With their infinite personality and motivational differences, people become entrepreneurs for any number of reasons. Some, like Lillian Lincoln, Andrew Carnegie, and Ray Kroc, had secure—even well-paying—jobs but saw an opportunity to do things better. Others, like John Sandridge, Beth Stewart, Cornelius Vanderbilt, Steve Jobs, and Bill Gates, recognized a need in the market that was going unfilled. Still others, like Sam Walton, Nevada banker George Wingfield, and Henry Ford all declared bankruptcy, had their first enterprises fail miserably, or were unceremoniously kicked out of their own companies before attaining ultimate success. For some, destitution and the demands of everyday living provided incentive enough, while others needed to reestablish their business to gain a measure of self-vindication. Then we have observed a group of entrepreneurs loosely called "dreamers"—people such as James J. Hill, Kemmons Wilson, Walt Disney, and Berry Gordy—who wanted to improve the lives of the community in specific ways and founded exceptional businesses in the process.

Of course, entirely different people come to mind when critics of capitalism cite examples of entrepreneurs. They often refer to "robber barons" such as Rockefeller, Fisk, Gould, and Andrew Mellon, or modern-day "Gordon Gekkos" such as Michael Milken, Ivan Boesky, or Donald Trump. Frequently, as we have seen, the reality is much different from the myth. Rockefeller provided cheap fuel for millions, jobs for thousands, and gave away each year more than most people earn in a lifetime. Mellon paid off one-third of the national debt, lowered the tax burden on the poor and middle-class, and generated a decade of prosperity unparalleled in many ways, not to mention giving away millions of dollars to charity, education, and art institutes.

But even many of those cited as modern-day robber barons do not at all fit the description. The controversial Michael Milken is an individual with two distinct images. On the one hand, he followed Charles Merrill in trying to provide investment opportunities for people other than elites, ignoring the traditional securities markets and going to an entirely new tier of American investors.[2] He almost single-handedly opened a bond market for businesses created by women and minorities who did not qualify for higher bond ratings. As Milken put together his deals, including a phenomenal $365 million raised in thirty-six hours for the Triangle–National Can merger, he developed entirely new investment concepts, including one considered highly unethical called the "air fund"—an offering based entirely on the "confidence" of Milken to raise the anticipated capital.

On the other hand, Milken skirted the law throughout much of his career because no regulations covered the new securities he had developed.[3] He incurred no small amount of hostility partly because he received such astronomical fees, which ranged in the millions for a single deal. "Old" Wall Street hated him because he abandoned New York for Beverly Hills. His operations were so novel, and relied so heavily on comments from corporate heads to Milken's firm, Drexel Burnham, that in 1989 Milken was indicted on "insider trading" charges in New York City. New York City District Attorney Rudolph Guliani, supported by a settlement with Milken competitor Ivan Boesky, who turned "state's evidence," indicted Milken's brother Lowell, thought by most observers to be merely "leverage" to bring Milken to heel. In 1990, Milken changed his plea to guilty in return for the release of Lowell, paying a fine of $600 million and receiving a prison sentence four years longer than the infamous "wilding" rapists of Central Park.[4]

The war on Milken represented a much larger attack on the junk-bond industry, much the way Ralph Nader's assault on the Corvair was the skirmishing party in his movement to subjugate Detroit. But the critics of junk bonds ignored the fact that the default rate on Drexel-sponsored bonds from 1981 to 1986 was only *2 percent,* when the industry average approached 17 percent. The government had produced studies during Milken's prosecution showing that Drexel's default was 30 percent, but that data used extremely narrow trend lines. When the default rate for all junk securities was calculated over several years, it came to 3 percent.[5] For securities bearing such extreme risk, that represented a remarkably low default rate by historical standards. As Robert Sobel observes, "In taking the entire cycle into consideration . . . [one analytical service found] that for the ten years ending on September 30, 1990, the total return on junk bonds came to 145 percent, or 9.4 percent annualized."[6] Compared to Treasury bonds, which rose 10.7 percent over the same period, junk performed exceptionally well, and when keeping in mind that junk represented only the highest risk companies, junk was, well, anything but junk.[7]

At the time Milken financed the communications revolution and, specifically, the Internet, by channeling $26 billion into MCI, McCaw, Viacom, TCI, Time Warner, Cablevision Systems, News Corp., those companies had little net worth. Virtually none of them commanded capital acceptable to banks and could not have raised the money elsewhere. By the 1990s, though, the same companies were worth $224 billion.[8] Thanks to junk bonds, Disney, then worth $1.8 billion, was restructured and again became profitable, so that in eleven years it was worth $30 billion. But Milken represented only the most prominent of a group of buccaneering financial wizards who conducted more than 42,000 corporate restructurings between 1976 and 1993, worth a total of $3.1 trillion, generating almost $900 billion in constant-dollar gains to shareholders and pumping up the pension funds of average American retirees, schoolteachers, hospital workers, and garbage collectors. Harvard scholar Michael Jensen, who has analyzed those takeovers during the junk-bond era, concludes that far from disguising large wealth transfers from workers and communities, "junk-bond fever" made the United States much more competitive and caused the equity of public firms to rise by $1.6 *trillion* dollars.[9] Astoundingly, *Forbes* magazine estimated that the stock market gains from 1995 to 2000 could add another $2 trillion, especially as interest rates fall in response to the meltdown in the Far East.

Attacks on junk securities generally were subsumed into criticisms of the merger wave that struck American business in the 1980s.

Again, the evidence does not support the notion that the takeover frenzy of the decade was harmful: just the opposite. Michael Jensen found that corporate takeovers fostered by junk bonds benefited target shareholders; that acquiring firm shareholders earned a 4 percent return on hostile takeovers; that takeovers generated substantial gains—historically 8.4 percent of the value of both companies; and that the "golden parachutes" typically did not harm shareholders. Jensen and his colleague William H. Meckling identified the problem with the manager-dominated firm in their widely cited article, "Theory of the Firm," in which they noted that "agents," namely, managers who may not have the same interests as the owner, or "principals," can develop divergent interests and thus take the firm into directions that the principals might not desire.[10] The merger wave of the 1980s, especially, constituted a sustained effort by principals to regain the direction of their companies and monitor the aberrant activities of the agents, through the securities markets. When the "White Shoe" securities firms did not respond, entrepreneurs and shareholders alike turned to junk.

But the campaign against junk temporarily succeeded. After the late 1980s, new issues of high-yield securities and bank loans to "non-investment-grade companies dropped some 90 percent, while venture capital outlays sank some 40 percent."[11] The net losers in the onslaught were small entrepreneurial firms—many minority-owned and often involving cutting-edge technologies. Fortunately, the damage was temporary. An interest in low-cost securities had been established, impervious to either government regulations or Wall Street bluster, and, ironically, the NYSE itself was the biggest winner. By the 1990s, Americans surged into the stock market as never before, driving it to unprecedented levels. Among the factors driving the new investment surge were an ocean of new entrepreneurs, pressing in on the market from unorthodox and unusual perspectives.

Unorthodox and Unusual: Paths to Entrepreneurial Achievement

Arnold Schwarzenegger's name constituted only one barrier to his success. What was it that made a skinny Austrian kid with an unintelligible German accent become the best bodybuilder in the world, a top American movie star, and a well-respected businessman? While most people consider Schwarzenegger (usually simply referred to as Arnold) an actor—and many joke about his talent—he has approached his product with an entrepreneur's vision and faith. At first, he concentrated entirely on being the best bodybuilder in the world; and when he accomplished that, he studied acting and worked on his accent.

Schwarzenegger carefully selected his roles, choosing those that had little dialogue while he improved his speaking, and at the same time picking movie vehicles that allowed him to display his (at the time) only asset, his physique. When offered the role of the hero in the smash hit *Terminator,* Schwarzenegger instead realized that the robot would dominate the movie. He tweaked scripts to make his accent believable, such as in *Red Heat,* where he played a Soviet cop, or in futuristic science fiction scenarios like *Running Man* and *Total Recall.* He parlayed his million-dollar paychecks into a Colorado real-estate bonanza, and few in the business community doubt his capabilities when it comes to commerce. Is Arnold Schwarzenegger an entrepreneur?

What about Michael Jordan? Although his basketball career comes to mind immediately, Jordan was much more than a basketball player, and indeed, Nike's Air Jordan commercials emphasized that he is a "corporation." Think of all the hundreds of baseball, football, hockey, and basketball players who have received six- and seven-digit salaries for years, only to retire on a pittance. Michael Jordan, by contrast, crafted an image that allowed him to sell McDonald's, Air Jordan basketball shoes, cologne, and his own high-fashion line of ties. Jordan, like Schwarzenegger, realized that his image was his product. Is Michael Jordan an entrepreneur?

Historians and economists frequently ignore the entrepreneurship inherent in the panorama of human activities, a failing J. R. T. Hughes hoped to correct. Even Hughes's efforts, however, have been inadequate in capturing the spirit of enterprise. Robert J. Loewenberg, for example, a professor of history at Arizona State University, had grown frustrated over the snail's pace of publishing in the academic world. His ideas appeared in print only years after he formulated them, and through the review process, books or articles could be "killed" before they ever reached publication. Loewenberg resigned his university position and created a nonprofit think-tank in Jerusalem, the Institute for Advanced Strategic and Policy Studies, raising virtually all of the capital himself. After five years, the Institute's policy papers were cited regularly in the European *Wall Street Journal;* within eight years Loewenberg opened a branch of the Institute in Washington; and in 1998 the Institute celebrated its tenth anniversary. Such an operation required more than $1 million annually to run, turning out a stream of policy papers and funding student interns to work with Israeli and American lawmakers—in the process reminding their mentors about the value of the free-enterprise system. Ultimately, Loewenberg's goal is to turn the Israeli economy from a socialist model to a market model, and to that end, the Institute was instrumental in shaping legislation in the Israeli parliament to create the first "enterprise zone" in that nation. When Benjamin Netanyahu was elected prime minister,

IASPS suddenly found itself playing an active role in remaking the Israeli economy. Is Robert Loewenberg an entrepreneur?

Minority Entrepreneurship

More than ever, entrepreneurship includes athletes, academics, consultants, writers, movie stars, music personalities, and nonprofit foundation leaders. Lines have blurred between employers and employees, between entrepreneurs and managers. Traditionally, entrepreneurs had to be "self-employed." Is that definition appropriate anymore, especially when people cross over through different situations frequently, and occasionally several times in one day? Michael Jordan, for example, was an "employee" when he played a two-and-a-half-hour basketball game for the Bulls, but when he promoted his ties in the postgame talk show, he worked for his own company.

The "crossover" phenomena renders less meaningful statistical analyses of participation rates among different ethnic groups. Surveys showed blacks defined themselves as "self-employed" only one-fourth as often as whites and only one-half as often as Asians.[12] But for those groups with a history of low business participation, the crossover phenomena would be even harder to detect, because individuals themselves tend to identify with their "steady" job. Moreover, the data diverges significantly when Jamaicans, Haitians, and Dominican blacks are considered separately: Jamaicans had business participation rates of over 21 percent, and Haitians, over 15 percent, both percentages far above that of whites.

Part of the dilemma for minorities has been to target a market. One approach, such as that taken by John H. Johnson, involved providing products aimed at other blacks. Johnson, *Black Enterprise* magazine's "Entrepreneur of the Decade" in the 1980s, published *Ebony, Jet,* and *Ebony Man.* Johnson Publishing Company was the largest U.S. black-owned business, with $175 million in sales in 1987, when Johnson was honored.[13] Whereas Johnson prospered by tailoring publications to the black community, the most popular businesses among the top 100 black-owned companies in America were auto dealerships, which had no special ethnic focus. In the mid-1980s, for example, two of the top five black-owned firms in growth were auto dealerships.[14] And Reginald Lewis became one of *Forbes's* wealthiest Americans by acquiring undervalued companies and making them into marketable commodities.[15] When he bought Beatrice Foods for $1 billion in 1987, investors quickly knew it would be valuable; his earlier purchase of McCall Pattern Company had fetched a 90-to-1 return!

Debates about the "dependency mentality" imposed by slavery peaked in the 1960s and have shifted somewhat to arguments over whether the New Deal/Great Society programs created a culture of dependency. The lingering effects of slavery during the late 1800s and into the 1900s were obvious and widespread. No economic historians deny that blacks, especially the freedmen, had little in the way of education or skills and virtually no possessions. Discrimination prohibited blacks from equal access to many public facilities, even though they paid taxes on those facilites. Laws against blacks entering a variety of professions, occupations, institutions, and other avenues of economic advancement existed until the 1960s in some cases. Professional sports were segregated until the 1950s, and most large corporations, in any genuine sense, have opened career paths to minorities only in the last two decades. Nevertheless, government policies have also hindered minority entrepreneurship, especially among blacks.

Liberals have contended that slavery and racism created long-term structural barriers to blacks that the market could not overcome, and that government intervention to "level the playing field" was necessary. The perpetuation of segregated facilities and businesses only symbolized, according to some, the larger problem of a "two-track" society, with opportunities for some but not others. In the 1960s, civil-rights legislation ended most segregation officially, although social, cultural, and residential segregation continues to occur—some by deliberate design, some by personal choice. The federal government also enacted so-called affirmative action or equal-opportunity laws. In their original form, equal-access laws specifically prohibited denying anyone a job or access to public programs on the basis of skin color. Over time, government used quotas to ensure that certain numbers of minority groups would be hired—a point vehemently renounced at the time of the adoption of such laws. Then the government used equal opportunity laws to mandate that private businesses have equal access, but the only way the federal agencies could guarantee proper "distributions" was to institute quotas; and when business did not institute such quotas voluntarily, it opened itself to litigation from the government. By the 1990s, then, the solution to discrimination had become . . . discrimination.

Meanwhile, welfare, designed (as proponents were fond of saying) to be a "hand, not a handout," quickly became a trap of its own. Welfare incentives tended to accelerate marriage dissolution and illegitimacy.[16] Reformers tended to focus on "workfare" programs that emphasized working as a solution to receiving welfare, while the issue of marriage largely went unaddressed.[17] By the 1990s, studies had shown quite conclusively that welfare and illegitimacy were linked and that illegitimacy was linked to low employment rates and poor work habits.[18] Perhaps more surprising to some, government regulations designed to lift people out of poverty have in some cases specifically harmed minorities, as in the case of minimum wage laws.[19] Other government regulations enacted on behalf of unions have limited the mobility of minorities into such occupations as beauty and hair care and taxi and transportation services. In some cases, as with the armed forces and school admissions, government has played an important role in ensuring equal access to public facilities. In the private sector, though, important breakthroughs had little to do with government. Jackie Robinson desegregated baseball because the Dodgers had not beaten the St. Louis Cardinals and needed to overcome the magic of Stan Musial. They desperately wanted to win. Certainly the Dodger organization had no more racial sensitivity than other clubs, and government did not mandate hiring minorities. Instead, the private sector, with its incentives for gaining a competitive edge, gave Jackie Robinson a chance.[20] And markets, even in the post-Civil War South, have shown a propensity to be "color blind" *if* the return was high enough: Jennifer Roback, for example, found that southern streetcar businesses were desegregating on their own (for profit) until local governments segregated them.[21]

Since most small entrepreneurs do not receive start-up capital from banks, entrepreneurship remains the best opportunity for minorities to advance economically. Such entrepreneurship relies more heavily on the values a child inherits from the family than on inherited financial assets. Studies have shown that family income only marginally affects children's life chances, especially once extremely basic needs are met, which is the case with most Americans in poverty. As Susan Meyer found, "The parental characteristics that employers value and are willing to pay for, such as skills, diligence, honesty, good health, and reliability, also improve children's life chances, independent of their effect on parents' income. Children of parents with these attributes do well even when their parents do not have much income."[22] An intact family can capitalize a business with its labor, but a broken family will find it much more difficult. As a result, minorities other than American-born blacks, with higher success rates of keeping families together, especially Asians and Jamaicans, have moved in to establish groceries, laundries, and other businesses in inner cities by using family labor.

Despite these hurdles, evidence suggests that American-born blacks have started to engage in entrepreneurship at higher rates. According to reports from *Black Enterprise* magazine, sales for the nation's top black-owned businesses rose almost 12 percent in 1995, outperforming both the *Fortune* 500 and the *Forbes* 500 lists, representing a revenue jump of almost 10 percent.[23] Black-owned firms stressed innovation—"striving to meet their entrepreneurial mission in ways that they may not have considered or attempted in the past," noted Alfred Edmond Jr., the executive editor of *Black Enterprise*.[24]

Still, entrepreneurship within the American-born black community has lagged behind other groups. One reason has been the high employment of blacks in nonprofit occupations. Working *in* a business— as opposed to working for a government agency or nonprofit firm— has been identified as a crucial component in the training of minority entrepreneurs.[25]

Achieving such training comes hard when up to one-half of the rising black middle class, according to one study, worked in some way for government at the state, local, or federal level. Even when blacks engaged in private enterprise, government often was a central client. For example, in 1987, the fastest growing black business in America, Lawson National Distributing Company in Chicago, growing at an annual rate of 100 percent, made buses for the city of Chicago. Such dependence on the government as a client is detrimental to black-owned businesses, especially in an age when state and local governments are experiencing budget constraints. Overall, it may well be that black employment in the public sector constitutes the single largest impediment to black entrepreneurship since slavery.[26]

On the other hand, the tax cuts of the 1980s proved especially beneficial to blacks. The U.S. Civil Rights Commission found that the number of black-owned businesses rose at record rates during the period 1978–1987, nearly doubling in the period that top capital gains tax rates were cut from 49 percent to 20 percent. Public policy, however, could provide only a framework for entrepreneurship. The creation of thriving businesses still required what it always has in America: faith, family, work, and service.

It is not surprising, then, to find that outstanding black entrepreneurs like Herman Cain, the CEO of Godfather's Pizza, started with a firm spiritual grounding.[27] "My father never looked for a government program, a government handout," Cain recalled. Instead, Herman Cain saw his father work hard and heard his mother teach him about God. "Success," he remembered her saying, "is not a function of what you start with materially but what you start with spiritually." Cain grew up in a tiny duplex, sleeping on a foldup cot in the kitchen with his brother, and while growing up he shined shoes, waxed cars, and latched on to a job at Coca-Cola, where his father was a chauffeur. He put himself through Morehouse College, then worked as a civilian statistician for the navy. Demanding more of himself than merely a comfortable life, Cain earned a master's degree in computer science at Purdue and eventually worked as an analyst at Pillsbury. He knew, however, that the path from the computer division ended well below the top, and he met with a former boss, Win Wallin, by then the Pillsbury president, to ask for advice. Boldly, Cain told the president he wanted his job. "I can't get to your job from where I am. What do you recommend?"

For many modern black youths steeped in the rebellious "gangsta" culture, what Cain heard—and did—next would have been unfathomable. Wallin told Cain he had to quit his position and go to another department, starting absolutely at the bottom and learning the operations from the ground up at the corporation's subsidiary, Burger King. Cain had to resign his title, give up a company car and privileges, and forgo stock options to flip burgers and cook fries. Understandably, Cain prayed about the decision, receiving assurance that he could do anything he put his mind to. Herman Cain joined the sixteen-year-olds at the Burger King assembly lines and front counters, mopping floors and cleaning toilets. But he persisted, learning the two-year program in nine months, impressing management so much that he was named a vice president of the Philadelphia region—perhaps, not coincidentally, the worst-performing region in the chain. Cain launched a restructuring, restoring morale and turning the region into Burger King's best in growth, sales, and profits at the end of four years.

Pillsbury had seen all of Cain it needed to see; in 1986, at only forty years of age, Cain was named president of the Godfather's Pizza chain of 911 stores. Like the Philadelphia Burger King, however, Godfather's had lost money. Cain chopped 300 locations, standardized menus, and sought advice from the local managers. In 1988, he formed a group of Godfather's executives to buy out the company for $50 million, putting his life's work on the line. Within two years, the value of the company had doubled, but Cain knew what made it work: "Service is the driving force in any restaurant business. . . . Our No. 1 rule is the customer is always right. Rule No. 2 is, if he is not right, go back to rule No. 1." Cain conducts outreach programs to inner-city youth, trying to impress on them the potential for entrepreneurship. "Many blacks in America today show disdain for the food-service trade. . . . But I saw it as a chance to run something, to own something. Black people should get over the idea that serving people carries a stigma. . . . More than half of current restaurant-owners began their careers in hourly positions like dishwashers and servers. . . . I just decided not to use segregation and racism and color as an excuse."[28]

As the ranks of blacks in entrepreneurial positions swelled, women also have become entrepreneurs like never before. By 1997, according to one study, one out of every four American workers is employed by a female-owned business.[29] Sales in women-owned firms had risen 235 percent over a nine-year period, while employment nearly tripled. According to Julie Weeks, research director for the National Foundation for Women-Owned Businesses, the influx of women into business schools had women "thinking of entrepreneurship right off the bat."[30] The report found service-sector businesses made up more than half of the female-owned companies, while, surprisingly, the number of women-owned construction firms rose by 171 percent since 1987.

Female entrepreneurs have benefited from the expansion of computer technology into the homes, especially the advent of desktop publishing operations. Like black entrepreneurs, however, they also have appreciated the service aspect of business. Firms such as Patti-Maids and other house- and office-cleaning businesses have thrived, as have in-home day-care facilities that require little start-up capital and which have enormous, consistent demand.

Cable television and the Internet have made millionaires of other women who found that they could market their products or expertise directly without going through a layer of male supervisors. Susan Powter, the guru of diet "infomercials," and Tamilee Webb, who advertised a tape series primarily on cable television that has become memorable even if only for its title, "Buns of Steel," reached unimagined heights for a once-fat divorcee and an aerobics instructor, respectively.

Bank Mergers and Capital Growth

Most small businesses capitalized themselves out of the savings of entrepreneurs and their friends and families. But midsized and larger firms often relied on bank loans, and the banking structure also expanded during the 1980s and 1990s through a series of mergers. Leading acquiring banks included Banc One of Columbus, Ohio, which completed takeovers with Valley National Bank in Arizona, as well as large institutions in Texas, Colorado, and West Virginia; BankAmerica of San Francisco, California, which by 1996 had banks in eleven states; Norwest out of Minneapolis, Minnesota, with operations in twelve states; and NationsBank, with a presence in nine states. Banc One rose in the 1980s from $3 billion in assets to $48 billion, with over 862 branches. BankAmerica capped the biggest turnaround in the history of American banking, going from virtual bankruptcy to an asset base of $188 billion to become the second-largest bank in the United States. In 1991, BankAmerica acquired Security Pacific Bank. NationsBank, the country's number four bank in size, was created from a merger of North Carolina National Bank (NCNB) and Georgia's C&S Sovran. Those merely constituted a few of the many mergers during the 1990s, including Chemical Bank/Chase ($10 billion, August 1995), First Union/First Fidelity ($5.4 billion, June 1995), and First Chicago/NBD Bancorp ($5.3 billion, July 1995). Meanwhile, the S&L industry had stabilized and even recovered a little; total tangible capital was rising, and problem assets were declining.[31]

Nevertheless, the banking structure itself remained somewhat backward. By 1995, federal regulations still did not permit interstate branch banking, considered a much more effective way to move funds to new areas of demand. Regional branch banking had been approved in the 1980s and had undergone a test case in Maine in 1975 when Maine offered out-of-state holding companies the opportunity to purchase Maine banks if their home state reciprocated by allowing Maine banks into the home state of the acquiring bank. A similarly successful regional compact occurred in North Carolina and Georgia, where North Carolina National Bank and Citizens and Southern expanded their operations in each other's states.[32]

At that point, most banking experts and many CEOs fully expected that the momentum would result in a national interstate banking law. Large New York banks had already purchased small independent banks in the West and South, while unit banks continued to oppose interstate branch banking, fearing they would be put out of business. Once again, however, the computer played a role. Money moved electronically, instantaneously, and, at the same time, credit cards from the major New York and California banks blanketed the nation. "On-line" banking loomed just around the corner in the neural networks of computers. Bank executives suddenly spoke of "tellerless" banks, where individuals conducted most of their transactions by automated teller. The drive for interstate branch banking lost its impetus, its force dissipated by the computer revolution, and perhaps the banking system has overcome the most deleterious effects of branching regulations. As Charles Calomiris has pointed out in several articles, American banks have entered an era of "universal banking," in which they offer a wide menu of services, particularly the securitization of risk, and relationship economies of marketing products.[33]

Legislation had not caught up with the reality of banking in the modern economy, but it hardly mattered. American banks had rebuilt themselves without government help, survivng what Calomiris called a "costly detour" of regulatory policy that led to "financial fragmentation."[34] With the financial structure restored and growing again, American banks returned to competitiveness in the world market, where Japan held a substantial lead. Eight of the world's top ten banks were Japanese by the 1990s, replacing what used to be exclusively an American domain. It reflected, though, the fact that by the mid-1990s the United States had more than $40 *trillion* in assets, with little of it in foreign hands. (Domestic debt—"*the*" national debt—was held overwhelmingly by Americans, with more than 85 percent in the hands of U.S. securities owners). The restored competitiveness of U.S. banks again highlighted the increasing global competition in which American companies found themselves.

Thus, as incredible as it would have seemed just a decade earlier, American banking actually stood poised to recapture much of the world market in 1998 when the Japanese financial structure started to implode. By November 1997, Japanese banks had reached a "danger zone," saddled with more than a quarter of a trillion dollars in bad loans.[35] The Tokyo stock market in 1997 alone fell by 22 percent, and six of Japan's largest financial institutions faced the prospect of substantial losses. By December 1997, two brokerage houses and the third-largest bank had collapsed, but an estimated $265 billion in bad loans still remained in the "strong" institutions. As the economy shrank at a rate of over 11 percent annually, it threatened to take with it several of its neighbors. Thailand, South Korea, and Malaysia all saw their economic structures eroding, in many cases reaping the harvest of two decades' worth of government support and subsidies. South Korea's composite index dropped almost 60 percent in 1997; Indonesia's fell more than 62 percent; and Thailand's stock exchange lost 70 percent of its value.[36] Critics of Americans' savings habits had pointed to Japan as the model saving nation, without noting that where savings are placed is at least as important as to how much one saves. Japanese tended to put their money into the real estate market, which lost between 50 percent and 75 percent of its value in a ten-year period, depending on the location of the properties. Even with a national savings rate of 15 percent, the real retained value of the savings by 1998 was only 3–5 percent, or possibly even below that of the United States. Developments in the Far East led Fed Chairman Alan Greenspan to note in 1998 that "elements of central planning [used by the Asian governments] turned out to be their Achilles' heel."[37]

The Competitive Advantage of Nations

Revitalizing the entrepreneurial spirit, dampened by decades of inflation, regulation, and bloated managerial bureaucracies, was all the more important as American business neared the twenty-first century. More than ever, foreign competitors challenged U.S.-made goods and services in almost every arena. A weakened but still competitive Japan remained the primary economic challenger, but Germany, plus the "seven dragons" of Korea, Malaysia, Thailand, Singapore, Hong Kong, the Philippines, and Taiwan also had wedged their way into markets previously dominated by the United States.

Often, American businesses responded to the competition—as business often has in the past—by appealing to the government for quotas or concessions from foreign governments to "level the playing field." In the summer of 1995, for example, the United States threatened massive tariff increases on Japanese luxury-car models unless the Japanese "opened their markets" to American autos. A June agreement, on the surface, prevented a dreaded trade war. Under the agreement, the Japanese planned voluntary measures to allow more U.S. auto dealerships in the country and to purchase more American-made parts. But such agreements had accomplished little in the past, for the simple reason that Japanese consumers culturally had much higher standards for cars and electronic devices than do American consumers. Merely allowing dealerships to open in no way guarantees that Detroit will sell more cars in Japan. Indeed, historically, the last thing the large U.S. automakers have wanted was a "level playing field." Fortunately for consumers, when the market has approached an equality of sorts, Detroit has been forced to radically improve its products, and has responded.

Nevertheless, industry—not just auto companies—frequently has complained that the Japanese have "managed trade" through MITI that puts American firms at a disadvantage. In the 1980s, a significant number of policy makers in the Democratic Party, including then-Senator Al Gore, Robert Reich, Ira Magaziner, Charles Ferguson, Chalmers Johnson, and Lester Thurow, all advocated that the United States adopt an "industrial policy." Members of the Bush administration, including Robert Mossbacher, also supported such a policy. Specifically, the industrial policy advocates called for the government to support consortia activities, such as the Sematech computer consortium, the National Aerospace Plane program, and High Definition Television (HDTV).[38] Repeating the mantra that the Japanese had an industrial policy, the advocates succeeded in getting President Bush to create a council on competitiveness, and under President Clinton, they turned the Defense Advanced Research Projects Administration that developed futuristic military weapons into a civilian-oriented Advanced Research Projects Administration with only the broadest of mandates.

Only one problem existed: Japan achieved success *in spite of its government's involvement,* not because of it. A recent study of MITI, for example, concludes with a much different assessment of Japan's success, especially in the 1980s. Scott Callon, in *Divided Sun,* maintains that "Whatever the validity of this notion of a *cooperative* and *functional* Japanese industrial policy, it is now seriously out of date" [italics in original].[39] Contrary to the view that the substitution of government industrial policy for market principles gave the Japanese an advantage, Callon concluded that "there *are* costs and there *are* dramatic failures in Japanese industrial policy, and these costs and failures appear to have increased substantially since Japan became an advanced industrialized economy" [italics in original].[40] Most analysts, some reluctantly, have blamed MITI and the special "government relationships" with Japanese corporations for their collapse in the 1990s, and by 1998, virtually no policy makers held up Japan as a model for industrial policy. And as Callon pointed out, the Japanese government's policies may have killed its only hope of long-term competition, computers: Far from focusing the Japanese computer companies on exports, government subsidies had the perverse effect of

turning them inward, to fight for an overpriced and profitable protected domestic market.

But wherever Japanese companies did take the lead from American firms—as in electronics and autos—it was because the Japanese
created more competitors, not fewer. Among the industries in which
the Japanese prevailed, they "created three times as many shipyards,
four times as many steel firms, five times as many motorcycle manufacturers, four times as many automobile firms, three times as many
makers of consumer electronics, and six times as many robotics companies as the United States."[41] Often, Japan of the 1950s, '60s, and
'70s resembled America in the same decades exactly one century earlier; at various times the Japanese had fifty-three integrated steel
firms, fifty motorcycle companies, twelve auto companies (compared
to the "Big Three" in the United States), and forty-two makers of handheld calculators. As Japan surged ahead of America in robotics, it create 280 new robotics companies; in the area of videocassettes, eight;
thirteen fax machine manufacturers; and twenty copier companies. In
contrast, a study by economists Richard Beason and David Weinstein
indicated that Japan's most subsidized industries have not been its
most successful.

By comparison, where did the United States hold the lead? In
computer chip companies, America had a sizable lead, 280 to 20. But
in software and computer manufacturers, the United States had thousands more firms. An astounding investment of almost 300 billion yen
in Japanese computer consortia left it in a worse relative position to
U.S. firms than before the investment. One could point to other areas—recording studios (where Nashville alone likely exceeds Japan's
total) or independent movie companies, giving America the cultural
grip on the world's markets—and the facts are the same. Wherever a
country gains a competitive advantage, it has to have competitors.
And, not surprisingly, the United States has started to recapture market share in steel, where companies such as AK and Nucor plus re-
constructed old giants like USX and Bethlehem have once again
encountered a myriad of competitors, including the highly efficient
minimills. In computer video games, American programmers and
software manufacturers have taken advantage of Americans' love of
football to offer no fewer than a dozen different video football games,
using almost as many hardware formats. Even in computer games, the
Japanese possibly have focused on the short term while conceding the
long-term market. The expansion of Internet gaming and the establishment of "cyber cafes" that feature lines of PCs linked to common
"shooter" games have already started to expand. All of that, of course,
is due to the proliferation of software designers and the plummeting
prices of personal computers, modems, and fiber-optic wire.[42] Only in
autos, where the start-up costs even forty years ago could engulf a

multimillionaire like Kaiser, has American competition remained in the hands of three major manufacturers.

Of course, international barriers excepted, the automobile buyer has a choice, thanks not only to a half dozen Japanese firms but also several German, a few European, and a couple of British companies as well. Autos, however, may be the last of the old-style managerial hierarchies to fall, largely because the technology is still relevant. Until the next major transportation breakthrough—the personal jet-pack or the antigravity device—automobiles will remain the major form of individual transportation in the world. But within the auto industry, tastes, too, can change, as witnessed by the rapid ascent of trucks and minivans, of which the majority of purchasers were women—a completely unpredicted phenomenon. Perhaps the most amazing aspect of the automobile is that by the mid-1990s public transportation advocates had all but given up trying to "break" the American public of its car culture.

A fundamental, little-heralded fact of American trade activity was that the United States, after rebuilding its competitive base from 1978 to 1987, started again to increase its exports, and in 1988—the peak for measuring the impact of the Reagan tax cuts on U.S. productivity—exports skyrocketed by more than 23 percent. In 1981, exports stood at approximately $354 billion, then they tailed off, recovered, and by 1991 reached $416 billion (constant 1991 dollars).

The absolutely crucial role of competition in forging productive industries emerged as a powerful theme in the comprehensive study of international trade advantages by Michael Porter, *The Competitive Advantage of Nations.*[43] Examining the industries from ten nations (including the United States), Porter and his team identified those industries in which a nation had a significant international market position as of 1985. Overlaps could exist—for example, both Japan and Korea had significant international market positions in shipbuilding—but expectedly Singapore, the smallest of the ten nations, had the fewest competitive industries. Japan had the most. Porter's analysis differed from traditional approaches, though, when he argued that nations succeed in "clusters" of industries, connected through vertical and horizontal relationships, rather than in individual industries.

Among Porter's most important findings was that "few 'national champions,' or firms with virtually unrivaled domestic positions, that were internationally competitive. Instead, most were uncompetitive though often heavily subsidized and protected."[44] Japan, which was noted for its audio equipment, had 25 competitors in that field, and 112 in machine tools. In the United States, where soft drinks accompany virtually all fast-food meals, the two largest competitors, Coca Cola and Pepsi Cola, aggressively battle for the market, despite the fact that they are global competitors. Moreover, the presence of the two giants has not stopped a consistent stream of new soft-drink firms from launching alternatives, such as Snapple. In some cases, such as the production of ceramic tiles in Italy, 30 percent of the *world's* production comes from a number of competitors in a single town.

Competition alone, however, will not ensure entrepreneurship. The business climate, including taxes, regulation, education, and public support for commercial ventures, must be favorable. Recent evidence suggests that, despite the high-tech promise of computers, *basic* education in reading and math makes a substantial difference in earnings—up to $30,000 a year for a high school graduate. Indeed, the authors of *The New Basic Skills* maintain that much of what accounts for a "wage gap" between college graduates and high school graduates can be learned before students even finish high school.[45] Wiring every classroom to the Internet thus becomes far less important than learning to add, multiply, read, write, and speak in public.

Fortunately, despite the decline in American education and other burdens that still afflict business in the United States, it has the most favorable business climate of any nation in the world, including Japan. For years, Japan's success was supported artificially—as many have argued—through protective tariffs, government policies, and high domestic housing and food costs. In the mid-1990s, the protective bubble burst under a wave of collapsing financial institutions. The United States, having (in general) never adopted such insulation, stood atop the competitive world.

Compared to Europe (with the recent exception of Ireland), America remains a business mecca. Unemployment in Germany has risen to 10.5 percent, in Italy to 11.5 percent, and in France to 11.7 percent. A central factor in that performance is that the share of gross domestic product (GDP) absorbed by government remains lower in the United States than in any other advanced country except Japan, which trails by a small margin (see Figure 13.1). Research at universities continues to lead the world, as evidenced by the 76 Nobel Prize laureates in chemistry, physics, and physiology/medicine just between 1970 and 1989. In the 1970s, Americans took 57 percent of the Nobel Prizes in those fields; in the 1980s, the Americans' share had risen to 62 percent. Whatever the failings of the elementary educational system in the United States, its colleges still excel in the hard sciences. The University of California–Berkeley alone claimed more prizes than the former Soviet Union had in its entire history.

Taxes and regulation form dual threats to any business, as data from cities demonstrates. A study of economic performance of several Michigan cities, correlated with the tax burdens they levied, appears in Figure 13.2. Clearly those cities that had lower tax burdens had much higher growth rates during the decade.

FIGURE 13-1 *Government Expenditures as Percent of GDP, 1955–1982*

	1955–1957*	1967–1969*	1974–1976*	1978–1982†
Belgium		35.6	43.0	52.0
Canada	25.1	33.0	39.4	41.3
Denmark	25.5	35.5	46.4	56.3
France	33.5	39.4	41.6	47.8
Germany	30.2	33.1	44.0	48.8
Italy	28.1	35.5	43.1	48.6
Japan		19.2	25.1	32.8
Netherlands	31.1	42.6	53.9	60.3
Norway	27.0	37.9	46.6	50.3
Sweden		41.3	51.7	63.8
Switzerland		25.0	33.5	
United Kingdom	32.3	38.5	44.5	45.8
United States	25.9	31.7	35.1	35.3
OECD average‡	28.5	35.5	41.1	45.3

*Three-year averages.
†Five-year average.
‡Unweighted and for 1955–1976, excludes Greece, Ireland, New Zealand, Spain, and Switzerland.

Sources: OECD (1978), 14–15, for 1955–1957, 1967–1969, and 1974–1976.
　　　　OECD (1985b), 41–42, for 1973–1982.

Sources: From Henry R. Nau, *The Myth of America's Decline: Leading the World Economy into the 1990s*, p. 175. Copyright © 1992 by Oxford University Press, Inc. Reprinted by permission.

FIGURE 13-2 *1980 Michigan Tax Burden and Per Capital Revenue*

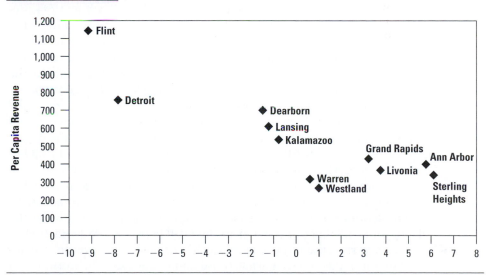

Source: Adapted from Stephen Moore and Dean Stansel, *A Prosperity Agenda for Michigan Cities*. (Midland, Mich.: Mackinac Center for Public Policy, 1993), pp. 7-13. Reprinted by permission of the Mackinac Center for Public Policy.

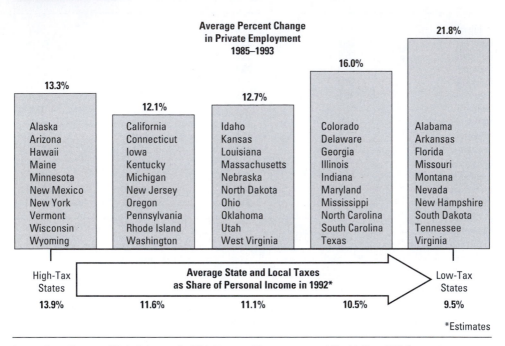

FIGURE 13-3   *Low-Tax States Create More Jobs*

Average Percent Change
in Private Employment
1985–1993

	13.3%	12.1%	12.7%	16.0%	21.8%
	Alaska	California	Idaho	Colorado	Alabama
	Arizona	Connecticut	Kansas	Delaware	Arkansas
	Hawaii	Iowa	Louisiana	Georgia	Florida
	Maine	Kentucky	Massachusetts	Illinois	Missouri
	Minnesota	Michigan	Nebraska	Indiana	Montana
	New Mexico	New Jersey	North Dakota	Maryland	Nevada
	New York	Oregon	Ohio	Mississippi	New Hampshire
	Vermont	Pennsylvania	Oklahoma	North Carolina	South Dakota
	Wisconsin	Rhode Island	Utah	South Carolina	Tennessee
	Wyoming	Washington	West Virginia	Texas	Virginia

High-Tax
States   **Average State and Local Taxes**   Low-Tax
              as Share of Personal Income in 1992*   States

13.9%   11.6%   11.1%   10.5%   9.5%

*Estimates

Source: From *Business Week,* February 7, 1994. Reprinted by permission of The McGraw-Hill Companies.

The same was true at the state level. *Business Week* in 1994 presented data showing starkly that "Low-Tax States Create More Jobs" (see Figure 13.3). Of course, cities and states could only affect business climates just so much. The federal government still had the capacity to levy far more burdensome taxes on business, both in the form of income taxes and the more destructive capital gains taxes. Tracking the incredible increase in capital gains after the top marginal rate was cut from 70 percent in the early 1970s to 20 percent under Reagan, Warren Brookes found that gains reported by the top 1 percent of all taxpayers rose from under $20 billion in 1976 to $176.3 billion in 1986, while the amount of taxes paid by that group increased by a factor of *eight.* Between 1979 and 1986 alone, gains rose by 467 percent, and taxes paid rose by 305 percent. Tax cuts, in fact, have been identified as the leading cause of increasing participation in the labor force, adding 6–7 percent to the GDP between 1982 and 1989.[46]

At any rate, the term "capital gains" seriously misleads anyone interested in understanding what those sums represent: In truth, it is a "capital earnings" that is reinvested into new factories, more jobs, and wealth creation. There is virtually no way to keep the capital earnings from expanding wealth for all. Wealth, once created, is a lightning bolt that must touch ground somewhere, and it will ground at the most receptive point on the horizon.

Lessons from Silicon Valley

The critical role of government policies in enhancing or deterring entrepreneurship applied to local businesses as well as international trade. A comparison of Silicon Valley and Route 128, two "high-tech" centers, underscored the importance of having the right policies, and highlighted the virtues of decentralization on the micro level. When compared to the other significant computer region in the United States, Route 128 in Boston, Silicon Valley, California, had all but buried its cross-continental rival. The once-hailed "Massachusetts Miracle" went bust, while Silicon Valley, home in 1990 to more than one-third of the 100 largest technology firms created since 1965 in the United States, saw the market value of its companies soar by $25 billion between 1986 and 1990. Route 128 companies, in contrast, increased in value by only $1 billion. What was so different about the two regions?

First and foremost, Silicon Valley epitomized the decentralized industrial system organized around regional networks. In doing so, the companies demonstrated the further breakdown of the classical Chandlerite model: Instead of growing vertically to control all sources of raw materials, supply, distribution, and sales, the Silicon Valley companies for the most part prided themselves on staying small, mobile, and nimble.[47] Whereas large managerial hierarchies impeded change, the Silicon Valley stars embraced it. Boundaries between companies remained highly porous, and the culture encouraged risk-taking. Silicon Valley entrepreneurs, according to one study, differed sharply from their Boston counterparts in that they were entrepreneurs as opposed to financial professionals. Able to use their "human capital" of ideas to start over with far less material capital than was required by the traditional steel or railroad companies, the Silicon Valley capitalists made money creating and selling firms, then starting over. Instead of cherishing continued, steady growth, the Silicon Valleyites thrived on the excitement of rapid surges and sudden plunges, because they understood that nothing could destroy their greatest assets—their ideas and concepts for chips and computers.

Route 128 businesses—in the more classical Chandlerite mold—emphasized long-term growth, and the regional organization "devoted most of its efforts to lobbying for state and local tax cuts that undermined the ability of the public sector to contribute to industrial development."[48] As a result, by 1992, only thirteen of the Route 128 region's start-ups surpassed $100 million in revenues, as opposed to forty-seven in Silicon Valley. Lotus, Sun, Silicon Graphics and dozens more firms pioneered new markets and explored interactive educational products. Silicon Valley surged past 128 because it had developed dynamic relationships between firms, not between firms and government. At the regional level, companies and, when necessary, local governments, could tailor policies for local conditions. Federal policies, on the other hand, were too far removed and responded too slowly to have any positive effect. For example, the 1986 Semiconductor Trade Agreement, "was disastrous for U.S. computer makers," as noted in our discussion of chips above.[49]

The traditional managerial hierarchies were on their way out, but that is not to say that a somewhat traditional path of entrepreneurs taking on partners through stock does not still occur. A clear example can be seen in the experience of Sandy Lerner and her husband, Len Bosack, two computer administrators at Stanford University. In the mid-1980s they found that their respective departments could not exchange e-mail or swap software because the computer networks could not "talk" to each other. Bosack designed a system that linked the computer networks to share databases and software, and when he and Lerner could not interest an existing company in their product, they quit their jobs to start Cisco Systems in their garage.

They received a good reception for their product but suffered constantly from a cash shortage, living on credit cards and taking a second mortgage on their house. With each new order that rolled in, so did a stack of bills. In 1990, after selling stock to raise cash, they lost control of Cisco, in the process selling their stock for $200 million. The company went on to be valued by Wall Street at $5 billion.[50]

When Capital Gains, Stocks Boom and People Gain

One of the major reasons the 1980s provided a renaissance for so many American industries was that as tax cuts placed more investment capital in the hands of large investors, they put that money to use in the financial markets to fund MCI, Microsoft, Apple, Ford, Boeing, and thousands of other companies. At the same time, typical consumers had more money to purchase goods because their tax burden fell while the tax burden on the wealthy—after the cuts— rose (see Figure 13.4). Even after two "adjustments" that raised rates on the rich slightly and eliminated deductions (in 1986 and 1990), the top 1 percent, the top 5 percent, the top 10 percent, and the top 50 percent *all* paid more in taxes, while the bottom 50 percent paid less in taxes (see Figure 13.5). If the 1981–1984 trends had continued, without the 1986 and 1990 tax increase, it

| FIGURE 13-4 | *Percentage of Total Tax Burden by Income Class, 1981–84* |

ADJUSTED GROSS INCOME ($)	1981	1982	1983	1984	PERCENT CHANGE, 1981–84
0–9,999	2.8	2.6	2.3	2.1	− 26.1
10,000–19,999	14.0	12.5	11.5	10.4	− 25.9
20,000–29,999	19.7	18.7	16.9	14.8	− 24.7
30,000–49,999	30.6	30.6	30.1	28.9	− 5.6
50,000–74,999	12.8	12.9	14.0	15.7	22.5
75,000–99,999	5.2	5.3	5.6	6.2	20.6
100,000–199,999	7.5	7.9	8.0	8.5	13.9
200,000–499,999	4.4	5.1	5.7	6.2	41.9
500,000 and over	3.1	4.5	5.9	7.2	134.7
Total		100.0	100.0	100.0	

Note: Totals may not add up to 100 percent because of rounding.

Source: Internal Revenue Service. From David Boaz, ed., *Assessing the Reagan Years.* (Washington, D.C.: CATO Institute Press, 1988), p. 73. Copyright © 1988 by CATO Institute Press, Washington, D.C. Reprinted by permission.

| FIGURE 13-5 | *Tax Shares and the Rich* |

Percent of Federal Individual Income Taxes Paid by the Richest and the Poorest

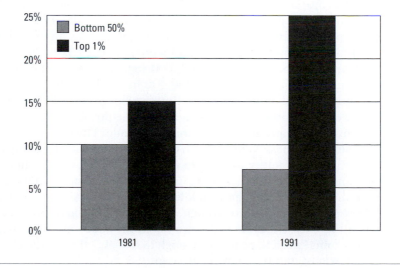

is likely that the percent change of taxes paid by those earning $500,000 and over would have finished the decade up by more than 200 percent!

Nevertheless, the effect of the lower tax rates sent investment soaring and spurred demand at the same time. Families gained like never before, contrary to dire commentaries that the middle class was disappearing. There was some truth to the statement that the middle class had gotten smaller, however. In the years following World War II until the mid-1970s, millions of American families moved into the middle class, to such an extent that the 1950 median male income of $13,768 did not extend as high as the federal poverty level in the 1990s (over $15,000 for a family of four). Then, around 1975, the middle class stopped growing, causing the percentage of households earning $25,000 to stagnate at approximately 40 percent. As the tax cuts wound their way into the framework of economic life, the proportion of households earning $25,000 to $75,000 actually dropped.

Aha! cried the critics. Tax cuts caused the "rich to get richer and the poor to get poorer." Except that the percentage of "poor"—those earning under $25,000—still had not changed. Rather, a silent boom occurred as the top rank grew broader, welcoming millions of nouveau riche into its ranks. Consider that in 1950, "fewer than one million American families earned as much as $60,000 in today's money."[51] It needs to be reinforced that this measure is in *constant* (1993) dollars—adjusted for inflation—so that rising prices do not have any effect on the value of earnings. By 1967, just over one million families earned more than $100,000 a year (1993 dollars). Then came the boom. In 1980, 2.7 million households had incomes of more than $100,000, and in 1993, 5.6 million households had attained that income level. Proportionally, the population had not risen that rapidly, meaning that a larger portion of the population was becoming rich by any standard. Indeed, one million households had incomes of over $200,000—that is, the number of people earning $60,000 (constant dollars) in 1950 and the number of people earning $200,000 in 1993 are the same. Or, put another way, the nation got three times richer in the 1980s than it had in the entire 1950–1980 period, adding the equivalent of the output of the entire German economy during the decade. The rich did get richer, but the middle class gained wealth even faster, causing the group of people defined as wealthy to swell to unprecedented levels. Although this remains a topic to be taken up again in the final chapter, suffice it to say that the analysis that had middle-class people losing ground in the 1980s measured "peak to trough" periods in the business cycle, and when the business cycle years are taken into account, with measurements going "peak to peak" or "trough to trough," the middle class benefited by any standard of measurement.

A key to wealth creation and upward mobility remained marriage. Stagnation of overall middle-class incomes have much to do with the fact that the percentage of households made up of married couples fell between 1980 and 1992, from 61 percent to 55 percent. Nor does there appear to be a link between increased workforce participation and marriage breakup: Just the opposite, when tax rates fell in the 1980s, many one-earner families became two-earner families.[52] And contrary to evidence that women were pushed into the workforce by higher taxes, many entered the workforce voluntarily because of lower taxes; and the question of participation in the workforce at all—not just the number of hours worked—was highly sensitive to progressive taxes.[53]

With more wealth in the hands of the public, and with the middle class moving into the lower echelons of the wealthiest class, securities provided a natural outlet for savings. Meanwhile, stock prices, long an indicator pointed to by corporate raiders as undervaluing corporate assets, finally started to catch up to the companies whose assets they represented by the late 1980s. A spectacular crash in 1987 did not seriously detour the boom, and analysts as late as December 1994 still posted dire predictions about the market: "Double-digit returns simply aren't there," one Merrill Lynch strategist said.[54] As of late 1997, the market reached a new peak weekly. Only months earlier, in October 1996, the Dow rose to 6,000; then passed that mark, representing a gain of $1 trillion for investors just since November 1994 and a total capitalization of *$10 trillion!*[55] Clear Channel, a company operating television and radio stations, gained 2,975 percent after October 1990.[56] Japan's stock market, by comparison, had plummeted in value by two-thirds in the 1990s, bringing Japanese property values down by up to 75 percent and threatening to drag under the nation's most stable banks.[57] In 1999, the Dow topped 11,000.

The astounding gains in the securities markets reflected an underlying—and totally fantastic—rise in American assets in the Reagan years, to the tune of a $23 trillion increase (from $17 trillion to $40 trillion). American dominance is nothing short of astounding: U.S. companies earned almost 47 percent of all the profits in the world economy by the mid-1990s. Yet much of the merger mania reflected the view of investors that the stock prices of American companies did not match what those firms were actually worth. Why was that the case?

Many of the corporations, as the corporate raiders well knew, often had quality workforces and excellent equipment but were poorly run at the top (Jensen's "agency costs" at work). Consequently, during the 1980s, a new wave of acquisition had occurred, capped by 1985, when the total value of the fifty largest mergers and acquisitions reached $94.6 billion. That year, Philip Morris acquired General Foods for $5.7 billion and General Motors bought Hughes Aircraft for $4.7 billion. The previous year, Chevron purchased Gulf Oil for $13.2 billion, and in 1986 General Electric absorbed RCA, USX acquired Texas Oil & Gas, and Burroughs merged with Sperry. In part, the relaxed regulatory environment encouraged mergers, and several of the mergers, such as USX's and GM's acquisitions, represented attempts to diversify and thus stabilize the companies against market fluctuations.

Other purchase offers, however, came when corporate raiders identified a stock that had not performed well, compared with what the raider thought was the true value of the company. Raiders such as T. Boone Pickens, Saul Steinberg, and Carl Icahn usually began by purchasing a small stake in a company; making a tender offer (using borrowed funds, with help from investment banks like Drexel Burnham) to the other shareholders for enough additional stock to gain a controlling interest in the firm; and either acquiring control or striking such terror in the hearts of managment that it paid a huge premium to reacquire stock. The latter practice, called "greenmail," occasionally had beneficial results for a company: When Saul Steinberg's Reliance Group made a bid to take over Disney in 1984, Disney management brought onto its board Stanley Gold and Sid Bass, who in turn demanded a decisive management change that led to the hiring of Frank Wells and Michael Eisner and literally turned the Disney company around.[58]

Raiders performed a valuable function. They enforced stricter accountability on management by stockholders, who frequently had little impact on how companies directed their affairs. Giants such as GM were immune to such tactics, and thus were able to merge with weak companies like Hughes or absorb ticking time bombs (with potentially difficult entrepreneurs such as Ross Perot and his Electronic Data Systems). But most companies had to take care that management did not diversify without rhyme or reason or pay too much when they did find a fit. In 1989, for example, Ford took over Jaguar after it had substantially improved itself, giving Ford a foreign, top-end auto producer. But Ford seriously overpaid, giving the British stockholders approximately $2.5 billion.

Entrenched, high-salaried managers, of course, complained that takeover tactics forced them to ignore the legitimate interests of customers and employees in the long run to focus on short-term takeover defenses. In fact, however, GM lost its profitability and productivity at the very time it overinvested in capital. Its state-of-the-art robotic Hamtramck plant had more robots than any Japanese factory, yet was woefully unproductive, as robot paint sprayers routinely doused each other.[59] Michael Jensen found that during the 1970s and 1980s one-quarter of the firms in a study (including Ford, ITT, Du Pont and

Goodyear) invested more in physical plant and R and D than traditional margins demanded.[60] As the authors of another study suggest,
"Detailed corporate financial reports do not support the assertions
that U.S. companies faced a high cost of capital. . . ."[61] Rather, the "internal systems for profit planning and capital budgeting tended to
work against attempts to invest in the organizational capabilities
needed for long-run survival."[62] Or, the managerial revolution in the
1800s spawned a financial and budgeting system that in the twentieth
century did not account for managerial talent very well because those
organizational capabilities were not easily quantifiable in the cash-
flow financial systems.

If the takeover wave did not detract from companies' ability to
raise capital, did it nevertheless have other negative effects? Managers
often explained that they were so busy fighting takeovers they could
not deal with foreign competitors, yet productive companies never
seemed to face the problems that afflicted the poorly managed businesses. The most serious criticism of the 1980s "merger mania" in the
United States involved the charge that companies assumed more debt
with each new takeover attempt. Warnings that the American corporate structure was "overloaded with debt" completely missed the
point; by 1990, the worth of corporate equity in the United States exceeded its debt by $1 trillion! The level of equity increased during the
so-called decade of debt, rising by $160 billion after 1980.

Instead, a second boom in the 1990s occurred. The market, rather
than seeing weak companies teetering with debt and ripe for Japanese
acquisition, found restructured firms made more efficient by raiders
and competition. During the 1980s and early 1990s, for the first time
in decades, the boards of directors of major U.S. companies demanded
that CEOs—not just faceless middle managers—be held responsible
for company performance. At GM, Compaq Computer, Kodak, Westinghouse, American Express, and IBM, boards had revolted, no longer
rubber-stamping CEOs' decisions. At GM, the board even separated
the position of CEO from the position of chairman of the board when
it fired Robert Stempel, a step that none of the other major companies
took. But it sent a clear signal that American business had entered a
new era, or, as a Kodak executive called it, the "post-Stempel world."[63]

Then, in 1997, when Wall Street felt several shocks that took the
Dow down more than 1,000 points—more than 500 in a day!—critics
crowed that the debt had finally exacted its tribute. No sooner had
such claims surfaced than the stock market again climbed upward—
hardly racing as it had, but steadily recovering virtually all of its losses,
which at worst totaled about 4 percent. In comparison, the losses that
could be accounted to inflation since 1989 totaled more than 29 percent, not counting the capital gains taxes that immediately consumed

20 percent of any profit. By 1998, the market had recovered almost entirely, in the process capitalizing American industry afresh, resulting in a remarkable 4.5 percent productivity increase by the third quarter of 1997, with manufacturing productivity soaring almost 10 percent.[64]

Changes at the top sometimes followed, but usually led, a turnaround in the production of quality goods in America. Early in the 1980s the precarious position of steel, autos, electronics, and other industries generated an orgy of productivity-enhancing and management-improvement books. Some derisively referred to "management by best-seller" as authors offered instant solutions. One of the first, and genuinely most insightful, was *In Search of Excellence* by Tom Peters and Robert Waterman Jr. The book examined the corporate traits of several highly successful, or "excellent," companies, urging managers to stay close to their customers and to demand quality in every endeavor.[65] Some authors, such as William Ouchi, in *Theory Z,* recommended copying Japanese management methods, and some corporations, such as Xerox, found the Japanese models appropriate. Referred to as the "American Samurai," Xerox's share of worldwide copier revenues fell by half, from 82 to 41 percent, during the 1970s. Canon, Ricoh, Minolta, and Sharp had cut into the American giant's business. But Xerox introduced the ten series of copiers in 1982, gained a few market share points back in 1983, and by 1985 had regained more than a dozen points in key middle-range copiers, where it counted the most. Xerox at that time had done what no other U.S. company had done in reestablishing itself, and the famous 1075 won the Japanese Grand Prize for Good Design. Much of Xerox's success came from Japanese-style "just-in-time" manufacturing that eliminated excess parts and storage bins full of spares, allowing more employee participation in the processes and reiterating the emphasis on quality by designing quality into the product rather than developing an extensive warranty and repair network.[66]

Japanese-Style Management and Managerial Efficiency

At least one study of transplanted Japanese industries in America has heralded a new epoch in capitalism, that of "innovation-mediated production."[67] The authors found that in heavy industry, Japanese-style management has transferred well to U.S. systems, but in electronics the record is less favorable. An increasing synthesis of innovation, production, and research has resulted from the socialization of the work process, demanding far more skilled and educated workers capable of thinking abstractly. Meanwhile, as of 1998, Japan entered its sixth year of severe stagnation, with growth at the 1 percent level and record unemployment rates.

There has also been evidence to suggest that Japanese-style "reengineering" has not been a roaring success in American companies. Jack Stanek, who runs the International Survey Research Corporation, compiled the most comprehensive database on U.S. workers ever assembled, containing 12.5 million workers and more than 300,000 managers of the top American companies. Stanek's analysis of the database showed that more than half of the managers reported that the restructuring to make the companies more competitive, based on the new "empowerment culture," has actually made firms less flexible and more inefficient.[68] American workers and managers are not Japanese or Germans, and they have a completely different view of life, work, and leisure. Still, the productive record of the Japanese companies between 1970 and 1990 led most management professionals to at least investigate *kaizen* principles.

In the quest for the Holy Grail of management perfection, corporate leaders have left no example unexamined. Some management experts suggested copying the leadership traits of Attilla the Hun, Abraham Lincoln, or Jesus; others referred to their own thriving businesses in hair salons or greeting cards. In most cases, the advice either was so company-specific as to be irrelevant to other types of businesses or such common sense that managers *should* intuitively know it. What manager really needed, for example, to be told to focus on what the customer wanted?

Instead, the real change in American business in the 1970s and 1980s involved the end of the managerial revolution. The layers of managerial hierarchies that once had served American industry well acted as a bottleneck to information flow instead of a filter. Finance departments increasingly passed along not the wrong data but the wrong types of information. Belatedly, business recognized that it was bloated. The same hierarchies that once gave America its competitive advantage had become part of the problem. Consequently, in the late 1970s and 1980s, major steel companies, soon followed by autos, computers, communications, and other companies, slashed thousands of managerial positions from their payrolls.

While management shouldered much of the blame—made more visible by whopping bonsuses and multimillion-dollar "golden parachutes" bestowed on executives such as Roger Smith—labor had contributed to the doldrums with outrageous contracts and declining productivity. Problems in individual industries have been discussed already, but by the 1980s American workers had improved their productivity. Contentions that the work ethic had eroded may have had some application in specific situations, including highly unionized "featherbedded" jobs. Strangely, at the same time some analysts complained about the decline in the work ethic, others lamented the plight of the "overworked American." Who was right?

A March 1969 issue of *Psychology Today* pointed out that in the 1950s sociologists had predicted that America would become a "leisure society," with people increasingly abandoning work in favor of pleasurable activities. By 1973, however, other analysts warned that "work has become our intoxicant. . . . Americans are working harder than ever before."[69] A Roper poll that year found that 85 percent of the American public was satisfied with its field of work, and the number rose to 87 percent in 1988. One poll posed the following question: "If you received enough money to live as comfortably as you like for the rest of your life, would you continue to work?" Those answering "yes" rose steadily over time, from 70 percent in the 1970s to 74 percent in the period 1983–1987 and 85 percent in 1988. More than 90 percent of Americans polled stated that it was important to work. Perhaps more surprising, data collected over a twenty-year period in the 1960s to 1980s revealed little change in sick-leave rates. Even more shocking, whereas Japan's absenteeism rates stood at a minuscule 2 percent, America's were only slightly higher, at 3.5 percent, or second lowest in the world.[70] Surveys asking "How much pride, if any, do you take in the work that you do?" found that Americans had the highest "pride" rate of any nation: 84 percent said "a great deal," while only 36 percent of Japanese responded "a great deal."[71]

The raw numbers were impressive. In 1980, 97.6 million Americans were employed, and a decade later 117.7 million had full-time jobs. Employment increased 20 percent in a decade when population increased only 10 percent. Since 1973, U.S. employment rose an unbelievable 40 percent, compared to *zero* net new job growth in Europe (although, again, there were pockets of job growth, as in Ireland).[72]

As management corrected itself, and as heavily unionized companies had to adapt to the realities of foreign competition, U.S. business not only regained productivity, it recaptured percentages of world trade. Although statistics on international trade often must take into account the fact that nations use different accounting methods and that currencies fluctuate against each other, Henry Nau, using data from the United Nations and estimates from Walt Rostow, showed that the share of world trade commanded by the United States rose by two percentage points between 1978 and 1985.[73] That increase came mostly because American exports rose, and continued to rise, during the 1980s.

Ironically, increasing exports came at a time when the United States supposedly was becoming a "debtor nation." Several factors led to that widespread, widely reported notion that America was a net debtor, some of them statistical manipulations and some simply irrelevant. Official statistics contributed to some inaccuracies. For example, the Commerce Department had put America's international investment position at $4.4 billion in 1984, minus $111.9 billion in 1985, and minus $263.3 billion by 1986. But as the U.S. economy grew and increased the values of foreign-held assets in the United States, those assets grew (and were counted against some trade indicators) as opposed to the declining values of American-held assets abroad, which, on the whole, were older assets. Worse, the older assets were still valued at purchase prices rather than at current market values. Adjusting the assets for real, current market value, the RAND Corporation found that in 1985, rather than a negative $111 billion, an adjusted market value of the same assets would leave the United States with a $177 billion surplus. Likewise in 1986, RAND's adjusted data showed that the United States had a $49 billion surplus instead of a $263 billion deficit.[74]

At the same time, new alarms went off related to foreign purchases of American firms, highlighted when, in December 1988, CBS televised "America for Sale," a "news" special that showed Japanese purchasing land in Hawaii and touring the Grand Ole Opry. Typically, the media missed the story: Great Britain owned 40 percent of all foreign-held assets in the United States, while Japan held only 5 percent. Between 1983 and 1988, there were only seventeen hostile takeovers of American firms by foreigners, of which only one involved a Japanese purchase.

Another way in which the account balances made it appear that the Unites States had become a debtor already had taken place in the period 1973–1982. When OPEC hiked prices and petrodollars flowed into American banks, Chase, Citibank, BankAmerica, and other giants had nowhere to put those deposits where they could generate income. American industry was languishing. Thus, the banks sent the loans abroad, mostly to Latin America and Mexico. At one time, U.S. banks had more than $110 billion in loans to companies in those areas. By the late 1970s, however, the big banks realized that Latin American and Mexican growth had stalled; it looked as though the loans never would be repaid. Consequently, quietly, the banks individually dipped into their profits and set up "loan loss reserves" that they used to pay down the debts. More important, they quit making new Latin American and Mexican loans, choosing instead to invest in the then-booming American economy. But the foreign-trade balance sheet reflected only that in 1979 U.S. banks contributed more than $100 billion to the asset side of the ledger, and five years later that $100 billion had disappeared. For all accounting purposes, it looked like the United States had gone from being a "creditor" to a "debtor." In fact, though, the loans simply moved from overseas to America, from Columbia to Cleveland, and from Argentine to Albuquerque. Had anything really changed in America's international position? Hardly. If anything, the fact that U.S. banks again found investment opportunities at home better than in Mexico was an encouraging fact. After passage of the North American Free Trade Agreement (NAFTA) in 1993, the pattern started to reverse itself, as U.S.-Mexican trade rose especially fast, from $80 billion in 1993 to $100 billion in 1994, creating more than 100,000 new jobs by the most conservative estimates.

Finally, as the RAND report noted, even the Commerce Department data represent *American* calculations of Japanese data, and the Japanese tended to double- or even triple-count some trade items. For example, if an auto had certain microchips in it, the value of the auto was counted, but in some cases so was the value of the microchips. The inability to ensure that data remained consistent across national barriers further worked in Japan's favor.

For debating purposes, however, assume that the critics' view (the anti-NAFTA/Ross Perot/Pat Buchanan view) of free trade was correct and that free-trade agreements like NAFTA actually did increase imports. There is no connection between rising imports and unemployment; the U.S. could import 100 percent more bananas, of which it grows almost none domestically, but that would not put out of work one orange grower or rice planter, let alone a single computer engineer or telecommunications software designer. (NAFTA, however, showed no ill effects. A 1998 survey of 361 senior executives revealed that 28 percent said that NAFTA had increased business significantly, and 42 percent said it had no effect. Only 4 percent said that NAFTA hurt their business, and a vast majority—91 percent—said that NAFTA had not affected labor costs).[75]

The Deficit Debate, Again

Supposedly, American business in the 1980s not only suffered from a trade deficit but also from domestic budget deficits. According to popular theory, those deficits arose from the 1982–1984 Reagan tax cuts. That was not the case, however, as seen in the Office of Management and Budget statistics table (Figure 13.6). Federal revenues rose after the tax cuts and continued to rise substantially every year until the 1990 "deficit reduction plan" actually raised taxes. Clearly, excess spending, which rose from $800 billion to $1.4 trillion over the same period, caused the deficits. Between 1955 and 1995, as Figure 13.7 illustrates, the real growth in the budget occurred not in national defense, which rose only 12 percent, but in education and social

FIGURE 13-6 *Spending Caused the Deficit, Not Tax Cuts (in Billions of Dollars)*

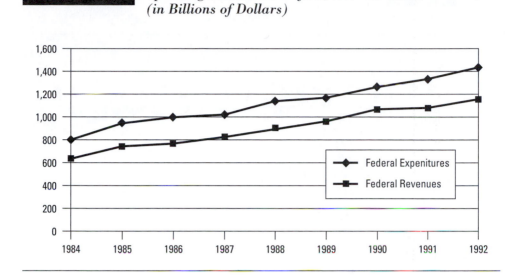

FIGURE 13-7 *Growth in the Federal Budget*

	BILLIONS OF 1995 DOLLARS		
	1955	1995	REAL GROWTH 1955–95
National defense	$242.8	$271.6	11.9%
Health	1.7	272.4	16,374.2
Income security	28.8	223.0	674.0
Social security	25.2	336.1	1,236.4
Education and social services	2.5	56.1	2,117.4
Veterans' benefits	26.6	38.4	44.5
Community development	0.7	12.6	1,618.8
Interest	27.6	234.2	750.0
International affairs	12.6	18.7	48.2
Science and technology	0.4	17.0	3,937.8
Agriculture	20.0	14.4	− 27.9
Justice/general government	5.2	32.4	523.4
Transportation	7.1	39.2	453.1
Energy/natural resources	7.2	26.5	268.4
Offsetting receipts	− 19.8	− 41.4	108.6
Total outlays	$388.9	$1,558.9	2,957

Source: Budget of the U.S. Government. Fiscal Year 1996. Historical Tables. From *National Review*, December 25, 1995, p. 21. Reprinted by permission.

FIGURE 13-8   *Deficits as a Share of GNP, 1930–1990 (in Real Dollars)*

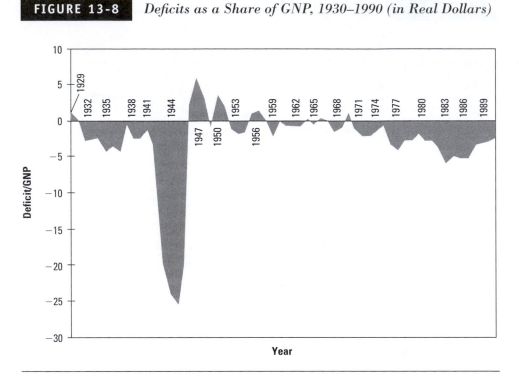

Source: From author's calculations, based on *Historical Statistics of the United States* and *Statistical Abstract of the U.S.* (1991)

services (2,117 percent), health (16,374 percent), and science and technology (3,937 percent).

Contrary to popular presentations of deficits, current deficits are not high by historical standards and have fallen since 1987. Usually, deficits are reported in *nominal* dollars, meaning the dollars reflect inflation. Similarly, deficits are discussed in isolation. But if told that "Mr. X has a Visa/Mastercard debt of $1,000," can you tell if that is a "heavy" debt for him to pay? It is impossible without knowing what Mr. X makes. If he makes $1 million a year, his debt is meaningless, but if he makes $2,000 he has a problem. Thus, the only accurate way to present deficit data is in *real* (constant) dollars as a share of GNP. Figure 13.8 depicts this data, and reveals that, not only are current deficits lower than seven years ago, but they are *lower than the deficit levels in the 1970s,* and far below those run by Franklin Roosevelt during the New Deal.

The "national debt"—often referred to as a "bomb" waiting to go off—has been treated with similar hysteria. When expressed in

FIGURE 13-9   *Debt as a Share of GNP, 1930–1990*

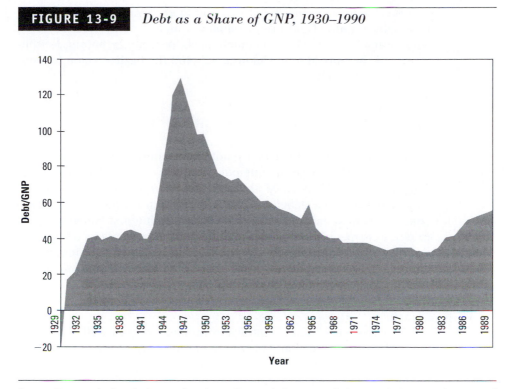

Source: From author's calculations, based on *Historical Statistics of the United States* and *Statistical Abstract of the U.S.* (1991)

real dollars as a share of GNP (i.e., how much we as a nation owe, compared to how much we earn), debt levels, while high, are lower than debt levels under John Kennedy, Dwight Eisenhower, and Harry Truman—all of whom had reputations as fiscal conservatives, and, of course, Franklin Roosevelt, who did not (see Figure 13.9). Once again, "gloomsters" warned that Americans as a society were taking on too much debt. Yet consumer debt rose 25 percent slower than charitable giving in the United States!

Two indicators used by economists and the business community to signal excess debt, and its more significant corollary, inflation, have been the price of gold and interest rates. Just as the body's temperature is a symptom of illness, so too have those indicators signaled an inflationary economy. For example, prior to the 1973 oil crisis, a Krugerrand sold for under $180. A few years later Krugerrands sold for $950 a coin. If the American economy had entered a period of consumer binging and excess debt, one would expect to find during the

1980s evidence of rising gold prices and interest rates. In fact, neither rose substantially. Gold prices remained as low in 1990 as in 1980, while interest rates fell by as much as six percentage points. Neither indicated that any kind of sickness afflicted the basic economic foundation of the nation.

Business and the Global Economy of the 1990s

Deficits and the national debt are not at the ominous levels many suggest, and neither pose an immediate threat to American business. They are, however, a signal about intentions and direction, which is why rising nominal deficits in the 1980s did not generate any deep concern in financial markets, as reflected in interest rates and gold prices. Most people knew, with conservative presidents in office, that the nation would not spiral out of financial control. More important, businesses were outgrowing inflation and the GNP outpaced deficit growth. Had everything else stayed the same, the deficits were on track to eliminate themselves, albeit slowly, through sheer economic growth.

Nowhere did the new realities of financial responsibility show up faster than in financial and currency markets, which instantaneously rendered its verdict on every fiscal move by every major government in the world. No longer could governments contain their inflation domestically or protect it from world pressure. Walter Wriston, who led Citibank into the top position in world financial markets in the 1970s, observed, "The entire globe is linked electronically, with no place to hide."[76] Money and information could move across borders at the speed of light. During the Gulf War, Kuwaiti banks faxed their entire account ledgers, representing virually all of their wealth, to Bahrainian banks in a period of less than forty-eight hours. Governments fretted about losing their power to inflate, and the crash of the dollar against the yen between 1986 and 1995 illustrated that productivity relationships and fiscal policy will face an accounting in the international arena. As Wriston often pointed out, money went where it was wanted and would not stay where it was not welcome.

Russia was a case in point. Long before communism officially expired, the Communist Party school presented the movie *Wall Street* in Moscow as an object lesson in the evils of capitalism. An American observer, however, noted that "the young acolytes, presumably the next generation of Leninist priests, reacted to this morality play . . . in a way that would have made poor Oliver Stone weep. . . . They audibly lusted after the goods on display: the stretch limo (with bar and TV), the sushi-making machine [and Michael Douglas's Turnbull & Asser shirts]. God, they loved those shirts."[77] Lenin Hall then fell silent as Douglas (Gordon Gekko) delivered his classic line, "Zhdanost—eto khorosho!" ("Greed is good!"), and the "Communists went wild. There were whoops of approval."[78] One could hear the sound of the lid on the garbage dumpster slamming on Marxism as it was confined to the slag heap of history. In practical terms, a lesson in enterprise zones was delivered in the October Region of Moscow, where the regional council passed measures that made it easier for businesses to register in the area, thus reducing bribes and bureaucracy. The Russian "enterprise zone" soon showed the results: More than 4,500 small enterprises registered within a year, including restaurants, research labs, construction businesses, electronics firms, and so on. Placing a small tax on the license fees, the regional council increased its annual income from 73 million rubles to 250 million rubles.[79]

The message was clear: The market would expose any nation engaged in fiscal shenanigans, and fluctuations in American currency values represented a reaction to domestic policies. Under Reagan, however, inflation disappeared, leading to a quandary: If there was no domestic inflation, how could the dollar fall against foreign currencies? Foreigners recognized that dollars did not buy their own goods as in the past; that represented increased productivity in those countries, and, in the case of Japan, a very strong yen due to the extremely low Japanese inflation rate in the 1990s—well below our own. Yet Wriston's words still ring true, because much of the Japanese surplus ended up in American investments. Japan financed a great deal of our debt in the 1980s and early 1990s (although Americans still held 85 percent of the total national debt, putting to rest any idea that the Japanese somehow had a "dagger pointed at our hearts"). Instead of reflecting poor fiscal policies in the United States—and they could have been still better—the rise of the yen attested to Wriston's maxim that money went where it was wanted, namely, to the United States.

The astounding fact of American business in the late 1980s and early 1990s is that, even with Japanese investments, junk bonds, and the booming stock market, the entrepreneurial explosion could have absorbed still larger sums of capital. Part of the problem stemmed from the old Latin American loans written off in the 1980s, where the major banks had taken a beating. BankAmerica (BofA), once the number one bank in the world, slid down the ladder, replaced by Japanese giants. BofA restructured and cut staff and offices while focusing on domestic lending. It revived in 1990, just as books were written about its funeral.[80]

Japan's banks surged to the forefront largely because the culture and tax rates in Japan had encouraged personal savings. Furthermore, Japanese consumers were "cash rich and goods poor." The absence of available land for housing meant that citizens there could not expect to own even the most modest American-sized family home. Whereas Americans put money into their houses, "saving" in essence as much as 30 percent of their salary a year, and into forced savings such as Social Security—viewed by many as a retirement fund—and high-quality private health insurance systems, the Japanese had no such automatic deductions from their paychecks. Likewise, one recent study of workers' compensation in America showed that it caused reductions in private savings by as much as 25 percent when all other factors were held constant![81] When all of the varieties of "forced" savings and the cost of home mortgages are factored into the savings rates, America compared favorably with Japan or any other nation in real savings.

The New Competition in Quality Service

Perhaps no challenge looms larger for American business than that of maintaining quality in the service sector. And perhaps that is why local companies and small businesses hold a qualitative edge over the managerial corporations involved in services, and should continue to do so in the immediate future. That point is well illustrated with the example of two health and fitness gyms, one in Phoenix, Arizona, and the other in Dayton, Ohio. In the 1980s, fitness became a major market in the United States, featuring large chains such as L.A. Fitness and Ballys, which, as of 1994, was the largest health and fitness chain in America. Yet employee turnover at Ballys and other chains was staggering—a local club might change managers every six months. Worse, the large chains experienced general employee turnover of close to 100 percent a year. High-volume chains were less fitness clubs than credit operations, running "lifetime" memberships sold at high initial fees with the promise of very low "annual dues," and, as their corporate reports made clear, their real business was in financing the contracts, not in building bodies or burning fat.[82]

By comparison, a relatively small gym in Phoenix, Weider's Gym, opened for business in the mid-1980s to tackle the giants. Originally planned as part of a chain that did not materialize, but keeping the Weider name, Weider's fostered a total social atmosphere in addition to providing the most up-to-date workout equipment and programs. The co-owners and managers, Alan Rosen and Jon Perryman, competing in a large urban market of almost 2 million against well-financed national chains such as Ballys, L.A. Fitness, Moore's Nautilus, World, and Powerhouse Gyms, knew they had to offer more than just barbells and aerobics. They targeted families as well as singles; sponsored desert nature walks; threw Friday-night social hours at the gym with catered refreshments; held fitness contests; and encouraged members of the Phoenix Cardinals and Arizona Rattlers indoor football team to join for "celebrity" appeal. Aware that they knew almost nothing about aerobics, Rosen and Perryman hired the top aerobics coordinator in the state, Faye Stenerson, to create and run a program that featured traditional aerobic workouts, kids fitness classes, yoga, and her own fitness invention, Karobics, a combination of karate and aerobics. The employees made follow-up "satisfaction" calls to new members, knew members by their first names—usually after one visit—and solicited suggestions about all aspects of the business.

Weider's Gym was typical of a small business, which can suffer sudden shocks. Although after four years management and major front-office staff had not changed once, and although Weider's had double the usage rate of other area gyms, meaning that the owners had to refurbish equipment and facilities at a faster rate, it had started to lose members in the face of relentless competition. Then, one of those events that strikes a partnership hit Weider's: A death in one of the owner's families caused a reassessment of the entire business, followed shortly by the sale of Weider's to a chain, L.A. Fitness, which hired many of the Weider personnel, including Stenerson.

But in the cycle of entrepreneurship, no vacuum goes unfilled. The Phoenix gym market witnessed the appearance of other aggressive businesses, including Mountainside Health and Fitness, whose owner, Tom Hatton, was named "Arizona entrepreneur of the year" by a local business magazine. Mountainside, started in 1991, appealed to a more downscale clientele—students, power lifters—and grew from sales of $186,000 to $1.3 million in 1996 to become the seventh-largest gym in Phoenix, with a membership of 5,000. More relevant to Hatton's competitors, the gym had signed up 1,000 new members in a two-month period, mostly from other fitness clubs, including Weider's.[83] Whether Mountainside can become another L.A. Fitness or is doomed to follow Weider's into obscurity is the ongoing entrepreneurial saga.

More than halfway across the country, in Dayton, Ohio, a slightly different entrepreneurial story unfolded. Former bodybuilder and world bench-press champion Larry Pacifico took a different approach to the problem of competing with the "big boys" in the health and fitness industry. In 1980, while working as a vice president for another fitness company, Pacifico opened a small gym on Dayton's north side with $20,000 in savings. Competing against Holiday, Moore's, and others, Pacifico focused on a market not reached by the all-purpose gyms—bodybuilders and weight lifters. He worked full-time at his fitness company job, then spent an additional four hours a day at his

Tested, Literally, by Fire: Aaron Feuerstein and the Destruction of Malden Mills

AARON FEUERSTEIN FELT COMPLETELY DEpressed when his family's company, Malden Mills, in Lawrence, Massachusetts, declared bankruptcy in 1981. Like other textile mills in the area, it had laid off workers and struggled, with one after another leaving the area. Fuerstein refocused, gathered himself, and poured more money into R & D, creating new synthetic fabrics such as Polartec and Polarfleece for outdoor wear, like L.L. Bean.

Suddenly, Malden Mills had business like never before. A family-owned firm started almost a century earlier, Malden had the patents for the fabrics and the machines needed to make them. Lines ran all day and all night, turning out products that had quality above all. It produced 130,000 yards a week, employing more than 3,000 people. By that time, Feuerstein, then seventy years old, must have thought he had been through the fire and seen it all. Christmas was approaching, and, as he always had, Feuerstein could be counted on to hand out generous bonuses. The employees could never have guessed how great their bonus would be that year.

On December 11, 1995, a catastrophic fire swept through the main manufacturing facility at Lawrence. More than thirty people were injured and trapped until rescued by fellow workers and firefighters. Through Herculean efforts, one small building remained, and Feuerstein, watching from the parking lot, fought back tears as he said, "This is not the end." But few believed it. As Bill Cotter, a Malden worker for nineteen years, recalled, "We thought we'd just collect our last check and then go on unemployment." Instead, Feuerstein informed the employees that he intended to rebuild the plant and that they would all get paid that month. When the next month's payday came along, Feuerstein met that payroll, too. And the next. Personally supporting 3,000 workers while the factory was recreated, Feuerstein literally brought his company through the fire. All but 400 of the employees had come back to work, but he guaranteed them new jobs when the new plant opened in 1997 and kept them on health benefits while appointing full-time employees to help them find work until that time.

Within ten days, the factory was in operation, and within a few weeks, the lines turned out 230,000 yards a week—100,000 a week more than before the fire. So impressed were his employees, that they willingly gave more than their alloted time, occasionally twenty-four hours a day. "They wanted a miracle to happen and it did," Feuerstein humbly observed. In truth, Aaron Feuerstein was the miracle.

Source: Michael Ryan, "They Call Their Boss a Hero," *Parade Magazine,* September 8, 1996, 4–5.

own gym. Pacifico soon quit his job to put his full efforts into his enterprise, and in the process of rehabilitating an injured Cleveland Browns safety, Kyle Kramer, Pacifico found a partner. Although still catering to weight lifters and bodybuilders, the newly named Champions expanded its client base. Pacifico and Kramer encouraged "drop-ins" from the World Wrestling Federation tours or from the Christian "Power Team" that came to town. Emphasizing personal training as much as annual memberships, Pacifico and Kramer virtually memorized individual trainees' weight programs. In 1993 Champions opened a new facility in Moraine, a blue-collar section of Dayton that bordered wealthy Oakwood, and thus the gym featured a unique clientele, with gray-haired socialites training next to grungy bodybuilders or boxers lifting alongside pro athletes such as Hugh Douglas, a number one draft pick of the New York Jets. By 1995, they opened a brand-new Champions facility, capitalized at $1 million, across town to replace the original location.

Once again, though, the challenges of growth demanded change. In 1997 Kramer had exploited his football contacts to lay the groundwork for expanding a franchise-type of arrangement with Cincinnati Bengals football players in other cities, which involved substantial travel, and Pacifico, who did not want to travel any longer, amiably split with Kramer. Champions remained Pacifico's gym, while Kramer named his facility, "Kyle Kramer's Pro Fitness."[84] With his NFL contacts, would Kramer take his franchise to the levels attained by Ballys? Or would it go the way of Weider's, absorbed by a larger firm? The saga continues.

The difficulty of maintaining quality while expanding was common to virtually all small businesses. By the 1990s, with its emphasis on service, it promised to be the most important challenge to the success of any enterprise. Consumers had enough money that price competition seldom worked, but not for the reasons that critics suggested. Instead of huge corporations foisting goods on unsuspecting buyers through mass advertising, the modern consumer has so many choices that quality has emerged as a central concern. Lee Iacocca had recognized as much with his revolutionary five-year warranty on Chryslers. In addition to the search for quality control, however, business enterprise in the 1990s and beyond must overcome several challenges, some of them institutional. It is to those we turn in closing.

Notes   1. In 1990 a British company called Instanet introduced the first fully computerized securities trading terminals, allowing brokers to bypass brokerage houses and further democratizing securities exchanges. See Robert J. McCartney, "Computer Network Lets Traders Bypass Exchanges," *Dayton Daily News,* July 8, 1990.

2. Larry Schweikart, "Michael Milken," in *The Encyclopedia of American Business History and Biography: Banking and Finance, 1913–1989* ed., Larry Schweikart, (New York: Facts on File, 1990), 291–301, and Connie Bruck, *The Predators Ball* (New York: Simon & Schuster, 1988). For a contrary view, see James B. Stewart, *Den of Thieves* (New York: Touchstone, 1992 [1991]), and Benjamin J. Stein, *A License to Steal* (New York: Simon and Schuster, 1992). Stein is unique—a conservative who thinks financial institutions have too much freedom. Robert Sobel's *Dangerous Dreamers* offers an insightful explanation of, if not defense of, Milken's activities in the context of the government's attacks on him. See 178–179, for example.

3. Glenn Yago, *Junk Bonds: How High Yield Securities Restructure Corporate America* (New York: Oxford University Press, 1991).

4. Paul Craig Roberts, "Insider Journalism," *Commentary*, March 1992, 54–57.

5. See Paul Asquith, David Mullins Jr., and Eric D. Wolff, "Original Issue High Yield Bonds: Aging Analysis of Defaults, Exchanges, and Calls," *Journal of Finance*, 44 (September 1989): 923.

6. Sobel, *Dangerous Dreamers*, 188.

7. George Anders and Constance Mitchell, "Milken's Sales Pitch on High-Yield Bonds Is Contradicted by Data," *The Wall Street Journal*, November 20, 1990.

8. George Gilder, "Michael Milken and the Two Trillion Dollar Opportunity," taken from the Internet on "http://forbes.com/asap/gilder/telecosm," and published in *Forbes*, April 10, 1995.

9. Michael Jensen quoted in Gilder, "Milken"; Michael C. Jensen, "The Takeover Controversy: Analysis and Evidence," Harvard University Graduate School of Business Administration Division of Research, reprint series, from the *Midland Corporate Finance Journal*, v 4, no. 2 (1986).

10. Michael Jensen and W. H. Meckling, "Theory of the Firm: Managerial Behavior, Agency Costs and Ownership Structure," in Michael C. Jensen and Clifford W. Smith Jr., *The Modern Theory of Corporate Finance* (New York: McGraw Hill, 1984), 78–133.

11. Gilder, *Recapturing the Spirit of Enterprise*, 181.

12. Statistics by Timothy Bates, "An Analysis of Minority Entrepreneurship," (1985), cited in Shelley Green and Paul Pryde, *Black Entrepreneurship in America* (New Brunswick, N.J.: Transaction Publishers, 1990), 25. Also see Joel Kotkin, "The Reluctant Entrepreneurs," *Inc.*, September 1987.

13. "The Top 100," *USA Today*, May 6, 1987.

14. Harriet C. Johnson, "Fast-Growth Firm Makes Buses," *USA Today*, May 6, 1987.

15. Reginald F. Lewis and Blair S. Walker, *"Why Should White Guys Have All the Fun?": How Reginald Lewis Created a Billion-Dollar Business Empire* (New York: John Wiley & Sons, 1995). When Lewis died of brain cancer just six years after the Beatrice purchase, former Dallas Cowboy tight end Jean Fugett took over the management of the conglomerate.

16. Edward D. Berkowitz, *America's Welfare State: From Roosevelt to Reagan* (Baltimore, Md.: Johns Hopkins University Press, 1991), 100–101.

17. Daniel Patrick Moynihan's report is reproduced in William L. Yancey and Lee Rainwater, *The Moynihan Report and the Politics of Controversy* (Boston: MIT

Press, 1967). Also see Moynihan's *Maximum Feasible Misunderstanding* (New York: Free Press, 1969).

18. Stuart Butler, *Out of the Poverty Trap* (New York: Free Press, 1987), and Charles Murray, *Losing Ground* (New York: Basic Books, 1984). A different interpretation appears in William Julius Wilson, *The Truly Disadvantaged: The Inner City, the Underclass, and Public Policy* (Chicago: University of Chicago Press, 1987), and David T. Ellwood, *Poor Support: Poverty in the American Family* (New York: Basic Books, 1988). A somewhat middle ground is presented by Bradley R. Schiller, *The Economics of Poverty and Discrimination,* 5th ed., (Englewood Cliffs, N.J.: Prentice-Hall, 1989 [1973]).

19. Thomas Sowell has numerous books with this and other evidence about the non-impact of racism on economic matters. See his works, cited earlier, *The Economics and Politics of Race, Knowledge and Decisions, Ethnic America: A History* (New York: Basic Books, 1981), and *Preferential Policies: An International Perspective* (New York: William Morrow, 1990). Walter William's work is best captured in *The State Against Blacks* (New York: New Press, 1982). Other material can be found in Gilder, *Wealth and Poverty,* as well as Dinesh D'Souza, *The End of Racism* (New York: Free Press, 1995).

20. Steve Sailer, "How Jackie Robinson Desegregated America," *National Review,* April 8, 1996, 38–41.

21. Jennifer Roback, "The Political Economy of Segregation: The Case of Segregated Streetcars," *Journal of Political Economy,* 46 (December 1986): 893–917.

22. Susan E. Mayer, *What Money Can't Buy: Family Income and Children's Life Chances* (Cambridge, Mass.: Harvard University Press, 1977), 2–3.

23. "Black Businesses Excel: Outperform 'Forbes' 'Fortune' Top Companies," *Dayton Daily News,* May 7, 1996; "24th Annual Report on Black Business," *Black Enterprise,* June 1996, 103–195 and, in the same issue, Eric L. Smith, "Is Black Business Paving the Way?" 194–206.

24. "Black Businesses Excel."

25. Green and Pryde, *Black Entrepreneurship in America,* 100; Carol Hymowitz, "Taking a Chance: Many Blacks Jump Off the Corporate Ladder to Be Entrepreneurs," *The Wall Street Journal,* August 2, 1984.

26. Welfare remains an impediment to entrepreneurship, though, and not just in the United States. See "A German Who Offers Low-Pay Service Work Dismays Countrymen," *The Wall Street Journal,* March 3, 1998.

27. The following material comes from Wallace Terry, "I Chose to Change My Life," *Parade,* October 13, 1996, 4–5.

28. All quotations from Terry, "I Chose to Change My Life."

29. "1 of 4 U.S. Workers Employed by Women," *Dayton Daily News* (from AP), March 27, 1996, quoting the National Foundation for Women Business Owners "1996 Facts on Women-Owned Businesses" and Census Bureau data.

30. "1 of 4 U.S. Workers Employed by Women."

31. Paul Wiseman, "Thrifts Strain to Rise from the Ashes," *USA Today,* June 29, 1992.

32. An excellent overview of these changes appears in Charles Calomiris, "Regulation, Industrial Structure, and Instability in U.S. Banking: An Historical Perspective," in

Structural Change in Banking eds., Michael Clausner and Lawrence J. White, (New York: New York University/Business One, Irwin, 1993), 19–116.

33. Charles W. Calomiris, "The Role of Financial Relationships in the History of American Corporate Finance," *Journal of Applied Corporate Finance,* 9 (Summer 1997) 52–73.

34. Charles W. Calomiris, "Universal Banking and the Financing of Industrial Development," in Gerard Caprio, Jr., and Dimitri Vittas, eds., *Reforming Financial Systems: Historical Implications for Policy* (Cambridge: Cambridge University Press, 1998), 113–127 (quotation on 124).

35. Rich Miller, "Japan's Banks 'in a Danger Zone,' Analysts Warn," *USA Today,* November 17, 1997.

36. "The Asian Crisis: How it Started, What Happens Next," *USA Today,* December 9, 1997.

37. "Greenspan Sees Asian Crisis Speeding Worldwide Move to Market Capitalism," *The Wall Street Journal,* April 3, 1998.

38. On the Aerospace plane, see the author's *National Aerospace Plane and the Quest for the Orbital Jet,* passim.

39. Scott Callon, *Divided Sun: MITI and the Breakdown of Japanese High-Tech Industrial Policy, 1975–1993* (Stanford: Stanford University Press, 1995), 2.

40. Ibid., 201.

41. Gilder, *Microcosm,* 341.

42. These and other projections from Gilder, based on his forthcoming book, *Telecosm,* are available (appropriately enough) on the Internet at http://www.forbes.asap.com/gilder/telecosm.

43. Michael Porter, *The Competitive Advantage of Nations* (New York: Free Press, 1990).

44. Ibid., 117.

45. Richard J. Murnane and Frank Levy, *Teaching the New Basic Skills: Principles for Educating Children to Thrive in a Changing Economy* (New York: Free Press, 1996).

46. Reynolds, "Ominous Decline in Work Incentives," 15.

47. For a further discussion of the collapse of these hierarchies, see Penzias, *Harmony,* passim.

48. Annalee Saxenian, "Lessons from Silicon Valley," *Technology Review,* July 1994, 42–51 (quotation on 47).

49. Ibid., 51

50. Penzias, *Harmony,* 50.

51. David Frum, "Welcome, Nouveau Riches," *New York Times,* August 14, 1995.

52. Reynolds, "Ominous Decline in Work Incentives," 15.

53. Robert Triest, "The Efficiency Cost of Increased Progressivity," National Bureau of Economic Research *Working Paper,* #4535, November 1993.

54. "Markets Are Unfazed by Slow Economy," *USA Today,* June 23, 1995.

55. See the October 23, 1996, edition of the *Washington Post* for details.

56. "Running of the Bull Market," *USA Today's Market Scoreboard,* October 11, 1996.

57. See Lester C. Thurow, "The Revolution is Upon Us," *Atlantic Monthly,* March 1997, 97–105, as well as William Greider, *One World, Ready or Not: The Manic Logic of Global Capitalism* (New York: Simon & Schuster, 1996).

58. The Disney story appears in John Taylor, *Storming the Magic Kingdom* (New York: Alfred A. Knopf, 1987), and Ron Grover, *The Disney Touch* (New York: Irwin, 1991).

59. See Ingrasia and White, *Comeback,* 87–121.

60. Michael Jensen, "The Modern Industrial Revolution: Exit and the Failure of Internal Control Systems," *Journal of Finance,* 48 (July 1993): 831–880. Also see Michael Jensen, "Eclipse of the Public Corporation," *Harvard Business Review* (Sept.-Oct. 1989), 61–74.

61. Carliss Y. Baldwin and Kim B. Clark, "Capital-Budgeting Systems and Capabilities Investments in U.S. Companies after the Second World War," *Business History Review,* 68 (Spring 1994): 73–109 (quotation on 76).

62. Ibid., 79.

63. John E. Rigdon, "Contrasting Images: The New Finance Chief at Kodak Has a Style Quite Unlike His Boss's," *The Wall Street Journal,* April 28, 1993.

64. Beth Belton, "U.S. Worker's Productivity Jumps 4.5%," *USA Today,* November 14, 1997.

65. Tom Peters and Robert Waterman Jr., *In Search of Excellence: Lessons from America's Best Run Companies* (New York: Harper, 1982).

66. Gary Jacobsen and John Hillkirk, *Xerox: American Samurai* (New York: Macmillan, 1986).

67. Martin Kenny and Richard Florida, *Beyond Mass Production: The Japanese System and Its Transfer to the U.S.* (New York: Oxford University Press, 1993).

68. "Re-engineering Not a Roaring Success," *Dayton Daily News,* January 28, 1996.

69. George Harris and Robert Trotter quoted in Seymour Martin Lipset, "The Work Ethic—Then and Now," *Public Interest,* Winter 1990, 61–69 (quotation on 63).

70. Ibid., passim.

71. Gallup Poll, May 21, 1982, cited in Ben Wattenberg, *The First Universal Nation* (New York: Free Press, 1991), 370.

72. Michael Barone and Grant Ujifusa, *The Almanac of American Politics* (Washington, D.C.: National Journal Inc., 1992), xxv–xliv.

73. Henry R. Nau, *The Myth of America's Decline.* fig. 6.2.

74. RAND Corporation report R3610, 1986.

75. William Flannery, "NAFTA Is No Disaster," *Arizona Republic,* April 7, 1998.

76. Walter Wriston, "Technology and Sovereignty," *Foreign Affairs* (Winter 1988\1989): 63–75 (quotation on 71).

77. David Remnick, *Lenin's Tomb: The Last Days of the Soviet Empire* (New York: Random House, 1993), 307.

78. Ibid., 307.

79. Ibid., 312.

80. See Gary Hector, *Breaking the Bank: The Decline of BankAmerica* (Boston: Little, Brown, 1998), for example.

81. Shawn Everett Kantor and Price V. Fishback, "Precautionary Saving, Insurance, and the Origins of Workers' Compensation," *Journal of Political Economy,* 104 (April 1996): 419–442.

82. Interview with Jon Perryman, July 5, 1995.

83. Interview with Tom Hatton, October 29, 1996.

84. Interview with Larry Pacifico, July 5, 1995.

The Enterprising Spirit, Reprise

AMERICAN BUSINESS CONFRONTED A NUMBER OF CHALLENGES AND ISSUES as it anticipated the twenty-first century. For the first few years of the 1990s, the U.S. economy stumbled along at a rate of growth of 2.5 percent, leaving most citizens to conclude that they were "getting by," but hardly "getting ahead." Robert Heilbroner asserted in the most recent edition of his economics textbook that "Not since the Great Depression have economic problems been so insistent, so worrisome. . . . International competition, unemployment, and the fear of inflation have brought economics into the center of our lives."[1] Bill Clinton had won his election in 1992 largely on the basis of the claim that the economy was the worst in the past thirty years, and expressions about economic insecurity grew so bad that the July/August 1996 issue of *The American Enterprise,* a magazine published by the free-market American Enterprise Institute, dedicated an entire volume to "economic anxiety." James Glassman of the *Washington Post* wrote several columns examining the disparity between how the economy really was and how people perceived it. Even as late as 1998, most public opinion surveys suggested that Americans did not think their children would be as well off financially and materially as they were.

In March 1996, the *New York Times* ran a series of "scare" articles called "The Downsizing of America"—a seven-part series produced by more than twenty writers and researchers that represented the longest piece of journalism by the paper since 1971—with the conclusion that wages were falling, job security had disappeared, and the middle class had started to fall out of the "middle."[2] But this constituted only one of a torrent of stories about bad news: One search of 2,500 media outlets over a sixteen-month period for the first half of the 1990s revealed more than 19,000 stories on plant closings, but only 5,000 stories mention plant openings. Likewise, job losses dominated more than 38,500 stories, but job gains appeared in only 11,399 stories—almost a 2 to 1 ratio of bad news to good, even though total net job gains during that period exceeded 2.5 million.[3] That didn't keep other critics from complaining. In *The Overworked American,* Juliet Schor, complained that "capitalism involved a tremendous expansion of human effort. People began to work longer and harder."[4] Lamenting that Americans do not have time for unpaid, "caring," work, she contends that leisure time has declined in recent decades. According to the gloomsters, the U.S. national debt was a "bomb," looming on the horizon and permitting foreigners to buy into America.[5] The 1980s have been lambasted as a "decade of greed," supposedly reflecting the fact that the tax cuts had turned people into a mass of selfish misers. And, of course, the most common complaint, that the rich got richer and the poor got poorer in the 1980s, frequently resurfaces.

The scare tactics began in the early 1980s, when it was clear that a free-market revolution was under way. Those enamored of "planning" and "industrial policy," most notably Ira Magaziner (the guru of Hillary Clinton's failed government takeover of the health care system) and Robert Reich (President Clinton's secretary of labor), as well as high-tech gloomsters such as Chalmers Johnson and foreign-takeover fearmongers like Susan Tolchin, gained prominence with a number of books warning that the American economy was in a state of decline, that government planning was the central solution, and that free trade would destroy U.S. competitiveness.[6] Claiming that U.S. productivity had eroded, for example, Magaziner and Reich faulted business strategy and called for strategic governmental policies designed to improve American competitiveness. Surely if the views of the gloomsters were correct, the U.S. economy—and especially productivity—should have hit all-time lows by the early 1990s (before the Clinton administration enacted some of Reich's suggestions). Moreover, business should never have experienced growth in the late 1980s, when the Reagan-era tax cuts started to have their effect. What has been the result of policy changes on business by the 1990s?

The State of the U.S. Economy, 1998

Several myths had developed about the 1980s that must be corrected in order to examine modern trends. Critics argued along three basic lines: (1) the federal debt, resulting from consistent deficits in the

1980s—related to the tax cuts—had gown beyond all reasonable levels; (2) the United States serviced this debt—often described as a "consumer binge"— by borrowing from foreign governments, thus "selling out" America; and (3) whatever capital the tax cuts did produce went into consumer buying of foreign products, made by cheap labor, not into investment and productivity growth in American industry. When the growth rate of the U.S. economy indeed slowed down in the early 1990s, critics thought they finally had validation of their view that tax cuts had come home to roost. But several problems have emerged with the proposition that either deficits or the debt of the 1980s caused the slowdown, effectively rendering the contention null and void.

First, as economist Robert Eisner has demonstrated in *The Misunderstood Economy,* the notion that the U.S. is the largest debtor nation in the world is a myth. Much of it derives from an inaccurate—indeed, flatly false—measurement of American-owned assets abroad. Those assets have been measured using traditional accounting statistics, which uses "book value" of assets. When Eisner measured U.S. assets abroad, he found that traditional measures undercount those assets by *half a trillion dollars*—a single adjustment that removes more than 10 percent from the national debt.[7] Other accounting errors were equally egregious. For example, the U.S. Treasury and Federal Reserve's gold supply had a nominal value of $42 an ounce, yet gold on the open market brought just under $400 an ounce, adding yet another trillion dollars to America's asset position and lopping another 10 percent off the debt. Similar accounting problems existed with virtually all U.S. assets, from lumber in national forests to office buildings. Thanks to publications such as Eisner's, the Bureau of Economic Analysis stopped publishing the bottom line of the international investment position, admitting that it was comparing apples to oranges. Eisner has suggested that the United States essentially had no national debt at the peak of the debt scare in 1989.[8] By 1996, meanwhile, the United States had assets of as much as $40 trillion dollars, a fantastic sum that dwarfs any genuine debt that might exist.

Immediately, some critics will shout, "Does this mean that we should sell the Washington Monument?" Of course not, but it does mean that the federal government could sell unused land, such as the ghost town of 442 acres at Wilshire Boulevard and the San Diego Freeway, which had a market value in 1988 of $2 billion.[9] (Students should keep in mind that Jefferson only retained 4 out of 30 sections in a township for the government, with the intention that eventually the government would sell most of those 4!) Private business would not hesitate to unload an expensive office building like the Rayburn Building if it could turn a profit and still put its employees in an equivalent facility, but the federal government in the twentieth century has become a land hog: By the late 1980s, Uncle Sam held 727 million acres, containing more than 27,000 separate properties, of which independent appraisers concluded that 5,000 could be sold. Cities also controlled substantial public assets that could be sold, including golf courses for the upper classes. Privatization of civic services represents the wave of the future, as sewers, fire protection, security, and even road building—all of which once were privately financed and operated—again are turned over to the market.[10] Houston privatized some of its streets in the early 1980s, raising $4.3 million a year; Laredo sold 150 streets, with the buyers including a church and a trailer park and revenues going to pave the remaining streets; and entire planned communities now provide their own streets.[11] Of course, this was nothing new. St. Louis had a sixty-year history of privatized residential streets, which proved a model for private developers and public planning agencies.[12]

A second myth of the American economy is that foreign investment constitutes a devious plot to "take over" America. The United States attracts money from all over the world because it represents the single best, safest, and most promising place in which to invest. Who wants to start a new car dealership in downtown Beruit? Or build a shopping mall in downtown Sarajevo? The answer is obvious: Those are not safe areas, and one's capital would be in danger. Less obvious, though, is why people do not hurry to invest in, say, Uganda or Guatemala. The answer again is that those areas are not safe, but for other reasons. Governments in many nations have long histories of "nationalizing" (i.e., stealing) the investments of foreigners. Foreign investors simply take their marbles and go home—or, rather, flock to the game going on in the USA.

But even the trade deficits, touted by critics as evidence that the United States had lost its edge, were the result of statistical manipulations. Measured as a share of output, the trade deficit indeed rose from 1980 (when Carter was still in office) to a peak in 1986, when it reached 3.5 percent of GDP, then shrank consistently from 1986 to 1990 (when George Bush was president), almost to its 1980 levels. Then, from 1990 to 1996, the trade deficit took off again.[13]

As for the domestic budget deficits, it has been shown that (1) they were the result of increased domestic (especially welfare) spending, not decreased tax revenues in the 1980s, and (2) little scholarly evidence has tied deficits per se to higher interest rates or inflation.[14] Eisner and a colleague, Paul Peiper, have shown that the deficits (what the country owes on an annual basis) relative to what the country makes (the GNP or GDP) fell under Reagan and Bush. Indeed, the nation owed more (relative to what it made) during the Truman, Eisenhower, Ford, and Carter years than at any time after 1980. However, after 1990, when the second of two tax hikes came into play—both intended to help eliminate deficits—the ratio of deficits to GNP reversed itself and started to grow.[15] These concepts are easily understood when placed in a personal context: If a person owes $1,000 on a Visa bill, is that a great deal, or not? Typically the answer is, "Who knows? It depends on what the person makes." Exactly the point: If a person makes $300,000 a year and has a Visa bill of $1,000, it is barely a nuisance; if the person makes $10,000 a year, the bill is a severe drain on household finances.

On the other hand, it should be kept in mind that the Social Security Trust Fund has been running a steady surplus for years as the "baby boom" generation reaches its prime earnings decades, and Congresses consistently have counted that trust fund surplus into budget considerations, when in fact it should be considered entirely as an "off-line" item. In other words, to the extent that Social Security is excluded—as it should be—the United States has had severe deficits at least since Lyndon Johnson. Likewise, in the 1997–98 "budget surplus," no real surplus existed, because the budget contained projections that relied entirely on money from the tobacco settlement that, as of mid-1998, will likely not materialize.

Neither the national debt nor the deficits—whatever their size—shape economic behavior by themselves. Rather, deficits and the perceived debt level work their way into politics as a justification for taxes, and scholarship is suggesting that anticipation of taxes changes business and economic behavior rather than the anticipation of inflation or the ill effects of the deficits themselves. Or, more bluntly, people fear increased taxes and respond accordingly when they suspect politicians will raise them. The 1990 and 1993 tax increases under Republican George Bush and Democrat Bill Clinton dampened an otherwise robust economy, leaving it limping along. Then, after 1994 when the Republican "Contract With America" signaled a return to low taxes and a recommitment to property rights, the entire discussion shifted to tax cuts and even abolition of the Internal Revenue Service. Perceptions play an important role in economic activity.

Nevertheless, some still argue that the United States is "undertaxed" among developed nations. Such an approach overlooks the fact that other nations have national health-care systems. If the contributions Americans made to their private health care was included, the United States would be among the most highly taxed nations— among those with rising productivity—in the world. U.S. capital gains taxes are higher then anywhere except Australia, which has eroded economic incentives. In the 1990s, the notion that Americans are undertaxed, when combined state, local, and federal taxes take a larger share of wages and earnings than ever before in history, is unsupportable. Until the 1980s, taxes were not even indexed, meaning that they rose automatically with inflation. A family that found its income blasted into a higher bracket paid more taxes, regardless of the fact that its income "growth" was entirely the result of 1970s-era inflation.

Even the tax arguments, however, become distorted by straight-line comparisons to other nations, because France, Germany, and Britain have unemployment rates at or near 10 percent, which the United States would find completely unacceptable. (Recall that under Calvin Coolidge, in a time of peace, unemployment reached 1.6 percent!) Further, only Japan has maintained higher productivity rates than U.S. industry, and that margin started to fall in 1997 and 1998 with the collapse of the Asian economies. A 1992 study by the Federal Reserve Bank reported that "labor productivity in U.S. manufacturing soared in the 1980s [growing] at an annual average of five percent . . ."[16] Further, the study found "some evidence of a positive relationship between high-tech capital usage and productivity in manufacturing industries. The relationship is sufficiently large to account for a non-trivial fraction of the growth of productivity in manufacturing industries from the first to the second half of the 1980s. . . ."[17] Put another way, the capital that was saved and imported from foreign nations in the 1980s went heavily into improving the productivity of U.S. manufacturing, and it was the capital investments—not labor inputs, as Robert Reich suggests—that were crucial to giving American industries a rising productivity rate. Indeed, Japanese experts admit that U.S. workers are 1.6 times more productive than their own laborers, and the Kinsey group, surveying managerial attitudes toward productivity, reported even more striking disparities between Japanese and American productivity.[18] More recently, new government calculations showed that productivity may have grown even faster than was estimated previously. The Bureau of Labor Statistics revised its estimates to correct for seasonal distortions, leading to even greater productivity gains.[19] In addition, a long-term analysis by Henry Nau aptly captured the misconceptions in the title of his book, *The Myth of America's Decline.*[20] The entire dynamic of America's declining, then recovering, then triumphant productivity is understandable in light of Henry Dethloff's comment about Americans' reaction to competition. Americans follow a "classical psychological pattern: 1) ignore it, 2) discount it, 3) repulse it, 4) acknowledge it, and 5) adapt to it."[21]

The fallacious "decline" in American productivity, which in turn was blamed on the trade deficit and the budget deficits, has not been supported in recent research, most notably by the studies of Michael Jensen, or an analysis by Morgan Stanley that revealed that between 1987 and 1992, U.S. corporations snared 47.7 percent of *global* profits and 37 percent of *global* sales.[22] Again, it should be pointed out that this occurred during a time that then-candidate Clinton called the worst economy in the last fifty years, and during a recession year of 1991–1992.

Another standard complaint lodged against the American economy, emerging from the 1980s backlash against the Reagan tax cuts, was that the United States was a nation of consumers and spenders. That view blamed a supposedly low national savings rate on consumers, who had a "party in the 1980s." In part, the interpretation revived the scare of foreign ownership of U.S. assets as a way of "paying" for the party.

The entire view was utterly false. Americans do not have savings rates as statistically high as other nations because in the United States, people provide for their own health insurance (while other nations, with socialized medicine, charge that to the government). That factor alone accounts for a large block of savings. On the other hand, people of all nations save for specific purposes: to buy large- ticket items, such as houses; to educate children; and for retirement. In modern America, however, the federal government subsidizes borrowing for homes (through home mortgages), requires participation in a retirement system (Social Security), and offers federal guarantees to student loans. Or, put another way, the federal government "saves" for the average American, or provides incentives not to save. Meanwhile, the U.S. savings rate of 3.9 percent (1997) is above that of Canada (3.4 percent), but somewhat below that of France (6.1 percent). If savings was as important as the critics make it out to be, France should not have an unemployment rate more than twice that of the United States.

Nor have foreign investors acquired the U.S. debt, 85 percent of which is held domestically. Foreigners account for approximately 8 percent of acquisitions and mergers in the United States but pay "phenomenal prices for U.S. assets," indicating that they fail to get bargains.[23] High-priced acquisitions by the Japanese of Rockefeller Center and the Aladdin Casino, for example, proved horrible flops, eventually prompting the Japanese to unload their purchases at substantial losses. Contrary to the perception, the most prominent foreign investor remains Great Britain, with Canada second, and Japan barely third, only recently catching the Dutch. By far, the single largest area of investment was in capital goods, not consumer goods. In the early 1980s, a media hysteria arose over Arab purchases of farmland; yet at its peak, Arab land purchases came to only *1 percent* of foreign land purchases in the United States. Foreign purchases of U.S. assets rose from 1982 to 1987, but hardly in the way the "gloomsters" contended: British purchases accounted for 40 percent of the total acquisitions, while Japan purchased only 5 percent, an amount lower than Australia and slightly ahead of Switzerland![24] More significant, between 1984 and 1989, the General Accounting Office could find only seventeen hostile takeovers of U.S. companies, and only one of those by a Japanese firm.

A Nation of Spenders or Givers?

Obviously, then, the American economy has been better than suggested; Americans save more than critics contend; and foreign investment in the United States constitutes a small part of the capital market. Did that mean Americans selfishly held on to their cash? No. Quite the contrary, the "decade of greed" was a decade of giving, by any measure (total gifts, dollar value of gifts, number of givers—all adjusted for inflation).[25] Perhaps more surprising, using a projection trendline of levels of giving during the previous twenty-five years, philanthropists actually contributed 55 percent more than predicted had then-current trends continued. Still more startling, as people's income rose, they gave at a faster rate than they consumed! Giving rose faster than expenditure on "selfish" items such as new autos, jewelry, and personal services, and giving by the "rich" rose faster than by other income groups. Charitable Americans continued their philanthropy in 1997, when donations to charity topped $130 billion—up almost 10 percent since 1995—and yet half of all donors earned less than $50,000 annually.[26]

One traditional explanation for increases in giving was that higher tax rates encouraged charity as a tax shelter; but the evidence suggests that as tax rates fell, people contributed more. When government's share of paychecks dropped, people grew more generous. Much of that charity went to churches, where people could supervise its use and reflecting the gnawing concern that money sent to Washington disappeared in a bottomless pit of bureaucracy. (Indeed, less than 30 percent of funds targeted to welfare ever reaches welfare recipients. Two-thirds of welfare funds went to, among other things, pay government employees making salaries far above that of typical working Americans.) If, on the other hand, churches saw it as part of their job to help the poor, it certainly would be possible. One recent study of tithing by Christians found that, depending on the definition of "devout," the number of "devout" tithing Christians in America, giving 10 percent of their income, could yield $370 billion—far more than enough to run all churches and a sum 225 percent higher than all federal, state, and local welfare spending.[27]

Regardless of what was possible, the real experience of the 1980s was that Americans made more, saved more, and gave more, as people moved upward, out of the middle class and into the wealthiest classes at unprecedented levels. Less than ever, the path to upward mobility was heavy industry, autos, steel, or the physical/material sector; instead, it was through ideas, services, and talent. Nevertheless, by the mid-1990s, public opinion polls seemed to reflect the attitude that the economy was in decline or that the standard of living for today's children would be far below that of their parents. But was this view either widely held or accurate?

Misplaced Anxiety?

Media treatments of "downsizing" and force reductions by American industry in the 1990s, highlighted by the famous *Newsweek* "Corporate Killers" cover, fueled a general impression that the U.S. economy was in a state of malaise. Growth rates had slowed after the Bush and Clinton tax hikes; but the phenomenal productivity of the nation's entrepreneurs and industrialists overcame the tax drag, plunging the United States into the information revolution of the twenty-first century. Nor were the charges by the media true. James Glassman, debunking the notion that corporate downsizing had brought on the new anxiety, offered the following observations in his columns:

✦ Since 1979, 43 million jobs were lost, but 70 million new jobs were created, for a net gain of 27 million.

✦ The number of working Americans has increased by 32 percent since 1982.

✦ When AT&T employment shrunk, MCI grew, adding 36,000; Sprint added 25,000; the number of cable operators and programmers rose by 88,000 since 1978 alone.

✦ Baby boomers have inflation-adjusted incomes 50 percent higher than their parents at the same age.

Or, as Glassman noted, "The Me Generation has become the Woe is Me Generation . . . never mind the facts or context."[28]

Glassman rejected the notion that the economy was poor, and *Newsweek* economics writer Robert Samuelson contended that the media had created a "hysteria over downsizing—whipped up in part by Labor Secretary Robert Reich" and the *New York Times*.[29] The concept that companies owed economic security to employees, which represented an idea tried and found wanting in the "welfare capitalism" of the 1920s, is an expectation of the private sector that arose in the period 1960–1980 but that proved unconnected to the real world. Distortion by the press covered the fact that almost half of all Americans rated themselves better off in 1996 than a year earlier, and the overall rating was higher than at any time since 1976. While the *Times* focused solely on layoffs, it ignored the rate of rehires, with case studies showing that most of those laid off find themselves better off in a short period.[30] Or, as historian Otto Bettmann noted in the title of his book, *The Good Old Days: They Were Terrible!*[31]

Several factors account for the media's inability to get the story right or even report accurately the data that was used. First, the official data on job loss and unemployment is extremely complex and often inaccurate. As a new study on job creation and destruction by Steven J. Davis, John Haltiwanger, and Scott Schuh reveals, existing measurements are misleading or entirely unreliable.[32] They found that one of the most significant factors influencing job creation and destruction was "idiosyncratic factors"—in other words, those things no one could predict or capture.[33] Second, recent polls of economic and financial reporters showed not only that were they politically biased in their reporting—almost completely identifying the themselves as "liberal" and their political affiliation as Democrat—but that they appear to be professionally lazy: Out of the 100 most-cited economists in the academic literature, only 3 were cited with any regularity by the reporters (Milton Friedman, Paul Krugman, and John Maynard Keynes—and Keynes is dead!)[34] Such slothful reporting works its way into discussions not only of employment but also so-called wealth inequality.

Inequality, or the gap between rich and poor, has grown only insofar as more people became rich in the 1980s, and thus the middle class shrunk. After a small spike in 1948, the share of total family income received by the top 5 percent has barely moved, remaining two times lower than in 1913. A slight rise occurred in the late 1980s, then remained at that level in the 1990s despite higher tax rates on the rich.[35] Remember, though, that even the Bureau of the Census researchers, who produced this data, did not adjust for age, and that older people almost always have higher income and wealth levels than younger people, so that any rate distorts the real levels of equality in the American system.

Another distortion that has fed the perception that the income gap rose during the 1980s is the "dirty little secret" that most measurements have compared "peak" periods in the business cycle to "trough" periods, and that when "peak" to "peak" is compared—1979–1989—or "trough to trough"—1982–1992—the middle class was better off in constant dollars by either measurement.[36] Only by "fudging" the data so as

| FIGURE 14-1 | *Real Median Family Income, 1970–1995* |

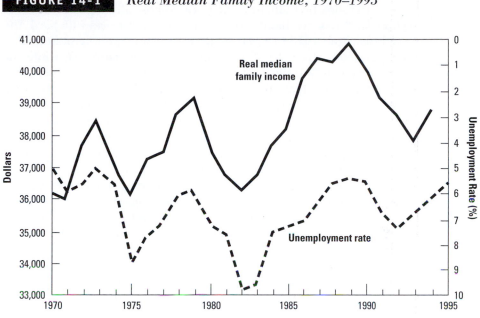

Source: From Richard Burkhauser et. al., *Income Mobility and the Middle Class.* (Washington, D.C.: American Enterprise Institute, 1996), p. 5. Copyright © 1996 by American Enterprise Institute, Washington, D.C. Reprinted by permission.

to compare a high to a low can the middle class be shown to have lost ground in the 1980s. As the authors of a study that examined income shifts from "peak to peak" and "trough to trough" concluded, "The great increase in income inequality [in the 1980s in both the United States and England] was not primarily the result of the rich getting richer and the poor getting poorer. It was the result of the unequal income gains *in the middle of the income distribution* [emphasis added]."[37] The majority of younger working families and older families in the middle of the distribution found themselves better off in 1989 than in 1979, and even better off in 1992 than in 1982. Only those younger families living on social assistance lost ground (see Figure 14.1).

In a similar study, Benjamin Zycher has analyzed the effect of such "income streams" and found that in 1975, of those in the lowest quintile of income earners, only 5 percent were still in the lowest quintile by 1991 while 29 percent had moved into the *highest* quintile. Conversely, of those in the highest quintile in 1975, more than one-third had dropped out by 1991. When measured by income averages, every quintile improved in real dollars, but the lowest groups improved faster than the top. In short, "These data suggest that the rich have become richer, and the poor richer faster."[38] There were reasons different groups had different incomes, almost all of them related to age. Federal Reserve Bank researchers Michael Cox and Richard Alm found that from 1975 to 1991 the lowest income quintile increased in average income from $1,500 to $26,400 (2,196 percent), while the highest income quintile rose from $45,700 to $49,600 (9 percent). Cox and Alm then identified six "secrets" of higher income growth: get married (because 83 percent of the top fifth of households are married couples, while only one-fifth of the bottom group are married); get an education (20 percent of the top, compared to 4 percent of the bottom); get a job (top income households have an average of 1.5 more workers than lower fifth households); work full-time (80 percent of the top bracket worked fifty hours a week or more, compared to 84 percent of lower fifth groups who reported working only part-time or not at all); save money; and stick to it—with age and work comes wealth.[39]

Charles Murray points out that inequality has less to do with income and everything to do with culture and behavior, and that such life decisions as whether or not to live in a large city can produce the *effects* of substantial changes in wealth, afflicting a group he labels the "high-income struggler."[40] At the other end of the spectrum are a group with enough income but who have a terrible standard of living. Indeed, studies suggest that a huge amount of income in low-income neighborhoods is unreported—the result of the steady stream of drug money, reflected in the visual evidence of $1,000 gold necklaces and $300 jackets. Murray calls these the "people with enough money who don't know how to spend it." In between are the working Americans who are comfortable or who do not live in large cities and therefore get by on far less income. That group can even report incomes at the poverty level but have a standard of living equal to that of middle-class groups in larger urban areas.

The End of the Visible Hand?

Much of whatever "anxiety" that existed in the 1990s stemmed from the radical transformation that had begun in the 1980s. While large corporations appeared to wield great power and control substantial numbers of jobs, it is entirely possible that they will be dinosaurs in the twenty-first century economy—huge, lumbering beasts incapable of adapting to their environment, losing the life struggle to smaller, quicker creatures. As they seek to survive, one of the major casualties appears to be the managerial hierarchies that gave them their strength for so long. Certainly in their current form, the managerial hierarchies appear somewhat obsolete.

It is therefore ironic that the "visible hand" theory of Alfred Chandler gained widespread acceptance at the very time that the computer started to render the managerial hierarchies he described less efficient, and occasionally downright out of date.[41] In the nineteenth century, when communications were slow, expert and educated managers sorted and transmitted relevant information that individual on-site employees could not obtain or lacked the education to understand. For want of a better term, managers had the "big picture" because of their access to information. By the 1980s, however, computers transmitted information far faster than humans could, with workplaces wired for electronic mail, providing instantaneous communication with employees. While managers still had much of the authority for making the decisions as to which information was important, they could not begin to function quickly enough to process it. They became bottlenecks for information rather than sources of information transmissions. The result often was a blizzard of "net" messages spewed out to everyone's computers or, worse, a torrent of paper memos.

Equally paradoxical, just as Chandlerite thought started to dominate the academy, American industries from autos and steel to aircraft and electronics had come under sharp competition from more efficient foreign rivals. U.S. businesses found that they had become bloated with the very bureaucracies Chandler celebrated, and they no longer could adapt quickly to meet emerging markets or rapid shifts in demand. Instead, American business hesitated, then launched itself into a remarkable downsizing, relying on automation and computers to improve efficiency. Companies literally shrank into profitability. At the same time, business searched for new and different ways to manage, discarding the traditional managerial hierarchies in favor of unconventional structures touted by highly sought-after consultants like Tom Peters or popular economic writers like Peter Drucker.

Again, it was George Gilder who predicted the paradigm shift. In his history of computers, *Microcosm* (1989), Gilder observed that the computer freed humanity from natural resources. Made of silicon and glass—essentially sand—computer chips increasingly got more powerful as they got smaller, marking a major departure from the industrial paradigm of "bigger is better." They also required little in the way of fossil fuels to produce. More relevant, Gilder argued, the computer, when used in conjunction with the modem or fax machine, could transform the workplace itself into a tiny site employees only occasionally needed to visit from their primary places of work, their homes. That restored to individuals much of the autonomy they had ceded to managers over the previous 120 years. Automation performed most of the routine labor, causing work to be increasingly individual rather than collective, as a cog in an industrial machine.

The implications for the restoration of individual freedom from the government were also extensive. No longer could government automatically tax people through withholding if an ocean of consultant, work-at-home "free agents" dominated the economic landscape. While still possessing the terrifying potential to become "Big Brother," the central government in a decentralized post-Chandler era would lose much of its mission and power. Government—federal, state, and local—still retains an important influence over the economy in that it remains the only substantial sector for the growth of union jobs. Overall, union membership had dropped to under 15 percent of the workforce in the 1990s, but the proportion of all union members holding a government job has increased. This formidable alliance between organized labor, with its dues-rich pot of AFL-CIO funds, and politicians bent on government expansion poses severe problems for further improving the efficiency of government and, thus, the economy. In the budget battles of 1995, according to memos leaked to the press, the federal employee's union, AFSME, promised to aid President Clinton in shutting down the government and blaming it on the Republicans, who had sought budget cuts in several agencies. That deal was in place in July 1994—almost a year before the "government shutdown" occurred, providing the union with considerable preparation time to secure a "war chest" for its members. Likewise, the powerful teachers' unions, the American Federation of Teachers and the National Education Association, have successfully stalled attempts by public school systems to introduce any form of competition into the education system. As a result, many districts have turned to newly emerging "for-profit" education businesses to run schools.

But the message remains constant: improve productivity, or disappear. And increasingly, whether at the Social Security Administration or the local public school, the quickest way to improve processing of information is with the new computer technologies. Indeed, in many ways, it can be argued, the computer won the cold war. In the late 1980s, the USSR, finding itself unable to either purchase or steal computer technology on the one hand, or to yield independence to people at personal workstations outside the iron hand of the government on the other, simply fell apart. The most exaggerated form of the "visible hand" on the planet thus went out with a whimper.

The "deconstruction" of the "visible hand" in American business was all the more remarkable, though, because it occured even while management thought it was "retooling" itself for the twenty-first century. Again, the "agency gap" arises, having originated the managerial revolution more than 130 years earlier. During times of dramatic business change, the agency gap widens into a gulf, and the skills of the managers and executives become out of synch with the needs of the corporation. General Motors, as has been shown, invested more than $120 billion in R&D and capital equipment in the 1980s during a time that the company's value dropped to under $23 billion, while IBM invested more than $100 billion while its value fell under $65 billion (and continued to plummet to $41 billion by 1995). Clearly, it was not lack of investment or research that had caused those companies to become unprofitable, but rather, according to Jensen, the wrong investments. Meanwhile, in brokerage and finance firms, while employment merely doubled between 1973 and 1987, the number of shares traded in those companies rose twelvefold! Managers steeped in statistics and flowcharts mostly missed the sea-tide change brought on by the unimagineable fall in computing costs. The government, for example, in its Bureau of Labor Statistics, reported annual price drops for the cost of computers at somewhere between 15 percent and 6 percent, yet during the past twenty years the real price of computers has dropped one millionfold! Most important of all, the productivity of capital rose during the 1980s for the first time in thirty years, moving from a minus 1.03 percent since 1950 to a positive 2.03 percent in the so-called decade of greed.[42] What had happened, of course, was that the stodgy, management-heavy dinosaurs had sliced out level after level of middle executives who had merely served as bottlenecks to information that could be acquired by employees directly at computer stations. The value added by managers in the nineteenth century had reversed itself, and many layers of management started to drain value or block its creation. The corporate raiders forced American industry to abandon much of its skeleton of managerial hierarchies by coming to grips with the computer.

Overturning the Chandler thesis also opened the door for other fascinating theories to emerge, often advanced by so-called pop economists such as Jude Wanniski or David Warsh, a journalist with the *Boston Globe*. Warsh, studying inflation trends over several centuries, noticed that there were huge periodic inflationary "blips" when prices ratcheted up significantly. Those blips corresponded almost perfectly with the major business "revolutions" in European and American history—the commercial revolution, the capitalist/industrial revolution, and the computer revolution. Warsh challenged traditional definitions of cost and value, pointing out that a modern house may cost four times as much as a house in 1950, but the expected standard items (including dishwasher, garage, energy-efficient windows, air conditioning, and so on) make the *value* of the house perhaps ten to twenty times greater than the 1950 version. As Michael Cox and Richard Alm of the Dallas Federal Reserve Bank show, the differences in the standard of living in 1970 and 1990 are

	1970	1990
FIGURE 14-2 *Measures of Living Standard*		
Average size of a new home (square feet)	1,500	2,080
New homes with central air-conditioning	34 percent	76 percent
People using computers	<100,000	75.9 million
Households with color TV	33.9 percent	96.1 percent
Households with cable TV	4 million	55 milion
Households with VCRs	0	67 million
Households with two or more vehicles	29.3 percent	54 percent
Median household net worth (real)	$24,217	$48,887
Housing units lacking complete plumbing	6.9 percent	1.1 percent
Homes lacking a telephone	13 percent	5.2 percent
Households owning a microwave oven	<1 percent	78.8 percent
Heart transplant procedures	<10	2,125*
Average workweek	37.1 hours	34.5 hours
Average daily time working in the home	3.9 hours	3.5 hours
Work time to buy gas for 100-mile trip	49 minutes	31 minutes*
Annual paid vacation and holidays	15.5 days	22.5 days
Number of people retired from work	13.3 million	25.3 million
Women in the workforce	31.5 percent	56.6 percent
Recreational boats owned	8.8 million	16 million
Manufacturers' shipments of RVs	30,300	226,500
Adult softball teams	29,000	188,000
Recreational golfers	11.2 million	27.8 million
Attendance at symphonies and orchestras	12.7 million	43.5 million
Americans finishing high school	51.9 percent	77.7 percent
Americans finishing four years of college	13.5 percent	24.4 percent
Employee benefits as a share of payroll	29.3 percent	40.2 percent[†]
Life expectancy at birth (years)	70.8	75.4
Death rate by accidental causes	714.3	520.2

*Figures are for 1991. †Figure is for 1992.

Source: From Michael Cox and Richard Alm, *These Are the Good Old Days: A Report on U.S. Living Standards.* (Dallas, Texas: Federal Reserve Bank of Dallas, 1994), table 1, p. 4. Reprinted by permission of the Federal Reserve Bank of Dallas.

staggering (see Figure 14.2). Or, put another way, would anyone confuse a modern Pentium-chip computer with Windows 95 with an early 1970s antique, despite the fact that they might have had the same price tag in constant dollars?[43] Putting together a single price index of "consumables" in England, David H. Fischer showed a price trend line that supported the Warsh thesis (see Figure 14.3), although Fischer wanted to credit (or blame) social and moral factors for long-term changes in prices.[44]

This, of course, is the weakness of so-called stage theories of history. Seldom do they capture the comprehensive sweep of the business scene,

FIGURE 14-3   *The Price of Consumables in England*

Three Series, 1201–1993

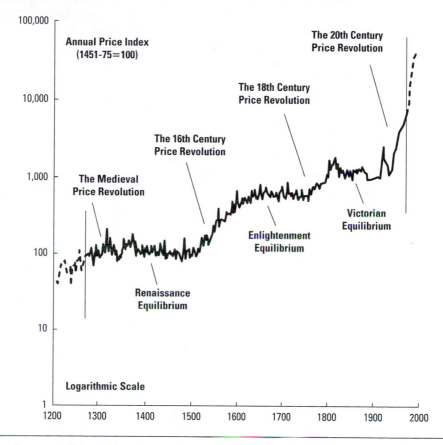

Source: From David Hackett Fisher, *The Great Wave.* (New York: Oxford University Press, 1996), p. 4. Copyright © 1996 Oxford University Press. Reprinted by permission.

or, conversely, the specific contributions of individuals. After all, that is where this entire discussion started, with the entrepreneur. Or, to reference a popular song by Emerson, Lake, and Palmer, "Welcome back my friends to the show that never ends" . . . the entrepreneur's show!

Welcome Back, My Friends

More than ever, entrepreneurs remain the essence of enterprise. Exceptions exist to most characterizations, but generally men and women in business who experience success work hard, serve others, get married, save and invest, and, most important, break new ground. Kenneth Tuchman worked at a bicycle shop at age thirteen, then started importing puka shells "to meet women."[45] After selling used cars, he started working for his dad, where he learned that customers could not get answers to questions about air conditioners, roofing, and other systems. In 1982, he started TeleTech at age twenty-two to handle customer questions and complaints for big companies such as ITT, Herbal Life, and others. Despite only two years of community college, Tuchman, worth $1 billion, had attended "the university of life."[46]

Ted Schwartz, who founded APAC (All People Are Customers) TeleServices, handled 200 million phone calls a year, acting as a middleman to firms such as United Parcel Services. A college dropout, Schwartz sold time for a small Colorado radio station, beating the streets to drum up business. In 1973 he founded Radio America in Chicago, then, in 1985 secured a contract with Xerox calling for subscriptions to the *Weekly Reader* through a phone bank he established. Worth over $1 billion, Schwartz and his family owned the majority of stock in APAC.[47]

Or consider the phenomenal rise of the manicure/nail business in America. Whereas two decades earlier manicurists were confined almost entirely to exclusive hotels and corners of hair salons, the number of nail salons in the United States blossomed into a $6 billion industry—equivalent to video games—and more than 400 manufacturers made nail-related products.[48] With more than 239,000 people in the industry, manicurists and nail specialists represented a growth business that was not even listed in the Bureau of Labor Statistics in 1979. Nail stylists, while licensed, did not have to pass batteries of tests or EPA inspections, thus providing an opening for the newest and least educated of citizens. In Los Angeles County, for example, 80 percent of the more than 15,000 nail stylists were Vietnamese-born. The nail business also offers an interesting view of the productivity paradox, in that productivity gains—through falling prices and stronger nails—were going to consumers, not the producers. Yet nail technicians make $475 a week for thirty-five hours in air-conditioned, comfortable surroundings, working at what are often derided as "low-wage jobs."

On the other end of the spectrum is Dennis Washington, a billionaire who worked at a gas station to buy his first car. Washington was diagnosed with polio, then a fatal disease, yet survived, only to be bounced around through several family members when his mother decided she did not want him.[49] Working construction in Alaska, Washington started a construction business, pouring everything he and his wife could save into the firm. Convinced that the Anaconda copper mine in Butte had potential, he purchased the closed mine for

$5 million and was losing $800,000 a month when an English investor offered him $50 million for the property. Suspicious, Washington held on to the mine as the price of copper rebounded, making Washington a billionaire. Washington then turned to philanthropy, setting up a 64,000-acre ranch for the Christian Young Life group.

Perhaps the most amazing story of entrepreneurship, one not captured in the *Forbes 400*, occurred in the least likely place, with a tradition steeped in socialism, the Indian reservation. The Choctaw Indians in Mississippi had for decades operated like most other Indian tribes, receiving government aid, eschewing business enterprise (except for government-subsidized activities, such as gambling casinos or tax-free cigarette stands), and eking out a living by farming. Then, in 1975, after a long campaign to give the tribal council executive authority over all activities, Chief Philip Martin led a drive to put private enterprise on an industrial park that the tribe had built with a seed grant from the government. Of 150 letters Martin sent to companies, only one respondent, a purchasing agent for the Packard Electric Division of General Motors, expressed interest. When George Gibbons, the purchasing agent, visited the site he was shocked, finding that the Choctaws had paved parking lots, cleared land for plant construction, and electricity. A contract was finalized in which the Choctaws purchased component parts and assembled wire harnesses for instrument panels. Under the aegis of the MBCI (Mississippi Band of Choctaw Indians) economic development program, the tribe received a $1.3 million loan to build a 42,000-square-foot plant that turned out its first products in 1979. Within another two years, the Choctaws moved into greeting-card manufacturing, raising money for a second plant for cards. By that time, production at the original facility had expanded so much that still another facility was needed. Ford Motors, requiring the same electric harnesses as General Motors, signed a contract for $4.3 million worth of harnesses.[50]

Each contract was managed by a separate Choctaw company, responsible for manufacture of that product and under the direction of a CEO with full autonomy over the business. A board of directors, appointed by the tribal council and chief (popularly elected) supervised the CEOs. The CEO and boards decided how much profit to reinvest and how much to distribute. For the Choctaws, the results were nothing short of miraculous.

Previous generations of Choctaws had lived with unemployment rates of 75 percent. Under Chief Martin, they fell below 20 percent—still too high by the standards of most capitalists, but an accomplishment of fantastic proportions given the tribe's history. Martin admitted that the tribe benefited from government minority status but pointed out that its performance had to retain any customers once brought in by special privilege. Ford gave the Choctaw plants awards for quality in excellence. By 1993 the tribe had a portfolio of businesses constructing circuit boards for Chrysler, Ford, Navistar, AT&T, as well as the American Greeting Card factory, most of them owned by the tribe, accounting for more than $271 million in sales and making the tribe the tenth-largest business in the state. As Senator Ben Nighthorse Campbell noted, "Indians now see private enterprise as the best way out of poverty."[51] And, he could add, away from government dependence: Of the $90 million in capital investment in the MBCI projects, less than 4 percent came from the government. Employment reached 5,000 by 1995, with an additional 2,000 jobs coming on-line with the opening of a new casino. Meanwhile, annual per capita income increased 201 percent between 1979 and 1990, while only 2.7 percent of household income came from welfare or other social assistance.

Although the Choctaws were the most successful of the tribes, they were not alone. In Arizona, the Yavapais in Prescott took advantage of their proximity to the resort community to build a resort hotel, securing the assistance of Phoenix developer William Grace. With his help and a bond sale from the city of Prescott, the tribe completed a 160-room Sheraton hotel in 1988, later home to the first casino in the state. The tribe then leased some of the reservation to Grace, who built a shopping mall anchored by Wal-Mart. Only 130 miles away, the Ak-Chin tribe farms two-thirds of its 22,000-acre reservation, bringing in revenues of $10 million annually. Private enterprise had driven the unemployment rate to 3 percent, prompting the tribe to tell the local welfare office to send back any of the tribe who come for welfare, telling them "We have plenty of jobs." In reclaiming their place in modern society and regaining their independence, several Indian tribes have decided instead of getting even to get rich.

Ultimately, if enterprise can thrive in a culture that has known little but government intervention and socialism for over a century; if college and high-school dropouts can become millionaires; if most of the 400 richest Americans were not on the list a decade earlier; if elderly entrepreneurs like Lydia Pinkham and middle-aged failures like C. W. Post can found large-scale enterprises; if immigrants account for large segments of the most rapidly growing sectors of business; and if people can shake off failure after failure, lose it all, only to start again and demand nothing less than success from themselves, then truly business enterprise in the free market captures the essence of the American dream. In every case, faith was the key—faith in one's own creative powers, in the basic fairness and good judgment of consumers, and, often in God.

As often is said of democracy, the free market is not perfect, and it is the worst system on earth except for all the others. The market certainly offers its share of degradation and evil, much of it available on cable television or over the Internet. Approached the right way, however—the way Adam Smith wanted his theory to be applied—the free-enterprise system appeals to the most noble human elements of the human character, requiring sacrifice, commitment, service to the wants and needs of others, and, above all, hard work. It is anti-elitist in that the taste or view of the average citizen in purchasing products carries as much weight as that of the wealthiest blue blood. What the market does not care about is intentions. That accounts for much of the media and cultural hostility toward business, because a person can have no higher aspiration than to get rich and still be successful. In a society that celebrates feelings over actions and deals more with intentions than results, entrepreneurs can seem removed. Even when acting out of noble motivations, most entrepreneurs disdain having to explain themselves to CNN or *Time* magazine, which accounts in part for the high visibility in the media given to those few entrepreneurs who publicly champion their efforts for the environment, social justice, or animal rights.

Debates in the mid-'90s over welfare policy bore out this tension between intentions and results, as the political parties battled over whether welfare that has insidious effects—but good intentions—should be maintained. The "War on Poverty" was lost when it was declared in the 1960s, with its casualties now in the millions. Reclaiming the offensive requires government policies dominated by demonstrable results, not altruistic feelings. (As Henry David Thoreau wrote, "If you see a man approaching you with the obvious intent of doing you good, run for your life.") Policies alone, however, can do little except free American entrepreneurs to wage the real war on poverty and homelessness in the market. It is an astounding phenomena to observe, because as entrepreneurs take risks, employ others, cherish work, and exhibit faith, they infect those around them, including their employees and family, who themselves soon embark on their own to take risks, employ others, and exhibit faith. The "enterprise infection rate" is thus geometrical, spreading throughout families and neighborhoods.

Lest the reader be left with the impression that the United States has entered a "golden age" of entrepreneurship, a warning is in order. For all the freedoms that make possible economic growth, personal fulfillment, and business enterprise, many have come under attack in recent years. Attempts to regulate the Internet, censor television through government-imposed "V-chips," eliminate firearms under the guise that they are a "health problem," destroy the tobacco industry, mandate entire products from existence (freon-based air conditioners, perfumes and colognes) or regulate them so strictly that they become inaccessible (vitamins) have already occurred. Federal departments have floated plans—again, under the best of intentions—to reduce auto emissions by having the Global Positioning Satellites transmit "kill" signals to auto engines that do not comply (while in use on the road!) or censoring free speech through campaigns to eliminate advertising of "unworthy" products. Still other discussions already have occurred in Congress to penalize companies (designated "bad companies") that do not reward their workers or provide child-care or offer other benefits that the government deems socially just, or even prevent (at taxpayer expense) a company from closing an unprofitable location.

The great danger is that most of the laws and regulations that permit such incursions of human freedom are carried out by government officials and supported by a media elite called by economist Thomas Sowell "the anointed." As a class, that group fosters a deep-seated hostility to business enterprise and entrepreneurs—although some are given a "free pass," who embrace their social agenda like Ted Turner. An even worse danger is that the intrusion of those laws and regulations into American life occur on an incremental basis, so only when they become so completely reprehensible does the public respond. Meanwhile, attempts to rein in government have met with only minor success.

Thus, the entrepreneurial adventure continues, confronted with new challenges to market freedoms. However, history is not progressive—it is not constantly improving toward perfection, as huge chasms in the material well-being of humanity attest. (A case in point was the Soviet Union, which, for the first time in the history of industrialized nations, had a declining life expectancy rate.) Therefore, the continued operations of free markets and the economic liberties enjoyed by entrepreneurs are not guaranteed, but must be maintained and protected.

Yet the market is resilient, and entrepreneurs relentless. Few places on earth offer the same opportunities for achievement as the United States, even with its growing restrictions. Americans still achieve, in part, thanks to low taxes among all the developed nations; the most favorable climate toward property rights in the world; and a vibrant class of entrepreneurs bent on accomplishments, regardless of the odds. Despite its handicaps, the path to achievement in the United States, especially through business, remains open for the ambitious and the talented, the hardworking and the dreamers. Success is available for all who choose to embrace it. Ask Marty Grunder, who at age twelve began mowing yards as a high-school student. He had a capital investment of $25 in a lawn mower and did yard work because "I liked plants and the idea of having a little money in my pocket."[52] That year—1981—Grunder's total sales came to $1,800, hardly placing him on the *Forbes 400* but setting him on a career path far ahead of his high-school contemporaries. Along with his brother Rich, Grunder started a two-man mowing operation in 1983 that used a small tractor, initiating a cycle that expanded the business steadily over time: "We would save money, buy equipment, save money, employ people, go to school, buy equipment. . . ."[53] A $10,000 contract with a doctor's office complex solidified the seasonal nature of the business. Within three years after getting his driver's license, Grunder's yard-cutting operation had swelled to $19,000 in sales, and he and Rich had employed a friend.

Even then, Marty Grunder did not think of himself as a landscape artist, but instead envisioned a career in sports broadcasting. To that end, he attended the University of Dayton, continuing to run the business on the side. Working from 7:00 A.M. to 10:00 or 11:00, then going to classes, then working again, Grunder maintained a hectic pace, but also attracted attention when the 1989 *New York Times* included him in a story on student entrepreneurs. When local papers picked up the story, his business took off. While in school, for a class assignment he had interviewed motivational speaker Zig Ziglar, which helped convince him to devote himself full-time to his landscaping career. He also took a partner, cousin Dave Rado, who impressed on Grunder the value of goodwill in marketing. As a result, Grunder's employees received rewards when they stopped to help motorists or perform acts of charity, providing testimony to the company motto, "Where Service Is Always in Season."

A self-taught horticulturist, Grunder learned as the business grew to trust his specialist-employees and to focus on delegating responsibility. He still motored from site to site, overseeing work and meeting clients to select the most appropriate shrub or bush for a yard; yet he well understood the necessity of moving beyond the direct daily involvement of the owner in field operations if the business was to reach the next echelon. One of the keys to landscaping in cold-weather climates is to manage the cyclical nature of the business. That prompted Grunder to move into snow removal, deck construction, and corporate landscaping. In 1993, Grunder Landscaping opened a 6,500-square-foot facility in Miamisburg, Ohio, and had a fleet of a dozen trucks, staffed by eighteen full-time and seven part-time employees. Sales had reached $1.5 million by 1995, and, of course, for Grunder, the best was yet to come, with plans to move into the Cincinnati market. He had even written his own landscaping book yet never lost sight of the fact that the central goal was satisfied customers. Clients not only received personal thanks but at Christmas found a beautiful Grunder Christmas wreath delivered to their residence or business.

For the entrepreneurial business to grow to the next level, it had to operate beyond the constant input of a single individual on matters of detail. That is why the story of Sam Walton, with whom we started chapter 12, is so appropriate. Walton managed to run a billion-dollar business like a local store. Ultimately, small entrepreneurs who want to see businesses grow must make that leap—enter the "Walton zone"—and expand outside the personal, daily control of the founder. It requires trust in subordinates, valuing their opinions and decisions. Grunder had a close network of assistants and partners, just as, on a different scale, Andrew Carnegie molded a core of trusted lieutenants who implemented his vision, developing a powerful management team. A. P. Giannini's family built a world-class banking institution on such simple principles that it took "professional" managers more than thirty years to forget them. Ray Kroc used franchising and strict product testing to expand, finding a way to routinize and standardize quality control in such a way that franchisees could oversee the quality issues themselves. Lee Iacocca, for a brief time, was able to convince the entire vast corporate ships of Ford and Chrysler to follow his new course. Bill Gates, Steve Jobs, and Steve Wozniak all tapped into the hacker's mentality, offering their designers independence and creative outlets in return for new ideas.[54]

Yet Sam Walton, perhaps, was the master at entrepreneurial management of a giant corporation, walking into a store before hours in his Wal-Mart cap and congenially talking to the people upon whom the quality of the business rested, the employees. As he knew, computers could facilitate ordering and inventory control, management structures could improve efficiency in operations, but in the end it took vision, faith, and hard work to realize a dream. Even more: As Abe Karatz, Preston Tucker's right-hand man in the movie *Tucker,* observed, people who associate with entrepreneurs catch their dreams. The entrepreneur must be infectious, to the extent that employees "catch his dreams."

To the extent that America still leads the world in entrepreneurship, it still leads in business. And while the auto, steel, electronics, and other heavy industries have staged remarkable comebacks in recent decades, success in the competitive markets of the twenty-first century will not go to the nation that dominates today's existing technology but the one whose entrepreneurs break through into the next technologies and service ideas. Detroit's comeback is noteworthy but of more importance than the entrepreneur working on the hydrogen-based auto engine or even—yes, this *is* far out—the "antigravity device." The point is, the future belongs to those able to discern those businesses that no one else has even heard of today and to invent those products not even thought necessary now. No one can do that better than American entrepreneurs. If the American past is a guide to our future, the entrepreneurs of the world will be seeking to catch our dreams.

Notes

1. Robert Heilbroner, *The Making of Economic Society,* 9th ed. (Englewood Cliffs, N.J.: Prentice Hall, 1993), xiii. See also, for this type of "gloomsterism," Kevin Phillips, *The Politics of Rich and Poor: Wealth and the American Electorate in the Reagan Aftermath* (New York: Random House, 1990); and Robert Kuttner, *The Economic Illusion: False Choice Between Economic Prosperity and Social Justice* (Boston: Houghton Mifflin, 1984).

2. See the *New York Times,* March 3, 1996, and various dates, spring 1996.

3. Richard B. McKenzie, *The Paradox of Progress: Can Americans Regain Their Confidence in a Prosperous Future?* (New York: Oxford, 1997), 45.

4. Juliet B. Schor, *The Overworked American: The Unexpected Decline of Leisure* (New York: Basic Books, 1991), xvi.

5. Benjamin Friedman, *Day of Reckoning* (New York: Random House, 1988).

6. Ira C. Magaziner and Robert B. Reich, *Minding America's Business: The Decline and Rise of the American Economy* (New York: Vintage, 1983 [1982]); Martin and Susan Tolchin, *Selling Our Security: The Erosion of America's Assets* (New York: Knopf, 1992); Marc Levinson, "The Hand Wringers," *Newsweek,* October 26, 1992, 44–46; Chalmers Johnson, *MITI and the Japanese Miracle* (Stanford, Calif.: Stanford University Press, 1982); Robert Reich, "Members Only," *New Republic,* June 26, 1989, and his *Tales of a New America* (New York: Times Books, 1987) and *The Work of Nations* (New York: Vintage, 1992), in which he includes Arkansas in a list of nations [!]; Alfred Eckes, "Trading American Interests," *Foreign Affairs,* Fall 1992, 135–152; Otis L. Graham, *Losing Time: The Industrial Policy Debate* (Cambridge, Mass.: Harvard University Press, 1992); Stephen Cohen and John Zysman, *Manufacturing Matters: The Myth of the Post-Industrial Economy* (New York: Basic Books, 1987); Michael J. Borrus, *Competing for Control: America's Stake in Microelectronics* (Cambridge, Mass.: Ballinger, 1988); Clyde V. Prestowitz, Jr., *Trading Places: How We Allowed Japan to Take the Lead* (New York: Basic Books, 1988); and, less strident, Lester Thurow, *The Zero-Sum Society* (New York: Basic Books, 1980).

7. Robert Eisner, *The Misunderstood Economy: What Counts and How to Count It* (Boston: Harvard Business School Press, 1994), 76.

8. Ibid., 77.

9. Randall Fitzgerald, *When Government Goes Private* (New York: Universe Books, 1988), 183.

10. David T. Beito, "From Privies to Boulevards: The Private Supply of Infrastructure in the United States during the Nineteenth Century," in *Development by Consent: The Voluntary Supply of Public Goods and Services* eds., Jerry Jenkins and David E. Sisk, (San Francisco: Institute for Contemporary Studies Press, 1993), 23–48.

11. David T. Beito with Bruce Smith, "Owning the 'Commanding Heights': Historical Perspectives on Private Streets," in *Essays in Public Works History: Public-Private Partnerships: Privatization in Historical Perspective* (Chicago: Public Works Historical Society, 1989, 1–47.

12. Marc A. Weiss, *The Rise of the Community Builders: The American Real Estate Industry and Urban Land Planning* (New York: Columbia University Press, 1987), 3; David T. Beito with Bruce Smith, "The Formation of Urban Infrastructure Through Nongovernmental Planning: The Private Places of St. Louis, 1869–1920," *Journal of Urban History,* 16 (May 1990):263–301.

13. Michael R. Darby, "The Resurgent Trade Deficit: A Cause for Alarm?" *Jobs and Capital,* Summer 1997, 20–25.

14. See the work of Paul J. Peiper, "Measurement and Effects of Government Debt and Deficits," in *Economic Policy and National Accounting in Inflationary Conditions, Studies in Banking and Finance,* no. 2, 1986, North Holland, cited in Eisner, *Misunderstood Economy,* 86–87, and Eisner and Peiper's "The World's Greatest Debtor Nation?" *The North American Review of Economics and Finance,* 1 (Spring 1990): 9–32. Also see Eisner's *How Real Is the Federal Deficit?* (New York: The Free Press, 1986).

15. *Economic Report of the President, 1993* (Washington, D.C.: Government Printing Office, 1993), Table B–74.

16. Charles Steindel, "Manufacturing Productivity and High-Tech Investment," *Federal Reserve Bank of New York Quarterly Review,* Summer 1992, 39–47 (quotation on 39).

17. Steindel, "Manufacturing Productivity," 39.

17. Karl Zinmeister, "MITI Mouse," *Policy Review,* Spring 1993, 28–35.

18. Beth Belton, "Productivity May be Higher Than Figured," *USA Today,* May 7, 1998.

19. Henry R. Nau, *The Myth of America's Decline* (New York: Oxford, 1990).

20. Henry C. Dethloff, *The United States and the Global Economy Since 1945* (Fort Worth, Texas.: Harcourt Brace, 1997), 110.

21. Quoted in George Gilder, "Telecosm," Internet print of Gilder's book available for downloading at "forbesasap.com," quotations from "Washington's Bogeymen," first published in *Forbes,* June 6, 1994. I deliberately cite the Internet version here because of the predominance of the net as an economic tool.

22. Norman J. Glickman and Douglas P. Woodward, *The New Competitors: How Foreign Investors Are Changing the U.S. Economy* (New York: Basic Books, 1989), 38.

23. Warren Brookes, "That 'Foreign Invasion' Canard, Up Close," *Washington Times,* February 20, 1989.

24. Richard B. McKenzie, "Was It a Decade of Greed?" *Public Interest,* 91–96, and his *Giving USA: 1990* (New York: American Association of Fund Raising Council Trust for Philanthropy, 1990).

25. James K. Glassman, "From Art to War," *Washington Post,* January 6, 1998.

26. Larry Schweikart and Robert Gressis, "Charity Begins at Home: Christianity, Tithing, and the Welfare State," paper presented to the 1996 Economic and Business Historical Society Meeting, in author's possession.

27. James K. Glassman, "Jobs: The (Woe Is) Me Generation," *Washington Post,* March 19, 1996, and "Far From Doomsday," March 5, 1996.

28. Robert J. Samuelson, "Downsizing for Growth," *Newsweek,* March 25, 1996.

29. Robert Samuelson, *The Good Life and Its Discontents* (New York: Times Books, 1995).

30. Otto Bettmann, *The Good Old Days: They Were Terrible!* (New York, Random House, 1974).

31. Steven J. Davis, John Haltiwanger, and Scott Schuh, *Job Creation and Destruction* (Cambridge, Mass.: MIT Press, 1996).

32. Davis, Haltiwanger, and Schuh, *Job Creation,* 160.

33. Beverly Burr, "Economics and the Public," *Jobs and Capital,* 3 (Summer 1996): 4.

35. Eugene Smolensky and Robert Plotnick, *Inequality and Poverty in the United States: 1900 to 1990: 1947–1994* (Washington, D.C.: U.S. Bureau of the Census).

36. Richard Burkhauser, Amy Crews, Mary Daly, and Stephen Jenkins, *Income Mobility and the Middle Class* (Washington, D.C.: American Enterprise Institute, 1996).

37. Burkhauser et. al., *Income Mobility,* 10.

38. Benjamin Zycher, "Conventional Wisdom Review: The Rich and the Poor," *Jobs and Capital,* 3 (Summer 1996): 30–31 (quotation on 31).

39. W. Michael Cox and Richard Alm, *By Our Own Bootstraps: Economic Opportunity and the Dynamics of Income Distribution* (Dallas: Federal Reserve Bank of Dallas, 1996), 8 and passim, and their *Myths of Rich & Poor: Why We're Better Off Than We Think* (New York: Basic Books, 1999).

40. Charles Murray, "A Stroll Through the Income Spectrum," *American Enterprise,* 40–42.

41. A recent examination of the state of scholarship, by Richard John ("Elaborations, Revisions, Dissents: Alfred D. Chandler, Jr.'s *The Visible Hand* after Twenty Years," *Business History Review,* 71 [Summer 1997]: 151–200), despite updating the discussion, fails to address the rather radical departures outlined by George Gilder and Walter Wriston and the effects of those changes on the "Visible Hand." See also Dwight R. Lee and Richard B. McKenzie, "Countervailing Impotence," *Society,* November/December 1992, 34–40.

42. Gilder, "Telecosm: Michael Milken and the Two Trillion Dollar Opportunity," *Forbes,* April 10, 1995.

43. A variation on this theme appears in David H. Fischer, *The Great Wave: Price Revolutions and the Rhythm of History* (New York: Oxford University Press, 1996).

44. Fischer, for example, offers comparisons of prices to such variables as illegitimate births (see his Figure 4.25).

44. "Kenneth D. Tuchman," *The Forbes Four Hundred,* 192.

45. Ibid., 192.

46. "Ted Schwartz," ibid., 188.

48. Virginia I. Postrel, "The Nail File," *REASON,* October 1997, 4–8.

49. Elliot Blair Smith, "Montana Billionaire's Legacy Is Biggest Burden," *USA Today,* October 27, 1997.

49. Peter Michelmore, "Uprising in Indian Country," *Reader's Digest,* November 1984, reprint.

50. Andrew E. Serwer, "American Indians Discover Money Is Power," *Fortune,* April 19, 1993, reprint from Choctaw tribe.

51. Interviews with Marty Grunder, various dates 1996; Carol Mattar, "Grunder Discovers Green in Landscaping," *Dayton Business Reporter,* October 1993, 4.

52. Mattar, "Grunder Discovers Green," 4.

53. The reverse also is true, as large corporations seek to maintain the entrepreneurial attitude. See "How Can Big Companies Keep the Entrepreneurial Spirit Alive?" *Harvard Business Review,* November-December 1995, 183–192.